# Quarterdeck and Bridge

# Quarterdeck and Bridge

*Two Centuries of*
**AMERICAN NAVAL LEADERS**

EDITED BY JAMES C. BRADFORD

NAVAL INSTITUTE PRESS ☆ ANNAPOLIS, MARYLAND

LIBRARY OF CONGRESS CATALOGING-IN-PUBLICATION DATA

Quarterdeck and bridge : two centuries of American naval leaders /
    edited by James C. Bradford.
        p.    cm.
    Includes bibliographical references and index.
    ISBN 1-55750-073-8 (hc). — ISBN 1-55750-096-7 (pbk.)
    1. United States. Navy—Biography.    2. United States—History,
Naval.    I. Bradford, James C.
E182.Q37    1996
359'.0092'273—dc20
[B]                                                        96-43106

Printed in the United States of America on acid-free paper ♾

08  07  06  05  04  03  02  01    PBII  10  9  8  7  6  5  4

William M. Fowler, Jr., "Esek Hopkins"; James C. Bradford, "John Paul Jones"; John H. Schroeder, "Stephen Decatur"; John K. Mahon, "Oliver Hazard Perry"; and Harold D. Langley, "Robert F. Stockton," appeared in slightly different forms in James C. Bradford, ed., *Command under Sail: Makers of the American Naval Tradition, 1775–1850* (Annapolis: Naval Institute Press, © 1985).

John H. Schroeder, "Matthew Calbraith Perry"; William N. Still, Jr., "David Glasgow Farragut"; Warren F. Spencer, "Raphael Semmes"; and Tamara Moser Melia Smith, "David Dixon Porter," appeared in slightly different forms in James C. Bradford, ed., *Captains of the Old Steam Navy: Makers of the American Naval Tradition, 1840–1880* (Annapolis: Naval Institute Press, © 1986).

John B. Hattendorf, "Stephen B. Luce"; Vernon L. Williams, "George Dewey"; David F. Trask, "William Sowden Sims"; and Clark G. Reynolds, "William A. Moffett," appeared in slightly different forms in James C. Bradford, ed., *Admirals of the New Steel Navy: Makers of the American Naval Tradition, 1880–1930* (Annapolis: Naval Institute Press, © 1990), as did a much longer version of Robert Seager II, "Alfred Thayer Mahan."

Lloyd J. Graybar, "Ernest J. King"; John B. Lundstrom, "Chester W. Nimitz"; John F. Wukovits, "William F. Halsey"; David Alan Rosenberg, "Arleigh Burke"; Francis Duncan, "Hyman G. Rickover"; and Thomas J. Cutler, "Elmo R. Zumwalt, Jr.," were written especially for this volume.

*For Judy*

# Contents

# Preface

STRATEGICALLY AN ISLAND, THE UNITED STATES HAS ALWAYS REQUIRED A NAVY to bar enemies from its shores. Economically a trading nation, it has also needed a navy to defend its trade. The size and type of navy have always been debated. So has the way in which a navy should carry out its responsibilities. Prior to the twentieth century, the U.S. Navy did not need to exercise command of the sea or naval mastery, or even to vie for such exalted strategies, but it had a key role to play in defense of the Republic and the protection and expansion of its commerce.

The Continental Navy was established during the Revolutionary War with the anticipation that it could help win independence and because Americans knew that sovereign nations have navies. Similar thoughts led most of the states to establish navies of their own and both state and national governments to license privateers. The nation's founders did not discuss naval strategy. They simply assigned tasks to the fledgling service—capture supplies for George Washington's army, transport diplomats to Europe, bring munitions from the West Indies, raid British commerce, help to defend American ports—and the officers of the navy responded as best they could with the limited resources available to them. Independence achieved, many Americans believed that a navy was no longer needed or at least that the nation could not afford one. For a decade, the Stars and Stripes were carried to sea only by merchant vessels.

When attacks on those trading vessels became more than Americans could bear and a new constitution gave the government the ability to support a navy, one was reestablished. At virtually the same time, Europe returned to war. Coalitions led by Britain and France fought a life-and-death struggle, in which neither side showed much respect for the rights of neutral commerce espoused by the United States. The young Republic was not a passive observer of that great war but followed a policy of belligerent neutrality, which twice led it into the European conflict, first into the Quasi-War against France, then into the War of 1812 against Britain. Because the war with France was conducted entirely at sea, the burden of defense fell on the U.S. Navy. The war against Britain was fought equally on land and sea, but it was the Navy's frigate actions in 1812 that avenged the nation's honor and earned its enemy's respect, and its victories on Lakes Erie and Champlain in 1813 and 1814 that helped to secure the status quo antebellum Treaty of Ghent, which ended the war.

During the decades following peace with Britain, the United States obtained Florida, settled its northern and western borders, and marked the Caribbean as within its sphere of influence. The Monroe Doctrine proclaimed the principles of U.S. foreign policy to the rest of the world, and Britain gave tacit recognition to the equality of U.S. interests and authority in the Western Hemisphere by signing the Clayton-Bulwer Treaty in 1850.

It fell to the U.S. Navy to execute this policy and to protect American commercial interests around the world. From the 1770s to the 1840s, most of the Navy's squadrons, cruising the Atlantic, Mediterranean, and Caribbean, showed the flag, and suppressed piracy and the slave trade. When periodic visits by naval vessels failed to deter infringement of American rights, officers turned to retribution and punished those who mistreated shipwrecked mariners, seized the property of merchants, discriminated against American commerce, or dishonored the American flag.

During the 1850s, various interest groups demanded that the Navy do more and its officers eagerly accepted increased responsibilities. The Navy's role was expanded from merely defending commerce to exploring new lands and trade routes, identifying opportunities for trade, collecting nautical and commercial information, negotiating diplomatic agreements, and opening areas previously closed to American merchants. Matthew F. Maury's collection of data on wind and ocean currents; Charles Wilkes's United States Exploring Expedition of 1838–42; Matthew Calbraith Perry's "opening of Japan" and conclusion of the Treaty of Kanagawa in 1854; the North Pacific Surveying and Exploring Expedition of 1853–55; and Robert Shufeldt's globe-encircling voyage of 1878–80, during which he opened U.S. trade relations with Korea, epitomize these new roles.

The Civil War interrupted but did not change American policy or significantly alter how the Navy operated. When the South seceded from the Union, all U.S. Navy squadrons, except the one operating off Africa, were called home. Additional ships were leased, purchased, and constructed, and the U.S. Navy grew exponentially. During almost four years of operations, its forces made significant contributions to Union victory by blockading the Southern coast and

joining with U.S. Army troops to subdivide the Confederacy along the Mississippi River and to capture all of its major ports. After Appomattox came a return to traditional U.S. policies, the maintenance of stability, and the reestab-
lishment of the Navy's squadrons.

By the middle of the nineteenth century, the Age of Sail was drawing to a
close. For three centuries, ships and weapons had remained basically unchanged and developments had been evolutionary in nature. Then, in only a
few decades, propulsion changed from sail to steam, hulls from wood to iron
and steel, armaments from muzzle-loading smoothbore cannon to breech-
loading rifled guns, and projectiles from solid shot to exploding shells. Such
revolutionary developments appeared to demand changes in both strategy and
tactics, but the nature of the changes required was unclear. Fifty years of uncertainty followed.

Before the impact of technology could be clarified, the Navy was called on
to assume new and quite different roles. During the previous century, the
Navy's expanding commercial role had been neither planned nor envisioned
by naval officers or government leaders, though a foreign visitor, Alexis de
Tocqueville, divined the future. The observant French traveler predicted the
twentieth century when he observed, "When I contemplate the ardor with
which the Anglo-Americans prosecute commerce, the advantages which aid
them, and the success of their undertakings, I cannot help believing that they
will one day become the foremost maritime power of the globe. They are born
to rule the seas, as the Romans were to conquer the world."[1] By the 1880s and
1890s, Americans were beginning to look outward, beyond the Western Hemisphere, and both political leaders and naval officers began to measure the U.S.
Navy by comparing it with the navies of Europe's great powers, rather than by
its ability to defend and serve American commerce. America's maritime empire had developed without the benefit of a clearly defined peacetime naval
policy.

During the 1880s and 1890s, American naval and political leaders began debating what types of vessels should be built and where and how they should be
deployed. The ABCD ships (the protected cruisers *Atlanta*, *Boston*, and *Chicago* and the dispatch vessel *Dolphin*) of the 1880s represented new technological developments but not a new role. They remained—like the sloops and
frigates of the sailing Navy—primarily commerce defense and raiding vessels
to be scattered among the Navy's several squadrons during peacetime. A
decade later, the United States built its first true capital ships. Alfred Thayer
Mahan lobbied for keeping them together in a battle fleet whose primary role
was to engage the enemy's fleet, not its commerce. By the turn of the century,
the Navy developed a systematic body of thought that would guide it for at least
the next fifty years. It was a heady time for American naval officers as their ser-

vice competed with the navies of Britain, Germany, and Japan for supremacy. At the same time, they sought to protect America's new possessions in the Pacific; police its informal empire in the Caribbean; and expand the economic and political interests epitomized by the Open Door Notes, in which the United States committed itself to maintaining the equality of trading and investment opportunity for all foreign nations in China plus defending the territorial and administrative integrity of China.

Victory in the Spanish-American War brought the Navy great popularity at home, and the writings of Mahan achieved great influence abroad. Leaders in all maritime nations read and, with only a few exceptions, accepted the ideas of Mahan, the "Prophet of Sea Power." His writings provided the intellectual underpinning of American maritime strategy. Though he was neither the first nor the only person to identify "timeless principles" from the study of naval history, he stated them well and often in his trilogy on Anglo-American naval history and in scores of magazine and newspaper articles. Indeed, Mahan's ideas or the inferences drawn from them by world leaders led to actions that resulted in some historians blaming them for the naval race that helped to precipitate World War I. The United States entered that race with gusto. By 1910, it had twenty-seven battleships in service and six more building, which made it the world's second or third strongest naval power. Less than a decade later, President Woodrow Wilson served notice of American intent to build "a navy second to none" and, with World War I in progress, Congress appropriated funds toward that end.

American participation in the war was relatively brief and its direct contribution to Allied victory modest, but the nation emerged from the conflict with its economy strengthened, ready to challenge all nations for naval supremacy. But, support for a large navy evaporated as the American people demanded a return to "normalcy." That meant a reduction in taxation and, consequently, the curtailment of naval building. A return to normalcy also implied a retreat from international involvement, which, together with the desire for retrenchment in naval expenditures, led to the Washington Conference of 1921–22 and naval arms limitations. For the next decade, the Navy appeared to languish, just as it had following most previous wars. The U.S. Navy did not even build to the level allowed by the Five Power Pact of the Washington Conference, but its failure to do so did not mean that no progress was made; there were advances, particularly in the field of aviation.

The rise of aggressive regimes in Italy, Germany, and Japan and pressures to create jobs in the depression-stricken United States led to the construction of new ships during the 1930s. Funds had been appropriated for most of the major combatants used by the U.S. Navy to wage World War II even before Japan attacked Pearl Harbor. During the first six months of that global conflict, the Navy reeled before the onslaught of German U-boats in the Atlantic and Japanese advances in the Pacific. Then it reorganized, identified effective commanders, developed sound tactics, and devised a winning strategy. Taking the offensive in late 1942 and early 1943, it began to rid the Atlantic of the Nazi submarine menace and to drive Japan backward until the United States and its Allies triumphed over the Axis Powers in mid-1945.

The United States emerged from World War II with unchallenged supremacy at sea. The war destroyed the multipower system of the past, as Germany, Italy, and Japan were vanquished and the economies of Britain and France were ruined. There emerged a bipolar world, in which for half a century the United States used its navy to counter the land-based power of the Soviet Union and to support friendly governments around the world. Ever more rapid technological change brought nuclear weapons, atomic-powered submarines, and intercontinental ballistic missiles, which, combined with other factors, escalated the cost of defense immensely. Those costs contributed to the implosion of the Soviet Union in the 1980s that laid the basis for a new world order, one whose contours will take time to clarify. Nor is the role of the U.S. Navy in that new order clear. What is certain is that the Navy will continue to be more than machines. Innovations in technology, or even new roles and missions, do not change everything. "Without officers what can be expected from a navy?" Thomas Truxtun asked Secretary of War James McHenry in 1797. "The ships cannot maneuver themselves."[2] Almost two centuries later, Admiral James Calvert expressed a similar thought, "Important as ships are, naval history is made by men."[3]

These words speak to the purpose of this book, whose biographical essays trace the history of the U.S. Navy from its roots in the War for Independence to the postnuclear present. They tell the Navy's story through the lives of the officers who forged its traditions and stand today as the models against whom the leaders of tomorrow will be measured. Selection of subjects for this volume was not easy. The officers chosen were neither "representative," in the sense of being average or common, nor were they only the "great men" that a Thomas Carlyle or Sidney Hook might choose. Influence and importance are not necessarily linked to fame or battle command, and a number of the selections, Esek Hopkins and Robert F. Stockton, for example, are not obvious. The exclusion of other officers, such as Thomas Truxtun, Raymond Spruance, and George W. Anderson, Jr., is not a judgment of their importance. The selection criteria focused on choosing individuals who set precedents, reached particular heights of achievement, or had careers reflecting the main currents of naval development and the roles played by the U.S. Navy during its two centuries of operations. In selecting the subjects, an effort was made to avoid Whiggish anachronism. That is to say, the events of the Navy's early history did not lead inexorably to the present. The U.S. Navy was not predestined to become the world's supreme sea power. The adoption of nuclear power and the wedding of its use in submarines to ballistic missiles was not preordained. Lessons of seamanship, strategy, and tactics drawn from events of more than a century ago are unlikely to be directly applicable to conditions today, but there are connections, however allegorical, between the eras.

Few would deny the crucial importance of leadership in naval affairs or that many of the qualities of effective leadership—moral courage, technical competence, trustworthiness, loyalty upward and downward, self-confidence—are timeless. The question of whether leadership is innate or learned is insoluble, and no attempt is made here to answer it.[4] The men of the Continental Navy received their training in the merchant marine and only entered the Navy in time of national peril. The next generation of leaders, men such as Stephen Decatur, David Glasgow Farragut, and David Dixon Porter, also learned their profession at sea while serving as midshipmen during the Barbary Wars and the War of 1812. The establishment of the Naval Academy in 1845 was a turning point in officer education. For the first time, young officer candidates received the rudiments of their education and training on shore before serving at sea. Four decades later, the Naval War College was founded by Stephen B. Luce, and henceforth most senior officers received a postgraduate professional military education to prepare them for high command. Seniority and command at sea were virtually the only avenues to promotion in the Old Navy, but within the last century, Luce, Mahan, William A. Moffett, and Hyman G. Rickover rose through special talents in education, training, and engineering. Thus, this collection contains essays on a variety of officers.

The victors in great battles—John Paul Jones at Flamborough Head, Oliver Hazard Perry at Lake Erie, Porter at Vicksburg, Farragut at Mobile Bay, George Dewey at Manila Bay, and William F. Halsey at Leyte Gulf—are included, as are such dashing characters as Decatur battling the Barbary Corsairs, Raphael Semmes raiding Union commerce, and "31-Knot" Arleigh Burke devising destroyer tactics in the Solomons. But, the Navy is more than broadsides and battles. Essays on reformers (Matthew Perry, William Sowden Sims, and Elmo R. Zumwalt, Jr.), thinkers (Luce and Mahan), those who exercised high command (Hopkins, Chester W. Nimitz, and Ernest J. King), and technical innovators (Stockton, Moffett, and Rickover) round out the volume.

The essays are not merely short biographies but also interpretive studies that assess the roles of their subjects as establishers, practitioners, and exemplars of the American naval tradition. For this reason authors have been selected whose knowledge of America's naval heritage extends beyond the individuals about whom they write. Some have written on their subjects before, but all offer more than distillations of views presented elsewhere. I made no attempt to impose a uniformity of interpretation on the essays. The authors' views are their own, and each contributor provides suggestions for additional reading to guide those whose interest they arouse.

Certain patterns do emerge. All the officers had great self-confidence. In combat or times of danger, most had courage and were aggressive, as illustrated by John Paul Jones uttering "I have not yet begun to fight," Matthew Perry sailing boldly into Tokyo Harbor to "open Japan," and Arleigh Burke leading his destroyers against superior Japanese forces. Such personality characteristics are to be admired in times of danger, but, at other times, they can lead to less desirable traits, such as the hypersensitivity exhibited by Stephen Decatur, which ended in a tragic duel, and the impetuosity of the sort demonstrated by Raphael Semmes when he rashly pitted his *Alabama* against the more powerful *Kearsage*. Many of the officers, and not just the reformers, faced strong opposition within the Navy but refused to retreat from foes. Jones fought the parochialism and nepotism represented by Hopkins; Moffett opposed the entrenched admirals of the "Gun Club."

Navies, like other institutions, reflect the societies they serve. Few individuals better illustrated the spirit of the young republic than Decatur, the romanticism of the Confederacy's "Lost Cause" than Semmes, or the hatred of the Japanese brought by Pearl Harbor than Halsey. The officers who guided the Navy, shaped its character, and set its course for two centuries were products of their times. Much has been demanded of them by the American people. Some met the challenges, and others did not, but all were makers of the American naval tradition. This book presents their stories and, in doing so, tells the story of one of the finest military services that the world has ever known.

NOTES

1. Alexis de Tocqueville, *Democracy in America*, 2 vols., edited by Phillips Bradley (New York, 1945 [1835]), 1:447.

2. Truxtun to McHenry, 3 March 1797, James McHenry Papers, Huntington Library, San Marino, California.

3. James Calvert, *The Naval Profession* (New York, 1965), 6.

4. Early in this century, Alfred Thayer Mahan, *Types of Naval Officers* (London, 1904), and Charles B. Davenport, *Naval Officers: Their Heredity and Development* (Washington, D.C., 1919) investigated the problem. Influenced by the social science thinking of the day, Davenport classified officers by "temperament," "juvenile promise," and "hereditary traits." More recent studies include Oliver Warner, *Command at Sea: Great Fighting Admirals from Hawke to Nimitz* (New York, 1976), and John Horsfield, *The Art of Leadership in War: The Royal Navy from the Age of Nelson to the End of World War II* (Westport, Conn., 1980).

# Acknowledgments

THIS BOOK, LIKE ANY COLLECTION OF ESSAYS, IS A COOPERATIVE EFFORT. I could not have had a more congenial group of authors to work with and to them goes my deepest debt of gratitude. Fourteen of the essays first appeared in previous collections that I edited: *Command under Sail: Makers of the American Naval Tradition, 1775–1850* (1985); *Captains of the Old Steam Navy: Makers of the American Naval Tradition, 1840–1880* (1986); and *Admirals of the New Steel Navy: Makers of the American Naval Tradition, 1880–1930* (1990). The authors of those essays made minor revisions where necessary, particularly in adding to the suggestions for further reading the works that have appeared since they wrote their essays. Robert Seager so revised his essay for this book as to make it virtually a new work. The authors of the six essays especially written for this book bore with good humor my sometimes heavy-handed commentary and acquiesced to my pleas for brevity. At the Naval Institute Press, our editor, Paul Wilderson, provided encouragement, and our manuscript editor, Terry Belanger, saved us from infelicities and inconsistencies of style, and our proofreader, Barbara Johnson, caught a number of errors which eluded the contributors and the editor.

During the 1995–96 academic year, the Air War College provided an atmosphere most congenial to this undertaking. David Curtis Skaags shared his knowledge of the early navy, Mark L. Shulman offered his views of the "New Navy" of the late nineteenth and early twentieth centuries, and both applied their critical eye to the preface. Our dean, Rear Admiral Ronald Kurth, USN (Ret.), contributed more than he realized through stimulating conversation shared over lunches. Alexander Cochran, chairman of the Department of Strategy, Doctrine, and Air Power, saw to it that I had time for this and other projects.

At my home institution, Texas A&M University, Judy Mattson typed the revised sections on "Further Reading" and Joseph G. Dawson made valuable suggestions to improve the preface.

This book is dedicated to my wife, Judy, who makes all possible and all worthwhile.

# Quarterdeck and Bridge

# ☆ ☆ Esek Hopkins

## ☆ Commander-in-Chief of the Continental Navy

*by William M. Fowler, Jr.*

IN THE SUMMER OF 1797, JOHN ADAMS, THE NEWLY INAUGURATED
President of the United States, was on his way home to Quincy, Massachusetts.
En route he decided to spend an evening in Providence, Rhode Island. The
arrival of the President caused quite a stir. A company of dragoons escorted him
to the Golden Bull Tavern where a gala reception, complete with pealing bells
and sounding cannon fire, was offered. Never indifferent to public accolades,
Adams was pleased at his warm reception.

After an evening of innumerable toasts and endless feasting, Adams and his
family retired to their quarters. An unexpected knock at the door brought a servant who announced that a gentleman begged to see the President. In the an-
teroom, the President "found an old man bowed with years and infirmities."
His visitor was Esek Hopkins, late commander-in-chief of the Continental
Navy.

He came, he told the President, to pay his respects and to tell him how
grateful he was that Adams had stood in his defense twenty years before when
his enemies in Congress had sought to destroy him. Old, wan, and barely able
to walk, this man was hardly the vigorous and sharp-tongued seaman Adams
remembered from those heady days of the Revolution. The veil of age obscured the traces of a naval career that had begun most promisingly many
decades earlier.

Esek Hopkins was born on 26 April 1718 into a large and well-known Rhode
Island family. Two of his older brothers had gone to sea before him, when, at
age twenty, upon the death of his father, young Esek left the family farm and
signed on board a merchantman out of Providence. Within a very few years he
had his own command in the West Indies trade and was a frequent visitor to

Surinam and the neighboring sugar islands. Married at twenty-three to Desire Burroughs, daughter of a prosperous Newport merchant and shipmaster, Hopkins moved to his wife's town and continued his voyaging. Two years later, in 1743, sensing greater opportunities in Providence, he returned home.[1]

By 1750, Hopkins had settled easily into the predictable lifestyle of a Yankee shipmaster: frequent voyages to the West Indies; a good and respectable marriage at home; numerous children (five in the first seven years of marriage); and growing investments and responsibilities shoreside. In 1754 he joined many of his Rhode Island shipmates and went "a privateering" against the French during the French and Indian War (1754–1763). He quickly proved to be as good a warrior as a trader, increasing both his fame and fortune.

Like most other colonials, Hopkins celebrated the peace and looked forward to reestablishing the old trade. Events in America and England precluded that, and, in the dozen tumultuous years from the end of the war to the battles at Lexington and Concord, Esek Hopkins found himself enmeshed in local affairs. He served on several town committees and in the General Assembly. Most important, however, his elder brother Stephen was elected governor, and, in the rough and tumble of Rhode Island politics, Esek became his close ally, sharing both his friends and his enemies.

At the summons for the First Continental Congress in the fall of 1774, Rhode Island, not surprisingly, elected Stephen Hopkins one of its delegates. From the moment the body came to order, it was clear that sectionalism would play a pivotal role in decision making. For his part, Stephen Hopkins was loyal to Rhode Island and New England. He allied himself closely with his New England colleagues and struck up a particularly close association with John and Samuel Adams. Never one to forget his friends, Hopkins emerged as a key member of Congress, accustomed to using his influence on behalf of his constituents.

With the outbreak of hostilities, Rhode Islanders quickly discovered their vulnerability by sea. In Newport, Captain James Wallace had been busy terrifying the populace from his frigate, HMS *Rose*. In reaction to Wallace, the Assembly commissioned two small vessels to patrol the waters of Narragansett Bay and, in October, appointed Esek Hopkins a brigadier general and placed him in command of Rhode Island's defenses. In Philadelphia too there was action. On 26 May 1775 Congress resolved that the colonies be put in a state of military readiness so that they might be able to defend their rights and liberties; on the twenty-ninth it called upon the people of Canada to join the rebellious colonies in their common cause. By the end of June, Congress had voted to raise and equip an army, appointed George Washington as commander-in-chief, and voted to issue two million dollars in bills of credit to finance the new government's operation. In July, Congress entered into negotiations with the

Indians and elected Benjamin Franklin postmaster general.[2] Although the Declaration of Independence was still more than a year away, the Continental Congress was taking on the power of a sovereign body. In one noticeable area, however, its members held back. They did not authorize a navy.

Congress was skeptical of creating a navy. It was one thing to appoint a commander-in-chief over a rabble in arms surrounding "ministerial Butchers" in Boston. After all, that could be justified on strictly defensive grounds. But a navy was another matter, for the mobility and striking capability of armed vessels give them an inherent offensive character. This factor, plus sectional politics and concern over the high cost of a navy, prevented Congress from acting on a naval program.

Congress's inaction distressed Rhode Island, and, on 26 August, the General Assembly resolved:

> this Assembly is persuaded, that building and equipping an American fleet, as soon as possible, would greatly and essentially conduce to the preservation of the lives, liberty and property, of good people of these Colonies and therefore instruct their delegates, to use their whole influence at the ensuing congress, for building, at the Continental expense, a fleet of sufficient force, for the protection of these colonies, and for employing them in such manner and places as will most effectively annoy our enemies, and contribute to the common defense of these colonies.[3]

On 3 October 1775, the Rhode Island delegation presented the resolution to Congress. Four days later, when the resolve was put on the floor for debate, it was obvious Rhode Island had set off a powder keg. Samuel Chase of Maryland called it "the maddest Idea in the World to think of building an American fleet." Others, mainly southerners, chimed in, calling attention to the huge expense involved while alluding to the fact that the region most likely to benefit from the creation of a navy was New England, whence both ships and men might come.[4]

As tempers in Congress heated up, events were taking place at sea that made some kind of action unavoidable. Washington's forces were in desperate need of supplies. The quickest and most direct source for the Americans were the British themselves, who, believing the rebels could not harm them at sea, were sending out unarmed and unescorted store ships. These were ideal targets, and, on 13 October, Congress agreed to fit out two vessels "to cruise eastward, for intercepting such transports as may be laden with warlike stores."[5]

A committee was appointed to prepare a plan. With a bit of clever politicking, the pro-navy faction took control and brought back a report that startled Congress. Instead of two vessels, the committee called for ten. It was too bold a plan for the temper of Congress; instead of ten, it authorized four. Nevertheless, this was a great victory for the New England navalists, who had secured twice the number of vessels originally debated and, more important, now had a naval commitment from Congress.

To manage this fleet of four, Congress elected a seven-man committee. The Naval Committee consisted of Stephen Hopkins, Joseph Hewes of North Carolina, Richard Henry Lee of Virginia, John Adams of Massachusetts, Silas Deane of Connecticut, John Langdon of New Hampshire, and Christopher Gadsden of South Carolina.

Eager to get under way, the committee arranged for quarters in a local tavern and agreed to meet every evening at six to conduct its business. The meetings were productive, lively, and convivial. John Adams remembered his service on the committee as "the pleasantest part of my labors . . . in Congress." With unusual nostalgia he recalled the men he had met with on those fall and winter evenings of 1775, especially Stephen Hopkins, "Old Grape and Guts" as some called him. According to Adams, the old gentleman greatly enlivened the meetings with his wit and wisdom, and after adjournment many remained behind with him until very late—smoking, drinking, and swapping stories in a room swimming with the heavy warm odor of port and rum.[6] These sessions were more than social, however. In the weeks to come, Hopkins's influence in the committee would become abundantly clear as Rhode Island reaped the benefits of those late-night meetings.

On 2 November, Congress granted the committee one hundred thousand dollars to fit out four vessels and "to agree with such officers and seamen, as are proper to man and command said vessels."[7] As the committee scouted for commanders, the assignment turned out to be a family affair, the jovial storyteller Hopkins displaying all his political dexterity. Esek, still busy in Rhode Island, was made commander-in-chief of the fleet. His son, John Burroughs Hopkins, was commissioned a captain, as was another Rhode Islander and kinsman, Abraham Whipple. Whipple and Esek Hopkins had sailed together on many privateering voyages. A third captain was a Connecticut mariner, Dudley Saltonstall, brother-in-law to Silas Deane. The fourth and only non-New Englander and unrelated officer was Nicholas Biddle, a well-known Philadelphia captain. All in all, the appointments were a marvelous manifestation of Hopkintonian influence.

Having appointed officers, Congress next needed to provide rules and regulations by which the infant navy was to be governed. For reasons that are not altogether clear, the Naval Committee assigned that task to John Adams. Although a lawyer and a man reasonably acquainted with maritime law, he had no seagoing experience. Nevertheless, with his usual passion for detail, Adams undertook the duty, and, on 28 November, Congress approved Adams's "Rules for the Regulation of the Navy of the United Colonies." In general, they followed the pattern of the Royal Navy but tended to be less severe.[8] In Rhode Island, Esek Hopkins received the news of his appointment with glee. However, it can hardly be said that he rushed to his post. He spent several weeks tending to private and public business and did not arrive in Philadelphia until very early in January.

In the absence of the commander-in-chief, Congress had not been idle. Neither time nor funds permitted the construction of new warships, so the Naval Committee sent agents on the prowl seeking likely merchantmen to be converted to warships. They found four: the *Black Prince*, renamed the *Alfred* and given to the command of Saltonstall; the *Sally*, renamed the *Columbus*, given to Captain Whipple; the *Andrea Doria*, given to Nicholas Biddle; and the *Cabot*, given to John Burroughs Hopkins. These four, considered to be the most powerful members of the fleet, were joined by four additional lightly armed vessels: the *Wasp* and the *Fly*, eight-gun schooners; the *Hornet*, a ten-gun sloop; and the twelve-gun sloop *Providence*, formerly the *Katy* of the Rhode Island navy.

On 4 January 1776, with Hopkins on board the *Alfred*, of twenty-four guns, the fleet cast off and moved out into the Delaware. This first movement lasted only long enough—about four hours—to get over to Liberty Island, where they tied up again to avoid ice flows coming down the river. The next day Hopkins received two sets of orders from the Naval Committee.[9] The first were general in nature, setting out procedures and protocols. He was addressed as "Commander in Chief of the Fleet of the United Colonies," leading some to suggest that Congress intended to place him on a par with Washington. However, closer scrutiny reveals otherwise, for in a key paragraph he was told: "You are by every means in your power to keep up an exact correspondence with the Congress or Committee of Congress aforesaid, and with the Commander in chief of the Continental forces in America."

Clearly, in Congress's mind Hopkins was subordinate to Washington, though the relative rank of the two officers was never seriously contested and thus not clearly defined.

The second set of orders Esek opened on 5 January were his sailing instructions, outlining his first mission. For reasons of strategy and politics, this Yankee fleet was being sent south to rid those coasts of British raiders.

> You are instructed with the utmost diligence to proceed with the said fleet to sea and if the winds and weather will possibly admit of it to proceed directly for Chesapeake Bay in Virginia and when nearly arrived there you will send forward a small swift sailing vessel to gain intelligence. . . . If . . . you find that they are not greatly superior to your own you are immediately to enter the said bay, search out and attack, take or destroy all the naval force of our

enemies that you may find there. If you should be so fortunate as to execute
this business successfully in Virginia you are then to proceed immediately to
the southward and make yourself master of such forces as the enemy may
have both in North and South Carolina. . . . Notwithstanding these particular orders, which it is hoped you will be able to execute, if bad winds, or
stormy weather, or any other unforseen accident or disaster disable you so to
do, You are then to follow such Courses as your best Judgment shall suggest
to you as most useful to the American Cause and to distress the Enemy by
all means in your power.

It took more than six weeks to get the fleet to sea. Ice in the river as well as
difficulty in filling out the crew delayed Hopkins until 18 February, when, with
a fair wind blowing, men were sent aloft to "loose the Fore topsail and sheet it
home."

An experienced mariner, Hopkins knew the risks of a winter sail. He was
not disappointed. Gale force winds out of the north bore down on the fleet.
The *Hornet* and the *Fly* proved to be poor heavy weather boats and were separated from the remainder of the fleet. The other six plowed on.

Ignoring his orders, Hopkins bypassed both Chesapeake Bay and the southern coast; instead he laid a course offshore that took him to the Bahamas. Because nowhere in his orders were the Bahamas mentioned (unless one con-
strues them to be included in the "best Judgment" clause), it is difficult to
divine the commodore's motives. Later, when he was questioned about his
change of plans, he laid his decision to the fact that so many of his crew were
sick. A far more likely explanation is simply that sailing the southern coast was,
in his judgment, too risky. In Chesapeake Bay, Lord Dunmore, former royal
governor of Virginia, was busy terrorizing the folks along the shore. Although
the governor's force was technically inferior to Hopkins's, the American commodore knew full well that in combat his ersatz navy would most likely collapse at the first sight of the Royal Navy. As for the southern coast, Hopkins had
already taken a beating just getting off soundings; coming along the shore
would have meant hazarding Cape Hatteras. Esek Hopkins had no desire to
challenge either the Royal Navy or nature.

It was a bad decision. Hopkins was behaving more like a privateersman
whose main concern was to minimize danger and maximize profits. By completely bypassing the southern coasts, he displayed a callous disregard for southern interests and reinforced southern suspicions about a Yankee navy. Hopkins's
insensitivity to sectional and political concerns ill-suited him for command of
a navy created by a Congress where these elements counted so heavily.

On 1 March, the fleet came to anchor on the lee side of Abaco Island, where
for the next two days the Americans took on water and made preparations for

an assault against Nassau on New Providence Island, only a few more miles to the south. Hopkins hoped to catch the garrison by surprise and carry away its reportedly large supply of gunpowder.

On Sunday, 3 March, the Americans landed on the northeast tip of New Providence about four miles to the west of Fort Montague.[10] After firing a few token shots, the garrison left the fort and retired to the town of Nassau. The Americans spent the night in the fort and the next day marched on the town and Fort Nassau; neither offered any resistance.

With everything secured, Hopkins brought his ships into the harbor and went looking for gunpowder. Herein lay disappointment. While the Americans were spending their evening at Fort Montague, the governor of the Bahamas had been busy moving his gunpowder out of the magazine and into the hold of a commandeered sloop that had taken off for another island. By the time Hopkins's men broke into the fort, all they found were twenty-four barrels. However, some solace could be taken from the fact that their opponents had not had enough time to remove their cannon and various other military supplies. It took two weeks to load the booty.

On the same day that the British were evacuating Boston, 17 March 1776, Esek Hopkins evacuated Nassau. At first, according to his testimony, the commodore gave thought to taking his fleet to Georgia to help rid that coast of enemy ships. Whether he really intended to undertake such a cruise is questionable; at any rate, he gave up the idea when he learned that the enemy was there in force. Instead of Georgia, the American captains were ordered to keep company with the *Alfred* and, if separated, then to sail alone and rendezvous in Block Island channel. Clearly Hopkins was headed home to Rhode Island.

Homeward bound, the men and the commodore stayed alert for any signs of enemy shipping. They saw none until 4 April, when the fleet drew near to the east end of Long Island. Cruising in the same area was the schooner *Hawk*, tender to the *Rose*. She was spotted and easily overtaken by the American force. The next day, a second British vessel, the bomb brig *Boston*, was sighted and pursued. She proved to be a tartar and put up a fierce resistance until, finally, the Americans overwhelmed her.

The *Hawk* and the *Boston* were only small fry. On 6 April, a truly worthy foe came into view: HMS *Glasgow*, a twenty-gun ship under the command of Captain Tyringham Howe.[11] Howe, apparently unaware that the Americans were in the area, came down toward the rebel fleet. It was not until they were within hailing distance that he realized his mistake. He then made a run for it, with Hopkins in hot pursuit. Although the *Glasgow* was greatly outnumbered and outgunned, she managed to inflict heavy damage on the Americans, to elude them, and to escape into the safety of Newport. Captain Howe had shown himself to be not only a fine fighter, but a clever ship handler as well.

The engagement with the *Glasgow* showed the Americans, for their part, to be neither.

In the first place, Hopkins had not bothered to disperse his ships in a proper squadron formation. If he had done that, he might well have trapped the *Glasgow*. Furthermore, during the battle, which lasted for several hours, Hopkins made no attempt to control or coordinate the movement of his fleet. It was a typical privateering operation—that is, every man for himself.

After breaking off the engagement with the *Glasgow*, Hopkins ordered the fleet onto a southwest course intended to bring them into New London. Despite thick fog, on Sunday afternoon, 7 April, the Americans came abreast of New London Light and dropped anchor, and the commodore finished his dispatches for Congress.

His report was well received, as it deserved to be. After all, with marginal warships and inexperienced men, he had managed to sail into enemy waters, land his forces, and return with a considerable store of material. The brush with the *Glasgow* was not a particularly proud moment; but, considered in the context of the entire cruise, it was, if not excusable, at least understandable to members of Congress.

What was neither excusable nor understandable was the commodore's subsequent behavior ashore. Unlike Washington, who once he took command of the army seemed to rise above sectional politics and petty disputes, Esek Hopkins never was able to make that leap. Whatever he might have thought about Congress, the commander-in-chief of the army always consulted with it and kept its members informed of his decisions. Hopkins, on the other hand, seemed more inclined to find ways to annoy them. At New London his ships were crammed with military stores that were continental property. Instead of asking Congress for its pleasure, Hopkins went ahead and wrote to the governors of Rhode Island and Connecticut and offered those gentlemen the stores for the defense of their colonies. It was a foolish and graceless move.

Compounding his problems with Congress were mounting vexations within the fleet. Only a day after the ships arrived at New London, the first wisp of trouble appeared when the crew of the brig *Cabot* presented Hopkins with a round-robin petition asking to be paid. That stir among the enlisted men was soon followed by a storm among the officers.

Ever since they had landed, rumors had circulated about the alleged cowardice or incompetence of certain captains during the engagement with the *Glasgow*. Among them was Hopkins's old and dear friend Abraham Whipple. In the face of these allegations, Whipple asked his commander to summon a court-martial to clear his name. Hopkins agreed, and in its finding the court determined that, indeed, Whipple had made an error during the battle but the fault was "in Judgment and not from Cowardice."[12]

Whipple's trial was only the beginning. Two days after rendering the decision on him, the same court, with the acquitted captain now joining it as a member, heard charges against John Hazard. Hazard was not so fortunate; after hearing the evidence, the court found "The Prisoner, John Hazard Esqr., had rendered himself unworthy of holding his Commission in the Navy of the United States of North America. . . . "[13]

Deserved or not, the spate of courts-martial, petitions, and nagging rumors of unrest put Hopkins in a poor light. Nor was his situation improved when, on the same day that Hazard was being cashiered, Congress had decided to conduct its own investigation into Hopkins's conduct. By congressional order, Hopkins's orders of 5 January were read on the floor and then sent to a special committee to determine if the commodore had in fact complied with them. Southern resentments over his failure to protect the coasts were surfacing and slowly merging with an already festering anti-New England sentiment.

Had Hopkins been able to point to a naval success, he might well have survived the gathering storm. Such was not the case. His fleet was so weakened by disease that he had to "borrow" nearly two hundred soldiers simply to bring his fleet around from New London to Providence. When Washington, who was facing a disaster of his own at New York City, asked for the return of his men, the commodore naturally complied but had to report that their loss made his fleet "useless." He did manage, by stripping all his other ships of men and supplies, to get the *Andrea Doria* and the *Cabot* to sea.

Not the least of Hopkins's problems was the fact that he had moved his fleet to Providence. Aside from the obvious reason that it was home, it is not clear why he decided to make the move. In fact, he probably would have been better off had he remained at New London. In December 1775, Congress had authorized the construction of thirteen frigates; two of these, later to be named the *Providence* 28 and the *Warren* 32, were ordered built in Providence. The construction of these vessels, among the largest yet built in America, consumed huge amounts of money, men, and supplies. Within a short time, the Providence waterfront witnessed a threeway struggle for men and material among Hopkins's fleet, the frigates abuilding, and voracious privateersmen. With such competition, the opportunities for profiteering were enormous, and the local merchants were not slow to take advantage. In the face of such greed, Hopkins was helpless; while others outbid and outmaneuvered him, he could only lament "that Private Interest bears more sway than I wish it did."[14]

Having invested heavily in the Navy, Congress was in no mood to listen to Hopkins's excuses explaining why he and his fleet were still snug in the harbor. After all, other continental captains—John Paul Jones, Nicholas Biddle, and Abraham Whipple—had managed to get to sea during this time. On 14 June, President of the Congress John Hancock, acting on the instructions of the full body, summoned Hopkins, Saltonstall, and Whipple to appear in Philadelphia to answer for their "frequent Neglect or Disobedience of Orders" and the "numberless Complaints against them."[15]

Saltonstall appeared and was let off, the charges being not "well founded." Whipple received a mild rebuke and was told "to cultivate harmony with his officers." It was for Hopkins that Congress saved its full fury. Having been forced to cool his heels for several days, on 12 August he was finally called to defend himself. It was an unpleasant experience. Recalling the scene, John Adams remarked that the affair was yet another example of the rising "Anti New England Spirit, which haunted Congress." Still, even in defending the commodore, Adams had to admit that while he "saw nothing in the Conduct of Hopkins, which indicated Corruption or Want of Integrity . . . Experience and Skill might have been deficient, in several Particulars. . . ."[16]

Lawyer Adams and other New Englanders skillfully defended Hopkins. They were successful in preventing the commodore from being cashiered but not in preventing a grave humiliation: on 16 August, Congress voted "That the said conduct of Commodore Hopkins deserves the censure of this house, and the house does accordingly censure him."[17] With that, Congress sent the commodore back to Providence to resume command. It might better have dismissed him from the service, for his authority and reputation were now so severely eroded that his effectiveness as a commander was reduced to virtually nothing.

For his part, Hopkins vented his wrath on Congress. With great indiscretion, he referred to the gentlemen in Philadelphia in highly unflattering terms, cursing them and calling them "ignorant fellows — lawyers, clerks, persons who don't know how to govern men." He even went so far as to swear that he would not obey the orders of Congress. Naturally, such actions were quick to come to the attention of Congress, where not even his friends could defend the old man's intemperance."[18] On 26 March 1777, Hopkins was suspended from command. He was kept in that limbo until 2 January 1778, when he was summarily dismissed from the service.

Bitter at his firing, but hardly surprised, Hopkins retired to his farm in North Providence. He continued to serve his state as a member of the Assembly from 1777 to 1786 and served as a trustee of Rhode Island College, later renamed Brown University, from 1783 until his death. Never again, though, did he go to sea, and by the time of his death on 26 February 1802, few aside from his neighbors and friends remembered him as the commander-in-chief of the Continental Navy.

Esek Hopkins was an ordinary man who had the misfortune to live in extraordinary times. He was, at heart, a provincial person, loyal to his relatives, friends, and state. His localism blinded him to the greater needs of the revolutionary cause and made him insensitive to the legitimate concerns of other regions, as well as the prerogatives of Congress. Hopkins's decision to attack New Providence rather than the enemy forces harassing the southern colonies, together with his presenting the captured munitions to Connecticut and Rhode Island rather than to the continental government, combined to heighten southern hostility toward the Navy. His infelicitous manner of dealing with Congress compared very unfavorably to Washington's deference, a comparison many were wont to make.

As a commander, Hopkins failed in many respects, but nowhere were his shortcomings more apparent than in his inability to bridle his temper and tongue in the face of congressional control. It was his intemperate behavior toward his civilian superiors more than his failures at sea that eventually caused his professional demise.

Despite his failures, Hopkins ought not to be judged too harshly. His provincialism was perhaps no greater than that of many of his contemporaries. Most of those who fought in the Revolution thought of themselves as Virginians, Georgians, Rhode Islanders—the concept of being an American was still in its infancy. Furthermore, it is difficult to imagine how any officer in Hopkins's position could have effectively controlled the pack of rascally privateersmen put under his command. The debacle with the *Glasgow* was a product of both his and his officers' inexperience, whereas the scandalous business in Providence was not of his doing.

In attempting to create a naval force, Congress was trying to build a preposterous structure on a pitiful foundation. Navies are expensive and complex; the Americans had neither the material resources nor the manpower to put an effective force to sea. It is true that the American Revolution was decided at sea but not by the American cockleshells; rather, the decisive battles were fought by the wooden giants of Great Britain, France, and Spain.

If the Continental Navy had never existed, it is hard to see how the outcome of the Revolution could have been any different. But a citation of failures should not be read as a condemnation of effort. As a contributor to the American naval tradition, Esek Hopkins ought to be remembered as a man who was asked to do the impossible and failed.

FURTHER READING

There is only one full-length biography of Esek Hopkins: Edward Field, *Esek Hopkins, Commander-in-Chief of the Continental Navy during the American Revolution, 1775–1778* (Providence, R.I., 1898). It is, unfortunately, a very uncritical work written more as a defense of Hopkins than as an examination of his life. This ought to be supplemented by William James Morgan, *Captains to the Northward: The New England*

*Captains in the Continental Navy* (Barre, Vt., 1959), a series of very good biographical sketches.

Field drew quite heavily upon the Hopkins manuscripts at the Rhode Island Historical Society, which were later edited by Alverda S. Beck and published as *The Letter Book of Esek Hopkins, Commander-in-Chief of the United States Navy, 1775–1777* (Providence, R.I., 1932), and *Correspondence of Esek Hopkins, Commander-in-Chief of the United States Navy* (Providence, R.I., 1933). These papers also provide the source material for several articles written about Hopkins, but none of these is particularly useful. The best brief treatment on Hopkins and the Nassau expedition is John J. McCusker, Jr., Alfred: *The First Continental Flagship* (Washington, D.C., 1973).

Published documentary material for the Continental Navy is in good supply. First among these sources is the superb William Bell Clark and William James Morgan, eds., *Naval Documents of the American Revolution*, 10 vols. to date (Washington, D.C., 1964–). Scholars interested in Hopkins should also consult Charles Oscar Paullin, ed., *Out-Letters of the Continental Marine Committee and Board of Admiralty, August, 1776–September, 1780*, 2 vols. (New York, 1914), and W. C. Ford, ed., *Journals of the Continental Congress, 1774–1789*, 34 vols. (Washington, D.C., 1904–1936), supplemented by the National Archives microfilm edition of the *Papers of the Continental Congress*, The Rhode Island Continental Congress political settings are discussed in the author's *William Ellery: A Rhode Island Politico & Lord of Admiralty* (Metuchen, N.J., 1973).

NOTES

1. Edward Field, *Esek Hopkins, Commander-in-Chief of the Continental Navy during the American Revolution, 1775–1778* (Providence, R.I., 1898) 1–35.

2. W. C. Ford, ed., *Journals of the Continental Congress, 1774–1789*, 34 vols. (Washington D.C., 1904–1936) 2:15, 68–70, 89, 91, 93, 209 (hereafter cited as JCC).

3. John R. Bartlett, ed., *Records of the Colony of Rhode Island and Providence Plantations in New England*, 10 vols. (Providence, 1856–1865) 7:347.

4. L. H. Butterfield, ed., *Diary and Autobiography of John Adams*, 4 vols. (New York, 1964) 2:198.

5. JCC, 3:293–94.

6. Butterfield, *Diary*, 3:350.

7. JCC, 3:315–18.

8. Ibid., 378–87.

9. William Bell Clark and William James Morgan, eds., *Naval Documents of the American Revolution*, 10 vols. to date (Washington, D.C., 1964–) 3:636–38 (hereafter cited as NDAR).

10. John J. McCusker, Jr., "The American Invasion of Nassau in the Bahamas," *The American Neptune* 25 (1965): 189–217.

11. For reports detailing the *Glasgow* engagement, see NDAR, vol. 4, passim.

12. Court Martial of Abraham Whipple, NDAR, 4:1419–21.

13. Court Martial of John Hazard, NDAR, 4:1458–59.

14. Hopkins to Marine Committee, 2 November 1776, in NDAR, 7:17.

15. John Hancock to Hopkins, 14 June 1776, in NDAR, 5:528–30.

16. Butterfield, *Diary*, 3:405–6.

17. JCC, 5:660–62.

18. Field, *Esek Hopkins*, 189.

# ☆ John Paul Jones
☆
## ☆ Honor and Professionalism
☆

*by James C. Bradford*

As the strains of "The Star-Spangled Banner" died, Secretary of the Navy Charles J. Bonaparte rose, walked to the lectern, and began to speak. "We have met to honor the memory of that man who gave our Navy its earliest traditions of heroism and victory." With these words, the Secretary began his introduction of the President of the United States, Theodore Roosevelt, the first of several dignitaries to deliver addresses at the 1906 commemorative exercises held in honor of John Paul Jones at the U.S. Naval Academy. Before the podium stood a star-draped casket containing the body of John Paul Jones, recently returned to the United States after lying for more than a century in an unmarked grave in France. Upon the casket lay a wreath of laurel, a spray of palm, and the sword presented to Jones by Louis XVI of France in honor of his victory over the *Serapis*.

The ceremony's date had been selected by President Roosevelt—24 April, the 128th anniversary of Jones's capture of the *Drake*—and the observance in Annapolis capped a series of activities that included a White House reception and an official visit by a French naval squadron. Congress ordered the publication of a commemorative volume whose introduction stated, "There is no event in our history attended with such pomp and circumstances of glory, magnificence, and patriotic fervor."[1] This may have verged on hyperbole, but there can be no doubt that the splendor surrounding America's reception of the remains of John Paul Jones, and their reinterment in a crypt below the chapel of the U.S. Naval Academy, contrasted sharply with the treatment accorded him at the time of his death in Paris.

*The author wishes to thank Dale T. Knobel for his advice and comments on this essay.*

In July 1792, as Jones lay mortally ill in rented rooms near the Luxembourg Palace, America's Minister to France, Gouverneur Morris, seemed to have trouble finding time between social activities for a visit to his deathbed. In his diary, Morris recorded: "A Message from Paul Jones that he is dying. I go thither and make his Will. . . . Send for a Notary and leave him struggling with his Enemy between four and five. Dine en famille with Lord Gower and Lady Sutherland. Go to the Minister of the Marine's. . . . I go to the Louvre. . . . Take [my mistress] and Vic d'Azyr [a physician] to Jones's Lodgings but he is dead, not yet cold."[2]

Morris ordered Jones's landlord to arrange for as private and inexpensive a burial as possible, but others interceded, and the French Legislative Assembly, wishing to "assist at the funeral rites of a man who has served so well the cause of liberty," took charge of the arrangements. Two days later, a cortege of soldiers, representatives of the Assembly, and Masonic brethren from the Lodge of the Nine Sisters accompanied Jones's body to the Protestant cemetery outside the city walls for interment. Gouverneur Morris was giving a dinner party that evening and did not attend. Such was the sad ending to the life of the man whom Benjamin Franklin had once considered the chief weapon of American forces in Europe and whom Thomas Jefferson had described as the "principal hope" of Americans in their struggle for independence. What kind of a man was Jones to be so heralded during his lifetime, ignored at the time of his death, and honored a century later?

The answer is complex, just as Jones was complex. From humble origins he rose through sheer force of character and combat success to prominence in the Continental Navy. More than any other American of his era, he wrote about naval policy and offered suggestions to foster professionalism in the service; but congressional leaders refused to heed his advice. When the war ended, the Continental Navy was disbanded and its officers returned to civilian endeavors. The transition was difficult for Jones. For a few years, he served the United States as a diplomat, but he was a military man whose ambition focused on naval command. When he accepted service in the Russian navy of Catherine the Great to increase his naval knowledge, there were those who mocked his earlier contention that he fought in the American Revolution for the cause of liberty. When he died in Paris, he seemed a man passed by time.

If Jones feared he would be forgotten by history, he need not have. His image might change, but his name was etched on the Anglo-American memory. For a century, Americans would recall him as a battle leader, a brave, almost foolhardy captain who inspired his men with "I have not yet begun to fight." To Britons his name conjured up images of treason and piracy. But this would change. At the start of the twentieth century, when the United States was building a modern navy and Britain and America were drawing closer together, this image began to shift. Britons began to view Jones more positively, and Americans rediscovered his ideas. With these changes came a desire to know more about all aspects of Jones's life, a life of enough adventure to satisfy any biographer.

John Paul Jones rose from humble stock, a fact he seems never to have forgotten. Born in 1747, the fifth child of a gardener, John Paul, as he was then known, received only a rudimentary education. His father worked for William Craik, owner of "Arbigland," an estate on the Scottish shore of the Solway Firth. Young Paul's contacts with Craik and other area landowners helped instill in him a desire to better his position in society. There being little chance for advancement at home, John Paul was apprenticed at age thirteen to a shipowner from Whitehaven, a town on the Cumbrian coast of the Solway.

His first voyage took him to Fredericksburg, Virginia, where his older brother, William, was a tailor. A number of voyages between England, the West Indies, and the Chesapeake followed until his master went bankrupt and released Paul from his apprenticeship. At least his next two voyages were on board slavers, but he could not long abide what he called that "abominable trade," and in 1768 took passage home from Kingston, Jamaica. En route, both the ship's master and mate died of a fever, and Paul assumed command. The owners rewarded him by giving him permanent command of the vessel, the sixty-ton brig *John*.

Only twenty-one years old, John Paul had risen quickly. His biggest handicaps were his temper and his inability to get along with people whom he considered incompetent or lazy. In 1770, on a voyage from Scotland to Tobago, he had Mungo Maxwell, the son of a prominent resident of Kirkcudbright, Scotland, flogged for neglect of duty. Maxwell lodged a complaint against John Paul with authorities in Tobago, but it was dismissed. Maxwell then boarded a packet ship for home but died from a fever en route. Learning of his son's death, Maxwell's father had Paul arrested on a charge of having inflicted fatal wounds on his son. John Paul was jailed briefly before being allowed bail to gather evidence that cleared his name.

In the meantime, he joined the Masons in Kirkcudbright, probably with the knowledge that membership was a step up socially and that it could help clear any blemish on his character left from the Maxwell affair. Years later, his Masonic membership would open doors to him in Boston, Portsmouth, Philadelphia, and Paris.[3] By age twenty-five, John Paul formed a partnership with a merchant-planter in Tobago and commanded ships in the triangular trade between Britain and her colonies in North America and the Caribbean. In 1773 his crew mutinied and he killed the ringleader in self-defense. Friends in Tobago advised him to "retire incognito to the continent of America and remain there until an Admiralty Commission should arrive in the Island" to hear his case. The young captain took their advice, fled to Virginia, and adopted the surname "Jones" as a precaution.[4]

Still in Fredericksburg at the outbreak of the Revolution, Jones traveled to Philadelphia where he became friendly with Joseph Hewes, a congressman from North Carolina, whose partner was a brother of Jones's sponsor when he joined the Masons. Through Hewes, he obtained a commission as senior lieutenant in the Continental Navy on 7 December 1775. When offered command of the sloop *Providence* (of twenty-one guns), he refused and chose instead to serve on board the frigate *Alfred* (with thirty guns) in the hope that he could expand his knowledge of ship handling and fleet maneuvering. It was characteristic of Jones throughout his career to seek such opportunities to add to his professional education. In this capacity he took part in the New Providence raid and the squadron's engagement of HMS *Glasgow*. The latter convinced him that he had nothing to learn from Esek Hopkins, the commander-in-chief of the Continental Navy. When he was again offered command of the *Providence* in the shuffling of positions that followed the *Glasgow* affair, he eagerly accepted.

Assigned to convoy and transport duty in May and June 1776, Jones set sail on his first independent cruise in August. Operating off the Grand Banks, he captured sixteen British prizes and destroyed the local fishing fleets at Canso and Isle Madame in Nova Scotia. In recognition of his achievement, he was promoted to the rank of captain on 10 October 1776 and transferred to command of the *Alfred*. In a second cruise to the Grand Banks, Jones took seven more prizes, including the armed transport *Mellish* and her much needed cargo of winter uniforms.

Upon his return to port, Jones learned that he had been placed eighteenth on the seniority list established by Congress and that he had been reassigned to the *Providence*. Incensed, Jones wrote letters of complaint to congressmen, charging in one of them that several men placed senior to him were "altogether illiterate and utterly ignorant of marine affairs."[5]

Congress had not purposely slighted Jones when it compiled the list; clearly, he was the most successful officer to date. Family relationships and place of residence, not ability, were the main criteria. The four most senior officers on the 1775 list were related to members of the congressional committee that directed naval affairs. The 10 October 1776 list was drawn up shortly after Congress had ordered the building of thirteen frigates, and, in order to enlist local support in the construction of the vessels and to facilitate the recruitment of sailors, local men were assigned to command the vessels. Jones was an outsider. He had no relative in Congress to press his appointment, no shipyard interest to support him, and no local community to put forward his name. This may have saved him from the provincialism of an Esek Hopkins, but it certainly did not help him gain advancement.

It is perhaps of more note that his name appears on the list at all than that it appears so low. But it is also natural that Jones should resent what he took to be a slight. That he should continue to complain throughout the war of what he considered to be an insult is a testament to his personal sense of honor, though he also believed that there was a principle involved. Jones regarded the existing system as unfair and wanted to replace it with one based on merit and seniority. "Perhaps it would have been good policy to have commissioned five or seven old mariners who had seen War, to have examined the qualifications of the candidates . . . ," he wrote. At the least, no officer should have been superseded by another unless such a change in seniority was based on the proven abilities of the men involved.[6]

Jones traveled to Philadelphia and pressed his case without success. He also proposed a strategy for carrying the war beyond American waters. Specifically, he suggested a voyage along the unprotected coasts of Africa to prey on British trading outposts and the India fleet. Robert Morris, speaking for Congress, endorsed such an overseas strategy but suggested that the Caribbean was a better place to attack the British than Africa.[7] When plans for the Caribbean expedition were canceled—through the jealousy and backwardness of Esek Hopkins, Jones suspected—he was given command of the *Ranger,* a sloop-of-war under construction in Portsmouth, New Hampshire.[8]

For months, Jones worked to ready the *Ranger* for sea. Cordage, sails, and cannon were collected from all over New England.[9] Though he anticipated only a single voyage in the ship—once in Europe his orders called for him to take command of a frigate under construction in Holland—Jones took great pains in his work. A perfectionist, he was rarely satisfied with the condition of a ship when he took command. His seasoned eye told him that the *Ranger* was too lightly built to carry the twenty guns her sides were pierced for, and he reduced the number to eighteen.

On 1 November 1777, the outfitting and alterations complete and a crew enlisted, Jones set sail for Europe. The passage was not used for resting after the months of work on the ship but for exercising his officers and crew. Jones was a hard but fair commander who had the best interests of the entire ship's company at heart. "The care . . . of our seamen is a consideration of the first magnitude," he wrote to Robert Morris soon after his arrival in France.[10] Before proceeding to Paris, Jones advanced spending money to the crew from his own account, ordered the purchase of fresh meat and vegetables for them, purchased new sails for the *Ranger,* altered her rig, and reballasted her.

In mid-December he was summoned to the capital by the American commissioners to France. Jones quickly became friends with the first two of them, Benjamin Franklin and Silas Deane, but, probably because of this, did not enjoy good relations with Arthur Lee. The divisions among the commissioners reflected political alignments in Congress. Because of the friendships he had developed with Morris, Franklin, and other members of the Middle States faction, Jones became almost anathema to many of the Adams-Lee faction, of which Arthur Lee and John Adams, who succeeded Deane, were principals.

Jones was disappointed to learn that the ship promised to him would not be available because the British had learned of her intended use and convinced the Dutch not to deliver her to the Americans. He then sought and obtained orders from the commissioners allowing him to retain command of the *Ranger* and to "proceed with [her] in the manner you shall judge best, for distressing the enemies of the United States by sea, or otherwise."[11] The final phrase reflects Jones's strategic ideas. The Continental Navy could best contribute to victory by preying on British commerce and raiding Britain's coast. The Royal Navy should be left to the French, who had a fleet capable of engaging it in a pitched battle. Thinking in broad strategic terms, Jones proposed a plan to bring the war to a speedy close:

> Were any continental marine power in Europe disposed to avail of the present situation of affairs in America . . . a single blow would now do the needful. Ten or twelve sail of the line with frigates . . . would give a good account of the fleet under Lord Howe. . . . Small squadrons might then be formed to secure the coast and cut off the enemies supplies while our army settled the account current.[12]

Jones's ideas were ahead of their time. The French had greater interests in the West Indies, but his belief that a French fleet in American waters could bring victory was correct.

In February and March, Jones cruised the Bay of Biscay to prey upon British commerce and familiarize himself with the area. On 14 February 1778, during a visit to Quiberon Bay, he arranged the first official salute of the American flag by a foreign power. Early in April he set sail for the Irish Sea with plans to raid a coastal town to repay Britain for her raids on towns in Connecticut and to seize one or more prisoners who could be exchanged for American seamen held in British prisons. Jones was always concerned about Americans so incarcerated. One of his objections to the use of privateers was the fact that they captured so few English seamen who could be used to gain prisoners' release.[13]

Within a month Jones fulfilled both his goals, though not in the way he had planned. On the night of 22 April, he led an attack on Whitehaven where he spiked the guns of the fort and set fire to colliers in the harbor. The damage was minimal in financial terms, but the alarm it spread was great. Not for over a century, since the Dutch burned Sheerness in 1667, had foreign forces so treated a British seaport.

On the following day, he led a party ashore on St. Mary's Isle in Kirkcud-bright Bay, across the Solway Firth. Jones planned to seize the Earl of Selkirk as a hostage to force the release of Americans held prisoner by Britain. To a boy raised in a nearby gardener's cottage, the earl seemed worthy of such a price. In fact, he was a minor Scots peer at best and by his own admission "scarce known" to the king. When Jones learned from a servant that the earl was away, he ordered his men back to their ship, but the men "were disposed to pillage, burn, and plunder all they could," and refused to obey. Faced with mutiny, Jones proposed that a small group go to the house and "politely de-mand the family plate." His plan was accepted, the silver taken, and violence averted. In a letter to Lady Selkirk written upon his return to France, Jones in-formed her of his original plan to kidnap the earl, promised to purchase and return the plate, and explained his motives:

> It was my intention to have taken [the earl] on board the Ranger, and to have detained him till thro' his means, a general and fair Exchange of Pris-oners, as well in Europe as in America had been effected. . . . I have drawn my Sword in the present generous Struggle for the right of Men; yet I am not in Arms as an American, nor am I in pursuit of Riches . . . I profess my-self a Citizen of the World.

Some of Jones's contemporaries and many historians since have discount-ed his claim to have fought for the "rights of men" and to be a "Citizen of the World," sentiments he would repeat on a number of occasions. To do so is wrong. Such statements were common during the Enlightenment. Thomas Jefferson, Samuel Adams, and Edward Gibbon expressed similar ideas, and James Otis adopted "Ubi Libertas, Ibi Patria," meaning "Where liberty is, there is my country," as his motto. Jones was as serious as any of them when he stated the idea, though he may have been a bit naive in stating it thus in a let-ter. He certainly made himself appear foolish when, later in the letter, he said to Lady Selkirk: "Let not therefore the Amiable Countess of Selkirk regard me as an Enemy. I am ambitious of her esteem and Friendship, and would do any-thing consistent with my duty to merit it." It was important to him that the Selkirks consider him a gentleman. In his biography of Jones, Admiral Mori-son speculates that Jones might have even thought of returning to live in the area after the war.[14]

The Earl of Selkirk did not prove to be the key to gaining the release of American prisoners, but the action of the next day did effect the freedom of some of them. On 24 April 1778, Jones crossed the Irish Sea to Carrickfergus where he enticed HMS Drake into battle. It was an even match: the Drake mounted twenty, six-pounders and the Ranger eighteen, nine-pounders, but the Drake had more men. Jones concluded that it was in his interest to disable the *Drake* with cannon fire and prevent her from closing, so that her larger crew could not board the *Ranger*. Such tactics would also preserve the value of the sloop as a prize.

In an hour-long action described by Jones as "warm close and obstinate," the captain of the *Drake* was killed, her second in command mortally wounded, and her rigging virtually cut to pieces. When the *Drake* surrendered, a more cautious captain might have burned his prize and sailed away before the Royal Navy could send ships after them, but not Jones. Understanding the impact that a British prize would have on the French if brought into port, he calmly remained in sight of the coast for most of the next night and day and refitted the badly damaged *Drake*. Finally, on 8 May, he led the prize ship into Brest "with English Colours inverted under the American Stars." On board were two hundred prisoners, who were later exchanged for Americans held in Forton and Old Mill prisons in England.[15]

The entire cruise was a huge success. "What was done," Jones said later, "is sufficient to show that not all their boasted navy can protect their own coast, and that the scene of distress which they have occasioned in America may soon be brought home to their own shores." The Royal Navy and the British government might assail him as a pirate, but Americans knew better. John Banister, a Virginia delegate to Congress, called his attack on Whitehaven "intrepid & bold," saying that it gave the British "a small specimen of that Conflagration & distress, we have so often experienced from our Enemies, in a much higher degree." Fellow delegate James Lovell recognized the strategic value of the attack when he wrote that Jones's "conduct alone will make England keep her ships at home."[16]

If Jones expected immediate recognition and promotion as a reward for his actions, he was disappointed. The Continental Congress had few ships to assign, and Jones was too far away to press his claim, in any case. The American commissioners in France, especially Benjamin Franklin, appreciated his achievements but commanded even fewer resources, a fact not fully appreciated by Jones. In June, the French Minister of Marine called Jones to Paris to discuss various operations, but nothing was agreed upon, and Jones returned to Brest where he sought to make profitable use of his time.[17] He had by this time become proficient enough in French that he felt comfortable using the language. He undoubtedly brought to mastering it the same determination that characterized his self-study of every subject that he considered of value to a naval officer. When word arrived of the outbreak of war between Great Britain and France, Jones sought permission to join the French fleet as an observer to study fleet maneuvering and battle tactics firsthand. To his displeasure, permission did not arrive before the fleet sailed, and Jones missed the chance to observe the Battle of Ushant.

The search for a suitable command for Jones continued. The task was not easy. Several vessels were suggested but rejected. "I wish to have no connection with any Ship that does not Sail *fast* for I intend to go in harm's way," wrote Jones.[18] Finally, a ship was found. She was an old East Indiaman, the *Duc de Duras*, which Jones almost wholly rebuilt and transformed into the *Bonhomme Richard*, renamed in honor of his friend and patron Benjamin Franklin.

Jones proposed "several plans related to different important operations [that he] wanted to undertake" in the vessel, but "was not reluctant" when asked in early April to join the Marquis de Lafayette in launching a raid on Liverpool.[19] Work continued on the *Richard* and the ships assigned to join her, but in May, France and Spain agreed to a joint invasion of England and the Jones-Lafayette expedition, was canceled.[20] In June, Jones made a cruise of the Bay of Biscay, and, after some changes in the crew and recovery from the first illness to strike him in years, he was ready to execute his own plans.

On 14 August, he put to sea from L'Orient with a squadron composed of the frigates *Bonhomme Richard* (with forty guns), *Alliance* (with thirty-six guns), and *Pallas* (with thirty-two guns) and the corvette *Vengeance* (with twelve guns), the cutter *Cerf* (with eighteen guns), and two privateers that left the squadron soon after it sailed. Jones planned first to intercept ships expected from India, then to lay Leith, the port city of Edinburgh, under contribution, and finally to intercept the Baltic convoy laden with naval stores. He proceeded clockwise around the British Isles, taking seventeen prizes before he reached the southeast coast of Scotland. Two of the prizes were sent into the neutral port of Bergen in Norway.

Almost a month to the day later—on 13 September—Jones, with the *Richard*, *Alliance*, and *Pallas*, was off the Firth of Forth. Writing later, he assessed his position and stated goals in the enterprise:

> Though much weakened and embarrassed with prisoners, [I] was anxious to teach the enemy humanity, by some exemplary stroke of retaliation, and to relieve the remainder of the Americans from captivity in England, as well as to make a diversion in the north, to favour a formidable descent which [I] then expected would have been made on the south side of Great Britain, under cover of the combined [French and Spanish] fleet.[21]

His plan was to sail up the Firth to Leith where he would put a small party ashore and demand payment of two hundred thousand pounds, under the threat that otherwise the town would be burned. On the point of the plan's execution, Jones reported, a "sudden storm rose and obliged me to run before the wind out of the Gulf of Edinburgh."[22] Jones next attempted to convince his captains to attack the city of Newcastle-on-Tyne to destroy coal supplies destined for London. Seeing no profit in such a plan, his subordinates refused but, after further pleading from Jones, agreed instead to cruise along the Yorkshire coast to prey on British shipping.

On 23 September, between two and three in the afternoon, a fleet of forty-one sail was sighted off Flamborough Head. Jones realized immediately that this had to be the sought-after Baltic convoy and set course to engage. As the wind was very light, he was not able to close with the enemy until dark. There ensued one of the hottest naval engagements in the Age of Sail.

The opponents appeared to be evenly matched. The *Serapis*, rated at forty-four guns, actually carried fifty and was supported by the twenty-gun *Countess of Scarborough*. The *Bonhomme Richard* was rated at forty-four guns, like the *Serapis*, but, in fact, carried only forty. With the eighty guns, total, of the *Alliance*, the *Pallas*, and the *Vengeance* to support him, Jones should have had an advantage. However, the *Vengeance* took no part in the battle, and the *Alliance*, captained by the erratic Pierre Landais, did nothing to support the American effort; on the contrary, her only part in the battle was to fire three broadsides into the *Bonhomme Richard*.

In addition, the *Serapis* was a newer (less than six months off the stocks), faster, and more maneuverable ship, and her crew of Englishmen were almost certainly superior to Jones's polyglot mix of 174 French, 79 Americans, 59 English, 29 Portuguese, 21 Irish, and representatives of six other nationalities.

By seven o'clock, the *Richard* and the *Serapis* were within pistol range of one another and opened fire almost simultaneously. On the first or second broadside, two of Jones's eighteen-pounders exploded, killing their crews and blowing a hole in the deck above. Fearing the other eighteen-pounders would also explode, Jones abandoned his main battery. Now sensing that his only hope for victory lay in boarding the more powerful *Serapis*, Jones ran the *Richard* against the starboard quarter of the *Serapis* and ordered his men to board. The British drove the Americans back, and Jones sheered off to seek a better position. When Captain Richard Pearson of the *Serapis* tried to cross the *Richard*'s bow to rake her, Jones ran the bow into the *Serapis*'s stern.

Cannonading continued with, in Jones's words, "unremitting fury," the *Richard* receiving most of the damage. The American flag was shot away, and Captain Pearson shouted, "Has your ship struck?" Jones responded with his immortal, "I have not yet begun to fight."

Their ships entangled, the two captains continued to maneuver as best they could until Jones was able to get the two vessels lashed together bow to stern. With his own hands he tied a loose forestay from the *Serapis* to his mizzenmast. "Well done, my brave lads," he cried, "we have got her now." For two hours the ships lay in deadly embrace with the *Serapis* pouring devastating cannon fire into the *Richard* while the seamen and French marines of the *Richard* swept the enemy's deck with small arms and swivels. Remaining on the quarterdeck, Jones directed fire and worked with the gun crew of a nine-pounder. Near exhaustion, he rested for a moment on a hen coop. A sailor begged him, "For God's sake, Captain, strike." "No," responded Jones, "I will sink, I will never strike," and he jumped to his feet.

At ten o'clock the battle swung in favor of the Americans when a grenade thrown from one of the *Richard's* yardarms fell through an open hatch on board the *Serapis* and, exploding among a pile of loose cartridges, killed at least twenty British sailors, horribly burned others, and caused panic on the gun deck.

Jones then focused the fire of his three remaining nine-pounders on the enemy's mainmast. Growing desperate, Captain Pearson ordered his men to board the *Richard*. They were thrown back, and he sought to continue the battle, but within half an hour his mainmast began to tremble. Seeing no hope of victory, he surrendered. The casualties were high. Between seventy-five and eighty died in each ship during the three-and-a-half-hour battle, and some 100 others were wounded. Thus, almost half of the *Bonhomme Richard's* crew of 322 were casualties, and Captain Pearson lost almost the same number of the *Serapis's* 325-man crew. Lieutenant Richard Dale boarded the *Serapis*, and Jones, in a typical eighteenth-century gesture, invited Richard Pearson to his cabin for a glass of wine.[23]

Meanwhile, the crews of both ships worked frantically to extinguish fires and patch holes. In a memoir, Midshipman Nathaniel Fanning described the "shocking sight" of "the dead lying in heaps . . . the groans of the wounded and the dying . . . the entrails of the dead scattered promiscuously around, [and] the blood over ones shoes." For two days, Jones tried to save the *Bonhomme Richard*, but she was "mangled beyond my power of description," and "with inexpressible grief" he watched her sink into the North Sea.[24] For a week the battered ships drifted and sailed across the North Sea. Jones wanted to try to reach the French port of Dunkirk, but the captains of the *Alliance, Pallas,* and *Vengeance* insisted on going directly across the sea to the Texel in Holland and arrived there on 3 October. A combination of foul weather and good fortune allowed the squadron, including the *Countess of Scarborough,* which had been captured by the *Pallas* while Jones battled the *Serapis,* to escape the dozen British ships sent in their pursuit.

Most of the Royal Navy's ships searched the English and Scottish coasts in response to wild rumors and false sightings. When the Admiralty learned that Jones was in the Texel, ships were sent to blockade the port. Now something of a celebrity, Jones was both hated and admired in Britain. "Paul Jones resembled a Jack o' Lantern, to mislead our marines and terrify our coasts," said London's *Morning Post.* He is "still the most general topic of conversation," the paper said a month later. Poems and ballads celebrated his victory and attacked him as a traitor.[25]

In America, news of his victory was eagerly embraced; 1779 had not been a good year for American arms. The Dutch people greeted Jones as a hero. He was applauded when he attended the theater, and crowds gathered when he walked the streets. British ambassador Sir Joseph Yorke was appalled at his reception and demanded that Jones be forced to leave Holland and that the Dutch government turn the *Serapis* and the *Countess of Scarborough* over to the Royal Navy. Jones, supported by France's ambassador, asked that he be allowed to land his sick and wounded, send his 504 British prisoners ashore, and repair his ships so that he could put to sea. For the next two months Jones was the center of partisan political maneuvering in Amsterdam where the House of Orange was basically friendly to Britain and the Patriot Party favored France and sympathized with the United States. Some Dutch officials even suspected that Jones had been sent to Holland to try to provoke a war between Britain and the Netherlands.[26]

Jones had no desire to remain in Dutch waters and made his repairs as quickly as possible. He did try, unsuccessfully, to trade his English captives for Americans held in British prisons, but otherwise he focused his attention on his men and ships. Finally, he was forced to turn control of his prisoners and ships over to the French and set sail in the *Alliance* on 27 December. Leaving the Texel, Jones called his officers together and informed them that he planned to cruise for twenty days before going to L'Orient. "Gentlemen," he told them, "you cannot conceive what an additional honour it will be to us all, if in cruising a few days we should have the good luck to fall in with an English frigate of our force and carry her in with us. . . . This would crown our former victories, and our names, in consequence thereof would be handed down to the latest posterity."

His crew was hesitant, indeed near mutiny, but Jones imposed his will upon them, and the *Alliance* sailed through the English Channel and on to Corunna, Spain, where she took on supplies and made repairs before crossing the Bay of Biscay to arrive at L'Orient on 19 February. Jones immediately set the crew to making alterations in the ship that he felt had been shown essential by the cruise. Many of his crew did not believe the work was necessary and had an additional grievance: they had not been paid either wages or prize money since they left America almost a year before. This latter was not Jones's fault, but the crew blamed him, and, in mid-April, he set out for Paris to see if he could obtain funds either from the American commissioner or from Le Ray de Chaumont, the French agent who had handled the financial arrangements for fitting out the *Bonhomme Richard* squadron.[27]

Jones proved unable to obtain money but was flattered by the welcome he received. His capture of the *Serapis* contrasted sharply with the failure of the combined French and Spanish fleet. His personal conduct during the battle appealed to the French sense of valor, and all Paris lionized him. Louis XVI awarded him the Ordre du Mérite Militaire and presented him a gold-hilted sword. France's leading Masons, the brethren of the Lodge of the Nine Sisters, invited Jones to join and engaged the renowned Jean-Antoine Houdon to sculpt his bust. Crowds applauded him everywhere he went. A handsome war hero, fluent in French and genteel in manner, Jones was in great demand for dinners and receptions. His wit became famous. At a dinner given in his honor by the Duc de Biron, Jones was informed that the king of England had recently knighted Richard Pearson for his conduct during the battle with Jones; and Jones replied, "Let me fight him again and I'll make him a lord!" Women seemed to be irresistibly drawn to Jones, who often responded with poetry. His six weeks in the capital flew by.

In June, Jones returned to L'Orient with plans to sail to America with a cargo of military supplies. In his absence, Pierre Landais had been busy undermining Jones's command of the *Alliance* by telling the crew that Jones was acting in league with Chaumont to deny them their prize money. Arthur Lee was in L'Orient ready to sail to America and promised to use his influence with Congress to help them get their wages if they backed Landais. Benjamin Franklin warned Jones that trouble was brewing, but Jones seems to have underestimated the gravity of the situation and allowed himself to be outmaneuvered. Landais took control of the ship and sailed in June. Most of the sailors who had served on board the *Bonhomme Richard* under Jones were left behind and formed the nucleus of a crew for the *Ariel*, a sloop-of-war built for the British navy but captured by the French and lent to the United States to carry supplies to America. When given command of the *Ariel*, Jones was, as usual, dissatisfied with the ship and ordered her rerigged, thus further delaying his departure.

While the *Ariel* lay at anchor, the *Independence*, an American privateer, entered the harbor under the command of Thomas Truxtun. Like many other privateers, Truxtun had little respect for the Continental Navy and thus refused to accord to Jones and the *Ariel* the traditional signal of respect. Rankled, Jones sent an officer to remind Truxtun of the congressional resolution prohibiting privateers and merchant vessels from flying pennants when in the presence of ships of the Continental Navy. When Truxtun refused to remove the pennant, Jones wrote to him, "It is not me you have offended. You have offended the United States of America," and sent his first lieutenant, Richard Dale, and two boatloads of seamen to forcibly haul it down. When Truxtun again flew the pennant, Jones sent a letter to the Board of Admiralty describing the incident and asking, "Is not this bidding defiance to Congress and the Continental Flag?" There is no evidence that Congress took any action on Jones's complaint, but Truxtun's biographer believes that the incident had an effect on

Truxtun, who "put some of Jones's ideas away in the corner of his mind" and recalled them later when he became the commander of an American man-of-war.[28]

Work was finally finished on the *Ariel* in September, and Jones put to sea only to be caught in a vicious gale that destroyed ships along the entire Breton coast. The survival of the *Ariel* was due to Jones's consummate seamanship. The French commander of the port of L'Orient wrote: "The Commodore showed in this gale the same strength that he had exhibited in battle. . . . The crew and passengers all credit him with saving the ship."[29] The *Ariel* lost two masts, and repairs delayed Jones's departure so that he did not reach America until February 1781.

Upon his arrival in Philadelphia, a group of congressmen sought to launch an investigation of Jones's conduct in France to show that it had delayed the sending of supplies to America. They hoped through Jones to embarrass Benjamin Franklin but abandoned their plan when it appeared it might backfire. Instead, they decided to have Jones examined in private by the Board of Admiralty. The secretary of the board gave Jones forty-seven questions to which he skillfully responded, giving a detailed account of his triumphs and laying blame for any delays on Landais and Chaumont.

Governmental restraint soon turned to acclaim as France's ambassador formally invested Jones with the eight-pointed star of the Ordre du Mérite Militaire, the highest award the French could give to a foreigner. Congress showed its regard for Jones by voting "that the thanks of the United States in Congress assembled, be given to Captain John Paul Jones, for the zeal, prudence and intrepidity with which he has supported the honor of the American flag; [and] for his bold and successful enterprizes to redeem from captivity the citizens of these states." Jones was particularly pleased by the last section. Congress rewarded him more concretely by voting unanimously to give him command of the *America*, the Continental Navy's only ship-of-the-line, then building at Portsmouth, New Hampshire.[30]

In mid-August, Jones left Philadelphia for Portsmouth where he arrived on the last day of the month. For a year Jones struggled to find the supplies and skilled workmen necessary to ready the *America* for launching, but, just as she was ready for sea, command of the ship was taken from him. Peace negotiations were under way with the British, and the war seemed almost over. The Continental Congress, even shorter on funds than usual, doubted the need for the ship. When a French ship-of-the-line was lost on a sandbar outside Boston Harbor, Congress voted to give the *America* to the French navy as a replacement.[31] Jones supervised her launching on 5 November 1782 and, two days later, set out for Philadelphia. Unable to procure another command, Jones sought and was given permission to join a French fleet for a cruise to the Caribbean.

As in 1778, his goal was to increase his professional knowledge by firsthand study of fleet maneuvering and French naval tactics. Jones sailed with the fleet on Christmas Eve 1782 for what turned out to be a mixed experience. The wardroom company must have been pleasant, but for part of the voyage Jones was gravely ill. He was able to observe fleet evolutions, but there was no combat. When the fleet reached Puerto Cabello, Venezuela, it learned that a peace treaty had been signed with Britain. From there, Jones sailed to Cape Haitien, where, sick again, he left the ship.

By May, Jones was back in Philadelphia, his health so bad that Robert Morris feared for his life; and in July, he entered a sanatorium in nearby Bethlehem where he remained for more than a month — thinking, perhaps brooding, about the future. Back in March he had tried to purchase an estate in New Jersey, and, in August, he wrote to a friend that "I hope that I have occasion 'to learn War no more,'" indicating that he hoped to visit Portsmouth, New Hampshire, in the fall.[32]

Such thoughts of domesticity may have been induced by his illness. By fall, he had recovered and was planning far more ambitious enterprises. To Robert Morris he wrote suggesting that he be sent to Europe "in a handsome Frigate to display our Flag in the Ports of the different Powers," to negotiate commercial treaties, and to study the administration of foreign navies. In mid-October, he wrote to the President of Congress concerning prize money owed to the officers and men of the *Bonhomme Richard* squadron in France and Denmark. Jones was confident that he could succeed where others had failed. "I beg leave to acquaint you that I am ready to proceed to Europe in order to make the necessary application at those two Courts, provided I can go honored with the Sanction of Congress."[33] On 1 November 1783, Congress gave its sanction; nine days later, Jones boarded a packet ship for France.

Negotiations in France dragged on for two years. Jones's success in finally extracting money from the distressed French treasury is a mark of both his continued prestige in Paris and the tenacity with which he pursued almost all his objects. During this period "the Chevalier," as Jones was known in France, renewed old friendships and cast about for future employment. He considered several commercial ventures and invested in a few with mixed results. At the same time, he yearned for more active service.

In 1784, Thomas Jefferson joined Franklin and Adams in Paris as an American commissioner to France. The three were empowered to deal not only with France but also with the Barbary states, whose corsairs had been taking American ships captive under the pretext of war. The North Africans wanted tribute, and the American commissioners were divided on how to deal with them. Jefferson opposed such payments in principle: "We ought to begin a naval power, if we mean to carry on our own commerce. Can we begin it on a more honourable occasion, or with a weaker foe? I am of opinion Paul Jones with half a dozen frigates would totally destroy [the Barbary states'] commerce . . . by constant cruising and cutting them to pieces by piecemeal."[34] Jones would no doubt have welcomed such an enterprise.

Only a month before leaving America, he had addressed a long letter to Robert Morris, who as "Agent of the Marine" headed the Navy. "In the time of peace it is necessary to prepare, and be always prepared for war by sea," wrote Jones. In succeeding paragraphs he discussed strategy, the officer corps, and naval education and training. "It is the work of many years' study and experience to acquire the high degree of science necessary for a great sea officer," he wrote. He claimed that service in the merchant marine does not adequately prepare a man for naval command, nor does "cruising after merchant ships, (the service on which our frigates have generally been employed), afford . . . the knowledge necessary for conducting fleets and their operations." Officer candidates must be carefully selected and promoted on a merit basis. Jones recognized the financial constraints imposed on the young nation:

> My plan for forming a proper corps of sea officers, is by teaching them the naval tactics in a fleet of evolution. To lessen the expense as much as possible, I would compose that fleet of frigates instead of ships of the line: on board of each I would have a little academy, where the officers should be taught the principles of mathematics and mechanics, when off duty. When in port the young officers should be obliged to attend at the academies established at each dockyard, where they should be taught the principles of every art and science that is necessary to form the character of a great sea officer.

In addition to training officers, the fleet of evolution would provide an opportunity to develop and practice signals and tactics. In his draft of the letter to Morris, Jones analyzed current French and English signaling and maneuvering systems and concluded that the French system was far superior.[35]

Reform of the officer system was also necessary, he believed. The Continental Navy's ranks of midshipmen, lieutenants, and captains were inadequate. In 1775, Congress had established three grades of lieutenants, but Jones saw the need for "the same number of subaltern grades" below lieutenant. "The charge of the deck of a ship of the line should . . . never be entrusted to an officer under twenty-five years of age." The increase in the number of grades would allow the Navy "to raise young men by smaller steps" and thereby avoid the "uneasiness" of mind that results "when they are continued too long in any one grade." Regular promotions would also give officers a sense of accomplishment. In the same letter, he commented on Congress's failure to mention his name when transferring the *America* to France. "Such little attentions to the military pride of officers are always of use to a state, and *cost nothing.*" Perhaps Jones was learning. During the war he had not always been liberal in his praise of his subordinates in official reports.[36]

By the time Jefferson made his suggestion concerning the Barbary states, Jones appears to have given up hope of any immediate service in an American navy. As early as 1782 he had written to Hector McNeill that his voice was "like a cry in the Desert" when he made suggestions to improve the Navy.[37] During the fall of 1785 he wrote his "Memoir" for Louis XVI, probably with the hope that, should the threatening war with Britain become real, he might be offered a commission in the French navy. If so, he was disappointed. There was no war in 1785 or 1786, and Jones decided to return to America before proceeding to Copenhagen to press the claims of the *Bonhomme Richard* squadron before the Danish court.

Jones sailed from France to New York City in July 1787. There he presented his accounts for the French prize money negotiations to Congress and again sought to be named rear admiral. As in the past, officers senior to him blocked the promotion. Such an action would have been honorary at best because the United States lacked a navy at the time. Congress did honor Jones by unanimously voting him a gold medal and instructing that Thomas Jefferson have it executed in Paris. Jones was the only Continental Navy officer so recognized and was much pleased. Congress also asked the king of France, probably at Jones's request, to allow him "to embark with one of his fleets of evolution; convinced that he can no where else so well acquire knowledge which may hereafter render him more extensively useful." In addition, Congress renewed his authority to press the Danish government for payment for the prizes handed over to the British.

Jones left America for the last time in 1788. He arrived in Copenhagen in March and was received with ceremony. He met with the Danish foreign minister and dined with the royal family but could do nothing to obtain the money. By mid-April he was presented a far more appealing opportunity and gave up on the prize money. He certainly was not willing to devote two years to the project as he had in France.

The offer was a commission in the Imperial Russian Navy. Attracted by an opportunity to command a fleet, as well as the promise of adventure, glory, and profit, Jones accepted immediately and set out for Saint Petersburg. However, several British officers served in Catherine the Great's navy in the Baltic, and they threatened to resign rather than serve with a "pirate"; so Jones was ordered to the Black Sea.

Jones was commissioned a rear admiral, but the limits of his authority were not clearly delineated. Prince Potemkin, one of Catherine the Great's favorites, was the overall commander in the region. Jones thought that he was to command all naval forces, but there were three other rear admirals already serving in the Black Sea. One commanded the arsenal at Kherson, another the flotilla of galleys, and the third a separate fleet at Sevastopol. Jones was given command of the sailing ships and had to deal closely with only one of the other admirals, Prince Nassau-Siegen, an international adventurer who was very jealous of Jones and had the ear of Prince Potemkin, their common superior.

Jones boarded his flagship, the *Vladimir*, on 29 May 1788. With a Turkish attack imminent, Jones took strategic control of the Russian forces and deployed them across the Liman, an estuary of the Dnieper River. Eight days later the Russian forces repulsed an assault by the Turks. A second attack broke down when the Turkish flagship ran aground. During the following night, Jones personally reconnoitered the enemy fleet in a rowboat and skillfully shifted the position of his ships to meet the next day's onslaught. The Second Battle of the Liman lasted two days and resulted in the capture or destruction of ten large and five small Turkish vessels against the loss of only a single ship by the Russians. Nassau-Siegen, with the support of his friend Potemkin, took credit for the victory, although the strategy of fighting a defensive battle had been Jones's and was adopted over Nassau-Siegen's protests. In fact, the victory would have been greater had Nassau-Siegen followed Jones's orders during the battle.

After four months of political bickering over credit for the victory, Jones emerged the loser and was recalled to Saint Petersburg under the pretense of reassignment to the Baltic fleet. For several more months he languished in the capital, where he devoted much of his time to drafting plans for a Russian-American alliance, the reorganization of the Black Sea fleet, and Russian-led operations against the Barbary corsairs. He also compiled a "Narrative of the Campaign of the Liman," which he meant to submit to Catherine in the hope that it would regain her favor.

In April 1789, a trumped-up scandal linking Jones to a young girl ended any chance for his restoration to command, and he decided to leave Russia. It took him until the end of August to put his affairs in order and to obtain the necessary exit papers. From Saint Petersburg he went to Warsaw, Alsace, and Vienna before reaching Amsterdam in December. In May 1790, he visited London and finally settled in Paris. Jones was clearly drifting. His health was deteriorating. Without money or employment, he settled into rented rooms near the Luxembourg Palace. There he spent his final days, all but ignored. To the American Minister to France he became a bore. "Paul Jones calls on me," Gouverneur Morris recorded in his diary. "He has nothing to say but is so kind as to bestow on me all the Hours which hang heavy in his Hands. . . ." A few days later, Morris wrote "Paul Jones calls and gives me his Time but I cannot lend him mine."[38]

It was a sad ending to a career filled with highlights. Jones must have sensed the attitude of Morris and have been hurt by the inattention of men like Lafayette who had once sought him. When death claimed him in July 1792, just days after his forty-fifth birthday, he may have welcomed it as a relief after two months of suffering from jaundice and other diseases brought on by long exposure to the elements. Had he known that President George Washington and his Secretary of State Thomas Jefferson remembered him and valued his services, it would have been a great comfort. Only days before his death, the two leaders signed a commission appointing "John Paul Jones a citizen of the United States . . . a Commissioner . . . to confer treat and negotiate with the [Dey of] Algiers . . . concerning the ransom of all citizens of the United States of America in captivity with the Said Dey."[39]

Jones died before the commission was delivered. It was a strange and lonely death.

Jones's life paralleled that of the Continental Navy. Both rose from humble origins, appeared briefly on the world scene, and then passed with few mourners. Jones gave to it some of its brightest moments, including the capture of the two largest Royal Navy ships to strike their flags to Americans during the Revolution. He always made the most of the limited resources available to him. In the battle against the *Serapis*, he left a legacy of dauntless courage and unconquerable persistence in the most desperate of circumstances. Every fighting service needs a tradition of refusal to surrender in the face of seemingly overwhelming odds. "It was [John Paul Jones] who . . . created the spirit of my country's infant Navy," wrote a mid-nineteenth-century naval officer.[40]

This was the dominant image of Jones during a century when naval officers, in particular, shared his great sense of personal honor. The era of Jacksonian Democracy found much to admire in the rise of a Scots gardener's son to glory in the Continental Navy and to flag rank in the Imperial Russian Navy.

Early American naval officers were not an introspective group. Few conducted extensive correspondence, and fewer still left memoirs of their service. No account exists of the mundane contacts between Jones and those who served with him, of the long hours shared on the quarterdeck, the inspection tours of the ship, and the relaxing dinners in his cabin. Still, it is clear that he directly influenced such future officers as Richard Dale, Thomas Truxtun, and Joshua Barney.

At the start of the twentieth century, when the U.S. Navy took its place among leaders of the world, the image of Jones held by the general public and by naval officers began to change. The Navy's rising professionalism led it to value Jones not simply as a courageous leader in time of battle but as a complete naval officer. Jones understood the basics of his vocation. His grasp of naval architecture was demonstrated by his supervision of the construction of the *Ranger* and the *America,* the virtual reconstruction of the *Bonhomme Richard,* and alterations to the masts and rigging of almost every ship he commanded. His victories were not won by courage and superior tactics alone but were the result of careful preparation. Jones took a motley crew on board the *Bonhomme Richard* and welded it into a team. His letters and actions show the respect he had for his subordinates, though he often failed to give enough credit to the officers who served under him.

His writings also suggest a nascent professionalism. His opposition to nepotism and his desire to establish boards to evaluate officers for promotion were visionary for his time. His proposals for a fleet of evolution and naval academies predated the establishment of such institutions in the United States by over half a century. Consequently, quotations from his writings, sometimes imaginary, appeared on the fitness report forms of the Navy's Bureau of Personnel and on examination books at the U.S. Naval Academy in the early twentieth century.

Jones's strategic ideals were equally sound. As clearly as anyone, he understood the limitation of the Continental Navy and advocated operations congruent with its capabilities. The need for French assistance in ejecting the British army from America was apparent to Jones. It is not surprising that French Admiral François DeGrasse's biographer credits Jones with suggesting the strategy that ultimately brought victory at Yorktown.[41]

John Paul Jones's great fault was his egotism. He could express his gratitude to men such as Hewes, Franklin, and Morris, who appreciated his abilities and helped him, but he always resented anyone who did not measure up to his standards and was in a position to control his affairs. As an individual, Jones was jealous and vain. A man of strong opinions, he generated strong feelings in others. To some, he was an arriviste whose pride smacked of overweening hubris. This partly explains his nation's treatment of him at the time of his death.

That he was a man of talent cannot be denied nor can his patriotism. His disappointments in terms of recognition and command rivaled those of Benedict Arnold, but their reactions differed sharply. Jones's reputation rests on his exploits of 1778 and 1779, when he took the war to the British people and strengthened American morale at times when it was sinking. Sadly, he was destined never to test his talents on a broad scale. With the end of the war, America thought it no longer needed a navy and thus had no use for Jones as a naval officer.

But Jones never fully adapted to peace. His success as a diplomat was no compensation for his disappointment when his plans for an American navy were rejected. Throughout the Revolution he had remained optimistic, convinced that the Continental Navy, no matter how low its fortunes, could win respect from Europe for the new United States. That he sought personal fame at the same time is not surprising. His pursuit of glory as a reward for self-sacrifice and service to the nation was fully in keeping with the spirit of the time.[42] In the end, John Paul Jones's legacy rests not so much on what he accomplished as on how he did it. As the inscription on his tomb reads: "He gave to our navy its earliest traditions of heroism and victory."

FURTHER READING

John Paul Jones has been the subject of more than a score of biographies and even more works of fiction. Only four of the biographies are worthy of attention, however. These are John Henry Sherburne's *Life and Character of the Chevalier John Paul Jones* (New York, 1825); Anna DeKoven's *The Life and Letters of John Paul Jones*, 2 vols. (New York, 1913); Lincoln Lorenz's *John Paul Jones, Fighter for Freedom and Glory* (Annapolis, Md., 1941); and Samuel Eliot Morison's Pulitzer Prize–winning *John Paul Jones: A Sailor's Biography* (Boston, 1959). Other biographies contain so many errors that they should be avoided. Most important in this group is Augustus C. Buell's *Paul Jones, Founder of the American Navy: A History*, 2 vols. (New York, 1900), which served as the basis for later biographies such as Norman Hapgood's *Paul Jones* (New York, 1901) and M. MacDermot Crawford's *The Sailor Whom England Feared* (London, 1913). Valentine Thomas, *Knight of the Seas* (New York, 1939), accepts most of Buell's tales and adds several of her own. Gerald W. Johnson, *The First Captain: The Story of John Paul Jones* (New York, 1947), describes episodes, such as Jones's service in the Royal Navy and his career as an actor, for which there is no documentation.

A comprehensive addition of Jones's own writing was published on microfilm in 1986, *The Papers of John Paul Jones*, 10 reels (Alexandria, Va., 1986), edited by James C. Bradford. During the nineteenth century, Jones's niece, Janette Taylor, arranged for the publication of the *Memoirs of Rear-Admiral Paul Jones* (Edinburgh, 1830), probably by Sir John Malcolm, and Robert Sands's *Life and Correspondence of John Paul Jones, Including His Narrative of the Campaign of the Liman* (New York, 1830). William Bell Clark and William James Morgan, eds., *The Naval Documents of the American Revolution*, 10 vols. to date (Washington, D.C., 1964–), include Jones's most important papers for the first two years of the war, and Frank A. Golder's *John Paul Jones in Russia* (Garden City, N.Y., 1927) includes transcriptions of most of his important papers relating to his service in the Black Sea. John S. Barnes edited *The Logs of the* Serapis-Alliance-Ariel *under the Command of John Paul Jones, 1779–1780* (New York, 1911).

Louis F. Middlebrook edited *The Log of the* Bon Homme Richard (Mystic, Conn., 1936); Gerald W. Gawalt translated Jones's *Memoir of the American Revolution* (Washington, D.C., 1979) that Jones prepared for the king of France; and Joseph G. Sawtelle drew from these sources to edit *John Paul Jones and the* Ranger (Portsmouth, N.H., 1994).

Jones's operations are described in Gardner W. Allen's *A Naval History of the American Revolution*, 2 vols. (Boston, 1913); his command of the *Providence* is included in Hope S. Rider's *Valour Fore & Aft: Being the Adventures of the Continental Sloop* Providence, *1775–1779, Formerly Flagship* Katy *of Rhode Island's Navy* (Annapolis, Md., 1977); and the battle between the *Bonhomme Richard* and the *Serapis* is analyzed by John Evangelist Walsh in *Night on Fire: The First Complete Account of John Paul Jones'*

*Greatest Battle* (New York, 1978). Don C. Seitz's *Paul Jones, His Exploits in English Seas during 1776–1780, Contemporary Accounts Collected from English Newspapers with a Complete Bibliography* (New York, 1917) will guide the reader to eighteenth- and nineteenth-century works.

The administration of the Continental Navy and early naval policy and strategy have not received the attention they merit. Charles O. Paullin's *The Navy of the American Revolution: Its Administration, Its Policy, and Its Achievements* (Cleveland, 1906) has been superseded by Frank C. Mevers's doctoral dissertation, "Congress and the Navy: The Establishment and Administration of the American Revolutionary Navy by the Continental Congress" (University of North Carolina, 1972). Both works focus on administration rather than strategy and policy.

Three officers who served with Jones left varying accounts of their commander. *Diary of Ezra Green, M.D., Surgeon on Board the Continental Ship-of-War* Ranger *under John Paul Jones, from November 1, 1777 to Sept. 27, 1778 . . .* (Boston, 1875), edited by George H. Preble, pictures Jones in positive terms, as does Lt. Richard Dale's "Particulars of the Engagement between the *Bonhomme Richard* and the *Serapis*," which is printed in Sherburne's biography. Nathanial Fanning, author of *Fanning's Narrative: Memoirs of Nathaniel Fanning* (New York, 1912), edited by John S. Barnes, served as a midshipman on board the *Bonhomme Richard* and is more critical of Jones. His "memoir" and the sketch of Jones's life that follows contain a number of amusing but apocryphal stories.

NOTES

1. Charles W. Stewart, comp., *John Paul Jones Commemoration at Annapolis, April 24, 1906* (Washington, D.C., 1907), 13.

2. Gouverneur Morris, *A Diary of the French Revolution, 1789–1793*, 2 vols. (Boston, 1939), 2:468, 471.

3. Documents relating to the Mungo Maxwell episode, including the warrant for Jones's arrest, his petition for bail, dated 10, 13, and 15 November 1776, are in the Kirkcudbright Sheriff Clerk's Records, Scottish Record Office, Edinburgh. Jones's petition for admission to the Masonic Lodge is in the Naval Academy Museum.

4. Jones to Benjamin Franklin, 6 March 1779, Franklin Papers, American Philosophical Society, Philadelphia.

5. Jones to Joseph Hewes, 17 August and 1 September 1777; Jones to Robert Morris, 24 August and 30 October 1777 (from which the quotation is taken) and 10 October 1783; Jones to Jonathan Williams, 20 November 1780; Jones to John Ross, 23 November 1778, Jones Papers, Library of Congress (hereafter cited as Jones Papers, DLC).

6. Jones to R. Morris, 10 October 1783, Jones Papers, DLC; Jones to Franklin, 6 March 1779, American Philosophical Society.

7. Jones to R. Morris, 12 January 1777, and the Marine Committee to Jones, 1 February 1777, Jones Papers, DLC; R. Morris to Jones, 5 February 1777, Jones Papers, Papers of the Continental Congress, National Archives (hereafter cited as PCC 168).

8. Jones to R. Morris, 10 October 1783, Jones Papers, DLC.

9. Jones to John Brown, 31 October 1777, Pierpont Morgan Library.

10. Jones to R. Morris, 11 December 1777, Jones Papers, DLC. Also see Jones to William Whipple, 11 December 1777, Dreer Collection, Historical Society of Pennsylvania.

11. American Commissioners to Jones, 16 January 1778, Benjamin Franklin Letterbook, DLC.

12. Jones to American Commissioners, 10 February 1778, PCC, 193.

13. Jones to R. Morris, 11 December 1777, Jones Papers, DLC.

14. John Paul Jones's *Memoir of the American Revolution*, translated and edited by Gerald W. Gawalt (Washington, D.C., 1979; hereafter, Jones, *Memoir*); Jones to Lady Selkirk, 8 May 1778, original in possession of Sir David Hope-Dunbar, Kirkcudbright, Scotland. Virtually all of Jones's biographers quote the letter. And Samuel Eliot Morison, *John Paul Jones: A Sailor's Biography* (Boston, 1959), 186.

15. Jones to Commissioners, 9 May 1778, Jones Papers, PCC 168. William Bell Clark, *Ben Franklin's Privateers* (New York, 1969), discusses previous attempts by Americans in Europe to obtain British prisoners for use in an exchange for American prisoners.

16. John Banister to Theodorick Bland, Jr., 31 July 1778, and James Lovell to William Whipple, 14 July 1778; both quoted in Paul H. Smith, ed., *Letters of the Delegates to Congress*, 15 vols. to date (Washington, D.C., 1976–) 9:278, 376. Also, see G. J. Marcus, *A Naval History of England: The Formative Centuries* (Boston, 1969), 418.

17. Jones, *Memoir*, 25.

18. Jones to Le Ray de Chaumont, 16 November 1778, Jones's Letterbook, U.S. Naval Academy Museum.

19. Lafayette to the Comte de Vergennes, 1 April 1779, in Stanley J. Idzerda, ed., *Lafayette in the Age of the American Revolution*, 5 vols. to date (Ithaca, N.Y., 1977–1983), 2:251–53.

20. Lafayette to Sartine [16–20 April]; Lafayette to Vergennes, 26 April 1779; Lafayette to Jones, 27 April and 22 May 1779; Franklin to Jones, 27 April 1779; Jones to Chaumont, 30 April 1779; all in Idzerda, *Lafayette*, 2:255–68.

21. Quoted from the lost English copy of Jones's memoir in Robert Sands, *Life and Correspondence of John Paul Jones, Including His Narrative of the Campaign of the Liman* (New York, 1830), 171.

22. Jones, *Memoir*, 31.

23. All of Jones's biographers recount the battle. The most recent and most complete account is John Evangelist Walsh, *Night on Fire: The First Complete Account of John Paul Jones' Greatest Battle* (New York, 1978). Samuel Eliot Morison reconstructs Jones's words and actions that evening in *John Paul Jones: A Sailor's Biography* (Boston, 1959), 221–42.

24. Nathaniel Fanning, *Fanning's Narrative: Memoirs of Nathaniel Fanning*, edited by John S. Barnes (New York, 1912), 53; Jones to Franklin, 3 October 1779, Jones Papers, DLC.

25. Morison, *Jones*, 247–49, contains excerpts from several.

26. Jan Willem Schulte Nordholt, *The Dutch Republic and American Independence*, chap. 5, "Here Comes Paul Jones!" (Chapel Hill, N.C., 1982).

27. Fanning, *Narrative*, 78–79, 81.

28. Eugene S. Ferguson, *Truxtun of the Constellation* (Baltimore, 1956), 40–42.

29. Quoted in Morison, *Jones*, 306.

30. W. C. Ford, ed., *Journals of the Continental Congress, 1774–1789*, 34 vols. (Washington, D.C., 1904–1936), 27 February, 14 April, and 26 June 1781.

31. Ibid., 3 September 1782.

32. Jones to Major John Sherburne, 1 August 1783, U.S. Naval Academy Museum.

33. First quotation in Jones to R. Morris, 10 October 1783, Jones Papers, DLC; second quotation in Jones to Boudinot, 18 October 1783, PCC 168, 35.

34. Thomas Jefferson to James Monroe, 11 November 1784, in Paul L. Ford, *The Writings of Thomas Jefferson*, 10 vols. (New York, 1892–1899), 4:10–11.

35. Jones to R. Morris, 13 October 1783.

36. Ibid. The draft containing Jones's comments on the current state of the French and British navies is in the Jones Papers in the Library of Congress.

37. Jones to Hector McNeill, 25 May 1782, in Anna DeKoven, *The Life and Letters of John Paul Jones*, 2 vols. (New York, 1913), 1:195.

38. Morris, *Diary*, 2:59, 64.

39. The commission is in Jones's crypt at the U.S. Naval Academy.

40. Lieutenant Alexander B. Pinkham quoted by Edouard A. Stackpole, *A Nantucketer Who Followed an Ideal in a Far Country* (n.p., n.d.), 2–3.

41. Charles Lee Lewis, *Admiral DeGrasse and American Independence* (Annapolis, Md., 1945), 70–71.

42. This is the central theme of Douglas Adair's "Fame and the Founding Fathers," in *Fame and the Founding Fathers*, edited by Trevor Colbourn (New York, 1974). Every war produces individuals whose talents seem of little value or whose temperaments prevent them from achieving success in peace commensurate with that in war. George Rogers Clark and "Light-Horse Harry" Lee—as well as Jones—come to mind as examples for the American Revolution.

# ☆ Stephen Decatur
☆
☆ Heroic Ideal of the Young Navy

*by John H. Schroeder*

WHEN STEPHEN DECATUR DIED IN 1820, JOHN QUINCY ADAMS MOURNED
the nation's loss of a hero "who has illustrated its history and given grace and
dignity to its character in the eyes of the world." His spirit, noted the Secretary
of State, was "as kindly, as generous, and as dauntless as breathed in this nation, or on this earth."[1] Coming as they did from such a critical judge of character as Adams, these remarks reflected the tremendous impact that Decatur
had made on his generation. His career had combined stirring military exploits, providential good fortune, and exemplary personal attributes in a manner that captured the imagination of his fellow citizens. In an era of military
heroes, Decatur was the most heroic naval figure of his day. Congress, presidents, and public officials praised him. Banquets, speeches, toasts, and poetic
verses celebrated his achievements. Gifts, awards, and mementos flowed from
a grateful public.

From the time of his birth in 1779, Stephen Decatur, Jr., seemed destined
for a nautical career. Of maritime stock, he was born near the sea and grew up
in a seafaring environment. His paternal grandfather had served in the French
navy and migrated via the West Indies to Newport, Rhode Island, where he
married an American in 1751. Their son Stephen was born the following year
shortly before the family moved to Philadelphia, where he spent his childhood,
became a ship master, and married Ann Pine in 1774. During the Revolution,
Stephen Decatur, Sr., commanded several American privateers, made numerous captures, and collected a considerable amount of prize money.

In the meantime, Mrs. Decatur had left Philadelphia during the British occupation and moved to Sinepuxent on the Eastern Shore of Maryland, where
she gave birth to Stephen, Jr., on 5 January 1779. After the Revolution, Stephen
senior returned to Philadelphia, commanded merchant ships for the shipping

firm of Gurney and Smith, and became part owner with his business associates of the merchant vessels *Pennsylvania* and *Ariel*.[2]

Stephen, Jr., and his younger brother, James, enjoyed a pleasant and typical childhood in Philadelphia. When Stephen was eight, his father took him on a voyage to Europe to help him recover from an attack of whooping cough. That voyage seems to have imparted a strong desire in the boy for a career as a ship captain. His mother objected to additional cruises, however, and he spent his next few years as a student at the Protestant Episcopal Academy, where his classmates included Richard Rush and future naval officers Richard Somers and Charles Stewart. Although Decatur later entered the University of Pennsylvania, he was indifferent to academic study and remained only a year before accepting a position as a clerk for Gurney and Smith.

In addition to its commercial activities, the firm also built ships and served as the naval agent in Philadelphia. When Congress authorized construction of three frigates for the new Navy, the firm contracted to build the forty-four-gun *United States*. Decatur, whose pastime was the construction, sparring, and rigging of miniature ships, was sent to New Jersey to supervise the getting out of the keel pieces for the new warship and was on board when the *United States* was launched on 10 May 1797. Fortuitously, Decatur had played a minor role in the construction and the launching of a ship that would carry him to a great triumph fifteen years later.[3]

In the midst of a worsening diplomatic crisis with France in 1798, Decatur received his warrant as a midshipman in the U.S. Navy. The commission was obtained and delivered by Captain John Barry, a close friend of the family and the commander of the *United States*. In the process of supervising construction of the frigate, Barry had been impressed with young Decatur's desire to become a naval officer. Understanding the family's opposition, he did not consult them before obtaining the warrant. Stephen's mother withdrew her objections when Barry arrived in person to deliver it.[4]

Decatur was fortunate to be assigned to the *United States* and to serve under Barry, who as one of the most distinguished naval officers of the Revolution, provided excellent tutelage for the young officer. During the undeclared naval war with France, Decatur participated in a number of cruises on board the *United States* and one on board the brig *Norfolk*. Although these cruises provided excellent experience and resulted in the capture of several French prizes, the *United States* did not engage in any major naval action. Rather, it was Stephen's father who distinguished himself by volunteering for action, commanding the *Delaware* and capturing the French schooner *Croyable*, as well as several other prizes. Later, the senior Decatur commanded the frigate *Philadelphia* and captured five more French privateers.

As a young officer, Decatur advanced quickly. He became a lieutenant in 1799, a first lieutenant in 1801, and received his first command in 1803. From

the outset Decatur distinguished himself as a resourceful, able, and courageous officer and impressed others as a likable and exceptionally promising individual. A handsome, athletic man at five feet ten inches, he was a striking figure. Another officer later remembered Decatur's "peculiarity of manner and
appearance . . . I had often pictured myself the form and look of a hero, such
as my favorite Homer had delineated; here I saw it embodied."[5]

During these early years Decatur also demonstrated an acute sense of hon-
or, and this sensitivity to various slights involved him in several affairs of hon-
or as either principal or second. In 1799, the first mate of a merchant ship insulted Decatur and the Navy when the young officer came to collect several
seamen who had enlisted in the Navy and later signed on with the merchant
ship. Decatur held his temper and left with his enlistees, but he later demanded an apology after discussing the matter with his father. When the mate
refused to apologize, Decatur challenged the man to a duel and used his excellent marksmanship to wound rather than kill the offender, thus exonerat-
ing his own personal honor and courage.

Several years later, in the Mediterranean, Decatur served as the second for
Midshipman Joseph Bainbridge in a controversial duel with an Englishman
who was the secretary to the British governor of Malta. After a scuffle in a theater, the Englishman, who was an experienced duelist, challenged Midshipman Bainbridge. Decatur agreed to serve as a second but insisted on a distance
of only four paces because of Bainbridge's inexperience in duels. When Bainbridge killed the Englishman in the confrontation, the governor objected to
the affair and demanded that the two American naval officers be tried in civil
court for murder. Commodore Richard V. Morris responded by sending both
officers home as passengers on board the *Chesapeake*.

In spite of this potentially damaging incident, Decatur received command
of the brig *Argus* and returned to the Mediterranean in late 1803. By the beginning of 1804, Decatur commanded the schooner *Enterprise*, a part of Commodore Edward Preble's naval squadron waging war against Tripoli. The
young republic's problems with Tripoli and the other Barbary states dated back
to the 1780s, when the rulers of these states began to demand tribute from the
newly independent United States. The Barbary powers had long preyed on
merchant ships plying the Mediterranean trade. If a nation paid tribute, its
ships were unhindered. If it did not, the Barbary corsairs captured merchant
vessels and held their crews for ransom. For various reasons, the major naval
powers of Europe usually preferred to pay tribute rather than attempt to destroy the Barbary corsairs and impose peace on their rulers.[6]

Initially, the United States signed treaties with each of the four states and
continued to pay tribute during the 1790s. Humiliating to the young republic,
these agreements reflected American naval weakness in the Mediterranean.
When the Pasha of Tripoli demanded increased tribute and declared war

against the United States in 1801, the Jefferson administration decided to retaliate and sent a naval squadron to the Mediterranean. For two years, the successive commands of Commodores Richard Dale and Richard V. Morris proved ineffective. Although American naval vessels blockaded Tripoli, captured a number of ships, and scored several victories, their efforts were inconsistent and did not bring Tripoli to terms.

In September 1803, the Navy Department appointed Commodore Preble to command the squadron in the Mediterranean. Although he ranked low in the Navy's list of captains, Preble proved an excellent choice. He was a tough commander known for his foul temper and iron discipline, but he was also an energetic officer determined to prosecute the war vigorously, a quality that his younger officers understood and revered in him. His initial squadron in the Mediterranean consisted of six warships, all commanded by officers under thirty years of age, a group that became known as "Preble's Boys."[7]

Shortly after taking command, Preble suffered a serious setback when the Tripolitans captured the thirty-six-gun frigate *Philadelphia* on 31 October 1803. Under the command of Captain William Bainbridge, the *Philadelphia* had been blockading the port of Tripoli when she ran aground on uncharted rocks in the harbor while pursuing a Tripolitan ship. All attempts to free the American warship failed, and Captain Bainbridge finally surrendered after a four-hour gunboat attack. Two days later, the Tripolitans used a high tide to refloat the *Philadelphia*, recovered her guns, and moved the frigate into the harbor within range of their forts. In one stroke, the Bey had gained a powerful frigate to bolster his defenses as well as 307 captives who could be held for large ransom.

When news of the disaster spread, the idea of recapturing or destroying the ship surfaced immediately. From captivity, Captain Bainbridge also suggested the idea in a letter written in lemon juice, which was invisible until subjected to heat. Lieutenant Decatur offered to lead such an expedition, as did Lieutenant Charles Stewart. The *Philadelphia* held special significance for Decatur because she had been built and paid for by the citizens of Philadelphia and commanded in the naval war against France by Decatur's father. After the *Enterprise*, commanded by Decatur, captured the Tripolitan ketch *Mastico*, Commodore Preble decided to risk the plan and selected Decatur to lead the mission. The captured vessel offered an ideal means of entering the enemy harbor and approaching the *Philadelphia* without alarm.[8]

On 31 January 1804, Preble ordered Decatur to collect a force of seventy-five men and proceed in the captured ketch, renamed the *Intrepid*, to Tripoli in the company of the *Siren*. Decatur's party was then to "enter that harbor in the night, board the *Philadelphia*, burn her and make good your retreat in the *Intrepid*, if possible, unless you can make her the means of destroying the enemy's vessels in the harbor, by converting her into a fire-ship for that purpose."

Preble's instructions did not provide the option of recapturing and escaping with the *Philadelphia* from Tripoli.

Although Decatur's orders were simple, the task he faced was difficult and dangerous. The *Philadelphia* was fully armed, well manned, and anchored within range of more than one hundred shore guns, as well as Tripolitan gunboats in the harbor.[9] Decatur selected volunteers for his force and set sail in early February. After a two-week passage delayed by bad weather, the *Intrepid* entered the harbor on the evening of 16 February. Sicilian Salvatore Catalano piloted the ship to avoid suspicion while the American crew were either dressed as Maltese or concealed. When they approached the *Philadelphia* and were hailed, Catalano replied that the ship was Maltese and had lost her anchors in a recent storm, and he sought permission to moor alongside the frigate for the night.

Once the request was granted, a line was attached, and the concealed Americans began to haul the small ship toward the frigate. Not until the *Intrepid* was alongside the *Philadelphia* did the Tripolitans realize the ruse and shout an alarm. Within five minutes, however, the Americans, using no firearms, secured the ship from the startled enemy. Twenty Tripolitans died, one was taken prisoner, and the remainder were driven overboard in the attack. The Americans then set the ship on fire, returned to the *Intrepid*, and escaped from the harbor under fire from Tripolitan gunboats and shore batteries. In the attack, the *Intrepid* suffered only minor damage; no American was killed, and only one man was injured slightly. The courageous Decatur had been the second man to board and the last to leave the *Philadelphia*.[10]

The news of Decatur's triumph delighted Commodore Preble, who had written to the Secretary of the Navy only a short time before to emphasize that the *Philadelphia* had to be destroyed, but that the mission would "undoubtedly cost many lives." Now, almost miraculously, Decatur had returned, the *Philadelphia* had been destroyed, and not a single American life had been lost. Preble immediately wrote to the Secretary to praise Decatur's achievement and recommend his "instantaneous promotion to the rank of post captain."[11] No less a figure than Lord Nelson termed the feat "the most bold and daring act of the age." In May 1804, Secretary of the Navy Robert Smith conveyed President Jefferson's special thanks and promoted Decatur to the rank of post captain, thus making him the youngest captain in American naval history. At the same time, the President praised Decatur in a presidential message, and Congress passed a resolution lauding the men of the *Intrepid*, authorizing presentation of a sword to Decatur, and approving two months of extra pay to each man on the mission.[12]

Meanwhile, Preble had imposed a blockade on Tripoli and, in August 1804, began a series of naval attacks on the city. In the first of these actions, Stephen

Decatur commanded one of the two squadrons of attacking gunboats while James Decatur, a lieutenant, commanded a gunboat in the other squadron. Decatur was towing a captured Tripolitan gunboat out of the harbor when he learned that James had been killed by a Tripolitan commander, who had first surrendered and then shot the young lieutenant when he boarded the vessel. Accompanied by ten men, Stephen Decatur sought out and boarded the suspected enemy gunboat. In fierce hand-to-hand fighting, Decatur almost lost his own life before he finally shot and killed the enemy commander. Decatur had been saved only by the selfless action of a devoted sailor, who blocked a blow directed at Decatur with his own head, thereby suffering a serious injury. In the fighting, all twenty-four Tripolitans were either killed or wounded while the Americans suffered only four wounded. Although Decatur was exhilarated by these combat missions, the death of his brother and the subsequent loss of boyhood friend Lieutenant Richard Somers tempered much of his excitement.[13]

Shortly after these events, Decatur received notification of his promotion and assumed command of the *Constitution* and then the *Congress* in November 1804. After a peace treaty was concluded with Tripoli in June 1805, Decatur returned to Hampton Roads in the *Congress*. There he received a hero's welcome and in the process met his future wife, Susan Wheeler, the daughter of a wealthy merchant who was the mayor of Norfolk. During 1805 and 1806, Decatur was feted and honored on a number of occasions, including a banquet in Philadelphia during which his father commemorated the contribution of his two sons with the moving toast, "Our children are the property of their country."[14]

During the next several years, Decatur's career continued to advance as he performed various duties close to home. In addition to supervising construction of new Jeffersonian gunboats and commanding the Gosport naval yard, Decatur took command of the frigate *United States* in 1810 and helped to protect American shipping by cruising along the coast. Although he hoped to be excused from serving, Decatur was a member of the court-martial that suspended Captain James Barron for five years for his role in the *Chesapeake-Leopard* affair in June 1807. The court found Barron guilty of not clearing his ship for action once the American officer had received the British ultimatum to relinquish the alleged British deserters on board. Thus had been sown the seeds of a quarrel that would surface more than a decade later with tragic consequences.

In contrast to the findings of the Barron court-martial, Decatur presided over an 1811 court of inquiry that completely exonerated Commodore John Rodgers for his role as commander of the *President* in the near destruction of the smaller British *Little Belt* in May of that year.

When Congress declared war on England in June 1812, Commodore Rodgers had already prepared his five-ship squadron for action and was able to sail from New York within days. The squadron, which included Decatur's *United States*, sailed in pursuit of a large British merchant convoy, but it experienced a disappointing cruise and captured only a few British vessels. A few weeks later, the squadron returned to Boston, where it was reorganized into three small units under the commands of Rodgers, Bainbridge, and Decatur. Although Decatur's squadron consisted of the *United States* and the *Argus*, the two ships separated after sailing from Boston in October.

Dispersal of the Navy's few warships very much reflected Decatur's own strategic analysis of the manner in which the naval war should be conducted. To counter Britain's huge navy, the United States had only sixteen warships, eight of them frigates, in 1812. Like most of his naval colleagues, Decatur feared that the British navy would either destroy or blockade the small U.S. Navy if the United States concentrated its warships in one squadron or based them in one or two ports. Instead, Decatur believed that the American frigates should be fully provisioned and dispatched individually or in pairs without specific instructions as to their cruising grounds. Relying on the situation at hand as well as their good judgment and initiative, American naval commanders could then harass and raid British commerce around the globe. American attacks on British commerce worldwide would force the British, in turn, to disperse their own naval forces along their far-flung shipping lanes and thereby diminish British naval power in American waters. Although the potential efficacy of this strategy was exaggerated, the size of the U.S. Navy left the nation's military leaders few other options.[15]

After separating from the *Argus*, the *United States* sailed eastward and by the end of October was cruising between the Azores and the Canary Islands. In the early morning of 25 October 1812, Decatur's crew spotted an approaching ship that proved to be the British frigate *Macedonian*, commanded by Captain John Carden. Ironically, Decatur and Carden had met before the war and discussed the comparative merits of their two ships. Although the *United States* was larger and carried more heavy guns, Carden argued that the *Macedonian* would win an encounter because she had a battle-tested crew and her smaller eighteen-pound guns could be handled more rapidly and effectively than the twenty-four-pounders of the *United States*. In addition, the American frigate was known to be a poor sailer and was supposedly much less maneuverable than the *Macedonian*.[16]

In the battle that settled this argument, Carden enjoyed the wind advantage, but he apparently mistook the *United States* for the smaller American frigate *Essex*, which would have given him a marked advantage in long-range heavy guns. As a result, the British captain kept his distance and unwittingly played into Decatur's own tactics. With superior firepower, Decatur and his well-drilled gun crews capitalized fully and directed a destructive bombardment at the *Macedonian*. At one point, the firing of the American twenty-four-pounders became so rapid that the British mistook the solid sheet of flames for a fire on board the *United States*.

Decatur's superior seamanship prevented Carden from using his smaller guns effectively throughout the battle or from closing later to board the *United States*. Finally, with his masts destroyed, his guns disabled, and his decks a scene of carnage, Carden was forced to surrender. Of her 301-man crew, the *Macedonian* had lost 104 killed or wounded. The *United States* had lost seven dead and five wounded and had suffered only minor damage.[17]

Not wishing to risk losing his prize should he meet a superior enemy, Decatur decided to return to New London and arrived there on 4 December 1812. During the following weeks, Decatur and his crew were honored by a round of celebrations. The legislatures of Massachusetts, New York, Maryland, Pennsylvania, and Virginia expressed their appreciation, as did official bodies in the cities of New London, New York, Philadelphia, and Savannah.

During 1813, the British responded to the loss of several warships by tightening their blockade of the Atlantic coast and hampering American naval efforts. In New York the blockade posed a serious problem for Decatur, who, despite his best efforts, was unable to escape with his squadron. In 1814, the Navy Department transferred Decatur to command of the frigate *President*, but he still did not return to sea. During the summer of 1814, the British offensive in the Chesapeake Bay and the capture of Washington, D.C., created fears that the British might also attack Philadelphia or New York. In response, the Navy Department ordered Decatur to postpone a cruise in the *President* and to take charge of the naval defenses of New York.

After it became apparent that no British attack on New York was imminent, Decatur proposed an extended cruise against British commerce. With a squadron consisting of the *President* and the sloops *Peacock* and *Hornet*, Decatur would raid British commerce in either the area east of Bermuda or the Bay of Bengal. The Navy selected the latter plan, and Decatur again attempted to slip through the British blockade. On the evening of 14 January 1815, the *President* sailed past Sandy Hook in high winds but ran aground in the process. Nearly two hours of heavy pounding damaged the *President* and seriously impaired her sailing speed.

Unable to return to port because of strong westerly winds, Decatur sailed fifty miles along the Long Island coast in an effort to elude the British. Early the next morning, he encountered a British force of four warships, and a chase ensued with the British frigate *Endymion* closing to firing range by late afternoon. Decatur's plan of boarding and capturing the enemy frigate was foiled as the *Endymion* maintained a safe distance; the two ships exchanged shots, and the British ship was forced to retire with damage. Because the presence of the British warships precluded any attempt to capture the *Endymion*, Decatur made a last attempt to escape, but his efforts failed. He was unable to elude the enemy and was finally forced to surrender after two British frigates began to bombard the *President*. In the battle, the Americans lost twenty-four killed and fifty-five wounded, or more than twice the casualties of the British.[18]

Although some naval historians have contended that Decatur might have seriously damaged one or both of the British frigates had he not surrendered prematurely, his compatriots and his naval peers did not question either his performance or his courage. Decatur returned to the United States shortly after word of the Treaty of Ghent arrived and was received as a hero in both New London and New York.

In April 1815, a naval court of inquiry exonerated Decatur and praised him for his command of the *President*. The court found that misplaced beacon boats had caused the *President* to run aground and sustain damages that eventually led to her capture. Denying that different tactics might have produced success, the court concluded that Decatur had adopted the "proper measures" and made "every possible effort to escape." Moreover, the court considered "the management of the *President*, from the time the chase commenced till her surrender, as the highest evidence of the experience, skill, and resources of her commander, and of the ability and seamanship of her officers and crew." Noting that the *Endymion* had been disabled and would have been captured had other British warships not been present, the court asserted that "In this unequal conflict the enemy gained a ship, but the victory was ours."[19]

On 20 April, Secretary of the Navy B. W. Crowninshield conveyed to Decatur the approbation of the President and the Navy Department for "brilliant actions [which] have raised the national honor and fame even in the moment of surrendering your ship to an enemy's squadron of vastly superior force, over whose attack, singly, you were decidedly triumphant."[20] In the meantime, the Navy Department also signified its high opinion of Decatur by offering him his choice of positions.

Relations with Algiers had deteriorated during the war with England, as the Dey had demanded additional tribute in 1812 and then captured the brig *Edwin* and enslaved her crew. Only the fact that few American merchant ships plied the Mediterranean during the war prevented more ship seizures. In response, Congress approved President James Madison's request in March 1815 for measures against Algiers. Decatur was selected to command the first of two naval squadrons to be sent to the area, and he accepted on the condition that he could return to the United States immediately upon the arrival of the second squadron, which was to be commanded by his senior, Commodore William Bainbridge.

On 20 May, Decatur sailed from New York in the *Guerriere*, and on 15 June, he reached Gibraltar with a squadron of nine American warships. He immediately sailed in pursuit of an Algerian naval squadron that was rumored to be in the area under the command of Admiral Reis Hammida. On 17 June, the American squadron captured the forty-six-gun Algerian frigate *Mashuda* and killed the admiral in battle. In addition, thirty other Algerians were killed and more than four hundred taken captive. Two days later, the American brig *Epervier* ran the twenty-two-gun *Estedia* aground and captured her. In this encounter, another twenty-three Algerians died and eighty were taken prisoner.

Decatur then proceeded to Algiers, where he and American Consul-General William Shaler opened negotiations through the Swedish consul on 28 June. Decatur, whose military reputation was well known throughout the region, informed the Algerians of their naval losses and delivered a letter from President Madison that offered the Dey a choice of either peace, on terms of equality, or war. Decatur and Shaler added a note emphasizing that the terms of any settlement must be based on perfect equality between the two nations, inclusion of the most-favored-nation principle, and an end to the payment of any form of tribute to the Dey. In addition, the Americans refused to accept a temporary truce during the negotiations and insisted that the negotiations be concluded on board the *Guerriere* rather than on shore.

The following day, the Algerians agreed to discuss the model treaty, presented by the Americans, that ended all forms of tribute, provided for the return of all prisoners without the payment of any ransom, and specified that the Dey would pay ten thousand dollars, plus a quantity of cotton, to indemnify Americans for their losses. In addition, the treaty included a most-favored-nation clause and provided that captives taken in future wars were to be treated as prisoners of war, not slaves. Although he refused to return the captured Algerian ships to the Dey as part of the treaty, Decatur agreed to restore them to Algiers as a gift to the Dey.[21]

When the Algerians pleaded for a temporary truce to make final arrangements, Decatur refused and set off in pursuit of an approaching Algerian cruiser. In the face of such pressure, the Algerians quickly agreed to final terms and, within a matter of hours, returned to the American squadron with the signed treaty as well as all ten American prisoners. On that same day, 30 June 1815, Consul-General Shaler was received on shore with full honors. Only two weeks after sailing into the Mediterranean, Decatur had, in less than forty-eight hours, concluded a landmark agreement with one of the Barbary states.

Decatur's remarkable success can be attributed in large part to the size of his squadron and the commodore's experience in the Mediterranean. Although negotiations moved with alacrity and the Algerians proved most cooperative, Decatur harbored no illusions about his adversary's motives. In his report to Secretary of the Navy Crowninshield, Decatur noted that the treaty "had been dictated at the mouth of the cannon, has been conceded to the losses which Algiers has sustained, and to the dread of still greater evils apprehended." Decatur added that "the presence of a respectable naval force in his sea will be the only certain guarantee for its observance."[22]

From Algiers, Decatur sailed to Tunis. There, he exacted an indemnity of forty-six thousand dollars for two American merchant ships that Tunis had permitted British men-of-war to capture in the harbor of Tunis during the recent war. Then, in early August, Decatur proceeded to Tripoli where he imposed a similar indemnity of twenty-five thousand dollars and insisted that ten Christian slaves be released. After sailing through the Mediterranean, Decatur touched at Gibraltar, met the second squadron, and returned to New York on 12 November 1815.[23]

As on previous occasions, Decatur's successes in the Mediterranean in 1815 produced a new round of honors and celebrations. Secretary of State James Monroe commended Decatur, and President Madison praised his achievements in a December 1815 message to Congress. Congress also expressed its appreciation by appropriating one hundred thousand dollars to indemnify Decatur and his crew for the losses they sustained when the Algerian prizes were returned to the Dey. In 1815 and 1816, Decatur again enjoyed a series of banquets, speeches, and toasts. It was during a banquet in Norfolk, in April 1816, that he added to his legend by uttering his famous toast: "Our Country. In her intercourse with foreign nations, may she always be in the right, but our country, right or wrong." Although long criticized in some circles as a dangerous expression of patriotic duty, Decatur's adage subsequently became a virtual motto of the Navy.[24]

When the resignation of Isaac Hull created a vacancy on the three-man Board of Navy Commissioners, Secretary of the Navy Crowninshield selected Decatur for the prestigious position. With the board located in Washington, Decatur and his wife settled there, bought a home, and then built a mansion facing Lafayette Park across from the White House. In their new residence, Decatur and his wife soon assumed a prominent social role in the official life of the capital. Decatur brought the same talent and energy to his new position that he had shown in his previous commands at sea.

In its role of providing professional expertise to the Secretary of the Navy, the board played an active administrative role in the construction of warships, the development of ordnance, the purchase of naval supplies, the creation of numerous regulations, and the supervision of various sensitive personnel matters. The commissioners also provided important advice on strategic questions, as in 1817 when Decatur submitted a report on the best site for a naval depot within the Chesapeake Bay and the best means of defending the bay by the use of stationary batteries.[25] The department largely adopted Decatur's recommendations.

Although he much preferred the challenge of active sea duty in wartime, Decatur seems to have been relatively content during these postwar years and might have maintained his style of life had not a tragic duel ended his life prematurely. That duel's origin dated back to the court-martial that suspended Captain James Barron for five years for his role in the *Chesapeake-Leopard* affair. Barron subsequently served as a merchant ship master and was out of the country when the War of 1812 began. After his suspension ended in 1813, Barron requested reinstatement to active duty but did not return to the United States. Although the Navy Department placed Barron on half pay as an officer on leave, it did not reinstate him because of additional incriminating charges that another naval officer had levied against Barron in the *Chesapeake* incident.

Here the matter stood until Barron returned to the United States near the end of 1818 and applied in person to Secretary of the Navy Smith Thompson for restoration the following February. When these efforts failed, an increasingly embittered Barron blamed Decatur for the failure. As a navy commissioner, Decatur had actively opposed Barron's reinstatement because of his conduct since the *Chesapeake* affair. Moreover, Decatur had stated his position in an outspoken and vigorous manner a number of times.[26]

After he received reports of these statements, Barron, encouraged by other officers who were resentful of Decatur, opened an extended correspondence with his adversary. He began by accusing Decatur of insulting his honor as a naval officer. In the ensuing exchange, which lasted more than seven months, Decatur denied that he had any "personal differences" with Barron but admitted that he had openly opposed Barron's reinstatement because his "conduct as an officer since the affair of the *Chesapeake*, has been such as ought to forever bar your readmission in the service. . . . In speaking thus, and endeavoring to prevent your readmission, I conceive I was performing a duty I owe to the service; that I was contributing to the preservation of its respectability." Although he had not actually insulted Barron, Decatur's strong opinions, sense of honor, and standards of conduct led Decatur to assume a position that, while technically correct, did not help avoid a duel.

The friction between Barron and Decatur was compounded by the role of Captain Jesse D. Elliott, who resented Decatur's support of Captain Oliver Hazard Perry in a quarrel with Elliott over the latter's role in the Battle of Erie. At any rate, Elliott apparently falsely reported Decatur's remarks to Barron and encouraged him to call Decatur to the field of honor.[27]

In January 1820, Barron issued the challenge, which Decatur promptly accepted. After arrangements were made by Commodore Bainbridge and Elliott, acting as seconds for Decatur and Barron, respectively, the two antagonists met at Bladensburg, Maryland, on 22 March 1820. Firing from a distance of eight paces, Barron was wounded in the hip and Decatur mortally wounded in the hip and abdomen. Decatur was carried back to his home, where he lingered briefly but died that same evening.[28]

News of Decatur's death stunned the capital. The nation's loss of a beloved hero created an outpouring of grief as Congress adjourned on the day of his funeral. The services were attended by all of official Washington, including the President and the Chief Justice. With full honors, Stephen Decatur, Jr., dead at age forty-one, was buried at Kalorama, the estate of a close friend in Washington.

During a relatively brief naval career, Stephen Decatur, Jr., was a central figure in a series of naval actions that elevated him to the stature of an authentic national hero. His role in the destruction of the *Philadelphia* captured the imagination of a nation frustrated by months of indecisive activity in the Mediterranean and the recent loss of an American frigate to Tripoli. Decatur's immediate avenging of his brother's death in hand-to-hand fighting embellished his reputation for personal valor. In 1812, the defeat and capture of the *Macedonian* by the *United States* fueled national pride in the Navy and reaffirmed Decatur's exceptional seamanship. In 1815, the dramatic successes of Decatur's naval squadron in the Mediterranean further enhanced both his stature and the republic's confidence during the months after the War of 1812. Even the surrender of the *President* to the British in January 1815 did not diminish Decatur's legendary heroism because of the skillful manner in which he commanded his damaged frigate against a numerically superior force. In a young republic with only a brief military history, Decatur's were daring exploits indeed.

Of particular significance in these triumphs were Decatur's flawless character and exceptional personal qualities, which seemed to make these achievements possible. As with other military heroes, fortune placed Decatur at the right place at the right time. But, in each instance, Decatur's own attributes allowed him to overcome difficult obstacles and achieve victory where lesser men would have failed. With Decatur, a rare combination of courage, resourcefulness, determination, kindness, and judgment produced an exceptional leader revered by his men. Even when he failed and had to surrender the *President*, naval peers and contemporaries agreed that his superior talents had brought him close to success and only very bad luck had prevented his escape. In *The Life of Stephen Decatur* published in 1846, naval officer Alexander Slidell Mackenzie summarized those qualities that made Decatur such an appealing figure to nineteenth-century Americans:

The fortune of Decatur, like that of Caesar, was dependent mainly upon himself, upon the happy ascendancy within him of the qualities essential to success, of a spirit prone to hardy enterprise, and accurate judgment . . . upon a steady confidence in his own intrepidity and force of character . . . upon his own matchless courage and prowess; upon his celerity of thought and action; and upon that imperturbable calmness of temper which left him, in critical situations, master of himself, of others, and of events.[29]

In addition to these personal characteristics, Decatur manifested an intense sense of honor, a passion for glory, and a love of country. In an age that romanticized such values, Decatur stood as an exemplary military figure to be emulated and a patriot to be idolized.

Embellishing the Decatur legend were a number of coincidences and fortuitous events that seemed to verify his providential destiny. That the *Philadelphia* had been built by the citizens of his hometown and commanded by his father was auspicious. Decatur's role in the birth of the *United States*, which he would first serve in as a midshipman and later command against the *Macedonian*, follows this pattern. Providence also seems to have had a role in the willingness of a loyal seaman to take a blow directed at Decatur in Tripoli in 1804, as well as in Decatur's conversation with Captain John Carden prior to their battle in the War of 1812.

Still, in spite of his dramatic deeds, exemplary character, and heroic stature, historians have not accorded Decatur a place among the top rank of American naval officers. Rather, his historical significance is confined largely to his individual achievements and to the high standards of conduct that he set for the Navy. Although studies of the period and naval histories tend to note his exploits, they do not dwell on Decatur's importance. Moreover, Decatur has not been the subject of a serious biography in almost half a century.

Stephen Decatur's historical significance as a secondary figure is attributable to several factors. First, the luster of his valorous actions has dimmed considerably as subsequent generations of Americans have adopted new heroes and celebrated more recent military triumphs.

Second, his victories tended to be in actions of limited military or strategic significance. Stirring as they were, his successes in Tripoli had little effect on the outcome of that conflict, and his capture of the *Macedonian* did not alter the strategy or the outcome of the War of 1812. His expedition to the Barbary states in 1815 occurred in a secondary diplomatic arena and only hastened the end of hostilities that many thought should have been concluded long before.

Third, Decatur had little long-range impact on the development of American naval policy or strategy. In fact, to the extent that he championed commerce raiding by single warships, some naval historians would consider Decatur's ideas an impediment to the development of a more realistic strategy of naval warfare.[30] At the same time, it is likely that, had he enjoyed the long career then common in the Navy, Decatur would have left his imprint on American naval development after 1820.

Finally, Decatur later came to symbolize some of the flaws as well as the positive attributes associated with the officer corps in the early Navy. His passion for military glory was widely accepted by contemporaries living in an era of romanticism, but subsequent generations have tended to be more cognizant of the dangers inherent in a quest for personal military glory. Decatur's exaggerated sense of honor and acute sensitivity to slights against himself, his uniform, and his country involved him in a series of affairs of honor and eventually led to his senseless death.

Although duels over questions of honor were then common in American naval affairs, Decatur's death stirred a sharp public reaction and encouraged efforts to end the practice of dueling. By 1850, duels among American naval officers had become rare, and the Navy finally made dueling a violation of law in 1862. Clearly, this highly individualized code of conduct and means of settling real or imagined personal differences had no place in a modern navy.

Likewise, although Decatur's adage "Our country, right or wrong" was initially extolled in the Navy and even suggested as the official motto when the Naval Academy was established in the 1840s, his brand of unquestioning loyalty long has been criticized in nonmilitary circles as a dangerous form of false patriotism. In comparison with the character and achievements of his naval contemporaries, Decatur's shortcomings appear minor, indeed, and his illustrious record of naval combat is unsurpassed. Without peer, Decatur stands as the most exemplary naval hero of his time, and that, in and of itself, remains a considerable historical legacy.

FURTHER READING

In spite of his stature as an early American naval hero, Stephen Decatur has attracted little attention from historians in recent decades. The most authoritative biography remains Charles Lee Lewis, *The Romantic Decatur* (Philadelphia, 1937). In this well-written and scholarly study, Lewis notes that Decatur lived in "the period of romanticism" and stands as "one of the most romantic characters in American history." Developing Decatur's life and career as a "romantic drama," Lewis concludes that his "heroic deeds, and even his untimely death, have made his the most romantic figure of his generation — the very embodiment of chivalrous patriotic youth."

A popular biography is Irwin Anthony, *Decatur* (New York, 1931), which extolls Decatur and claims that the "full facts in his case lead on to lyricism." Unfortunately, this narrative lacks critical analysis and is marred by a florid style that is imprecise and often misleading. The standard nineteenth-century biography is Alexander Slidell Mackenzie, *The Life of Stephen Decatur* (Boston, 1846). Although this biography necessarily lacks historical perspective, it details the various anecdotes, stories, and incidents that comprise the full Decatur legend and, as such, is an interesting source of further reading.

Given the paucity of recent material on Decatur, those interested in further reading should consult studies dealing with the most prominent events and personalities associated with Decatur's career. Among the most noteworthy biographies treating aspects of his career are David F. Long, *Nothing Too Daring: A Biography of Commodore David Porter, 1780–1843* (Annapolis, Md., 1970); Christopher McKee, *Edward Preble: A Naval Biography, 1761–1807* (Annapolis, Md., 1972); and Charles O. Paullin, *Commodore John Rodgers, Captain, Commodore, and Senior Officer of the American Navy, 1773–1838* (Cleveland, 1910). For an excellent popular account of Decatur and his contemporaries, see Leonard F. Guttridge and Jay D. Smith, *The Commodores* (New York, 1969).

A number of solid accounts exist on the Navy's role in the Barbary Wars. James A. Field, Jr., *America and the Mediterranean World, 1776–1882* (Princeton, N.J., 1969), is an extensively researched and well-written study that traces the Navy's role as one of the four themes that the author develops regarding the American role in the Mediterranean. Fletcher Pratt, *Preble's Boys: Commodore Preble and the Birth of American Sea Power* (New York, 1950), and Glenn Tucker, *Dawn Like Thunder: The Barbary Wars and the Birth of the U.S. Navy* (Indianapolis, 1963), present solid accounts of the Navy and the Barbary states. For the diplomatic role of the Navy in these wars see Charles O. Paullin, *Diplomatic Negotiations of American Naval Officers, 1778–1883* (Baltimore, 1912). William Shaler, who helped to negotiate the 1815 agreement with Algiers, is treated in "On the Shores of Barbary," in Roy F. Nichols, *Advance Agents of American Destiny* (Philadelphia, 1956).

For the Navy's role in the War of 1812, the two standard studies are Alfred T. Mahan, *Sea Power in Its Relation to the War of 1812*, 2 vols. (Boston, 1919), and Theodore Roosevelt, *The Naval War of 1812* (New York, 1882). An excellent basic history is Reginald Horsman, *The War of 1812* (New York, 1969). In addition to the accounts of the Barron-Decatur affair in the biographies of Rodgers and Porter, the duel is treated in Hamilton Cochran, *Noted American Duels and Hostile Encounters* (Philadelphia, 1963), and Don C. Seitz, *Famous American Duels* (New York, 1929).

NOTES

1. Charles Francis Adams, ed., *Memoirs of John Quincy Adams, Comprising Portions of His Diary from 1795 to 1848*, 12 vols. (Philadelphia, 1874–1877), 5:32, 36.

2. For detailed narratives of Decatur's life and career, see Charles Lee Lewis, *The Romantic Decatur* (Philadelphia, 1937), and Alexander Slidell Mackenzie, *The Life of Stephen Decatur* (Boston, 1846).

3. Mackenzie, *Life of Decatur*, 17–18.

4. Lewis, *Romantic Decatur*, 19–20.

5. Remarks of Captain Robert S. Spence as quoted in Mackenzie, *Life of Decatur*, 35–36.

6. For background on American diplomatic relations with the Barbary powers, see James A. Field, Jr., *America and the Mediteranean World, 1776–1882* (Princeton, N.J., 1969), and Ray W. Irwin, *The Diplomatic Relations of the United States with the Barbary Powers, 1776–1816* (Chapel Hill, N.C., 1931).

7. See Christopher McKee, *Edward Preble: A Naval Biography 1761–1807* (Annapolis, Md., 1972).

8. Ibid., 190–91; Mackenzie, *Life of Decatur*, 65.

9. Captain Edward Preble to Lieutenant Stephen Decatur, 31 January 1804, in *Naval Documents Related to the United States War with the Barbary Powers*, 7 vols. (Washington, D.C., 1939–1944), 3:376–77 (hereafter cited as *NDBP*).

10. For descriptions of the action, see Decatur to Preble, 17 February 1804; Lieutenant Charles Stewart to Preble, 19 February 1804; and Preble to Secretary of the Navy, 19 February 1804, *NDBP*, 3:414–15, 415–16, 440–41.

11. Preble to Secretary of Navy, 19 February 1804, *NDBP*, 3:441.

12. *Annals of Congress*, 2d Session, 8th Congress (1804–1805), 16, 17, 682–83.

13. For accounts of these actions, see Preble to Secretary of the Navy, 18 September 1804; Narrative of Attacks on Tripoli by Richard O'Brien; and Decatur to Preble, 3 August 1804, *NDBP*, 4:293–310, 341–43, 345.

14. Mackenzie, *Life of Decatur*, 136–38.

15. Decatur to Secretary of the Navy, 8 June 1812, Captains' Letters, Record Group 45, National Archives. On the question of strategy, see Alfred T. Mahan, *Sea Power in Its Relation to the War of 1812*, 2 vols. (Boston, 1919), 1:314–19.

16. Mackenzie, *Life of Decatur*, 156–58.

17. For Decatur's account of the battle, see Decatur to Secretary of the Navy, 30 October 1812, Captains' Letters; and Decatur to Susan Decatur, 30 October 1812, in Mackenzie, *Life of Decatur*, 371–72. For descriptions of the battle, see Mahan, *Sea Power*, 1:416–22, and Theodore Roosevelt, *The Naval War of 1812*, (New York, 1882), 144–56.

18. Decatur to Secretary of the Navy, 18 January 1815, Captains' Letters. Also, see Mahan, *Sea Power, 1812*, 2:397–403; and Roosevelt, *Naval War*, 144–49.

19. Mahan, *Sea Power*, 2:401–3; Roosevelt, *Naval War*, 144–54; and Report of the Court of Inquiry, 17 April 1815, *Niles Weekly Register* 8 (29 April 1815): 147–48.

20. Secretary of the Navy to Decatur, 20 April 1815, *Niles Weekly Register*, 8 (29 April 1815), 148.

21. Decatur to Secretary of the Navy, 19 and 20 June and 5 July 1815, in *American State Papers*, ser. 8: Naval Affairs, 4 vols., class 6 (Washington, D.C., 1834), 1:396.

22. Decatur to Secretary of the Navy, 5 July 1815, in ibid. Also, see Charles O. Paullin, *Diplomatic Negotiations of American Naval Officers, 1778–1883* (Baltimore, 1912), 110–15; "On the Shores of Barbary," in Roy F. Nichols, *Advance Agents of American Destiny* (Philadelphia, 1956), 113–24.

23. For correspondence that describes Decatur's activities in Tunis and Tripoli, see *American State Papers*, Class 6, 1:397–99. Also, see Paullin, *Diplomatic Negotiations*, 115–16.

24. Mackenzie, *Life of Decatur*, 294–96; and Lewis, *Romantic Decatur*, 182–83. Also, see Peter Karsten, *The Naval Aristocracy: The Golden Age of Annapolis and the Emergence of Modern American Navalism* (New York, 1972), 194–95.

25. Decatur to Secretary of the Navy, 2 January 1817, in Makenzie, *Life of Decatur*, 386–98.

26. Lewis, *Romantic Decatur*, 201–22; and Mackenzie, *Life of Decatur*, 303–34. Also, see Don C. Seitz, *Famous American Duels* (New York, 1929), 176–226.

27. The correspondence between Barron and Decatur is contained in Mackenzie, *Life of Decatur*, 398–440.

28. Lewis, *Romantic Decatur*, 223–37; and Seitz, *Famous Duels*, 222–25.

29. Mackenzie, *Life of Decatur*, 350–51.

30. Harold Sprout and Margaret Sprout, *The Rise of American Naval Power*, rev. ed. (Princeton, N.J., 1967), 83–85.

# ☆ Oliver Hazard Perry
☆
☆ **Savior of the Northwest**

*by John K. Mahon*

OLIVER HAZARD PERRY'S SHORT LIFE IS ALMOST EXCLUSIVELY A NAVAL one. He came into the world with navy in his blood. His father, Christopher Raymond, was in naval combat during the American Revolution and in British prisons for long stretches; when the Navy Department was created in 1798, he was commissioned captain. Oliver, born 20 August 1785, was the oldest of four sons and three daughters. All of the sons became officers in the Navy, and two of the daughters married naval officers.[1] Oliver's brother Matthew Calbraith, junior to him by nine years, became famous for commanding the U.S. expeditionary squadron during the Mexican War and for opening Japan to American trade.

In 1799, fourteen-year-old Oliver went on board the U.S. frigate *General Greene* (of twenty-eight guns) as a midshipman, under his father's command. Thereafter, he remained in the service until his premature death at age thirty-five. From the start, he learned his profession well; both afloat and ashore, he studied navigation, seamanship, and mathematics, and read Hackluyt. He worked with the guns too and became as fine an ordnance officer as there was in the service.

Apart from professional manuals, he read Shakespeare and Montaigne. He became an accomplished flutist, horseback rider, and fencer. The distinguished officers under whom he served contributed to his development: his father, Edward Preble, James Barron, Charles Morris, and, above all, John Rodgers. These and other senior officers were impressed with young Perry and took pains to advance his career. But, he owed more to diligence and to the consequent mastery of skills for his rise in the profession than to other contributants.[2] When he became a captain, he closely supervised the education of the young midshipmen under his command.

Perry rose rapidly in the young Navy. He was commissioned lieutenant at age seventeen while serving in the Mediterranean squadron; took command of the schooner *Nautilus* (with twelve guns) when he was twenty years old; and was chosen to direct the building of seventeen of Jefferson's gunboats two years later. Each of the gunboats was to be armed with a long twenty-four-pound gun and manned by thirty persons.[3] In 1809 he took command of the schooner *Revenge* (with twelve guns). But that ship came near to interrupting his upward mobility when, on 2 February 1811, she ran aground in a heavy fog and broke up on the rocks off Newport, Rhode Island. Perry was suspended from command pending a hearing on this loss. The panelists of the inquiry charged the grounding to the pilot, who was supposed to know the coastal waters, and exonerated Perry; but the loss of a ship marred his record nonetheless.[4]

Throughout the *Revenge* affair Perry seems to have tried to spare the feelings and protect the reputation of his second in command, Lieutenant Jacob Hite, notwithstanding that he had suspended Hite from duty for reasons that are not known. In spite of Perry's protection, the panelists decided that Hite's performance during the wreck was discreditable, and they broke him to midshipman and suspended him from active duty.[5] This episode reveals a tendency in Perry to shelter subordinates from their just deserts. One who was thus sheltered plagued the later years of Perry's life and did his best to destroy his superior's image in history.

The same day that President James Madison proclaimed a state of war against Great Britain, 18 June 1812, the Secretary of the Navy directed Perry to take command of the gunboats that he had helped to build at Newport. Perry instituted a rigorous training, putting the gunboats and their crews through fleetlike maneuvers and engaging them in sham battles.[6] But in time of war, this was not enough; like his peers, Perry needed the glory and honor that were to be attained only in combat. Accordingly, he steadily sought assignment to a seagoing fighting ship and, as steadily, failed to receive it. Finally, therefore, he requested transfer to the Great Lakes theater where John Rodgers assured him that, saltwater or not, there would be brisk fighting.[7]

On 8 February 1813, the Secretary of the Navy ordered Master Commandant Perry to proceed with 150 of his best gunboat sailors to report to Captain Isaac Chauncey, commander of the Great Lakes. Eager to see action, Perry lost no time in carrying out this directive.[8] On 28 February, only twenty days later, he met his new commanding officer, not on the Great Lakes but in Albany, New York. Chauncey—who was to be a central character in the events that placed Perry prominently in American history—personified one strain in the officer corps, Perry the opposite. Chauncey was an administrator, Perry an operational commander. Chauncey, the manager, ordered Perry, the combat officer, to travel westward with some of his Rhode Island men to Presque Isle on the south shore of Lake Erie, and there to build a naval squadron with which to wrest control of the lake from the British, who, at that time, dominated it. In carrying out this gigantic task, Perry was able to draw on his experience in building the Jefferson gunboats. After building the squadron, it was his task to become supreme on the lake, two hundred miles long and sixty miles wide, and over both tips of the Ontario Peninsula.[9]

Perry traveled in the bitter cold, partly by sled on the frozen lake, to reach Presque Isle on 27 March. The spot was one of natural beauty, with a fine but virtually undefended harbor. The garrison was insignificant, having but one cannon. As for building materials, the wood stood in the forest: cedar, black oak, white oak, chestnut, and pine for the decks. Nonwood materials had to come from Pittsburgh, Pennsylvania, 130 miles away, or Philadelphia, farther yet, via a series of small rivers and creeks. With the aid of army ordnance at Pittsburgh, Perry collected a few artillery pieces and some essential building materials. Authorities canvassed homes in the town for iron that could be put to naval use. At this time, as at all others, Perry doggedly held to his duty, and the building went forward.

Manpower was even scarcer than materials. A few blacksmiths could be drawn from the local militia, but more were needed and had to be trained as they worked. "Give me men, Sir," Perry wrote to Chauncey, "and I will acquire both for you and myself glory and honor ... or perish in the attempt."[10] Chauncey, who was hardpressed to hold his own against Sir James Lucas Yeo on Lake Ontario, sent small detachments but often retained the best sailors for his own command. Perry suspected as much, and, desperate as he was for reinforcements, he complained about one of the detachments sent to him. Had the Commodore ever seen these men? Chauncey, it happened, had had to curb his own operations to make that particular shipment and replied sharply. Perry was offended by the tone of the response and wrote to the Secretary of the Navy to request a transfer. "I cannot serve," he said, "under an officer who has been so totally regardless of my feelings."[11]

Here, Perry displayed the hypersensitivity common to the officer corps. Feelings were deep within these men, and they were touchy on matters of honor, glory, and pride. Chauncey became conciliatory, the Secretary denied the transfer request, and Perry characteristically stood to his duty. Although he continued to believe that his crews were composed of Chauncey's rejects, he did his best with them.[12]

Such supplies as reached Presque Isle came at prices so high that the Secretary often required Perry to justify them. For example, it cost a thousand dollars to ship one cannon from Albany to the lake region; this was the price of five hundred acres of good land around Pittsburgh. A barrel of flour came at one hundred dollars. Small wonder that the Secretary demanded to know why

Perry requisitioned expensive lead for ballast when big heavy stones lay about free of charge. Perry made the rational and plausible response that the runs (i.e., the shape of his ship's underbodies) were such that sufficient stones could not be placed in them, that pig iron, the usual ballast material, was not available; and that the lead he purchased for ballast, at any time, could be sold for the price that he had paid for it and the money returned to the treasury.[13]

With the advent of spring Perry surveyed his resources for the upcoming campaign season. His Lake Erie command included, in addition to the vessels he was building, five small craft at Black Rock on the Niagara River. The problem lay in uniting his squadron. The Black Rock ships were immobilized by the guns at Fort Erie on the Canadian side of the Niagara, and it would be difficult to get them out of the river and up the eighty miles to Presque Isle because the British dominated the lake. In addition, the harbor at Presque Isle was blocked by a bar at its mouth. Even at times of high water, no more than seven feet of water passed over it; at other times, as little as four. The two brigs building there would draw nine feet. Jesse D. Elliott, soon to loom large in Perry's life, had told his supervisors that the place was unsuitable for the American base on Lake Erie because of the bar. Perry, who did not create the situation, accepted it as part of what he must overcome to do his duty and earn honor and glory.[14]

The opportunity to free the vessels at Black Rock came late in May 1813. Chauncey, for the Navy, and General Henry Dearborn, for the Army, agreed to assault Fort George, which sat at the northern end of the Niagara River. Chauncey summoned Perry to take part and turned the naval action ashore over to him. Perry had scant respect for the Army but found himself able to work well with Colonel Winfield Scott, to whom Dearborn had delegated the Army's role. Perry planned the river crossing and personally led the landing party that established the beachhead. The joint American force captured Fort George on 27 May, whereupon the British evacuated Fort Erie at the other end of the Niagara without a fight.

Now the Black Rock ships could emerge onto Lake Erie, but only after a herculean effort in which sailors yoked up with oxen and two hundred soldiers sent by General Dearborn dragged them against the swift current of the river as it rushed toward Niagara Falls. By 12 June, the vessels were on the lake and hugging the south shore for the eighty miles to Presque Isle in order to elude the British.[15]

Why had the enemy not wiped out Perry's precarious base when it was virtually defenseless? One part of the answer is that the British, like the Americans, were at the tip of their line of communications; supplies had to come up the Saint Lawrence, go through Lake Ontario, and only then reach Erie. Perforce, the end-of-the-line forces were chronically short of everything they needed. Added to this difficulty was another, the complicated layers of command interposed between a commander on Erie and supplies, men, and strategy.

Sir John Borlase Warren, British naval commander in North America, sent Captain Robert Heriot Barclay, a veteran who had lost an arm at Trafalgar, to the Great Lakes in February 1813, but some of his superiors retained Barclay on Lake Ontario too long. Finally he was told to go to Erie and take charge, but it was 3 June before, with the utmost effort, he could reach Amherstburg. There, he joined the ships of the British squadron and took to the lake at once to try to intercept the Black Rock vessels. Because the vessels were on the lake on 12 June, he had scant time for preparations.

In any case, Perry got them inside the Presque Isle bar on 19 and 20 June. Barclay reported that the Americans had slipped by him in heavy fog. He knew now that added forces were necessary to attack Presque Isle, and he pleaded for them to every commander, army and naval, who might help. His requests ricocheted around among Brigadier John Vincent, Governor General George Prevost, Brigadier Henry Procter, Major General Francis DeRottenburg, and Sir James Yeo, but none of them could find soldiers or sailors to wipe out Perry's menacing establishment.[16] Perry, who would have resisted, however futilely, any attack, never stopped putting together an American squadron to contest for the control of Lake Erie.

There is an ingredient in martial achievement that—combined with diligence and determination in the commander—must be present: luck. Perry was lucky that the British did not strike him when he was all but defenseless. Nor did luck desert him later.

By 10 July, Perry's squadron was ready, except for a shortage of sailors, to cross the bar. His twin brigs were 141 feet long by 30 feet wide, with two masts. Each mounted twenty guns, two of them long, the rest carronades, shorter in range but able to throw heavier projectiles. Perry knew that Barclay was hurrying to finish one ship equal to one of his brigs and that whoever got onto the lake first with a superior squadron might dominate it afterward. Sometime in July Perry learned that his closest friend in the Navy, James Lawrence, had been killed on board the *Chesapeake* in a battle with the frigate *Shannon* on 12 July. Consequently, Perry named the brig he had chosen as his flagship the *Lawrence*, and he saw to the sewing of a battle flag with Lawrence's last words worked onto it: "Don't Give Up the Ship!" Her twin brig received the name *Niagara*.

Noah Brown, who had supervised building the two brigs, said they were good for one battle, no more. Constructed as they were of green wood, a musket ball could penetrate their two inches of planking.[17]

It was a mile from deep water in the harbor to deep water in the lake. The two brigs would have to be mounted on "camels" to pass over the bar and the shoal water beyond it. The camels would be filled with water in the harbor and pumped dry at the bar, at which time they would lift the vessels high enough to pass over. Because of their weight, the guns would have to be dismounted; thus, while in transit, the vessels would be utterly helpless. In spite of this vulnerability, and in spite of being short about 250 men, Perry decided that he must go over. He positioned the dismounted guns and the light craft to give as much defense to the operation as was possible and started the movement on Sunday, 1 August. The country people from far and near came to watch, and the local militia pitched in to help with the heavy hauling. By Monday the five Black Rock vessels were over and posted defensively.

On 4 August, the *Lawrence* was afloat on the lake, but the *Niagara* was stuck in the shoals. At that critical moment, Barclay's squadron—minus his big ship, which was not yet finished—appeared. Perry now demonstrated the audacity that marked him as a combat commander by sending the *Ariel* and the *Scorpion* out to sail straight at the foe as they fired their long twenty-four-pounders. Thinking he saw a formidable squadron over the bar, Barclay failed to realize the Americans' vulnerability and sailed back toward Amherstburg, not to emerge again until his flagship, *Detroit*, was able to join.

For his part, Perry remounted the armament on his big ships and prepared them to cruise. His audacity, supported by luck, had brought him success. Barclay had always asserted that he could prevent Perry's crossing the Presque Isle bar.[18]

During the second week of August 1813, Master Commandant Jesse D. Elliott reported to Perry. He brought with him about a hundred men and the letter from Chauncey that caused Perry to ask for transfer. Perry's sailing master, William V. Taylor, noted that Elliott detailed the best of the replacements to the *Niagara*, which he was to command. Taylor protested to Perry, but the latter, showing his tendency to avoid ruffling the feelings of subordinates, let the matter pass.[19]

Perry now pointed his squadron up the lake toward the British base, 150 miles away. Illness appeared to be draining away his luck. Half of his crews were down with typhoid or malaria, and he, himself, was too sick to be on deck during the latter part of August. Good fortune returned, however, and he resumed active control on 1 September.[20]

As Perry's place on the roster of American military immortals depends on one battle, the details of that fight bearing on his leadership are here essential. Major General William Henry Harrison, commander of the land forces across the lake from Amherstburg, had been waiting many months for American domination of Erie so that he could cross and invade Upper Canada. It was grievous to Perry to have to tell Harrison from time to time that he must wait longer. Now he informed the general that a lack of manpower held him up. Harrison offered soldiers, and Perry accepted those who could be of help. The Secretary of the Navy rebuked Perry mildly for informing an army officer of his deficiencies. Such shortcomings, he said, ought to be kept within the naval service.[21]

Perry and Harrison together reconnoitered the upper lake and selected South Bass Island as the staging point for action against the British. Thirty-five miles from the enemy's base, the island has a good harbor—later designated Put-in-Bay—and it was a logical place to move the army from the American mainland if and when it could invade.[22] While Perry positioned his squadron to ensure that there would be a climactic battle, his superior, Captain Chauncey, was maneuvering on Lake Ontario in such a way as to virtually ensure that there would be no battle. For ten weeks or so, he and Sir James Yeo engaged in Virginia-reel-like action, falling back, and advancing, over and over. Neither commander was willing to bring on the climactic battle on the lake. Chauncey, for example, would never risk his fast ships to overtake the enemy while trusting the laggards to catch up in time to turn the tide. Instead he caused the swift ones to take the dullards in tow.[23]

Developments on the British side of Lake Erie were pushing toward the showdown that Perry sought. Supplies had piled up at Long Point that were desperately needed at the head of the lake, 150 miles away. They could not be transported by land, only via the lake. Barclay launched the *Detroit*, without stores or crew, on 20 July, and armed her with nineteen long guns of four different calibers and two howitzers removed from the forts. Filling out his crews with men from the foot regiments, he prepared for combat.

Perry knew in general terms of Barclay's preparations and took pains to avoid being taken by surprise. Should Barclay attack his squadron at anchor, the ships should weigh anchor and form a line with the *Lawrence* in the lead. Should there not be time for such a maneuver, the ships should cut their cables and make sail behind the leewardmost vessel. Passwords were devised to avoid confusion during darkness. Twice Perry reconnoitered Barclay's fleet at Fort Malden and surveyed the coast for suitable places to land Harrison's army.

By the beginning of September, Barclay had to act. Perry's anchorage in the Bass Islands virtually blockaded the British at Malden and cut their supply lines from the east. With twenty thousand troops and Indian allies to feed, Barclay's stores ran low, and he was forced to put his men on reduced rations. On 6 September, he informed his commanders that he was prepared to leave his base and fight. He knew that his squadron was inferior but not to what degree, and his only alternative was to abandon his ships and withdraw overland. The obvious choice was to fight.

The balance of forces slightly favored the Americans:[24]

|         | Ships | Brigs | Schooners | Sloops | Men | Guns | Weight of Broadside |
|---------|-------|-------|-----------|--------|-----|------|---------------------|
| U.S.    | 2     | 1     | 5         | 1      | 530 | 54   | 896 lb.             |
| British | 2     | 2     | 1         | 1      | 440 | 63   | 459 lb.             |

Barclay's advantage lay in his superiority in long guns, but Perry knew this and planned to bring his squadron into close action rapidly, where his superior weight of broadside would count. Thus, he directed each ship captain to close with the opposite of his class and engage at close range. The *Lawrence*, Perry commanding, would duel the other flagship, the *Detroit*, and the *Niagara*, Jesse Elliott commanding, would fight the *Queen Charlotte*.[25]

American lookouts sighted the British squadron nine miles west of Put-in-Bay and nine miles from the U.S. mainland. The direction of the wind made it difficult for Perry to leave harbor, but so determined was he to engage that he ordered the line to move anyway, working from the lee side. He made the rounds of the gun crews, and his visit strengthened their determination. Forty-seven of his guns were manned by Rhode Islanders, for whom he had special encouragements. Next he ran up the banner, "Don't Give Up the Ship," and urged the sailors to follow the motto; they responded with a great shout.

Then the Perry luck reasserted itself, as the wind swung around ninety degrees to give him the weather gauge. His squadron straightaway fanned down upon the enemy at an angle of about twenty-five degrees in order to get within carronade range the fastest way. The oblique approach subjected the *Lawrence*, in the lead, to heavy fire before she could bring her own broadsides to bear. Moreover, Barclay, who had decided that his best tactic was to knock out the American flagship, concentrated thirty-five of his sixty-three guns on the *Lawrence*. Beginning at a range of one and a half miles, the British long guns began to take effect. Because, for some reason, Elliott did not bring up the *Niagara* to close, the *Queen Charlotte* could also concentrate on the *Lawrence*.

In spite of the punishment, Perry got his vessel to within three hundred yards of the *Detroit* and pounded away at her. For two and a half hours the American flagship absorbed as severe a shelling as any ship ever has. By 1:30 P.M. the *Lawrence* was dead in the water, but still fighting. Thirty minutes later, only 19 of her crew of 142 men were fit for duty. In the midst of the maelstrom, however, the Perry luck was holding. Dressed as a common sailor in order to deceive marksmen, Perry stood at his post, where he was slightly wounded once, while men fell all around him and spattered him with their blood and brains.[26]

Elliott finally brought the *Niagara* forward, but he kept the *Caledonia*, which had closely supported Perry throughout the battle, and the shattered *Lawrence* between his ship and the enemy broadsides. When the *Niagara* was about half a mile from the flagship, Perry decided to shift to her, perfectly unharmed as she was. He boarded the gig, providentially intact, and with five sailors and his brother Alexander, made for the *Niagara*. Once the British saw the movement, they opened fire on the little boat, but, in fifteen minutes, Perry was across the bullet-churned water and on board his new flagship. Although there were precedents for this transit in the English-Dutch wars, it was rare enough to be astonishing. Numerous pictures of it have been painted by artists who were not there, more than one of which depicts Perry standing upright in full-dress uniform with his sword pointed straight out like a lance. Perry, who knew better than to posture in this critical moment, was, of course, still in common sailor's garb, and sitting because the rowers begged him to sit.[27]

It can never be known for sure what passed between the two master commandants when Perry came on board. There are several versions of the conversation, all of them suspect because of bias.[28] It is certain, however, what took place next. Elliott got into a small boat and was rowed to the lesser warships to bring them into closer action. His passage, like Perry's, was hazardous. Perry curbed the speed of the *Niagara*, which seemed to him about to run out of the battle, and turned into what was left of the British line so as to cross the "T" on both broadsides. The *Niagara* raked the vessels to her left and right from stem to stern. At three o'clock, fifteen minutes after Perry's transit, the *Detroit* struck her colors, and the other British ships soon did the same. Here, for the first time in history, a full British squadron was surrendered.[29]

That great historian Henry Adams said of the result, "More than any other battle of the time (this) was won by the courage and obstinacy of one man."[30] Perry reported his victory in simple, powerful words. To the Secretary he wrote, "It has pleased the almighty to give the arms of the United States a signal victory over our enemies on this Lake . . ."; and to General Harrison, "We have met the enemy and they are ours, two ships, two brigs, one schooner and one sloop."[31]

This tiny action, involving fifteen vessels, 117 guns, and about one thousand men, ranks as one of the decisive battles in American history when one considers the results. By gaining control of Lake Erie, and with it the waterways between Upper Canada and Michigan, it transferred the initiative to the Americans. The British found their position in Michigan and Ohio untenable; they were forced to withdraw, and the Northwest was preserved for the United States. William Henry Harrison was now able to invade Upper Canada. Beginning on 20 September, Perry transported Harrison's troops to Canada. Thereafter, his squadron kept the invading army supplied, while Perry himself joined the general and, on 5 October 1813, was in the forefront of the Battle of the Thames, which broke the fighting power of the British west of the Niagara River.[32]

Only ten days after his great achievement, Perry requested to be relieved from the Erie command. Why he did so is not known. He had found it trying to work under Chauncey and, perhaps, to function as Elliott's superior. Moreover, little honor seemed available while Chauncey continued his combat-free maneuvering on Ontario. In any case, the Navy Department granted his request. On 25 October, he transferred the Erie command to Elliott and began a hero's progress across the northeastern United States to his home in Newport. Chauncey protested the department's decision to release Perry because it would make it difficult to hold competent officers in the lake zone. To him, Perry was deserting his post, and, to a degree, he was.[33]

In reporting the battle, Perry had made a grave mistake. Dissatisfied as he had been with Elliott's performance, he yet wrote in his official account, "At half past two, the wind springing up, Captain Elliott was enabled to bring his vessel . . . gallantly into close action." Without adding that he had personally assumed command of the *Niagara*, Perry went on to say, "In this action, [Elliott] evinced his characteristic bravery and judgment."[34] Later, he acknowledged that it was foolish of him to have written this because it was not true. He explained his lapse thus: "At such a moment, there was not a person in the world whose feeling I would have hurt."

Almost immediately after the battle, Elliott began to demand more recognition than was in the after-action report. In response, just nine days from the fight, Perry informed Elliott that his conduct had his commander's "warmest approbation."[35] This distortion of what Perry really believed, in order to spare the feelings and the record of a subordinate, dogged him the rest of his life. Elliott persisted in his demand that the report be changed. Finally, in 1818, he challenged his former commander to a duel.[36] By this time Perry no longer cared about the man's feelings. He replied that he could fight only a gentleman, which Elliott had proved he was not, and that he would file formal charges against him. If the resultant court-martial exonerated him, then, and only then, would there be a duel.

The charges went to the Secretary of the Navy on 10 August 1818, nearly five years after the battle. They stipulated that Elliott had disobeyed his orders; had hung a mile behind the *Lawrence*; had handled his sails to keep clear of the melee; and through "cowardice, negligence, or disaffection" had not done his utmost to destroy the vessel he had been assigned to attack. The Secretary, not wishing to divide the officer corps on a matter so far in the past, passed the papers along to the President without recommendation. James Monroe, for political reasons, chose to pigeonhole them; so there never was a trial. As a consequence, years after Perry had died, Elliott was asserting that he, not Perry, had really won the battle.[37]

Elliott's campaign did not dislodge Perry from his pedestal in American history, nor did it perpetuate Elliott's own name, but it poisoned relations within the Navy's officer corps for thirty years. Only the Sampson-Schley controversy at the turn of the twentieth century rivals it for acrimony and longevity. Writers, such as the novelist-historian James Fenimore Cooper and the naval officer-biographer Alexander Mackenzie, were drawn into the fray. More recent historians have preferred to overlook the bitter dispute between the naval hero and the officer who wished to replace him as hero. The one place where Elliott nearly got even was in the distribution of prize money. Congress appropriated $250,000 to distribute among officers and sailors for the capture of the British squadron. At the start, Elliott received $7,140, the same sum as Perry. Chauncey, who was in overall command on the lake though not present at the battle, received more than either of the participants, his share being $12,750. Later Congress voted five thousand more for Perry.[38]

The balance of Perry's short life is quickly told. In 1814, when the British fleet moved up the Potomac River, Perry, with John Rodgers and David Porter, was sent by the department to delay the British in any way possible. They put naval guns ashore and commanded batteries that harassed the invading ships as they returned down the river.[39] Perry was assigned to supervise the completion of the *Java*, a frigate of forty-four guns, and command her when at sea. The ship was built like a fine piece of cabinetwork, but what Perry did not know was that some of the wood used was substandard. It was 1816 before the *Java* was ready to sail for the Mediterranean. During that voyage, one of the yards broke, pitching five sailors to their death on the deck and revealing rotten wood.

That year continued to be a bad one for Perry. While serving with the Mediterranean squadron, he made a second serious error; he struck Captain John Heath, the commander of marines on board the *Java*. Perry reported his violation of regulations to his superiors at once, acknowledging that he had lost control of himself. There was a court of inquiry; the judges censured Heath and gave a light reprimand to Perry. Some of his oldest associates, senior captains, protested that Perry's sentence was too lenient. To condone striking a junior officer, they said, opened the way to arbitrary, dictatorial conduct by senior commanders. Others of Perry's peers defended him to the point of demanding that the protesters be dismissed. The sentence stood, and no one was let go.[40]

In the Marine Corps an officer could not allow a blow, whoever struck it, to go unrevenged. Therefore, Heath persisted in demanding satisfaction. Finally, on 19 October 1818, two years after the event, Heath and Perry met in a duel at Weehawken, where Alexander Hamilton had been killed by Aaron Burr in 1804. Like Hamilton, Perry let it be known that he would not fire at all; while he stood with his arms at his side, Heath shot and missed. Perry's second proposed to Heath that what had occurred ought to satisfy his honor; Heath agreed, and the matter ended there.[41]

In Perry's naval career, very little of historical note had occurred for some time. Then, in 1819, the Secretary of the Navy directed him to sail in the frigate *John Adams*, accompanied by the schooner *Nonsuch*, to find the leaders of Venezuela, a new nation freshly created by Simon Bolívar, and negotiate a treaty with them not to molest American merchantmen. To find the Venezuelan government, Perry had to work his way 150 miles or so up the Orinoco River in the *Nonsuch* because the frigate drew too much water. At the town of Angostura, the captain found a vice president, Francisco Zea, who seemed competent to negotiate, because Bolívar himself, the head of state, was off fighting for independence from Spain in another area. By the time Perry had secured an agreement from Zea and started down the river, it was August, with fearful heat and clouds of insects.

The Navy Department, one supposes, had no way of knowing that to order a voyage into the jungle at that season was the equivalent of issuing a death warrant. Among the swarming insects were mosquitoes, carriers of deadly yellow fever. Perry's crew was decimated. The captain wrote his reaction to the conditions: "I meet this danger as I do all others, simply because it is my duty; Yet I must own that there is something more appalling in the shape of death approaching in a fever than in the form of a cannon ball." The Perry luck had finally run out. It was his fate to accept death in the more appalling form: yellow fever killed him at the mouth of the Orinoco River on 23 August 1819, just three days after his thirty-fourth birthday.[42]

The family he left behind consisted of his widow, three sons, and one daughter. Congress voted Elizabeth Mason Perry four hundred dollars per year through her life and all of the children fifty dollars per year until they were of age. The daughter's annuity was to run for life if she did not marry. Congress here exceeded its previous provision for dependents, which ended with the life of the veteran himself.[43]

This concern for Perry's heirs reflected the commodore's treatment of others while he was alive. Perry was generally conciliatory and humane, reserved in public but warm with close associates. His best friends in the Navy were James Lawrence and Stephen Decatur, two of its finest officers. Midshipmen who were fortunate enough to serve with him received an excellent professional beginning. Perry opened his library to them, and they remembered his guidance in later life. Other subordinates, including Sailing Master William V. Taylor and Surgeon Usher Parsons, considered him a brave officer; they respected not only his ability as a fighter but also his humanity toward the sick and wounded. Among the latter, Perry's prisoner, Captain Robert Barclay, who had been terribly wounded, recorded that his captor treated him like a brother.

Perry expected the best from common sailors and got it by visiting them at their battle stations, by appealing to their pride, and by standing under the same hail of bullets that they endured. After the war, while recruiting a crew for the *Java*, Perry had to turn away good seamen who had flocked to serve with him because he was the sort of hero who reflected credit upon them.

Better than many of his peers, Perry worked effectively with competent army officers. He and Winfield Scott shared in the capture of Fort George, and he and William Henry Harrison cooperated to bring about the final defeat of the British army in Upper Canada.[44]

Perry is remembered in the Navy, however, not as a hail-fellow-well-met, but for winning one of the decisive battles in American history. In doing so he became a national hero. While the memory of his achievement was fresh, citizens named nineteen towns and nine counties after him. Painters executed a dozen or more heroic portraits of Perry and at least as many canvases of the Battle of Lake Erie, most of them featuring the transit from the *Lawrence* to the *Niagara*. A massive monument to him stands on South Bass Island and another, less massive but more artistic, in Newport, Rhode Island, his hometown. A third statue stands in Buffalo, New York. A replica of the *Niagara*, containing some fragments of the original, is placed on a hillside overlooking the harbor at Erie, Pennsylvania. The U.S. Naval Academy displays the sword Perry wore during the battle and spreads the pennant, "Don't Give Up the Ship," in Bancroft Hall. During the past half century, seven articles in which Perry is mentioned, some of them featuring him, have been printed in the *Proceedings* of the United States Naval Institute.[45]

Part of the Perry legacy is the imbroglio between him and Jesse D. Elliott. This demonstrates to all generations that it never pays to gloss over a poor performance in order to protect the feelings or the record of any person. Too late, Perry himself recognized this. When his relationship with Elliott had deteriorated as far as it could go, he wrote him: "I shall never cease to criminate myself (for giving a favorable report of your conduct) for the sake of screening you from public contempt."[46]

Perry was not a managerial officer. When caught in an inactive theater, he sought transfer to the combat zone. Once there, he bent all his energy to engage the foe in a climactic battle. In his day, it was still possible to win a campaign, even a war, in a day. He drew on his reserve strength to be ready for the decisive moment; for example, when dragging the ships across the bar at Presque Isle, he went without sleep for three days and three nights. Although he stood throughout the action, he took pains, as noted earlier, to keep from being foolishly conspicuous. Perry was basically a kind man, but in battle he became so preoccupied with the outcome as to be unconscious of the misery about him. He was prepared to lose his life for three intangibles: duty, honor, and glory.

Certainly he was not indifferent to material rewards, yet he would not accept the percentages of the cost of ships built under his supervision, to which he was entitled by regulation. He feared this sort of financial gain might warp his judgment as a fighting officer. It is no small part of his legacy to his profession that he was first and foremost a combat officer.[47]

FURTHER READING

Biographers have widely differed in their evaluations of Oliver Hazard Perry. James Fenimore Cooper, *Lives of Distinguished American Naval Officers*, 2 vols. (Philadelphia, 1846), is less favorable to Perry than is any other biographer, whereas the most recent biography of Perry, Richard Dillon's *We Have Met the Enemy: Oliver Hazard Perry, Wilderness Commodore* (New York, 1978) is one of the most positive. The latter contains neither footnotes nor bibliography, but it is apparent that Dillon has used well the Perry Papers in the William L. Clements Library, Ann Arbor, Michigan. It is not clear if he used the Perry Collection at the Northwest Ohio Great Lakes Research Center at Bowling Green State University or Perry's correspondence with the Secretary of the Navy, which is in the National Archives. He has not, however, consulted British Admiralty Records or Colonial Office records in Kew or the manuscripts in the Public Archives of Canada in Ottawa. If the reader has time for only one volume, this is the one to read. Charles J. Dutton's *Oliver Hazard Perry* (New York, 1935) is not a first-class biography, but it is the second choice after Dillon's. Alexander S. Mackenzie's *The Life of Commodore Oliver Hazard Perry*, 2 vols. (New York, 1840) is essential reading for the inquirer who wishes to get below the surface. Much of the second volume is taken up with documents, among them the charges Perry made against Elliott five years after the action. Frederick L. Oliver's "Commodore Oliver Hazard Perry of Newport, Rhode Island," U.S. Naval Institute *Proceedings* 80 (1954): 777–83, is a tidy summary if the reader has only a short time to read.

Much has been written about the Battle of Lake Erie, Perry's major claim to fame. Theodore Roosevelt covers the battle in *The Naval War of 1812* (New York, 1882). He says that James Fenimore Cooper's critical analysis of the battle in *History of the Navy of the United States of America*, 2nd ed., 2 vols. (Philadelphia, 1840) is inaccurate. Roosevelt also believed William James's *Full and Correct Account of the Chief Naval Occurrences of the Late War between Great Britain and the United States*, 2 vols. (London, 1818) to be unreliable on the lake war, but it does provide the British point of view. Benson J. Lossing's *Pictorial Field-Book of the War of 1812* (New York, 1868) may be the best short summary of all. It contains diagrams of the ship positions and pictures of the sites and participants. Alfred Thayer Mahan, *Sea Power in Its Relation to the War of 1812*, 2 vols. (Boston, 1919), is especially good in contrasting Perry's dash with Chauncey's excessive caution. On naval matters, it never pays to neglect Mahan. James H. Ward's *Manual of Naval Tactics* (New York, 1859) is very instructive because it includes a technical examination of the battle and the handling of the sails and sailing accessories. James C. Mills's *Oliver Hazard Perry and the Battle of Lake Erie* (Detroit, 1913) was issued as a centenary tribute and tells a straightforward story but is too eulogistic and condemns Elliott without reservation.

Richard J. Cox, "An Eye-Witness Account of the Battle of Lake Erie," U.S. Naval Institute *Proceedings* 104 (1978): 72–73, published the account of Samuel Hambleton, who was Perry's purser during the battle. The papers of another participant, Daniel Dobbins, who was sailing master under Perry, were used by his son to produce a very useful account entitled *History of the Battle of Lake Erie (September 10 1813), and Reminiscences of the Flagship "Lawrence" and "Niagara"* (Erie, 1876).

Several collections of primary sources have been published. *Anecdotes of the Lake Erie Area: War of 1812* (Columbus, Ohio, 1957), transcribed from the original sources by Richard C. Knopf, contains extracts from the court-martial proceedings of Robert

Heriot Barclay, the British commander, and accounts of participants Usher Parsons, David C. Bunnell, and Isaac Roach.

In 1835, a volume entitled *A Biographical Notice of Commodore Jesse D. Elliott Containing a Review of the Controversy between Him and the Late Commodore Perry* was anonymously published in Philadelphia. It was written or prepared by Elliott himself and contends that Elliott, not Perry, was the true victor in the Battle of Lake Erie. Stephen Decatur's widow had *Documents in Relation to the Differences Which Subsisted between the Late Commodore O. H. Perry and Captain Jesse D. Elliott* (Boston, 1834) published from papers that were left with Decatur by his friend O. H. Perry. Elliott had been James Barron's second in the duel in which Barron killed Decatur in 1820. These documents do not spare Elliott.

Charles O. Paullin, ed., *The Battle of Lake Erie: A Collection of Documents* (Cleveland, 1918), contains the proceedings of the court-martial of Robert Heriot Barclay and the court of inquiry of Jesse D. Elliott.

NOTES

1. John M. Niles, *Life of Oliver Hazard Perry*, 3d ed. (Hartford, 1821), 16, 17; Richard Dillon, *We Have Met the Enemy: Oliver Hazard Perry, Wilderness Commodore* (New York, 1978), 1.

2. Dillon, *We Have Met the Enemy*, 4, 6, 16, 18; Niles, *Life of Perry*, 23, 25; and Charles J. Dutton, *Oliver Hazard Perry* (New York, 1935), 17.

3. Dutton, *Perry*, 24, 28, 41; Niles, *Life of Perry*, 31, 57, 223; Dillon, *We Have Met the Enemy*, 13, 28, 38, 39; and Frederick L. Oliver, "Commodore Oliver Hazard Perry of Newport, Rhode Island," U.S. Naval Institute *Proceedings* 80 (July 1954): 778.

4. Dutton, *Perry*, 24, 28; Alexander S. Mackenzie, *The Life of Commodore Oliver Hazard Perry* (New York, 1840), 1:99.

5. Dillon, *We Have Met the Enemy*, 39ff.

6. Dutton, *Perry*, 50; and *Appleton's Cyclopaedia of American Biography*, 6 vols. (New York, 1887–1889), 4:735.

7. Dillon, *We Have Met the Enemy*, 54; and Mackenzie, *Life of Commodore Perry*, 1:122.

8. Secretary of the Navy to Perry, 8 February 1813, Record Group (RG) 45; Letters Sent by the Secretary of the Navy to Officers, National Archives (hereafter cited as Secretary of the Navy Letters).

9. Mackenzie, *Life of Commodore Perry*, 1:130–33, 170, 171; and Dutton, *Perry*, 56ff, 63, 73.

10. Quoted in Dillon, *We Have Met the Enemy*, 101.

11. Chauncey to Perry, 14 July 1813, RG 45, Letters Received by the Secretary of the Navy: Captains' Letters, National Archives; Perry to Secretary of the Navy William Jones, as quoted in Alfred Thayer Mahan, *Sea Power in Its Relation to the War of 1812*, 2 vols. (Boston, 1919), 2:63–66; and Dutton, *Perry*, 113.

12. Richard J. Cox, "An Eye-Witness Account of the Battle of Lake Erie," U.S. Naval Institute *Proceedings* 104 (February 1978): 73.

13. Dillon, *We Have Met the Enemy*, 64, 66, 67, 113, 114; George D. Emerson, comp., *The Perry Victory Centenary* (Albany, 1916), 158; and Mackenzie, *Life of Commodore Perry*, 1:208, 209.

14. Dillon, *We Have Met the Enemy*, 58; Fletcher Pratt, *The Navy* (Garden City,

N.Y., 1938), 178; Glenn Tucker, *Poltroons and Patriots: A Popular Account of the War of 1812*, 2 vols. (Indianapolis, 1954), 1:316; and Barclay to Yeo, 1 June 1813, printed in Richard C. Knopf, trans., *Ancedotes of the Lake Erie Area: War of 1812* (Columbus, Ohio, 1957), 17.

15. Mahan, *Sea Power*, 2:38, 41; Dillon, *We Have Met the Enemy*, 85–92, 94; and Chauncey to Secretary of the Navy, 29 May 1813, RG 45, Captains' Letters.

16. Dillon, *We Have Met the Enemy*, 94, 95; Barclay's narrative in Charles O. Paullin, ed., *The Battle of Lake Erie: A Collection of Documents* (Cleveland, 1918), 159–61; Barclay to Yeo, 4 June 1813 and 10 July 1813, in Knopf, *Anecdotes*, 23–24; Brigadier Vincent to Lieutenant General Sir George Prevost, Governor and Military Commander of all Canada, 18 June 1813, Public Archives of Canada; and Brigadier Henry Proctor to Prevost, 11 July 1813, Public Archives of Canada.

17. Mackenzie, *Life of Commodore Perry*, 1:136; Mahan, *Sea Power*, 2:62; Dutton, *Perry*, 86; and Dillon, *We Have Met the Enemy*, 98, 99, 116, 131. On carronades, see Spencer C. Tucker, "The Carronade," U.S. Naval Institute *Proceedings* 99 (August 1973): 65–70.

18. Dutton, *Perry*, 98, 105; Tucker, *Poltroons and Patriots*, 1:316, 317; Mackenzie, *Life of Commodore Perry*, 1:178; Mahan, *Sea Power*, 2:72; James C. Mills, *Oliver Hazard Perry and the Battle of Lake Erie* (Detroit, 1913), 86, 88; Dillon, *We Have Met the Enemy*, 108, 109; and Barclay's narrative in Paullin, *Battle of Lake Erie*, 161.

19. Dillon, *We Have Met the Enemy*, 112; and Mills, *Perry*, 91.

20. Mackenzie, *Life of Commodore Perry*, 1:203; Mills, *Perry*, 109; and Dr. Usher Parsons, in Knopf, *Anecdotes*, 53.

21. Mackenzie, *Life of Commodore Perry*, 1:210.

22. Mills, *Perry*, 107; and Dillon, *We Have Met the Enemy*, 97.

23. Mahan, *Sea Power*, 2:51, 55ff, 61.

24. Ibid., 2:71; and Barclay to Yeo, 6 September 1813, in Knopf, *Anecdotes*, 37. The strength figures come from William James, *Full and Correct Account of the Chief Naval Occurrences of the Late War between Great Britain and the United States*, 2 vols. (London, 1818), 292.

25. Mills, *Perry*, 119, 125.

26. Ibid., 122, 125, 130; Dillon, *We Have Met the Enemy*, 133–36, 149, 150; Mackenzie, *Life of Commodore Perry*, 1:229, 230, 234; Mahan, *Sea Power*, 2:72; Dutton, *Perry*, 145, 149, 154; Oliver, "Commodore Perry," 777; and James H. Ward, *Manual of Naval Tactics* (New York, 1859), 77.

27. C. S. Forester, *The Age of Fighting Sail: The Story of the Naval War of 1812* (New York, 1956), 183; Mackenzie, *Life of Commodore Perry*, 1:245; Mills, *Perry*, 130; and Emerson, *Perry Victory Centenary*, 147.

28. Elliott's version is carried in full in *A Biographical Notice of Commodore Jesse D. Elliott Containing a Review of the Controversy between Him and the Late Commodore Perry* (Philadelphia, 1835), 34; Cox, "Eye-Witness Account," 72; Emerson, *Perry Victory Centenary*, 158; Mackenzie, *Life of Commodore Perry*, 1:283; and Mahan, *Sea Power*, 2:97.

29. Mahan, *Sea Power*, 2:64, 76; Mackenzie, *Life of Commodore Perry*, 1:229; Mills, *Perry*, 145; Oliver, "Commodore Perry," 777; and Kenneth J. Hagan, ed., *In Peace and War* (Westport, Conn., 1978), 59.

30. Henry Adams, *The War of 1812*, edited by H. A. De Weerd (Washington, D.C., 1944), 69.

31. Perry to Secretary of the Navy, 10 September 1813, RG 45, Captains' Letters; and Perry to Harrison, 10 September 1813, in Logan Esarey, ed., *Messages and Letters of William Henry Harrison*, 2 vols. (Indianapolis, 1912), 2:539.

32. Perry to Secretary of the Navy, 24 September 1813, RG 45, Captains' Letters; Harrison to Secretary of War, 9 October 1813, RG 107; Letters received by Secretary of War, National Archives; and Henry Bathurst, Secretary of State for War and the Colonies, to Prevost, 5 November 1815, in *House of Lords Sessional Papers*, 1815, vol. 4, 332.

33. Mackenzie, *Life of Commodore Perry*, 1:303; Dutton, *Perry*, 218; Dillon, *We Have Met the Enemy*, 164, 182, 183; Perry to Secretary of Navy, 25 October 1813, RG 45, Captains' Letters; and Chauncey to Secretary of the Navy, 13 October 1813, RG 45, Captains' Letters.

34. Quoted in Dudley W. Knox, *A History of the United States Navy* (New York, 1936), 118.

35. Mackenzie, *Life of Commodore Perry*, 1:286.

36. Elliott to Perry, 7 July 1818, in *Biographical Notice*, 207.

37. Dillon, *We Have Met the Enemy*, 209–11; Mahan, *Sea Power*, 2:78; and *Biographical Notice*, 35, 207–13. The charges are printed verbatim in Mackenzie, *Life of Commodore Perry*, 2:251, 252. Elliott published his last attack in *Address . . . to His Early Companions* (Philadelphia, 1844). The controversy among nineteenth-century writers can be seen in James Fenimore Cooper, *History of the Navy of the United States of America*, 2d ed., 2 vols. (Philadelphia, 1840); Paullin, *Battle of Lake Erie*; and Mackenzie, *Life of Commodore Perry*. Compare these with Edward Channing, *History of the United States* (New York, 1917), 4:521–22.

38. Secretary of the Navy to Perry, 18 April 1814, RG 45, Secretary of the Navy Letters.

39. Dillon, *We Have Met the Enemy*, 187, 188; and Robert G. Albion, *Makers of Naval Policy 1798–1947* (Annapolis, 1980), 186.

40. Niles, *Life of Perry*, 270; Park Benjamin, *United States Naval Academy* (New York, 1900), 94; Mackenzie, *Life of Commodore Perry*, 2:128, 139; and Dillon, *We Have Met the Enemy*, 192–203.

41. J. Robert Moskin, *The U.S. Marine Corps Story* (New York, 1977), 100, 101.

42. Niles, *Life of Perry*, 279, 289; and Mackenzie, *Life of Commodore Perry*, 2:197, 206.

43. Niles, *Life of Perry*, 303, 304.

44. Cox, "Eye-Witness Account"; Dillon, *We Have Met the Enemy*, xii, civ, 27, 88–92, 182, 192; William V. Taylor to his brother, 17 October 1813, in Emerson, *Perry Victory Centenary*, 157; and Mackenzie, *Life of Commodore Perry*, 1:76, 229, 2:140, 141.

45. Ellery H. Clark, Jr., "United States Place Names Honoring the Navy," U.S. Naval Institute *Proceedings* 74 (April 1948): 452–55, and "Famous Swords at the United States Naval Academy," U.S. Naval Institute *Proceedings* 66 (December 1940): 1769–75; Ruby R. Duval, "The Perpetuation of History and Tradition at the United States Naval Academy Today," U.S. Naval Institute *Proceedings* 64 (May 1938): 660–77; and Emerson, *Perry Victory Centenary*, 8, 9, 80.

46. Perry to Elliott, 18 June 1818, in *Documents in Relation to the Differences Which Subsisted between the Late Commodore O. H. Perry and Captain Jesse D. Elliott* (Boston, 1834), 22.

47. Dutton, *Perry*, 104, 209; Dillon, *We Have Met the Enemy*, xii–xiv, 181; and Knox, *History of United States Navy*, 119.

# ☆ Robert F. Stockton
## ☆
## ☆ Naval Officer and Reformer

*by Harold D. Langley*

ROBERT FIELD STOCKTON (1796–1866) WAS ONE OF THE MOST INTELLI-gent and versatile officers of the U.S. Navy during the Age of Sail. His background, education, philosophy, and personal qualities all contributed to making him an effective and highly esteemed officer and man. He was the first career naval officer to be elected to the U.S. Senate, and he was also mentioned as a candidate for President. But Stockton did not find political life particularly appealing, nor would he consent to any compromise of the principles that he believed to be right. He returned to private life and devoted himself to his family. He is well remembered for his contributions to the development of steam power in the Navy and to ending the practice of punishment by flogging.

The Stockton family had a long and honored association with New Jersey. Robert Stockton's immigrant ancestors were Quakers who acquired a large tract of land in the Princeton area. His paternal grandfather, Richard Stockton, was a member of the first graduating class of Princeton College, a lawyer, a member of the Executive Council of the Colony, and an associate justice of its Supreme Court. When the Revolution began, he sided with the rebels and was a signer of the Declaration of Independence. While a chairman of a committee of the Continental Congress, he was captured by the British in New York and imprisoned for a month. The hardships that he endured in prison undermined his health and he never fully recovered. He died in 1781.[1]

The future commodore's father, Richard Stockton, was the eldest son of the signer of the Declaration of Independence. A prominent lawyer, and a Federalist, he had a political career that included a term in the U.S. Senate (1796–1799), four unsuccessful bids for the governorship of New Jersey (1801–1804), and a term in the U.S. House of Representatives (1813–1815).[2]

From the experiences of his grandfather and his father, young Robert F. Stockton learned of the demands and obligations of public service and a sense of duty to his country. From his lawyer father, he learned to think critically and to get to the heart of every question. His father's example in politics and in law taught him the virtue of patience and discretion and the importance of principles. Robert was raised in a Federalist environment and much admired the men of that persuasion whom he met through his father. In later life he said that if he had been of age in those days, he would probably have been a Federalist himself.[3]

As a young man Robert Stockton led a rather sheltered life. Much of the time, he was privately tutored, and, for the most part, his contacts with other boys his age was limited to those who lived near his home.

During the brief period that Robert attended a local school, he proved himself among his peers and gained a reputation for personal courage and for coolness and self-possession in times of crisis. He made an effort to be respectful and courteous to all whom he met, but he was quick to repay any insult or act of aggression. He cultivated a high-minded and generous attitude. For school bullies, he had nothing but contempt. Whenever he found one of them preying on a weaker boy, he assisted the victim.[4]

In 1808, at the age of thirteen, he entered Princeton College where he distinguished himself in mathematics, languages, and elocution. He does not seem to have had a clear idea of what he wanted to do in life. No doubt he gave some thought to following in his father's footsteps, but the study of the law held no great appeal. In his more reflective moments Stockton might well have decided that it would be hard to surpass his grandfather and his father in the field of law. Possibly he was looking for a more active career. Whatever the case, this was the time when the English-speaking world was reading about the life and exploits of Horatio Lord Nelson, the British naval officer who died in the act of defeating the combined French and Spanish fleets in 1805. Young Stockton was inspired by Nelson's exploits and dreamed of emulating him.[5]

For a long time, there seemed to be little hope of a naval career in the United States. Under President Thomas Jefferson the naval force had been cut back, and a heavy reliance was placed on gunboats. With no Navy to protect them on the high seas, American merchant ships were caught in the middle of a war between France and Great Britain and were seized by both sides for blockade violations. The impressment of American seaman by British naval officers was a further gross abuse of national pride and honor. These events undoubtedly fanned the patriotic ardor of young Stockton.

It was not until 1811 that he was able to apply for a midshipman's warrant. When he was accepted, he still had a year and a half to go to finish college. Why his father let him drop out of school is not known. Very possibly his father felt that a little time at sea would be a maturing experience. Ordered to join the frigate *President*, then at Newport, Rhode Island, Stockton left Princeton in February 1812 and reported to Commodore John Rodgers, the most widely known senior officer of the Navy.[6] So began a long and important association for young Stockton.

The *President* and the *Essex* sailed for New York on 28 March, and Stockton got his first taste of sea duty when the ships encountered a heavy gale that carried them south of the Delaware Bay. When war was declared in June, Rodgers promptly took his squadron to sea. Six days later, off Nantucket, they sighted the British thirty-two-gun frigate *Belvidera* and gave chase. A running fight ensued. On board the *President* a bow gun exploded, killing one midshipman and wounding fourteen men, including Rodgers. The *President* lost ground and sustained some damage from British shot. Rodgers was unable to overtake the enemy vessel. The pursuit was called off and the rest of the squadron came up to join the flagship.[7]

Ever since reporting for duty, Stockton had observed Rodgers and the other officers on board the ship and noted their strengths and weaknesses. He could not help but be impressed with Rodgers, especially after he was wounded. With a fractured leg, Rodgers was supported by two of his men while he continued to command.[8] Here was an officer whom Stockton could emulate.

Rodgers had also taken the measure of Stockton. The military deportment and coolness in battle of this young and inexperienced officer were impressive. Rodgers and other officers noted that Stockton was prompt in his discharge of every duty; that he was quick to anticipate what was needed in every given situation; and that he was courteous, respectful, and had a sprightly disposition. Stockton's brief experience in battle had whetted his appetite for more excitement. The young midshipman's outlook and manner also made him a favorite with the crew, to whom he became known as "Fighting Bob."[9]

At the time of the British campaign against Baltimore, Rodgers was ordered to report to Washington, and he brought Stockton with him. Impressed with Stockton, Secretary of the Navy William Jones had the young man assigned to him as an aide. While on this duty, Stockton volunteered to ride over to British-occupied Alexandria, Virginia, to investigate some cannonading. His coolness and willingness to take chances added to the regard with which he was held by his civilian superior.[10]

But the life of an aide to the Secretary did not commend itself to Stockton. He requested and received permission to return to Rodgers, who was then involved in preparing the defense of Baltimore. A part of those preparations involved the training of seamen to execute the rudiments of military drill and maneuvers. Although they were eager to fight, Rodgers had great difficulty in fashioning the men into an effective land force.[11] Stockton undoubtedly reached Baltimore in time to participate in some of the training. Many years later, in California, Stockton would be called upon to transform another body of sailors into infantry and would draw upon the experience of Rodgers.

Stockton took part in the defense of Fort McHenry and exposed himself to enemy fire on several occasions to carry messages to and from Rodgers's headquarters. When Rodgers learned that barges carrying British troops were headed for the Lazaretto, he sent Stockton with a detachment of Pennsylvania riflemen to the site of the suspected landing. For his gallantry in action at Fort McHenry and in other battles, Stockton received honorable notices from his superiors. On 9 December 1814 he was promoted to lieutenant.[12]

It had long been obvious that Stockton would never return to college to complete his studies. His early years in the Navy were spent mastering the details of his profession, then he turned to educating himself through books. He read history, international law, ethics, moral philosophy, and religion. His favorites were the Bible and the works of Cicero, Shakespeare, and Lord Bacon. A Princeton professor who knew him well, later, said that Stockton was one of the best-informed men he had ever met. No matter what the subject under discussion, Stockton could make some worthwhile observations on the topic. Princeton gave him an honorary master's degree in 1821.[13]

In the war with Algiers, Stockton showed an unusual interest in the effects of naval gunnery. While the frigate *Guerriere* was closing to attack the Algerian frigate *Mishouri*, Stockton, in the accompanying schooner *Spitfire*, requested permission to station himself on his ship's bowsprit to observe the effect of the broadside. His request was approved. The *Spitfire* moved close to the stern of the enemy ship. From his precarious perch, Stockton observed two of the *Guerriere*'s broadsides. To his commanding officer he reported that the *Guerriere* was firing widely and suggested that the *Spitfire* aim her long thirty-two-pound cannon on the cabin windows of the pirate vessel. This was done, and in half an hour the Algerian ship was taken.[14]

The incident was an early indication that Stockton was studying the most effective way to use guns in a manner well beyond the other lieutenants. It was also a way of bringing himself to the attention of his superiors.

After the war with Algiers, Stockton returned to the Mediterranean in the new ship-of-the-line *Washington*, the flagship of Commodore Isaac Chauncey. Peacetime routine was dull, and officers had few opportunities to advance themselves. Frustration often prompted younger officers to utter hostile, unguarded remarks that led to duels. Discipline among the officers deteriorated. Two events that took place in the squadron greatly influenced Stockton.

First, Captain John Orde Creighton of the *Washington* was brought to trial for striking a midshipman, accusing him of lying, and threatening to throw him overboard. The court-martial board, with Commodore Oliver Hazard

Perry presiding, did not allow the midshipman to present the testimony of two lieutenants and arbitrarily ended the trial. The court found Creighton not guilty. This verdict so outraged the midshipmen of the squadron that fifty-one of them sent a petition to Congress asking for protection from tyrannical officers. It was the view of members of Congress that the petition was insubordinate, and they took no action on it.[15]

Another outrage took place when Commodore Perry, acting in an arbitrary manner, removed from command John Heath, the captain of the marines on *Java*. When the relief from command was not followed by charges, Heath sent a note to Perry and asked what the next step was to be. Perry summoned Heath to his cabin, and, during a high-pitched discussion, struck the marine. Heath proffered charges, with Perry making countercharges. The same court that had tried Creighton now tried Perry, and Creighton was one of the judges. The court found both men guilty but sentenced them only to a reprimand. Once again, the verdict outraged the junior officers. Fifty of them—midshipmen, lieutenants, and marines—sent a memorial to Congress that protested the partiality of the court-martial.[16]

Stockton signed this memorial, which marked the real beginning of his interest in naval reform.

Although Stockton could do little to reform the Navy as a whole, he could do something about those under his immediate command. He set about teaching his subordinates his philosophy of command. Stockton believed that a commander must inspire his officers to respect him and to be deferential to his position and sense of honor. It was the commander's obligation to demonstrate to everyone his dedication to justice and fairness. An officer was expected to be a gentleman, and a gentleman should not do wrong himself or allow anyone else to do it without punishment. As for the subordinates, they must respect and obey their superiors. One of the basic lessons that all officers must learn, according to Stockton, was that they remain cool under all circumstances. "Remember, Gentlemen," he would say, "that there is always time enough to fight; keep cool; never get in a passion, under the grossest provocation."[17]

The young lieutenant applied this principle in an effort to curtail dueling. Stockton himself was a good shot, and he fought duels with British officers in the Mediterranean in the interest of demanding respect for the officers of the U.S. Navy, not to avenge his personal honor. When an American midshipman challenged him to a duel, Stockton met the man ashore at the appointed place. The midshipman fired and missed. Stockton fired into the air. The seconds determined that honor had been satisfied. All involved in this encounter became firm friends of Stockton, and the midshipman became a zealous upholder of shipboard discipline.

Increasingly, Stockton devoted himself to compromising disputes between officers and discouraging duels. His success in this effort led others to enlist his effort to arbitrate questions. In Stockton's view, it was rarely necessary for a gentleman to fight a duel. A gentleman was always willing to make whatever explanations were proper. If the offended person was also a gentleman, he would be satisfied with honest explanations.[18] This code of conduct was palatable to junior officers because it came from someone who had proved his personal courage on a number of occasions.

Because he had some knowledge of the law and was a good speaker, Stockton found himself in demand as a counsel in courts-martial. In this, as in other affairs, he was a conscientious officer, and he had some successes in this area as well. It may well have pleased him to reflect that by a strange quirk of fate he was now acting as a lawyer, as his father and grandfather had done before him.[19]

As a result of several disciplinary problems in the squadron, Commodore Charles Stewart relieved four officers and sent them to the sloop-of-war *Erie*, under Stockton's command, for passage home. Stockton made the journey during the winter and arrived in late January 1820 without any mishaps. Secretary of the Navy Smith Thompson expressed his satisfaction with Stockton's report of his voyage and added that it was "evidence of your active exertion, and prudence as commander of the ship."[20]

For his next assignment, Stockton asked the Secretary "for the most dangerous, the most difficult and the most unpromising employment at the disposal of the government." This turned out to be an assignment in the schooner *Alligator* to the west coast of Africa, where Stockton was to seize any American ships that were involved in slave trade.

While he was in Washington on official business, Stockton was approached by two leaders of the American Colonization Society and asked if he would acquire some land on the west coast of Africa that could become a colony for the resettlement of ex-slaves. He was willing to undertake the mission, provided that he was not bound by detailed instructions and was free to exercise his own discretion. The society agreed to these terms. Stockton was to work with Dr. Eli Ayres, the society's agent in Africa, who also held a commission as a naval surgeon.

In the fall of 1821, Stockton went to sea again in the *Alligator*.[21] Given the humanitarian nature of the enterprise, it seemed appropriate to Stockton to put into action some of his ideas on leadership. He decided to see whether discipline could be maintained without the use of the cat-o'-nine tails. Remembering Captain Creighton's penchant for flogging men, Stockton was determined to have none of that on board his ship. So, while the ship was still within sight of the shore, he ordered that the cat-o'-nine tails be thrown overboard. He would command obedience and discipline by other means. The experiment proved to be a success, and thereafter Stockton became an advocate of the abolition of flogging.[22]

As for the mission of the American Colonization Society, Stockton explored the coast of Africa and determined that the region around Cape Mesurado would be suitable for the proposed colony. With some difficulty and using the threat of force, he persuaded the local tribal rulers to cede the area. The colony subsequently established became the Republic of Liberia. Stockton developed a strong interest in the work of the society, and a few years later, when he returned to New Jersey, he organized a branch of the society in his native state and served as its first president.[23]

Turning his attention now to the slave trade, Stockton zealously seized ships that he suspected were American vessels operating under foreign flags. Unfortunately, four of them turned out to be French, and a minor diplomatic crisis resulted. A Portuguese slaver made the mistake of firing on him, and he seized that as a prize as well. The Secretary of the Navy was obliged to tell Stockton to restrict his activities to ships flying the American flag.[24]

The *Alligator*, under Stockton's command, was next assigned to the West Indies as a part of the government's effort to eliminate piracy in that area. The ship became a part of the newly created West India squadron under Commodore James Biddle. In the course of this duty Stockton went to Charleston, South Carolina, where he met and fell in love with Harriett Maria Potter, the only daughter of John Potter, a wealthy merchant. His overtures were encouraged, and the couple was married in Charleston on 4 March 1823. The marriage brought Stockton control of property in the South and close ties with his wife's father and friends. As a result, Stockton developed a great sympathy for the people and problems of the South.[25]

When Stockton took his bride to Princeton, and while on leave from active service, he found himself caught up in the politics of the day. The question was who would succeed James Monroe in the presidential election of 1824. The Federalists had ceased to be a force on the national scene but were still active in some states. In the dominant Democratic-Republican Party of Monroe, five major figures were competing for the office. Secretary of State John Quincy Adams was the candidate from the Northeast. Senator Andrew Jackson of Tennessee and Representative Henry Clay of Kentucky were the candidates of the West. There were two candidates from the South: Secretary of War John C. Calhoun of South Carolina and Secretary of the Treasury William H. Crawford of Georgia.

No clear victor emerged in the election, and the question was referred to the House of Representatives. As a result, Adams became the President and Calhoun the Vice President. Clay was subsequently appointed Secretary of

State in the new administration. The Jacksonians charged that the will of the people had not been done and that Adams had won the office through bargain and corruption. Thus, the campaign of 1828 started four years early.[26]

In 1824, Stockton favored John Quincy Adams, but he was disappointed in his actions as President. At Princeton, Stockton established a newspaper and began to write occasional editorials for it. Not surprisingly, he was drawn into politics. He became an ardent supporter of Andrew Jackson and shared the widespread enthusiasm that followed the triumph of the general in the presidential elections of 1828 and 1832.[27]

Meanwhile, Stockton was recalled to active duty in November 1826 and given the job of superintending the survey of the harbors of Savannah, Georgia, and Beaufort, South Carolina. Southerners were eager to see a naval base established in Georgia or the Carolinas, and the survey was a part of that effort. While engaged in this work, Stockton received word of the death of his father in March 1828. He requested and received a leave of absence to settle his father's affairs. So began a decade of activity in New Jersey.[28]

With the death of his father, Stockton came into possession of the family homestead, "Morven," as well as land and other capital. This inheritance, together with other property that he inherited and that which he acquired by purchase and by marriage, made him quite comfortable.[29] He was now prepared to risk it all to support internal improvement in his native state.

The people of New Jersey noted New York's success with the Erie Canal and believed that they could reap similar benefits by linking the Delaware and Hudson Rivers. Several groups sought governmental assistance for at least three competing routes. When Congress refused to provide aid, the state legislature turned to private investors and chartered several canal companies. The first one, chartered for the New Brunswick-to-Bordentown route, was unable to sell its stock, and the second one, the Delaware and Raritan Canal Company, was doing little better when Stockton bought a controlling interest in 1830.

One of the major problems facing the company was the legislature's chartering of the Camden and Amboy Railroad Company at the same time. Stockton knew that the canal could not succeed if it had to compete with a virtually parallel railroad from the very beginning. To meet the challenge, he applied to the state for the right to build another railroad from Trenton to New Brunswick. He argued that unless he could build the proposed route, the Camden and Amboy Railroad would be a monopoly. The state responded by consolidating the two companies and by giving the combined company the authority to build the Trenton–New Brunswick connection. As a result, both the canal and railroad lines were built, and New Jersey enjoyed a system that not only did not incur any public debt, but actually paid large sums to the state for charter rights and transit duties.[30]

Before all this became a reality, however, the very difficult problem of rais-ing capital had to be overcome. Rebuffed by New York and Philadelphia in-vestors, Stockton turned to his father-in-law, John Potter, who raised between a third and a half of the required funds in Charleston, South Carolina. On the New Jersey front, the struggle to build and maintain the company developed Stockton's political and managerial skills to a high degree. Yet, for the rest of his life, he was quite defensive about his association with a monopoly.[31]

In 1838, Stockton traveled to England to obtain a loan to help the compa-ny to weather the financial crisis caused by the panic of 1837. His success in negotiating a large loan at a low interest rate added to his reputation in the busi-ness community. The trip was also to have enormous implications for the U.S. Navy because at that time he met John Ericsson, a Swedish engineer.[32]

Ericsson was trying to convince the officials of the Royal Navy of the value of his iron-hulled steam vessel powered by a screw propeller. A ride in the craft convinced Stockton that it was just what his company needed. He ordered one of the boats and had Ericsson design a fifty-horsepower engine for it.[33]

A few months after Stockton returned from Europe, the Navy Department ordered him to sea as the executive officer in the ship-of-the-line *Ohio*, under command of Commodore Isaac Hull. Stockton was now a master comman-dant, having been promoted to that rank on 27 May 1830.[34] After his many years ashore, the return to active duty must have had its difficult moments. Stockton was forty-two years old and had been used to a comfortable existence. Now he must adjust once again to the rigor and discomfort of shipboard life.

During the crossing of the Atlantic Ocean, Stockton had additional oppor-tunities to observe the state of naval discipline. Commodore Hull was a hu-mane officer who enjoyed the respect and affection of the crew; it was his habit to reduce the sentences of men convicted of offenses. The ship itself was in the charge of Captain Joseph Smith, a tall officer, with a penetrating eye, who had a strong interest in temperance and who called himself the seamen's friend. But in his zeal to stop drunkenness and other evils, he punished the men se-verely by flogging. As a result, he lost the respect of the men and failed in his efforts to improve them. It seems likely that this experience simply reinforced Stockton's view that flogging could be eliminated and that there were better and more effective ways to lead men.[35]

In Europe, Stockton was detached from the ship to carry dispatches to the American Minister to Great Britain. While in that country he studied the lat-est improvements in naval architecture and visited navy yards, depots, and manufacturing plants. The trip to England provided an opportunity to witness the trials of the iron screw steamer he had ordered from Ericsson. They were most impressive. Named the *Robert F. Stockton*, the completed vessel crossed the Atlantic under sail in 1839 and was used for many years as a tugboat on the Delaware and Raritan Canal.[36]

Stockton was most impressed with Ericsson's work and saw opportunities for the application of his genius in America. His encouraging comments came at a time when the British Admiralty rejected Ericsson's design for a screw steamer. Stockton had Ericsson build a model of a screw steamer for naval use that was sent to the Navy Department. The warm encouragement of Stockton led Ericsson to emigrate to the United States. Meanwhile, Stockton learned that he had been promoted to captain on 8 December 1838. He returned to the United States full of enthusiasm for modernizing the Navy.[37]

Back home, Stockton found resistance to his ideas in official circles. Some of the older naval officers and even the Secretary of the Navy were hostile about moving toward steam-powered warships. The only thing that Stockton could hope for was a change in administration, and the election of 1840 was approaching.

Thoroughly disenchanted with the Van Buren administration, Stockton took a leave of absence and worked actively in New Jersey to support the Whig Party candidate, General William Henry Harrison. Harrison died in April 1841, and the new President, John Tyler, and his Secretary of the Navy, George E. Badger, were more receptive than their predecessors to building steam vessels and improving the naval forces of the nation.[38]

Much encouraged by the change, Stockton sent the model of the steam warship to Secretary Badger in April 1841. As a result, the Navy Department authorized the construction of "a steamer of six hundred tons on the plan proposed by Captain Stockton; steam to be the main propelling power upon Ericsson's plan." Thus, Ericsson's genius and Stockton's connections and sponsorship combined to produce the first steam-powered screw vessel in the U.S. Navy. When completed, the vessel was a full-rigged ship of 954 tons that used steam as auxiliary power. For armament, it carried twelve forty-two-pound carronades and two 12-inch wrought iron guns reinforced by tiers of hoops. One of these, known as the "Oregon," had been designed by Ericsson in England and brought to the United States. The other gun, known as the "Peacemaker," was forged for Stockton by Hamersley Forge and bored and finished under Ericsson's direction. The names of the guns had a special significance at a time when there was a diplomatic crisis with Great Britain over the Oregon Territory.[39]

In the process of building the ship, additional funds were required, and Stockton put his own money into the project. By the time the vessel was finished, he had developed a proprietary attitude toward it and considered it "his" ship. It was named the USS *Princeton* in honor of the captain's hometown. An unfortunate change took place in Stockton at this time: he encouraged the notion that the ship was the product of his ideas alone. Evidence of this is contained in Stockton's 5 February 1844 letter to the Secretary of the Navy, in which he described the virtues of the *Princeton* and her guns without mentioning John Ericsson. When the *Princeton* went to Washington to demonstrate her capabilities to government officials, Ericsson, left in New York, was angry at his exclusion from the official party.

On 28 February 1844 the *Princeton* made a cruise down the Potomac River to show the power of her large guns. On board were the President, members of his cabinet, members of Congress, and a number of ladies. Earlier, Ericsson had suggested that the demonstration be done with a gun of his own design, but Stockton preferred the one with which he was associated. The assembled guests were impressed by the power of the cannon. On the way back to Washington, the captain was requested to fire it one more time. He consented, but on this occasion, the gun exploded and killed the Secretaries of State and Navy, as well as four other persons. Stockton himself was badly scorched, but he continued to give his attention to all around him. Subsequently, he asked for a court of inquiry to investigate the accident.

Shortly after the news of the explosion reached Ericsson in New York, he received a letter from one of the *Princeton*'s officers requesting that he come to Washington for the investigation. This Ericsson refused to do, nor would he accept any responsibility for the accident. The court exonerated Stockton of any blame for the explosion of the gun, but Stockton never forgave Ericsson, and in retaliation for what he considered Ericsson's failure to support him, he used his influence to prevent the government from paying Ericsson for his services in building the *Princeton*. This was the most petty and dishonorable aspect of Stockton's naval career, and it tarnished his reputation as an exponent of the new technology in warfare.[40]

Before the diplomatic crisis with Great Britain over the Oregon Territory was settled, a new threat of war with Mexico emerged as a result of efforts to bring the republic of Texas into the Federal Union. The problem for Mexico was that Texas, in arguing that its border was the Rio Grande, was asserting control over a region well beyond the actual settlements of the republic. For anti-slavery-minded Northerners, the admission of Texas ran a risk of increasing the power of the Southerners in the Senate, as well as bringing on a war. The decision on Texas was so controversial that it was not until the closing days of the Tyler administration that it was admitted to the Union by a joint resolution of Congress. A troublesome issue was thus removed from the public agenda before newly elected President James K. Polk took office.[41]

From Stockton's point of view, the admission of Texas was a highly desirable thing. A thoroughgoing expansionist, he believed that God had ordained the Americans to occupy the areas of the West.[42] Given this point of view and his close association with the outgoing administration, it is not surprising that Stockton was chosen by President Tyler to carry to Texas the news that Congress had approved the annexation. It was now up to the Texas legislature to accept this and to enter the Union as a state. The business was not without risk. At the news of the passage of the joint resolution in Texas, the Mexican government broke off diplomatic relations with the United States. The Mexican minister at Washington went home to his country to help organize resistance to the United States.[43]

As Stockton saw it, the new Democratic administration headed by President Polk had come into office on a platform that promised the reoccupation of the Oregon Territory and the annexation of Texas. These actions might provoke a war with Great Britain, with Mexico, or with both. If war came with both and Stockton had a chance to make a choice, he wanted to test his skill against the British on the high seas. He had not forgotten the thrill of combat under John Rodgers. Of the two contestants, Britain was the bigger threat. Therefore, it seemed wise to resolve the Mexican question as quickly as possible in order to be free to cope with Great Britain, if necessary.

In Texas it was reported that the Mexicans were preparing for war and might possibly have the assistance of a European power. There seemed to be no time to lose. Why wait until the Mexicans were ready to fight? Why not resolve the question according to the United States' own time table?[44]

For Stockton this meant that someone in Texas had to take the initiative. When he arrived in Texas, he found that Texan politicians were quibbling over the terms of the annexation and that European diplomats were trying to convince them not to accept the incorporation. Fearing that Texas might yet be lost to the Union, Stockton suggested to Texas President Anson Jones that Texas should become more hostile toward Mexico. He argued that if Mexico went to war, the United States could neutralize the threat before any Europeans got invoked. Jones hoped to establish more friendly relations with Mexico and rejected Stockton's suggestion that Texas manufacture a war for the convenience of the United States.

Although there was strong pro-annexation sentiment among the Texas people, their leaders were not enthusiastic about risking war. Most likely, Stockton talked about his ideas with the American chargé d'affaires in Texas. If so, he learned quickly that Polk's administration was committed to resolving the problems with Mexico through diplomacy. Disgusted at the turn of events, Stockton returned to the East and reached Philadelphia in June 1845.[45]

The commodore's action in Texas was an example of his boldness. The record shows that he had no authorization from the President or the Navy Department to do as he did. Stockton was prepared to take risks because he was convinced that, if he were successful, the administration would overlook some irregularities. Also, he believed that Mexico would fight, and he communicated these thoughts to his superiors.

In the fall of 1845, Stockton was given the command of the frigate *Congress* and instructions to carry a U.S. commissioner to the Hawaiian Islands. The captain also carried sealed orders that were not to be opened until he was beyond the Virginia Capes. Stockton was very much afraid that he was being sent to the Pacific just as war with Mexico was about to break out. His old ship, the *Princeton*, had been assigned to Commodore David Conner in the Gulf of Mexico. If war should come instead with Great Britain, he would be far from that as well. But orders were orders, and Stockton was determined to do his best in any situation into which fate cast him.[46]

While the *Congress* was preparing for sea, her chaplain, Walter Colton, received a consignment of some three hundred to four hundred books for the ship's library. These were on religious as well as miscellaneous subjects, and they came from the American Tract Society, the Sunday School Union, and the Presbyterian Board of Publications. Knowing that there was no appropriation for such books, Stockton purchased them himself for his crew. In addition, the American Tract Society supplied Bibles for the crew. Delighted with this windfall, Chaplain Colton wrote in his journal: "No national ship ever left a port of the United States more amply provided with books suited to the habits and capacities of those on board."[47]

Religious ideas were important in shaping Stockton, so it followed in his mind that they could influence others. Born a Presbyterian, he became an Episcopalian at the time of his marriage and subsequently served as a vestryman at Trinity Church in Princeton. As a naval officer, he insisted that religious services be performed on board his ship every Sunday. He cultivated the friendship of chaplains and supported their work.

Among the people he was close to was Charles S. Stewart, who had a strong opinion about the degrading effects of punishment by flogging. His ideas reinforced Stockton's own views. In human affairs, Stockton believed that people responded to reason and that kindness begat kindness. He was not above flogging if all other possibilities were exhausted, but, unlike many other officers in his day, he did not consider it his first recourse. He took pains to make his men believe that, as their commander, he was like a parent, stern and demanding at times but always concerned, sympathetic, and forgiving. This approach was quite effective on board his ships.[48]

Stockton's efforts to promote harmony in the *Congress* included keeping the men informed of their mission. When Stockton opened his sealed orders, he learned that after he discharged his passengers in Hawaii, he was to sail for Oregon and California. He promptly shared this information with his crew. No one knew what to expect when the *Congress* anchored in Monterey Bay, California, on 15 July 1846 and found a squadron under the command of Commodore John D. Sloat in control of the area. Stockton promptly went to confer with the senior officer.[49] So began one of the most controversial aspects of Stockton's career.

The meeting between Sloat and Stockton produced some surprises. The senior commander told Stockton that his health was bad and that he intended to transfer the command as soon as possible. It developed that the previous May, while Sloat's squadron was at Mazatlán, Mexico, he had received a message from the squadron's surgeon, then in Guadalajara, Mexico, that there had been fighting between Mexican and American troops along the Rio Grande. Sloat promptly relayed this information to the American consul at Monterey, California, by way of Captain William Mervine in the sloop-of-war *Cyane*. Sloat remained in Mazatlán until he learned of General Zachary Taylor's victories at Palo Alto and Resaca de la Palma in northeastern Mexico.

Further confirmation of the war came from Mexico City by way of another message from the squadron's surgeon. It was not until 8 June—twenty-two days after the first report of fighting—that Sloat sailed for Monterey in the *Savannah*, arriving there on 1 July. Five days later he learned that a small group of soldiers under Brevet Captain John C. Fremont of the Topographical Engineers had abandoned their scientific survey work and were actively supporting a revolt by American settlers. Sonoma and San Francisco were under control of this group. What was Sloat to do?

It probably seemed reasonable to Sloat that Fremont had acted under orders from Washington. If so, it was important to have a meeting with him as soon as possible to determine what was to be done. Meanwhile, Sloat was concerned that the British had their eyes on California, and he wanted to forestall any movement by them in that direction. Accordingly, he ordered the seizure of Monterey and San Francisco, and this was accomplished on 7 and 9 July, respectively. Sonoma was also occupied.

Fremont hastened to Monterey and conferred with Sloat in a meeting unsatisfactory to both. Fremont wanted an official endorsement of what he had done thus far and support for further operations in California. Sloat was surprised and shocked to learn that Fremont had acted on his own authority and without knowing about the war with Mexico. This news induced Sloat to break off the meeting. He was delighted when Stockton arrived and was only too happy to turn the naval and land command over to the younger officer. Arrangements for the change of command were completed on 29 July, and Sloat departed for home.[50]

While seizing Monterey, Commodore Sloat had issued a proclamation announcing the outbreak of war and the annexation of California. It spoke of the advantages that the area would have as a part of the United States and promised that all who did not wish to remain there could return to Mexico after the war. The real estate titles of the Californians and the church would be recognized.

Items furnished to the Americans would be bought at a fair price. This moderate and statesmanlike document was in accord with American Consul Thomas Larkin's hopes that the conquest of California would be peaceful. Larkin knew that long before the arrival of Fremont or Sloat, Californians had been discontented under Mexican rule.[51]

Stockton's assessment of the situation was different. He knew that the U.S. government was anxious to acquire California. He was suspicious of the British naval vessel in California waters and thought the British might support Mexican efforts to resist the American occupation. Even if no British support were forthcoming, however, Mexico was bound to react to the loss of California. Stockton thought it wise to complete the conquest as soon as possible, before the Mexicans discovered how small and scattered the American forces were.[52]

Stockton's force consisted of the *Portsmouth* at San Francisco, with her men holding the garrisons ashore; the frigate *Savannah* at Monterey; and the *Warren* at Mazatlán. This left only the frigate *Congress*, the sloop-of-war *Cyane*, and 160 men under Fremont to seize and control the rest of California. To Stockton it seemed clear that he must move quickly with all the men he could muster.

On his own authority, he designated Fremont's organization "the California battalion of United States troops" and promoted their leader to the rank of major. Arrangements were made to establish volunteer garrisons at Sutter's Fort, Sonoma, San Juan Batista, and Santa Clara. Stockton informed Chaplain Colton that he would function as the mayor of Monterey until further notice.[53]

The commodore's supreme confidence in his own judgment and his "take charge" personality led him to issue a rather arrogant and bombastic proclamation that blamed the Mexicans for the war and for outrages against Fremont and his scientific group. To avenge these wrongs, points had been seized in California. Mexican officials had departed, and anarchy reigned until Stockton brought order. General Jose Maria Castro, the Mexican commander in California, was to be driven out of the country; local officials must recognize American authority. Consul Larkin told the authorities in Washington that the assertions in the proclamation did not come from him. One of Stockton's subordinate officers considered the proclamation rather unintelligible.[54] It was not a happy note on which to begin. One can only assume that Stockton was trying to intimidate the Mexicans with rhetoric.

Stockton's strategy was to increase Fremont's strength as quickly as possible by moving Fremont's battalion via the *Cyane* to San Diego, California. After acquiring horses there it would move inland to prevent Castro's retreat from Los Angeles. Then, Stockton would land his sailors and marines at San Pedro and move against Castro. While Stockton was transforming his men into infantry, Larkin tried to arrange a truce and a conference between the commanders. Stockton refused to talk to Castro unless California declared its independence under the protection of the United States. Castro could agree to no such terms, but his force was too small to oppose the Americans. He left California. Stockton's force marched to Los Angeles where it was joined by Fremont's followers.[55]

In Los Angeles Stockton issued a new proclamation, stating that California belonged to the United States and would soon have a government and laws similar to those of other American territories. An election date for civil officers was announced. Meanwhile, a civil and military government would be in power with Stockton as governor. In forming a civil government the commodore exceeded his instructions and the provisions of the Constitution. Stockton justified his actions on the grounds that it was important for the tranquillity of the area to have a functioning civil government that could protect civil property rights, maintain the American presence, and free his forces for an attack on Mexico. He was also concerned about the influx of Mormons into the area. As events later proved, neither the President nor the Secretary of the Navy accepted these arguments.[56]

No sooner had Stockton reported to the Secretary of the Navy that peace reigned in California than a revolt broke out in Los Angeles and spread to other points. All the territory south of San Luis Obispo reverted to Mexican control. An army expedition under General Stephen Watts Kearney marched overland from New Mexico, suffered a defeat in a battle with the Mexicans in California, and joined Stockton at San Diego. The balance of power in California now shifted; the combined army and naval units, along with Fremont's forces, defeated the Mexican troops that opposed them, and the reconquest of California was completed in January 1847.[57]

When the fighting stopped, a smoldering feud between Stockton and Kearney intensified over the issue of who was in control of the area. Kearney pointed to his instructions from the President stating that he was to establish a new territorial government in California, as he had already done in New Mexico. Stockton based his claims on the Navy Department's orders to Sloat. The commodore argued that the general's orders had been superseded by events. Stockton then proceeded to appoint Fremont the governor. In February, new orders from Washington placed the authority in Kearney's hands.[58]

The commodore left California on 20 June and traveled overland to Washington where he visited President Polk on 25 November. Later, Stockton returned to Washington to give testimony in court-martial proceedings against Fremont. The court found Fremont guilty of mutiny, disobedience, and prejudicial conduct and sentenced him to be dismissed from the service. Polk approved all but the mutiny finding and restored Fremont to duty. Instead, Fremont resigned.[59]

It had become clear to Stockton that the authorities in Washington disapproved of his actions in California, but the general public did not. On his return from the West, he was cheered by crowds and offered testimonial dinners, which he declined until after he returned home; then he attended a reception in his honor in New Jersey and a banquet in Philadelphia.[60]

Although all this was personally gratifying, Stockton was worried about the debate on Negro slavery and Southern threats to secede from the Union. Stockton believed that God had plans for the United States and the breakup of the Union would retard them. He was, therefore, willing to support any compromise that would hold the states together. The commodore did not believe that the federal government had a right to interfere with slavery in the states. His own connection with the South through his wife naturally gave him a good insight into the views of Southerners, but his own views of the blacks and their future was unique.

As Stockton saw it, God intended to use the blacks in America as the means of civilizing Africa. He believed that no white man could survive there. The slaves and their ancestors had been taken from their tribal environment and exposed to the superior civilization of the Anglo-Saxons. Slavery was a time of suffering, but it was an ordeal through which the blacks must go to prepare them for the work ahead. Their situation was similar to that of the Jews in Egyptian bondage before Moses led them to the promised land. The establishment of Liberia was a step toward the development of Africa, and as such, freed blacks should be encouraged to settle there. Slavery would end when God was ready to use the blacks for his work in Africa. Until that time, slaves had to be trained to be self-supporting. This comfortable philosophy allowed Stockton to believe that there was cruelty and injustice in the institution of slavery, but that slavery itself was not a sin. It was the duty of the states to correct injustices. Abolitionists would drive the Southern states out of the Union and would not free any slaves.[61]

These views and his national stature made Stockton an appealing compromise candidate in some circles, but he was not interested in political office. He resigned his commission in the Navy on 28 May 1850 to devote himself to private affairs. In a letter to a Trenton newspaper in November 1850, Stockton turned down the suggestion that his name should be placed in nomination for the U.S. Senate. He hoped that the honor would go to someone who was pledged to uphold the Union. Members of the New Jersey state legislature believed that no one had a stronger dedication to the Union than Stockton. He was elected as a Democrat to the Thirty-second Congress, which met in special session on 4 March 1851.[62]

During his time in the Senate he made speeches advocating improved harbor defenses and against intervention in European affairs, but his most famous effort came about as a result of an attempt to reintroduce punishment by flogging in the Navy.[63]

Flogging in the Navy and merchant marine had been abolished by a provision in an appropriation bill passed on 28 September 1850. The President signed the bill into law, and Congress adjourned on the same day. Because no substitute punishments were indicated, there was a feeling in some parts of the Navy that the measure was hasty and ill conceived. The Secretary of the Navy received letters from officers who asked for instructions on how to deal with unruly seamen. The Secretary of the Navy asked Congress to revise the whole system of punishments at once. On 17 December 1851, Senator Richard Broadhead of Pennsylvania introduced a memorial, signed by a large number of citizens, urging that punishment by flogging be reintroduced. This stirred Stockton to action. After expressing his amazement that any group of people would advocate such a thing, Stockton gave notice that he would oppose the suggestion.

When the proposition was considered on 7 January 1852, Stockton was ready. He spoke with feeling about the superiority of the American sailor and how he had proved his worth in war and peace. Stockton protested: "The theory that the Navy cannot be governed, and that our national ships cannot be navigated, without the use of the lash, seems to me to be founded in that false idea that sailors *are not men* — not American citizens — have not the common feelings, sympathies, and honorable impulses of our Anglo-American race." The commodore related how men would undergo all sorts of hardship for a commander they loved and who they believed cared for them. Punishment by flogging destroyed a sailor's self-respect, pride, and patriotism. A new and more civilized age had dawned. In the state prisons, the worst offenses were no longer punished by flogging. Why then, he asked, did people want to restore "this relic of barbarism" to the Navy?

Stockton went on to describe his own quarter century of association with seamen in various parts of the world. He told what they had done as infantry in the California campaigns. "American sailors, as a class," argued Stockton, "have loved their country as well, and have done more for her in peace and war, than any other equal number of citizens." Yet the sailor enjoyed little in the way of comfort; was treated as an outcast on shore; and often died poor. Some now argued that he should again be flogged like a felon. As far as he was concerned, said Stockton, he would rather see the Navy abolished than to see flogging restored. Officers of the Navy who thought that the sailor was more influenced by fear than by affection were wrong. "You can do infinitely more with him by rewarding him for his faithfulness than by flogging him for his delinquencies," Stockton asserted. It was much more effective to punish minor infractions by stopping the sailor's allowance of tobacco, tea, sugar, or coffee.

To improve the Navy and its discipline, Stockton recommended a system of rewards and punishments, the abolition of the grog ration, and a restructuring of the recruiting service.

Efforts to refute Stockton's arguments were made by George E. Badger of North Carolina, a former Secretary of the Navy, and by Stephen Mallory of Florida, but they were futile. No one could bring to the subject the range of firsthand experience and conviction possessed by the commodore. The petition to reestablish flogging was referred to the Committee on Naval Affairs, where it died. The Congress now had to consider a new code of discipline. This code was not completed and enacted into law until 1862.[64]

In beating back the effort to restore flogging, Stockton reached the apex of his career as a naval reformer. He was the right man in the right place to win the battle. No one could match his credentials. He had had a wide-ranging and full career and had proved himself successful in business, in politics, and as a naval officer. On board his own ship, he had demonstrated that a system of humane discipline was not only possible but also efficient. It was now up to other officers to learn how to apply those lessons. He had repaid his own men for their devotion. In the Senate of the United States, he had proclaimed the virtues of the American sailor. By his action in stopping the restoration of a cruel punishment, he helped to start a systematic reexamination of the whole body of regulations. The result was both a new code and a fresh perspective on how the Navy should function.

By the time the new regulations came about, Stockton was long gone from the Senate. He had been a reluctant candidate for the honor, and, when his wife's father died, he found himself obliged to deal with many additional questions in regard to the estate. Accordingly, he resigned his seat in the Senate on 10 January 1853 and served from then until his death as president of the Delaware and Raritan Canal Company. He was mentioned as a possible presidential candidate by the new American Party in 1856, but he seems to have given little encouragement to such talk. The widening sectional rift of the following years worried him. By 1859, the extreme positions of the Democrats and Republicans on the slavery issue led him to return to politics. Now embracing the American Party, Stockton argued that, if it immediately reorganized itself and softened its stand against immigrants, it could attract the conservative, patriotic, and moderate men who loved the Constitution and wished to preserve the Union.[65]

When remnants of the American and Whig Parties later combined to form the Constitutional Union Party, they accepted Stockton's ideas but turned to others for candidates. After Lincoln and the Republicans won the election of 1860 and secession of the Southern states was threatening the future of the

Union, Stockton tried to help. As a delegate to the Peace Conference in Washington that year, he tried unsuccessfully to work out a compromise solution to the crisis. During the Civil War, Stockton was deeply distressed by the suffering on both sides and withdrew from active participation in public affairs. The nation was in the midst of determining a reconstruction policy for the South when Stockton died on 7 October 1866.[66]

Stockton's naval career had been a checkered one, broken by various leaves of absence. He had the typical experiences of the day: combat against the British during the War of 1812; tours in the Mediterranean and chasing pirates in the Caribbean; and surveying expeditions along the coast. In addition, Stockton shared the aggressive spirit of his contemporaries as demonstrated by his belligerent actions against Mexico. It is for these things that he is best remembered, but in a way this is wrong, for Stockton was not a typical or average officer. He was unlike most of his fellow officers in that the sea was not his entire life. Ashore, he had a highly successful business career, was a popular — if reluctant — politician, and was active in reform movements such as the American Colonization Society. An early advocate of "white man's burden," Stockton believed that Americans were divinely ordained to inspire the "lesser peoples" of the world. Within the Navy, he was an early exponent of steam propulsion. Through his influence, John Ericsson, the future designer of the *Monitor*, came to America. With Ericsson, Stockton supervised the construction of the USS *Princeton*, the first American screw-propeller-driven sloop-of-war.

Stockton was also a reformer. He ran the ships under his command without the lash, thus serving as an example of a new style of leadership; in the Senate, he prevented the reintroduction of flogging. In these and other ways, Stockton was a link between the Old Navy of sailing ships and men driven to their work and the New Navy of steam propulsion and professionalism.

FURTHER READING

There are only two biographies of Stockton, one published and one unpublished. The first, by his friend and neighbor Samuel J. Bayard, *A Sketch of the Life of Com. Robert F. Stockton* (New York, 1856), is a campaign biography prepared for the presidential election of 1856. It is uncritical, but it contains information found in no other source. It also reflects Stockton's ideas about aspects of his career and on public issues. The book amounts to a summing up of his life when Stockton was at the height of his career.

The second biography is an unpublished typescript manuscript by Alfred Hoyt Bill, titled "Fighting Bob: The Life and Exploits of Commodore Robert Field Stockton, United States Navy," in the Princeton University Library. The work is not documented but was prepared with the help of information from Stockton's descendants, and it shows some signs of reliance on published and unpublished sources. The biography is only mildly critical of Stockton on a few matters, such as the fight with Ericsson. Bill completed the manuscript sometime in the late 1950s or early 1960s and doubtless intended to publish it in book form with sources before he died. Earlier he had produced a book on the home of the Stocktons, now the residence of the governors of New Jersey. That book, *A House Called Morven: Its Role in American History, 1701–1954* (Princeton, N.J., 1954), contains brief sketches of the commodore and his father, among others, in relation to the history of the house.

Brief accounts of aspects of Stockton's career can be found in Charles O. Paullin's *Commodore John Rodgers, Captain, Commodore, and Senior Officer of the American Navy, 1773–1838* (Cleveland, 1910); David F. Long's *Ready to Hazard: A Biography of Commodore William Bainbridge, 1774–1833* (Boston, 1981); Philip J. Staudenraus, *The African Colonization Movement, 1816–1865* (New York, 1961); John Elfreth Watkins, *Biographical Sketches of John Stevens, Robert I. Stevens, Edwin A. Stevens, John S. Darcy, John P. Jackson, Robert F. Stockton* (Washington, D.C., 1892); William Conant Church, *The Life of John Ericsson*, 2 vols. (New York, 1890); Frank M. Bennett, *The Steam Navy of the United States* (Pittsburgh, 1896); Donald L. Canney, *The Old Steam Navy*, vol. 1: *Frigates, Sloops, and Gunboats, 1850–1885* (Annapolis, Md., 1990); Spencer Tucker, *Arming the Fleet* (Annapolis, Md., 1989); James Phinney Baxter, *The Introduction of the Ironclad Warship* (Cambridge, Mass., 1933); and Richard P. McCormick, *The Second American Party System: Party Formation in the Jacksonian Era* (Chapel Hill, N.C., 1966). For details on the development of the *Princeton*'s guns, see Lee M. Pearson, "The 'Princeton' and the 'Peacemaker': A Study in Nineteenth-Century Naval Research and Development Procedures," in *Technology and Culture* 7 (1966): 163–83. An excellent contemporary account of the tragedy in the *Princeton* by Representative George Sykes of New Jersey may be found in St. George L. Sioussat, ed., "The Accident on Board the U.S.S. 'Princeton,' February 28, 1844: A Contemporary New-Letter," *Pennsylvania History* 7 (1937): 1–29. A general overview of the policies and personalities of the various Secretaries of the Navy under whom Stockton served may be found in Paolo Coletta, ed., *American Secretaries of the Navy, 1775–1972*, 2 vols. (Annapolis, Md., 1980), 1:93–361.

Stockton's ideas on reform are most easily studied in his speeches in Congress, published in the *Congressional Globe*, 32d Congress, many of which were also reprinted as separate items, and in the open letters published in his biography.

Stockton's role in the Mexican War is treated in a very critical manner in Glenn W. Price, *Origins of the War with Mexico: The Polk-Stockton Intrigue* (Austin, Texas, 1967). Price's conclusions are disputed by Charles Sellers in his *James K. Polk: Continentalist, 1843–1846* (Princeton, N.J., 1966); in David M. Pletcher, *The Diplomacy of Annexation: Texas, Oregon, and the Mexican War* (Columbia, Mo., 1973); and in K. Jack Bauer, *The Mexican War, 1846–1848* (New York, 1974). The fullest account of the California campaign is in Hubert Howe Bancroft, *History of California*, 7 vols. (San Francisco, 1884–1890). Briefer accounts are in Justin W. Smith, *The War with Mexico*, 2 vols. (New York, 1919); K. Jack Bauer, *Surfboats and Horse Marines: U.S. Naval Operations in the Mexican War, 1846–1848* (Annapolis, Md., 1969); Allan Nevins, *Fremont, Pathmaker of the West*, 2 vols. (New York, 1955); and Dwight L. Clarke, *Stephen Watts Kearney: Soldier of the West* (Norman, Okla., 1961). A modern popular account of the war in California is in David Nevin, *The Mexican War* (Alexandria, Va., 1978), a volume in the Time-Life series on the Old West.

An excellent, balanced account of the California campaign and the war is Bauer, *The Mexican War, 1846–1848*. The most recent study of the California campaign is Neal Harlow, *California Conquered: War and Peace on the Pacific, 1846–1850* (Berkeley, Calif., 1982). Most modern writers tend to be very critical of Stockton's personal traits, especially his arrogance and quest for glory in California. My own feeling is that in most things except his attitudes toward his men, his outlook and stance were very similar to those of many wealthy civilians of his times. Stockton describes day-to-day matters in letters written from California. These can be read in a photostat copy of the letterbook of Captain Robert F. Stockton, August 1843–February 1847, Record Group 45, Entry 395, National Archives. For a naval chaplain's favorable view of Stockton, see Walter Colton, *Three Years in California* (New York, 1850), and his *Deck and Port; or, Incidents of a Cruise in the United States Frigate* Congress *to California* (New York, 1860). For an enlisted man's view of Stockton, see Joseph T. Downey, *The Cruise of the* Portsmouth, *1845–1847: A Sailor's View of the Naval Conquest of California*, edited by Howard Lamar (New Haven, Conn., 1958).

For a full account of the efforts of Stockton and other reformers to abolish flogging in the Navy, see Harold D. Langley, *Social Reform in the U.S. Navy, 1798–1862* (Urbana, Ill., 1967). On Stockton's efforts to save the Union, see Robert Gray Gunderson, *Old Gentlemen's Convention: The Washington Peace Conference of 1861* (Madison, Wis., 1961).

NOTES

1. Richard B. Morris, "Richard Stockton," in Allen Johnson and Dumas Malone, eds., *Dictionary of American Biography*, 20 vols. (New York, 1928–1936), 17:46–47 (hereafter cited as *DAB*).

2. Walter R. Fee, "Richard Stockton," *DAB*, 17:47–48.

3. Alfred Hoyt Bill, *A House Called Morven: Its Role in American History, 1701–1954* (Princeton, N.J., 1954); Samuel J. Bayard, *A Sketch of the Life of Com. Robert F. Stockton* (New York, 1856), 131.

4. Bayard, *Sketch of Stockton*, 11; Alfred Hoyt Bill, "Fighting Bob: The Life and Exploits of Commodore Robert Field Stockton, United States Navy," unpublished typescript manuscript, Princeton University Library.

5. Bayard, *Sketch of Stockton*, 11–12.

6. Edward W. Callahan, ed., *List of Officers of the Navy of the United States and of the Marine Corps from 1775 to 1900* (New York, 1901), 524. Stockton's service record is in the Records of the Bureau of Naval Personnel, Record Group (RG) 24, Abstracts of Service of Naval Officers 1798–1892, Microcopy M-330, roll 19, 73, National Archives; and Bayard, *Sketch of Stockton*, 13.

7. Charles O. Paullin, *Commodore John Rodgers, Captain, Commodore, and Senior Officer of the American Navy, 1773–1838* (Cleveland, 1910), 246–56.

8. Ibid., 255.

9. Bayard, *Sketch of Stockton*, 15.

10. Paullin, *Commodore Rodgers*, 260–61, 284–89; and Bayard, *Sketch of Stockton*, 18–19.

11. Paullin, *Commodore Rodgers*, 290–91.

12. Ibid., 294–95; Callahan, *List of Officers*, 524; and Bayard, *Sketch of Stockton*, 20–22; Scott S. Sands, *The Rockets' Red Glare* (Centerville, Md., 1986), 100.

13. Bayard, *Sketch of Stockton*, 12; and Bill, "Fighting Bob," 43.

14. Bayard, *Sketch of Stockton*, 2; and Leonard F. Guttridge and Jay D. Smith, *The Commodores* (New York, 1969), 278.

15. Guttridge and Smith, *Commodores*, 283; U.S. Congress, *American State Papers; Naval Affairs*, ser. 8, Naval Affairs, 4 vols. (Washington, D.C., 1834–1861), 1:453–55.

16. Congress, *State Papers*, 1:502.

17. Bayard, *Sketch of Stockton*, 28–29.

18. Ibid., 29–36.

19. Ibid., 36.

20. Ibid., 36–38; RG 45: Letters Sent by the Secretary of the Navy to Officers, National Archives (hereafter cited as Secretary of the Navy Letters).

21. RG 45: Letters Received by the Secretary of the Navy: Officers' Letters (hereafter cited as Officers' Letters); RG 24, Abstracts of Service of Naval Officers, 1798–1892, National Archives. Stockton was given the command of the *Alligator* on 21 August 1821. Also, see Bill, "Fighting Bob," 43, and Bayard, *Sketch of Stockton*, 39.

22. Bayard, *Sketch of Stockton*, 40; and Bill, "Fighting Bob," 44.

23. Bill, "Fighting Bob," 40–47, 54; and Philip J. Staudenraus, *The African Colonization Movement, 1816–1865* (New York, 1961), 50–51. Stockton's letter to the American Colonization Society on the selection of the site is dated 16 December 1821 and is in the Peter Force Collection, Library of Congress, Series 9, roll 110.

24. Bayard, *Sketch of Stockton*, 48–53. Stockton's seizure of the Portuguese ship *Marrianna Flora* was subsequently upheld by the U.S. Supreme Court. See Henry Wheaton, *Reports of Cases Argued and Adjudged in the Supreme Court, 1816–1827*, 12 vols. (Philadelphia, 1816–1827), 11:50–52. A court also upheld Stockton's seizure of the French ship *Jeune Eugenie*; see William Powell Mason, *Reports of Cases in the Circuit Court of the United States for the First Circuit*, from 1816–1830, 5 vols. (Boston, 1819–1831), 2:409–63. On the diplomatic aspects, see Charles Francis Adams, ed., *Memoirs of John Quincy Adams*, 12 vols. (Philadelphia, 1874–1877), 6:21–23, 27–29, 31. Additional information on Stockton's seizures is in RG 45, Correspondence of the Secretary of the Navy Relating to African Colonization, 1819–1844, Microcopy M-205, National Archives, which includes letters sent and received. Other correspondence is in Secretary of the Navy Letters, M-149, roll 14. The letter of the Secretary of the Navy cited is on page 202. For an overview of the slave trade problem, see Peter Duignan and Clarence Clendenen, *The United States and the African Slave Trade, 1819–1862* (Palo Alto, Calif., 1963).

25. Bayard, *Sketch of Stockton*, 53–54; Bill, "Fighting Bob," 49–55; and Secretary of the Navy Letters, M-149, roll 14, 261.

26. Robert V. Remini, *The Election of Andrew Jackson* (Philadelphia, 1963), 11–20.

27. For a succinct account of political developments in New Jersey, see Richard P. McCormick, *The Second American Party System: Party Formation in the Jacksonian Era* (Chapel Hill, N.C., 1966), 124–34. The newspaper that Stockton owned was *The Princeton Courier*. Stockton was a delegate from Somerset County to the Democratic-Republican (the dominant party of President Adams) state convention in September 1826. See Bayard, *Sketch of Stockton*, 56–64; and Bill, "Fighting Bob," 52.

28. Secretary of the Navy Letters, M-149, roll 17, 52, 56, 177, 328, 469, 504.

29. When his great-uncle Elias Boudinot died in 1821, Stockton received a bequest of ten thousand dollars. In 1826, Stockton built a house a hundred yards east of Morven. On the death of his father, the bulk of the estate was left to Robert. A trust fund of between sixty- and eighty-thousand dollars was established with Stockton and Samuel

Bayard as trustees to provide for Richard Stockton's widow and four daughters. According to Bill, some provisions in the father's will were so complicated that the courts were still trying to resolve them fifty years after Richard's death. When Robert was in Georgia in 1827, he bought a large sugar plantation near Cumberland Island and eighty or ninety slaves to work it. See Bill, "Fighting Bob," 51–53, 55–57.

30. Bayard, *Sketch of Stockton*, 65–68; and Bill, "Fighting Bob," 59–64.

31. George R. Taylor, *The Transportation Revolution 1815–1860* (New York, 1951), 51. Potter had made his own fortune in Anglo-American trade between the American Revolution and the War of 1812; see Bill, "Fighting Bob," 49–50. For Stockton's reply to a published letter from the citizens of Toms River, New Jersey, on the monopoly, see Bayard, *Sketch of Stockton*, 68–75. McCormick points out that in New Jersey the Jacksonians became identified with the Camden and Amboy Railroad and the Whig Party with the New Jersey Railroad; see McCormick, *Second American Party System*, 131.

32. Bayard, *Sketch of Stockton*, 66; and Bill, "Fighting Bob," 64.

33. Bayard, *Sketch of Stockton*, 66; Bill, "Fighting Bob," 74; William Conant Church, *The Life of John Ericsson* (New York, 1890) 1:92–93; and John Elfreth Watkins, *Biographical Sketches of John Stevens, Robert I. Stevens, Edwin A. Stevens, John S. Darcy, John P. Jackson, Robert F. Stockton* (Washington, D.C., 1892), 16.

34. Callahan, *List of Officers*, 524.

35. For an enlisted man's view of life in the *Ohio* under Captain Smith, see F. P. Torrey, *Journal of the Cruise of the United States Ship* Ohio, *Commodore Isaac Hull, Commander in the Mediterranean, in the Years 1839, '40, '41*, 48–50; and R. F. Gould, *The Life of Gould, an Ex–Man-of-War's Man with Incidents on Sea and Shore* (Claremont, Calif., 1867), 137–38.

36. Bayard, *Sketch of Stockton*, 76–77; Church, *Life of Ericsson*, 1:94–96; and James Phinney Baxter, *The Introduction of the Ironclad Warship* (Cambridge, Mass., 1933), 12–13.

37. Church, *Life of Ericsson*, 1:121, 123; and Callahan, *List of Officers*, 524. The *Ohio* sailed for the Mediterranean on 6 December 1838, two days before Stockton was promoted to captain. He learned of this later when he was in England.

38. Bayard, *Sketch of Stockton*, 77–79; and Bill, "Fighting Bob," 78–79. Bill points out that Stockton cultivated the friendship of President Tyler and entertained him at Morven. Tyler offered Stockton the post of Secretary of the Navy, which the captain declined.

39. Church, *Life of Ericsson*, 1:117–24; and Frank M. Bennett, *The Steam Navy of the United States* (Pittsburgh, 1896), 61–63.

40. Church, *Life of Ericsson*, 1:125–54; Bennett, *Steam Navy*, 70–71; and Baxter, *Introduction of Ironclad*, 13–14. In 1853, the U.S. Court of Claims decided the issue in favor of Ericsson, but Congress never appropriated the money to pay him.

41. For a recent study of the domestic and foreign implications of the annexation, see David M. Pletcher, *The Diplomacy of Annexation: Texas, Oregon, and the Mexican War* (Columbia, Mo., 1973), 139–207.

42. Bayard, *Sketch of Stockton*, Appendix, 70–71.

43. Ibid., 93; and Pletcher, *Diplomacy of Annexation*, 184–85.

44. Bayard, *Sketch of Stockton*, 93–95. In a letter to Secretary of the Navy George Bancroft of 24 October 1845, Stockton spoke of his hopes. Among other things, he wrote: "My great object in the first place was to be prepared, in the event of a war with Mexi-

co, to try to do something creditable to the Navy," RG 45, Letters Received by the Secretary of the Navy, Captains' Letters, M-125, roll 324, 205.

45. For a highly critical assessment of this episode, see Glenn W. Price, *Origins of the War with Mexico: The Polk-Stockton Intrigue* (Austin, Texas, 1967).

46. Bayard, *Sketch of Stockton*, 95–96; Bill, "Fighting Bob," 91–95; and K. Jack Bauer, *Surfboats and Horse Marines: U.S. Naval Operations in the Mexican War, 1846–1848* (Annapolis, Md., 1969), 8–10.

47. Walter Colton, *Deck and Port: or, Incidents of a Cruise in the United States Frigate* Congress *to California* (New York, 1860), 19; and Harry R. Skallerup, *Books Afloat and Ashore: A History of Books, Libraries, and Readings among Seamen during the Age of Sail* (Hamden, Conn., 1974), 94–96.

48. Harold D. Langley, *Social Reform in the U.S. Navy, 1798–1862* (Urbana, Ill., 1967), 184–85; and Colton, *Deck and Port*, 44–45.

49. Bayard, *Sketch of Stockton*, 97–98; Bauer, *Surfboats*, 158; and Justin W. Smith, *The War with Mexico*, 2 vols. (New York, 1919), 1:336. Smith says of Stockton: "The new Commodore seems to have been a smart, but vain, selfish, lordly and rampant individual, thirsting for glory; and little glory could be seen in following after his predecessor under so mild a policy."

50. Bauer, *Surfboats*, 158–63; Bauer; *Mexican War*, 164–73; Allan Nevins, *Fremont, Pathmaker of the West*, 2 vols. (New York, 1955), 1:253–89; and Hubert Howe Bancroft, *History of California*, 7 vols. (San Francisco, 1884–1890), 5:199–214, 224–54.

51. Bancroft, *History of California*, 5:234–38.

52. Bayard, *Sketch of Stockton*, 118; Bancroft, *History of California*, 5:251–54; and Bauer, *Surfboats*, 161–62.

53. Bauer, *Mexican War*, 168–74; Bancroft, *History of California*, 5:253–54; and Walter Colton, *Three Years in California* (New York, 1850), 17.

54. Bancroft, *History of California*, 5:255–60. Bancroft says that the proclamation "was made up of falsehood, of irrelevant issues, and of bombastic ranting in about equal parts." He says it was "unworthy" of Stockton, and was dictated by Fremont and Lieutenant Archibald Gillespie, USMC, to advance their own interests. Stockton adopted their views because they exaggerated the problems he faced and the glory that success would bring. It would make a good impression in the United States, and in the event that war had not been declared, it would help to lay a foundation for his own defense and that of the U.S. government. For the reactions of Larkin and others to the proclamation, see the study of the war by Neal Harlow, *California Conquered: War and Peace on the Pacific, 1846–1850* (Berkeley, Calif., 1982), 142.

55. Bancroft, *History of California*, 5:261–81; Smith, *War with Mexico*, 1:336–37; Bauer, *Surfboats*, 165–68; Bauer, *Mexican War*, 174–76; and Harlow, *California Conquered*, 142–54.

56. Bancroft, *History of California*, 5:281–85; Smith, *War with Mexico*, 1:336–37; Bauer, *Surfboats*, 165–68; Bauer, *Mexican War*, 174–76; and Harlow, *California Conquered*, 151–54. Stockton's proclamation is published in Congress, House, *Message from the President . . . at the Commencement of the Second Session of the Twenty-ninth Congress*, 29th Cong, 2d Sess., H. ex. doc. 4, 669–70.

57. Bancroft, *History of California*, 5:288–407; Smith, *War with Mexico*, 1:238–346; Bauer, *Surfboats*, 171–200; Bauer, *Mexican War*, 183–93; and Harlow, *California Conquered*, 159–232.

58. Bancroft, *History of California*, 5:411–31; Bauer, *Surfboats*, 202–4; Bauer, *Mexican War*, 194–95; Harlow, *California Conquered*, 235–41; Dwight L. Clarke, *Stephen Watts Kearney: Soldier of the West* (Norman, Okla., 1961), 256–78; Bill, "Fighting Bob," 139–41; and Congress, Senate, *Report of the Secretary of the Navy, Communicating Copies of Commodore Stockton's Despatches Relating to the Military and Naval Operations in California*, 30th Cong., 2d Sess., 16 February 1849, S. ex. doc. 31, 1–37.

59. Bayard, *Sketch of Stockton*, 154–67; Bill, "Fighting Bob," 143–51; and Nevins, *Fremont*, 1:327–42.

60. Bayard, *Sketch of Stockton*, 169.

61. Stockton's ideas are set forth in his letter to Daniel Webster of 25 March 1850, which is printed in the appendix to Bayard, *Sketch of Stockton*, 70–79.

62. Bayard, *Sketch of Stockton*, 185–86; and Bill, "Fighting Bob," 162–64. Bill says that Stockton was elected "by means of a secret bargain with the Whigs in the legislature," 162.

63. Stockton's speeches are in the *Congressional Globe*, 32d Cong., 1st Sess. vol. 24, pts. 1, 2.

64. *Congressional Globe*, 32d Cong., 1st Sess., vol. 24, pt. 1, 218–23. Mallory's speech is in the appendix to vol. 25, 108–19. On 2 March 1855, Congress passed "An Act to Provide a More Efficient Discipline for the Navy, that established a system of summary courts martial for minor offenses." This, in turn, led to a major revision of the regulations of 1800 and to the enactment of a new code on 27 July 1862. See *U.S. Statutes at Large*, vol. 12, chap. 204, 603. Stockton's views on flogging while he was an officer are set forth in his letter of 6 February 1850 to Secretary of the Navy William B. Preston, in Corporal Punishment and the Spirit Ration, RG 45, Reports of Officers, 1850, no. 17, National Archives.

65. Bill, "Fighting Bob," 164–69. Bill says that it was believed that Stockton resigned in anticipation of being named Secretary of the Navy in the incoming administration of Democrat Franklin Pierce. If so, it did not seem to affect Stockton's friendship with the President. Subsequently, Pierce was entertained at Morven. Bill also states that Stockton was hurt by association with the canal company monopoly in New Jersey and by his reactions to a collision of two trains on his line in New Jersey. Stockton refused to pay any compensation for the casualties or the loss of property. The commodore embraced the principles of the American Party in anticipation of getting the nomination of that group for the presidency. But, says Bill, public response to his name was so lukewarm that he withdrew it. Millard Fillmore became the party's nominee. Stockton never sought public office again, although he returned to the Democratic Party after the election of 1856.

66. Robert Gray Gunderson, *Old Gentlemen's Convention: The Washington Peace Conference of 1861* (Madison, Wis., 1961), 12, 64, 67–70. Bill, "Fighting Bob," 176–80, points out that during the Civil War Stockton kept away from all public demonstrations as much as he could. In 1863, his wife died, and he spent increasing amounts of time at his beach house in Sea Girt. Although loyal to the Union, he was largely a "silent and melancholy spectator" of the war.

# ☆ Matthew Calbraith Perry
☆
☆ Antebellum Precursor of the Steam Navy

*by John H. Schroeder*

BETWEEN THE WAR OF 1812 AND THE CIVIL WAR, THE PEACETIME ROLE of the U.S. Navy expanded dramatically. The primary peacetime mission of the Navy continued to be the protection of American overseas commerce, but accelerating American economic activity around the world transformed the operational definition of that duty by creating an array of additional demands and pressures for increased naval support. In the years after 1815, the protection of commerce meant that the Navy combated pirates, policed smuggling, showed the flag in major ports around the globe, maintained a continuous presence on various overseas stations, and performed limited diplomatic duties. Government officials and most politicians, regardless of their partisan faction, believed the Navy should play a limited peacetime commercial role and defined that mission in a rather narrow and defensive manner. Americans also assumed that most of the Navy's activities would occur in the Caribbean, the Mediterranean, and the Atlantic. To perform its roles, the Navy Department maintained a small, active force of fewer than two dozen wooden sailing warships and existed on a budget that averaged less than $4 million per year.

By the 1850s, the protection of commerce had been redefined and meant a great deal more than it had three decades earlier. The Navy now played a positive and expansive role in the nation's burgeoning overseas commerce. It not only protected and defended American lives, property, and trade overseas; it now also helped identify new markets, collected valuable commercial and nautical information, concluded diplomatic agreements, and opened new areas to American enterprises. In the Navy, the Mediterranean Squadron continued to be the most prestigious duty station, but American naval forces in Latin America, the Pacific, and the East Indies now carried out activities that

were more challenging and more valuable to American overseas commercial interests.

The Navy's far-flung activities required an active force of steam as well as sail vessels numbering between forty and fifty, and an annual budget of more than $12 million per year. On the eve of the Civil War, the Navy still had fundamental problems, and it hardly resembled the modern naval force of the late nineteenth century; but the nation's staggering overseas commercial expansion had already transformed the Navy's peacetime mission. And, in the process, the Navy had assumed an important diplomatic and commercial role in shaping the nation's overseas economic development.

The naval career of Matthew Calbraith Perry spanned this period, and he stands as a key transitional figure between the Navy of the early nineteenth century and the new commercial Navy that was beginning to emerge at the time of the Civil War. His early career embodied the values and the traditions of the old navy, dominated by its magnificent wooden sailing warships. At the same time, Perry was an early proponent of the type of technological innovation and naval reform that would transform the peacetime role of the Navy and the character of its warships by the end of the century.

Matthew Calbraith Perry was born into a distinguished American naval family. His father had been a naval officer in both the American Revolution and the undeclared naval war with France; his four brothers also joined the Navy, and one, Oliver Hazard, became one of the fighting heroes of the War of 1812. Matthew himself entered the Navy at age fourteen and served under the legendary John Rodgers and Stephen Decatur in the War of 1812. He subsequently served on various duty stations, mastered the intricacies of seamanship in wooden sailing vessels, rose to the rank of captain, and eventually commanded the Africa Squadron. During the Mexican War, Perry commanded the Gulf Squadron and distinguished himself in battle during several engagements, including the expeditions against Tabasco and the capture of Vera Cruz. By 1850, Perry had compiled an impressive record of command and service similar to other top naval officers in the Age of Sail.

Unlike most of his naval peers, however, Perry had long been an energetic proponent of technological innovation, improved education, and progressive reform within the Navy. In a navy of wooden sailing vessels, Perry had become an early advocate of steam power and explosive ordnance. Throughout his career he had demonstrated a notable intellectual curiosity and wide range of educational interests. Perry had also compiled an exceptional record of diplomatic experience in different capacities. Yet these attributes might well have represented nothing more than interesting sidelights to an impressive and traditional antebellum naval career had Perry not been chosen to command the American expedition to Japan. His selection permitted him to combine and fully utilize his varied naval, diplomatic, and intellectual talents in commanding an undertaking that developed into a major diplomatic expedition.

The dramatic success and far-reaching significance of the expedition captured the nation's imagination and elevated Perry to his place as one of the Navy's most distinguished nineteenth-century officers. In retrospect, Perry's understanding of the broad significance and implications of his Far Eastern exploits, as much as the achievements themselves, made the commodore an exemplary harbinger of a coming epoch when the Navy and its officers would play an instrumental role in forging an overseas colonial empire for the United States.[1]

Born on 10 April 1794 in Newport, Rhode Island, Matthew Calbraith Perry was one of the eight children of Christopher Raymond and Sarah Wallace Perry. Christopher Perry was a seafaring man who served in several ships and was taken prisoner four times during the Revolution. He later served in the American merchant marine and, in June 1798, entered the Navy as captain in command of the yet unfinished frigate *General Greene*. During the naval war with France, the warship helped to suppress pirates, conveyed American merchantmen, and patrolled the Caribbean. In 1801, Perry returned to the merchant service, but he later received a temporary appointment as commandant of the Charlestown Navy Yard.

Matthew Calbraith was the fourth child and third son of the family. All five of the boys became naval officers, and two of the three daughters married naval officers. Matthew entered the Navy as a midshipman in January 1809 and served on the schooner *Revenge* under the command of his brother Oliver Hazard Perry. During the next six years, Matthew also served under Commodores John Rodgers and Stephen Decatur, but he was not involved in any of the dramatic naval engagements of the War of 1812. In fact, the British blockade bottled up Decatur's frigate *President* in New York and allowed Perry enough time ashore to court and marry Jan Slidell, the daughter of a prominent New York merchant, in December 1814.

The marriage was a happy one, providing Perry with nine children as well as important political contacts through his brother-in-law John Slidell, an influential Jacksonian Democrat during the 1830s and 1840s. One of Perry's sisters, Anna Maria, provided another family tie of professional importance through her marriage to the younger brother of Commodore John Rodgers.[2] These family connections aided Perry's social stature and professional career. Later, his social connections were further enhanced by the marriage in 1848 of his daughter Caroline to August Belmont, the wealthy, German-born financier who was active in New York Democratic Party circles.

After a brief tour of duty with the Mediterranean Squadron in 1815, Perry took a furlough from the Navy and commanded merchantmen owned by his in-laws before returning to the Navy in 1819. During the next eleven years,

Perry received several assignments, including his first two commands, and his career progressed steadily. He served with the naval squadron that escorted a group of free blacks to West Africa to found a free colony at the site of Monrovia at Cape Mesurado. He served with the West Indies Squadron in the effort to end piracy in the Caribbean. He also received valuable experience as first lieutenant, or executive officer, of the 102-gun *North Carolina*.

In 1830, the Navy Department ordered Perry to assume command of the new sloop *Concord*. This assignment proved to be a frustrating but worthwhile experience for Perry as he was first forced to deal with the personal demands of an eccentric politician and later allowed to view firsthand the effect that naval power could have on diplomatic disputes. Perry's initial assignment on board the *Concord* was to convey John Randolph of Roanoke, Virginia, to Russia as the republic's new Envoy Extraordinary and Minister Plenipotentiary. The cruise provided a trying but useful lesson in patience and self-restraint for the thirty-six-year-old officer. Randolph embarked with a mountain of luggage, an entourage of personal servants, and his well-known cantankerous personality. The new minister insisted that Perry make several stops en route, and once Randolph reached Russia, he remained there only briefly before having Perry convey him and his entourage back to England.[3]

When finally rid of Randolph, the *Concord* joined the Mediterranean Squadron, where Perry served for the next two years. Here, Perry was able to pursue his intellectual interests in the culture and history of the region as well as to play an instructive role in resolving a claims dispute with Sicily in 1832. When discussions stalled, Commodore Daniel T. Patterson entrusted temporary command of the squadron to Perry. In concert with the *Brandywine* and the *Constellation*, Perry sailed to Naples in July 1832, then departed, and reappeared in September in command of the *Concord*. With the sloop *John Adams* already in port, all this naval activity had the desired effect, and a treaty resolving the claims issue was signed in October 1832.[4]

By the mid-1830s, Perry found himself among a number of energetic and farsighted younger officers who wanted to introduce various progressive ideas into the Navy. Perry, his brother-in-law Alexander Slidell, Robert F. Stockton, and Franklin Buchanan were officers whose further advancement and ideas for change had been stifled by the Navy's seniority-based promotion system and by the number of officers in their sixties and seventies who clung to positions of power in the department because there was no retirement system. These senior officers dominated the Board of Navy Commissioners, which directed naval affairs, and generally opposed progressive reform and technological innovation because they held very traditional ideas about the Navy and its role. For example, the board conceded a limited place for steam power in the Navy but detested the very thought of a navy dominated by cumbersome steam vessels that did not demand a high level of seamanship and created endless noise and dirt.[5]

In contrast, the younger group of career naval officers advocated extensive changes to improve the Navy and urged the application of steam power and other technological advances. These officers admired the changes then beginning in Europe, where serious experiments had begun with steam power, iron hulls, and explosive shells. Perry, Slidell, and others also sought a much expanded peacetime diplomatic and commercial role for the Navy. To protect and extend American commerce, they wanted more ships deployed overseas and engaged in an increased array of peacetime activities. Thus, Perry, Charles Wilkes, Matthew F. Maury, and other officers actively supported the proposed naval exploring expedition to the South Seas. In endorsing the project, these officers emphasized that the gathering of scientific, commercial, and nautical information would immeasurably enhance the nation's overseas maritime and economic interests in the Pacific. In essence, they sought an active role for the Navy in the creation of an overseas American commercial empire.[6]

Perry soon emerged as a leader in the group. During a decade as second in command and then as commandant of the Brooklyn Navy Yard, Perry advocated an array of reforms and innovations. He sought improvement in the recruiting of seamen and in the education of officers. He had long taken the shipboard instruction of officers seriously and now supported the establishment of a naval academy. In 1833, he was instrumental in founding the United States Naval Lyceum, an organization formed "to promote the diffusion of useful knowledge, [and] to foster a spirit of harmony and a community interest in the service." For officers in New York, the Lyceum held regular meetings and lectures, recorded weather data, and maintained a library. Perry served as its first curator and later became its president. He also helped found the *Naval Magazine*, served on its editorial board, and contributed occasional articles. When the Naval Academy was founded in 1845, Perry served on the board of officers that organized the new institution and designed its first curriculum.

During this period, Perry developed an interest in the improvement of coastal lighthouses as important aids to navigation. In 1837, he wrote a report that recommended improvements in navigational aids for the New York area. Then, after a trip to Europe and England in 1838, he prepared a report recommending the creation of an independent lighthouse board and the application of the superior lens of Augustin-Jean Fresnel to replace the older reflectors then in use in American lighthouses. Although his recommendations were practical and well advised, they were not widely adopted in the United States until the 1850s.[7]

Perry had a more immediate impact in the area of naval technology. He long had been interested in steam power and wanted to develop a genuine steam warship rather than the harbor-bound floating steam batteries authorized by Congress and favored by some senior officers. After the construction of a steam warship was authorized in 1834, the Navy Department placed Perry in charge of construction of the *Fulton II*, which was launched in 1837. Although serious problems existed with the vessel, Perry worked hard to demonstrate the practicality of an oceangoing steam warship.

In 1838, he sailed the *Fulton II* to Washington, where President Martin Van Buren and numerous congressmen toured the ship. Resistance to steam power remained intense in the Navy and the Van Buren administration, but this venture helped persuade numerous politicians of the potential of steam power and proved to be one factor in Congress's 1839 decision to authorize three war steamers, including two—the *Mississippi* and *Missouri*—that followed Perry's designs. For his efforts, Perry has been credited with being the "father of the steam navy."

Although the label is perhaps an exaggeration, Perry nevertheless deserves recognition as the founder of the Navy's engineering corps, whose organization he outlined and championed. In 1839 and 1840, Perry also experimented with different cannons and types of shells. As a result, he demonstrated the superiority of the Paixhans type sixty-four-pound shell artillery and the comparative inaccuracy of grapeshot. Perry also advocated the use of iron warships and endorsed construction of the propeller-driven steam frigate *Princeton*, which was built under the supervision of Robert Stockton.[8]

Many of the ideas of the Navy's progressive young officers were embodied in an influential 1837 article, "Thoughts on the Navy," published in the *Naval Magazine*. Although it bore the name of Perry's brother-in-law, Alexander Slidell, the article was coauthored by Perry and expressed his ideas about the need for a more modern, efficient, and powerful American Navy. Its authors asserted that "all of our misfortunes as a nation, from the day we became one," have proceeded from the "mistakes and disasters of the past," and the nation must establish the principle that attacks on our commerce and "our national honor shall be prevented at the time by a prompt display of power." To accomplish this, the United States needed to build a navy commensurate with the "extent and value" of its commerce in "relative proportion" to the navies that other maritime nations maintained to protect their respective foreign trades. The Navy could then "follow the adventurous trader, in his path of peril, to every sea with cruisers ready to spread over him the protecting flag of the republic!" The United States had the world's eighth largest navy, but to meet its peacetime responsibilities, the Navy would need to be expanded to three times its size, a goal that Slidell and Perry endorsed enthusiastically.[9]

In spite of Perry's vision and achievements, relatively little progress had been made in the movement for naval reform by the early 1840s. The Van Buren administration remained indifferent to the need for changes in the Navy. Secretaries of the Navy Mahlon Dickerson and James K. Paulding both held very conservative naval attitudes and opposed technological innovation. The administration also demonstrated little interest in the peacetime commercial and diplomatic potential of the Navy. For example, the United States Exploring Expedition, which had been authorized during Andrew Jackson's presidency, almost did not sail at all, owing to administration inertia and indifference, before finally departing in 1838.

In early 1843, orders to command the Africa Squadron ended Perry's term of shore duty. The assignment was a difficult one not highly coveted by experienced naval officers because service in African waters was characterized by bad weather, difficult conditions, the constant threat of yellow fever, and the absence of recreational or leisure outlets for the men. The squadron under Perry was dispatched to police the slave trade, in accord with the recently negotiated Webster-Ashburton Treaty, to protect the black settlements established by the American Colonization Society and to provide "all the aid and support" that lawful American trade required. "It is the chief purpose, as well as the chief duty of our naval power," wrote the Secretary of the Navy, "to see that these [commercial] rights are not improperly abridged, or invaded."[10]

In Africa, Perry attempted to police the slave trade in a conscientious manner, but the size of his four-ship squadron limited its effectiveness. The commodore had much better fortune in combating yellow fever among his crews. He instituted a number of measures that dramatically reduced the effect of the disease. All men were required to wash their bodies every week, to wear a flannel undershirt during nights as well as days, and to sleep in a cloth jacket and pants. In addition, fresh air was dried and circulated below the decks of the ships, and smudge pots were burned to repel insects.

Under Perry's leadership, the Africa Squadron provided effective naval support for American commerce along the West African coast. In previous years, legitimate American trade and black American settlements had been subjected to constant danger and periodic attacks by various native African tribes. In 1841, at the village of Little Berebee on the Ivory Coast, the American schooner *Mary Carver*, carrying a cargo valued at twelve thousand dollars, had been captured and her crew murdered. Although the Secretary of the Navy had issued instructions in August 1842 for Commodore William Ramsey to obtain reparation, it was Perry who finally took action. On 13 December 1843, Perry's entire squadron anchored off Little Berebee. Two hundred sailors and marines landed and pitched a tent on the beach so that the Americans would not have to enter the hostile village to hold a conference with the local ruler, King Ben Krako.

Krako, a man of great size and strength, attended the meeting accompanied by several subordinates and an interpreter. In regard to the *Mary Carver* outrage, Krako provided an explanation that Perry found preposterous, and a general melee ensued. The American sailors killed the king and several natives in the scuffle and burned the village. The following day, Perry proceeded to Grand Berebee and held a conference with several other local chiefs, all of whom disclaimed any part in the *Mary Carver* attack and praised the killing of the feared King Krako. To appease Perry, local authorities signed a treaty specifying that natives in the area would not plunder trading ships or molest missionaries.[11]

In September 1845, several months after Perry returned to the United States from Africa, Secretary of the Navy George Bancroft informally offered Perry command of the Gulf Squadron. The deterioration in Mexican-American relations and the likelihood of war made this command highly attractive, but complications soon arose. The secretary did not identify a specific date for the appointment to become effective and indicated that Perry would take over as soon as Commodore David Conner relinquished his command of the Gulf Squadron. Because Perry sought additional time at home in 1845, and Conner was known to be in poor health, neither Perry nor the Navy Department anticipated any problem with the transition of commanders. In spite of his health, however, Conner had no intention of relinquishing his choice command and, in fact, remained as commodore of the squadron until he was finally removed in March 1847, more than eighteen months after Bancroft had first offered the command to Perry.

In the meantime, Perry languished in the United States until August 1846, when he received command of the steamer *Mississippi* and joined the Gulf Squadron. Once on station, Perry flew the red broad pennant of vice commodore until he finally took full command of American naval forces in the Gulf in March 1847.[12]

Once hostilities with Mexico began in May 1846, the U.S. Navy played an essential military role in the war. American naval forces prevented Mexican gunboats and privateers from disrupting American commerce, captured a number of Mexican seaports, transported troops, carried supplies, and provided additional logistical support for the American armies of Zachary Taylor and Winfield Scott. Although the enemy's weak naval forces proved to be no match for the United States, the U.S. Navy's achievement was rendered more impressive by the severe obstacles that had to be surmounted.

In Washington, the Polk administration had not prepared for naval warfare and provided minimal support once hostilities began. The administration never assigned high priority to the Navy, and Congress responded to the Navy's needs in a piecemeal manner. Officers complained frequently of inadequate supplies, poor facilities, and long delays in the arrival of war material. The Navy also required more warships, and many of those provided were unsuitable for effective use in the shallow waters along the Mexican coast.[13]

After he joined the Gulf Squadron in September 1846, Perry assumed an active part in the war effort. In October, he led the first expedition into Tabasco, Mexico, which produced the easy conquest of Frontera and a seventy-mile expedition up the Grijalva River to Villahermosa. Although he could have occupied the town, Perry withdrew after a brief truce and limited fighting because he lacked sufficient forces to occupy and hold the town. After participating in several other actions, including the capture of Tampico, Mexico, Perry returned briefly to Norfolk, Virginia, and Washington, D.C., in early 1847. This visit finally produced the Navy Department's decision to remove Conner and install Perry as commander of the Gulf Squadron. Although Conner had proved to be rather ineffective as a fighting commander, his removal produced bad feeling among his own partisans and criticism of Perry's presumed political machinations in Washington.

Conner's removal was especially controversial because it came in the midst of the American offensive against Vera Cruz, Mexico, on 20 March 1847. The overall operation was commanded by General Scott, who relied on the Navy for logistical support and control of the coast. In addition, Scott urgently needed artillery, but Perry insisted that naval forces would provide the guns that Scott required only if the gun crews came as well. In this way, Perry ensured a significant combat role for naval forces in the invasion and capture of Vera Cruz. His well-drilled gun crews fought valiantly and earned special praise from Scott himself. Subsequently, Perry's forces captured Tuxpan, Mexico, in April and then returned to Tabasco in June. There, with the river approach blocked by enemy forces, Perry led a naval landing force that marched overland several miles and forced the surrender of the town of Villahermosa.[14]

By the end of the war, Perry had achieved a reputation as one of the Navy's most capable officers. Known as "Old Bruin" for his gruff way of barking out orders, Perry was widely respected for his diligent, serious, and efficient manner. "In many respects he is an astonishing man," wrote fellow officer Franklin Buchanan in 1847, "the most industrious, hardworking, energetic, zealous, preserving, enterprising officer of his rank in our navy. He does not spare himself or *anyone* under him . . . his great powers of endurance astonish everyone; all know he is by no means a brilliant man but his good common sense and judgment, his sociable manner to his officers, no *humbuggery* or *mystery*, make him respected and esteemed."

Never a dashing or romantic figure, "Old Bruin" inspired neither great love nor hero worship. Instead, he earned the respect and admiration of his contemporaries through hard work, sound judgment, and effective performance.[15] Although his family ties and political connections might have been resented, Perry's talent and achievements could not be denied.

After he returned to the United States and was honored for his wartime exploits, Perry relinquished command of the Home Squadron in the fall of 1848 and began more than three years of shore duty as general superintendent of mail steamers. Perry's most important responsibility in his new role was to supervise construction of government-financed mail steamers being built for several private steamship lines. Congress had approved subsidies for the steamers with the specification that the ships would be built in such a way that they could be converted to naval vessels in wartime. Perry's instructions and authority were vague, however, and he exercised little control over the new steamships in spite of the energy and commitment he brought to the assignment. Although Perry was an enthusiastic proponent of steam warships, he doubted that the new mail steamers ever could be converted into effective steam fighting ships.[16]

Near the end of 1851, the Navy Department selected Perry to command the East India Squadron and to lead a major diplomatic mission to Japan. An exotic, remote, secluded land in Asia, Japan had long held a fascination for Europeans and Americans. After initial contact with Westerners, the Japanese suppressed Christianity and excluded all foreigners during the seventeenth century. The only contact occurred at the small island of Deshima, off Nagasaki, where the Dutch maintained a small settlement that provided the few items Japan sought from the outside world. During the Napoleonic Wars, the Dutch chartered a number of American ships to fly their colors and visit Deshima, but this early and trifling American commerce with Japan ended once the Dutch resumed trade in their own ships in 1813. For the next three decades, Americans had virtually no contact with Japan.

During the 1840s, American interest in Asia and Japan grew in the aftermath of the signing of the Treaty of Wanghia with China. In 1845, the Polk administration dispatched Alexander H. Everett to exchange treaty ratifications with China and to negotiate a treaty with Japan. When Everett died en route, his naval escort, Commodore James Biddle, continued the mission, exchanged ratifications with China, and then proceeded to Japan in the ninety-gun *Columbia*, accompanied by the sloop-of-war *Vincennes*.

Arriving in the Bay of Yedo (Tokyo) in July 1846, Biddle achieved little and committed a number of blunders in the process. He permitted dozens of armed guards to surround his ships and Japanese sailors to board and inspect them. Without an interpreter, he dealt directly with minor Japanese authorities, showed himself freely on board, and entrusted President James K. Polk's official letter to one such minor official. The Japanese refused to accept the letter and ordered the American ships to depart with a curt note from a local official. To receive the reply, Biddle boarded a Japanese guard boat, and in the process, was rudely pushed or bumped by a Japanese sailor. Although the Japanese offered to punish the offender, the damage was done. Lacking explicit instructions that would have permitted retaliation, Biddle departed with the embarrassing assistance of a tow from the Japanese.

In 1849, the Navy sent Commander Thomas Glynn to Nagasaki to pick up fifteen American whalemen who were being held there. Unlike Biddle, Glynn demanded respect for the American flag and the return of the Americans. He sailed his *Preble* through a cordon of guard boats and anchored within cannon-shot range of the city. In subsequent negotiations, he threatened to bombard the city if the Americans were not released, and they were freed within two days.[17]

When he returned to the United States in 1851, Glynn urged the Fillmore administration to send another mission to Japan and thus added his name to a growing movement to open relations with the Japanese. By this time, the United States had emerged as a Pacific power eager to expand its political influence in the Pacific Basin, increase its economic activity in the area, and establish close ties with the Far East. Although various factors were involved, the main pressures were economic and commercial, as different American interests sought to protect the nation's extensive whaling fleet, expand existing trade, and open new markets. The Treaty of Wanghia had only quickened American commercial interest in Asia and whetted the American appetite for the fabled commercial wealth of the Orient. In response to active lobbying, the Fillmore administration agreed in 1851 to send a new mission to Japan and selected Commodore John H. Aulick for the assignment. With a squadron of three ships, Aulick experienced difficulties soon after his departure, quarreled with one of his captains, suffered a breakdown in health in Canton, China, and ended up being removed from his command in November 1851.[18]

Perry's selection as Aulick's replacement was exceptional. Perry's vision, initiative, experience, and influence transformed the mission into a major naval and diplomatic project of far-reaching significance for the United States. Although he would have preferred command of the Mediterranean Squadron, Perry informed the Navy Department that he would accept command of the East India Squadron if the sphere of action and size of the squadron were "so enlarged as to hold out a well grounded hope of its conferring distinction upon its commander."[19]

From the outset, Perry's command contrasted sharply with that of his predecessor, Aulick, because of the great care, time, and energy that Perry devoted to preparations for the expedition. He also requested and received a much enlarged squadron, with three additional ships assigned immediately and others to follow. Eventually, Perry would command ten ships, an American squadron of unprecedented size in Asian waters. He also selected first-rate officers, whom he had known previously, to assist him. They included Commanders Franklin Buchanan, Sidney S. Lee, and Joel Abbot, who commanded the *Susquehanna*, *Mississippi*, and *Macedonian*, respectively.

During 1852, Perry collected as much information and learned as much about Asia and Japan as he could. He met with naval officers who had sailed in the western Pacific and he visited New Bedford, Massachusetts, in April to talk to whaling captains familiar with the area. He read extensively and conferred with German scholar Philipp Franz von Siebold. As a result, Perry was exceptionally well versed in Japanese history, culture, and customs by the time he sailed. Perry also took great care in purchasing various presents for the Emperor of Japan and other dignitaries. He selected gifts to demonstrate the culture and technological advancement of American civilization. In addition to volumes by John J. Audubon, Perry included an assortment of champagne, cordials, and perfumes. More important were the gadgets and machine products, including rifles, pistols, carbines, farming implements, a daguerreotype camera, a telegraph, and a quarter-sized railroad complete with locomotive, tender, coach, and track.

Perry also reshaped the expedition by convincing the administration to make the mission to Japan his primary duty, in contrast to Aulick's instructions, which had specified that the Japan mission was supplemental to his regular duties as commander of the East India Squadron. After receiving general instructions in March 1852, Perry conferred with Secretary of the Navy John P. Kennedy and Secretary of State Daniel Webster, who suggested that the commodore be permitted to draft his own diplomatic instructions. When he departed, Perry carried detailed instructions from Kennedy, diplomatic instructions from the State Department, and a letter from President Millard Fillmore to the Emperor of Japan.[20]

Most specific in regard to Japan were the instructions that Perry himself had written for the State Department. Signed by Acting Secretary of State C. M. Conrad, this document outlined the background, three main objectives, and conduct of the mission to Japan. First, the treaty was to provide protection for American seamen and ships wrecked or endangered by weather in Japanese waters. Second, the agreement should permit American vessels to obtain provisions, water, and fuel and, if necessary, to refit in Japanese ports. Third, the treaty should allow American vessels to use one or more Japanese ports to trade their cargoes.

In addition, the squadron was instructed to explore and survey the coastal waters of Japan. To achieve these objectives, the Navy authorized Perry to use his "whole force" but reminded him that the mission was to be of a "pacific character." The commodore's conduct was to be "courteous and conciliatory, but at the same time, firm and decided." He would resort to force only in "self defense" or "to resent an act of personal violence" against himself or one of his men.[21]

In November 1852, after months of preparation, Perry sailed in his flagship, the *Mississippi*, and arrived at Hong Kong via the Cape of Good Hope route in April 1853 to find three of his ships already in port. To his chagrin, the *Susquehanna* had sailed to Shanghai to protect American merchants under the threat of violence from the Taiping Rebellion. When he reached Shanghai, Perry ignored pressure from the merchant community and the American minister to remain there with his squadron. Although he agreed to leave a sloop at Shanghai, Perry transferred his flag to the *Susquehanna* and departed in mid-May for Naha on Great Lew Chew (Okinawa) in the Ryukyus.

Earlier, Perry had written to the Navy Department to emphasize the importance of establishing "ports of refuge and supply" as bases for the mission to Japan. Lew Chew seemed an ideal choice for such a base because the harbor was good, and it was accessible to Japan. Although nominally under Japanese control, the islands were semiautonomous. Moreover, the people were docile, unarmed, and backward, with their only defense being their considerable ability to evade, procrastinate, and ignore foreigners and their demands. The proximity of Lew Chew to Japan ensured that Perry's actions and the size of his squadron would be reported to the Japanese. Lew Chew, then, provided an excellent place for a dress rehearsal.[22]

At Naha, Perry refused to meet with natives or local officials who greeted the American ships. Only when the regent for the ruler of the island visited the *Susquehanna* did Perry receive him and announce that he would visit the royal palace at Shuri. The horrified officials of Lew Chew attempted, without success, to divert Perry. On the appointed day, Perry and an impressive entourage landed, rejected further attempts to divert them, and proceeded to Shuri. The commodore rode in an elaborate sedan chair constructed for the occasion to emphasize his exalted station. After visiting the palace and feasting at the regent's residence, Perry and his party returned to the American ships.

During the next two weeks, the Americans visited Naha frequently, procured a shelter for Americans on shore, and dispatched a party to explore the island while other Americans surveyed the coastal waters.

In early June, the *Susquehanna* and the *Saratoga* sailed for the Bonin Islands to the northeast. At Port Lloyd, Perry found a small colony of thirty-one residents headed by Nathaniel Savoy, a native New Englander who had settled the island with a small group from Hawaii. Although he had no intention of using the islands as a base for his Japanese operations, Perry understood the potential value of the port, which stood directly on the great circle route from Hawaii to the south China ports. Perry himself purchased a small tract of land to serve as a possible waterfront coal depot. He also raised the American flag, drew up a code of laws, and had Savoy elected chief magistrate. Later, Perry would assert an official American claim to the islands and recommend establishment of an open port for whalers, steamers, and merchant ships of all nations.

Perry then returned to Naha, where he drilled American forces on shore and dispatched more parties to collect a range of information on the islands.

As subsequent events would demonstrate, the commodore intended Lew Chew and the Bonins to serve as much more than a temporary base for his own mission. He believed that he had taken the initial steps in establishing two permanent American "ports of refuge and supply" for American whalers, merchantmen, transpacific steamers, and naval vessels.[23]

On 2 July 1853, the *Susquehanna* and three other warships departed on a six-day journey to Japan. At the entrance to the Bay of Yedo, Japanese junks and guard boats immediately appeared and surrounded the American ships. But the Japanese ships were prevented from tying lines to the American ships and Japanese sailors were not permitted to board. Only when a man identified as the vice governor appeared was he permitted to board the flagship, where he was received by Perry's subordinates rather than by the commodore himself. The Americans informed the Japanese that Perry had a letter from the President for the Emperor, and they refused to deliver the document at Nagasaki as the Japanese specified. Operating through his subordinate officers, Perry insisted that the President's letter be delivered to appropriate authorities at Uraga and indicated that the American fleet would proceed directly to Yedo and the royal palace if the Japanese refused. To underline his claims, Perry had already initiated surveys of the area.

Finally, the Japanese agreed to receive the President's letter in special ceremonies at Kurihama near Uraga. At daybreak on 14 July, the *Susquehanna* and the *Mississippi* steamed into the bay at Kurihama, anchored, and positioned themselves to command the Japanese shore fortifications. Because thousands of Japanese troops had congregated on shore, Perry sent 250 armed marines and sailors in several launches.

Once they were ashore, the ceremony itself was brief. The American couriers opened the elaborate box containing the American document and received a Japanese scroll in return. The Japanese reply acknowledged receipt of the President's letter, explained that negotiations could not occur at this spot, and informed Perry that he could now depart. In response, the commodore explained that he would sail in two or three days and would be pleased to convey any messages to Lew Chew or Canton. When the Japanese did not reply, Perry explained that he planned to return the following spring with at least four naval vessels and possibly more.

The conference then ended, the Americans returning to their ships without incident. The next day, Perry transferred to the *Mississippi* and steamed up the bay to the outskirts of Yedo before turning back. A final ceremony was held on 16 July, in which small presents were exchanged, and the American squadron departed for Naha the following day.[24]

Perry based his decision to return to Japan later, rather than wait for the Japanese response to the President's letter, on several considerations. By departing for China, Perry could reprovision his squadron, add warships, give the Japanese time for deliberation, and address any problems that might have arisen in China. When he left Japanese waters, Perry could take considerable satisfaction in his initial achievements. He had avoided Biddle's earlier mistakes and established contact with the Japanese on a basis of equality without provoking an incident or engaging in hostilities. He had insisted on proper respect for his official authority, refused to deal directly with lower Japanese officials, and delivered the President's letter in an appropriate ceremony. Perry had also refused to permit the Japanese to swarm over his ships, insisted that all provisions be paid for, and exchanged gifts with the Japanese only on an equal basis.

In addition, American forces had navigated the Bay of Yedo without hindrance, conducted surveys of the area, and approached the outskirts of the capital. Perry's firmness, careful preparation, and conciliatory manner also left the unmistakable message that he was a determined man who would not be easily diverted by traditional Japanese tactics.[25]

Back at Naha the reports that he received displeased Perry. During his absence, provisions had proved difficult to obtain and numerous spies and police plagued Americans on shore. At a dinner on 28 July, Perry insisted that a free market be established, that Americans be left unmolested on shore, that use of a rest house be continued, and that a coal shed be erected for use by Americans. When the regent demurred, Perry replied that he would again march to the palace at Shuri unless he received a satisfactory response within twenty-four hours. For effect, he dispatched a carpenter to inspect and repair the sedan chair he had used on his initial visit. The regent complied with each request the next day, however, and Perry departed for China on 1 August.

In China, the arrival of additional naval vessels strengthened Perry's forces, and, by the end of 1853, his squadron numbered ten ships. Although he had originally planned not to return to Japan until the spring of 1854, rumors in China led Perry to fear that a Russian squadron was preparing to visit Japan before he returned, and he hastened his departure. By late January 1854, his entire squadron had assembled at Naha, where it remained for two weeks. Although Perry found relations with the natives at Naha more amicable, he protested to the regent about various difficulties. The commodore also recommended American occupation of Great Lew Chew should his mission to Japan fail. In February, the squadron departed for Japan and anchored near Uraga, where Perry prepared for a long stay.

Local Japanese officials welcomed the Americans hospitably and informed them that five Japanese commissioners had been appointed to negotiate with Perry at Uraga. Perry countered by suggesting that the negotiations be held at the Japanese capital. Thus began several weeks of disagreement over exactly where the formal negotiations would be held. Finally, the Japanese proposed and Perry accepted Yokohama, fifteen miles south of the capital, as the site.

Formal negotiations began with an elaborate ceremony on 8 March 1854, after Perry came ashore with an entourage of three bands and five hundred marines, sailors, and officers. In the initial meeting, the Japanese delivered the Emperor's reply and agreed to protect shipwrecked Americans and American ships in distress, as well as to provide provisions, water, and coal to American ships at one designated harbor. According to the Japanese, preparation of the harbor would take five years, and, in the meantime, coal would be available at Nagasaki. The Japanese also agreed to sell or barter anything ships might want that could be furnished from their empire.

Negotiations continued through March, as Perry and the Japanese differed on the extent of commercial privileges and the number of ports to be opened. On 13 March, Perry formally presented the American gifts to the Japanese and provided a full demonstration of the miniature railroad and telegraph. On the twenty-fourth, the Japanese reciprocated with gifts of their own. Relations between the two groups continued to be cordial and free of hostility. On 31 March 1854, the Treaty of Kanagawa was signed in a formal ceremony. The agreement guaranteed protection for shipwrecked American sailors and American ships in distress and specified that the ports of Shimoda and Hokadate would be open to American ships to purchase wood, water, coal, and provisions at a fair price. At these two ports, shipwrecked American sailors were also permitted to reside temporarily and to move freely within designated areas. In addition, the treaty included a most-favored-nation clause and allowed the United States to send "consuls or agents" to reside at Shimoda anytime after eighteen months.[26]

Although the concessions granted in the treaty did not approximate those enjoyed by the United States in its relations with China, the agreement constituted a dramatic achievement. Not only had Perry accomplished the basic objectives outlined in his instructions, but the commodore had also placed diplomatic relations between the two nations on a formal and equal basis. Such status had never been granted to the Dutch at Nagasaki or to any other nation. Subsequently, the commercial concessions would prove to be inadequate for the United States, but Perry's treaty nevertheless provided the basis for later expansion of commercial privileges.

As soon as the treaty was signed, Perry dispatched Commander H. A. Adams to the United States in the *Saratoga* with a copy of the treaty, while the main body of the expedition remained in Japanese waters, continued to survey the coastline, and visited the treaty ports of Shimoda and Hokadate. In July, Perry returned to Naha and signed a treaty of friendship with the regent. The commodore then returned to Hong Kong before leaving for the United States in September 1854.

Although contemporary attention focused on the "opening" of Japan, Perry's own goals and achievements were not limited to the treaty with Japan. He himself conceived of his mission in broad strategic terms and attempted to provide the basis for an American commercial empire in the western Pacific. In addition to the concessions wrested from Japan and the substantial scientific and nautical activities of the expedition, Perry sought American maritime superiority in the area.

In the Lew Chew Islands, he had insisted on a treaty that guaranteed water, wood, and provisions for American ships, native pilots to guide American captains safely into the harbor, land access for Americans on Great Lew Chew, an American burial ground there, and construction of an American coal shed. In the Bonin Islands, Perry had formally asserted an American claim to the islands, helped to establish a small independent community headed by a native New Englander, and purchased land at Port Lloyd to serve as a coaling station. He also dispatched two vessels to investigate reports that shipwrecked American sailors were being held captive on Formosa and to explore coal deposits there. Although no sailors were found, the coal proved to be abundant. The treaty with Japan, then, represented but a part of Perry's visionary Far Eastern program.[27]

Perry used the period after his return to the United States to outline his views on the nation's Far Eastern policy in two articles, as well as in an address to the American Geographical Society. Like many other Americans of his time, Perry predicted a new era of commercial enterprise for the United States in the Pacific Basin. The recent treaty with Japan represented only a "preliminary" step toward a more advanced commercial agreement that could be concluded once Japan was better prepared to enter the international community. To encourage American commerce, Perry urged formal diplomatic and commercial treaties with Siam, Cambodia, Cochin China, and parts of Borneo and Sumatra. Perry also endorsed creation of a government-supported steamship line from the Pacific ports of the United States to China, Japan, and the main islands in between. Finally, Perry emphasized the value of naval power in Asian diplomacy. "In all negotiations with China and other eastern nations," wrote Perry, "the display of a respectable armed force is necessary . . . in most cases, the mere presence of such force will answer the purposes desired."[28]

Although such views were popular during the 1850s, Perry went far beyond his contemporaries in advocating the creation of a European-style empire in the Pacific. He believed that the United States should take control of Lew Chew and the Bonin Islands, and he wanted the United States to take the initiative on the "magnificent island" of Formosa by establishing an American colony at the port of Kelung. Once established through a land grant, the American settlement would soon increase its area, wealth, and power until it rivaled the ports of Hong Kong and Singapore in importance.

In addition to the rich coal deposits on Formosa, American settlement there would provide an "entrepot for American trade" in Asia and give the United States an excellent "naval and military position . . . directly in front of the principal ports of China." Like most other Americans of his day, Perry also embraced the idea of American intervention in the internal affairs of Asia as part of the "responsibilities which our growing wealth and power must inevitably fasten upon us." Because "the advance of civilization and the industrial arts" could be achieved only when the Asian peoples joined the "new family of commercial" nations, the commodore argued that military intervention might "be fully justified," to force "the empires of China and Japan into the family of nations."[29]

Perry envisioned continued American expansion in the Pacific as Americans reached for their ultimate destiny by settling the remote islands of the Pacific and creating their own governments there. But Perry well understood that the development of an American empire in the Pacific would not be a benign process. Forceful military and political action would be necessary to combat European rivalry and establish American supremacy. Eventually, the American people would extend "their dominion and their power until they shall have . . . placed the Saxon race upon the eastern shores of Asia." There, predicted Perry, the American "exponents of freedom" would eventually confront the Russian representatives of "absolutism" in a "mighty battle" that would determine "the freedom or the slavery of the world."[30] These visionary ideas placed Matthew Perry far ahead of his time and attracted little serious support in the 1850s. In this respect, the commodore's prescience made him much more an ideological contemporary of Alfred T. Mahan's generation than of his own antebellum era.

In the United States, Perry received a hero's welcome and lavish praise for the expedition's achievements. Congress gave Perry a vote of thanks and a twenty-thousand-dollar grant for serving as the diplomatic envoy as well as the naval commander of the expedition. The commodore received a gold medal from the merchants of Boston and a 381-piece silver service from the New York Chamber of Commerce. In a ceremony at Newport in June 1855, the governor and the General Assembly of Perry's native Rhode Island presented him with a large silver salver. In the meantime, Perry had begun work on the official narrative of the expedition, with Volume I appearing in 1856 and Volume II in 1857.

By the end of 1857, Perry seemed ready for a new assignment, and he was rumored to be the next commander of the Mediterranean Squadron. But in early 1858, Perry caught a severe cold, became seriously ill, and died on 4 March.

Although his death denied him the chance for further distinctions in the upcoming Civil War, Matthew Calbraith Perry's legacy was already secure. In nearly a half century of service, he had distinguished himself as a professional officer, wartime commander, naval reformer, and effective diplomat. The breadth of his achievements was unmatched in the antebellum Navy. As a professional naval officer and commander, Perry was one of the best of his day. He was courageous in battle, and, during the Mexican War, he proved to be an energetic and effective commander.

In addition to these attributes, Perry also distinguished himself as a naval reformer and diplomat. Throughout his career, he sought ways to modernize and improve the efficiency of the Navy and better educate its men. Perry also became a skilled diplomat during his career, and the combination of his personal talent, energy, and intelligence was largely responsible for the spectacular success of the expedition to Japan. Equally important is the fact that Perry fully understood the long-term significance of his activities in the Far East. He realized that he was not merely opening formal relations with one island nation but was helping to shape a maritime empire as well. Thus representing the best qualities of the Old Navy, Matthew Calbraith Perry also manifested the very attributes that would be demanded by the navy of the new American empire several decades later.

## FURTHER READING

The standard scholarly biography of Perry is Samuel Eliot Morison, *"Old Bruin": Commodore Matthew C. Perry, 1794–1858* (Boston, 1967). In spite of some distracting digressions, Admiral Morison's biography is typically well written and extensively researched, and it presents a full account of Perry's life. An old, still useful but inaccurately titled study is William E. Griffis, *Matthew Calbraith Perry: A Typical American Naval Officer* (Boston, 1887). A more recent biography of little value is Edward M. Barrows, *The Great Commodore: The Exploits of Matthew C. Perry* (Indianapolis, 1935).

Aspects of Perry's career have also been treated in a number of studies. His contributions to antebellum naval development are analyzed in John H. Schroeder, *Shaping a Maritime Empire: The Commercial and Diplomatic Role of the American Navy, 1829–1861* (Westport, Conn., 1985). Perry's service in the African Squadron is discussed by Donald R. Wright, "Matthew Perry and the African Squadron," in Clayton R. Barrow, Jr., ed., *America Spreads Her Sails: U.S. Seapower in the 19th Century* (Annapolis, Md., 1973). K. Jack Bauer, *Surfboats and Horse Marines: U.S. Naval Operations in the Mexican War, 1846–1848* (Annapolis, Md., 1969), is an excellent study that details Perry's role in the conflict.

On the development of steam power in the United States, see Frank M. Bennett, *The Steam Navy of the United States* (Pittsburgh, 1896). Also, see David B. Tyler, *Steam Conquers the Atlantic* (New York, 1939), and John G. B. Hutchins, *The American Maritime Industries and Public Policy, 1789–1914* (Cambridge, Mass., 1941).

An abundant literature exists on the expedition to Japan, but good starting points are Morison's *"Old Bruin,"* Schroeder's *Shaping a Maritime Empire,* and Arthur Walworth, *Black Ships off Japan: The Story of Commodore Perry's Expedition* (New York, 1946). Perry's own account is found in the official narrative, F. L. Hawks, ed., *Narrative of the*

*Expedition of an American Squadron to the China Seas and Japan*, 3 vols. (New York, 1856). Also insightful is Earl Swisher, "Commodore Perry's Imperialism in Relation to America's Present-Day Position in the Pacific," *Pacific Historical Review* 16 (1947): 30–40. Perry's difficulties in China are detailed in Curtis T. Henson, *Commissioners and Commodores: The East India Squadron and American Diplomacy in China* (University, Ala., 1982).

NOTES

1. Although the study is not directly cited in the notes, this article is based to a considerable extent on the research and material in John H. Schroeder, *Shaping a Maritime Empire: The Commercial and Diplomatic Role of the American Navy, 1829–1861* (Westport, Conn., 1985). For detailed treatments of Perry's life, see Samuel Eliot Morison, *"Old Bruin": Commodore Matthew C. Perry, 1794–1858* (Boston, 1967), and William E. Griffis, *Matthew Calbraith Perry: A Typical American Naval Officer* (Boston, 1887).

2. Detailed treatments of the Perry family and Matthew's early years are found in Morison, *"Old Bruin,"* and Griffis, *Matthew Calbraith Perry.*

3. Morison, *"Old Bruin,"* 104–17. Also, see William Cabell Burce, *John Randolph of Roanoke, 1773–1833: A Biography Based Largely on New Material*, 2d ed., 2 vols. (New York, 1922), 2:634–61.

4. Morison, *"Old Bruin,"* 121–23.

5. W. Patric Strauss, "Mahlon Dickerson" and "James K. Paulding," in Paolo E. Coletta, ed., *American Secretaries of the Navy*, 2 vols. (Annapolis, Md., 1980), 1:160–62, 165–71.

6. House of Representatives Report No. 94, 23d Cong., 2d Sess. (1834–35).

7. Morison, *"Old Bruin,"* 124–39.

8. Ibid., 127–32. Also, see Frank M. Bennett, *The Steam Navy of the United States* (Pittsburgh, 1896).

9. Alexander Slidell [Mackenzie], "Thoughts on the Navy," *Naval Magazine* 2 (1837): 5–42.

10. Abel P. Upshur to Perry, 30 March 1843, Record Group (RG) 45, Letters Sent by the Secretary of the Navy to Officers, 1798–1868, vol. 34, National Archives.

11. Donald R. Wright, "Matthew Perry and the African Squadron," in Clayton R. Barrow, Jr., ed., *America Spreads Her Sails: U.S. Seapower in the 19th Century* (Annapolis, Md., 1973), 80–99.

12. Morison, *"Old Bruin,"* 179–89.

13. K. Jack Bauer, *Surfboats and Horse Marines: U.S. Naval Operations in the Mexican War, 1846–1848* (Annapolis, Md., 1969), passim, describes naval operations.

14. Morison, *"Old Bruin,"* 230–38.

15. Description by Buchanan as quoted in Charles Lee Lewis, *Admiral Franklin Buchanan: Fearless Man of Action* (Baltimore, 1929), 121–22.

16. David B. Tyler, *Steam Conquers the Atlantic* (New York, 1939), 204–07.

17. David F. Long, *Sailor-Diplomat: A Biography of Commodore James Biddle* (Boston, 1983), 209–20; and Merrill L. Bartlett, "Commodore James Biddle and the First Naval Mission to Japan, 1845–1846," *American Neptune* 61 (1981): 25–35.

18. Charles O. Paullin, *American Voyages to the Orient, 1690–1865* (Annapolis, Md., 1972), 123–24.

19. Perry to W. A. Graham, 3 December 1851, as cited in Griffis, *Matthew Perry*, 289–91. Perry's preparations for the expedition are described in detail in Morison, "*Old Bruin*," 270–90. Also, see Arthur Walworth, *Black Ships off Japan: The Story of Commodore Perry's Expedition* (New York, 1946).

20. John P. Kennedy to Perry, 13 November 1852, C. M. Conrad to Kennedy, 5 November 1852, Fillmore to His Imperial Majesty, The Emperor, 33d Cong. 2d Sess. (1854–1855), S. ex. doc. 34, 2–11.

21. Conrad to Kennedy, 5 November 1852, ibid., 4–9.

22. Perry to Kennedy, 14 December 1852, ibid., 12–14. Perry's own account of the expedition is F. L. Hawks, ed., *Narrative of the Expedition of an American Squadron to the China Seas and Japan*, 3 vols. (New York, 1856).

23. Earl Swisher, "Commodore Perry's Imperialism in Relation to America's Present-Day Position in the Pacific," *Pacific Historical Review* 16 (1947): 30–40; *Extracts from the Rough Journal of Commodore Perry*, 24 June 1853, S. ex. doc. 34, 33–39; and "Report of an Examination of the Bonin Group of Islands," in Hawks, *Narrative of Expedition*, 2:127–33.

24. *Notes Referring to . . . the Preliminary Negotiations of Commodore M. C. Perry with the Authorities of Japan in July 1853*, S. ex. doc. 34, 45–57.

25. Morison, "*Old Bruin*," 336; and Walworth, *Black Ships off Japan*, 115.

26. Perry to J. C. Dobbin, 25 January 1854, Dobbin to Perry, 30 May 1854, S. ex. doc. 34, 108–10, 112–13.

27. Hawks, *Narrative of Expedition*, 1:343–92; and Perry to Dobbin, 1 April 1854, S. ex. doc. 34, 145–50. A copy of the treaty is contained in ibid., 174–75.

28. *Extracts from Rough Journal*, 39; and Hawks, *Narrative of Expedition*, 2:153–54, 167–70, 180. Vol. 2 of the latter contains various reports on aspects of the expedition, including "Remarks of Commodore Perry upon the Expedience of Extending Further Encouragement to American Commerce in the East," 173–82, and "Remarks of Commodore Perry upon the Probable Future Commercial Relations with Japan and Lew Chew," 185–87.

29. Ibid., 178, 180, 177, 176.

30. *A Paper by Commodore M. C. Perry, U.S.N.* (paper read before the American Geographical and Statistical Society, New York, March 6, 1856).

# ☆☆☆ David Glasgow Farragut

## ☆ The Union's Nelson

*by William N. Still, Jr.*

BRITISH MILITARY HISTORIAN CYRIL FALLS DESCRIBES DAVID GLASGOW Farragut as "a great naval commander with something of the dash and inspiration of Nelson."[1] Farragut, however, was not so romantic a figure as the famous British admiral. His personal life was above reproach, and he was not mortally wounded during his most famous battle. Nevertheless, to the generation of naval officers that came of age during the Civil War and to the Northern public in general, he was a genuine hero, rightfully compared to the victor of Trafalgar.

Farragut was born on 5 July 1801 at Campbell's Station, outside of Knoxville, Tennessee. His family moved to New Orleans in 1807. Following the death of his mother and the enlistment of his father in the Navy, David was taken into the family of Commander David Porter, who was in charge of the New Orleans Naval Station.[2] After a brief period in school, David, at the age of nine and a half, was appointed a midshipman in the Navy.

When Porter was given command of the frigate *Essex* in 1811, Farragut sailed with him. After war broke out with Great Britain in 1812, the *Essex* captured a number of prizes in the Pacific, and Farragut, as prize master, took one of them into Valparaíso, Chile. He was twelve at the time. In 1814, Farragut became a prisoner of war when the *Essex* was taken after a long and bloody engagement with two British warships. Porter was extremely pleased with Farragut's performance during the battle and would have recommended him for promotion except for his youth.

After the war, Farragut served in various ships, primarily in the Mediterranean and the West Indies. In 1821, he was promoted to lieutenant; shortly afterward, he briefly commanded the *Ferret*, his first naval command. In 1823, he

married Susan C. Marchant of Norfolk, Virginia. She died in 1840 after an extended period as an invalid, and, three years later, he married Virginia Loyall, also of Norfolk. They had one child, Loyall. From the end of the War of 1812 until the time of the Civil War, Farragut's career was varied but unspectacular. He received his first important command, the sloop *Decatur,* in 1842 and his last, the *Brooklyn,* in 1860. In between, he commanded the *Saratoga* during the Mexican War. Of his shore assignments the most important was the period from 1854 to 1859, which he spent in California establishing the Mare Island Navy Yard. In September 1855 he was appointed captain. When the Civil War broke out, he was awaiting orders at home in Norfolk. Then sixty years old, he had spent nearly half a century in the Navy.

Career officers with the prospect of promotion on the horizon are usually delighted with the coming of war, yet this was not generally true in 1861. Certainly it was not true for Farragut. His residence was Norfolk when Virginia seceded in mid-April; he then moved his family to New York. There he remained, cooling his heels for nearly four months. As an officer of Southern descent he was under suspicion. In September, he was made a member of a naval board to select incapacitated officers for retirement. Farragut's chances for active employment were not promising. He was close to retirement age, had been passed over three times for squadron commander, and had spent very little time at sea since the Mexican War. In fact, his greatest accomplishment had been the establishment of the Mare Island Navy Yard.[3] Yet, through fortuitous circumstances, he would be given command of the most important naval expedition to be mounted during the war, the opening of the Mississippi River and the capture of the port of New Orleans.

Secretary of the Navy Gideon Welles appointed Farragut to this prestigious command for several reasons. Welles was impressed that Farragut had left Norfolk when Virginia seceded and moved his family to New York. He was also familiar with the naval officer's plan to capture a fortification at Vera Cruz during the Mexican War. Perhaps most important was the endorsement from Commander David Dixon Porter, the son of Farragut's guardian, who with Assistant Secretary of the Navy Gustavus Fox and Welles, strongly urged Farragut's selection. Finally, Farragut was the most likely candidate in order of seniority not already assigned to an important command.[4]

At times, Welles would ignore strict seniority, but he decided to adhere to it in this case. According to the Secretary's most recent biographer, Welles believed that President Abraham Lincoln would insist on giving the command to Commander John Dahlgren, in charge of the Washington Navy Yard and a favorite of the President, unless seniority were followed. A number of officers consulted by the Secretary had reservations concerning Farragut's ability to command a large force. Nevertheless, Welles decided to appoint him. "All who knew him gave him credit of being a good officer, of good sense," Welles wrote.[5]

On 21 December 1861, Farragut journeyed to Washington, D.C., where he met with Fox and Welles. That night, he elatedly wrote his wife the news of his appointment: "I am to have a flag in the Gulf and the rest depends upon myself."[6] Two days later, he received his official orders to the command with the *Hartford* as his flagship. Within a month, on 19 January 1862, the *Hartford* was commissioned and left Philadelphia for the Gulf of Mexico.[7]

A month later, the *Hartford* arrived at Ship Island, an islet lying approximately thirty miles to the south of Biloxi, Mississippi. Here, Flag Officer W. W. McKean transferred to Farragut thirty vessels that would comprise the nucleus of his force, the West Gulf Blockading Squadron. Farragut would need far more ships, however, to carry out his responsibilities, which included not only the capture of New Orleans, Louisiana, but the blockade of the Gulf region from Saint Andrews Bay in the east to the Rio Grande in the west. Fox had already written him, "We are crowding everything into your hands so as to give you enough to make sure work." This would include additional shallow-draft steamers, mortar boats to be commanded by David D. Porter, and even the recently completed revolutionary warship, the *Monitor*.[8]

By the beginning of April, Farragut commanded a heavily increased squadron. He had forty-seven warships, not counting mortar boats, with which to carry out the Mississippi River operation while enforcing the blockade throughout his station. A military force of some eighteen thousand men under Major General Benjamin F. Butler had arrived to cooperate in the attack.[9] Throughout March, Farragut had concentrated on getting his heavier ships over the bar at Southwest Pass and into the Mississippi River. He had reluctantly delayed the attack until the larger vessels were in the river. There is little doubt that he would have attacked with only his smaller ships and avoided several weeks' delay had the choice been his, but it was not. The Navy Department expected him to mount the attack not only with his larger vessels but with the support of Porter's mortar boat flotilla as well.

The department's orders called for him to reduce the two forts, Saint Philip and Jackson, by using Porter's mortar boats as long as necessary and then to place New Orleans under his guns until troops could arrive and assault the city. On 18 April, the mortar boats, in position below the forts and supported by the gunboats, opened fire. Almost immediately, Farragut realized that he did not have enough ammunition for a lengthy bombardment. On 20 April, at a conference of officers, he informed them of his decision to run past the forts, even though they had not been rendered ineffective. To the assembled officers, many of whom had strong reservations about his plan, including Porter, he replied: "Something must be done immediately. I believe in celerity."[10]

At 2:00 A.M. on 24 April, red lanterns hoisted to the mizzen peak in the *Hartford* signaled the fleet to get under way. Detachments from two of the smaller gunboats had already cleared an opening in a barrier of dismantled hulks across the river between the forts. Farragut's original plan called for the sortie to be in two columns with the lighter gunboats shielded by the heavier ones, but the passageway in the barrier was too narrow for ships to pass through two abreast — the advance instead would have to be in one long single column of three groups. The first group, under the command of Captain Theodorus Bailey, consisted of six gunboats and two sloops-of-war. The second was led by the *Hartford*, followed by the *Brooklyn* and *Richmond*. Six gunboats brought up the rear. The battle began immediately after the second vessel, the *Pensacola*, passed through the barrier. As both forts opened fire and the Union ships replied, Confederate vessels joined in the fight.

The small Confederate naval force above the forts consisted of four wooden gunboats and one ironclad ram, the *Manassas*. Only the *McRae* and *Manassas* posed a serious threat to Farragut's ships. The Confederates had hoped to reinforce this flotilla with two large armored vessels, the *Mississippi* and *Louisiana*, but both were still under construction when Farragut attacked, with only the *Louisiana* far enough along to be used. On the day that the mortar boats opened fire on the forts, she was towed down the river and moored to the bank above Fort Saint Philip. The day before Farragut's attack, six guns were mounted on her gun deck facing the river.[11]

As with so many plans, Farragut's soon collapsed during the smoke and confusion of battle. Most of the ships got through the barrier safely, although the *Brooklyn* strayed into a hulk, then into a raft of logs, before emerging in front of Fort Saint Philip. The *Kennebec*, one of the smaller gunboats, leading the third division, fouled the barrier, and along with two others in this division — the *Winona* and *Itasca* — remained below it. Some of the vessels, passing the others, fired on one fort and then the other before finally emerging from the smoke above the forts. There, the Confederate vessels added to the confusion by entering the fray. The *Manassas* rammed the *Brooklyn*; the *Hartford* was set ablaze by a fire raft; first the *McRae* and then the *Manassas* attacked the *Iroquois*.

The *Cayuga*, challenged by three of the Confederate vessels, escaped unharmed, but the *Varuna* was not so fortunate; seven miles above the forts, the *Governor Moore* sank her after a running fight. Shortly afterward, the *Governor Moore* was herself disabled and run aground by several Union ships. The fleet, less the three vessels that remained below the barrier and the sunken *Varuna*, assembled at Quarantine Station, seven miles above the forts.

Farragut had won his first major engagement as a fleet commander. Since observing French warships in action against a Mexican fort in 1838, he had been convinced that ships with sufficient speed could bypass forts without sustaining appreciable damage. This laid the basis for his plan of action, and the results justified his expectations. He lost only one ship, with minor damage to the others, and he suffered only 37 killed and 146 wounded. The forts were isolated; with their line of communication cut, it would be only a matter of time before they must surrender. New Orleans was next.[12]

Shortly after noon on 25 April, Farragut's fleet rounded the last bend in a drizzling rain and appeared within sight of New Orleans. The spectacle appalled the flag officer. "The levee of New Orleans was one scene of desolation; ships, steamers, cotton, coal, etc., were all in one common blaze and our ingenuity much taxed to avoid the floating conflagration."[13] Shortly after anchoring, Farragut sent his second in command to demand the city's surrender. After some defiance by Confederate military and civil officials, New Orleans surrendered to the Navy. Farragut then ordered a detachment of marines to raise the American flag over the U.S. Mint. Although the citizens remained hostile, with curses and threats following the U.S. uniforms, the city was taken. That night, Farragut wrote his wife and son: "I am so agitated that I can scarcely write and shall only tell you that it has pleased almighty God to preserve my life and limb. . . . I took the city at Meridian today."[14]

Farragut's haste to take New Orleans without waiting for Butler's troops had one unfortunate consequence: it allowed the Confederates to remove most of their stores and railroad rolling stock and to dismantle factories. The flag officer's decision may have been for personal achievement and a race for glory, as Butler hinted in a letter to his wife, but more than likely it was simply a product of Farragut's aggressiveness, self-confidence, and impatience. Farragut's victory clearly was important, but just how important it is difficult to say. A modern study has concluded that "without question the capture of New Orleans was the most important Union conquest of the war—strangling Southern commerce on the river and along the Gulf coast." Another author, in obvious agreement, titled his book-length study of the campaign *The Night the War Was Lost.*[15]

It is doubtful, however, that the battle and capture of New Orleans were that decisive, certainly in terms of the war's outcome. Southern morale was shaken by the fall of the largest city and most important port in the Confederacy; trade virtually ceased to flow on the Mississippi River. But Confederate morale was still resilient, and it would be another year and a half before it would begin to collapse. Also, closing the Mississippi had little effect on trade elsewhere along the Gulf Coast. Yet, Liddell Hart correctly maintained that running past the forts and thereby gaining "the bloodless surrender of New Orleans . . . was the thin end of a strategical wedge which split the Confederacy up the vital line of this great river." It was the capture of the lower Mississippi, along with

Port Hudson, Louisiana, and Vicksburg, Mississippi, that proved decisive. James D. Bulloch, a Confederate naval officer, wrote years after the war, "I have always thought that the consequences which resulted from the operations of [the Union Navy] . . . in the waters of the Mississippi were more fatal to the Confederacy than any of the military campaigns."[16]

After New Orleans, what next? Farragut's original instructions had stressed that he reduce the forts, capture New Orleans, continue up the river possibly as far as Memphis, Tennessee, link up with Union forces descending the river, and finally seize Mobile, Alabama. With New Orleans in Union hands, Farragut initially decided to attack the forts guarding Mobile Bay, but, informed of Farragut's plan, the Navy Department reacted negatively. Although the capture of Mobile had been in Farragut's instructions, the evidence is clear that the Navy Department expected him to complete the river campaign before attacking Mobile. On 17 May, Fox wrote to Porter: "Somebody had made a most serious blunder in persuading the Flag Officer to go at Mobile instead of obeying his instructions to go up the Mississippi. . . . It seems extraordinary how Farragut could have committed this terrible mistake. . . . Mobile and the whole Gulf will fall at any time, but the Mississippi is a golden opportunity that I fear is fast slipping through our fingers."[17]

Before Fox could communicate his concerns to Farragut, the flag officer had already changed his mind and ordered vessels up the river "to keep up the panic as far as possible." Why had Farragut reconsidered? One biographer suggests that the flag officer had second thoughts about his orders and realized the priority of moving up the river. Rowena Reed in *Combined Operations in the Civil War* argues that Butler persuaded the flag officer to change his mind. On 29 April, he wrote to the Secretary of War that he hoped to convince Farragut "to pass up the River as far as the mouth of Red River if possible, so as to cut off [the Confederates'] supplies," and added that he believed Mobile was not so important as this.[18] Whatever the reason, the decision was correct. Opening the Mississippi was far more vital to ultimate victory than the capture of Mobile.

On 7 May, Farragut left New Orleans with the *Hartford*, two large steamers, and eight small gunboats and arrived below Vicksburg on 24 May. Some two thousand men under the command of General Thomas Williams accompanied the naval force. Convinced that more troops were needed to attack Vicksburg successfully, Farragut awaited reinforcements. When no additional troops materialized, the flag officer left for New Orleans determined to begin the Mobile campaign. Within a few weeks, however, a reluctant Farragut returned upstream under orders to pass Vicksburg and take Memphis if possible.

By the time Farragut reached Vicksburg, Memphis had fallen, and the Union Mississippi Squadron was approaching Vicksburg from upstream. Farragut determined to link up with the descending squadron. On 28 June, his vessels, once again in two columns, got under way and, under the cover of fire from mortar boats, made their way slowly past the fort. Although several vessels were hit, none was seriously damaged, and all but the *Brooklyn* and two gunboats made it past the city. Farragut's conviction that ships could run past forts and fortifications without receiving serious damage again proved correct.[19] On the last day of June, the Union Mississippi Squadron under Flag Officer Charles Davis joined Farragut at anchor above Vicksburg.

Farragut wanted to return downstream as quickly as possible. Additional troops were still unavailable, the river was beginning to fall, and he feared for the health of his crews in the unhealthy river lowlands. On 4 July, he wrote his wife, "If I can retain my health and get out of this river . . . I shall be most thankful."[20] He felt that he had accomplished the department's major objectives with the exception of capturing Vicksburg, and it could not be taken without more troops. His officers and men overwhelmingly concurred. Lieutenant George H. Preble, commanding the *Katahdin*, complained that the "Squadron has no business up the river at all . . . and for once President Lincoln made a mistake in ordering it."[21]

Farragut delayed his decision, however, partly because of news of a Confederate ship under construction up the Yazoo River. On 15 July, a small reconnaissance force was sent up that stream. A few miles above the river's mouth, the Union ships encountered the Confederate ironclad *Arkansas*. In a running fight back downstream, one of the Union vessels ran ashore while the other two fled toward the anchored fleets.

Approximately halfway between Vicksburg and the mouth of the Yazoo, the thirty-odd vessels that made up the squadrons of Davis and Farragut were anchored generally in two lines, one on each side of the river. At 7:15 A.M. the two Union ships were observed rounding a bend, followed by the *Arkansas*. The Confederate ironclad fired broadsides at the anchored Union vessels as she steamed slowly between the lines. Some of the ships returned the fire; others did not. Aroused by the cannonade, Farragut appeared on the flagship's deck in his nightgown and "seemed much surprised."[22] After running the union gauntlet, the *Arkansas* successfully reached the protection of the Vicksburg batteries.

The presence of the ironclad between his squadron and the Gulf prompted Farragut to end his indecision and take his vessels back downstream. They would attack and destroy the *Arkansas* in their descent. "No one will do wrong who lays his vessel alongside of an enemy or tackles the ram," Farragut said in orders reminiscent of Nelson.[23] The attack failed; by the time the vessels got under way, it was twilight, and the ironclad could not be seen. Thus ended what was probably the most humiliating day in Farragut's career.

On 22 July, a final and futile effort was made to destroy the Confederate ship. The Union warships *Essex* and *Queen of the West* attempted to ram the *Arkansas*, moored below Vicksburg, but heavy fire from the Confederate iron-clad and the land batteries forced the two ships to retire, leaving the Southern vessel battered but seaworthy. This failure was the last straw. Two days after the abortive attack, the entire fleet was standing down the river. Farragut went all the way to New Orleans but left several vessels at Baton Rouge to watch for the *Arkansas* in case she came down. On 6 August, the Confederate ironclad approached Baton Rouge but broke down and was destroyed by her crew.[24]

Arriving in New Orleans on 10 August, Farragut received official word that he had been promoted to rear admiral, the first in terms of seniority and the first admiral in the U.S. Navy. According to one officer, "a prouder or a happier or more boy like exhilarated little man you never saw." The following day, the admiral wrote to his wife, "Yesterday I hoisted my flag on the main, and the whole fleet cheered."[25] On 13 August, as the *Hartford* got under way for the Gulf, the squadron recognized his promotion with a fifteen-gun salute.

Farragut went to Pensacola, Florida, for a period of rest and, during the following weeks, devoted much of his time to improving the blockade. Prior to this time, he had generally neglected this responsibility, though the neglect was not altogether his fault. The Navy Department had made it clear that as important as the blockade was, he was to concentrate his energies on the Mississippi River campaign. In April, Farragut had deployed the bulk of his steamers on the Mississippi but left five steamers plus a dozen or so sailers to blockade the Gulf from Pensacola to the Rio Grande. By the end of the year his squadron had increased to nearly seventy vessels. A third of them, however, were still sailing vessels, of little use in chasing fast blockade runners. During the fall of 1862 and early 1863, Farragut had between twenty-five and thirty steamers on blockade station, approximately half stationed off Mobile and Galveston, Texas, with the remainder scattered throughout the Gulf.[26]

The Union blockade in the Gulf was not effective, at least not until late 1864. According to one authority in 1862, 65 percent of the vessels attempting to run through the blockade of the Gulf ports succeeded.[27] Like blockaders on the Atlantic coast, those in the Gulf were frustrated by their apparent inability to stop blockade runners. In October 1862, one officer wrote from a ship patrolling off Mobile, "Two steamers and seven schooners have run through the blockade last month, and it is a shame." He blamed Farragut: "It makes me feel cross . . . that our Commodore does not keep up the blockade more strictly." Although Farragut would insist that few blockade runners were getting through, one British observer thought otherwise. In May 1863, he noted, "Blockade running goes on very regularly at Mobile, the steamers nearly always succeed, but the schooners are generally captured."[28]

Farragut was not solely to blame for his squadron's problems with blockade running; there simply were not enough vessels available. Nevertheless, he had little faith in an outside blockade. Quite early in the war he had advocated blockading ports from inside a harbor, bar, or inlet. In a letter to his wife written before his ships crossed the bar into the Mississippi River the first time, Farragut wrote: "I shall endeavor to keep at the Head of the Passes a sufficient force to hold it against the Rebels without Blockading outside. You know my idea was always to Blockade inside, not outside, and when I show the example I feel satisfied that others will follow."[29]

Farragut hoped to employ this tactic at the other Confederate Gulf ports, particularly Mobile and Galveston. In September, Sabine Pass fell to Union forces; early in October, four gunboats under Commander W. B. Renshaw closed Galveston by capturing the harbor's entrance. The Galveston blockade was effective—that is, until Confederates on New Year's Eve defeated Renshaw's flotilla by capturing one vessel, destroying another, and forcing the remaining Union ships to retire outside the bar. Although Farragut immediately reinforced his force off Galveston, the port remained in Confederate hands. To add to the admiral's distress, one of his ships off Galveston, the *Hatteras*, gave chase to a suspicious-looking craft and paid the penalty for failing to identify her as the raider *Alabama* until it was too late. After a brief engagement, the Union vessel was sunk, and the *Alabama* escaped.[30]

Farragut was also deeply concerned about another Confederate raider that had entered his area. In September, the *Florida* slipped past the blockaders and entered Mobile Bay. When Welles dismissed the officer in command of the ship nearest the *Florida*, Farragut protested to his wife that "almost any man would have been deceived by a vessel coming right down to him with the English flag flying." The admiral, however, was not so understanding when the *Florida* again successfully eluded his vessels and escaped from the bay in January 1863. Farragut's son, Loyall, who was acting as his father's secretary at this time, wrote his mother: "Pa has been very much worried at these things but still he bears it like a philosopher. He knows that he has done all in his power to avert it with the vessels he has, if the government had only let him take Mobile when he wished to, the [*Florida*] would never have run out."[31]

Farragut was in New Orleans preparing to deploy again up the Mississippi when the incidents at Galveston and Mobile Bay occurred. Jim Dan Hill, in his excellent biographical essay of the admiral, suggests that Farragut decided to return to the river because his ships had been overhauled; the winter was far healthier than the summer along the river; and, most important, a combined expedition was again threatening Vicksburg from upriver.[32] Farragut certainly recognized these changes, but given the choice, he would have preferred to concentrate on Mobile.

The problem was that the Army would not commit troops to attack Mobile. Late in November 1862, Farragut had written to Captain Henry H. Bell: "I will not take another place without troops to hold it. . . . As to Mobile I have but little hopes of getting troops for the attack."[33] A few days later, he informed Bell, "By the indications of [General] Butler's letters [the next operation] will be in the River," adding that "they appear to be anxious for us to keep the River open up to Red River." Then on 15 December, he informed Bell that "Porter is knocking at the open door to Vicksburg and we must go to work at the lower door — Port Hudson."[34]

In mid-December, Major General Nathaniel Banks replaced Butler. Banks's orders were vague and conflicting, but Farragut was convinced that he was to cooperate with the general in attacking Port Hudson.[35] During the winter months, Farragut assembled his fleet at New Orleans for the movement upriver, but Banks continued to vacillate. Unknown to the admiral, Banks had decided not to attack Port Hudson because of its supposed strength.

As Farragut waited, passing his time in social activities, Rear Admiral Porter, in command of the Mississippi Squadron, ran two of his vessels past the Vicksburg batteries to secure the river between there and Port Hudson. The apparent Union success was mitigated in less than a month when the Confederates captured one of the vessels. Hearing the news, Farragut informed his flag captain: "The time has come; there can be no more delay. I must go, army or no army."[36]

Early in March, Farragut led his fleet of eight warships and a flotilla of mortar boats some 135 miles upstream to Port Hudson. There the Confederates had heavily fortified the bluffs overlooking the river with light field pieces and heavy guns, and the garrison numbered more than six thousand men. Banks had promised to provide troops to make a diversion while Farragut's ships ran by the fortifications, but, unfortunately, the "diversion" consisted of some fifteen thousand troops bivouacking a few miles outside of the Confederate stronghold. Banks had been convinced by a deserter that more than thirty thousand troops occupied Port Hudson.[37]

On 13 March, Farragut arrived below Port Hudson and intended to take his fleet past the fortifications the following night. As Mahan points out in his biography of Farragut, it was at Port Hudson that the admiral for the first time experimented with "a somewhat novel tactical arrangement," lashing his weaker vessels to the protected side (the side away from the fortifications) of the more powerful warships. Not only would this protect the lighter gunboats, but it gave each pair of ships the maneuverability of a twin-screw steamer. If one vessel were damaged, the other hopefully could carry it on upstream out of danger.[38]

It was nearly 10:00 P.M. when Farragut got his vessels in a column and under way. The *Hartford* led the line with the *Albatross* lashed to her side, followed in order by the *Richmond* and the *Genessee*, the *Kineo* and the *Monon-gahela*, and the old side-wheeler *Mississippi* bringing up the rear. The Confederates were expecting the Union vessels to attempt to pass Port Hudson and opened fire as soon as the leading vessels got in range.

The Union guns thundered in reply. Gunners on board the ships and in the land batteries had difficulty in spotting targets because of smoke from several hours of mortar fire. Port Hudson was built on a ninety-degree turn in the river, so the admiral feared that poor visibility would result in one or more of his vessels missing the turn and running aground directly under the batteries. The *Hartford* and her consort barely made the turn; the following ships did not. The *Richmond*'s machinery was put out of action by a lucky shot, and she drifted back downstream with the *Genessee* lashed to her side. The smaller gunboat, with merely a single screw, was unable to stem the current. The *Monongahela* did run aground and, in breaking free, damaged her machinery, a mishap that forced her and the *Kineo* back downstream. The *Mississippi* also ran aground and had to be abandoned under fire from several batteries. She burst into flames and was destroyed with heavy loss of life—sixty-four killed out of a complement of nearly three hundred men.

Although the Confederates achieved something of a victory at Port Hudson, it was certainly a mixed one. Farragut was able to get only his flagship and one other ship above the fortified town, but they were sufficient to control the river south of Vicksburg and blockade the mouth of the Red River. Much to his relief, the Navy Department did not censure him for what happened at Port Hudson, although Fox apparently referred to it as a disaster in a letter to Samuel F. Du Pont. Du Pont himself mentioned Farragut's "repulse" and later wrote, "I am worried about Farragut; he did not know, poor fellow, the difference between running forts and engaging them direct."[39]

Farragut was unusually depressed by what happened at Port Hudson. "Oh, how I feel the failure of my ships to get past," he wrote to his wife, and added, "but it was God's will and I must submit and be happy that it was no worse." He wrote to Du Pont the same day, admitting that he had had some "sad disasters, but as the Frenchman said, 'you can't make an omelet without breaking eggs.'"[40]

Farragut would remain above Port Hudson for nearly two months, patrolling the river, before returning to New Orleans. He had hoped that Porter would send one or two ironclads below Vicksburg to reinforce him, but the Mississippi Squadron commander refused, stressing that he had none "fit for service." Nevertheless, two of the Army's "Ram Fleet" did attempt to run the Vicksburg batteries and join Farragut. The *Lancaster* was sunk, but the *Switzerland*, under Colonel C. R. Ellet, was successful. Although Ellet wrote that "Farragut and all his officers have treated me with the utmost kindness and cordiality," he was not happy when the admiral ordered him to blockade the Red River.[41]

On 6 April, the Navy Department instructed Porter to "occupy the river be-low Vicksburg" so that Farragut could return to the Gulf. Ten days later, his fleet ran the batteries. This move not only carried out the department's wishes, but it fitted Ulysses S. Grant's plan of attacking Vicksburg from be-low.[42] On 4 May, Porter conferred with Farragut; four days later, Farragut left for New Orleans and turned over command of the *Hartford* to Captain James S. Palmer.

The admiral was not free of the river campaign, however. For two months longer he remained at New Orleans and kept close watch over the river up to Port Hudson. Porter's squadron, concentrated near Vicksburg, was cooperat-ing with Grant's army. Banks was laying siege to Port Hudson, and Farragut's vessels had to support him until either Vicksburg or Port Hudson fell. Vicks-burg's surrender on 4 July finally freed his vessels to return to the Gulf.

Early in August, Farragut, whose health had deteriorated, obtained leave and sailed with the *Hartford* for New York. During the fall months, while the admiral recuperated, his flagship was overhauled. On 30 December, a telegram from the Navy Department brought Farragut the intelligence that the Confederate naval force in Mobile planned to attack the blockaders off Mobile Bay in the near future. Farragut was urged to expedite his departure. Within a week, he sailed south, with Mobile, finally, his major objective.

While on the East Coast, Farragut had requested that monitors be assigned to his squadron. Ironically, he preferred wooden to iron-armored ships, in-cluding monitors. It was not altogether because of "ignorance" or "inexperi-ence," as a Confederate naval officer later wrote, but because he considered monitors undependable, unseaworthy, and frequently inoperable. Less than a month before the Battle of Mobile Bay, Farragut wrote to his wife, "Monitors and Rifled Guns are in my opinion demoralizers to men—they make them think that men should only fight in Iron cases or at 3 or 4 miles distance."[43] He preferred ships with broadside guns, "high speed, and all good fighting men."

Monitors were primarily to be used against the forts guarding the bay; against enemy warships, including ironclads, Farragut was quite willing to haz-ard his wooden ships. "I am tired of watching [the vessels of Confederate com-manders Franklin] Buchanan and [Thomas J.] Page, and wish from the bot-tom of my heart that Buchanan would come out and try his hand upon us," he wrote his son. "This question has to be settled, iron *versus* wood; and there nev-er was a better chance to settle the question." Farragut's opinion of ironclads was common knowledge, but not accepted, in the Navy. His friend Du Pont wrote, "Farragut will [have to learn] that iron vessels are required to meet iron vessels."[44]

Returning to his squadron, Farragut expected to attack Mobile within the next month or so, as soon as troops and the monitors arrived. The troops were tied up in Banks's Red River expedition, however, and it would be more than six months before the first monitor joined Farragut's force off Mobile. The admiral's queries to the Navy Department about ironclads for his squadron finally brought a response from Fox in late March: "I have three letters from you. . . . I have held on to the last moment . . . in hopes to be able to say exactly what we can do for you about iron-clads." The Assistant Secretary then went on to say that Grant's campaign—just getting under way in Virginia—would determine when monitors could be assigned to the Gulf. "If [Grant] goes to James River, of course we shall have to keep a force of iron-clads to keep his communications open," Fox wrote. Finally, in what must have been a bitter pill for Farragut, Fox mentioned, "We have the summer before us and I trust you will not act until you oblige us to give you everything you require."[45] Once again, the Mobile attack was to be delayed.

The Confederate States Navy's growing strength in the Mobile area finally persuaded the Navy Department to order monitors to the Gulf. The Confederates there had four ironclads either completed or under construction. On 18 May, they succeeded in getting the *Tennessee* over the bar and into Mobile Bay. From then until a monitor finally arrived, Farragut was worried about the possibility of a surprise attack. Every night, half the crew of each ship remained at battle stations with the batteries cast loose. On 10 May, he informed his ship commanders that leave would no longer be granted "for the next two months." Later that month, he wrote his wife, "My life is now one of anxiety—I cannot leave here to go beyond a few miles."[46]

When the news that the *Tennessee* was in Mobile Bay reached Washington, Welles ordered the monitor *Manhattan* at New York to "proceed with all possible dispatch" to the Gulf, and instructed Porter to send the double-turreted monitors *Chickasaw* and *Winnebago* from his squadron immediately.[47]

Even if ironclads had been available earlier in the year, it is doubtful that Farragut would have attempted to enter Mobile Bay without the support of troops. The Army did not consider Mobile Bay to be a priority until the Red River campaign had ended and Sherman's movement on Atlanta was under way. In June, Grant, who favored an attack on Mobile, ordered that troops be assigned to cooperate with Farragut; however, the first contingent of twenty-four hundred men did not arrive from New Orleans until 3 August.[48]

In July, with the *Manhattan* at Pensacola, Farragut received word that a second ironclad, the *Tecumseh*, was en route, and that the two river monitors from Porter's squadron had reached New Orleans. On 31 July, the admiral wrote his wife, "My monitors are all here now so that I am the one to attack, and no longer expect to be attacked."[49] On 3 August, the various ship commanders assembled in the *Hartford* for final instructions. Farragut planned to use the same tactics employed at Port Hudson: each large wooden ship would have a smaller gunboat secured to her disengaged side, while the monitors would move past the forts in a separate column, on the starboard side of the wooden ships. As the channel approached the bay at right angles to Mobile Point where Fort Morgan was situated, the wooden vessels firing broadsides would be unable to fire until nearly opposite the fort. Monitors, with their uninhibited field of fire, would be able to open fire much sooner.

The main channel into the bay, approximately three miles wide, ran between Mobile Point to the east and Dauphin Island to the west. Fort Morgan on the end of Mobile Point and Fort Gaines on the eastern end of Dauphin Island guarded the channel. To the west of Dauphin Island was Grant's Pass, a smaller, shallower channel used only by light-draft vessels and guarded by Fort Powell, a small earthwork fortification. The main channel was partially obstructed by pilings jutting eastward from Fort Gaines and a mine or torpedo field extending an additional four hundred yards into the channel. The narrowed channel forced ships to pass within relatively close range of Fort Morgan's powerful batteries. Because of the "configuration of the bottom," Farragut believed he would have to stay in the main channel. He hoped to make the attack on a flood tide going into the bay, which would help the vessels pass through the channel as swiftly as possible.[50]

On 3 August, the ships were readied for action. One young officer, flushed with the anticipation of battle, wrote in his diary, "This has been the most exciting day on the blockade . . . sand bags have been piled up around the machinery, guns shifted to the starboard side, shot and shell rooms and magazines placed in readiness." Anchor chains were ranged along the exposed side of the larger vessels to protect their machinery. These preparations continued after sunset while heavy rains, accompanied by fierce lightning, covered the area.[51]

During the night, Farragut postponed the attack because the *Tecumseh* had not arrived from Pensacola. The attack on Dauphin Island to invest Fort Gaines went ahead, however. Under the protection of gunboats, fifteen hundred soldiers were landed on the island and began a fifteen-mile march to the fort. In the afternoon, while another squall was blowing in, the *Tecumseh* arrived. The attack would be made the following morning.

The fifth of August dawned beautiful and cloudless, with ideal conditions for the attacking force. An early morning flood tide would carry damaged vessels past the fort and into the bay, and a breeze blowing out of the southwest would carry the smoke of battle toward Fort Morgan. At 5:30 A.M., the fleet got under way in two columns. The main column consisted of seven large ships, each with a gunboat lashed to her port side; to starboard of these ships a second parallel column was formed, with the *Tecumseh* in the lead, followed by the *Manhattan*, *Winnebago*, and *Chickasaw*. Farragut had relinquished the lead position in the main column to the *Brooklyn*—the only vessel with bow chasers and a minesweeping device on her bow. After the *Brooklyn*, with the

*Octorara* lashed to her side, came the *Hartford* and the *Metacomet*, the *Richmond* and the *Port Royal*, the *Lackawanna* and the *Seminole*, the *Monongahela* and the *Kennebec*, the *Ossipee* and the *Itasca*, and, at the end of the column, the *Oneida* and the *Galena*.

At 6:30 A.M. the battle began when the *Tecumseh* fired a 15-inch shell in the direction of Fort Morgan. The fort's guns replied, and, by seven o'clock, the engagement had become general—each vessel firing as she came within effective range. After firing twice at the fort, the *Tecumseh* turned toward the Confederate ironclad *Tennessee*, which was moving slowly into the bend in the channel just clear of the mine field. The monitor crossed the main column about three hundred yards in front of the *Brooklyn* on a collision course with the enemy ironclad. Farragut's instructions required the vessels to pass east of buoys marking the end of the mine field, but the *Tecumseh*, turning to port, penetrated the field.

An hour after the battle began she struck a mine, reeled to port, and went down within two minutes, bow first. Commander Thomas H. Stevens, in command of the *Winnebago*, wrote that as his ship steamed by the spot where the *Tecumseh* had sunk, all that could be seen was "the top of the smoke stack and the seething water beneath which she had gone down."[52] The crews of the flagship *Hartford* and the *Metacomet* cheered as they observed the three remaining monitors steaming unhesitatingly by the sunken monitor into the bay.

Meanwhile, a lookout on board the *Brooklyn* sighted suspicious objects in the water ahead. Her captain immediately backed his engines to avoid them. Earlier, Farragut had climbed into the rigging for better visibility, where he was lashed to the after shroud by a piece of line fastened around him, and upon seeing his lead ship apparently backing down, he ordered the flagship to pass her and take the van. As the *Hartford* steamed by the port side of the *Brooklyn*, the flagship's captain informed Farragut that there was a "heavy line of torpedoes ahead." The admiral is then supposed to have shouted "Damn the torpedoes!" or something to that effect, and the *Hartford*, followed by the rest of the column, steamed directly across the mine field and into the bay. As most authorities rightly imply, this was the decisive moment in the battle, for the admiral's courageous decision to ignore the mines—a calculated risk, for he had earlier suspected that if there were any, they were inactive from long immersion—prevented the development of a chaotic situation that might have caused the attack to fail.

As Farragut's ships entered the bay, they engaged a small Confederate naval force under the command of Rear Admiral Franklin Buchanan. In the ensuing battle, they captured or destroyed every Confederate warship, with the exception of one small wooden gunboat. The ironclad *Tennessee* continued to fight until rammed by three Union ships, and, with the *Chickasaw* pounding her mercilessly, she surrendered. By noon, the battle was over and Farragut's fleet was at anchor in the bay.

Alfred Mahan, an admirer and biographer of Farragut, wrote that "the Battle of Mobile Bay was to the career of Farragut what the Battle of Copenhagen was to that of Nelson." Mahan was right. As Jim Dan Hill said: "Farragut's public was not even academically critical. It considered Farragut greater than Nelson." Yet, Hill himself wrote that the battle was "void of major strategic significance."[53] It had little or no effect on the war's outcome.

Farragut's plan of attack was carefully thought out. The decision to place the ironclads in a column nearest to Fort Morgan generally worked as expected despite the *Tecumseh's* unfortunate move and demise. The monitors did attract most of the fort's fire. The tactic of lashing two vessels together had not worked well at Port Hudson; yet Farragut had adopted the same plan again, and, in this instance, it was far more successful. All of his warships except the *Tecumseh* made it into the bay.

There has been some criticism of Farragut's tactics. Hill suggests that it was a mistake to have rammed the *Tennessee* with wooden vessels. "This repeated ramming injured the cruisers much more than they did the hostile armored craft." Carroll S. Alden wrote: "Certain English tacticians asserted, and with some show of reason, that Farragut had placed his fleet in an untenable position. For so long as three Confederate forts controlled the approaches to Mobile Bay, the fleet could not be reached by the transports and was cut off from supplies."[54]

This criticism is unfounded. Farragut was aware that Grant's Pass was guarded by a small earthwork fort, and, on 4 August, an amphibious force was landed to take it. The fort was captured the same afternoon as the Battle of Mobile Bay. Supply ships used this entrance until the forts guarding the main channel were taken. Fort Gaines surrendered on 7 August, but it was not until Union troops invested Fort Morgan from the landward side, with a heavy bombardment from both siege artillery and ships' guns, that the fort finally yielded on 23 August.

Farragut's victory at Mobile Bay created something of a dilemma for the Navy Department. Fox was urging Welles to place the admiral in command of a naval force to take Wilmington, North Carolina. On 18 August, the Assistant Secretary wrote Farragut, "I do not see the necessity of you remaining to blockade," and added, "Wilmington . . . is the most important point remaining." Welles, however, resisted. He was convinced that the city of Mobile should be taken as soon as possible. Farragut was opposed to taking Mobile; he considered it unnecessary "except for the morale effect."[55] Finally, Welles gave in to Fox's insistence and ordered Farragut to take command of the Wilmington attack force.

Farragut accepted these orders but requested leave to return to the North before assuming the new command. In fact, the admiral was most reluctant to undertake the Wilmington operation. He questioned the suitability of a naval attack up the shallow Cape Fear River, and he also felt that the season was far too advanced to begin such a campaign. Perhaps his greatest reservation, however, was himself. He was physically and emotionally worn out. He recognized this and so did his officers. On 24 August, Lieutenant George Perkins wrote: "I was talking to the Admiral today . . . when, all at once, he fainted away. He is not very well, and is all tired out." In September, Percival Drayton wrote to Du Pont that Farragut "has not been well."[56] Farragut finally informed the department that he had to have an extended leave of "four or five months," and Welles assigned the Wilmington operation to Porter.

With the *Hartford*, Farragut arrived in New York on 13 December. Ten days later, President Lincoln signed a bill creating the office of vice-admiral, and Farragut was immediately named to fill it.[57] The admiral would not command an active naval force again during the war. During the final months, he served as president of an officers promotion board. After the war ended, he continued to head the board but spent most of his time at home in New York City. In July 1866, Congress established the rank of admiral, and he was appointed to this office. Early in 1867, he assumed command of the European Squadron.[58]

Farragut's appointment to this command surprised many. He was sixty-six years old, a full admiral, and not in good health. Welles does not say in his diary why he appointed Farragut, but the reasons seem obvious: he was the most prestigious officer; the European Squadron was at that time the most important peacetime command; it was a traditional appointment for a senior officer about to retire; and Farragut clearly wanted it. On Bastille Day, 14 July 1867, Farragut arrived in Cherbourg, France, in the flagship *Franklin*. The following day he relieved Rear Admiral Louis Goldsborough of the command.[59]

During Farragut's seventeen-month tour with the European Squadron, no serious problems required attention; in fact, it was one triumphal visit after the other to various countries. On 18 October 1868, the *Franklin* left for the United States, and for all practical purposes Farragut's active service in the Navy came to an end.

While Farragut was in Europe, Grant won the presidency.[60] The admiral, however, would have little to do with the new administration. He was displeased with the new Secretary of the Navy, Adolph Borie, as well as the influence that Porter had with both Grant and the Secretary. He was also ill during the spring of 1869; in fact, his health, which had been poor since the river campaign in 1863, would continue to be delicate for the remainder of his life. In May 1869, Mrs. Farragut wrote that "the Admiral continues very miserable and I can scarcely leave his side. . . . I am very much discouraged about him."[61] He recovered and visited the Mare Island Navy Yard, which he had started some eleven years before. On the way home, however, he had a heart attack. He again recovered, but, in August 1870, while visiting the Portsmouth Navy Yard in New Hampshire, he died. Farragut had a premonition of his approaching death; when Mrs. Farragut protested his activities, he said that "he would just as well die in harness as any other way."[62]

Farragut was the most competent naval officer on either side during the Civil War. He was, as Bern Anderson wrote, "head and shoulders above them all." He had all the attributes of a great commander: intelligence, knowledge, self-confidence, enormous energy, and courage. "Farragut has always been my ideal of the naval officer," Admiral George Dewey related in his autobiography. Other officers would reiterate this sentiment. Alfred T. Mahan and Winfield Scott Schley would favorably compare him to Nelson. Army officers and even former Confederates would voice their admiration. Major George C. Strong, who met the admiral in New Orleans, wrote "Farragut is as gallant a man as ever walked a ship's deck." James Bulloch agreed that "Farragut showed that he had the qualities . . . which make a great naval commander."[63]

Senior officers in the Navy, Farragut's peers—Du Pont, Goldsborough, Davis, Dahlgren, and others—generally admired and liked him. Even Porter, who was clearly envious of Farragut, had a grudging respect for "his half brother." Farragut had no particular enmity for Porter, although he was aware of his jealousy. Rear Admiral Charles Davis mentioned in a conversation with Farragut that Porter would give him trouble, and Farragut replied, "Of course he will."[64]

S. Phillips Lee is the only Civil War flag officer who is known to have been critical of Farragut's abilities and performance, but according to one authority, Lee was at times hypercritical of all the senior officers. On 28 May 1862, Lee wrote his wife that Farragut "is a worthy man and gallant officer but deficient in judgment." Less than two weeks later he declared to her that "for [Farragut's] want of military mind and knowledge we shall earn some dear experience." Then, in July, he wrote that "Dr. [Jonathan] Foltz who is on good terms with the Flag Officer says to me *privately*, that he has served . . . under 3 Flag Officers . . . and that [Farragut] . . . has less mind than either of the others. That Farragut is wholly unstable, not having the same opinion from hour to hour."[65]

Farragut and Lee developed an intense dislike for each other that would continue throughout the war. Farragut blamed Lee for the *Florida*'s success in slipping through the blockade into Mobile Bay in September 1862. Nevertheless, Lee would be promoted to captain and shortly afterward acting rear admiral in command of the South Atlantic Blockading Squadron.

Farragut had complete confidence in his own judgment and in his opinion of naval officers, operations, tactics, and just about anything else related to naval affairs. Before the Battle of New Orleans he wrote: "As to being prepared for defeat, I certainly am not. Any man who is prepared for defeat, would be half defeated before he commenced." Mahan mentions in his biography that Farragut admitted his "unusual self-esteem"—a characteristic that at times irritated both his superiors and subordinates. Irritated or not, they valued his advice, as is demonstrated by the impact on Welles of his recommendation of Porter to command the Mississippi Squadron.

Samuel Eliot Morison, in his biography of Matthew C. Perry, suggests that Farragut "had an irascible side [and that he] disliked being subordinated to anybody."[66] It is true that Farragut was impatient with anyone questioning his judgment and became angry when they persisted. At the same time, he did not get along with Perry, but there is no evidence that any of his other commanding officers considered him insubordinate. This "supreme self-confidence" possibly explains why he failed at times to award credit to his subordinates; at least many of Farragut's officers, who otherwise admired him, believed this.[67]

Farragut's self-confidence was perhaps partly a natural trait, but it also evolved from his intelligence, knowledge, and penchant for careful and thorough planning. Even before the war he was noted for his organizational ability. John M. Brooke, who would head the Confederate Bureau of Ordnance and Hydrography, served with Farragut in the *Delaware*. Brooke later recalled "that he never saw greater skill in administering affairs than Farragut displayed." Mahan mentions that before Mobile Bay, Farragut "spent hours with his flag lieutenant, studying by the aid of little wooden models, the different positions in which the ships might be placed. Afterwards he had the squadron get underway several times to practice keeping close order, and changing formation and course."[68]

The tactics that he employed at New Orleans, Port Hudson, Mobile, and elsewhere were carefully worked out, based on an analysis of his weaknesses and those of his opponent. The lashing of weak vessels to the sides of more powerful warships was a brilliant innovation. He grasped the limitations of land fortifications in naval actions and, on the Mississippi River and in Mobile Bay, utilized this tactical understanding successfully. He also believed very strongly in maximum fire power. "The best protection against the enemy's fire is a well-directed fire from our own guns."[69]

Finally, he had an extremely energetic and aggressive nature, which is absolutely essential for a successful military commander. Farragut's mental and physical energy was indeed prodigious, particularly during the Civil War years when the strain of conflict seemed to tap new reservoirs of strength. Although in his sixties, he enjoyed demonstrating his physical strength and agility by running up the ratlines or doing handstands before astonished junior officers. His mental vigor was apparent and remarked on by various observers. Nor was it confined to work or professional matters. He was a very social person and took considerable pleasure in conversations. Lord Clarence E. Paget wrote that Farragut was "a great but very agreeable talker." Commodore Schley agrees that the admiral was an "animated and interesting talker," and adds that "his information and experience were general, and upon almost all subjects."[70]

Farragut was an aggressive commander—in the opinion of Admiral George Dewey, perhaps too aggressive at times. J. C. Watson, the admiral's flag lieutenant at Mobile Bay, told his son in later years that when the *Tennessee* "was reported underway and *standing out,* Farragut at once said to [Percival] Drayton, 'Get underway and follow him (Buchanan) out' . . . Never was an order more unwelcomed. Coming over the minefield was enough. They [none of them in the fleet] wished to go out over them."[71]

Farragut's personal courage undoubtedly influenced his aggressive nature. Mahan and Schley, among others, attribute his extraordinary courage to his strong religious beliefs. Yet, his devoutness does not adequately explain his boldness, his willingness to "Damn the torpedoes." A more acceptable explanation was his sense of duty and his unusually strong desire to succeed in the Navy. Rear Admiral Bradley Fiske wrote, "Duty, in whatever form it came, was sacred" to a naval officer. And Farragut himself said that "He who dies in doing his duty . . . has played out the drama of life to the best advantage."[72]

Comparing Farragut to Nelson is probably a meaningless exercise. They were products of their time. Nelson was a brilliant tactician in utilizing sailing ships-of-the-line; Farragut was equally successful in using steam warships. Yet, they both stand out in their chosen profession. As Bern Anderson wrote, the Navy would not produce another officer as gifted as Farragut until the naval leaders of World War II.[73]

FURTHER READING

Although David Glasgow Farragut is one of the best known and most successful admirals of the U.S. Navy, few full-length biographies have been written about him. Only two are worthy of attention: Alfred T. Mahan, *Admiral Farragut* (New York, 1905), and Charles Lee Lewis, *David Glasgow Farragut*, 2 vols. (Annapolis, Md., 1941–1943). Loyall Farragut's biography of his father, *The Life and Letters of Admiral Farragut, First Admiral of the United States Navy* (New York, 1879), should be mentioned because it is the primary source for Mahan's study and most of the other biographies published before Lewis's.

Mahan was embarrassed by his biography and considered it mediocre. "The great defect in my *Farragut*," he later wrote, "was that I had no data with which to depict the *man*" (quoted in Robert Seager II, *Alfred Thayer Mahan* [Annapolis, Md., 1977], 234). Historians have generally agreed with this assessment. Despite the overall quality of the book and Mahan's assertion, his characterization of Farragut is the most perceptive of any to date.

Lewis's two-volume work is the more comprehensive. Although deficient in analysis, it is impressively researched and well written. No attempt has been made to duplicate his exhaustive research for this essay. Rather, an effort has been made to supplement Lewis's work by locating relevant manuscripts that were not available when he wrote it. Few were found. Perhaps the most important are the Farragut Collection, on loan to the Naval Historical Foundation and located at the foundation's office in the Washington Navy Yard, and a number of Farragut letters acquired in recent years by the Henry P. Huntington Library. Lewis's bibliography is thorough, but it should be supplemented by works written since its completion in 1943.

There are a large number of biographical sketches of Farragut, the best of these being the ones in Allen Johnson and Dumas Malone, eds., *Dictionary of American Biography*, 20 vols. (New York, 1928–1936), and in Jim Dan Hill's *Sea Dogs of the Sixties* (Minneapolis, 1935). Although brief, Hill's essay well might be the most balanced analysis of Farragut's Civil War campaigns.

NOTES

1. Cyril Falls, *A Hundred Years of War* (London, 1953) 104.

2. For Farragut's early life and career, see Charles Lee Lewis's two volumes, *David Glasgow Farragut: Admiral in the Making* (Annapolis, Md., 1941), and *David Glasgow Farragut: Our First Admiral* (Annapolis, Md., 1943), and David F. Long, *Nothing Too Daring: A Biography of Commodore David Porter, 1780–1843* (Annapolis, Md., 1970).

3. Howard K. Beale and Alan W. Brownswood, eds., *The Diary of Gideon Welles, Secretary of the Navy under Lincoln and Johnson,* 3 vols. (New York, 1960), 2:116, 134; and John Niven, *Gideon Welles: Lincoln's Secretary of the Navy* (New York, 1973), 383.

4. Bern Anderson, *By Sea and by River* (New York, 1962), 118.

5. Niven, *Welles,* 383–84.

6. Quoted in Lewis, *Farragut: Admiral in the Making,* 13.

7. Farragut to his wife, 23 December 1861, David G. Farragut Papers, Henry P. Huntington Library (hereafter cited as Farragut Papers, HPH).

8. Fox to Farragut, 11 February 1862, David G. Farragut Collection, Naval Historical Foundation (hereafter cited as Farragut Col., NHF).

9. Hans L. Trefousse, *Ben Butler: The South Called Him Beast* (New York, 1957), 101–2; and Robert S. Holzman, *Stormy Ben Butler* (New York, 1954), 74–75.

10. Quoted in Lewis, *Farragut: Admiral in the Making,* 47.

11. William N. Still, Jr., *Iron Afloat: The Store of the Confederate Armorclads* (Columbia, S.C., 1985), 55.

12. Anderson, *By Sea and by River,* 124.

13. Quoted in Still, *Iron Afloat,* 58.

14. Farragut to his wife and son, 25 April 1862, Farragut Col., NHF.

15. Clark Reynolds, *Command of the Sea* (New York, 1974), 386; and Charles L. Dufour, *The Night the War Was Lost* (New York, 1968), 246, 284–85. Rowena Reed is critical of the decision in her *Combined Operations in the Civil War* (Annapolis, Md., 1978), 195. In a letter to his wife written on 25 April, Farragut makes a statement that suggests his intense ambition to take the city: "God has permitted me to make a name for my Dear Boy's inheritance as well as for my own comfort," Farragut Col., NHF.

16. James D. Bulloch, *The Secret Service of the Confederate States in Europe,* 2 vols. (Liverpool, England, 1883), 2:193–94.

17. R. M. Thompson and R. Wainwright, eds., *Confidential Correspondence of Gustavus Vasa Fox, Assistant Secretary of the Navy 1861–1865*, 2 vols. (New York, 1920), 2:101–2. Also, see Lewis, *Farragut: Our First Admiral*, 78.

18. Reed, *Combined Operations*, 196.

19. Lewis, *Farragut: Our First Admiral*, 102–4. Farragut relieved the *Brooklyn*'s commanding officer, T. T. Craven, for his failure to pass the batteries. Farragut wrote his wife a detailed account of the incident and reminded her, "I always told you I knew T. T. Craven." 4 July 1862, Farragut Col., NHF.

20. Farragut Col., NHF.

21. George H. Preble to Molley, 11 July 1862, George H. Preble Papers, Massachusetts Historical Society (hereafter cited as Preble Papers). Also, see Reed, *Combined Operations*, 211–12.

22. Still, *Iron Afloat*, 70.

23. Ibid., 72.

24. Ibid., 76–78.

25. Farragut to his wife, 11 August 1862, Farragut Col., NHF. Also, see Preble to his niece, 19 August 1862, Preble Papers.

26. Diary of H. H. Bell, entry 12 April 1862, *Official Records of the Union and Confederate Navies in the War of the Rebellion*, edited by Richard Rush, et al., 31 vols. (Washington, D.C., 1894–1922) (hereafter cited as ORN), ser. 1, vol. 18, 690. Also, see Farragut to Welles, 1 January 1863, ORN, ser. 1, vol. 19, 478.

27. Marcus Price, "Ships That Tested the Blockade of the Gulf Ports, 1861–1865," *American Neptune* 11 (1951): 262–97; Stephen R. Wise, *Lifeline of the Confederacy: Blockade Running during the Civil War* (Columbia, S.C., 1988), 370–435.

28. Walter Lord, ed., *The Fremantle Diary* (New York, 1954), 105–6; and Carroll S. Alden, *George Hamilton Perkins, Commodore, U.S.N., His Life and Letters* (Boston, 1914), 106.

29. Farragut to his wife, 15 March 1862, Farragut Papers, HPH.

30. Farragut, extremely critical of Renshaw, wrote to his wife that none of the blockaders were where they were supposed to be. "I cannot make people do their duty when they are demoralized. . . . I suppose that must have been the case with Renshaw." 1 February 1863, Farragut Col., NHF. He placed Henry H. Bell in charge of the Texas blockade; "don't have any other disaster if possible for they are abusing us enough at home," he wrote Bell, 6 February 1863, Farragut Col., NHF.

31. Quoted in Lewis, *Farragut: Our First Admiral*, 161.

32. Jim Dan Hill, *Sea Dogs of the Sixties* (Minneapolis, 1935), 41.

33. Farragut to Henry H. Bell, 30 November 1862, Farragut Col., NHF.

34. Farragut to Henry H. Bell, 15 December 1862, Farragut Col., NHF.

35. Reed, *Combined Operations*, 241; and Farragut to Bell, 30 January 1863, Farragut Col., NHF.

36. Quoted in Lewis, *Farragut: Our First Admiral*, 168.

37. Reed, *Combined Operations*, 246. The most detailed account of the battle of Port Hudson is David C. Edmonds, *The Guns of Port Hudson*, vol. 1, *The River Campaign (February–May, 1863)* (Lafayette, La., 1983).

38. Alfred T. Mahan, *Admiral Farragut* (New York, 1905), 212; and Hill *Sea Dogs*, 43.

39. Du Pont to his wife, 23 March 1863, in John D. Hayes, ed., *Samuel Francis Du Pont: A Selection from His Civil War Letters*, 3 vols. (Ithaca, N.Y., 1969), 2:508. Also, see Fox to Du Pont, 18 March 1863, in Hayes, *Samuel Du Pont*, 2:507.

40. Farragut to his wife, 20 April 1863, Farragut Papers, HPH; and Farragut to Du Pont, 20 April 1863, in Hayes, *Samuel Du Pont*, 3:47–48.

41. Ellet to cousin, 3 May 1863, William D. Cabell Papers, University of Virginia Library.

42. Reed, *Combined Operations*, 250.

43. 12 July 1864, Farragut Papers, HPH; and Bulloch, *Secret Service*, 2:205–6.

44. Du Pont to Davis, 29 March 1864, in Hayes, *Samuel Du Pont*, 3:324–25. Also, see Loyall Farragut, *The Life and Letters of Admiral Farragut, First Admiral of the United States Navy* (New York, 1879), 402. Franklin Buchanan, former captain in the U.S. Navy, was in command of Confederate Naval Forces, Mobile. Richard L. Page, formerly of the U.S. Navy, was in command of Fort Morgan.

45. Fox to Farragut, 24 March 1864, Farragut Col., NHF.

46. Farragut to his wife, 30 May 1864, Farragut Papers, HPH. Also, see Farragut to Jenkins, 10 May 1864, Farragut Papers, HPH, and Still, *Iron Afloat*, 204.

47. Lewis, *Farragut: Our First Admiral*, 246. There is an unsigned letter in the Farragut Col., NHF, dated 24 June 1864, apparently from a naval officer intimately associated with the construction of these ships. The writer assured Farragut of their seaworthiness and that he had convinced Welles of this.

48. Still, *Iron Afloat*, 204.

49. Naval History Collection, Naval War College.

50. Bartholomew Diggins, "Recollections of the War Cruise of the USS *Hartford*, January to December, 1862–1864," New York Public Library. Also, see G. M. Brady, "Damn the Torpedoes, Full Speed Ahead," *Manuscripts* 31 (1979): 86–96.

51. Still, *Iron Afloat*, 204.

52. Thomas H. Stevens to F. A. Parker, 24 April 1877, Thomas Stevens Papers, Private Collection.

53. Mahan, *Admiral Farragut*, 239–40; and Hill, *Sea Dogs*, 61.

54. Quotations in Hill, *Sea Dogs*, 61, and Alden, *George Hamilton Perkins*, 195–96.

55. Quoted in Lewis, *Farragut: Our First Admiral*, 298. Also, see Fox to Farragut, 18 August 1864, Farragut Papers, HPH.

56. Alden, *George Hamilton Perkins*, 149–50; Drayton to Du Pont, 8 September 1864, in Hayes, *Samuel Du Pont*, 3:380; and Drayton to Mrs. Farragut, 20 October 1864, Farragut Papers, HPH.

57. On 14 December, Welles had written to Farragut suggesting that he hold off visiting Washington as Congress was considering "a new naval grade" that would affect him. Welles to Farragut, 14 December 1865, Farragut Col., NHF.

58. Farragut to Jenkins, Farragut Papers, HPH.

59. William N. Still, Jr., *American Sea Power in the Old World: The United States Navy in European and Near Eastern Waters 1865–1917* (Westport, Conn., 1980), 35.

60. While in Europe, Farragut was approached as a possible Democratic Party candidate in the 1868 presidential election, but the admiral was not interested. See John Cisco to Mrs. Farragut, 7 March 1868, Farragut Papers, HPH; and R. H. Kern to Samuel Jackson Randall, 7 April, 26 May, 3 June, and 6 June 1868, Samuel Jackson Randall Papers, Van Pelt Library, University of Pennsylvania, Philadelphia.

61. Mrs. Farragut to Thomas Welles, 17 May 1869, Thomas C. Welles Papers, Duke University (hereafter cited as Welles Papers).

62. Mrs. Farragut to Welles, 19 January 1870, Welles Papers. Also, see Lewis, *Farragut: Our First Admiral*, 374–75.

63. Anderson, *By Sea and by River*, 292; George Dewey, *Autobiography of George Dewey, Admiral of the Navy* (New York, 1913), 49; Mahan, *Admiral Farragut*, 307–9; Winfield Scott Schley, *Forty-five Years under the Flag* (New York, 1904), 28, 50–51; Strong to [unknown], 20 May 1862, Gratz Collection, Historical Society of Pennsylvania, Philadelphia; and Bulloch, *Secret Service*, 2:192.

64. 5 March 1864, in Hayes, *Samuel Du Pont*, 3:435.

65. Lee to Elizabeth Lee, 28 May, 10 June, and 12 July 1862, in the Blair-Lee Papers, Princeton University Library. For Farragut's attitude toward Lee, see letter to his wife, 10 October 1862, Farragut Papers, HPH. Foltz is not critical of Farragut in his autobiography, *Surgeon of the Seas: The Adventurous Life of Surgeon General Jonathan M. Foltz in the Days of Wooden Ships*, edited by Charles S. Foltz (Indianapolis, 1931).

66. Farragut, *Life and Letters of Admiral Farragut*, 218; Samuel Eliot Morrison, *"Old Bruin": Commodore Matthew C. Perry, 1794–1858* (Boston, 1967), 240; and Mahan, *Admiral Farragut*, 327–28.

67. T. Bailey to his nephew, 22 May 1869, Theodorus Bailey Papers, Duke University; Mrs. Farragut to Welles, Welles Papers; and Paulding to Dahlgren, 12 May 1868, John Dahlgren Papers, Duke University.

68. George M. Brooke, Jr., *John M. Brooke: Naval Scientist and Educator* (Charlottesville, 1980), 12; and Mahan, *Admiral Farragut*, 327.

69. Farragut to Du Pont, 20 April 1863, in Hayes, *Samuel Du Pont*, 3:47. Also, see Robert S. Browning III, *Two If by Sea: The Development of American Coastal Defense Policy* (Westport, Conn., 1984), 116; Lewis, *Farragut: Our First Admiral*, 316; and Henry N. Sulivan, ed., *Life and Letters of the Late Admiral Bartholomew James Sulivan* (London, 1896), 428.

70. Sir Arthur Otway, ed., *Autobiography and Journals of Admiral Lord Clarence E. Paget* (London, 1896), 306–7; and Schley, *Forty-five Years*, 50–51.

71. Edward Watson to William Rodgers, 14 March 1901, Rodgers Family Papers, Library of Congress.

72. Quoted in Peter Karsten, *The Naval Aristocracy* (New York, 1972), 250, 261.

73. Anderson, *By Sea and by River*, 293.

# ☆ Raphael Semmes
☆
☆ **Confederate Raider**

*by Warren F. Spencer*

DURING THE CIVIL WAR, CONFEDERATE ADMIRAL RAPHAEL SEMMES was the most successful practitioner of the traditional American naval strategy of commerce raiding. At sea for a total of twenty-five months on board the CSS *Sumter* and the CSS *Alabama*, Semmes destroyed or bonded seventy-six U.S. commercial ships.[1] As early as November 1862 cargo owners began to ship by neutral vessels, and this "flight from the flag" as it continued throughout the war crippled the U.S. merchant fleet permanently.[2]

Semmes's wide-ranging cruises—from the West Indies into the North and South Atlantic Oceans, across the Indian Ocean to the China Sea and back— made him world renowned. Newspapers in the Americas, London, Paris, Cape Town, and Singapore traced his movements and reported his victims. He became a romantic figure to millions throughout the world and a national hero to Southerners, but, in the United States, he was castigated as a pirate and a beast.

Aware of his fame and infamy, Semmes nonetheless was only fulfilling instructions from his superior, Confederate Secretary of the Navy Stephen R. Mallory. To compensate for the superior Northern naval power, Mallory developed a twofold policy: draw Union ships from blockade duty by striking at Northern commercial ships with privateers and regularly commissioned naval vessels, then force the weakened blockade by warships purchased or built in Europe. His strategy anticipated cooperation of the European maritime powers, but in the spring and early summer of 1861, a series of international proclamations appeared from both sides of the ocean that affected both Mallory's naval strategy and Semmes's career as a commerce raider.[3]

On 17 April 1861, Confederate President Jefferson Davis announced that in "accordance with international law" his government would issue letters of marque for privateers to prey on Northern commercial shipping; two days later, U.S. President Abraham Lincoln proclaimed a blockade of Southern ports and further stipulated that if any person should molest a U.S. vessel or a cargo on board her, he would be held under U.S. laws of piracy. The European maritime powers accepted Lincoln's threat against possible Confederate privateers because, in the Declaration of Paris (1856), they had outlawed privateers. If Lincoln simply had closed Southern ports as a sovereign act, other governments could have accepted that also without response. But a blockade of a port is an act that affects other nations, and the same Declaration of Paris had established international law concerning blockades. The British and French governments had already adopted a common policy to pursue toward the American secession crisis, and Lincoln's blockade proclamation elicited from them proclamations of neutrality, the British on 14 May 1861 and the French on 10 June 1861. Other European nations soon issued similar proclamations.

The neutrality proclamations forbade belligerents from recruiting neutral subjects, equipping or arming warships on neutral territory or in neutral territorial waters, or in any way enhancing the war-making powers of such vessels. Belligerent use of neutral dock facilities was limited to repairing damage that resulted from "acts of God." To discourage privateering, the domestic laws also forbade subjects from adjudicating belligerent prizes.[4]

These proclamations both enhanced and hindered the South's war-making efforts. The neutrality proclamations gave de facto recognition to the Confederate States as a belligerent engaged in legitimate warfare and extended to them the same belligerent rights enjoyed by the United States. Confederate warships, but not privateers, could purchase coal and food in neutral ports and use neutral shipyards to repair damage to their ships caused by nature. Neither belligerent, however, could purchase warships from the neutrals, as Mallory had expected to do, or take prizes for adjudication into a neutral port, as Mallory had expected his commerce raiders to do.[5] This latter provision forced Semmes to remain at sea for more than two years and to destroy his captures, an act he regretted.

The U.S. government, maintaining that the Civil War was a rebellion and not legitimate warfare, never officially accepted the neutrality proclamations. That is why Northern officials constantly referred to Semmes as a pirate or privateer.[6]

Thus, before the first battle was fought at Manassas, Virginia — 21 July 1861 — the Southern secession, based primarily on anticipated naval activities, had become a worldwide event. Before Appomattox, people in the West Indies, Brazil, Australia, South Africa, and Indochina, as well as Europe, would be drawn into the American conflict because ships flying the Confederate flag would sail in their adjoining waters. The man whose ships touched most of these people was Raphael Semmes, commander (1861), captain (1862), then admiral (1865) of the Confederate States Navy. What kind of man was he?

The circumstances of his youth foreshadowed the introspective and self-reliant captain of the *Alabama*. Born in Piscataway (Charles County), Maryland, on 27 September 1809, into a Roman Catholic family, Semmes descended on his father's side from an early (1640) French settler and on his mother's side from a signer of the Declaration of Independence, Arthur Middleton of South Carolina. Orphaned at an early age, he grew up in the Georgetown (District of Columbia) home of his uncle, Raphael Semmes. He had some formal education in private schools and with tutors, where he learned Latin and natural history.

When he was about fifteen years old, young Raphael decided to pursue two careers, those of lawyer and naval officer. The influence to study law undoubtedly came from his brother and intense family discussions on the nature of the U.S. Constitution. The reasons for his attraction to a naval career are not so clear, but perhaps he viewed it as one of travel, excitement, and learning. At any rate, his congressman uncle obtained for him an appointment as midshipman in the U.S. Navy from President John Quincy Adams, dated 1 April 1826.

A second career was almost a necessity in the pre-Civil War navy because there were more officers than officer slots. A young officer could expect many enforced and long leaves of absence during his slow rise through the ranks. For five years, Raphael Semmes served as a trainee-officer in five different ships, sailing the Caribbean Sea, the Gulf of Mexico, and the Mediterranean Sea. He spent much time studying navigation and naval regulations and developing an appreciation for the varieties of tropical nature—different plants, sunsets, and sudden storms. Finally, on 28 April 1832, having passed at the head of his class, he was promoted to passed midshipman and placed on extended leave.[7]

Interspersed with the long leaves, Semmes's naval career developed slowly during the years prior to the Mexican War. For eighteen months he was acting mate on board the USS *Constellation*, a ship that decades later would pursue the CSS *Alabama*. He was promoted to lieutenant on 9 February 1837, eleven years after his appointment as midshipman. His longest continuous duty was from May 1841 to April 1845 as a surveyor of the Gulf Coast while based at the Pensacola Navy Yard in Florida. In performance of that duty, he sailed in the USS *Warren* and commanded the USS *Poinsett* (1843–1845), one of the few steamers in the U.S. Navy. Survey duty was not demanding, and the Navy used officers and ships for occasional duties such as transporting diplomats. On one such journey to Mexico, Semmes navigated the treacherous waters of the approaches to Vera Cruz and accompanied his passenger to the Mexican capital, thereby gaining two types of knowledge that he would use during the Mexican War.[8]

Semmes's personal life developed more rapidly than his military career. During a two-and-a-half-year leave after his promotion to passed midshipman, he read law in his brother's office, and he passed the Maryland bar examination in early 1835. Later, he established a law practice in Cincinnati, Ohio, where he met and married Ann Elizabeth Spencer in 1837. She was Protestant and of New Jersey origins, "a stately, handsome woman with regular chiseled features, brilliant brunette complexion and hazel eyes."[9] In a move indicative of their strong mutual bonds, or perhaps Raphael Semmes's strong personality, or both, Ann Spencer joined the Catholic Church prior to the wedding, and later she adopted Semmes's ardent Southern sentiments. Their marriage, marred only by his absences at sea, was a happy and long one, blessed with three sons and three daughters.

Raphael Semmes moved his family to be near him while he served at Pensacola Navy Yard and rented property just across the Perdido River in the state of Alabama. It was a symbol of passing because, afterward, he considered himself a citizen of Alabama, and Ann followed him. His commitment to the Southern cause was both intellectual and emotional.

Semmes's experiences in the Mexican War seem almost to have been a dress rehearsal for his later duties during the Civil War. As flag-lieutenant to the commander of the Home Squadron, he was privy to the U.S. government's policies and close to the fleet commander's interpretations and applications of the government's directives. Later, as commander of the USS *Somers* on blockade assignment of Vera Cruz harbor, he experienced firsthand the intricacies of neutral and belligerent rights, as well as the boredom, frustrations, and dangers of blockade duty. More important, he learned how a blockader must think and exploited that knowledge later during the Civil War when he escaped two federal blockades on board the CSS *Sumter*. He dealt with problems, both real and potential, of Mexican privateers, whom he condemned as nothing more "than licensed pirates."[10]

The few months of blockade duty led Semmes to complain that the conflict had become "a war, for the navy, of toils and vigils, without the prospect of either excitement or glory."[11] But, excitement seemed to attract Raphael Semmes, and it inspired in him an eloquence that characterized his writing ever after.

As commanding officer of the brig *Somers*, on blockade duty, which he so detested, he lost his ship to a gale. Semmes's report to his superior officer candidly recounted the loss of thirty-nine men and re-created as well the excitement of the life-and-death struggle, the necessity of making split-second decisions to save lives, and the ability to discern the moment when nature had won and man had lost: "I gave the order 'Every man save himself who can!'" His report, so filled with heroic imagery, completely overshadowed any question that Semmes might have contributed to the fate of his ship by failing to provide proper ballast or to order the correct sails carried. Semmes was not simply "rather lucky," as another officer put it, that the court of inquiry found for him; he had, unconsciously, manipulated it by the force of rhetoric.[12] He would later, in June 1864, swim off from another sinking ship under his command and be promoted to admiral.

Semmes was reassigned as flag-lieutenant to the fleet commander, a duty he considered boring. But within six months—after General Winfield Scott's successful landing at Vera Cruz and march to Jalapa on the road to Mexico City—excitement once again beckoned. Semmes was assigned to take a message from Washington through the military lines to the Mexican government. He was delighted. "There was romance in the idea!" On 28 April 1847, he left the Home Squadron to spend the remainder of the war with the Army.[13] His account of the journey is spiced with vivid word pictures of the Mexican landscape and of the plant and animal life.[14]

General Scott was jealous of civilian interference in the war and took out his resentment on Semmes. Only after a sharp exchange of letters did the general finally permit the persistent Semmes, who could write more convincingly, to remain with the Army.[15] When his mission "was suddenly brought to a close," Semmes "had no thought of returning to the squadron" because the Army was "on the eve of commencing our glorious campaign."[16] To fight with the Army was much more exciting than blockade duty.

Semmes was, as he said, an onlooker. He observed, he took notes—his memoirs are based more on these notes than on memory—and ever inquisitive, he described and characterized all that he saw. As a Catholic, Semmes was drawn to the Cathedral in Puebla, and his description reveals a clear understanding of architecture and its symbolism. In Mexico, he seemed to discern social inequities more clearly than he did in Alabama, and he deplored the squalor of Mexican poverty, which he blamed on the government and the country's socioracial history.

But his favorite topic was people—beautiful women, leaders of men, and even the common sailor and soldier. A product of the age of romanticism and nationalism, Semmes firmly believed in the superiority of the Anglo-Saxon race and the great-man theory of history.[17] From all these observations, Semmes developed a view of history and of man's role in it based on a concept of the proper order of things, in which the higher element had the responsibility to protect and nourish the lower element, but not the power to coerce it. By the end of the Mexican War his mind-set had matured; he was the man who in thought and action would become the world-renowned captain of the CSS *Sumter* and the CSS *Alabama*. Although his was not a unique attitude in the mid-nineteenth century—he shared it with English aristocrats, French notables, and thousands of Americans, North and South—his age of preparation was complete, and the stage for greatness was set.

In 1849, the peacetime Navy placed Lieutenant Raphael Semmes on extended leave. He moved his family to Mobile, Alabama, and settled into a quiet practice of law and reflection upon his Mexican experiences. Using his wartime notes, and adding long digressions that grew from his reflections, he published *Service Afloat and Ashore during the Mexican War* in 1851. It became a best seller, as much perhaps because of its flowing and flowery language as for its revelations of Americans at war.

The U.S. Navy seemed to have forgotten Semmes. But his name gradually rose on the promotion list. On 8 October 1855, he was promoted to commander, effective 14 September 1855.[18] Recalled to duty the following month, Semmes began the longest continuous stretch of active naval service of his career. For ten months he commanded the mail steamer *Illinois*, the last U.S. ship to which he was assigned. In December 1856, Commander Semmes became lighthouse inspector of the 3d District, conveniently based in Mobile. From 1858 into 1861, Semmes served as secretary to the Lighthouse Board in Washington, D.C.[19]

Viewing the developing secession crisis from the nation's capital as it moved to its climax, Semmes rejected the arguments of early advocates of secession. Although he considered the tariff to be economic suppression of the South and the abolition movement a violation of states' rights, he expected a solution to be reached, and he believed that Stephen A. Douglas's popular sovereignty theory was the best possible solution. A Douglas man in the election of 1860, he regarded the election of Abraham Lincoln as President as the final blow to the Union. Semmes thus became a secessionist; his *"Alabama"* mind-set was complete.

If his change of mind about secession was difficult, his personal break with the U.S. Navy was even more soul wrenching. "Civil war," he wrote, "is a terrible crucible through which to pass character."[20] Loyalty to the flag, love of country, old friendships, career advancement and security, care of family—all of these practical factors shouted for Semmes to remain in the U.S. Navy and loyal to the United States, but his personal psychology demanded allegiance to his state. During the congressional session of 1860–1861, Semmes informed members from Alabama of his "intention of retiring from the Federal Navy, and of taking service with the South" should the state of Alabama join other Southern states in secession. Although the Alabama secession vote passed on 11 January 1861, Semmes waited for more than a month to resign his position.

During that interlude, Semmes was promoted from secretary of the Lighthouse Board to membership on the board, which he accepted on 12 February 1861. Only two days later, he received a telegram from the Committee on Naval Affairs of the Provisional Government in Montgomery, Alabama, requesting him to "repair to this place at your earliest convenience." Semmes replied on the same day, "I will be with you immediately." The next day, he resigned his commission in the U.S. Navy and informed the new secretary of the Lighthouse Board that because of that resignation he was "no longer a member" of the board. All official commitment to the U.S. government thus dissolved, Mr. Raphael Semmes took a sorrowful leave from his wife and children on 16 February and embarked by train for Montgomery.

Semmes arrived in the provisional capital on 19 February 1861, consulted with the chairman of the Committee on Naval Affairs and with provisional President Jefferson Davis, and departed for New York on 21 February. His first duty for the Confederacy, on Davis's request, was a shopping trip in the North. En route, he stopped in Washington to inspect machinery in the U.S. Arsenal and to recruit skilled machinists, so scarce in the South. In New York City, where he arrived on 5 March, he purchased "large quantities of percussions caps," which he sent without disguise to Montgomery, "made contracts for batteries of light artillery, powder, and other munitions," and purchased a complete set of machinery for rifling cannon. Although he found no ships suitable for conversion to warships, he did manage to visit his eldest son, who was a cadet at West Point.[21]

Semmes returned by ship to Savannah, Georgia, and thence by train to Montgomery, where he arrived on 4 April 1861, just eight days prior to the firing on Fort Sumter, South Carolina. It had been a whirlwind trip and more successful than those of other Southern agents sent on similar missions.[22]

In Montgomery, Semmes found the Confederate government to be organized on a regular basis. Stephen R. Mallory, a former chairman of the U.S. Senate Committee on Naval Affairs, was Secretary of the Navy. He was one of only two of the original Davis cabinet appointees to serve throughout the war, and he directed the Confederacy's Navy and naval policy with a firm hand.[23] He and Semmes worked well together, and Mallory had the good sense to allow Semmes complete freedom during the cruises of the *Sumter* and *Alabama*. Mallory immediately appointed Semmes a commander in the Confederate States Navy and chief of the Lighthouse Bureau.

With the firing on Fort Sumter on 12 April 1861, Semmes realized it was "time to leave the things of peace to the future." He went immediately to Mallory and urged the use of privateers to strike at the enemy's commerce. Semmes saw no contradiction in recommending the use of "licensed pirates," as he had called privateers early in the Mexican War, because now his country was the weak naval power fighting an enemy with an established navy. Mallory agreed fully with the commander, and, on 17 April, President Davis announced his intentions to issue letters of marque.

But Semmes did not intend to serve as a privateer; he asked Mallory at the same time for command of a regularly commissioned Confederate naval vessel suitable for commerce raiding. Mallory despondently showed him a file on a ship examined by a naval board in New Orleans, Louisiana, and condemned as unfit for commerce raiding. Examining the file, Semmes saw that, with modifications, the ship could be converted into a suitable raider. "Give me that ship," he said to the secretary. "I think I can make her answer the purpose." Thus was conceived the CSS *Sumter*, the first war vessel of the Confederate States Navy.[24]

Semmes arrived in New Orleans on 22 April and immediately took possession of his new ship. He found her to be "as unlike a ship of war as possible. . . . Still, . . . her lines were easy and graceful, and she had a sort of saucy air about her."[25] It took two months of hard work to convert the ship. Semmes removed the superstructure, provided crew and officer quarters, acquired ordnance from as far away as the Norfolk Navy Yard, designed new gun carriages, bought clothing, and recruited a crew.

The officers, all natives of Confederate states, received their assignments to the *Sumter* from Mallory's office, and all except the marine officer had experience in the U.S. Navy. The enlisted crew consisted of seventy-two seamen and twenty marines. The seamen, as was the custom in most navies, were recruited from among sailors who were between voyages and happened to be in the New Orleans port. Only about half a dozen were native Southerners, a situation that reflected the scarcity of seafaring men in the South and imposed upon Semmes special problems of discipline and constant recruiting in neutral ports. Most of those recruited in New Orleans were English and Irish, whom Semmes considered generally to be good sailors.[26]

Finally, on 3 June 1861, Semmes formally commissioned the converted packet as the CSS *Sumter*, named after the fort in Charleston harbor. She was a small screw steamer of 499 tons, length only 152 feet, beam 27 feet, and draft 12 feet. She had a coal capacity for only eight days; her propeller was stationary and therefore a drag when she was under sail only; her top speed under sail and steam was from ten to twelve knots.

After some trial runs, Semmes dropped the *Sumter* downriver, where he put the crew through training exercises and awaited an opportune moment to run the Union blockade. Drawing on his own blockading experiences, he knew the Union blockader had large stretches of water to watch. Given a few miles distance, Semmes calculated that the *Sumter* could make a fairly safe run for the open waters, so he stationed a small boat just beyond Pass à l'Outre to signal the location of the blockader. On 30 June 1861, with a little luck and superior seamanship, he narrowly escaped the faster and larger USS *Brooklyn*.

In the evening, as the sun was setting, Semmes stood on the poop deck and mused about the past few months—how "hurried and confused" they had been, how "family ties were severed," and how war was "arraying a household against itself." He thought of the American flag flying on board the *Brooklyn* and was startled to realize how he "now hated that flag!"[27] Nonetheless, he slept soundly that night.

Free of the USS *Brooklyn*, Semmes was beginning a new naval career for which his previous naval experience had little prepared him. He knew that destruction of the enemy's merchant fleet was common naval duty, and he knew the glory that it had brought to his predecessors during the American Revolution and the War of 1812; he also knew that he had no open home ports where he could take his prizes for adjudication and that neutral nations prohibited the adjudication of prizes taken by either belligerent. That was a problem he would have to solve in his own way. There were other problems: to develop a technique of prize taking, to finance and provision his own ships and crew, to deal with neutral port authorities, and to sail in strange seas. He was fully aware of the dangers implicit in Mallory's twofold strategy. If he succeeded in destroying Northern merchant ships and in luring federal vessels from blockade duty, he risked his own destruction by those faster and larger warships. The success of his mission and the safety of his ship and crew depended more on Semmes's seamanship, cunning, and innovation than it did on his naval experiences.

The study of law was Semmes's most useful prewar experience for his career as a commerce raider. It enabled him to master the intricacies of international law concerning belligerent and neutral maritime rights and obligations. At sea during the war, he consulted his ever handy copy of 3Phillimore, *Commentaries upon International Law*, and presented legal briefs to neutral port authorities. He successfully argued that as a belligerent he had rights to buy coal and provisions and to repair his vessel. Otherwise, he never could have kept constantly at sea for over two years.

Legal knowledge, however, was not enough. Semmes was also an excellent naval strategist who possessed the nautical knowledge necessary to execute that strategy. He knew that prevailing winds and currents created crossroads at sea for merchantmen carrying goods between certain markets and the fishing and whaling grounds where other ships congregated. The crossroads-at-sea just off the south end of Cuba served Semmes in the same strategic sense that Marye's Heights above the Rappahannock River in Fredericksburg, Virginia, served General Robert E. Lee in December 1862. In two days off Cuba in the CSS *Sumter*, Semmes captured seven Northern merchantmen. When Semmes commissioned the *Alabama* off the Azores in September 1862, he immediately sought out the New England whaling fleet, whose Azores season ended about 1 October. Within three weeks, he destroyed eight whalers that sat low in the water, heavy with the season's catch. Then he changed his hunting grounds to the Newfoundland fishing banks. He followed the strategy of sea-position throughout his career as a commerce raider.

Semmes's successful strategy was adopted by other Confederate commerce raiders. The total number of Northern merchant vessels destroyed by Confederate ships was about two hundred.[28] On board the *Sumter* and the *Alabama*, Semmes captured eighty-seven ships, of which he burned sixty-two, converted one into a Confederate raider (the *Conrad* into the *Tuscaloosa*, in June 1863), and sold another (the *Sea Bride*, in August 1863).

Semmes accounted for about 32 percent of all Union commercial ships lost during the war; however, that is not the full story. He captured 85 percent of his total prizes during the first year of his twenty-two-month cruise in the *Alabama*[29]; the *Florida*'s thirty-three and the *Georgia*'s five prizes after August 1863 were mostly coastal ships. Thus, by early fall in 1863, Semmes had driven the bulk of the U.S. merchant ships from the busiest sea-lanes. Many that he did not capture were sold to neutrals, and those still flying the Stars and Stripes were old or worthless craft used in coastal service.[30]

Marine insurance rates increased by a factor of three between 1861 and 1863. Cargo owners naturally shipped by neutral vessels, so much so that in November 1862, only 20 of 150 vessels loading in New York for European ports were under the U.S. flag; by 1864 neutral flags were "almost monopolizing European trade." More than half of the U.S. merchant fleet was lost during the Civil War, either directly to Confederate raiders (one hundred thousand tons) or indirectly by sale to neutrals (eight hundred thousand tons).[31] Semmes was mostly responsible for the success of one part of Mallory's strategy—to drive the Northern merchant fleet from the seas.

For the other half of that same strategy—to lure Union naval vessels from their blockading stations—Semmes was notably less successful. Counting both the *Sumter* and the *Alabama* voyages, records reveal that, from July 1861 to June 1864, Semmes encountered at most only ten to fifteen U.S. naval vessels, and none of these was from the blockading fleet. This was true partly because Semmes's mission was to sink commercial ships, not to fight naval battles. Despite these orders, Semmes did challenge and sink the USS *Hatteras* in January 1863. He searched for the USS *Wyoming*, which was seeking him in the China Seas in October 1863, but the two never met.[32]

Finally, in a kind of death wish, he sailed from Cherbourg, France, on 21 June 1864, precisely to fight the *Kearsarge*, but none of the Northern naval vessels was on blockade duty. Semmes's failure to help lift the Union blockade was more a failure of Mallory's strategy and of Confederate diplomacy, and particularly of Union naval policies, than of Semmes. Rapid expansion permitted the U.S. Navy, without weakening the blockade, to create the West Indies Fleet that guarded the Gulf area and occasionally sent ships to search the Brazilian coast for Confederate raiders; individual ships were dispatched to foreign stations such as the China Sea and, especially, to European waters. Union strategy against Confederate raiders, however, was to chase and destroy them, not to escort or defend Northern merchant ships, and this strategy failed as completely as did Mallory's. The Union Navy did not capture even one Confederate raider on the open high seas. Civil War naval strategy concerning commerce raiders was a failure on both sides because the North did not protect its commerce, nor did the South lure the blockaders away from the Confederacy.

The cruises of the *Sumter* and *Alabama* are detailed completely,[33] but no account explains how Semmes—a naval officer with much more sea time on coastal waters than on the high seas—could convert himself into the most proficient of commerce-destroying sea captains. In fact, his experiences on board the *Sumter* served as training for his much longer and more varied *Alabama* cruise.

Semmes had to develop a method of disposing of his prizes. Despite restraints imposed on him by the Union blockade of Southern ports and the refusal of neutrals to adjudicate belligerent prizes, Semmes did not want to destroy his captures. His first victim was the *Golden Rocket*, taken off the southeastern tip of Cuba on 3 July 1861 and burned. In the log he recorded simply that "she made a beautiful bonfire," but the moment was so etched in his mind that, seven years later, he recounted every vivid detail. Despite the thrill of his first capture, he found his duty "a painful one to destroy so noble a ship," and his officers felt badly enough about the burning ship to take up a collection for the *Golden Rocket's* captain.[34]

Semmes refused to destroy any of his next ten captures. Instead, he tested the neutrality prohibitions against adjudicating prizes. He took six into a Cuban harbor in the hope that the Spanish colonial officials would intern them until a Confederate court of admiralty could adjudicate them, and he took one to Venezuela in an effort to impose his will on a weak neutral. In both places, he submitted a lawyer's brief claiming that the neutral's position was, in fact, unneutral because Confederate captains had no ports to take their prizes to, whereas the federal captains had their own open ports. His pleas, however, fell on deaf ears, and he claimed the United States "not only bullied the little South American republics, but the whole world besides."[35]

Semmes had learned his lesson. Thereafter, he constituted himself to be a Confederate court of admiralty, and he tried, condemned, bonded, or released all merchant ships he hailed, in accordance with the rules established by the

Declaration of Paris in 1856: neutral cargo, except contraband, is free from seizure even when in an enemy ship; and enemy cargo, except contraband, is free from seizure when in a neutral ship. Of course, not all cases were as clear-cut as the Paris declaration would have them be—cargoes of mixed ownership and falsified papers gave Semmes difficulty. Without the leisure of contemplative time, Semmes made some debatable decisions, but he never again took a captured vessel into a neutral port. Although he regretted the necessity of burning ships, he performed his duty unhesitatingly, and his officers never took up a collection for another victim's captain.

In order to bring cases before his floating court of admiralty, Semmes developed his own techniques of capture. Seagoing merchant and war vessels were unmarked and similar in configuration. Only the flag indicated nationality. When Semmes sighted a sail, he gave chase under a British, French, or U.S. flag. If the merchantman did not haul to, Semmes fired a round or two across her bow, then hailed her captain to ask the ship's name and nationality. Only then did he raise the Confederate flag and order the ship to receive a boarding party. The boarding officer, usually a lieutenant, was ordered to bring the merchant captain with his ship's papers to Semmes's cabin. After an examination of the papers, Semmes questioned the captain and rendered his decision. If he condemned the ship, the crew and passengers, if any, were transferred to the *Sumter*, as were any usable supplies, such as food, fuel, clothing, and rigging. For all condemned ships, Semmes meticulously wrote a legal decision setting forth the evidence and the law.

Semmes's very success created problems of adjudication. Out of fear of the *Sumter* and the *Alabama*, shippers began to use false papers of registry or of cargo ownership. In such a case Semmes consulted legal references such as Phillimore, carefully detailed the circumstances, and then recorded his decision. Here is an excerpt from Semmes's *Alabama* journal, dated 6 July 1863: " . . . at 3:30 A.M. hove to a ship with a shot, she having disregarded two blank cartridges. She proves to be the *Express*, of Boston, from Callao to Antwerp. . . . Captured her . . . fired her at about 10:30 A.M. and filled away on our course." Noting that the French chargé d'affaires at Lima had certified the cargo to be neutral property, Semmes wrote the following legal justification for having destroyed the cargo:

> This certificate fails to be of any value as proof, for two reasons: First it is not sworn to, and secondly, it simply avers the property to be neutral . . . instead of pointing out the owner or owners. First, a consul may authenticate evidence by his seal, but when he departs from the usual functions of a consul and becomes a witness he must give his testimony under oath like other witnesses. . . . Now, the presumption of law being that goods found in an enemy's ship belong to the enemy, unless a distinct neutral character be given

to them by pointing out the real owner by proper documentary proof, and as neither the bill of lading nor the certificate . . . amounts to proper documentary proof, the ship and cargo are both condemned . . . as a distinct neutral character is not impressed upon the property by proper evidence. I must act under the presumption of law. (See 3d Phillimore, 596.)[36]

This tactic of enforcing international law strictly, even in the face of cleverly falsified documents, led Northern shipowners to sell their vessels legitimately to neutral nationals, thus reducing Union commercial shipping.

Not all cases were as easily accepted by the victims as was the case of the *Express*. Later, on his return trip from Singapore, just off the Strait of Malacca on 24 December 1864, Semmes hove to "an American-looking bark, under English colors, with the name *Martaban*."[37] Semmes ordered Master's Mate George Fullam, an Englishman, to board her. Fullam considered the bark to be "suspicious looking" and soon ascertained that she was originally the *Texan Star* out of Houston. The captain, Samuel B. Pike, who spoke with a Maine accent, refused to board the *Alabama* because he claimed to be a British subject.

So, for the first and only time, Semmes boarded a victim. From all appearances—freshly repainted name; ship's design; American captain, officers, and even "a black, greasy cook"—the transfer was recent and probably fraudulent. Although Captain Pike claimed the cargo to be neutral owned, there was no bill of sale and only the ordinary cargo bill of lading. The ship's papers were freshly written in the same handwriting, even to the crews' signatures. That was enough for Semmes. "I had no doubt," he noted in the log, "that the transfer was fraudulent and captured and burned her."

Semmes must have had some lingering doubt, however, especially because of the claim that the cargo was British owned. So he called Captain Pike into his cabin (Semmes typically getting in the last word on a cabin visit), placed him under oath, and asked if the transfer of the ship were bona fide. Pike then admitted that, out of fear of the *Alabama*, he had arranged "a sham sale in hopes of saving" his ship. Upon the "answer being recorded," Semmes wrote, "the court adjourned." Because the ship was American and there existed no legal evidence that the cargo was British owned, then, as in the *Express* case, Semmes had not violated a neutral's rights. But, although Semmes had closed the case by adjourning the court, British public and official opinion was not satisfied.

The *Martaban* incident aroused adverse feelings among the English in Singapore.[38] The Chamber of Commerce of the Straits Settlement put the issue clearly when it petitioned the governor and asked "whether the capture and destruction of a vessel possessed of a certificate of British Registry is legal or justified because suspicions may be entertained that she is not *bona fide* the property of a British subject."[39] This outcry from the commercial circles of Singapore, despite the U.S. consul's belief that the registry transfer was "a 'bogus' sale," reflected their concern for the safety of investments in merchant ships acquired by transferring the registry from the United States to Great Britain. Captain David McDougal of the USS *Wyoming* wrote to Washington that "nearly all of the American vessels in the China Seas have changed flags." When the *Alabama* had approached the Eastern waters, "fourteen American ships were sold in Calcutta in short order."[40]

British concern spread from Singapore to England and on to Sir James Hope, vice-admiral of the English Atlantic Fleet. Citing the case of the *Martaban*, Sir James instructed officers under his command "to capture and send to England for adjudication in the admiralty court every vessel by which a British vessel, *i.e.*, with legal British papers, is burned at sea."[41]

This naval interpretation of the British Proclamation of Neutrality, according to the records, was never applied, but it reflected growing British concern over the *Alabama's* destruction of ships on the high seas and, perhaps, the South's failing fortunes of war as well. The fact that Semmes was legally correct in the *Martaban* case, as he had been in the *Express* incident, illustrates the difference between dealing with a weak neutral state (Belgian ownership of the *Express* cargo) and a strong one.

Semmes seems never to have known of Sir James Hope's instruction because he never mentioned it in the *Alabama's* log or in his memoirs. He did, however, know the difference between dealing with a weak as opposed to a strong neutral state—he learned it at the end of the *Sumter* cruise. After a rough and long Atlantic crossing, the little *Sumter* was leaking badly, food and provisions were low, and Semmes had only one thousand of his ten-thousand-dollar cruising fund left. She limped into the harbor of Cádiz, Spain, on 4 January 1862, to seek repair facilities, food and provisions, and time to receive funds from Confederate Commissioner William L. Yancy in London. The harbor officials received him coolly, forced him to justify every request by legal brief, and delayed responses while they consulted Madrid. Finally, after allowing him to repair the *Sumter's* hull in a government-owned dry dock, they refused to allow him to remain in the harbor while awaiting funds from London. Disgusted with the Spanish treatment, Semmes blamed it on their fear of the United States and later noted "that all of the weak powers were timid, and henceforth, I rarely entered any but an English or French port."[42]

The Spanish officials' delays in responding to Semmes's request allowed him time to read and write. In January in Cádiz he read a copy of U.S. Secretary of the Navy Gideon Welles's report to Congress, which prompted him, on 9 January 1862, to write a long letter to the *Times* of London.[43] In it, he identified Welles as "the Secretary of the Northern fragment of what was formerly known as the United States of America," and noted that Welles wrote that the *Sumter* and Confederate privateers were engaged in "piratical warfare." Rejecting Welles's accusation of piracy, the *Sumter* commander refuted the charges. In his letter he employed logic and a style designed to appeal to English readers of the *Times*.

> Mr. Welles . . . calls me a privateer. He knows better than this. Privateers sail under a letter of marque, but he knows that I have been regularly commissioned as a ship of war of the Confederate States. If Welles insists on calling all Confederates rebels, then he might criticize me as a rebel man of war. But, if I am this, so were all the ships of the American colonies commissioned by that Virginian, George Washington.

In referring to the *Sumter*, Welles listed those U.S. ships assigned to search for her. Among them was the USS *San Jacinto*, which violated English neutral rights by stopping HMS *Trent* on the high seas and forcibly removing John Slidell and James Mason. European pressure and British preparation for war forced the federal government to release the two Confederate diplomatic commissioners, and news of their release had reached Europe just days before Semmes was writing. "I feel honored," Semmes wrote, "to have been pursued by six frigates, and one of them caught Messrs. Mason and Slidell instead of catching me." This was an effective stroke of Semmes's pen because it placed him and the English on the same side against the United States.

Also at Cádiz, twelve enlisted seamen deserted the *Sumter*, seduced, Semmes claimed, by the "agents, spies, and pimps" of the U.S. consul, but such problems were common to most ships in his day. Seamen signed on for a particular voyage, and most of them left the ship on completion of their contracts. At any given time, unemployed seamen in port cities throughout the world were ready to sign on board any ship. They had no allegiance to any flag. Semmes had a constant problem with his foreign seamen.

Although the *Sumter*'s crew were mostly non-Americans, they were homogeneous compared with the crew of the *Alabama*. By mid-cruise there were English, Irish, French, Portuguese, Spanish, and Oriental sailors on board the *Alabama*, and they were controlled only by strict discipline. Semmes read the Confederate Articles of War to the full crew every Sunday morning. Even so, he had to suppress a mutiny on 19 November 1862 while at Fort de France in Martinique.[44] Semmes nevertheless developed a strong attachment to his crew and often moderated discipline with mercy. His crew, in return, respected the captain and affectionately referred to him as "Old Beeswax." Semmes was particularly proud of the fact that of the twenty-five hundred men—officers, seamen, and prisoners—under his command from time to time, on board both ships, he "had not lost a single man by disease."[45]

On 17 January 1862, after the Cádiz governor, "a bull-head, stupid official," refused to allow him to stay any longer, Semmes sailed out of the port and turned the *Sumter*'s bow toward the British base at Gibraltar. En route, the

*Sumter* made her last captures, bonding one and burning the other,[46] and she anchored in Gibraltar Bay early the next evening. This was the effective end of the *Sumter* cruise. From 30 June 1861 to 18 January 1862, she had captured eighteen enemy merchant vessels—seven burned, two bonded, eight lost to Cuban internment, and one recaptured by the enemy—and had overhauled thirty-four neutral ships. Unable to procure coal or repair the *Sumter*'s boilers, and blockaded variously by three or four U.S. warships, including the *Kearsarge*, Semmes finally abandoned the ship. In mid-April 1862, Semmes and several officers boarded a passenger steamer for England.

Semmes and John MacIntosh Kell, his first lieutenant, took rooms together in Euston Square, London, where they remained through May. Semmes appreciated the "relaxation and ease" of London living compared with that of the past six months on board ship. Through James Mason, Semmes met many distinguished men—cotton brokers, shippers, shipbuilders—who had an economic interest in the Confederate cause. Normally a sharp judge of character, he misread their genial entertainment, flattery, and expressions of support for the Confederacy as reflecting British government policy. More important, he also conferred with James D. Bulloch and James North, Confederate naval purchasing agents, and learned of the recent sailing of the CSS *Florida* and the near readiness of the future CSS *Alabama*. Persuaded that no ship was available to him, however, Semmes decided to return immediately to the Confederate States and arrived at Nassau on 8 June 1862.[47]

By pure coincidence, Semmes met another officer fresh from Richmond with copies of letters from Secretary Mallory, who thought Semmes was still in England. From the letters he learned that Mallory had nominated him for promotion to captain and appointed him to command the *Alabama*.[48] Fearful that the British would seize the ship before he could return to England, Semmes wrote to Bulloch and suggested that the *Alabama* be sent to some rendezvous point to await her newly assigned captain. Not knowing whether Bulloch received his letter, Semmes spent "several very anxious weeks" before securing passage back to England.

Meanwhile, Captain Bulloch received the letters of Mallory and Semmes at the same time and put into effect a plan to evade British neutrality laws. He sent the *Alabama* under British colors and a British captain to the Azores to await her captain, crew, munitions, and supplies. Both Bulloch and Semmes expended great effort to prove that the building, equipping, arming, and manning of the *Alabama* were done within the boundaries of the British neutrality laws. But neither ever understood that England had adopted a strict policy of neutrality, found her own domestic laws inadequate, and acted thereafter on policy and not on law. Semmes devoted thirty-two pages of a tightly written and logical argument in his *Memoirs* to prove that the *Alabama* was a legitimate warship of the Confederate States Navy and operated in an accepted mode of naval warfare.

The postwar negotiations between London and Washington, however, concerned not the ship herself, but her origins and the British obligation to prevent a ship intended for war use — regardless of how or where she might later be armed, manned, and equipped — from leaving British territory. As a matter of principle, the British government accepted in 1861 its own responsibility for preventing a ship from leaving British territory if it were built in England by a belligerent power and intended to war on an enemy. That principle, incorporated into the Treaty of Washington (1871), served as the basis for the 1873 Geneva Tribunal's decision that Great Britain must pay an indemnity of $15,500,000 to the United States.[49]

Semmes, writing in 1867–1868, could not have known of the diplomatic principle accepted by England or that Great Britain, not the *Alabama*, was to be put on trial. Unfortunately, the writings of Semmes and Bulloch have influenced many scholars and still serve to cloud the origins and nature of the ship on whose decks Semmes would rise to greatness.

The *Alabama* sailed from England on 30 July 1862, several days before Semmes returned from Nassau (8 August 1862). He spent about a week gathering his *Sumter* officers and making financial arrangements for a cruise fund. Recalling his embarrassments in Cádiz, Semmes obtained a cruising fund, and there is evidence that he also had a "considerable sum of gold" in the ship throughout the cruise.[50] At no time while on board the *Alabama* did Semmes ever mention the need for money.

Bulloch had designed the ship, nursed her to completion, and now turned her over to Semmes, who saw her afloat for the first time on 20 August 1862 when he, his officers, and Bulloch arrived in the Azores. Semmes paid his great debt to Bulloch when he described the ship in words that convey across a hundred years his thrill and excitement: "Her model was of the most perfect symmetry, and she sat upon the water with the lightness and grace of a swan. She was barkentine rigged, with long lower masts, which enabled her to carry large fore- and aft-sails. . . . Her sticks were of the best yellow pine, that would bend in the gale like a willow wand, without breaking, and her rigging was of the best Swedish iron wire." She had a lifting device to raise her propeller out of water to prevent drag when under sail. "She was a perfect steamer and a perfect sailing ship at the same time."[51]

Semmes saw the *Alabama* as a love-partner, a home, and, once he took possession of her, he was pleased and legitimized their affair. "I had surveyed my new ship as we approached with no little interest, as she was to be not only my home, *but my bride*, as it were, for the next few years, and I was quite satisfied with her external appearance." Once on board, Semmes "was as much pleased with her internal appearance, and arrangements, as . . . with her externally."[52] The union was complete between man and ship, for that night Semmes slept in her bosom—a sound, restful, and peaceful sleep. It was a union that over the next twenty-two months would become ever more intimate as each learned more about the other, and they responded to each other's demands.

By Saturday night, 23 August 1862, all supplies were transferred to the *Alabama*. On Sunday, in international waters where no nation had jurisdiction, Semmes commissioned the *Alabama* as a regular warship of the Confederate States Navy. He read to the assembled officers and seamen his commission as a captain and his orders. The seamen who had signed on as merchant seamen had no obligation to the *Alabama*, so Semmes spoke to them in terms of fighting the "battles of the oppressed" and a cruise of "excitement and adventure." Then he offered them contracts at twice the going wage and "lots of prize money." Aroused by the ceremony they had just witnessed and greedy for the double wages and prize money, eighty of the assembled ninety sailors—English, Dutch, Irish, French, Italian, and Spanish—signed on. Semmes "felt much relieved in consequence."[53]

During the next few days Semmes exercised his crew and gave them gunnery practice. He then turned to his task. On 5 September 1862, the *Alabama* made her first capture, a whaling vessel off the Azores. This was the first of the 54 ships that she would capture and of the 447 that she would speak or board.[54] Thus, the *Alabama* began her career as the most destructive commerce raider in history.

Her captain, however, had greater ambitions for her. Even on board the *Sumter*, Semmes had resented the reputation that he "never fights, only plunders." When he first had seen the *Alabama* in England, still in the shipyard, he thought her to be "quite equal to encounter any of the enemy's steam sloops." Four months into the cruise he deliberately sought a battle with an enemy war vessel. Having learned from captured Northern papers that the United States was planning a combined operation under General N. P. Banks against Galveston, Texas, Semmes decided "to strike a blow" against the expedition in the Gulf of Mexico.

Accordingly, after recoaling and resting his crew at an island one hundred miles east of Vera Cruz—waters familiar to him from his Mexican War days— Semmes approached the Texas coast. On 11 January 1863, as he timed his speed to arrive before Galveston after dusk, the *Alabama*, turned huntress, flushed the enemy. Semmes soon realized that he had come upon three warships, not the Banks expedition. He tacked off, and, when one of the enemy ships got up steam to investigate, he tried to lure the enemy vessel away from her sister ships and to gain time for darkness to arrive.

Semmes had an advantage because he knew the ship was an enemy, but his antagonist proved to be the USS *Hatteras*, an eighteen-month-old iron steamer of eleven hundred tons, with airtight compartments. Still, the *Alabama* met her captain's demands as the two ships, standing from thirty to one hundred yards apart, exchanged fire. The close distance offset the effect of the *Hatteras*'s light cannon; but the *Alabama*'s shells "entered the *Hatteras* at the waterline tearing off entire sheets of iron." The water rushed in, and the *Hatteras* struck her flag. Within forty-five minutes, the first battle on the high seas between Confederate and Union warships was a victory for Semmes and his ship.[55]

Neither Semmes nor Homer C. Blake, captain of the *Hatteras*, made special comment on the fact that the *Alabama*'s shells tore off "sheets of iron" at the waterline of the *Hatteras*. Yet, the impact of the new ironclad ships on naval warfare was a constant topic among maritime people, especially after March 1862, when the ironclad CSS *Virginia* inflicted destruction on the Union's wooden warships in Hampton Roads and then fought the ironclad USS *Monitor* to a draw. Eleven months later, the wooden *Alabama* destroyed a Union iron warship in an exchange of shots at close range! It was a remarkable feat, yet Semmes made no remark on it. Why not? His omission is a mystery unless one suspects that he did not want to cloud his later argument that the *Kearsarge*'s captain surreptitiously armored his ship by covering the vertical chains that hung from deck to waterline.

After the battle with the *Hatteras*, Semmes could find no prey in American waters, so, in compliance with Mallory's suggestion, he decided to head for the East Indies. The life of a commerce raider was not easy. The loneliness of a sea captain, the strains of imposing discipline on a motley crew of several nationalities who depended on him for food and clothing, the challenges of rough seas, the thrills of the chase, and the climax of the capture all had a psychological effect on the introspective Semmes. He never confided in his men but wrote in his ship's journal. In June 1863, frustrated by bad weather, Semmes noted that his two years afloat had "produced a constant tension of the nervous system, and a wear and tear of body that . . , no doubt, would be quite obvious to my friends at home."

The introspection continued. On 8 September 1863, as he complained of the rolling and pitching in the sea, he confessed to his journal: "I am supremely disgusted with the sea and all its belongings. The fact is, I am past the age when men ought to be subjected to the hardships and discomforts of the sea."[56]

The man and the ship both needed rest and refurbishing. On 16 September 1863, they entered the anchorage at Simon's Town, South Africa, where they spent eight days. The *Alabama* took on a full provision of coal, repaired her copper hull sheathings, and refitted her fore-topmast. Semmes strolled into the countryside beyond Simon's Town, attended mass in the small Catholic church, and dined with British officers. Thus refreshed, ship, captain, and crew sailed from Simon's Town on 24 September, rounded the Cape of Good Hope, and headed into the Indian Ocean.[57] Semmes chose the southern route to avoid U.S. warships. The constant rainsqualls and gale winds imposed a dull routine on the man that tested his spirit and a stress on the ship that tested her timbers.

On the return voyage from the Far East, the chase that led to his last capture momentarily lifted the spirit of the still-despondent captain. The weather was good: the moon bright, the breeze gentle, and the sea smooth. "The Yankee worked like a good fellow to get away, piling clouds of canvas upon his ship . . . , but it was no use," Semmes wrote. "When the day dawned we were within a couple of miles of him. It was the old spectacle of the panting, breathless fawn, and the inexorable stag-hound." The thrill of the kill soon turned to despair, however, as Semmes read of Northern victories in recent New York newspapers that he had captured. "Might it not be," Semmes mused, "that after all our trials and sacrifices, the cause for which we were struggling would be lost? . . . The thought was hard to bear."

The ugly mood persisted. As he recrossed the equator northward toward Cherbourg, Semmes fell into a deep depression. Detached, he referred to himself in the third person—no longer the bright-eyed seaman who "gloated upon the spectacle" of the burning *Golden Rocket*—his first victim, thirty months earlier—and saw in those leaping flames the bright promise of a war easily won, but now only a man upon whom stress and strain "had laid, in the three years of war he had been afloat, a load of a dozen years on his shoulders." And he saw his ship just as clearly. She was no longer the "inexorable stag-hound," but only a "wearied foxhound, limping back after a long chase, footsore and longing for quiet and repose." Above his visions of man and ship, he saw "shadows of a sorrowful future," and knew that his cruise on board the *Alabama* was "drawing to a close" in defeat. The man and ship were beaten not by the enemy on the high seas, but by the seas themselves and by the enemy armies on land.[58]

The bent and beaten seaman had pushed his ship, his sea bride, too hard for too long. Answering his every demand, she had fought and defeated a U.S. war vessel; she had braved the storms of the Antarctic; she had survived the tropical waters of the East Indies. She had not been in dry dock since her launching into the River Mersey that fifteenth of May so many nautical miles ago in 1862. As she approached Cherbourg on 10 June 1864, she complained that her boilers were rusted and leaky, her copper sheathing was broken and dragging in the water, and her timbers—so tested by raging seas infested with icebergs—were wearied by her long journeys. Her captain, too, was exhausted, not only from the "vigils by night and by day," but even more by a new mental attitude: the lost cause for which he had "so struggled, . . . the shadows of a sorrowful future," his beloved *Alabama*'s cruise "drawing to a close."

It was in this depth of depression that, on 11 June 1864, Semmes in his well-worn ship dropped anchor in Cherbourg. Two days later, he learned that Com-

modore Samuel Barron was in Paris. He immediately wrote to his superior officer: "My health has suffered so much from a constant and harassing service
of three years almost continuously at sea, that I shall have to ask for relief [from
command of the *Alabama*]."[59] Semmes makes no mention of this request in
any of his writings because the USS *Kearsarge*'s arrival in Cherbourg harbor
on 14 June 1864 changed the situation. He had to reassess the *Alabama*'s role
in the new circumstances and, having done so, realized the necessity for quick
action. His depression left him as he prepared for the task at hand.

The *Kearsarge*, he knew, had been guarding Calais, France, where the CSS
*Rappahannock*, held by the French government, was slowly rotting away.[60]
Semmes could not permit his gallant staghound, tail between her legs, to be
bottled up in Cherbourg while the *Rappahannock* was in Calais. What an in-
glorious end to a glorious cruise that would be! No, better that, once again, she
ride the waves. She might win against the *Kearsarge*: the U.S. vessel possessed
no obvious overwhelming advantage over the *Alabama*; and if she failed, she
would die as she had lived—gloriously.

But Semmes was a realist as well as a romantic. He knew other U.S. warships would soon appear and confine him to Cherbourg harbor, as they had
done at Gibraltar Bay. The *Alabama*'s only chance to get to sea ever again was
to risk battle with the *Kearsarge* before the other ships arrived. It was a naval
captain's decision to take the proper action at the proper moment in order to
keep his ship afloat and in service against the enemy.

Departing from custom, Semmes summoned his first lieutenant and announced: "Kell, I'm going to fight the *Kearsarge*. What do you think of it?" Kell
dutifully reminded his captain that in target practice a few weeks earlier the
gunpowder appeared to be weak and that one in three shells had failed to explode because of the defective fuses. Semmes replied, "I will take my chances
of one in three."[61]

Semmes required four days to take on 150 tons of coal. Sailors holystoned
the *Alabama*'s decks, polished brass, and repaired or replaced the sails and rig-
gings. In the meantime, word of the impending battle spread, and the curious
and concerned took the train from Paris to Cherbourg. The artist Edouard
Manet came and painted the *Alabama* in her death throes; photographers and
newspaper reporters arrived to record the event. Confederate naval officers
from Paris tried to join the crew but were denied by the French officials who
were enforcing their neutrality obligations.

On Sunday morning, 19 June 1864, the *Alabama*, with her officers and crew
in dress uniform, sailed out of Cherbourg harbor as if en route to a gala naval
review. The crowds on quays, housetops, hills, boats, and even the breakwater
cheered as the proud ship steamed toward the waiting *Kearsarge*. The *Alabama*, responding to the occasion, once again rode the water with the grace of
a swan.

About three miles out of Cherbourg, Semmes called his crew together to hear a rousing speech, reminiscent of Napoleon's First Order to his army in Italy. "The name of your ship has become a household word wherever civilization extends. Shall that name be tarnished by defeat? The thing is impossible." And the sailors, aroused, at the word "defeat" answered, "Never! Never!" But Semmes himself was not so sure. Just earlier, he had asked his fifth lieutenant, "How do you think it will turn out today, Mr. Sinclair?" Surprised to be asked his opinion, the lieutenant replied, "I cannot answer the question, Sir, but can assure you the crew will do their full duty, and follow you to the death." Turning away, Semmes responded, "Yes, that's true." Did Semmes mean that the crew would literally, that day, "follow him to the death"?[62]

The story of the battle has been repeated often, from that day to this, by eyewitnesses, participants, popular writers, and scholars.[63] The plain facts—the "whats" of the battle—are clear: the two ships met about seven miles at sea, still in view of the spectators. Semmes opened fire about a mile from the Kearsarge, and the force of the fight threw the two ships into a circular pattern. After about sixty-five minutes of intense and continuous firing, the Alabama was foundering, and she sank stern first at 12:24 P.M. The "whys" of the battle are disputed still because eyewitnesses and participants recounted the events from their own scope of vision, personal allegiance, and mental conditions.

Depression struck Semmes early in the battle because he could see that the Alabama's shot and shell did little damage to the Kearsarge. He ordered his gunners to aim low so the shots would ricochet off the water into the enemy hull. Finally, about thirty minutes into the fight, a lucky shot embedded a shell into the Kearsarge's sternpost. A cheer went up from the Alabama's crew, but the shell failed to explode. As Semmes later wrote, that shell "was the only trophy they ever got of the Alabama! We fought her until she could no longer swim, and then we gave her to the waves." As the ship began to settle stern first and the water engulfed the taffrails, Semmes and Kell prepared to abandon ship. Once again, Semmes identified with his ship. At almost the last moment, in a gesture of defiance against the Yankee victor, Semmes cast his sword— symbol of command—into the sea. Then he and Kell jumped and, side by side, swam away to avoid the vortex of the waters.

It was an emotional moment for the two men as they swam in the water and saw their ship go down. Gallant losers often gain more renown than the winners. Whose name do we remember from the Battle of Thermopylae? And whose name comes to mind when we hear the word "Waterloo"? Who remembers the name of the Kearsarge's captain? It is from such stuff that legends grow.

Semmes later blamed his defeat on weak gunpowder and faulty percussion caps. But a sailor on board the Kearsarge claimed that the Alabama's shells failed to explode because the gunners had not removed the lead caps, which exposed the time fuses that, in turn, would cause the shells to explode.[64] If that were true, then the blame should be placed on the gunners, not the gunpowder. Only about 8.5 percent of the 370 shots fired by the *Alabama*'s gunners even touched the *Kearsarge,* and of those, more hit the rigging than the hull. Commander Bulloch, analyzing the loss, wrote that the *Alabama* crew had not been trained at judging distance nor had they practiced "firing at a visible target and noting effect." He concluded that "the result of the action was determined by the superior accuracy of the firing from the *Kearsarge.*"[65]

Semmes refused to criticize or lay blame on any of his officers or crew. Despite his earlier criticism of Jack Tar and the stern discipline imposed during the cruise, Semmes wrote of them after the battle with sentiments he had never before expressed: "When I looked upon my gory deck, toward the close of the action, and saw so many manly forms stretched upon it, with the glazed eye of death, or agonizing with terrible wounds, I felt as a father feels who has lost his children."[66]

It is true that of the twenty-one men who died in the action and in the waters, thirteen had served from the start of the cruise. It is also true that such a scene as the "gory deck" would impress itself on Semmes's mind as indelibly as that of his sinking ship. Semmes's memoirs are impressionistic, but do his impressions convey any less truth than Edouard Manet's impressionistic painting of the end of the *Alabama?* No. Semmes could not blame his crew any more than he could blame his ship.

> No one who is not a seaman can realize the blow that falls upon the heart of a commander, upon the sinking of his ship. It is not merely the loss of a battle—it is the overwhelming of his household, as it were, in a great catastrophe. The *Alabama* had not only been my battlefield, but my home, in which I had lived two long years, and in which I had experienced many vicissitudes of pain and pleasure, sickness and health.[67]

And so Semmes sought other causes for the catastrophe. Just two days after the event, from Southampton, England, Semmes composed his official report to Commodore Barron. In it, he referred to the slight damage done by shells exploding against the *Kearsarge*'s hull, but only in the context of his order to use shot alternately with shells; he did not mention weak gunpowder. Two paragraphs later, simply as a matter of information, he noted that his officers who went alongside the enemy's ship reported that "her midship section on both sides was thoroughly iron-coated" by perpendicular chains covered by a thin outer planking, but he made no critical comment about the iron coating. Ten days later, on 1 July, he wrote: "My defeat is due to two circumstances—the very thorough manner in which the enemy's ship was protected by her chain armor and the deterioration . . . of my powder and fuses." On 5 July, he placed the loss on the condition of the powder and referred to the *Kearsarge's* chain armor only by indirection.

In neither letter did he criticize Captain John B. Winslow for applying the chain armor or for covering it with planking. He did comment in the letters that he was "overwhelmed" and "oppressed" with "mortification" for the defeat. His humiliation grew with the passing years, so that he wrote in his memoirs: "The plain fact is, without any varnish, the *Kearsarge*, though as effectively protected as if she had been armored with the best of iron plates, was to all appearance a wooden ship of war." She really had "concealed armor."[68]

The battle, then, had been unfair, won by deceit and trickery. The Semmes who wrote those words was not the naval officer who took the *Sumter* through the Union blockade in 1861, who destroyed more Northern merchantmen than any other raider captain in history, who guided and molded a motley crew of replacements and various nationalities into fighting men who, despite defeat, left him glory. No, it was not Captain Raphael Semmes of the CSS *Alabama* but a broken man whose pride and, perhaps, self-respect had been destroyed on that Sunday off Cherbourg in 1864.

Although his years of greatness ended when the *Alabama* sank, excitement still beckoned Semmes. After several weeks of paying off the crew and settling the *Alabama's* affairs, he regained his self-confidence. He was feted by several pro-South British societies, one of which presented him with a new sword. Recovered from the ordeal of battle and his health restored, Semmes embarked on 3 October 1864 on his return journey to the Confederate States. Wartime necessity imposed on him a circuitous route: by ship to Matamoros, Mexico, thence to Brownsville, Texas, and by coach with a military escort to Shreveport, Louisiana, where he rested a few days and visited his son, whom he had last seen at West Point before the war. Traveling by horseback, eluding U.S. troops by sleeping in swamps and swimming rivers, the fifty-six-year-old Semmes, in good health and high spirits, greeted his wife and daughters in Mobile on 19 December.[69] Given the circumstances, a seven-and-a-half-week trip from England to Mobile was rather remarkable.

Semmes left his family on 2 January 1865 to report to Secretary Mallory in Richmond. For two weeks Semmes traveled in the wake of war, shocked at the "scene of havoc and destruction." In Richmond, he was received by President Davis and both houses of Congress, promoted to admiral, and given command of the James River Fleet. The breakdown of Confederate society was almost more than Semmes could bear. His concepts of social structure, privilege and responsibility, honesty, and loyalty were shaken. "The *Alabama* had gone to her grave none too soon. If she had not been buried with honors at war, with the howling winds of the British Channel to sing her requiem, she might soon be handed over to the exultant Yankee, to be exhibited at Boston as a trophy of war."[70] Time had stopped for the *Alabama*; now safe in her grave, she remained in her proper place in Semmes's concept of the order of things. It was a notion that, along with his family, sustained him during those last, horrible days of the war.

Semmes had to destroy his own fleet as Grant turned Lee's right flank; he fled with his officers and sailors to Danville, Virginia, where President Davis appointed him a brigadier general in the Confederate States Army. At the end of the war, he was with General Joseph E. Johnston in North Carolina and accepted that unusual military convention offered by General William T. Sherman to Johnston's troops. Later, he used its particular terms to refute charges of piracy and, after a four-month imprisonment, gained a pardon from President Andrew Johnson.

Forbidden from practicing law during the period of reconstruction, Semmes sustained himself and his family by teaching in an academy that later became Louisiana State University, editing a newspaper in Memphis, and lecturing on his wartime experiences. He also wrote the 833-page *Memoirs of Service Afloat during the War Between the States* (1869). He completed his life in Mobile as a lawyer, appropriately specializing in international law and maritime affairs. In 1877, short by a month of being sixty-eight years old, he died at Point Clear, his second residence, on the east side of Mobile Bay. The citizens of Mobile declared a full day of mourning, during which cannon sounded every half hour. After a military burial in the Catholic cemetery, Semmes had rejoined the *Alabama*.

What kind of man was Raphael Semmes? In one sense he was very ordinary, a typical product of his time. But he was also an extraordinary man because he tempered romanticism with the discipline of a naval career, and balanced nationalism with the logic of a legal mind. He accepted the decisions of the battlefield and adjusted to life after the Confederacy, but he always remained convinced that the South was constitutionally right. He also managed to retain, despite the Civil War, the mind-set about the proper order of things that he developed during the Mexican War.

As commanding officer of the *Sumter* and the *Alabama*, he gained world renown as a romantic sea raider, but he also applied imagination and resourcefulness to the unpleasant job that wartime circumstances assigned him. Whatever the task, he threw himself into it with conviction and intelligence. Imagery dominated his moods, reinforcing his aloofness as a sea captain and fostering occasional mental depressions that led him to identify with his ship so as to become one with her. If history associates "Semmes and the CSS *Alabama*," it is right; and if historians have romanticized the man and the ship, they are also right, because that is the way Semmes imagined himself—as one with her on a great adventure.

FURTHER READING

The best sources for the life of Raphael Semmes are the two memoirs he wrote. *Service Afloat and Ashore during the Mexican War* (Cincinnati, 1851) and *Memoirs of Service Afloat during the War between the States* (Baltimore, 1869) are autobiographical accounts that are self-serving but, at the same time, contain some documents, relate actual facts, and, most important, reveal Semmes's acute observations and inner thoughts. When compared with the logs of the CSS *Sumter* and the CSS *Alabama*, Semmes proves to be quite accurate, and even his acidulous comments about Northern leaders and issues of the Civil War cast much light on his mental attitudes.

While the war was still on, an English house published *The Cruise of the* Alabama *and the* Sumter, 2 vols. (London, 1864), based on "Private Journals and Other Papers of Commander R. Semmes, C.S.N. and other Officers," which Semmes considered to be only "a meager and barren record." A very helpful book on Semmes as captain of the CSS *Sumter* is *Rebel Raider* (Chapel Hill, N.C., 1948), composed of extracts from Semmes's *Memoirs*, with comments by Harper Allen Gosnell on points of international law and seamanship. In 1962, Indiana University Press published in its Civil War Centennial Series, *The Confederate Raider* Alabama (Bloomington, 1962), which consisted of selections from Semmes's *Memoirs*, edited with an introduction by Philip Van Doren Stern. Stern gives a sketch of Semmes's life and attempts a characterization of him as a person and ship commander. Perhaps the most valuable and straightforward memoir of Confederate naval activity in Europe, including Semmes's role there, is James D. Bulloch's *The Secret Service of the Confederate States in Europe*, 2 vols. (Liverpool, England, 1883). It contains the full story of the *Alabama* from design to commissioning at sea.

Other essential sources are those in United States Department of the Navy, *Official Records of the Union and Confederate Navies in the War of the Rebellion*, 31 vols. (Washington, D.C., 1894–1922). Series 1, vols. 1–2, contain the logs of Semmes's ships and correspondence pertaining to the ships' cruises; series 2, vols. 1–3, contain correspondence between the secretary of the Confederate Navy and his various agents and officers. For Semmes's personnel service record in the U.S. Navy, the listing of assignments and extended leaves is in the National Archives, Washington, Record Group 24, Records of the Bureau of Naval Personnel, rolls 4–7, and also in the National Archives, publication no. 19, "Treasury Department Collection of Confederate Records."

Two of Semmes's close associates in the Confederate Navy published memoirs. John McIntosh Kell's *Recollections of a Naval Life* (Washington, D.C., 1900) and Arthur Sinclair's *Two Years on the* Alabama, 3d ed. (Boston, 1896), although containing errors of fact, reveal attitudes about Semmes held by his subordinates. Both authors, however, ardently admired Semmes, and their accounts are uncritical and nonanalytical.

Biographers have all based their works on Semmes's own writings, and they are equally uncritical. The two best ones are W. Adolphe Roberts, *Semmes of the* Alabama (New York, 1938), which romanticizes Semmes's life and career, and Edward Boykin, *Ghost Ship of the Confederacy: The Story of the* Alabama *and her Captain, Raphael Semmes* (New York, 1957). Boykin presents his account of Semmes as "the best out-and-out adventure story of the Civil War," and that theme characterizes the whole book. The most recent biographical treatment is in Charles Grayson Summersell, *CSS Alabama: Builder, Captain, and Plans* (University, Ala., 1985). It also contains an account of Bulloch and the construction of the *Alabama*, including the building contract, specifications, and plans, and a detailed record of the *Alabama's* cruise.

Recently, some very good, scholarly works have appeared on Confederate naval officers who were associated with Semmes. Norman C. Delaney's *John McIntosh Kell of the Raider Alabama* (University, Ala., 1973) is an excellent study and clarifies the relationship between Semmes and his executive officer on board both raiders. Charles Grayson Summersell, *The Cruise of the C.S.S. Sumter* (University, Ala., 1965) reveals a good understanding of Semmes and details the full story of the ship. The same scholar has edited *The Journal of George Townley Fullam* (University, Ala., 1973), the English master's mate on the *Alabama*, and annotated it with invaluable detail gleaned from various other sources. This book, without doubt, provides more factual detail about the cruise of the *Alabama* than any other. William Stanley Hoole wrote *Four Years in the Confederate Navy: The Career of Captain John Low on the C.S.S.* Fingal, Florida, Alabama, Tuscaloosa, *and* Ajax (Athens, Ga., 1964). Low was fourth lieutenant in the *Alabama* until Semmes made him commanding officer of the *Tuscaloosa*. Hoole has also edited *The Logs of the C.S.S.* Alabama *and the C.S.S.* Tuscaloosa, *1862–1863* (University, Ala., 1972), with an introduction.

For an excellent study of Confederate naval activity in England, see Frank J. Merli, *Great Britain and the Confederate Navy, 1861–1865* (Bloomington, Ind., 1970), and for the diplomatic implications of Southern naval activities, see Warren F. Spencer, *The Confederate Navy in Europe* (University, Ala., 1983).

NOTES

1. W. Adolphe Roberts, *Semmes of the* Alabama (New York, 1938), 282–84.

2. George W. Dalzell, *The Flight from the Flag* (Chapel Hill, N.C., 1940), 237–48.

3. United States, Department of the Navy, *Official Records of the Union and Confederate Navies in the War of the Rebellion* (hereafter cited as ORN), ser. 2, 2:151, Mallory to Davis, first annual report, 27 February 1862. Also, see Warren F. Spencer, *The Confederate Navy in Europe* (University, Ala., 1983), 1–4, for the circumstances that necessitated Mallory's naval policy.

4. The Davis proclamation is in ORN, ser. 2, 3:96–97; the Lincoln proclamation is in James D. Richardson, comp., *A Compilation of Messages and Papers of the Presidents, 1789–1897*, 10 vols. (New York, 1896–1899), 7:3215. For the early French-English consultation, see Lynn M. Case and Warren F. Spencer, *The United States and France: Civil War Diplomacy* (Philadelphia, 1970), 50–57, and 59 for the French proclamation of neutrality. The British proclamation of neutrality is in Ephraim Douglas Adams, *Great Britain and the American Civil War*, 2 vols. (New York, 1925), 1:94–95.

5. For a more detailed discussion of the European neutrality proclamations and their effects on the Confederate Navy, see Spencer, *Confederate Navy in Europe*, 8–10, 212–16.

6. For Seward's reactions to the neutrality proclamation, see Norman B. Ferris, *Desperate Diplomacy: William H. Seward's Foreign Policy, 1861* (Knoxville, Tenn., 1976), 33–54, passim, and Case and Spencer, *United States and France*, 71–72.

7. For Semmes's early life, see Roberts, *Semmes*, 11–27, and John McIntosh Kell, *Recollections of a Naval Life* (Washington, D.C., 1900), 278–79. For his naval assignments, see Records of the Bureau of Naval Personnel, Record Group (RG) 24, National Archives, rolls 4-7, 9 (hereafter cited as Records of Naval Personnel).

8. For Semmes's naval leaves and promotion, see Records of Naval Personnel, rolls 5, 6. For his *Poinsett* services, see Harper Allen Gosnell, *Rebel Raider* (Chapel Hill, N.C., 1948), 4–5.

9. Roberts, *Semmes*, 18.

10. These quotes are from Raphael Semmes, *Service Afloat and Ashore during the Mexican War* (Cincinnati, 1851), 80–82. For the Mexican War and the Navy's role in it, see K. Jack Bauer, *The Mexican War, 1846–1848* (New York, 1974), especially chap. 7; Robert Selph Henry, *The Story of the Mexican War* (New York, 1950), and Charles L. Dufour, *The Mexican War* (New York, 1968), especially chap. 23. All of these authors cite Semmes, *Service Afloat and Ashore*, as an eyewitness account. It is difficult to discern whether Semmes reflects his ideas as of the time of the events or as of the time he wrote (1849–1850). Even in the latter case, this work reflects his ideas as a result of the Mexican War and as he held them prior to secession.

11. Semmes, *Service Afloat and Ashore*, 76.

12. Semmes's report is in ibid., 93–99. The critical comment is by Gosnell, *Rebel Raider*, 6.

13. Semmes, *Service Afloat and Ashore*, 158–96, passim. The quote is on 159, and the letters are on 159–61. Semmes's duty with the Army is also covered in Edward S. Wallace, *General William Jenkins Worth* (Dallas, 1953), 136–49, passim. Wallace cites Semmes's work frequently but supplements his accounts of Semmes with other original sources.

14. Semmes, *Service Afloat and Ashore*, 168, 169.

15. For the exchange of letters, see ibid., 198–202.

16. Ibid., 302.

17. See, in order, ibid., 255, 256, 379, 281, 282–83, 379.

18. This and the following information are in Records of Naval Personnel, roll 7, and "Treasury Department Collection of Confederate Records," publication No. 19, National Archives.

19. "Treasury Department Collection." The U.S. government took over the lighthouses from private owners in 1787; the Lighthouse Board, established in 1852, was under the Treasury Department; the Lighthouse Service, established in 1910 in the Department of Commerce, was transferred to the U.S. Coast Guard in 1939.

20. Raphael Semmes, *Memoirs of Service Afloat during the War between the States* (Baltimore, 1869), 72.

21. Ibid., 86–88. The younger Semmes later served as a major in the Confederate army.

22. For the purchasing mission of Lieutenant James North and for the travels of James D. Bulloch, see Spencer, *Confederate Navy in Europe*, 16–17, 19–20.

23. The best historical treatment of Mallory is J. T. Durkin, *Stephen R. Mallory: Confederate Navy Chief* (Chapel Hill, N.C., 1954).

24. The story of the birth, conversion, and fate of the CSS *Sumter* has been thoroughly detailed in Charles Grayson Summersell, *The Cruise of the C.S.S. Sumter* (University, Ala., 1965), and need not be repeated in this essay.

25. The quotes in this section all come from Semmes, *Memoirs*, 96–118, passim.

26. Ibid., 123–25.

27. Ibid., 121

28. Dalzell, *Flight from the Flag*, 240.

29. Ibid., 137; and Roberts, *Semmes*, Appendix II, 282–84.

30. Dalzell, *Flight from the Flag*, 247.

31. Ibid., 241, 247 (" . . . the only business American bottoms got consisted of evil-smelling, offensive cargoes that neutral vessels did not want").

32. *ORN*, ser. 1, 2:777–79.

33. For the CSS *Sumter* cruise, see Summersell, *Cruise of C.S.S.* Sumter, and Gosnell, *Rebel Raider*; for the two best secondary accounts of the CSS *Alabama*, see Norman C. Delaney, *John McIntosh Kell of the Raider* Alabama (University, Ala., 1973), and *The Journal of George Townley Fullam*, edited and annotated by Charles G. Summersell (University, Ala., 1973). Also, see the works of William Stanley Hoole: *Four Years in the Confederate Navy: The Career of Captain John Low on the C.S.S.* Fingal, Florida, Alabama, Tuscaloosa, *and* Ajax (Athens, 1964), and *The Logs of the C.S.S.* Alabama *and the C.S.S.* Tuscaloosa *1862–1863* (University, Ala., 1972).

34. *Sumter* log, *ORN*, ser. 1, 1:695; Semmes, *Memoirs*, 128–29; and Kell, *Recollections of Naval Life*, 150.

35. Semmes, *Memoirs*, 161–62. Summersell, *Cruise of C.S.S.* Sumter, 60–71, 80–82, details these two incidents.

36. *Alabama* log; *ORN*, ser. 1, 2:755.

37. Semmes's actions and reasons for his decision in the famous *Martaban* case are taken from the *Alabama* log, ibid., 792, and Semmes, *Memoirs*, 717–19, where he acknowledges the cargo to have been neutral owned, but without legal evidence. The case is presented fully in Summersell, *Journal of George Fullam*, 166–69. The accuracy of Semmes's *Memoirs* account is confirmed in "Statement of Samuel B. Pike . . . ," 30 December 1863, Governor's Papers: Miscellaneous Letters, Public Records Office (PRO), Singapore. I am indebted to my former colleague at Old Dominion University, Harold S. Wilson, for sharing with me his research notes from the Public Records Office, Singapore, and the *Straits Times*, Singapore.

38. *Straits Times*, 2 January 1864.

39. Chamber of Commerce to Captain Burn, 30 December 1863, Governor's Papers: Misc. Letters, PRO, Singapore.

40. In order, U.S. consul to U.S. State Department, 8 January 1864, RG 59: Despatches from the U.S. Consuls in Singapore, M-464, roll 2, National Archives; McDougal to Welles, 22 October 1863, *ORN*, ser. 1, 2:474; U.S. Consul to Seward, 10 January 1864, RG 59: Despatches from the U.S. Consuls in Calcutta, M-464, n. 3, National Archives.

41. Sir James Hope to Charles M. Morris (commanding officer of the CSS *Florida*), undated, enclosed in Morris to Mallory, St. George, Bermuda, 21 June 1864, *ORN*, ser. 1, 3:616.

42. Semmes, *Memoirs*, 304. Semmes never entered a port in England, only colonial English ports. Summersell, *Cruise of C.S.S.* Sumter, 146–51, details Semmes's experiences while at Cádiz. Also, see log of the *Sumter*, *ORN*, ser. 1, 1:734–37, and Semmes's correspondence while at Cádiz, *ORN*, ser. 1, 1:638–53. The Spanish did revoke the leave order, but Semmes in his fury refused to read it.

43. The letter is in *ORN*, ser. 1, 1:640–43, and appeared in the *Times* (London), 17 January 1862.

44. Summersell, *Journal of George Fullam*, 54; Delaney, *John Kell*, 137–38; and Semmes, *Memoirs*, 511–13.

45. Semmes, *Memoirs*, 750–51, 763–64; and Delaney, *John Kell*, 174.

46. *Sumter* log, *ORN*, ser.1, 1:737; Semmes, *Memoirs*, 306–46. The best secondary account of the *Sumter* at Gibraltar and of her later fate is Summersell, *Cruise of C.S.S. Sumter*, 152–78. Also, see Spencer, *Confederate Navy in Europe*, 34–37, for the *Sumter's* role in Confederate naval affairs in Europe.

47. Semmes, *Memoirs*, 375–81.

48. Semmes, *Memoirs*, 351–53. For Confederate confusion concerning *Alabama* command assignment, see Spencer, *Confederate Navy in Europe*, 48–55, and for the ship's preparation and sailing, 55–58. For an evaluation of Semmes's officer roster, see ibid., 58–60. Spencer's account is based largely on James D. Bulloch, *The Secret Service of the Confederate States in Europe*, 2 vols. (Liverpool, England, 1883); Frank J. Merli, *Great Britain and the Confederate Navy, 1861–1865* (Bloomington, Ind., 1970); and various documents in *ORN*, ser. 1, vol. 1, and ser. 2, vol. 2.

49. Spencer, *Confederate Navy in Europe*, 8–10, 212–16, and passim.

50. Bulloch to Mallory, 21 July 1862, *ORN*, ser. 2, 2:336; and Arthur Sinclair, *Two Years on the* Alabama, 3d ed. (Boston, 1896), 127.

51. Semmes, *Memoirs*, 402–5. I use Semmes's dimensions of the ship, which are given in round figures. It is through his eyes that we must meet the *Alabama*.

52. Ibid., 408–13.

53. Bulloch's report to Mallory, *ORN* ser. 1, vol. 1, 777, and Semmes, *Memoirs*, 413.

54. Summersell, *Journal of George Fullam*, Appendix, 197–98.

55. The battle is described by Lieutenant Commander Homer C. Blake, USN, in his report to Secretary Welles, *ORN*, ser. 1, 2:19–21; Semmes's firsthand account is in ibid., 721–22, and his later one in his *Memoirs*, 545–52. The two captains differed on the distance between the ships during the battle, Semmes giving a range of two- to five-hundred yards, while Blake gave twenty-five to one hundred yards. A sailor from the *Hatteras* confirmed Blake's figures, so I have used the shorter distance.

56. *ORN*, ser. 1, 2:753, 764.

57. Ibid., 765–67.

58. These and subsequent quotations are from Semmes, *Memoirs*, in order, 748, 749–50, and 746, 756, 765.

59. Semmes to Samuel Barron, Commodore, CSN, 13 June 1864, *ORN*, ser. 1, 3:651; Barron to Semmes, draft, 14 June 1864, Whittle Papers, Norfolk Public Library, folder X, no. 7. The commodore had already selected Commander Thomas J. Page to succeed Semmes.

60. Spencer, *Confederate Navy in Europe*, 191–92.

61. Kell, *Recollections of Naval Life*, 245. In 1883, a newspaper report quoted Kell as saying that Semmes had told him: "I have sent for you to discuss the advisability of fighting the *Kearsarge*" (Alfred I. Branham, reporter, reprinted in booklet form, "290": *Story of the Sinking of the* Alabama, 1930). Either version could be correct, although Semmes was not in the habit of discussing ship operations with the officers.

62. Sinclair, *Two Years*, 275–76.

63. The best accounts remain those by participants and by Bulloch. Captain Semmes rendered an impressionistic report, *ORN*, ser. 1, 3:649–51, and an even more

subjective account in his *Memoirs,* 751–65; Captain Winslow's reports were matter-of-fact, *ORN,* ser. 1, 3:59–82, especially 79–81; Lieutenant Arthur Sinclair of the *Alabama,* writing almost thirty years after Semmes, gave a subjective yet amazingly honest account in Sinclair, *Two Years,* 259–91; and Commander Bulloch, writing with the aid of documents, including the two captain's reports, presented an analytical and balanced account in *Secret Service,* 1:277–93. For accounts of eyewitnesses, see George T. Sinclair to Barron, Cherbourg, 20 June 1864, Whittle Papers, folder X, no. 9, and William M. Leary, Jr., "The *Alabama* vs. the *Kearsarge,*" *American Neptune* 29, no. 3 (1969): 167–68ff. Excellent illustrations are in Norman C. Delaney, "Showdown at Cherbourg," *Civil War Times Illustrated* 15, no. 3 (June 1976): 16–21. The best secondary accounts are Delaney, *John Kell,* 164–68, and Summersell, *Journal of George Fullam,* 190–96. Other good secondary accounts are Roberts, *Semmes,* 195–211, and Edward Boykin, *Ghost Ship of the Confederacy: The Story of the* Alabama *and her Captain,* *Raphael Semmes* (New York, 1957), 344–84. For the diplomacy of the pre- and postbattle days, see Case and Spencer, *United States and France,* 509–15.

64. Delaney, *John Kell,* 170, citing a newspaper report of the battle.

65. Bulloch, *Secret Service,* 1:279.

66. Semmes, *Memoirs,* 763.

67. Ibid.

68. In order: Semmes to Barron, 21 June 1864, *ORN,* ser. 1, 3:650; Semmes to Slidell, 1 July 1864, and to Barron, 5 July 1864, ibid., 663, 664; and Semmes, *Memoirs,* 754, 761, 762.

69. The story of the journey is based on Semmes, *Memoirs,* 790–98.

70. Ibid., 801.

U.S. NAVY

# David Dixon Porter

## ☆ Fighting Sailor

*by Tamara Moser Melia Smith*

DAVID DIXON PORTER LIVED IN THE SHADOW OF HIS FAMOUS FATHER, Commodore David Porter, an adventurous, independent officer whose annihilation of the British whaling fleet in the War of 1812 made him both a popular national hero and the most successful member of an old naval family. Commodore Porter, who had gone to sea with his own father at an early age, wanted sons to carry on the family tradition. His foster son, David G. Farragut, won the Navy's first admiralcy. Of the commodore's six natural sons, David Dixon— neither the eldest nor his father's favorite—became the second admiral of the Navy, both because of his father and despite him. From the first, he had to struggle to be noticed.

David Dixon, born while his father sailed the Pacific in the *Essex*, retained an idealized memory of his childhood. Commodore Porter was his greatest hero. Stimulated by his father's war stories and constantly aware of his heritage, Porter lived secure in the childlike belief that his father, a member of the Board of Navy Commissioners, literally ran the Navy. The commodore returned to sea duty in the West Indies in 1823. On one cruise, in 1824, he took along the entire family. David Dixon's first voyage lasted only a few months. He was away at school when, at Fajardo, Puerto Rico, Commodore Porter overstepped his authority by demanding an apology for disrespect to an American warship, was court-martialed, and received a six-month suspension. Incensed, David Porter resigned his commission and entered the service of the Mexican navy. He took with him David Dixon, age twelve; his favorite son, Thomas, age ten; and a nephew.

David Dixon watched his father sternly mold the Mexican seamen into a fighting unit and saw more action in a few months with the Mexican navy than he would during the next thirty-five years. On board his cousin David H. Porter's ship the *Guerrero*, in close combat with the Spanish frigate *Lealtad*, David Dixon received his first war wound, and he was captured and imprisoned in Havana Harbor. When paroled, he returned to the United States, where his maternal grandfather, Congressman William Anderson, wrangled him a midshipman's appointment in the U.S. Navy. His brother Thomas died in Mexico, and his other brothers distanced themselves from their father. Only David Dixon pleased his father, who, by the time of his death in 1843, found life and family disappointing. David Dixon Porter fought for naval distinction to earn his father's love and to restore his father's tarnished image.[1]

Porter's midshipman career was fairly routine. His father had taught him tradition, discipline, and seamanship; the Navy, technical skills and leadership. Porter became an expert channel surveyor and pilot in the Coast Survey and the Hydrography Department. He learned quickly and became known as a man who thought on his feet and who could be trusted with special operations. Detached to State Department service, he secretly surveyed Santo Domingo to determine its suitability as a naval base.

Porter participated in several major naval engagements of the Mexican War. His operational experiences, although totaling only a few hours of battle, demonstrated his inventiveness and courage. He planned and helped to execute the naval bombardment on the defenses of Vera Cruz and, leading a sailors' charge on the fort at Tabasco, captured the works and earned command of his first steamship, the *Spitfire*.

After the war, Porter sought to captain a modern steamer, but the peacetime Navy could afford only sail craft, and he was reassigned to the Coast Survey. Like many other young officers, Porter, anticipating a lifetime as lieutenant with little chance of advancement in rank or duty, chose a safe, attractive alternative: he obtained leave and captained mail vessels between New York and San Francisco, thus gaining valuable experience in commanding large ocean steamships. On board the *Panama*, *Georgia*, and *Crescent City*, Porter tried to instill naval discipline into civilian crews. Although he was a formalist like his father, Porter's disciplinary methods were less punitive than paternal. He also gained popular notice by nearly re-creating his father's Fajardo incident when, at Havana in 1852, he refused to accept the closure of the port to his mail vessel and almost provoked war between the United States and Spain.

Porter soon gained a reputation for speed, even at the expense of his mail route. Setting new world records in the remarkable *Golden Age*, he cut the voyage from England to Australia by a third; the Melbourne-Sydney run in half. Porter's Australian adventures netted him something more valuable than money and experience: fame made him a national figure and raised him from the ranks of "one of the Porters." He became known in his own right for his energy, perseverance, and clever direction of "unusual enterprises."[2]

Porter returned to naval duty in the spring of 1855 to command the storeship *Supply*, ferrying camels from the Mediterranean to Texas for the War Department, and later served as executive officer of the Portsmouth (New Hampshire) Navy Yard. After three years' administration of inert peacetime shipbuilding, he negotiated for a return to civilian duty. At the age of forty-seven, having spent twenty years as a lieutenant, Porter was fully aware that his childhood heroes had made their careers at nearly half his age. As he debated between captaining another mail vessel or a Coast Survey schooner, Abraham Lincoln won the presidency, and the Southern states began to secede. Members of the Navy Department eyed each other with distrust as more Southern ports fell into Confederate hands and officers resigned to go south.

Porter seized the moment. Along with his neighbor, Army Captain Montgomery C. Meigs, Porter formulated plans to reinforce Fort Pickens and recapture Pensacola, Florida. Secretary of State William H. Seward took their plans to the President. Lincoln agreed that Pickens, like Fort Sumter, should be saved if at all possible, and he allowed Porter and Meigs to write their own orders and attempt the mission without the knowledge of their superiors. In addition, Porter wrote a cryptic order, over Lincoln's signature, attempting to restructure civilian control of naval policy by effectively reorganizing personnel detailing within the Navy Department.[3]

Porter charged off to New York and quickly fitted out his ship, the *Powhatan*. The President had second thoughts and had Secretary of the Navy Gideon Welles order Porter to give up the *Powhatan* to her assigned duty with Gustavus V. Fox's expedition to relieve Sumter, but neither Porter nor Meigs was willing to let his chance for action and advancement go by. Proclaiming Welles's telegram "bogus," they stalled by wiring Seward to confirm the order while they went to sea. By the time Seward's terse reply reached Porter, he had left the harbor and would not put back. Rationalizing that presidential orders outweighed cabinet ones, he politely refused to comply. With his experience of short wars and stalled promotions, this chance, he feared, might be his only one.[4]

Porter steamed toward Pensacola in an unsound ship with an untrained crew. Organizing en route, he drilled the men at the guns and disguised the ship as a mail steamer. Arriving near Pickens on 17 April 1861, Porter prepared to steam straight in and retake Pensacola by surprise, but Meigs stopped him. The Army was unwilling to provoke a battle before ensuring its own invulnerability, and the commanders wavered at disobeying presidential orders calling for strictly defensive operations. Frustrated, Porter raged up and down the harbor, surveyed the bay for shelling positions, and planned a night attack at the Army's convenience. It never happened. The Union Army retained Fort Pickens and gave up any attempt to retake Pensacola, a decision that Porter later called "the great disappointment of my life."[5]

The *Powhatan* incident had several repercussions. Lincoln learned to confide in his cabinet officers, Seward to keep his hands off naval affairs, and Welles to watch Porter. Although Lincoln assumed all responsibility for the diversion of the *Powhatan* from Sumter, Welles never forgave Porter. He did recognize, however, that in Porter he had an asset, a brash, ambitious officer who would prove aggressive in battle. As for Porter, his inability to control events in Pensacola harbor taught him that he must command more than a ship to effect a victory; the single-ship actions of his father's day would not suffice. Subsequent ineffectual blockading duty at the mouth of the Mississippi convinced him of the need to capture New Orleans, Louisiana.

The campaign for New Orleans was both a victory and a defeat for Porter, who overconfidently projected that a fleet of boats firing properly aimed army mortars could reduce the strong forts below within forty-eight hours, which allowed ships to run up and capture the city. The Union desperately needed a victory in the spring of 1862, particularly at New Orleans. Porter recommended that his foster brother Farragut lead the expedition. Porter, who received independent command of the mortar flotilla over the heads of senior officers, did not impress the rest of Farragut's command, who looked down on his ragtag fleet and his use of merchant marine captains. Farragut himself had almost no faith in the mortar fleet but accepted it along with the assignment.[6]

Despite scientific placement of the mortars and highly accurate fire, the forts withstood six days of heavy bombardment. Farragut changed strategy and ran past the forts at night. Porter covered the attempt with mortar fire and received the forts' surrender three days after Farragut took New Orleans. The mortar boats failed to destroy the forts, but Porter's plan to capture New Orleans succeeded by adaption. The mortars kept Confederate gunners under cover, helped the fleet to pass the forts, and disabled several of the enemy's best guns. More important, the psychological effect of Porter's relentless attack caused the men in Fort Jackson to mutiny.[7] After the surrender, the forts were found to be as strong as ever; Porter had won by perseverance. Lincoln recommended Porter for the thanks of Congress, both as a member of Farragut's command and separately for "distinguished services in the conception and preparation of the means used for the capture of the Forts below New Orleans, and for highly meritorious conduct in the management of the Mortar Flotilla."[8]

Following up the victory proved more difficult. Porter pushed for an attack on Mobile Bay, but the Navy Department ordered the fleet to Vicksburg, Mississippi. The city's defending river guns were placed high on terraces, and Porter, minus his survey ship, had to aim his mortars by trial and error. It proved another futile effort. Farragut's fleet successfully ran the Vicksburg batteries, but several vessels were badly damaged and Porter's flotilla suffered heavy casualties while covering him. Low water and low morale led to dissension, as Farragut's captains and Army Major General Benjamin F. Butler warred with Porter over credit for the New Orleans expedition. Soon, Porter wanted release from the Gulf Squadron so badly that he swore he would even prefer "to serve any where else in a yawl boat."[9]

As politics played an increasing role in the war effort, Porter's distaste for civilian meddling grew. He loathed political generals, such as Butler, yet used politics to advance his own career. He cultivated congressmen and developed close ties in the Navy Department with Assistant Secretary Fox, a trusted member of the Lincoln administration. When Porter angered Welles with outspoken criticism of the Union high command, the Secretary reassigned him to obscurity inspecting gunboats under construction at Cincinnati, Ohio. Faced with exile, Porter, the politician went over his superior's head to Lincoln.

Lincoln twice before had given Porter major commands beyond his rank, the *Powhatan* and the mortar flotilla, with only partial success. Still, Porter had qualities that Lincoln could use. His persuasiveness and determination, along with Fox's influence, convinced Lincoln that Porter was exactly the fighter he needed, for he gave him command of the Mississippi Squadron, the fleet above Vicksburg. Welles made the assignment grudgingly, noting that recklessness and energy were Porter's primary qualifications.[10]

Porter's new assignment had its good and bad points. Given the temporary and local rank of acting rear admiral, he controlled nearly all naval forces on the upper Mississippi, truly a partner with Farragut this time. Porter saw his elevation to rank and command over the heads of some eighty senior officers as retribution for his father's suspension.[11] To uphold his father's image and to attain permanent rank, Porter had to succeed on the Mississippi, but Porter's orders required him to cooperate in the capture of Vicksburg with Major General John A. McClernand, a distinctly political general with whom few people got along. The upper Mississippi was, moreover, the dumping ground for unpredictable commanders: Porter's disreputable elder brother William David was there with a ship that he had named the *Essex* in memory of their father.

With funds, authority, and amenable subordinates, Porter reorganized his command and worked quickly to bring the fleet up to the Navy's standards. Hearing nothing from McClernand, recruiting in Illinois, Porter offered his services to Major Generals Ulysses S. Grant and William T. Sherman. Almost immediate affinity marked their relations.[12] All three, professionals in a war of volunteers, disliked civilian interference, and their personalities, although distinctly different, meshed. Grant, the taciturn commander, worked well with

Sherman, whose fiery, outspoken leadership complemented Grant's more me-
thodical style. Porter and Sherman were of the same mold: emotional, tem-
peramental fighters, considered brilliant yet difficult; both unrelentingly energetic, they were impatient with slower men.

Nevertheless, their combination did not thrive from the start. Porter and
Sherman assaulted the bluffs north of Vicksburg near Chickasaw Bayou. The
loss of Grant's supply line kept him from supporting Sherman, whose defeat
in December 1862 proved that route to Vicksburg impossible. Porter, energetically supporting Sherman's advance and worrying Confederate troops in the
northern rivers, could do little more to effect a victory. McClernand's arrival
to command after the battle did not help.

McClernand brought to the field raw troops, a political appointment, a
drive for personal fame, and a new bride. Porter disliked McClernand but
agreed to support him in capturing Arkansas Post, where Sherman had planned
to secure their supply line and achieve a victory. So determined was Porter to
win that, when McClernand's green troops left the post's Fort Hindman in retreat, Porter boarded troops and prepared to take the fort himself. The surrender of the fort to Porter earned him Lincoln's gratitude and another vote of
thanks from Congress.[13] Grant soon supplanted McClernand on the river and
sought other routes through the swollen wintry swamps to Vicksburg.

In an effort to circumvent the batteries at Vicksburg, Grant's army dug
canals as Porter and Sherman unsuccessfully attempted to turn the northern
flank of Vicksburg at Yazoo Pass and Steele's Bayou. While Porter was upriver,
two important vessels were captured by Confederates. Having nothing to send
down to save them, Porter and his men rigged up a dummy monitor from an
old barge and pork barrels. As it floated by in the dark, the monster frightened
Vicksburg and stampeded the Confederates into destroying the *Indianola* to
prevent her recapture. The effect of this ruse delighted Porter and he later used
another dummy monitor to draw fire at Wilmington, North Carolina. The
Navy Department fully appreciated Porter's often unusual attempts to recover
something from every loss.[14]

On 16 April 1863, under cover of darkness, Porter ran part of his fleet safely
past the Vicksburg batteries. While Sherman feinted north to Haynes' Bluff,
Porter bombarded Grand Gulf and covered Grant's crossing at Bruinsburg.
With three days' rations and no supply line, Grant set out overland to take
Vicksburg. Porter, eager for action, destroyed the abandoned Grand Gulf, then
assisted Farragut in a run up the Confederate supply line of Red River, capturing Fort De Russy and Alexandria, Louisiana. Grant and Porter opened a
concentrated attack on Vicksburg on 22 May before settling into a siege.

Porter maintained Grant's supply line, fired steadily on the city, fought guer-
rillas, and kept communications open to Washington. His passage of the Vicks-

burg batteries signaled the beginning of the end for the South. Confederate agents in London credited Porter with depressing their loan rate overseas. Porter's achievement and the anticipated fall of Vicksburg dominated all conversation in Washington, with most observers believing that success at Vicksburg would decide the war.[15] All Porter had to do for his coveted promotion was to support Grant, but he was too much of a fighter to wait patiently.

Within six weeks, Porter's forces captured fourteen Confederate forts above Vicksburg, destroyed more than $2 million worth of Confederate naval stores and ships building on the Yazoo, and assisted in demoralizing Vicksburg with desertion propaganda and constant shelling. The city surrendered on 4 July 1863, and Porter immediately followed up the victory with a series of raids on inland waterways to Yazoo City and up the Red and White Rivers. Lincoln shared the spoils of victory with those most responsible; he promoted Porter to permanent rear admiral to date from the fall of Vicksburg.[16]

Porter's last major campaign in the west, up the Red River in the spring of 1864, was the fiasco he expected it to be.[17] Ordered to command the naval arm of the attack toward Shreveport, Louisiana, in cooperation with Major General Nathaniel P. Banks, Porter doubted that the river would provide sufficient draft for his vessels and that he would want to attempt operations with another political general. He was right on both counts. There was little coordination between the two commands. When Banks finally arrived at the rendezvous point over a week late, he found Porter and the Navy chasing prize cotton on the river. Once operations began, Porter sent his largest vessel upriver first, and she grounded, further delaying cooperation. The water fell rapidly, and Banks abandoned the Navy after his repulse at Sabine Crossroads, Louisiana.

Porter's fleet had to fight its way downriver, but it was not the sort of fight he liked. Confederates with artillery ambushed the unprotected naval vessels. Porter got his fleet safely down to Alexandria, only to be stranded above the city in less than four feet of water. Without the support of Regular Army officers and an ingenious Army dam to float the boats over the bar, Porter would have been unable to extricate his command. The Army, the Navy, and his own men, by condemning Banks for his incompetency, preserved Porter's reputation despite his costly errors of judgment.[18]

Porter, ordered from one disaster to another, had no time to make up for this defeat. Welles brought him east to command the North Atlantic Blockading Squadron off North Carolina, where the only remaining port supplying General Robert E. Lee's army remained open at Wilmington. Porter used every stratagem he had learned in the war to tighten the blockade. He built up a powerful naval force, tightened cordon lines, and decoyed in $2 million worth of prizes, but only the capture of strategic Fort Fisher would close the port. Porter asked Grant for troops, and he agreed; when the Army finally appeared, Butler was leading. Porter, livid, treated Butler cordially, while privately damning Grant unfairly for sending the politician.[19]

Porter's and Butler's attack on Fort Fisher in December 1864 failed primarily because of distrust between the two commanders. Butler planned to destroy the fort by exploding an old ship loaded with gunpowder. Neither naval nor army engineers believed it would work, but Butler pressed, and Porter acquiesced. Butler kept most of his plans secret, which led to a long string of misunderstandings. The explosion failed, as expected.

Porter bombarded the fort to cover Butler's landing, but Butler chose not to assault, as Porter hoped he would, or to entrench, as Grant ordered him to. Instead, he retreated, leaving behind several hundred men. Lincoln relieved Butler of command, and Brevet Major General Alfred H. Terry replaced him in a second attempt at the fort.

The stakes were high. Lee believed that Union capture of Forts Fisher and Caswell would force the evacuation of Richmond, Virginia. A second failure would sustain Butler. As insurance, in case the Army should fail him again, Porter drilled a landing party of sixteen hundred sailors and four hundred marines to storm the fort. Porter and Terry cooperated fully. Between the two men there were no secrets, and their determination effected a true combination.[20]

The attack of the naval landing party failed, but it diverted the fort's defenders from the Army landing. Seven difficult hours later, the fort surrendered to Terry. The Confederates, forced to evacuate Caswell, fell back on Wilmington; pursued by Porter and Terry, they abandoned the last port in the Confederacy in January 1865. There was little left for the Navy to do. Porter went up the James River to Grant's headquarters at City Point, southeast of Richmond, where his final war duties included attending strategy conferences on board the *River Queen* with Lincoln, Grant, and Sherman, and escorting the President around captured Petersburg, Virginia, and Richmond.

Most of Porter's fame stems from his actions in combined operations. Although he was strategically clearsighted, his tactical plans, as first conceived, rarely worked. Luckily, he directed most maneuvers with enough personal autonomy to change course halfway and push the object through to success, at times by sheer force of will. Porter's strength was in special operations, and his fighting personality accentuated his ability to follow up nearly every setback with a victory.

Porter's campaigns depended on Army operations for success. At Chickasaw Bayou and then during the Yazoo Pass expedition, complete military cooperation would not overcome the barriers of geography, weather, and Confederate strength. Lack of coordination of forces up the Red River and in the first attack on Fort Fisher doomed the efforts from the start. Porter's successes, notably at Arkansas Post, Vicksburg, and the second attempt at Fort Fisher, were due in no small part to the personalities of the commanders involved. Porter worked well with those who fought but poorly with those who hesitated.

The war made Porter both famous and controversial. His ambition, hunger for publicity and prize money, and swift advancement offended many whom he had surpassed. Peace brought a new set of problems for Gideon Welles, among them the question of what to do with Porter. He could not be sent to sea: his oft-stated belief that those countries that had supported the Confederacy should pay, particularly Great Britain, might lead him to provoke a foreign war. Porter never made any secret of his wish to command the U.S. Naval Academy and "get the right set of officers into the Navy."[21] His wide fame and belief in strong discipline could only help the troubled institution, which, although removed north, had barely survived the war intact.

The wartime Naval Academy had taken scant notice of changing technology and encouraged no physical activities. Drinking sprees were the prime extracurricular recreation, and an antiquated demerit system proved ineffectual in controlling student abuses. The academy was, in fact, only slightly more than a secondary school and taught midshipmen little that they could use to command ships.[22] Porter believed that the academy's purpose was to train officers for naval war. Installed as superintendent in 1865, he imprinted the academy with his own philosophy of practicality and professionalism; he was determined to make it the rival of West Point, whose graduates had impressed him with just those qualities.[23]

Porter began his tenure by strictly enforcing discipline. Common infractions included hazing, drinking, and taking "French leave," none of which Porter took lightly. "The first duty of an officer," he taught, "is to obey."[24] He proved to the midshipmen that he was serious. On a single day in October 1865, Porter issued orders requiring regular small-arms drills, dress parades, an oath of allegiance, and an eight-year service obligation. Further, he repealed all upper-class privileges for those forced to repeat a year and organized recreation times, cleverly keyed to begin as soon as drill obligations were properly completed. Porter supplemented the demerit system with practical punishments; as at West Point, guard duty and drill, assigned by severity of the offense, were used to enforce discipline.[25]

Before Porter's arrival, few extracurricular activities had been organized to keep midshipmen out of trouble. Porter realistically decided that sports would give the young men an outlet for their frustrations. He built a gymnasium and especially encouraged fencing, boxing, bowling, shooting, and baseball. One never knew when Superintendent Porter might enter the ring to box the first classmen, and he especially hated losing a game of baseball. He encouraged competition within the academy and took his midshipmen to West Point for intercollegiate athletic trials.[26]

Porter also insisted on an honor system "to send honorable men from this institution into the Navy."[27] He designed uniforms, fostered music and drama clubs, invited midshipmen to test their gentlemanly behavior at tea, and led regular dancing parties. Lying and drinking earned his severest reproof, and he worked to close Annapolis brothels. He exhorted the midshipmen to act like officers and not "common sailors." Unashamedly elitist, Porter even recommended denying admission to candidates who were cross-eyed, "common looking," or too old. If he interfered with every aspect of the midshipmen's private lives, at least he stood by them, and occasionally directed a redress in grades or accepted an apology in lieu of punishment.[28]

Porter redesigned the academy curriculum. He emphasized lectures over textbooks and required courses in seamanship, gunnery, naval construction, practical navigation, and steam engineering. Midshipmen learned to operate fully rigged ship models, drill with mortars, run and repair steam engines, strip sails on ships in record time, and give exhibitions of steam tactics and seamanship. Porter enlarged the department of steam engineering with a new building housing a working engine and several boilers and required three years of courses and a practical knowledge of steam engines of each graduate.

He successfully dabbled in politics to keep the academy afloat. Seeking support for a growing school during intense fiscal retrenchment, Porter invited politicians to review dress parades and exhibitions of naval tactics. He never failed to publicize the academy or to impress visitors. As a result of his political influence and the growing prestige of the academy under his direction, appropriations increased despite national budget cuts. With ideological renewal, congressional appropriations, and stringent economy, Porter physically rebuilt the academy: he spent $225,000 for buildings and alterations and purchased more than 130 acres of adjacent land.[29]

Despite Porter's fame as an operational commander, his most enduring legacy was his whole philosophy of naval discipline and leadership, embedded in the academy and learned, he said, from his father. By strictly charging the midshipmen themselves with responsibility for their actions and the future of their institution, he made them aware of their elite status as naval leaders. Although Porter may have indeed "set the tone" for the modern-day Naval Academy, he did so by pinning that obligation on the midshipmen themselves, particularly on the first class.[30]

Porter restored pride to the academy. Grant and Sherman convinced him by their own examples that, despite West Point's reputation as the premier engineering school in America, it did not necessarily turn out only engineers and theoreticians but men trained in the basics of the military profession: discipline, duty, honor, obedience, command—principles transcending service divisions. Such basic officer training also suited Porter's daily expectations of foreign war.

Americans in peacetime have rarely supported a standing army or navy; the aftermath of the Civil War was no exception. Four years of expensive warfare put the United States ahead of its contemporaries in technology. Much of the rest of the world took America's advances and improved upon them. Naval vessels of the war period were soon outdated, and few Americans supported their replacement. The naval stagnation following the Civil War probably could not have been avoided short of the war that Porter anticipated. Americans, if anything, were sick of war, and believed peace to be permanent.

The Army fared better than the Navy in the postwar world. Battlefield brevet and volunteer rankings faded away with war's end and left in the service only those who had earned Regular Army promotions. The Army also had posts to maintain in the South and in the West, where Indians opposed the settlement by whites. Sherman, as lieutenant general and general, retained some active control over operations. Porter had no such power in his corresponding roles as vice admiral and admiral. With no offensive mission, the Navy had no role for ranking officers.

Congressmen, unwilling to fund advanced naval technology in peace, got only what they paid for—the U.S. Navy of their fathers, not that of their sons. Demobilization forced the Navy into a limited world mission until the 1890s, a rational approach to economic reality. Congress wanted a floating police force and saw no need to compete with European technology. Naval officers disagreed over the process of inevitable retrenchment and sought to protect their own definitions of a peacetime navy.[31]

Welles was proud of his success in directing the naval war and did not take kindly to any suggestions to share power in peace. Welles's burgeoning naval bureaucracy greatly expanded the powers of the Navy's bureau system. His raises in relative rankings and prerogatives for staff officers in support positions, and his recall of retired officers at high rank, bloated the officer class. Postwar retrenchment hit ranking line officers hardest, or so they perceived. With their ships laid up and promotion stagnant, staff officers and the bureau system, not Welles, bore the brunt of line officers' blame. The line/staff controversy, renewed and confused by technological issues and exacerbated by Welles's intransigence, erupted into war within the Navy. Behind the battles lay the real issue: who should control the Navy?

Porter's role in the naval controversies created his image as an operational progressive and a technological reactionary, while his fighting personality defined his perception of the naval establishment. Porter believed that the Navy's mission was war and that preparation for future wars was its peacetime occupation. Offensive purpose defined his view of naval administration, which he believed should remain strictly in the hands of experienced operational officers. "The Navy," he declared, "will be dead for many years to come unless we have another war."[32]

Technology, particularly steam engineering, was an important side issue in the controversy over control of the Navy. Neither Congress nor the American public would pay for advanced military technology. Between 1865 and 1869, the Navy's budget declined 84 percent. A great portion of that budget went to the Bureau of Steam Engineering, where Benjamin Franklin Isherwood still spent money at wartime levels.[33] Isherwood further offended line officers by seemingly placing the interests of machines over those of men. The attacks of Porter and the line officers on the status quo reflected the real anxieties of men who feared replacement by technology or by men of different abilities.

Porter did not hate engineers; he hated theoreticians—impractical, inflexible, wasteful men who built vessels but never sailed them—who understood machines but could not make them run. Isherwood's prize ship, the *Wampanoag*, was Porter's pet peeve, the symbol of technological inefficiency—the fastest ship in the world, built at an exorbitant cost, with insufficient room to house the men needed to run her, let alone those needed for naval maneuvers. That Isherwood, entrenched in the bureau, had sufficient power to control the direction of naval shipbuilding policy reaffirmed Porter's belief that the bureau system was faulty. Despite Porter's lengthy campaign to remove Isherwood and restore line supremacy, however, the two men remained friends and supported each other professionally in later years.[34]

Porter never hated Isherwood; his attacks were a means to an end. Porter wanted to revive and lead his father's old Board of Navy Commissioners and made several unsuccessful attempts to have Congress restore it. His insistence on the importance of line officers controlling the Navy had led him to replace staff officers with line officers in teaching positions at the academy.

In 1869, when Grant assumed the presidency, he appointed Adolph E. Borie as Secretary of the Navy and assigned Porter to special duty as his assistant, a rudimentary chief of naval operations. Porter took personal control of the Navy Department at the most visible levels and immediately issued a blizzard of sweeping general orders, twelve in one day, over Borie's signature. He reduced staff prerogatives and defined those of the line; he redesigned uniforms to reflect the staff's lower status and ranking. Further orders limited the power of the bureaus to internal matters, consolidated squadrons, renamed vessels, and organized a line board of ship examiners. Porter's most controversial orders were among his last. He delayed reducing the relative rankings of the staff officers to pre-Welles levels until a legal basis for it could be found. His orders requiring full sail power in all naval ships and strictly limiting the use of coal, along with the condemnation of Isherwood's ships by a board of line officers, were the parting shots of Porter's short administration.[35]

Behind Porter's attempted reforms of 1869 lay the threat of war with Great Britain. American diplomats were then negotiating reparations due the United

States for Britain's assistance to the Confederacy. Porter wanted war, especially with Great Britain, and he wanted a navy prepared for war. At the Naval Academy he prepared men for command and for war; in the department, he attempted to do the same. He endeavored to restore unity to a fragmented command structure by returning control to the Secretary and removing it from the bureaus. The Secretary, or his assistant, Porter, would command the naval forces in any coming war. Unfortunately for Porter, his war did not materialize. His reputation was the major casualty of his own administration.

Porter knew that the U.S. Navy could not match the Royal Navy, but he insisted on strengthening all natural advantages. General Orders 128 and 131 did no more than adopt international naval policies. British regulations requiring sails and restricting coal use were far harsher than Porter's—coal was expensive and engines were inefficient in 1869. In declaring steam auxiliary to full sail power, Porter capitalized on the natural resources of men and wind while directly overturning Welles's emphasis on steam over sails. Porter's orders prescribed readiness and constant exercise. He wanted the Navy to be ready for immediate action with maximum efficiency. A master at improvising, Porter convinced Congress to fund Naval Academy expansion through a combination of politics, prestige, and stringent recycling. He hoped, by using similar tactics, to convince Congress to fund a real naval fighting force.

Borie never wanted to run the Navy and was happy to sign over full authority to Porter, who issued orders in Borie's name until the furor over Porter's arbitrariness, impatience, and high-handedness made Borie's life miserable. After three months, Borie resigned, and Grant replaced him with George Robeson, who eased Porter from his position of power. Within one year, Porter's influence had so declined that he claimed he did not enter the Navy Department's headquarters more than four times between 1870 and 1876.[36]

Despite strong political opposition, Porter—promoted to admiral in 1870—remained on active duty until his death in 1891. During those last twenty-one years he wrote regular advisory reports, sat on inspection boards, and worked to develop naval higher education. His few duties were unimportant, and his opinions were generally ignored. Unhappy with semiretirement, he still sought to influence naval policy and continued to send in an unwanted yearly report.[37] Despite Porter's advocacy of a stronger coastal defense, he retained his vision of offensive naval purpose. His reports, in the form of incomplete, repetitive letters addressed to successive secretaries, sought immediate, effective answers to contemporary problems. Read as statements of policy, they seem foolish today; in the context of their intent, they are extremely revealing.

Porter, the product of a maritime nation, lived in an emerging industrial age. The Civil War destroyed America's commercial shipping industry whereas it strengthened the British carrying trade. The United States failed to recover its oceanic trade or its maritime reserve during Porter's lifetime. From 1870 until 1889, Porter fought a losing battle to restore U.S. maritime eminence, which enhanced his image as a reactionary against industrialization. He appreciated new technology but thought the training of men as important as the building of ships. Nothing in Porter's experience prepared him for an age when the needs of ships would outweigh those of men.

Machine dominance was by no means certain until after his death. Science and technology advanced slowly; not until 1880 were the first and second laws of thermodynamics usable in creating efficient steam engines. By 1884, steam predominated, which led the Navy to reduce sail power and, by 1889, to begin establishing the international fuel depots that Porter believed were necessary for a steam navy. Only as technology and foreign policy changed did Porter's advocacy of coastal defense and commerce raiding appear outdated; even Alfred Thayer Mahan supported such a program in 1885. Until instant obsolescence of naval vessels was controlled, the Navy remained transitional.[38]

What Porter advocated was naval diversification. He wanted improved forts; rams and monitors for defense; fast commerce raiders to cripple future enemy shipping; advanced submarine torpedo-firing boats for both offense and defense; and, ultimately, steel ships.[39] He opposed rebuilding the Navy around only one type of ship. Rather than returning the Navy to the age of sail, he sought to keep it flexible. He advocated constant exercise of existing ships and squadrons, development of new vessels, education of all naval personnel, modernization of armament, and subsidization of a new merchant marine. The 1874 sea trials in the West Indies following the *Virginius* crisis forced Porter into a more defensive position and convinced him that what little navy Congress allowed would be destroyed in the inevitable war; however, by 1881, he spoke of planning "a navy for *home defense,* but, of course, in time of war we should not be willing to rest quietly guarding our coast."[40]

On the eve of the New Navy, Porter reargued diversity, defense, and dedication and reasserted the necessity of rebuilding America's lost prestige as a maritime nation. He urged officers at the struggling Naval War College to exchange ideas about the new types of strategy and tactics needed for the battles of the future. Porter decried Congress's attempts to rebuild the Navy overnight, quoting from Mirabeau to express his own naval philosophy: "You cannot have a navy without sailors, and sailors are made through the dangers of the deep, from father to son, until their home is on the wave. You cannot build up a navy at once by a simple act of legislation."[41]

Despite his high rank, Porter had no voice in the Navy. Embittered, he turned to writing to gain an audience. His first and best work, *Memoir of Commodore David Porter* (1875), attempted to justify his father's career as well as his own. His later works, particularly his *Incidents and Anecdotes of the Civil War* (1885) and *Naval History of the Civil War* (1886), rank with some of his personal correspondence in the magnitude of their inaccuracy. Porter fired words like grapeshot, indiscriminately, in haste, and in often regretted rash comments.

The deaths of Porter and Sherman, one day apart, ended an era. Of the Union heroes of the Civil War, they were the last of the high command. Porter was excoriated by navalists of an expansionist, steam-powered world for advocating sails and a defensive strategy; by surviving political generals for his hatred of them; and by the many men with whom he argued in print in the pages of the various naval and maritime journals. They either damned him in print for his personality or mentioned him only for his operational victories.

Commodore Porter's sons never escaped their father. William David Porter, disinherited by his family, named his ship the *Essex* and, at his death, was buried next to his father, who had actively loathed him.[42] David Dixon Porter never saw the restoration of the maritime splendor of his father's age, but he surrounded himself with mementos of the commodore and retained many of his sociable habits. He easily eclipsed his father in the happiness of his relationships with his friends, his wife, and his children, but the Porter name advanced his career when his own actions failed to. Despite his rank and achievements, he never quite believed that his career was more successful than his father's.

One of Porter's subordinates said that it was a naval tradition that "the Porters were all brave and all braggarts," and David Dixon Porter was no exception.[43] He organized chaos into order, executed seemingly impossible tasks, cooperated well with anyone who respected him and gave him sufficient credit, and implacably hated those who did not. His boundless energy and pursuit of knowledge invigorated the Naval Academy. He helped found the U.S. Naval Institute and an experimental torpedo school (the progenitor of the Naval Underwater Systems Center), and influenced Stephen B. Luce's determination to make the Naval War College the home for the study of the art of war at sea.[44] Porter lived in the ages of both sail and steam, wooden ships and steel, and appreciated the qualities of each. His fighting spirit, the legacy of David Porter, for better or worse, affected all that he did.

FURTHER READING

David Dixon Porter has always provoked much comment in print. His associations with many of the nineteenth-century military and political figures have caused much speculation, and opinions concerning each facet of his life are often conflicting. The best and standard biography of Porter is Richard Sedgewick West, Jr.'s *The Second Admiral: A Life of David Dixon Porter, 1813–1891* (New York, 1937), which, although favorable, is realistic about many of his shortcomings throughout the Civil War period.

James Russell Soley's *Admiral Porter* (New York, 1903) and Noel Bertram Gerson's *Yankee Admiral: A Biography of David Dixon Porter* (New York, 1968) provide interesting insights but lack documentation. Porter's childhood is best illustrated in David F. Long's *Nothing Too Daring: A Biography of Commodore David Porter, 1780–1843* (Annapolis, Md., 1970). The "Camel Corps" of the 1850s has been the subject of several short books and articles, and, as it pertains to Porter, is outlined in Malcolm W. Cagle's "Lieutenant David Dixon Porter and His Camels," U.S. Naval Institute *Proceedings* 83 (December 1957): 1327–33.

Studies of the war period abound with references to Porter's activities, but West's *Second Admiral* remains the best source for the war as it relates to Porter. Porter's war career is ably related in several articles, particularly William N. Still, "'Porter . . . Is the Best Man': This Was Gideon Welles's View of the Man He Chose to Command the Mississippi Squadron," *Civil War Times Illustrated* 16, no. 2 (1977): 5; a chapter of Caroll Storrs Alden and Ralph Earle, *Makers of Naval Tradition*, rev. ed. (Boston, 1943); and Richard West's "The Relations between Farragut and Porter," U.S. Naval Institute *Proceedings* 61 (July 1935): 985–96. Ludwell H. Johnson's Red River Campaign: Politics and Cotton in the Civil War (Baltimore, 1958) goes beyond the normal campaign history to describe the outside influences that affected this operation, particularly as they relate to individuals, and ably describes Porter's errors of judgment.

Porter's postwar career is best discussed in Kenneth J. Hagan, *American Gunboat Diplomacy and the Old Navy, 1877–1889* (Westport, Conn., 1973) and "Admiral David Dixon Porter: Strategist for a Navy in Transition," U.S. Naval Institute *Proceedings* 94 (July 1968): 139–43; Charles O. Paullin, "A Half Century of Naval Administration in America, 1861–1911: Part IV. The Navy Department under Grant and Hayes, 1869–1881," U.S. Naval Institute *Proceedings* 39 (1913): 736–60; Lance C. Buhl, "Mariners and Machines: Resistance to Technological Change in the American Navy, 1865–1869," *Journal of American History* 61 (1974): 703–77; Park Benjamin's *The United States Naval Academy* (New York, 1900); and Edward William Sloan III's *Benjamin Franklin Isherwood, Naval Engineer: The Years as Engineer in Chief, 1861–1869* (Annapolis, Md., 1965). Porter's own writings, written mostly in reaction to his postwar inactivity, should not be relied on for specific facts, although they reveal clearly his personality.

NOTES

1. The chaotic Porter family relationships are best described in David F. Long, *Nothing Too Daring: A Biography of Commodore David Porter, 1780–1843* (Annapolis, Md., 1970), and Richard Sedgewick West, Jr., *The Second Admiral: A Life of David Dixon Porter, 1813–1891* (New York, 1937). For David Dixon Porter's idealized view of his father, see his *Memoir of Commodore David Porter, of the United States Navy* (Albany, N.Y., 1875).

2. West, *Second Admiral*, 63.

3. Lincoln to Porter, 1 April 1861, *Offical Records of the Union and Confederate Navies in the War of the Rebellion*, ser. 1, vol. 4, 108–9 (hereafter cited as ORN). Also, see Lincoln to Welles, 1 April 1861, in Roy P. Basler, ed., *Collected Works of Abraham Lincoln*, 9 vols. (New Brunswick, N.J., 1953–1955), 4:318–19. The appointment, over Lincoln's signature, of Samuel Barron to head the Office of Detail received much attention after the war by anti-Porter factions, who saw in it an attempt by Porter to place

a Southerner, and one who ultimately sided with the Confederacy, in a place of importance in the Navy Department. In reality, both Lincoln and Welles were also in the
process of appointing to responsible commands men who would later turn Confederate.
Welles certainly detested Porter's attempt to alter Navy Department policy, but he made
a public issue of Porter's selection of Barron only after the war, when politics intervened.
Porter had as many Southern connections as most officers in this war, but even Welles
admitted Porter proved his loyalty to the Union cause in action. Barron's appointment,
in Meigs's handwriting, with Porter's postscript, had the approval of Secretary of State
Seward. For Welles's postwar view, see Howard K. Beale and Alan W. Brownswood, eds.,
*Diary of Gideon Welles, Secretary of the Navy under Lincoln and Johnson*, 3 vols. (New
York, 1960), 1:16–21, and Gideon Welles, "Facts in Relation to the Expedition Ordered
by the Administration of President Lincoln for the Relief of the Garrison in Fort Sumter,"
*The Galaxy* 10 (November 1870), reprinted in *Selected Essays by Gideon Welles: Civil
War and Reconstruction*, compiled by Albert Mordell (New York, 1959).

    4. Porter to [A. H. Foote], [5 April 1861] ORN, ser. 1, vol. 4, 111–12; Seward to Porter,
6 April 1861, ibid., 4:112; and Porter to Seward, 6 April 1861, ibid.

    5. Porter to [Captain H. A. Adams], 24 August 1862, ibid., 130.

    6. West, *Second Admiral*, 114; Richard West, "The Relations between Farragut and
Porter," U.S. Naval Institute *Proceedings* 61 (July 1935): 989; and Loyall Farragut, *The
Life and Letters of Admiral Farragut, First Admiral of the United States Navy* (New York,
1879), 210.

    7. Lieutenant Colonel Edmund Higgins, CSA, to Lieutenant William M. Bridges,
CSA, 30 April 1862, David Dixon Porter Papers, Library of Congress (hereafter cited as
DDP, DLC).

    8. Lincoln to Senate and House of Representatives, 14 May 1862, in Basler, *Col-
lected Works of Lincoln*, 5:215n, and 11 July 1862, in ibid., 315–16.

    9. Porter to Fox, 22 June 1862, DDP, DLC.

    10. David Dixon Porter, *Incidents and Anecdotes of the Civil War* (New York, 1885),
120–22; and Beale and Brownswood, *Diary of Gideon Welles*, 1 October 1862, vol. 1,
157–58; ibid., 10 October 1862, 1:167. Welles glumly recorded his advancement of Porter
in his diary, noting many more of Porter's negative than his positive qualities, and questioning Porter's ability to succeed, sighing, "If he does well I shall get no credit; if he
fails I shall be blamed." Ibid., 1:157–58. Given his negativism and Porter's distinct mission to assist Lincoln's special forces under Major General John A. McClernand, it is
more likely that Fox and Lincoln decided on Porter's assignment and Welles acquiesced. Welles was later able to impress Lincoln with the first news of the fall of Vicksburg, making Welles briefly Porter's strong supporter.

    11. William N. Still, "'Porter . . . Is the Best Man': This Was Gideon Welles's View
of the Man He Chose to Command the Mississippi Squadron," *Civil War Times Illustrated* 16, no. 2 (1977): 5.

    12. Porter to Fox, 17 October 1862, in Robert Means Thompson and Richard Wain-
wright, eds., *Confidential Correspondence of Gustavus Vasa Fox, Assistant Secretary of
the Navy, 1861–1865*, 2 vols. (New York, 1920), 2:140; Porter to Fox, 21 October 1862, in
ibid., 2:143; and Sherman to [John Sherman], 14 December 1862, in Rachel Sherman
Thorndike, ed., *The Sherman Letters: Correspondence between General Sherman and
Senator Sherman from 1837 to 1891* (New York, 1969 [1894]), 174–75.

    13. William T. Sherman, *Memoir of William T. Sherman Written by Himself*, 2 vols.
(New York, 1875), 1:297; Lloyd Lewis, *Sherman, Fighting Prophet* (New York, 1932),

257–61; West, *Second Admiral*, 199; Fox to Porter, 6 February 1863, in Thompson and Wainwright, *Confidential Correspondence of Fox*, 2:156; Lincoln to Congress, 28 January 1863, in Basler, *Collected Works of Lincoln*, 6:82; and Lincoln to Congress, 19 February 1863, in ibid., 6:111–12.

14. Porter to Welles, 10 March 1863, in *War of the Rebellion: A Compilation of the Official Records of the Union and Confederate Armies* (hereafter cited as OR), ser. 1, vol. 24, pt. 3, 97–98; Porter to Fox, 19 February 1864, in Thompson and Wainwright, *Confidential Correspondence of Fox*, 2:200–01; and Fox to Porter, 16 July 1863, in ibid., 2:185.

15. Henry Hotze to Judah P. Benjamin, 9 May 1863, ORN, ser. 2, 3:760; Hotze to Benjamin, 14 May 1863, ibid., 3:768; West, *Second Admiral*, 229–30.

16. West, *Second Admiral*, 231–32; and Lincoln to the Senate, 8 December 1863, in Basler, *Collected Works of Lincoln*, 7:56–57.

17. Porter anticipated problems with the water level before the expedition. See Sherman to Grant, 4 January 1864, in John Y. Simon, ed., *Papers of Ulysses S. Grant* (hereafter cited as PUSG), 14 vols. to date (Carbondale, Ill., 1967– ), 10:20. Porter also knew Banks and had previously noted his unwillingness to assist other commands. See, for example, Porter to Grant, 14 May 1863, OR, ser. 1, vol. 24, pt. 3, 309, and Porter to Grant, 10 June 1863, PUSG, 8:335.

18. Ludwell H. Johnson, *Red River Campaign: Politics and Cotton in the Civil War* (Baltimore, 1958), 241; and Porter to Sherman, 14 April 1864, OR, ser. 1, vol. 34, pt. 3, 153–54. Examples of army opinions on Banks are in PUSG, 10:340, 351–52, and 429.

19. Porter's condemnation of Grant, soon regretted, was printed in newspapers and an anti-Porter tract in 1876. See Porter to Welles, 24 January 1865, in F. Colburn Adams, *High Old Salts: Stories Intended for the Marines, but Told before an Enlightened Committee of Congress* (Washington, D.C., 1876), 32–36.

20. West, *Second Admiral*, 288; Grant to Terry, 3 January 1865, PUSG, 13:219; and Porter to Grant, 14 January 1865, ibid., 13:227.

21. Porter to Fox, 28 March 1862, Thompson and Wainwright, *Confidential Correspondence of Fox*, 2:95.

22. Park Benjamin, *The United States Naval Academy* (New York, 1900), 266–71. Also, see Charles Todorich, *The Spirited Years: A History of the Antebellum Naval Academy* (Annapolis, Md., 1984).

23. Porter to Welles, 25 September 1866, U.S. Navy Department, *Annual Report of the Secretary of the Navy*, 1866, 76 (hereafter cited as *Annual Report*, [year]); and James Russell Soley, "Eulogy," in *A Memorial of David Dixon Porter from the City of Boston* (Boston, 1891), 63.

24. Porter Order, 14 October 1865, in Record Group (RG) 405, No. 48, Press Copies of Orders Issued by the Superintendent, 1865–1869, National Archives (hereafter cited as RG 405: Superintendent's Orders), 1:19–20.

25. Porter to Welles, 18 October 1865, RG 45, No. 34, Letters from Commandants of Navy Yards and Shore Stations, Naval Academy, National Archives (hereafter cited as RG 45: Naval Academy Letters), 246:48; Porter Order, 24 October 1865, RG 405: Superintendent's Orders, 1:43; and Porter Order, undated, ibid., 1:52.

26. Benjamin, *Naval Academy*, 266–67; Todorich, *Spirited Years*, 39; Walter Aamold, "Athletic Training at the Naval Academy," U.S. Naval Institute *Proceedings* 61 (October 1935): 1562.

27. Porter Order, 21 November 1865, RG 405: Superintendent's Orders, 1:82–83.

28. Porter Order, 11 January 1866, ibid., 1:125–26; Porter Order, 2 June 1867, ibid.,

1:540–42; Porter to Welles, 19 December 1865, RG 45: Naval Academy Letters, 246:110; Porter Special Order, 24 October 1865, RG 405: Superintendent's Orders, 1:45; and Porter Order, 21 November 1865, ibid., 1:82–83.

29. Report of Board of Visitors, 4 June 1869, *Annual Report*, 1869, 137.

30. Porter Order, [30] September 1867, RG 405: Superintendent's Orders, 1:582–88.

31. Lance C. Buhl, "Maintaining An American Navy, 1865–1889," in Kenneth J. Hagan, ed., *In Peace and War: Interpretations of American Naval History, 1775–1984* (Westport, Conn., 1978), 145–70.

32. Porter to John Barnes, 25 February 1869, quoted in Peter Karsten, *The Naval Aristocracy: The Golden Age of Annapolis and the Emergence of Modern American Navalism* (New York, 1972), 266.

33. Charles O. Paullin, "A Half Century of Naval Administration in America, 1861–1911: Part IV. The Navy Department under Grant and Hayes, 1869–1881," U.S. Naval Institute *Proceedings* 39 (1913): 744; Edward William Sloan III, *Benjamin Franklin Isherwood, Naval Engineer: The Years as Engineer in Chief, 1861–1869* (Annapolis, Md., 1965), 199.

34. Sloan, *Isherwood*, 240.

35. General Order No. 89, 10 March 1869; General Orders Nos. 90, 91, 94, 95, 96, 97, and 99, 11 March 1869; General Order No. 105, 13 March 1869; General Orders Nos. 108 and 109, 15 March 1869; General Order No. 124, 15 May 1869; General Order No. 130, 15 June 1869; and Circular, "Duties of Bureaus to Commence May 15, 1869," all in RG 45, No. 43, 'Directives,' DNA.

36. Although later navalists, notably Harold Sprout and Margaret Sprout, *The Rise of American Naval Power, 1776–1918* (Princeton, N.J., 1939), and Samuel W. Bryant, *The Sea and the States: A Maritime History of the American People* (New York, 1947), claim that Porter controlled naval policies under Robeson, there is no evidence to support this. Porter's lack of influence in naval matters is reported in Paullin, "A Half Century of Naval Administration," 750, and is mentioned in Porter to William C. Whitney, 30 November 1885, *Annual Report*, 1885, 280.

37. Porter to William H. Hunt, 19 June 1881, *Annual Report*, 1881, 95.

38. Lance C. Buhl, "Mariners and Machines: Resistance to Technological Change in the American Navy, 1865–1869," *Journal of American History* 61 (1974): 709; Kenneth J. Hagan, *American Gunboat Diplomacy and the Old Navy, 1877–1889* (Westport, Conn., 1973), 19–27; and Karsten, *Naval Aristocracy*, 312, 334.

39. Porter to Hunt, 19 June 1881, *Annual Report*, 1881, 102, 216; and Porter to William E. Chandler, 19 November 1883, *Annual Report*, 1883, 390–405. Porter early advocated abandonment of wood for all-metal shipbuilding. See "Lecture delivered before the 2nd Class of Midshipmen at the U.S. Naval Academy, January 22nd, 1870," DDP, DLC.

40. Porter to Hunt, 19 June 1881, *Annual Report*, 1881, 103.

41. Porter to the Secretary of the Navy, 6 July 1887, *Annual Report*, 1887, 53.

42. Dana M. Wegner, "Commodore William D. 'Dirty Bill' Porter," U.S. Naval Institute *Proceedings* 103 (February 1977): 44, 49.

43. Typescript, "Autobiography of Joseph Smith Harris," 12 August 1908, Naval Historical Foundation, Washington, D.C.

44. John B. Hattendorf, B. Mitchell Simpson III, and John R. Wadleigh, *Sailors and Scholars: The Centennial History of the U.S. Naval War College* (Newport, R.I., 1984), 5–6, 17; and Ronald Spector, *Professors of War: The Naval War College and the Development of the Naval Profession* (Newport, R.I., 1977), 21.

# ☆ Stephen B. Luce
☆
☆ Intellectual Leader of the New Navy

*by John B. Hattendorf*

REAR ADMIRAL STEPHEN B. LUCE WAS THE INTELLECTUAL LEADER AND the catalyst for professional naval thinking among the generation of officers who became the admirals of America's New Navy. Luce, himself, belonged to an earlier generation, but his contribution to the naval service became the legacy for the new era. As Rear Admiral Bradley Fiske wrote in an obituary in 1917:

> Luce taught the Navy to think, to think about the Navy as a whole. . . .
> More clearly than any other man in American history he saw the relations
> that ought to exist between the central government and its military and
> naval officers. . . . Luce saw strategy as clearly as most of us see a material
> object. To him, more than any other officer who ever lived, are naval offi-
> cers indebted for the understanding they have of their profession.[1]

It was with this point in mind that Fiske spoke for his own generation when he dedicated his autobiography to Luce, "who saw the light before others saw it and led the Navies toward it."[2]

Although Luce's impact was large, his contributions were for the most part intangible ones. The preeminent seaman in the navy of his day, he has won respect for his ability and accomplishment in command of ships at sea, yet his achievement was to go beyond that and to use his success and practical knowl-edge as the basis for a conceptual understanding of the navy as a profession. His greatest achievements were made in peacetime as an administrator, an or-ganizer, a writer, and a teacher. Most important, Luce may be credited with establishing a system of education and training within the U.S. Navy, ranging from the lowest apprentice seaman to the highest level of civil and naval command. His concept of education at the highest level was the basis for the Naval War College as an institution that would foster the continuing development and refinement of tactical and strategic theory, as well as the organizational concepts through which such theories and academic examination could be effectively translated into practice. Despite the intangible quality of his contribution to a rising generation of naval officers, there remain institutions within the U.S. Navy that derive their roles directly from the ideas that Luce championed. Under their present names, they are the Naval Recruit Training Command, the State University of New York Maritime College at Fort Schuyler, the Naval War College, and the office of the Chief of Naval Operations.

Stephen Bleecker Luce was born in Albany, New York, on 25 March 1827, the third son of Vinal and Charlotte Bleecker Luce. The original Luce family had come from England and settled in Martha's Vineyard, Massachusetts; his mother was from one of the old Dutch families of New York. In 1833, when Stephen was six years old, his father moved to Washington, D.C., where he obtained an appointment as a clerk in the Treasury Department through family connections with President Martin Van Buren. Family tradition has it that, at age fourteen, Stephen went to the White House with his father and personally requested a naval commission from Van Buren. Whatever the circumstances, Van Buren signed Stephen's appointment as a midshipman on 19 October 1841.

Assigned first to the receiving ship at New York, Luce spent his first five months in naval life on board the ship-of-the-line *North Carolina* during the winter of 1841. After his indoctrination, Luce reported to the newly commissioned frigate *Congress*, cruising on the Mediterranean and off the east coast of South America. In 1845, Luce was assigned to the ship-of-the-line *Columbus*, then preparing to sail as the flagship of Commodore James Biddle's squadron, which would bring to China the ratification of America's first treaty with that country and then make the first attempt to establish formal relations between the United States and Japan. On the return leg of the voyage, Luce spent six months in the *Columbus*, cruising on the California coast during the Mexican War. After two, three-year cruises at sea, Luce, with a number of his contemporary midshipmen, was sent to the newly established U.S. Naval Academy, where he became a member of the second class to be sent to the school. The early classes were not expected to follow a finely prescribed curriculum; for the most part, the midshipmen were at Annapolis to review information that they had learned from their seagoing mathematics professors and to prepare for promotion examinations. Luce spent the months between April 1848 and August 1849 studying for his examinations at Annapolis, Maryland.

In its early years, Annapolis lacked the formal program of education for which it later became known. In 1850, a year after Luce left the Naval Academy, it went through its first reform, during which it was remodeled along the lines of the Military Academy at West Point. The school's need for educational reform and its lack of discipline were readily apparent to Luce and were the cause of a punishment that hindered his career for years. In March 1849, the Secretary of the Navy had authorized midshipmen to participate in the inauguration ceremonies for President Zachary Taylor, but the superintendent of the academy decided not to take advantage of the opportunity. A number of midshipmen, including Luce, showed their displeasure by staging a demonstration, in protest. For his role in this event, Luce lost seventy-two places on the promotion list, which moved him from fourth in his class to near the bottom and delayed his promotion to lieutenant for six years.

As a passed midshipman, he then served from 1849 to 1852 in the sloop-of-war *Vandalia* on the Pacific station. Fortunately, part of his personal journal for this period is preserved among his papers. This ledger-sized book gives a good picture of the young officer in Honolulu, in San Francisco, and on board ship; it also provides an insight into his reading habits: Milton's *Paradise Lost*, Dickens's *Old Curiosity Shop*, works of Shakespeare, and George Grote's twelve-volume *History of Greece*. In addition, he read the Bible and knew it well. He became familiar with the writings of the French biblical scholar Augustin Calmet, the sailor-poet William Falconer, and such authors as Lord Byron, Theodor Mommsen, and James Fenimore Cooper. While studying these works, Luce provided for his own liberal arts education through broad reading, travel, and experience. As he became proficient in the practical skills of his profession, Luce developed an awareness of the type and quality of men that the naval service required. Understandably, this knowledge grew with the scope of his practical experience.

Following Luce's tour of duty in the *Vandalia* came four years in the Coast Survey. For a brief period in 1853, he assisted Lieutenant James M. Gillis with calculations made from Gillis's observations of Venus and Mars between 1849 and 1852. Luce was then assigned to various survey ships on the Atlantic coast, where he continued to gain experience in the scientific aspects of his profession: astronomy, oceanography, cartography, and hydrography. On 7 December 1854, Stephen married a childhood friend, Elisa Henley, daughter of Commodore John C. Henley and a grandniece of Martha Washington. Three children were born of the marriage: John Dandridge Henley Luce (1855–1921), Caroline Luce (1857–1933), and Charlotte Luce (1859–1946).

From 1857 to 1860, Luce served first as a lieutenant in the sloop-of-war *Jamestown* and then on the east coast of Central America. By this point in his career, he had gained a wide variety of experience from which he could draw sound observations about his profession and outline the general direction of his future career. In 1858, the thirty-one-year-old officer wrote in his private journal, "It is my opinion . . . that the navy should be re-organized."[3] These were significant words, for they expressed his early determination to reform the service. In the long journal entry that followed, he discussed the training and education required for officers to lead and organize men. These fields of interest seem unusual when compared with those of other officers at the time, but their selection was very much a product of his own experience.

Just before the Civil War—in 1860—orders to the Naval Academy as an instructor in seamanship and gunnery provided Luce with his first opportunity to write and to publish. His initial published effort was in the area of practical training: the compilation and revision of textbooks for the Naval Academy.

As part of this work, Luce first revised a small gunnery manual that had been written by Lieutenant W. H. Parker in 1859: *Instruction for Naval Light Artillery, Afloat and Ashore*. When Parker resigned his commission to join the Confederacy, Luce was asked to revise the "rebel" officer's work. Upon completion of that assignment, Luce saw the need for a text on seamanship; he perceived the inadequacy of the books on this important subject that were already in print and available in America. In recommending to the Commandant of Midshipmen that a seamanship text be prepared, he noted: "Compared to the Army with their wealth of professional literature, we may be likened to the nomadic tribes of the East who are content with the vague tradition of the past. Does it seem creditable then, Sir, to this Institution that it should possess no text book on the most important branch taught within its halls?"[4]

When his textbook was finally published a year or so later, it was not an original treatise on seamanship but a compilation from a wide variety of sources. Revised over the years, *Seamanship* became the standard American text for the late nineteenth century and appeared in nine different editions. In the area of practical sea training, this book was Luce's major contribution. As each edition appeared, Luce ensured that the new aspects of shiphandling in steamships were considered, along with guidelines for the newly popular fore-and-aft sailing rig. His attention to these details demonstrated his continuing interest in the practical aspects of the art, and his text provided up-to-date information on these matters to the academy's midshipmen.

At the same time, Luce was an advocate of training under sail as the most appropriate method of teaching practical maritime skills. Not one to be reactionary or anachronistic, Luce strongly believed that practical experience under sail would teach a young man more about the basic nature of ships than experience in any other type of vessel.

Luce's textbooks were all devoted to obtaining a standard routine for all drills, maneuvers, and evolutions at sea; but together, they form only a small part of Luce's literary contribution to training. Within a decade after his first text appeared, Luce had expanded the scope of his work to the broad problems of a training system. This too had its origins in Luce's experience during the period from 1861 to 1865.

Luce's service during the Civil War was divided between the Naval Academy and the South Atlantic Blockading Squadron. He participated in the early blockade, the operations at Hatteras Inlet, North Carolina, and the Battle of Port Royal, South Carolina. His most fruitful activity during this period, however, had nothing to do with the prosecution of the war. In the summer of 1863, he took his first command, the midshipman practice ship *Macedonia*, to Europe and visited the naval installations at Portsmouth and Plymouth, England, and Cherbourg, France. The French navy at this time was experiencing a resurgence, and the English were meeting the French challenge; both nations were developing efficient maritime administrations and excellent training systems. Luce compiled a comprehensive report on European naval training and later used this information as source material in his articles and letters recommending a system that would be appropriate for the United States. Shortly after returning from Europe, Luce was ordered to command the new monitor *Nantucket*.

The poor quality of many of the men in the U.S. Navy at this time was painfully evident to him. The situation was no better than the one that he had perceived in 1858. Wartime service in the Navy held few attractions for enlisted men. Blockade duty was arduous and boring, liberty ashore was infrequent, and the grog ration had been stopped in 1862. Even prize money was largely a delusion; only the crews of a few lucky ships received any.

The physical environment and pay were somewhat better for naval officers. A large number of officers was made necessary by the expansion of the Navy, and they were easier to recruit than were enlisted men. Drawn from both oceangoing ships and river steamers, these new officers performed credibly. The Navy would have been unable to perform its demanding task without them, but they did have their limitations.

While in command of the *Nantucket*, Luce resolved to search for remedies to deficiencies that he had found. During the war he wrote several articles on naval personnel and training for the *Army and Navy Journal*, and after the peace he developed a plan that included an apprentice system for the Navy and a parallel program of maritime schoolships for those aspiring to be officers in the merchant marine. Reform of the merchant training system was his first accomplishment, based on the 1862 Morrill Act, which established land-grant colleges "to promote the liberal and practical education of the industrial classes in the several pursuits and professions of life." This act was to be the source of the agricultural and mechanical arts colleges and many of the country's state universities. Luce expanded on the original concept and extended it to include the knowledge of nautical sciences among young men in the coastal states.

Luce wrote the draft bill that both extended the Morrill Act to nautical education and authorized the Secretary of the Navy to lend ships and to detail
officers to public maritime schools. This bill was enacted into law on 4 January 1874. By January of the following year, Luce had personally fitted out the
sloop-of-war *St. Marys* and drafted plans, rules, and regulations for her to function as the New York State Maritime School. Commander Robert L. Phythian
was chosen as the school's first superintendent. Other schools followed in
Massachusetts, Pennsylvania, California, Maine, and Texas. To meet the academic needs of these schools, Luce wrote a textbook, *The Young Seaman's
Manual.* Taken from *Seamanship,* it provided information needed in the new
curriculum that he had designed for merchant marine apprentices.

Once this program was effectively organized, Luce transferred his energies
to naval training and education. He spent the years from 1877 to 1883 in schoolships as he developed a naval apprentice program for training afloat. Eventually transferred ashore, with close-order drills added, this program became the
naval training system.

It was during this period that Luce produced a volume of *Naval Songs.* He
believed that singing was an effective means of instilling the traditions of the
sea and teaching the type of discipline that stresses interdependence.

By the mid-1870s, Luce had established himself well enough in Washington circles to exert some influence with regard to his ideas for reforming the
Navy Department. While in command of the *Hartford* at Norfolk, Virginia,
Luce met Congressman Washington C. Whitthorne when the Tennessee representative was inspecting the Norfolk Navy Yard in February 1876. Whitthorne, a former Confederate general, served as chairman of the Naval Affairs
Committee in the Democratic Party–controlled Forty-fourth (1875–1876) Congress; he was the first chairman of that committee. Although he came from an
inland state that had no navy yard, Whitthorne had become one of the nation's
chief spokesmen for naval preparedness. With other legislators, such as
Eugene Hale, Benjamin W. Harris, Charles Boutelle, Hilary Herbert, and
Henry Cabot Lodge, Whitthorne deserves credit for building the New Navy of
the 1880s.

Luce's meeting with Whitthorne marked the beginning of a relationship
that would be nurtured by fifteen years of correspondence and an exchange of
ideas on the state of the Navy and needed reforms. In 1878, Luce advocated reforming the Navy Department so that it would more successfully carry out government policy, complement the Army, and adequately represent the nation.
To achieve these goals, he recommended to Whitthorne the establishment of
a "mixed commission" made up of members of Congress and Army and Navy
officers, as well as other prominent citizens. For a time, success seemed likely,
but the attempt ultimately failed. It was to be thirty years before the Moody

Board would consider the basic issues behind this recommendation. Nevertheless, Whitthorne continued to listen to Luce's advice while serving in the House of Representatives and, later, the Senate. In this relationship, Luce had found an outlet in Congress for his views.

During this same fertile period in Luce's thought, he came into contact with Colonel Emory Upton, then at the Artillery School at Fort Monroe, Virginia. Through Upton, Luce came to appreciate more fully the practices of the Prussian General Staff, which would become a major factor in Luce's approach to professional education and staff work within the Navy. In 1877, Luce had been giving a considerable amount of thought to establishing an advanced school of naval officers. The opportunity came for Luce in 1882 with his assignment as the senior member of a commission to study and to make recommendations on the conditions of navy yards and naval stations. It was during the year that he was engaged in this work that he first came to associate closely with Secretary of the Navy William E. Chandler and to present to the Secretary his ideas on naval education, strategy, and administration.

In the 1880s the United States had just entered a period when rapid technological change would have a continuing and direct effect on the character of the Navy. The development of steam and electrical engineering, the screw propeller, the rifled gun, and the study of interior and exterior ballistics, together with the use of iron and then steel, provided a new fabric for sea power that spurred rapid and continued change in ship design, engineering, armor, and weapons.[5] These developments quickly altered the physical character of navies while, at the same time, they demanded new types of special expertise. It was the beginning of a period in American naval history, continuing to this day, in which new equipment would become obsolete almost as soon as it was put to sea. Luce saw that although naval professionals have nothing to gain from restricting technological development, surely their central interest should be in technologies that have a direct usefulness to their profession. For this reason, Luce believed that the most important education for naval officers to receive was that which developed their understanding of the purpose, character, use, and nature of navies.

For Luce, the highest aspect of the naval profession was the study of the art of warfare. This, he believed, was properly divided into several branches, in descending order of importance: statesmanship, strategy, tactics, and logistics. The study of diplomacy, or statesmanship, in its relationship to war, was so important to Luce's concept of education that he believed it needed "to attain any degree of proficiency, such an amount of careful reading as to leave little leisure for extra professional studies."[6]

Luce saw that diplomacy, strategy, tactics, and logistics were fundamental areas that together comprised the highest elements of professional naval thought. In order for naval officers to command effectively, all these areas must be in harmony and reflect even broader aspects of national interests, values, and economics. This, Luce believed, could be done only if a commander first had been given an education at a college dedicated to the broadest perspectives of professional thought.[7]

The Naval War College was Luce's answer to this need. On 8 March 1884, Luce presented to Secretary Chandler a draft of a general order establishing the school. Chandler appointed Luce to head a board that would elaborate on the subject and make specific recommendations. The board consisted of Luce, his sympathetic friend Commander W. T. Sampson, and Lieutenant Commander Caspar F. Goodrich.

The report of the board, submitted on 13 June 1884, concisely argued for establishing an advanced school of naval warfare, and it went on to consider the curriculum and location. Washington, D.C., Annapolis, New York City, Newport, Rhode Island, and Boston, Massachusetts, were all mentioned, but only the last two locations were critically examined. Newport was favored over Boston because in Rhode Island the college could be located close to a promising fleet base where a school of application could be established. At the same time, it would be distant enough from the daily pressures of policy making in Washington that it could allow for the proper academic atmosphere and broad reflection. It was also close enough to "the Hub" to ensure that eminent talent from Harvard, Yale, and Brown Universities, Massachusetts Institute of Technology, and other centers could easily visit the college. The Naval War College was established by General Order 325 of 6 October 1884, and the first course was presented from 4 to 30 September 1885.

When Luce first thought about a Naval War College, there were no books or studies on the theoretical character of a navy. One of his main objectives in establishing the college was to have its faculty create the philosophical and theoretical literature that related the basic elements of warfare to the naval profession. The essence of the body of literature could then guide practical application.

To create the fundamental underpinning of professional thought, Luce turned to the study of naval history as a key resource. He believed that from historical knowledge, officers could begin to generalize about the nature of navies and thereby provide the groundwork for professional thought. But, he warned, if this study were to be profitable, one had to be able to identify historical material that could be analyzed and reasoned upon with advantage. Here, Luce admonished officers to think broadly and to range freely over the centuries; he noted particularly that Thucydides and other ancient writers offered much valuable insight even for a technologically advanced culture.[8]

To stimulate a profitable examination of naval history, Luce proposed that

it be undertaken by individuals with an intimate knowledge of current practice as well as a wide-ranging theoretical understanding of the art of warfare.
Simultaneously, Luce suggested using the conclusions drawn from army history in a comparative way, as a guide to formulating naval theory. The basic
ideas in military studies were often directly applicable to the art of naval warfare, Luce believed; for these concepts to be assimilated properly, however,
someone needed to reformulate and modify them after making a detailed, thorough investigation of a broad variety of naval actions. Luce gave this job to Captain Alfred Thayer Mahan and suggested that Mahan use Jomini's ideas as a
basis in the work of creating naval theory through comparative study.

Luce believed that from a study of detailed cases in naval affairs, new naval
generalizations could be established by logical thinking. First, generalizations
would be established through inductive reasoning, that is, by proceeding from
particulars to generalization; then the process could be reversed, through deductive reasoning, by applying the generalizations as a guide to particulars in
the present and in the future.[9]

Luce's central and basic idea about the Naval War College was his belief
that a naval officer did something more than just perform a job. He carried out
his work as a highly educated, trained specialist operating within a clearly defined area with established procedures and ethical standards; further, the officer used a highly developed body of theoretical knowledge relating to his field,
and had a strong feeling of group identity and shared knowledge with others
performing similar work. In short, Luce saw the naval officer as a professional,
who, like a doctor, lawyer, or educator, should have both advanced education
and recognized credentials certifying his achievement in mastering the progressive levels of understanding needed for his chosen career.

The field of education was Luce's focus. In every sense of the word, he was
a teacher, and he devoted his entire career to the presentation of his concepts
to the naval profession and to the nation. In his thinking he drew a sharp distinction between practical training for specific tasks and the education of the
mind for creative functions. Representative of much that was popular among
the educational circles of his day, Luce's article "On the Study of Naval Warfare as a Science" best reveals the substance of his educational concepts.[10] Like
philosopher Herbert Spencer, Luce believed that education is an individual
process whereby each person has to discover for himself the nature of the world
around him. Largely for this reason, he established the methodology of the
Naval War College around individual reading and research. Teachers were not
to be sources of information, but, rather, guides in a cooperative search for
knowledge. For Luce and many others, truth was something to be found in
basic immutable laws of nature that were fully ascertainable by individuals.

At that time, the use of comparative study and analogy was popular in the arts, as it was among scientists. The scientists had demonstrated that there were basic laws of the physical universe, and it seemed logical to Luce that similar laws could be found in human nature. These were ideas that Luce brought together and applied in his own self-education and that he adapted to the Naval War College. They were not unusual ideas at this time, and they were not original with Luce; however, the depth of thought and the successful application of these ideas were unusual in a navy. Therein lies Luce's contribution.

The Naval War College was conceived as only part of Luce's larger scheme for the systematic development of the Navy, but during the latter portion of his lifetime, it became the aspect to which he devoted the majority of his attention. Even after its establishment, the development of the Naval War College along the lines that Luce had envisioned was not assured. The history of the Naval War College is the story of not only a battle for survival but also an effort to retain a conception of curricular study that emphasized the development of naval science and intellectual stimulation, rather than the mere training of officers in already preconceived ideas. In both these aspects, Luce led the effort and advised those who followed him.

After turning the presidency of the Naval War College over to Captain Mahan, Luce took command of the North Atlantic Squadron in 1886. Although markedly successful in this important command, Luce experienced some disappointment. The Naval War College comprised only the theoretical part of his plan, and it should have been supplemented by a permanent squadron of evolution, a sort of seagoing laboratory where the theoretical work of the college could be tested regularly. Luce tried to make the North Atlantic Squadron perform this function, but his hopes were not completely fulfilled for at least two reasons: the poor condition of the majority of ships, which made them unsuitable for such work; and the political situation in both Caribbean and Canadian waters, which kept the squadron scattered.

During Luce's command of the North Atlantic Squadron, he was able to achieve his objectives on several occasions, however, and these marked the high points of his command. During the late nineteenth century, the squadron was used as a squadron of evolution, and it was then that ships of the U.S. Navy were first exercised tactically as a fleet. Luce had first attempted this exercise while temporarily serving as commander of the North Atlantic Station in August 1884, when the squadron had made a surprise landing on Gardiner's Island in Long Island Sound. Given only two days of preparation, Luce issued orders for the landing while the squadron was at sea. He reported that such an exercise had never been previously attempted in secrecy. Luce's second major exercise took place at Newport on 10 November 1887.

In undertaking these exercises, Luce was particularly interested in linking fleet operations with the academic work of the Naval War College. In this endeavor, Luce saw a direct interaction between the work of the college and the fleet exercises. Both exercises were joint operations involving landings; Luce believed that such exercises gave realistic training for actual combat while, at the same time, supplementing the comparative study of military and naval subjects that Luce had stressed at the Naval War College. He vainly hoped that these beginnings would develop into an American equivalent of the annual exercises that were then common in Europe.

Closely linked to a broad understanding of statesmanship, policy, strategy, and the broad function of navies in Luce's mind was the need to investigate and to improve one's understanding in those additional elements that comprise the highest aspect of professional thought: tactics and logistics. As strategy is interwoven in the great issues of state that guide it, so an understanding of strategy is essential to and intertwined with logistics and tactics. Luce emphasized that none of the elements can be entirely separated or omitted if officers are to be educated in their profession. The concept of comprehensive control of armed force blends these areas into focus, showing the various elements as gradients of a single concept that forms the essence of the best professional thinking in high command.

Both tactics and logistics are practical matters that involve the direct employment of equipment. Whatever its conception, any military operation is a blend of the two, tactics being the immediate employment of forces to attain strategic objects, logistics being the provision of the physical resources for tactics to employ. Although practical in nature and dependent on new technology, both tactics and logistics require a theoretical underpinning that provides a basic understanding on which action can be taken. Far from being an unnecessary abstraction for practical naval officers, Luce saw that an understanding of theory in these areas sheds light on problems and provides guidelines for responsible executives who must attempt to make optimal decisions in the face of chance, a variety of possible solutions, and limited resources.

Although theory was an important consideration to him, and ought to be carefully developed at the Naval War College, Luce believed that the link between theory and practice was a key element that deserved equal attention at the college. "War," he wrote, "is no time for experimentation."[11] He commented: "That 'war is the best school of war,' is one of those dangerous and delusive sayings that contain just enough truth to secure currency: he who waits for war to learn his profession often acquires his knowledge at a frightful cost of human life."[12]

For this reason, Luce promoted naval war-gaming and encouraged the experimental use by the fleet of tactics and logistics concepts developed by the Naval War College. Peacetime, he believed, was the proper time to explore and to experiment with new methods and concepts in order to be prepared when war came.

Required to retire on his sixty-second birthday, 25 March 1889, Luce requested that for convenience the date be advanced by a month and a half. On 16 February, he ordered his flag struck on board his flagship, the USS *Galena*, at Key West, Florida, and he retired without ceremony to his home at Newport.

The next twenty-two years were spent in active retirement. During this period, Luce wrote more than sixty articles and maintained a close and active connection with the Naval War College. In 1892–1893, he served as commissioner general of the United States Commission for the Columbian Historical Exposition at Madrid, Spain. In 1901, Luce was ordered to active duty on the retired list at the Naval War College, and he remained in that status until he finally retired on 20 November 1910.

During these years, Luce devoted himself to a number of projects: promotion of the work of the Naval War College; prevention of the amalgamation of the U.S. Coast Guard and the U.S. Navy; improvement of the merchant marine; and, most important in his view, the installation of uniformed officers to direct the Navy from Washington. This last subject had been of long-standing interest to Luce, who took up the issue again in 1904 at the age of seventy-seven. In 1902 and 1903, the annual reports by the Chief of the Bureau of Navigation, Rear Admiral Henry C. Taylor, had pointed out that the bureau could not efficiently handle both the administration of naval personnel and the formulation of war plans. Secretary of the Navy William H. Moody and President Theodore Roosevelt concurred in Taylor's opinion, and both urged Congress to create a naval general staff similar to what had been provided for the Army. In April 1904, hearings were held before the House Committee on Naval Affairs to consider a direct link between the General Board and the Secretary. There was a great deal of opposition to this proposal. The bureau chiefs feared encroachment on their own departments, and members of Congress feared a decline in civilian control of the military.

In the midst of this rising controversy, Luce took a radical position. He proposed not merely an adviser, but an entirely new office that would have the responsibility for fleet operations. In a letter to Henry Taylor on 25 June 1904, Luce wrote:

> Up to the present time no Secretary has recognized the fact that naval operations should be included among his duties. Let this grave oversight be repaired at once by an Executive Order creating under the Bureau of Navigation the Office of "Naval Operations." . . . The Office should be placed in charge of an officer of rank and one of recognized qualifications for its duties. His relations with the Secretary will be close and confidential. He will be the Secretary's adviser on all questions of a military nature. . . . The duties of the office will be such as would have gone to the General Staff had one been created. Thus will the Secretary obtain, under the law, the substance of a General Staff without the empty shadow of the name. There is no such thing as spontaneous generation. Plant the seed now and let it grow.[13]

The seed grew into the aid for operations and eventually the chief of naval operations. Its development, however, was slow, and at first even Taylor had his doubts. He promised to bring the suggestion to the attention of Secretary Moody before he left office, but Taylor did have reservations, as he was also trying to establish the General Board as a naval staff. "If we plant this other seed that you suggest," Taylor wrote Luce, "I am afraid the two plants would not grow together well."[14]

Luce pressed forward; in March 1905 his article "The Department of the Navy" appeared after having been awarded an honorable mention in the U.S. Naval Institute's Prize Essay contest. On its publication, he sent a copy of this latest plea for an improved naval organization to Admiral of the Navy George Dewey. "The time for action has come," he wrote Dewey. "I have a plan of action which I would like to lay before the General Board."[15]

Appearing before the board on 31 March, Luce outlined his proposal in detail and urged the board to take immediate action in support of an executive order that would activate the plan without waiting for Congress. Legislative sanction, he believed, would follow as a matter of course, as it had for the Naval Academy, the Torpedo Station, the Naval War College, and the naval training services. The matter was considered, but no action was taken.

In November 1906, the annual report of Secretary of the Navy Charles J. Bonaparte stated that radical reform of the Navy Department was necessary. However, he soon left the Navy to become the attorney general. In April 1907, during a visit to Washington, Luce gave the new Secretary, Victor Metcalf, copies of his articles on naval administration and several papers on naval efficiency, all with little apparent effect. When Luce returned to Washington three weeks later, he found that the Secretary intended to rely on Congress, which, he felt, would certainly take up the matter at the next session.

Luce was not to be put off. In early October he took advantage of a general order soliciting "suggestions to improve the efficiency of the Navy" to again propose that an office of "Naval Operations" be established that would supervise the military operations of the fleet. Again, no action was taken, as politicians and bureaucrats thwarted the reformers. The climate improved in December 1907, however, as the Navy reentered the public spotlight. The Great White Fleet started its well-known cruise around the world, and the hearts of the nation sailed with it.

With the U.S. Navy in the forefront, *McClure's Magazine* published an article in January 1908 titled "The Needs of the Navy" by Henry Reuterdahl, the Swedish-American artist and American editor for *Jane's Fighting Ships*. Written at the encouragement of Commander William S. Sims, the outspoken inspector of target practice and recently appointed naval aide to President Roosevelt, the article summarized many of Sims's opinions on naval problems, particularly that the Navy's bureaus were responsible for design defects in ships under construction and that they had failed to correct such defects as too low freeboard and misplaced armor when the flaws were brought to their attention by officers serving at sea. Repercussions were heard in all quarters. In February, the Senate reacted by ordering an investigation into the problems brought to light by Reuterdahl and Sims.

Luce quickly saw that much of the trouble to which these men pointed could have been avoided if the Navy had had more effective central direction. In the spring, Luce took up correspondence with Sims. Here was an opportunity to transmit his views to President Roosevelt through a sympathetic naval aide. The Senate committee was dominated by opponents of reform; when its investigation began to indicate the need for far-reaching administrative reform, it went into executive session and then abruptly ended its investigation without recommendations. Thus, it seemed essential to procure presidential action.

While the Senate committee was falling into inaction, Sims and his predecessor as naval aide, Commander Albert L. Key, brought to the President's attention some serious design faults in the battleship *North Dakota*, then under construction. The President ordered the General Board, the Naval War College staff, and a group of junior officers with technical expertise to investigate the matter. This commission met in Newport in July 1908 and gave Luce and Sims the opportunity to talk at length about the basic problem of naval administration. In the midst of the conference, Luce wrote directly to the President and suggested the establishment of a commission to consider and to report on the reorganization of the Navy Department. Within two days President Roosevelt replied that he would carefully consider Luce's "very interesting suggestion."

In October 1908, Luce published his article "The Fleet" in the widely read *North American Review*. Interest in naval reform continued to grow. It appeared that by December a commission would be appointed to consider the matter. "Hope on hope Ever!" Luce wrote Sims, "We'll get there some time."[16] They did. On 27 January 1909, President Roosevelt appointed a board headed by former Secretary Moody and including former Secretary Paul Morton, Congressman Alston G. Dayton, and retired Rear Admirals Luce, Mahan, Robley D. Evans, William M. Folger, and William S. Cowles. Through Luce's urging, the board completed its work and submitted its recommendations to the President less than a week before he was to leave office. Roosevelt immediately forwarded the report to the Senate, but no action was taken.

When the administration of President William Howard Taft took office on 4 March 1909, the new Secretary of the Navy, George von Lengerke Meyer, immediately began to study the matter. Detailed plans were drawn up by a board headed by Rear Admiral William Swift, and in November 1909 Meyer ordered, without congressional authority, the establishment of a system of "aids" who would act as professional assistants to the Secretary and serve as an advisory council and general staff. The system was an improvement, although it did not represent the complete reformation that Luce and others had sought. From this beginning it would take more than five years for Congress to finally authorize a reorganization of the Navy Department and to provide for a chief of naval operations "charged with the operations of the fleet, and with the preparation and readiness of plans for its use in war."[17] Other individuals were responsible for bringing this idea to fruition. In early 1912, Luce became quite ill and ceased his work entirely. He died at his home in Newport on 28 July 1917, shortly after his ninetieth birthday.

First and foremost, Stephen B. Luce was a naval officer and seaman, but he was also a teacher, writer, organizer, administrator, and leader. During his career, he developed a perception of the Navy as a flexible tool for applying force. He believed that if a navy was to fulfill its function successfully, it must be efficiently controlled by leaders who not only were technically proficient but also understood the political limitations and implications of force. With this basic theme in mind, Luce worked for improvements in education and organization during a time of great technological innovation. He promoted standardized procedures throughout the service, established a basic training program for seamen, and initiated the Naval War College for educating officers who would establish naval policy, develop strategy, and manage the Navy's functions. He was greatly influenced by ideas of the scientific study of history in the works of T. H. Buckle and J. K. Laughton and by the military theories of E. B. Hamley, Emory Upton, and Jomini, as well as by the expansionist ideas of Theodore Roosevelt and Henry Cabot Lodge.

Luce appreciated the technological revolution of his age, but he saw such innovation only as an additional reason to improve education and organization in order to use and to control technology properly. He was the acknowledged leader of naval intellectuals and influenced a number of rising officers, among them Bradley Allen Fiske, William Sowden Sims, Henry C. Taylor, and Alfred Thayer Mahan. Luce was not an original theorist, but a subjective thinker, the leader of a reform faction that was strongly opposed by the technocrats within the Navy. In his own time, he served as a conduit for the new European military ideas, which became some of the fundamental impulses for the development of American naval education, organization, administration, and strategic theory in the twentieth century.

FURTHER READING

This essay is drawn from and summarizes John B. Hattendorf's earlier work on Luce. More detail can be found in *The Writings of Stephen B. Luce*, edited by Rear Admiral

John D. Hayes and John B. Hattendorf (Newport, R.I., 1975); John B. Hattendorf, B. Mitchell Simpson III, and John R. Wadleigh, *Sailors and Scholars: The Centennial History of the U.S. Naval War College* (Newport, R.I., 1984), chaps. 1–4; John B. Hattendorf, "Luce's Idea of the Naval War College," *Naval War College Review* 37 (September–October 1984): 35–53; and the entry for "Luce" in Roger L. Spiller, Joseph G. Dawson, and T. Harry Williams, eds., *Dictionary of American Military Biography*, 3 vols. (Westport, Conn., 1984).

Luce's midshipman cruise on board the USS *Columbus* is related in Charles Nordhoff, *Man of War Life*, edited by John B. Hattendorf in the Naval Institute Classics of Naval Literature series (Annapolis, Md., 1985), which includes Luce's article, "A Fo'castle Court Martial." In addition to the studies relating to other naval figures connected with Luce, see Albert Gleaves, *Life and Letters of Stephen B. Luce* (New York, 1925), which was written by a naval officer who knew Luce and his family well. Ronald Spector, *Professors of War: The Naval War College and the Development of the Naval Profession* (Newport, R.I., 1977), provides further detail on the early years of the Naval War College.

NOTES

1. B. A. Fiske, "Stephen B. Luce, an Appreciation," U.S. Naval Institute *Proceedings* 43 (September 1917): 1935–40.

2. B. A. Fiske, *From Midshipman to Rear Admiral* (New York, 1919).

3. Private Journal 1858, Stephen B. Luce Papers, Library of Congress (hereafter cited as Luce Papers).

4. Luce to Commandant of Midshipmen, 26 February 1861, Luce Papers.

5. Bernard Brodie, *Seapower in the Machine Age* (Princeton, N.J., 1941), 149–67.

6. S. B. Luce, "On the Study of Naval Warfare as a Science," reprinted in John D. Hayes and John B. Hattendorf, eds., *The Writings of Stephen B. Luce* (Newport, R.I., 1975), 65–66.

7. Ibid.; the modern and precise definitions of strategy, tactics, and logistics are from Henry E. Eccles, *Military Concepts and Philosophy* (New Brunswick, N.J., 1965), 69.

8. S. B. Luce, "Tactics and History," in Hayes and Hattendorf, *Writings of Luce*, 74–75.

9. Luce, "On Study of Naval Warfare," 53.

10. Reprinted in Hayes and Hattendorf, *Writings of Luce*, ibid., 45–68.

11. S. B. Luce, "The Naval War College," U.S. Naval Institute *Proceedings* 36 (March 1910): 685.

12. Luce to H. C. Taylor, 25 June 1904, Luce Papers.

13. Ibid.

14. Taylor to Luce, 29 June 1904, Luce Papers.

15. Luce to Dewey, 24 March 1905, George Dewey Papers, Library of Congress.

16. Luce to Sims, 29 December 1908, William S. Sims Papers, Library of Congress.

17. Act of 3 March 1915.

# ☆ Alfred Thayer Mahan
☆
## ☆ Navalist and Historian

*by Robert Seager II*

ALFRED THAYER MAHAN (1840–1914) WAS THE ELDEST SON OF MARY Okill and Dennis Hart Mahan (1802–1871), professor of civil and military engineering and dean of faculty at the U.S. Military Academy, and a highly regarded author of military treatises. Alfred was born at West Point on 27 September 1840, spent his first twelve years there, and was filled to the brim as a young boy with the absolute necessity of praying until blue in the face and reading until exhausted. His favorite books as a child and young man were "boarders-away!" naval biographies and other maritime adventure stories. He would become, sequentially, a history buff, amateur historian, world-acclaimed professional historian, and, in 1902–1903, president of the prestigious American Historical Association. He was raised an Episcopalian of the biblical literalist sort, and by his own later admission succeeded personally in finding and knowing God.

As a naval officer of heroic proportions, however, Mahan was an utter failure.[1] There was nothing swashbuckling about him. He thoroughly disliked the navy in which he served for forty years and was disliked by almost all who served with him, under him, or over him. His classmates at the U.S. Naval Academy "silenced" him during his first class year (1858–1859), his shipmates later avoided him in the wardroom, and his shoremates generally gave him wide berth. A tall, handsome, brilliant, and enormously vain young man, he was self-assured to the point of arrogance. Indeed, his contentious personality, his humorlessness, and his ill-concealed sense of social and intellectual superiority conspired to condemn him to a life of professional loneliness in the U.S. Navy. With the exception of Samuel ("Sam") A'Court Ashe, a midshipman who briefly befriended him at Annapolis, he had no close personal friends in or out

of the service. He was, as his daughter Ellen later observed, "The Cat That Walked by Himself."[2]

Further, he was a naval officer who was deathly afraid of the sea; and he was either a poor shiphandler or was incredibly accident-prone at the conn.[3] He never heard a naval gun fired in anger save during the closing moments of the action at Port Royal, South Carolina, in November 1861, and he spent many of his subsequent waking hours on shore trying to avoid or postpone reassignment to sea duty. His naval career, from tedious blockade duty during most of the Civil War until his assignment to the new Naval War College in 1885, was a dreary succession of antique vessels and underfunded shore installations.

Who, then, was this unusual, personally unpopular, ill-starred shiphandler who was prone to seasickness? He was the man who, between 1890 and 1914, did as much as or more than any other American to introduce his countrymen to new ways of looking at the U.S. Navy's role in American foreign policy decision making, the nation's proper role in world affairs, and the strategic implications and dimensions of national security. He published twenty-one books, eleven of them containing reprintings of many of his 137 articles or serving as the repositories of various preserialized magazine articles. He also penned 107 letters to newspaper editors, mostly to the *New York Times* and mostly contentious. His most important works by far are his seminal *The Influence of Sea Power upon History 1660–1783*, published in 1890, and its sequel, *The Influence of Sea Power upon the French Revolution and Empire, 1793–1812*, published in 1892.[4]

Mahan has been condemned as naval propagandist, imperialist, warmonger, racist, and social Darwinist. He has been praised as patriot, foreign policy realist, brilliant historian, founding father of the Anglo-American "special relationship," and strategic genius. What generally has been either overlooked or underestimated in evaluations of Mahan is that he was an intensely devout High Church Episcopalian, rooted in New Testament literalism, who combined into a single philosophical, theological, cosmological, and historical system conceptions that presented a Christian view of just war, pusillanimous peace, and Good Samaritan "imperialism." His was a cosmos filled with dialectical conflict, a history in which God continuously intervened, and an earth inhabited by inherently combative men and nation states.

Much of Mahan's adult life was spent as an Episcopal tither, lay-reader, sometime delegate to annual Episcopal Church general conventions, adviser to and lay president of the Seamen's Church Institute (Episcopal) of New York, and member of the Episcopal Church Board of Missions. He was also friend, counselor, and contributor to Boone University of Wuchang, China, and to St. Augustine School for Negroes in Raleigh, North Carolina; and frequent contributor to *The Churchman* magazine, as well as a leading figure in the controversy within the Episcopal Church concerning reform of *The Book of Common Prayer*. Episcopal Christianity in particular and Protestant Christianity in general were always in his heart and mind and were always a prism through which he viewed the secular world. His "spiritual biography," *The Harvest Within: Thoughts on the Life of a Christian* (1909), discloses the depth of this orientation, as does the revealing diary he kept while serving as executive officer in the *Iroquois* in East Asian waters in 1868–1869. The most important clue to understanding the mind of Alfred Thayer Mahan lies in his religion.[5]

There was nothing particularly original, however, in Mahan's eclectic cosmology. Nor was his major discovery (in 1884) of the influence of sea power on history original with him, a point he willingly conceded when he came later to realize that men, from General Pericles of Athens, Greece, to Representative Washington C. Whitthorne of Columbia, Tennessee, had earlier grasped the idea.[6]

Mahan participated in no stirring battles, chastised no duplicitous tribal chief by leveling his flimsy village, and opened no foreign port to U.S. trade at cannon mouth. On only two occasions (Osaka, Japan, in 1868 and Panama City in 1885) did he participate in putting small bodies of armed seamen on shore to protect American lives and property. Because he was totally unheroic, any analysis of his reputation as one of the most important and influential officers in the history of the U.S. Navy must turn almost entirely on his ideas and teachings: how and whence those ideas derived, how they applied to the nation and to the world in which Mahan lived, and to what extent, if any, they are still useful to the navy and the nation nearly a century later.

A summary of his ideas, to which the influence of sea power on history was basic, includes the following:

1. *Conflict, progress, and natural laws in the universe:* From his uncle, the Reverend Milo Mahan (1819–1870), professor of early Christian church history in the General (Episcopal) Seminary in New York City, Mahan derived his belief that motion in the universe and progress in human history could be explained in terms of the dialectical clashes of various cosmic forces inherently in opposition to one another. Whereas Milo Mahan was a Pythagorean numerologist and mystic who explained these forces as numbers that stood for conflicting ideas or principles, his nephew, without known assistance from Hegel or Marx, argued that progress in history was the result of "the conflict of two opposites, as in the long struggle between freedom and slavery, union and disunion in our own land; but the union nevertheless exists. It is not to be found in freedom, not yet in slavery, but in their conflict it is."

   From his uncle Milo also came the conviction that a universe fashioned and set in motion by an omnipotent, omniscient, and omnipresent Creator was, by definition, suffused with a logic and perfection that could be expressed in the form and fact of natural laws. Mahan therefore believed that there were "laws" of history, war (strategy and tactics), and human behavior. He held, further, that "the first law of states, as of men, is self-preservation," even if such preservation had to be achieved by national expansion.

2. *Inherency of war and just wars in human history:* Mahan viewed war as the earthly manifestation of dialectical conflict in the universe. Given the existence of sovereign states inhabited and governed by aggressive men (ample evidence for which he found in the Bible), and the fact that there was no recorded human history in which war was absent, he concluded that war was both constant and inevitable. Indeed, war was a corrective instrument placed in human hands by the Creator to enable God-fearing and God-loving men to defend that which is good, just, and righteous on earth and oppose forcibly that which is evil, unjust, and wrong. Modern nations in the service of God must be prepared at all times to fight just wars.

3. *Pacifism, arms limitation, and rules of war:* Mahan opposed all popular agitation for courts that would arbitrate international disputes, seek to control or outlaw particularly lethal weapons, or otherwise make rules and regulations designed to mitigate the horrors of war. Such activities foolishly denied the historical inevitability of war and compromised the necessity of fighting just wars. He felt, however, that modern wars might be rendered less protracted and less frequent if the profits reaped by nonparticipants were removed. Thus, as a U.S. delegate to the First Hague Conference in 1899 and a strident critic of American participation in the Second Hague Conference in 1907, he urged the abandonment of the seventeenth-century international rubric which held that in wartime "free ships make free goods, except contraband."

4. *Research and writing of history:* Mahan was convinced that his personal awareness of the influence of sea power on history came directly from God. It was clearly one of the laws (or central themes) of history because the creation and proper use of organized sea power in wartime to ensure "command of the sea" had clearly influenced the course of human history, certainly more than had any other single factor. His belief in the inerrancy of God-given central themes in the universe, themes that historians could discover through the favor of God and by the use of subordinationist historical methodology, underpinned his attitude toward researching and writing history.

Specifically, he believed, "Facts won't lie if you work them right; but if you work them wrong a little disproportion in the emphasis, a slight exaggeration of color, a little more or less limelight on this or that part of the grouping and the result is not truth, even though each individual fact be as unimpeachable as the multiplication table." By working them right, historians could achieve mystical oneness with God by verifying His laws; nor would historians ever err in matters of historical interpretation.

5. *Laws of naval strategy and tactics:* From Antoine-Henri Jomini (1779–1869) by way of Stephen B. Luce (1827–1917), Mahan derived the notion that a nation's "command of the sea" hinged on its recognition and scientific application of the laws of tactical and strategical concentration. These were cosmic laws that operated without reference to technological changes in naval vessels and ordnance. For this reason, fleets or armies, regardless of existing technology, that situated themselves at geographical positions in or near the "strategic center" of a given war—thus affording themselves the greatest amount of offensive mobility or the greatest measure of defensive flexibility—usually won the battles that determined the outcome of the wars and thus influenced the course of history. And a fleet in battle that could maneuver (concentrate) itself in such a way as to bring, for a decisive moment, a greater part of its firepower and personnel against lesser parts of the firepower and people of its enemy would invariably win the action—the decisive "Big Battle," that would establish "command of the sea" and bring victory. Indeed, as Mahan put it, again in dialectical terms, the very "Art of War consists in concentrating in order to fight and disseminating in order to subsist. . . . The problem is one of embracing opposites."

6. *Battleships as decisive naval weapons:* Finally, Mahan argued that mere commerce raiding during war at sea (*guerre de course*) could never be tactically or strategically decisive. Wars at sea could be settled conclusively, and "command of the sea" thereby established, only by concentrated fleets of battleships. But such vessels, he had come to believe by 1906, did not necessarily have to be copies of HMS *Dreadnought* and mount batteries composed solely of 10-inch or 12-inch guns. Modern navies, he argued, should maintain the operational flexibility inherent in "balanced" ship sizes and in the employment of "mixed batteries" of greater- and lesser-caliber guns. Whatever the size of the ships or caliber of the guns, however, battle fleets must obey the strategical and tactical laws governing war at sea. The projection of naval power ashore by amphibious or other means seems not to have concerned Mahan.[7]

Mahan's discovery of the influence of sea power on history occurred shortly after Commodore Luce had invited him to join the faculty of the proposed Naval War College, which was scheduled to commence operation in Newport, Rhode Island, on 4 September 1885. Luce told him only that he would be required to give lectures on the "certain general principles" adducing to success or failure in naval warfare.[8] Commander Mahan was no stranger to the scholarly Luce. They had sailed together briefly during the Civil War, and Luce also knew him as the author of *The Gulf and Inland Waters*, a credible volume in the Charles Scribner's Sons series on the Navy in the Civil War, which Mahan researched and wrote in five months in 1883 while serving as navigation officer at the New York (Brooklyn) Navy Yard. Why Scribner's picked Mahan for this task is not known, but why Mahan accepted such a pressure-packed assignment is clear: with a wife and three small children to support, he desperately needed the six hundred dollars the publisher was offering for the job. Competent as the book was, there was in it no hint of the sea power hypothesis to come. He did make plain, however, his view that the Civil War was in every respect a just war.[9]

The time, place, and circumstance of Mahan's great discovery of his sea power hypothesis are known precisely; it occurred in the library of the English Club in Lima, Peru, in November 1884, while he was reading Theodor Mommsen's *The History of Rome* in preparation for his War College lectures, and while his command, the decrepit *Wachusett*, lay at nearby Callao. Years later, in 1907, he described the exciting moment of his discovery in his autobiography, *From Sail to Steam*:

> He who seeks, finds, if he does not lose heart; and to me, continuously seeking, came from within the suggestion that control of the sea was an historic factor which had never been systematically appreciated and expanded. For me . . . the light dawned first on my inner consciousness; I owed it to no other man. . . . I cannot now reconstitute from memory the sequence of my mental processes; but while my problem was still wrestling with my brain there dawned upon me one of those concrete perceptions which turn inward darkness into light—and give substance to shadow. . . . It suddenly struck me, whether by some chance phrase of the author I do not know, how different things might have been could Hannibal have invaded Italy by sea, as the Romans often had Africa, instead of by the long land route.

Much earlier than this, however, in mid-1894, Mahan had privately assured his wife that he had been "guided to the work which is now so overwhelming praised," and that "the gift and call to write both came from outside."[10]

Whether the Creator had indeed nudged Mahan's mind, or a Gestalt experience of sorts had taken place, cannot be determined. Nonetheless, Mahan's blinding historical insight in November 1884 about sea power in history was destined to change the direction of his boring and lackluster naval career, revolutionize the study of naval history, and make his name a household word in U.S. naval and diplomatic circles and in the parlors of subscribers to such high-toned magazines as *Atlantic Monthly*, *Harper's Monthly*, and *North American Review*.

In mid-May 1885, Mahan informed Luce that preoccupation with the concerns of the *Wachusett* had rendered his sea power insight "a little vague" since November 1884, but that from "scanty notes" made at the time, his basic approach to his lectures would be, first, to "consider sources of maritime power or weakness—material, personnel, national aptitude, harbors with their positions relative to commercial routes and enemies coasts." He would then "bring forward instances from ancient and modern history, of the effect of navies and the control of the sea upon great or small campaigns," especially Hannibal's defeat in Italy in the Second Punic War. He hoped this approach would lead to the discovery of possible parallels "between the weapons or branches of land forces and those of the sea, if any hints can be drawn as to their use." As for the "subject of naval tactics," a primary theoretical interest of Luce's at this time, "I own I am awfully at sea; but in a study like the above I should hope for light."[11]

Mahan would soon learn that Luce had already discovered the source of that light and would urge Mahan to follow its gleam. Indeed, Luce was far ahead of Mahan in the conviction that naval officers should study history, especially that of great naval battles, to discover what scientific principles were illustrated in victorious combat, or where disregard for the accepted rules of war had led to defeat. Mahan would also learn that Luce had nothing less in view than to make of the new Naval War College the birthplace of the discovery of the laws and principles comprising the "science of naval warfare."

Indeed, Luce told the nine men in the first class to report to the college in September 1885 (Mahan was not yet present), and that their primary task there was "to raise maritime war to the level of a science." Moreover, he continued, "having established our principles by the inductive process, we may then resort to the deductive method of applying those principles to such a changed condition of the art of war as may be imposed by later inventions or by introduction of novel devices." Luce was also certain that although there was yet

> no authoritative treatise on the art of naval warfare under steam . . . we must, perforce, resort to the well-known rules of the military art with a view to their application to the military movements of a fleet, and, from the well-recognized methods of disposing troops for battle, ascertain the principles which govern fleet formations. . . . *It is by this means alone that we can raise naval warfare from the empirical stage to the dignity of a science.*

To make this last point quite clear, he suggested that "the existence of fundamental principles, by which all the operations of war should be conducted, has been placed beyond doubt by the researches of Jomini." Let us, Luce emphasized, as we search for "the science of naval warfare under steam . . . look for that master mind who will lay the foundations of that science, and do for it what Jomini has done for military science."[12]

So it was that through Luce, his commanding officer at the Naval War College, Mahan derived his conception of naval strategy and tactics from Jomini, whose numerous works (twenty-seven volumes of military history covering the wars of Frederick the Great, the French Revolution, and Bonaparte) dealt entirely with the strategy and tactics of land armies. In effect, Luce ordered Mahan to study Jomini's land-war tactics and apply their principles to hypothetical fleet combat maneuvers of ironclad vessels under steam. Mahan, of course, obeyed, even though Jomini had observed in his seminal *The Art of War* (1836) that "war in its ensemble is not a science, but an art. Strategy, particularly, may indeed be regulated by fixed laws resembling those of the positive sciences, but this is not true of war viewed as a whole."[13]

Mahan did not reach Newport until October 1885, after the brief twenty-six-day first session of the college had ended. He was delayed by the fact that the *Wachusett* was unexpectedly ordered to Central American waters during March and April 1885 to protect American lives, property, and transit-treaty rights during revolutionary and international disorders in the area. This enterprise forced Mahan to put a landing party ashore on the Isthmus of Panama in mid-March to maintain the nation's right of transit, an operation that involved seizing and holding the U.S.–owned railroad and cable station in Panama City. It also involved showing the flag in El Salvador and Guatemala in April during the chaos occasioned by Guatemala's invasion of El Salvador.

The detour of the *Wachusett* to the west coast of Central America was not without its educational advantages, however. If nothing else, Mahan learned from this experience that the U.S. Navy badly needed a coaling station on that coast, and that U.S. sea power, properly applied, had a critical role to play in sustaining U.S. diplomacy there. Further, the experience riveted in his mind an appreciation for the strategic importance of the isthmus, the chaotic political conditions within the weak little nations situated there, and the importance of the transit rights held by the United States. Indeed, the problem of the isthmus would play a major, almost disproportionate, role in Mahan's early studies of sea power and in the curriculum of the infant Naval War College after he became the institution's president in mid-1886.[14]

When Mahan finally conferred with Luce in Newport in October, they decided that Mahan (now captain) would spend the next ten months in New York to work up lectures on naval tactics and naval history to be given at the second session of the college, scheduled for a ten-week period commencing 6 September 1886. Three months before that session began, however, Luce (now rear admiral) was detached from the institution and assigned to command the North Atlantic Station, and Mahan became president of the school. Meanwhile, Mahan had been at work on his lectures in the Astor Library and the New York Lyceum.

It should be kept in mind that during this period of lecture preparation Mahan was attempting to accomplish two quite different research and writing tasks. First, he undertook a review of the tactical maneuvers employed by warring fleets of wooden sailing vessels in line-ahead formation during the seventeenth and eighteenth centuries with a view toward applying them to steel vessels under steam. To the practice of firepower concentration employed in line-ahead formations during the Age of Sail (usually employed without success or decision), he added Jomini's principles of unit or fractional concentration. His problem here was that in 1885–1887 there was no tactical combat doctrine for steel and steam vessels; also, with the exception of the Austro-Italian battle of Lissa in July 1866, which had been a tactically chaotic melee of ironclad vessels attempting to sink one another with close-in gunfire or by ramming, there was no body of combat experience to guide him.[15]

Second, he read broadly in the printed accounts of the naval dimensions of the great mercantilist wars for empire in which Britain, France, Holland, and Spain had participated in the period 1660 to 1783, with the clear intent to document and otherwise demonstrate the truth of the sea power hypothesis that he had stumbled on in Lima in November 1884. In this task he made no effort to consult primary sources or materials that might conflict with his conviction that the existence or nonexistence of sea power had been (and was) the most powerful factor in determining the course and direction of human history. "Original research was not within my scope, nor was it necessary to the scheme," he later confessed.[16]

The first of these dual historiographical enterprises to see the light was a curious manuscript titled "Fleet Battle Tactics." In its text and in the accompanying hypothetical battle diagrams, Mahan employed, as best he could, elements of Jomini's four main "maxims," or "principles" or "laws," of tactical concentration. As expressed in Jomini's *Study of the Art of War*, they are:

1. To throw by strategic movements the mass of an army, successively, upon the decisive points of a theater of war, and also upon the communications of the enemy as much as possible without compromising one's own.

2. To maneuver to engage fractions of the hostile army, with the bulk of one's own forces.

3. On the battlefield, to throw the mass of the forces upon the decisive point, or upon that portion of the hostile line which it is of the first importance to overthrow.

4. To arrange that these masses shall not only be thrown upon the decisive point, but that they shall engage at the proper times and with energy.[17]

These four "maxims," "principles," or "laws" of the "science" or "art" (Jomini's nomenclature varied) of tactical concentration lost something in persuasiveness when Mahan applied them to naval battle tactics in his "Fleet Battle Tactics" essay. As he viewed it, the battleship line, as it commenced action in either line abreast or echelon, would wheel, turn, and perform various precise, complex, and opportunistic geometric evolutions designed to secure, maintain, regain, or increase its concentration of fire ("the essence of scientific warfare," said Mahan) on selected smaller enemy units that would be sent gloriously to the bottom one by one. It was to be a "highly drilled" fleet operation executed by "reasonably perfect ships, reasonably drilled and commanded." In sum, said Mahan, "Perfection is our aim." But in reading "Fleet Battle Tactics" today, one gains the impression that the enemy fleet was expected to sit supinely in the water, watching in awe, as the U.S. battle line, directed by some brilliant naval choreographer, danced nimbly around it and destroyed it piecemeal and totally. Near the end, U.S. torpedo boats and rams, the equivalents of Jominian cavalry, would swiftly stand down on the sinking cripples and put them out of their misery.[18]

Luce did not think highly of his disciple's manuscript on tactics. He told Mahan, after reading the piece, that the main weakness in it was that it did not adequately link recent technological changes in ship design and ordnance with Jomini's principles of land tactics as applied to fleet maneuvers. Luce also informed him that he would be responsible for only two lectures on tactics during the 1886 session and that he had engaged someone else to do the rest. Mahan's "Fleet Battle Tactics" quickly disappeared from the sight and mind of man, a fate that seems not to have disturbed its author. Moreover, in his future books and articles Mahan never permitted the fact of technological changes in naval vessels and weapons to becloud or set aside his notions of fixed tactical and strategical principles, or laws, of naval warfare that were, he came to believe, inherent in the mathematical orderliness of the universe.[19]

Mahan's 1886 study of Jomini's tactical doctrines also influenced his conception of naval strategy, some elements of which he discussed in his Naval War College lectures in 1887, and which found their way into his two *Influence of Sea Power* books in 1890 and 1892. Not until 1911, however, did he finally bring together his scattered views on strategy in his *Naval Strategy, Compared and Contrasted with the Principles of Military Operations on Land.* "Naval Strategy," he assured the readers of that opaque volume, is based on "fundamental truths, which when correctly formulated are rightly called principles; these truths, where ascertained, are themselves unchangeable." He admitted that new light might be shed on the applications of these principles. But the appearance of the submarine, the long-range torpedo, wireless telegraphy, and the airplane by 1911 had not modified or illuminated his "fundamental truths" about naval strategy. These strategical "truths," all with Jominian overtones of tactical concentration, were, as Mahan viewed them, four in number:

1. To understand that the basic goal, and end purpose, of naval strategy is, by fleet action, to "break up the enemy's power on the sea, cutting off his communications with the rest of his possessions, drying up the sources of his wealth and his commerce, and making possible a closure of his ports." This produces "command of the sea."

2. To effect a deployment of battle fleet and support vessels in such manner as to bring a superior force of one's own to bear on an inferior though significant enemy force in one quarter, while elsewhere other enemy units are held in check long enough to permit the initial or primary strike force to produce victory; in short, the principle of "hit and hold."

3. To seek to commence naval war from a central position (or strategic center) so that one's own concentrated naval force can be dispatched offensively along interior lines outward against separated segments of the enemy's force. This positioning increases the likelihood of bringing successful hit and hold maneuvers into play. One must never divide his own main battle fleet or dispatch it on eccentric operations.

4. To appreciate and act on the fact that the main purpose and mission of battle fleets is to bring the enemy's main fleet (or a major segment thereof) to decisive battle, and to destroy it wholly with concentrated fire from guns of one's own capital ships (armored steel battleships). Battle fleets thus must operate offensively, not defensively (not as "fleets-in-being"), in bringing the enemy into a decisive "Big Battle" victory in which they are rewarded with "command of the sea," the fundamental strategic goal of naval warfare.[20]

The dubious relevance of his *Naval Strategy* volume and his "Fleet Battle Tactics" manuscript aside, it was Mahan's second task—to compose lectures that would clearly demonstrate the influence of sea power on history—that he wanted most to accomplish. These lectures would become, virtually unchanged, his famous *The Influence of Sea Power upon History, 1660–1783*. In November 1885, he had commenced reading the printed monographic, biographical, and autobiographical literature on the great European imperial wars of the seventeenth and eighteenth centuries. By May 1886 he had taken four hundred pages of notes and knew exactly what he wanted to prove and how to prove it. It was just a question of arranging his carefully selected facts to fit his thesis and getting it all down on paper.[21]

In analyzing Mahan's seminal volume, one should remember that the first and most influential chapter in the book, "Elements of Sea Power," was written last, that it was tacked onto the hefty manuscript at the very last moment at the request of the publisher to make the whole work "more popular." Mahan agreed to this bastard surgery because he knew history was not "an attractive subject to the public," and because he thought increased sales might encourage the publishers, Little, Brown of Boston, to gamble on a sequel that would carry the story up to 1812, as later they did.

In sum, "Elements of Sea Power" was primarily a summary of *European* national motives, opportunities, and aptitudes for the creation and employment of sea power, as Mahan conceived them to have related to the great mercantilist wars for empire fought in the seventeenth and eighteenth centuries. It was a précis of sorts to the rest of the book. The historical illustrations used in "Elements of Sea Power" to explain national motives, opportunities, and aptitudes for sea power were taken primarily from British and French military and naval experience in 1660–1783. How these examples might be applied to the United States in 1890 was treated briefly, tangentially, and diffidently.

"Elements of Sea Power," then, was not a prescription for or summons to U.S. imperialism, mercantilism, colonialism, or territorial expansion. Mahan sought only to awaken Americans to the need for a navy that could ensure national security in Gulf-Caribbean and eastern Pacific waters, if and when a canal was built across the Isthmus of Panama by a foreign power—a project that French interests indeed were attempting at that time. The essay was essentially a call to the American public to emerge from twenty-five years of isolation.[22]

The basic thing Mahan sought to demonstrate in the main body of the book was simply this: that among European nations with sea coasts, "in three things—production, with the necessity of exchanging products, shipping, whereby the exchange is carried on, and colonies, which facilitate and enlarge the operations of shipping and tend to protect it by multiplying points of safety—is to be found the key to much of history, as well as of the policy, of nations bordering upon the sea." Mercantilistic imperialism thus boiled down to the relationship of "(1) Production; (2) Shipping; (3) Colonies and Markets—in a word, sea power."[23]

It was sea power, therefore, that had made eighteenth-century European imperialism and mercantilism really work. Specifically, Mahan described the process whereby strong (usually absolute) monarchs exported the products and people of their kingdoms, in the numerous vessels of their national merchant marines, protected by their large navies, to overseas colonies that were designed to function as closed, monopolized markets. This policy produced favorable trade balances, thus generating the bullion or raw materials that made the imperial exporting nations and their ruling dynasties even richer and more powerful, as well as better able economically to launch and sustain the mercantilist wars on land and sea (mostly the latter) that served to expand their empires even farther. Britain, thanks to the early emergence of the superb Royal Navy, was Mahan's prime example of the crucial role that sea power (merchant and naval) had played in creating the national power, glory, and wealth that was the British Empire of 1890.

Mahan also set forth, in the "Elements of Sea Power" chapter, the six "principal conditions affecting the sea power of nations" and the potentiality of various coastal nations to develop such power, mainly citing illustrative comparisons from British, French, Dutch, and Spanish imperial history of the period 1660–1783. It was only in this comparative context, however, that the United States—with its tiny merchant marine and antiquated navy—was brought peripherally into the picture. The six conditions Mahan cited were geographical position, physical conformation, extent of territory, number of population, national character, and character of government.

As for geographical position, that of the United States was certainly conducive to the development of sea power should the nation choose to undertake such development. Mahan noted, however, that from a strategic and military defense standpoint, the relationship between the southern continental United States and the Gulf of Mexico was analogous to England's relationship to its channel, or that of the Mediterranean nations to Suez, especially if a Central American canal were to be constructed. If that occurred, Mahan warned, the Gulf-Caribbean, given a canal outlet, would become "one of the great highways of the world" along which "a great commerce would travel, bringing the interests of the other great nations, the European nations, close along our shores, as they have never been before." This magnetic attraction of world shipping, merchant and naval, to the Gulf-Caribbean would surely involve the United States in "international complications" eventually calling for "warships of the first class, without which ships no country can pretend to control any part of the sea." It would also demand bases in the Gulf-Caribbean sufficient to sustain U.S. naval operations in isthmian waters in the event of political crises in Central America. These bases should be positioned so as to control ingress and egress to and from the Mississippi River. It should be noted that, in this regard, Mahan was thinking almost entirely in terms of coastal strategic defense.[24]

He pointed out that the nation's physical conformation included numerous deep harbors with easy access to the sea like those that had been a source of maritime power and wealth in Europe, and that the United States had such assets on three coasts; but the country had no merchant marine, nor was it likely to have one in the foreseeable future. Further, the nation had no colonies because its investment capital found ample opportunity for profit in its economically underdeveloped interior. This would remain the situation for some time to come unless America's isolated "little corner" of the world was pierced by an isthmian canal—in which case the nation would be in for a "rude awakening."[25] In sum, of the three requisites for empire—production, merchant shipping, and colonies (closed markets)—America lacked two; the nation did have industrial productive capacity.

On the other hand, America's extent of territory and number of population were sufficient to achieve and sustain sea power capabilities. Also, the national character of Americans included a necessary amount of commercial aptitude and acquisitiveness; and Americans certainly had the ability to produce sufficient commodities for trade. But modern nations aspiring to sea power must also have a "capacity for planting healthy colonies." By healthy colonies, Mahan did not mean the kind of colonies planted by Spain, Portugal, and France in the sixteenth, seventeenth, and eighteenth centuries. These were simply mercantilistic "cows to be milked," upon which the home government had legislated "a monopoly of its external trade." He meant, instead, colonies like those the British had planted in North America, possessions that required minimum control from the mother country. They would be colonies settled by people with a "genius for independent action," not colonies rigidly controlled and monopolized by the home government. Therefore, if there were ever in the American future conditions "calling for colonization, it cannot be doubted that Americans will carry to them all their inherited aptitude for self-government and independent growth." He saw no such situation developing, however.

Finally, Mahan admitted that the character of government of most of Europe's great sea powers in the past had been absolutist or despotic; but he felt certain that democratic governments could also aspire to sea power, even though, "Popular governments are not generally favorable to military expenditure."[26]

What concerned Mahan most in all of this was that even with a great U.S. merchant marine, "it may be doubted whether a sufficient navy would follow," and even if it did follow, whether it would be strong enough and capable enough to meet a potential enemy far at sea, even close to foreign shores, rather than in American waters. Or would it be so weak that it would have to adopt a passive defense strategy and meet the enemy in U.S. coastal waters? The question, then, of the adequacy of the U.S. Navy, Mahan concluded, "is probably now quickening in the Central American Isthmus. Let us hope that it will not come to the birth too late."[27]

In general, Mahan did not in 1890 consider the United States a likely candidate for imperialism, colonialism, or militarism. "I dread outlying colonies," he had told Sam Ashe in 1884, "to maintain which large military establishments are necessary. I see in them the on-coming of a 'strong' central government . . . or perhaps a subversion of really free government." He worried too that neither the Republican nor Democratic Parties would have the political courage to respond to a foreign challenge at the isthmus, or even have the good sense to assume a sensible defense posture in the Gulf-Caribbean, but Mahan himself did little to change matters. He participated not at all in the political agitation for the New Navy in the 1880s, or in arguments in and out of Congress that linked naval expansion to forced commercial expansion abroad. He favored free trade, he had told Ashe in 1884. Indeed, he never advocated artificial U.S. government stimulation of overseas trade with tariffs, subsidies, drawbacks, or gunboats. Nor did he ever link the advent and growth of the New Navy to the advancement of his personal career.[28]

It thus seems reasonably clear that the principal thrust of Mahan's advice to his country on the nation's diplomacy and its defensive strategy at the advent of the so-called imperialist period in American history was not particularly imperialistic. He was an "imperialist," he said, because he was nonisolationist; and an "imperialist" United States, by his definition, was a nation that must abandon isolationism to the extent of aspiring to own, operate, fortify, or otherwise control any future Central American canal. The nation must also have a naval capability in warships, bases, and coaling stations in the Gulf-Caribbean with which to protect that canal and monitor international shipping to, near, and through its eastern approaches. Similarly, in the eastern Pacific the United States must annex Hawaii and establish there a naval presence capable of flanking and otherwise superintending international shipping to and from the future canal's western terminus. The new U.S. Navy, then, need be only large enough to maintain a protective shield in the northern and eastern Pacific for the purpose of defending the thinly populated, underdeveloped West Coast against threat from or attack by an increasingly aggressive Japan. As for the size of the nation's Pacific shield, Mahan was quite specific. In an *Atlantic Monthly* article in 1890, titled "The United States Looking Outward," he wrote:

> It should be an inviolable resolution of our national policy, that no foreign state should henceforth acquire a coaling position within three thousand miles of San Francisco—a distance which includes the Hawaiian and Galapagos islands and the coast of Central America. For fuel is the life of modern naval war; it is the food of the ship; without it the modern monsters of the deep die of inanition. Around it, therefore, cluster some of the most important considerations of naval strategy.[29]

True, Mahan also spoke in the 1890s of the possibility of increased American trade in the Pacific in future years; but he regarded this mainly as a desirable economic by-product of canal acquisition and Hawaiian annexation. It was far less important to him than was the strategic necessity of creating and policing an isthmian-centered, Caribbean-Gulf-Hawaiian-West Coast-Galapagos Islands defense perimeter. Indeed, the strategic importance of an American-controlled canal at the isthmus was almost always in his mind from 1890 to 1914. No other strategic subject engaged his attention with such frequency and intensity during these years.[30]

In November 1900, Mahan even suggested that, given the nation's commitment to China in its recently announced "Open Door Policy," Americans might well consider a "retrenchment of responsibility" and abandon insistence on the Monroe Doctrine in that sector of the Western Hemisphere south of the Amazon valley; or at least extend Open Door (free trade) principles there to all nations, principles of the sort that some Americans were then seeking to establish in China.[31]

This is not to say that the highly moralistic Mahan approved the tough methods employed by the Roosevelt administration against Colombia in November 1903 to acquire an acceptable canal right-of-way in Panama. After all, Christians do not steal—or should not. In any event, not until 1912 did he undertake a defense of the legality of U.S. behavior at the isthmus nine years earlier. In this belated exercise he argued that the Roosevelt administration had intervened to restore order in Panama so as to preserve the right-of-transit permitted in Article 35 of the 1846 treaty between the United States and New Granada (predecessor state to Colombia). He specifically separated the dubious morality of the U.S intervention from its legality.

Nor had Mahan been happy when Britain joined with Germany in a naval blockade of the Venezuelan coast—a blockade in which the Germans had actually bombarded a fort and a town on that coast—during December 1902, in an attempt to force Venezuela to pay its debts. He believed that the only good that could come of such arrogant European naval penetration of the Gulf-Caribbean so close to the isthmus was that Congress might be persuaded to authorize "two more battleships." Furthermore, Mahan did not think, as he made clear in February 1903, that the Monroe Doctrine should be used by the United States against Latin Americans to justify compelling them to make good their obligations to their European creditors, because "to do so which has been by some argued a necessary corollary of the Monroe Doctrine, would encroach on the very independence which that political dogma defends." The United States, he asserted, should be "preponderant" in Latin America, not "paramount."

Given these temperate views, Theodore Roosevelt's crude seizure of Panama in November 1903 was simply too much for Mahan. So too was the President's enunciation of the so-called Roosevelt Corollary to the Monroe Doctrine in December 1904, in which he justified unilateral preventive intervention by the United States in Latin America in order to forestall possible European intervention there. Not until 1908 did Mahan accept the principle underlying the corollary. In thus defending Roosevelt's 1904 policy in the Dominican Republic in 1908, and his 1903 policy in Panama in 1912, Mahan was tardily accepting the fait accompli of both situations. He had not contributed to or participated in the initial decision-making process in either instance, nor was he even consulted.[32]

In addition, it is well to note that Mahan's advocacy of an eastern Pacific defense perimeter, particularly his insistence that Hawaii be annexed, contained a distinct racial dimension that was related to his perception, as early as January 1893, that the Hawaiian Islands were being overrun by immigrant Chinese. He saw this as evidence of the beginnings of a "barbaric invasion" of Western civilization that could be contained only by "a firm hold on the Sandwich Islands by a great civilized, maritime power." An augmentation of U.S. naval power to protect underpopulated California from Oriental inundation (the "Yellow Peril") was clearly indicated, he insisted.

Four years later Mahan viewed increasing Japanese emigration to Hawaii and California in much the same light, and he saw the appearance of modern Japanese naval vessels in Hawaiian waters in 1897 as evidence that the "Yellow Peril" (Japanese manifestation) was about to engulf Hawaii. For the remainder of his life Mahan nursed the conviction, off and on, that there would someday occur a gigantic global military showdown between Orient and Occident, barbarism and civilization, yellow and white, heathen and Christian. That there would be an earlier war of lesser magnitude between the United States and Japan in the Pacific he had no doubt. Some day, in some way, and for some reason, Japan would attack the United States.[33]

Mahan's dogged insistence on Hawaiian annexation in the early 1890s earned him (so he claimed) exile to sea in 1893, by the antiannexationist Cleveland administration, as commanding officer of the USS *Chicago*. This banishment, however, led to his triumphal welcome in England, where his *Influence* books had been exceptionally well received in naval, political, and literary circles. His enthusiastic inclusion in such company was a social and professional success that increased his already enormous sense of Anglophilia, and cemented forever in his mind a firm belief in the absolute superiority of virtually everything British — parliamentary system, common law, navy, empire, Anglican Church, manners, and smug confidence in British racial superiority. His subsequent writing clearly reflects these unshakable biases.

His two-year cruise in the *Chicago* also convinced Mahan that the technology of the steel "naval monsters" of the New Navy had passed him by. The modern vessels truly frightened him. When he returned home in 1896, he retired; forty unhappy years in the U.S. Navy were enough. He had decided, meanwhile, that he could earn enough in a "second career" as a writer (at five to seven cents a word) to increase a retirement salary of $3,375 to a level necessary to support a wife and two unmarried daughters at home, put a son through boarding school and college, and sustain a gracious lifestyle of the sort that he had observed and admired in England.

Beginning in 1897 his literary output thus became increasingly voluminous; it also became increasingly commercial, popular, superficial, and repetitious, as he focused far less on history and much more on current events. Daily European and Asian diplomatic crises, conveniently spaced wars (Spanish-American, Boer, Russo-Japanese, Balkan), naval arms races, dangerous peace movements, and various Christian concerns soon became Mahan's principal subjects. "I have committed myself to pot-boilers," he confessed in June 1896. These potboilers—mostly magazine articles—subsequently collected and reissued in book form, however, helped to pay for a fine row house in New York City, an elaborate summer place in Quoque, Long Island, and a household staff of four or five servants in both residences. The "Philosopher of Sea Power" lived well from 1897 until his death in 1914.[34]

At the time of Mahan's retirement from the U.S. Navy in March 1897, many Americans had become aware that a bloody revolutionary war of independence against Spain was under way in Cuba. "Cuba Libre!" was the cry. In April 1898, the United States, for purposes of pacification and for reasons essentially humanitarian, intervened militarily in the conflict. This action brought on the 116-day war with Spain that secured the independence of Cuba and, incidentally (almost accidentally), resulted in U.S. annexation of Spain's colony in the Philippines.

Mahan had virtually nothing to do with the onset of the war. Neither his personal letters nor his publications from late 1897 to early 1898 indicate any interest in Cuba save as a strategic pawn in a hypothetical American-German naval war in the Gulf-Caribbean. He certainly visualized no actual war there.[35] Nor is there credible evidence that Mahan participated importantly in the U.S. Navy's routine contingency planning of naval war with Spain and other nations during the years 1894 to 1898. Three or four Mahan letters (now lost) written in March 1898 to then-Assistant Secretary of the Navy Theodore Roosevelt, do indicate, however, that he was consulted informally by Roosevelt on blockade strategy and tactics in Cuba in the event of war with Spain, and that he apparently recommended to Roosevelt a tight blockade of Havana, Mantanzas, and the western half of Cuba pending concentration of the U.S. battle fleet for a decisive action ("Big Battle") against the Spanish home fleet, if and when it arrived in the waters of the Western Hemisphere.[36]

There is no evidence that Mahan ever recommended a naval attack on the Philippines as part of a war with Spain. At no time during the prewar period did he agitate for war with Spain, contemplate or advocate territorial acquisitions as the result of such a war, or even speak out for a free Cuba. He was far too busy writing profitable articles for *Harper's Monthly* that addressed the possibility of future naval war with Germany or Japan and argued the need for creating eastern Pacific and Gulf-Caribbean defense zones in order to maintain U.S. naval preeminence near a possible future canal in Central America.

Thus, when the USS *Maine* mysteriously exploded in Havana harbor on 15 February 1898 and claimed the lives of 260 officers and men, Mahan was not among those splenetic Americans who irrationally blamed it on Spain and called loudly for war. Instead, he advocated a suspension of judgment in the matter and pointed out that the explosion might well have been caused by an accident within the vessel, which, in retrospect, now seems likely. Finally, on 26 March 1898, five weeks after the sinking of the *Maine* and sixteen days before McKinley read his war message to Congress, Mahan and his family departed the United States for a tour of Europe.[37]

Ordered back to Washington, D.C., on 25 April to serve on the Naval War Board, which was to advise Secretary of the Navy John D. Long on the conduct of the war in ways not made entirely clear, Mahan spent most of the brief war making various strategical and tactical suggestions dealing principally with operational problems associated with U.S. fleet concentration in Cuban, Caribbean, and Spanish home waters. By the time Mahan reached Washington on 10 May, however, the fleet was anything but concentrated, and Dewey had already sent Spain's decrepit Asiatic squadron to the bottom of Manila Bay. On 3 July, most of the remainder of Spain's little navy was demolished near Santiago, Cuba, thus severing the Spanish army in Cuba and the colony itself from the Madrid government. Responding to threats of bombardment of the Spanish coast by the U.S. Navy, Spain wisely asked for a cease-fire, and the fighting ended on 12 August. Meanwhile, U.S. infantry units, numbering about eleven thousand men, had occupied Manila in the Philippines. Guam, Wake Island, and Puerto Rico also had been seized—all without opposition—and Hawaii had been annexed at last (July 1898) by treaty with a compliant insular government that had been earlier (June 1897) negotiated by the equally willing McKinley administration.

Mahan's main contribution to these stirring events was his continued insistence on the annexation of Hawaii. A less obvious contribution was a lucrative ("at my price") contract, signed two weeks after joining the Naval War Board, with *McClure's Magazine* that called for a series of five articles on the war. These pieces ran monthly in *McClure's* from December 1898 through April 1899 and were reprinted in book format as *Lessons of the War with Spain* in September 1899 after Mahan's return from participation as an American delegate at the First Hague Conference. The articles remain a valuable primary source on the history of the naval operations of the conflict.[38]

The final report of the Naval War Board, written by Mahan during the third week in August 1898, saluted the nation's acquisition of Hawaii and called the islands "militarily essential, both to our transit to Asia, and to the defense of our Pacific coast." The report also called for a canal at the isthmus and for eight naval coaling stations—two in the Caribbean, one each in Hawaii, Samoa,

Manila, and Guam, and two in the Chushan Islands near the mouth of the Yangtze River in China. "Beyond these eight positions," Mahan wrote, "the Board is not prepared to recommend acquisitions." The proposed bases in the central, western, and southwestern Pacific, however, would contribute to the future protection of American commercial interests in and near a China suffering from "the intrusion of European control upon her territory, and the consequent effect upon her trade relations." Noticeably, the report did not call for annexation of the Philippines.[39]

Mahan accepted the idea of Philippine annexation with the greatest reluctance. He observed in the final report of the Naval War Board that, from purely a military standpoint, all that was needed by the United States in the archipelago was a naval station and coaling facility at the "city and bay of Manila, or Subic Bay, if all Luzon Island be not ceded." A month earlier, on 21 July 1898, he had explained that he had "not yet become wholly adjusted to the new point of view opened to us by [George] Dewey's victory at Manila," even though it had "opened a vista of possibilities which were not by me in the least foreseen," and in spite of the fact that he had long anticipated a massive conflict in the Pacific between East and West. Mahan finally decided that a beneficent God had delivered the Philippines into American hands to be civilized and uplifted. By early August 1898, he was reluctantly following the Republican Party line on annexation, which had moved gradually from merely acquiring a naval base in Manila, to taking only Luzon, to annexing all of the islands. His arguments, shared by many U.S. senators and other Americans at the time, pointed out that the Filipinos simply could not be returned to the brutal colonial rule of Spain; that they could not be subjected to the domestic political chaos inherent in Emilio Aguinaldo's ill-organized independence movement; and that to withdraw from the islands would "abandon" to other nations "the task of maintaining order in the land in which we have been led to interpose."[40]

This does not mean that Mahan suddenly had become an enthusiastic colonialist in 1898. He had not. The word *colony* so disturbed him that he referred to the Philippines and Puerto Rico as "dependencies." He hoped that Americans could administer them with the skill, benevolence, and beneficence generally shown by the British in their colonies, but he admitted that the "task is novel to us; we may make blunders."[41] He participated not at all in the public debate on annexation in 1899–1900. He scarcely mentioned the bloody guerrilla war fought by Americans and Filipinos in the jungles of Luzon, Mindanao, and Samar in 1899–1901. Instead, he turned his busy pen to a defense of the British cause in the Boer War in South Africa. He was convinced that the Philippines lay far outside the eastern Pacific defense perimeter that he considered the U.S. Navy capable of defending; further, he came to believe by

1911 that the loss of the archipelago by act of war would be no more significant to the United States from a material standpoint than the "loss of a little finger, perhaps a single joint of it. The Philippines to us are less a property than a charge." Moreover, in his 1911 critique of the Naval War College's contingency plan for war with Japan, Mahan roundly attacked the college's recommendation that the U.S. Navy should carry the war to Japanese home waters by way of the Philippines. The distant Philippines were simply indefensible, he argued.[42]

To be sure, Mahan did speak on occasion in 1899–1900 of the Philippines in American hands as a threshold to the markets of Asia as well as a gateway to the Christianization of China; but the fact is that he had little interest in American commercial successes in China. Certainly he had no personal stake in the nation's China trade. He was interested, however, in the thrust of Secretary of State John Hay's first "Open Door Note" on 20 March 1899, which proclaimed U.S. opposition to the increasingly successful efforts of Germany, Russia, France, Britain, and Japan to carve a militarily helpless and administratively hapless China into monopolistic economic spheres of influence. Hay naively asked the powers involved in these assaults on Chinese sovereignty to desist, and to extend to one another and to all nations equality of commercial opportunity in their respective spheres. Of course, they did not.

Mahan was convinced that American industry, thanks to abundant raw materials, superior management techniques, and the manufacture of quality products in great number, could compete effectively in the China market (or any foreign market) against the products of any other industrial nation if free trade (both import and export) were permitted and subsidies were not extended to the various foreign traders by their governments. He had no idea what the economic potential of the China market might be, however, and he wisely refrained from any statistical guesswork on the point. But as Paul A. Varg demonstrates, there was no market of any consequence for American goods in China in 1900–1912 and even less of a market in the United States for Chinese commodities, facts perceived by resident U.S. capitalists, commercial agents, consuls, and other "old China hands," then and later. The volume and value of U.S. exports to China, measured against total U.S. exports abroad in 1900–1912, were infinitesimal. The China market was a myth.[43]

In 1902, Mahan was elected president of the American Historical Association. From this prestigious podium he instructed his fellow historians in the art of writing and presenting history in a manner so simple that it would instruct "the man in the street" about the world in which he lived and would simultaneously serve the God who was omnipresent in history. History, after all, he said, was "the plan of Providence . . . in its fulfillment." It was incumbent upon historians, he told them, to search for, discover, and verify by subordinationist methodology those "central ideas" that by act of verification become central themes, or foundation stones, in the fashioning of the "great mosaic" that was God's continuing revelation of Himself to man. One such theme was Mahan's own concept of the influence of sea power on history; he was certain that he had verified this concept in his books.[44]

It is not surprising that an American naval officer of Mahan's national and international renown as the discoverer of the influence of sea power on history and a devout believer in its concomitant, the inevitability of war, would attract disciples, enemies, and skeptics during his lifetime and beyond. After all, he was also known as an advocate of U.S. naval preparedness and American expansion (limited principally to the acquisition of coaling stations for the purpose of enhancing national security), and as a spokesman for the conceptual fusion of free trade, free speech, free thought, and free missionary Christianity as a means of uplifting backward peoples in Asia who enjoyed none of these blessings. These controversial views, one and all, intensified the formation and expression of pro-Mahan and anti-Mahan schools of thought, both of which have attracted historians ever since.

Initially, Mahan was attacked by anti-imperialists, pacifists, and constitutional strict constructionists as Philippine annexation became the major presidential campaign issue in 1899–1900. Called a professional killer and worse, he was held solely responsible for the unnecessary annexation of Hawaii in 1898. His belief, then and later, that neither the First nor the Second Hague Conference could, should, or would bring perpetual peace to mankind was especially annoying to those pacifists who held that enough peace committees, pamphlets, and speeches, together with the sheer willpower of right-thinking people, could somehow usher in a peaceful millennium someday soon. Not so, countered Mahan: "There are no short cuts by which men may be made peaceful. If the world could have been saved by an organization it would have been saved a thousand years ago by the Christian church." Put another way, if the omnipotent God really wanted peace on earth, He had merely to decree it.[45]

On the other hand, disciples of Mahan were decidedly upset soon after World War I, when the United States took the lead in bringing about a naval arms limitation agreement at the Washington Conference in 1921–1922. William O. Stevens, one such true believer, was much distressed with American acceptance of the 5:5:3:1.75:1.75 capital ship tonnage limitation ratio, a decision that threw "overboard [Mahan's] whole philosophy of sea power." The Five Power Treaty, lacking enforcement provisions, was but a "scrap of paper" that left the nation naked in the western Pacific in the face of an aggressive Japan. The "world has scrapped more than battleships," Stevens warned; "[I]t has discarded Mahan's entire philosophy for an experiment in faith." Such clairvoyance, however, was but a weak zephyr blowing against the pacifist and isolationist gales of the 1920s and 1930s, the general directions of which were distinctly anti-Mahan.[46]

Nonetheless, Mahan's emphasis on the importance of sea power on history was substantially vindicated in World War II and after, even though the strategy and tactics used by the U.S. Navy to achieve "command of the sea" had little to do with Mahan's principles of naval warfare. There was no Mahanian concentration of battle fleets on either the Japanese or the American side. Both navies operated with fractional tactical task forces, often distributed over large areas of ocean. No decisive, war-ending big battle was fought at sea. It was a war of attrition in which American industry was more than able to replace and augment U.S. losses on, under, and over the sea while Japan's industrial plant lacked that capability. It was also a war in which naval air power played a decisive role, as did the U.S. submarine force, in bringing Japan to its knees industrially and economically. Aircraft carriers, submarines, mobile floating decks, amphibious landing craft, radar, variable time fuses, kamikaze tactics — one and all would have mystified Mahan.[47]

Indeed, Mahan's inexplicable disregard of the relationship between naval technology, tactics, and strategy has bewildered his supporters and critics alike — especially his underestimation of the submarine as a decisive *guerre de course* weapon and his overestimation of the battleship as the decisive fleet surface weapon. It was a costly misjudgment, as German U-boats demonstrated in both World Wars. Even when the obsolete *U-9* sank three old British armored cruisers on 22 September 1914, killing 1,460 sailors, Mahan dismissed the event as a freak accident. It did "not greatly impress me from a military standpoint," he wrote; "I have always held that torpedo protection is a matter of scouting — watchfulness, and lapses there will occur. The result will show if I am greatly wrong." He was totally wrong.[48]

During his final years in the public eye and in print, from the convening of the Second Hague Conference in June 1907 until his death in December 1914, Mahan spent much of his literary energy hurling verbal thunderbolts at the peace and arbitration movements, while simultaneously insisting that the U.S. Navy limit the tonnage of its battleships and the caliber of some of the guns mounted on them. Much of his literary activity during these years was also devoted to a gratuitous, almost tiresome campaign to warn the British that war with Germany was looming and to explain to them how the Royal Navy might best conduct the naval dimensions of that conflict.[49]

The four most significant of the controversial issues that he raised between 1907 and 1914, especially in terms of his personal relations with Theodore Roosevelt and his professional reputation within the U.S. Navy, were: (1) his contention that exempting neutral noncontraband private property from destruction at sea during wartime would simply lengthen the duration of conflicts, because of the excessive wartime profits inherent in the hoary U.S. maritime doctrine of "free ships make free goods"; (2) his belief that the tonnage of battleships should not exceed twelve thousand, as heavier vessels would be "larger than needed, and likely result in too few ships," the greater size of which would not provide a "commensurate gain in offensive power"; (3) his related recommendation that the U.S. Navy's annual tonnage construction allotment from Congress be spread over a "balanced" fleet of battleships, cruisers, and destroyer-torpedo vessels; and (4) his insistence that the all-big-gun (10-inch and 12-inch) batteries being built into the new U.S. battleships should be replaced with more operationally flexible mixed-caliber batteries mounting various combinations of 12-, 10-, 8-, and 6-inch guns. He went to the mat with Roosevelt on all these points, lost all four falls, and was gently nudged out of the President's inner circle for his trouble. By the time war in Europe loomed in 1913–14, Mahan was widely regarded as an eccentric, quarrelsome "back number" in the U.S. Navy. His main error was that although he was a "battleship navalist," he was not a *Dreadnought* purist.[50]

One must still ask, given the view that Mahan had become irrelevant by the time of his death, is he really worth reading and pondering today? Although there have been many other influences on history besides the existence or nonexistence of sea power, the relationship between the mastery of the sea and the rise, continuation, or fall of various seaboard nation-states since the beginning of recorded history is fairly obvious. And as long as there is no persuasive historical evidence whatever to contradict Mahan's insistence that war is inherent in the universe, in human history, and in the human condition, it is only prudent that the United States remains thoroughly and constantly prepared for war at sea, whatever the future technological dimensions of naval war might be. This may sound partly like advice from the grave at Quogue, as indeed it is.

## FURTHER READING

The most complete and important source for an understanding of Alfred Thayer Mahan is Robert Seager II and Doris D. Maguire, eds., *Letters and Papers of Alfred Thayer Mahan*, 3 vols. (Annapolis, Md., 1975). Mahan letters known by Seager or Maguire to have surfaced since 1975 have been directed to the attention of the curator of the Mahan Collection at the Naval War College Library in Newport, R.I. For information on the nature, content, and extent of the Mahan Papers at the War College, see John B. Hattendorf, comp., *Register of the Alfred Thayer Mahan Papers* (Newport, R.I., 1987). In addition, Professor Hattendorf and his sister-in-law, Lynn C. Hattendorf, have compiled *A Bibliography of the Works of Alfred Thayer Mahan* (Newport, R.I., 1986). Excellent in every respect, this work supersedes and renders obsolete all other bibliographical treatments of Mahan. Far from excellent is Mahan's autobiography, *From Sail to Steam: Recollections of Naval Life* (New York, 1907). It is uniformly self-serving and highly selective from a factual standpoint. Nonetheless, it is an important and unique historical document that also must be consulted.

Four full-length biographies of Mahan have appeared since his death in 1914. The first of these, *The Life of Admiral Mahan* (London, 1920), was written by Charles Carlisle Taylor, sometime British vice consul at New York. Based on interviews with Mahan family members, on conversations with a number of individuals who knew Mahan personally, and on a scattering of letters supplied by a few of Mahan's correspondents, Taylor's effort was superficial, episodic, and eulogistic, and he emphasized the Anglo-American dimension in Mahan's life and writings.

Taylor's book was followed two decades later by U.S. Navy Captain W. D. Puleston's *Mahan: The Life and Work of Captain Alfred Thayer Mahan, U.S.N.* (New Haven, Conn., 1939). The first extended evaluation by a fellow naval officer, it remains a solid, though somewhat dull, encyclopedic and narrowly conceived account of Mahan's professional naval life, which, in Puleston's view, was illuminated throughout by the brilliance and grandeur of Mahan's philosophy of sea power and its influence on history. Although Puleston's sources were far more numerous and more revealing than were Taylor's, his hagiographic account was essentially a glowing fitness report on Mahan into which nothing negative was permitted to intrude.

The first historiographically professional treatment of Mahan's life and works was William E. Livezey's *Mahan on Sea Power* (Norman, Okla., 1947). Utilizing the perspective of the naval and diplomatic aspects of the two World Wars and the historical antecedents of both conflicts, Professor Livezey produced a sophisticated evaluation of Mahan's doctrine of sea power viewed from a modern geopolitical, diplomatic, and technological standpoint, and he first questioned the usefulness of the doctrine in a militarily scientific world that Mahan never conceived.

Livezey's path-breaking account has been supplemented by Robert Seager II's *Alfred Thayer Mahan* (Annapolis, Md., 1977). Basing his work on much hitherto unused primary source material, Livezey's work, and factual data found only in Taylor, Puleston, and *From Sail to Steam*, as well as a growing body of scholarly monographs and articles about Mahan and the "New Navy," Seager attempted to humanize the man, to explain some of the forces and factors that apparently motivated him, and to evaluate his sea power doctrine in conjunction with U.S. imperialism at the turn of the century. Throughout his book, Seager emphasized Mahan's unorthodox Christian theology; his philosophy of history and of war in history; his Anglophilia in thought, word, and deed; his static conception of naval tactics and technology; his family life and personal financial problems; and his thoroughly controversial, contentious, and unpleasant personality. Of the latter, there is no suggestion whatever in Mahan's autobiography.

Although the body of Mahan, Mahan-related, and New Navy materials has expanded enormously since 1945, serious students of the "Philosopher of Sea Power" should not overlook Richard W. Turk's more recent *The Ambiguous Relationship: Theodore Roosevelt and Alfred Thayer Mahan* (Westport, Conn., 1988), or Richard S. West's enduring *Admirals of American Empire: The Combined Story of George Dewey, Alfred Thayer Mahan, Winfield Scott Schley and William Thomas Sampson* (Indianapolis, Ind., 1948). Nor should they overlook such important interpretative essays as

James A. Field, "Alfred Thayer Mahan Speaks for Himself," *Naval War College Review* 29 (Fall 1976): 47–60; Julius W. Pratt, "Alfred Thayer Mahan," in *The Marcus W. Jernegan Essays in American Historiography*, edited by William T. Hutchinson (Chicago, 1937), 207–26; and especially Philip A. Crowl's "Alfred Thayer Mahan: The Naval Historian," in *Makers of Modern Strategy from Machiavelli to the Nuclear Age*, edited by Peter Paret (Princeton, N.J., 1986), 444–77.

## NOTES

1. This interpretative essay is based substantially, although by no means entirely, on the following works and studies of Mahan by the present author, viz.: Robert Seager II and Doris D. Maguire, eds., *Letters and Papers of Alfred Thayer Mahan*, 3 vols. (Annapolis, Md., 1975) (hereafter cited as *LPATM*), and Robert Seager II, *Alfred Thayer Mahan* (Annapolis, Md., 1977), a biography based on *LPATM* (hereafter cited as Seager, *Mahan*). In greater or lesser degree, this essay also relies on material found in the author's several articles on Mahan, viz.: "Ten Years before Mahan: The Unofficial Case for the New Navy, 1880–1890," *Mississippi Valley Historical Review* 40 (1953): 491–512; "A Biography of a Biographer: Alfred Thayer Mahan," in *Changing Interpretations and New Sources in Naval History*, edited by Robert W. Love, Jr. (New York, 1950), 278–92; "Alfred Thayer Mahan," in *Dictionary of American Military Biography*, edited by Roger J. Spiller, Joseph G. Dawson, and T. Harry Williams, 3 vols. (Westport, Conn., 1984), 2:711–14; and "Alfred Thayer Mahan," in *Dictionary of Literary Biography: American Historians, 1866–1912*, edited by Clyde N. Wilson (Detroit, 1986), 162–73. It is also indebted conceptually to recent research by Philip A. Crowl, James A. Field, and Paul A. Varg. For a more traditional interpretation of Mahan, see Margaret Tuttle Sprout, "Mahan: Evangelist of Sea Power," in *Makers of Modern Strategy: Military Thought from Machiavelli to Hitler*, edited by Edward Mead Earle (Princeton, N.J., 1943), 415–45.

2. Rudyard Kipling, *The Cat That Walked by Himself* (New York, 1970), passim. For Ellen Kuhn Mahan's recollections of her father, see *LPATM*, 3:719–30.

3. For a conflicting view on Mahan's seamanship, see Captain Robert Brent, USN, "Mahan—Mariner or Misfit?" U.S. Naval Institute *Proceedings* 92 (April 1966): 92–103. Compare his account of the *Wachusett* collision, which he denies having happened, with Seager, *Mahan*, 140, 261; and *LPATM*, 2:160. It happened.

4. The useful bibliography of Mahan's publications found in William E. Livezey, *Mahan on Sea Power* (Norman, Okla., 1947), 301–19, has been substantially expanded by John B. Hattendorf and Lynn C. Hattendorf, comps., *A Bibliography of the Works of Alfred Thayer Mahan* (Newport, R.I., 1986), which is now the standard bibliographical source on Mahan.

5. Seager, *Mahan*, 575–77. See especially Alfred Thayer Mahan, "The Peace Conference and the Moral Aspect of War" and "War from the Christian Standpoint," in his *Some Neglected Aspects of War* (Boston, 1907); "The Apparent Decadence of the Church's Influence" and "Twentieth Century Christianity" in his *The Interest of America in Sea Power* (Boston, 1897), 229–30, 235–36, 243–46; and his 1913 and 1914 articles on "Freedom in the Use of the Prayer Book," *The Churchman* 108 (November 1913): 623–24, and "Prayer Book Revision," ibid., 110 (October 1914):465–66, 497–98. Also, see his "Christian Progress," *New York Times*, 16 August 1914, as well as his various state-

ments, addresses, and lay sermons on Christian and Episcopal Church themes and concerns in *LPATM*, 3:423, 590–91, 597, 598–602, 605, 644–56, 657, 682, 683–84, 693–97, 714–16. His intense religious experience while on board the *Iroquois* is printed in full in *LPATM*, 1:145–332.

6. For the derivation of Mahan's notion of the influence of sea power on history, see Lawrence C. Allin, "The Naval Institute, Mahan, and the Naval Profession," *Naval War College Review* 31 (Summer 1978): 29–48; A. T. Mahan, *From Sail to Steam: Recollections of Naval Life* (New York, 1907), 276; and J. M Scammell, "Thucydides and Sea Power," U.S. Naval Institute *Proceedings* 47 (May 1921): 701–14. See further, Kenneth J. Hagan's perceptive "Alfred Thayer Mahan," in *Makers of American Diplomacy*, edited by Frank J. Merli and Theodore A. Wilson, 2 vols. (New York, 1974), also, Seager, *Mahan*, 199–204, and his "Ten Years before Mahan," passim. Among others who flirted or consorted with the sea power hypothesis were ancient Greeks and Romans: Thucydides, Xenophon, and Tacitus; Englishmen: Francis Bacon, Walter Raleigh, and John Seeley; U.S. Navy Officers: Robert W. Shufeldt, Stephen B. Luce, and William Glenn David; and U.S. House members: John F. Miller and William G. McAdoo.

7. For Milo Mahan's theological influence on his nephew, see Seager, *Mahan*, 445–55, 555. Mahan's hostility to disarmament, arbitration, and international courts to end war or mitigate its horrors is expressed in, and the doctrine of 'free ships make free goods' is condemned in, his "The Peace Conference and the Moral Aspect of War," 433–37; "The Hague Conference: The Question of Immunity of Belligerent Merchant Shipping" and "Commerce and War," *New York Times*, 17 and 23 November 1898; "The Hague Conference and the Practical Aspect of War," *National Review* 49 (July 1907): 688–704; also in related articles, written in 1907 and 1911, which are reprinted in his *Some Neglected Aspects of War*, and in his *Armaments and Arbitration, or the Place of Force in the International Relations of States* (New York, 1912). Mahan's philosophy of history and historiography is discussed in detail in Seager, *Mahan*, 430–58, and briefly below in this essay. The influence of Jomini and Luce on Mahan in the realm of the "laws" of strategy and tactics is skillfully treated in Philip A. Crowl, "Alfred Thayer Mahan: The Naval Historian," in *Makers of Modern Strategy from Machiavelli to the Nuclear Age*, edited by Peter Paret (Princeton, N.J., 1986), 444–77. Mahan's arguments favoring "balanced" fleets and "mixed batteries" are presented in his "Retrospect upon the War between Japan and Russia," *National Review* 47 (May 1906): 383–405; "Reflections, Historic and Others, Suggested by the Battle of the Sea of Japan," U.S. Naval Institute *Proceedings* 32 (June 1906): 447–71; and "The Battleship of All Big Guns," *Worlds Work* 21 (January 1911): 13888–902. Also, see Seager, *Mahan*, 519–34, and note 49 below.

8. The quotation is Mahan's. Luce's letter of invitation, dated 22 July 1884, has not survived, nor is it clear just what he intended having Mahan cover in the lectures. See *LPATM*, 1:577–78; and Seager, *Mahan*, 141–42.

9. Seager, *Mahan*, 134–36.

10. *LPATM*, 1:577–78, 581–82; 2:276, 285; and Seager, *Mahan*, 144–47.

11. *LPATM*, 1:606–7.

12. Luce quotations in John D. Hayes and John B. Hattendorf, eds., *The Writings of Stephen B. Luce* (Newport, R.I., 1975), 45–68, 71–97, 190–91. Also, see John B. Hattendorf, B. Mitchell Simpson III, and John R. Wadleigh, *Sailors and Scholars: The Centennial History of the U.S. Naval War College* (Newport, R.I., 1984), 11–24. Luce had

also discovered that "Religion and war are the two great central facts of history. . . . Religion gave birth to education. War led the way to civilization." Mahan would soon come to accept this idea as well, if indeed he had not already embraced it.

13. Antoine-Henri Jomini, *The Art of War, 1836*, translated [1861] from the French by Captain G. H. Mendell, USA, and Captain W. P. Craighill, USA (Philadelphia, 1892), 321. This is a later edition of their 1862 English-language volume. It seems likely that of Jomini's many volumes, Mahan read only this one. See Crowl, "Alfred Thayer Mahan," 444–47.

14. Seager, *Mahan*, 149–58.

15. E. B. Potter and J. Roger Fredland, eds., *The United States and World Sea Power* (Englewood Cliffs, N.J., 1955), 383–87.

16. Mahan, *From Sail to Steam*, 168, 277–78.

17. Jomini, *Art of War*, 70–71; Crowl, "Alfred Thayer Mahan," 455–56; and Seager, *Mahan*, 168–70, 552, 555. The language here is Jomini's, as translated by Mendell and Craighill. See note 13 above.

18. A. T. Mahan, "Fleet Battle Tactics" [1886]. This lengthy, typewritten, unpublished study, containing critical marginal comments by Luce, is in the Mahan Collection, Naval War College Library. Also, see Seager, *Mahan*, 166–68, 171–73.

19. Mahan, *From Sail to Steam*, 284–85; and Seager, *Mahan*, 173.

20. A. T. Mahan, *Naval Strategy, Compared and Contrasted with the Principles of Military Operations on Land* (Boston, 1911), 1–3, 6–10, 15–18, 31, 49, 53–55, 189, 199, 254, 279, 386, 391–93, 415, 422–23, 428–29. Crowl, "Alfred Thayer Mahan," 457–61, contains an excellent synthesis and critique of Mahan's strategic concepts. Less persuasive is W. D. Puleston's attempt to identify those concepts with the strategic and tactical insights of Karl von Clausewitz in his otherwise useful *Mahan: The Life and Work of Captain Alfred Thayer Mahan, U.S.N.* (New Haven, Conn., 1939), 295–98. Jomini's views on land warfare strategy are set forth in his *Art of War*, 67–69. Most of his observations lend themselves imperfectly to naval warfare. For the difficult gestation of Mahan's volume, *Naval Strategy*, see Seager, *Mahan*, 548–53.

21. *LPATM*, 1:622–24.

22. Seager, *Mahan*, 205–6; and Mahan, *From Sail to Steam*, 324–25.

23. A. T. Mahan, *The Influence of Sea Power upon History, 1660–1783*, 14th ed. (Boston, 1898), 28, 53, 71.

24. Ibid., 33–34, 42, 88.

25. Ibid., 39, 42.

26. Ibid., 42–44, 49, 50, 53, 56, 57–58.

27. Ibid, 58, 67, 87–88. Indeed, as early as March 1880, Mahan had told Ashe that the coming of a canal in Panama would require American control of the isthmus. "To control at the Isthmus we must have a very large Navy — and must begin to build as soon as the first spadeful of earth is turned at Panama." That failing, "[W]e may as well shut up about the Monroe Doctrine at once," *LPATM*, 1:481–82.

28. *LPATM*, 1:572–74; Seager, *Mahan*, 122, 132–34, 140–41; and Seager, "Ten Years before Mahan," passim.

29. Reprinted in Mahan, *Interest of America in Sea Power*, 26. The population density per square mile of the three West Coast states in 1890 was: California, 7.63; Oregon, 3.28; Washington, 5.25. For the entire coast it was 5.83. For Mahan's definition of himself as an "imperialist" (i.e., nonisolationist), see his *From Sail to Steam*, 324.

30. See his articles in the *Atlantic Monthly* (1890, 1893), *The Forum* (1893), and *Harper's Monthly* (1895, 1897), as reprinted in Mahan, *Interest of America in Sea Power*, 3–104, 137–214, 271–314. The concept was later reiterated by Mahan in "The Panama Canal and Sea Power in the Pacific," *Century* 82 (June 1911): 240–48, and in "The Panama Canal and the Distribution of the Fleet," *North American Review* 200 (September 1914): 549–68. Also, see James A. Field's excellent "Alfred Thayer Mahan Speaks for Himself," *Naval War College Review* 29 (Fall 1976): 47–60, for a persuasive development and evaluation of Mahan's eastern Pacific defense perimeter concept.

31. "The Effect of Asiatic Conditions upon World Policies," *North American Review* (November 1900), in A. T. Mahan, *The Problem of Asia and Its Effects upon International Policies* (Boston, 1900), 201–2.

32. A. T. Mahan "Was Panama 'A Chapter of National Dishonor?'" *North American Review* 196 (October 1912): 549–68; A. T. Mahan, "Panama Unguarded Might be Seized," *New York Times*, 27 October 1912; and Seager, *Mahan*, 498–99. On the Monroe Doctrine and the Roosevelt Corollary thereto, see A. T. Mahan, "The Monroe Doctrine," *National Review* 40 (1903): 871–89. This article was revised in 1908 in order to change his hostile view of the Roosevelt Corollary and was reprinted in Mahan's *Naval Administration and Warfare, Some General Principles with Other Essays* (Boston, 1908). Also, see Seager, *Mahan*, 142, 492–94. For the numerous substantial differences of opinion between Mahan and Roosevelt on these and other so-called imperial matters, see Richard W. Turk, *The Ambiguous Relationship: Theodore Roosevelt and Alfred Thayer Mahan* (Westport, Conn, 1988), passim, but especially 49, 52–54.

33. *LPATM*, 2:92–93, 507; Mahan, *Interest of America in Sea Power*, 31; and Seager, *Mahan*, 248–50, 358, 465, 476–79.

34. *LPATM*, 2:461. For a view of Mahan from the perspective of his literary production, see Seager, "Alfred Thayer Mahan," in *Dictionary of Literary Biography*, 47:162–73. Also, see Seager, *Mahan*, 327–32. Save for his excellent two-volume life of Nelson, which he began while serving in the *Chicago* and finished soon after his retirement in March 1897, Mahan wrote but two more books. His two-volume *Sea Power in Its Relations to the War of 1812* (Boston, 1912), previously serialized in *Scribner's Magazine*, remains a solid study of naval operations in that conflict. It is Mahan's only book dealing substantially with U.S. history. It is also a fascinating interpretative exercise in how an American Anglophile decides that *both* Britain and the United States had simultaneously fought wholly just wars in 1812–1814. See Kenneth L. Moll, "Mahan: American Historian," *Military Affairs* 27 (Fall 1963): 132, 137; and Seager, *Mahan*, 506–8, 564–68. Mahan's other monograph, *Naval Strategy* (1911), is discussed elsewhere in this essay (see note 20).

35. Mahan, *Interest of America in Sea Power*, 182–84, 291–92, 295, 299, 307–10; *LPATM*, 2:505–6, 532; and Seager, *Mahan*, 357–59.

36. Livezey, *Mahan on Sea Power*, 133–37; *LPATM*, 2:37, 734; and Seager, *Mahan*, 358–59, 362. The best brief account of various U.S. Navy contingency war plans against Spain is in David F. Trask, *The War with Spain in 1898* (New York, 1981), 72–78. Also, see Turk, *Ambiguous Relationship*, 28–29, 34–35.

37. *LPATM*, 2:532, 3:592–94; Seager, *Mahan*, 357–58, 360–61; and H. G. Rickover, *How the Battleship "Maine" Was Destroyed* (Washington, D.C., 1976), 107–30.

38. For Mahan's service on the Naval War Board, see Trask, *War with Spain*, 67–68, 89–90, 119, 203, 280–83, 306, 339, 361, 377; A. T. Mahan, *Lessons of the War with Spain*

*and Other Articles* (Boston, 1899), 3–204; and A. T. Mahan, "The Work of the Naval War Board of 1898: A Report to the General Board of the Navy," 29 October 1906, in *LPATM*, 3:627–43. Also, see Seager, *Mahan*, 366–91.

39. *LPATM*, 2:538–39, 581–91; Livezey, *Mahan on Sea Power*, 170–74; and Seager, *Mahan*, 391, 395–96.

40. Seager, *Mahan*, 391–95; and Mahan, "Effect of Asiatic Conditions," in Mahan, *Problem of Asia*, 147–202, especially 175.

41. A. T. Mahan, "America's Duties to Her New Dependencies," reprinted under the title "The Relations of the United States to Their New Dependencies," in Mahan, *Lessons of War with Spain*, 241–53; A. T. Mahan, "Capt. Mahan on Expansion," *New York Times*, 1 December 1898. Also, see excerpts from a speech he gave on 30 November 1898, printed in *LPATM*, 3:596, under the title "A Distinction between Colonies and Dependencies." The distinction was that "A colony must be a country qualified by its natural conditions, climatic or otherwise, to become incorporated with the mother country." Therefore, he added: "We can't have colonies. The original Roman colony was an outpost of the mother country—an extended Rome in the fullest sense of the word."

42. Seager, *Mahan*, 394. He also later complained that the nation had been "pitchforked" into the Philippines and spoke of the "extreme repugnance" with which the United States had annexed the islands. The clash between the college's contingency war plan against Japan of 1911, and Mahan's critique, or counterplan, can be traced in *LPATM*, 3:380–88, 389–94, 395, 400–2; see also Naval War College, "Notes on Comments of Rear Admiral Mahan," ca. 25 February–1 March 1911, in the Naval War Collage Library, Newport, R.I., and Seager, *Mahan*, 483–86.

43. Mahan, *Problem of Asia*, 155, 166, 176–77, 189–90; and Paul A. Varg, *The Making of a Myth: The United States and China, 1897–1912* (East Lansing, Mich., 1968), 36–53; especially 50–52. In 1900, the value of U.S. exports to China ($7,000,000) was .005 percent of the value ($1,394,000,000) of all U.S. exports that year; it rose to a high ($53,000,000) of 3.5 percent in 1905 ($1,519,000,000) and slipped back to 1.1 percent ($24,000,000) in a total of $2,204,000,000 in 1912. See *The Statistical History of the United States from Colonial Times to the Present* (Stamford, Conn., 1965), 550.

44. A. T. Mahan, "Subordination in Historical Treatment," renamed "Writing of History," *Atlantic Monthly* 91 (March 1903): 289–98. For an earlier (October 1897) statement of his subordinational methodology, see Mahan, *Interest of America in Sea Power*, 284–85. Also, see Seager, *Mahan*, 448–51. For Mahan's predictably successful demonstration of the historicity of the resurrection of Jesus by similar methodological devices, see his *The Harvest Within* (Boston, 1909), 22–24, 3–41, 44–45, 49–52.

45. Wallace Rice, "Some Current Fallacies of Captain Mahan," *Dial* 28 (16 March 1900): 198–200; and Lucia Ames Mead, "Some Fallacies of Captain Mahan," *Arena* 40 (September 1908): 163–70.

46. William Oliver Stevens, "Scrapping Mahan." The Five Powers and their assigned ratios were Britain (5), United States (5), Japan (3), France (1.75), and Italy (1.75).

47. Bernard Brodie, "New Tactics in Naval Warfare,'" *Foreign Affairs* 26 (January 1946): 210–23.

48. Quoted passage in *LPATM*, 3:549; R. A. Bowling, "The Negative Influence of Mahan on Anti-submarine Warfare," *Journal of the Royal United Services Institute for Defense Studies* (December 1977), 52–59; A. T. Mahan, "The Submarine and Its Ene-

mies," *Collier's Weekly* 39 (6 April 1907):17–21; Seager, *Mahan*, 535–38, 554; and Dan van der Vat, *The Atlantic Campaign: World War II's Great Struggle at Sea* (New York, 1988), 15–16.

49. See, particularly, his "The Hague Conference and the Practical Aspect of War," "Germany's Naval Ambition," "The Battleship of all Big Guns," and the first six articles, initially published in *North American Review* in 1911–1912, that are reprinted in Mahan, *Armaments and Arbitration*, 1–154.

50. Seager, *Mahan*, 506–10, 521–33. Also, see Turk, *Ambiguous Relationship*, 57–61, 71, 76, 82–96, 101–8.

# ☆ George Dewey
☆
☆ **Admiral of the Navy**

*by Vernon L. Williams*

HE HAD COMPILED A GOOD RECORD, BUT ONE THAT LACKED DISTINC-
tion. He had spent very little time at sea during the previous twenty years,
played only a minor role in the development of the New Navy, and was not
considered a member of that brash new group of scientific officers determined
to modernize the navy; nor was he a contributor to the school of naval theo-
rists led by Stephen B. Luce and Alfred Thayer Mahan. There was little in
George Dewey's record to suggest that he had much hope for further promotion and leadership opportunities in the emerging navy of the twentieth
century.[1]

His prospects changed markedly in the early morning hours of 1 May 1898,
however, when Dewey turned to the captain of the *Olympia* in Manila Bay
and said quietly, "You may fire when ready, Gridley." From that fateful moment on, Dewey's star ascended dramatically as the nation sought to recognize
this new hero of America's war of manifest destiny. Some might debate the degree of Dewey's contribution to the modernization of the U.S. Navy, but no
one can ignore Dewey's administrative presence in that modernization process
from the turn of the century until his death in 1917.

George Dewey was born in Montpelier, Vermont, on 26 December 1837.
His father, Julius Y. Dewey, was a well-to-do physician whose entrepreneurial
pursuits led him to found a successful insurance venture that later would give
Dewey a more than comfortable lifestyle in the Navy. Dewey spent his child-
hood with two older brothers and a younger sister, as his mother, Mary Perrin
Dewey, had died early in his life. According to Dewey, his relationship with his
father was close and remained so throughout the rest of the elder Dewey's life.
Much in the character of George Dewey seems to have been drawn from his

father: "He was one of those natural leaders to whom men turn for unbiased advice. His ideas of right and wrong were very fixed."[2]

Of the years before he attended the U.S. Naval Academy, Dewey left little behind to indicate what kind of boyhood he had enjoyed. After his fame was won at Manila Bay, all kinds of wonderful stories were published in the newspapers and in popular histories that exploded on the scene in 1898 and 1899. As Dewey biographer Ronald Spector suggests, "Old residents of Montpelier, at the urging of eager newspapermen, found little difficulty in 'remembering' many colorful and prophetic incidents from Dewey's early years."[3] Earlier biographers noted that "it is curious how the wording of many passages in the autobiography follows so closely the phrases of eulogistic volumes on Dewey published in 1899."[4] From all indications, it appears that Dewey was no shy, withdrawn boy, but one who was active and, at times, difficult to control. Later, as a young cadet at the Naval Academy, Dewey would be hard-pressed to refrain from mischievous pranks.

Dewey entered the Naval Academy in 1854 despite his desire to go to West Point. No appointments were available to either West Point or Annapolis, but a last-minute change of heart by a Naval Academy appointee gave Julius Dewey the opportunity to use his influence with Senator Solomon Foote to name George as the substitute.[5] During the next four years, Dewey compiled a solid academic record while leaving behind a handsome list of demerits. He graduated fifth in a class of fourteen.[6]

Emerging from four years of "hell and discipline,"[7] Dewey was assigned to the USS *Wabash*, flagship of the Mediterranean Squadron. With no opportunity for leave, he sailed with the *Wabash* on 22 July 1858 en route to her station in the Mediterranean. Despite bouts of homesickness, Dewey came to appreciate the Mediterranean and the opportunity to observe European politics at each port of call. Impressionable and idealistic, Dewey spent the next three years in the region, developing his maritime skills and attending to his naval and diplomatic duties as he successively served in the *Wabash*, *Powhatan*, and *Pawnee*. In 1861, he was ordered back to the academy to take the examination for lieutenant.[8]

Dewey stood third in his class on the examination and would be commissioned lieutenant in April 1862. Immediately after taking the examination, however, he went home to Montpelier on leave. When word reached Dewey that hostilities had begun at Fort Sumter, South Carolina, he proceeded to a new assignment, the steam frigate *Mississippi*. The ship had had a distinguished career, having fought in the Mexican War and having accompanied Matthew C. Perry to Japan in 1853; but the introduction of screw propulsion had rendered her obsolete, and she was not expected to play an important role in the impending conflict. In the middle of May 1861, the *Mississippi*, with

Lieutenant Dewey on board, left Boston and steamed down the Atlantic coast to Key West, Florida. During the rest of 1861, Dewey participated in blockading activities and support of the Union Army along the southern Gulf Coast.[9]

Following the indecisive battle at Bull Run and a series of naval successes at Cape Hatteras, North Carolina, and Port Royal, South Carolina, Secretary of the Navy Gideon Welles and Assistant Secretary of the Navy Gustavus Fox convinced President Abraham Lincoln that the Union must secure control of the mouth of the Mississippi River and that David Glasgow Farragut was the man to command the naval forces sent there.[10] Years later, Dewey considered the New Orleans campaign to have been the most important training he received as a young officer. "Valuable as the training at Annapolis was, it was poor schooling beside that of serving under Farragut in time of war."[11]

Shortly before beginning operations against New Orleans, the *Mississippi* received a new commander, Captain Melancthon Smith. Because of transfers and a lack of trained officers, the *Mississippi* had on board only four line officers, including the captain, and, by a process of elimination, Dewey was the second ranking officer. Farragut informed Smith "that there was complaint on the part of some officers on the Navy list" that Dewey, who was very low on the list, held a "position higher than theirs." Although Smith had the reputation of being a difficult captain to serve under, Dewey apparently worked well with him and had won his trust. Persuading Farragut to let Dewey remain as his executive officer, Smith said: "Dewey is doing all right. I don't want a stranger here."[12]

Formidable obstacles stood between Flag Officer Farragut and his objective, the most important being two forts, Jackson and Saint Philip. The forts were located midway between New Orleans, Louisiana, and the mouth of the Mississippi, and the Confederates had built a boom of cypress logs and chain at Fort Jackson to block passage upriver. Ordered to use his gunboats to bombard the forts into submission before attacking New Orleans, Farragut doubted that he had the ammunition or the manpower to capture them. In spite of repeated warnings from his commanders that attacking New Orleans without control of the forts would bring disaster, Farragut proposed to bypass the forts and move against New Orleans.[13]

The first problem facing Farragut was getting all his vessels—including the *Mississippi*, to which Dewey was still assigned—across the bars at the entrance to the river. On 18 March 1862, using shallow-draft mortar boats, Farragut began towing his ships across the bar at the deepest point in the streams leading into the Mississippi River. For eight laborious hours the *Mississippi* was pulled through mud until she finally cleared the bar on the other side. A month later, on 17 April, the mortar boats opened fire on Forts Jackson and Saint Philip; on the twentieth, two gunboats forced an opening through the boom that was wide enough for Farragut's ships to pass through, one at a time.[14]

On board the *Mississippi* on 24 April, Smith received orders to begin an early morning cruise past the two Confederate forts. His ship was assigned to the first division, behind the *Cayuga* and the *Pensacola*. Farragut was hoping to get as many ships as possible past the two forts before the rebel gunners noticed his intention to bypass the gun positions and attack New Orleans. Explaining that his night vision was poor, Smith ordered young Lieutenant Dewey to take the helm while he supervised fire control.

According to Dewey, the *Pensacola* stopped as she came abreast of each fort to fire a broadside, each time causing Dewey, just behind with the *Mississippi*, to reverse engines to prevent a collision. Dewey later remarked that "for a man of twenty-four I was having my share of responsibility." All during this time, the *Mississippi* was "under fire and returning it." To complicate matters, the Confederate ram *Manassas* appeared, and Dewey, seeing an opportunity to run down the ironclad, quickly maneuvered the ship toward the ram. The rebel commander reacted in time to avoid the crush of the *Mississippi*, and at the last minute, "sheering in, he [the captain of the ram] managed to strike us a glancing blow just abaft the port paddlewheel." The damage to the *Mississippi* proved not to be fatal, and Dewey continued on past the forts out of range of the Confederate guns.[15]

As dawn was breaking, the *Manassas* was spotted astern of the fleet as she bore down on Farragut's ships in a second attempt to disrupt the Union attack. Smith was back in command on the bridge of the *Mississippi* and reacted swiftly to the sudden appearance of the ram. He was in the act of requesting permission to attack when Farragut appeared on the scene; hanging out of the rigging of the *Hartford*, he cried out to Smith to "run down the ram."

Turning to Dewey, Smith asked if he could turn the ship around. Dewey replied that he could but later admitted, "I did not know whether I could turn her or not, but I knew that either I was going to do so or else run her aground." On the first try, the *Mississippi* came around and faced the ram. Realizing that the cruiser bearing down on his ship would inflict a fatal blow, the Confederate captain evaded the collision and ran aground on the riverbank. The *Mississippi* "so riddled her [the stationary target *Manassas*] with shot that she was dislodged from the bank and drifted below the forts, [where] she blew up and sank." In his report to Farragut, Smith praised Dewey for his "efficient service," which "kept the vessel in her station during the engagement, a task exceedingly difficult from the darkness and thick smoke" that crowded the scene.[16]

Dewey's initial battle experience indelibly influenced him. The unforgettable image of Farragut hanging onto the rigging of the *Hartford* with blood in his eyes and screaming for attack remained with Dewey the rest of his life. Dewey confided later that when hard-pressed for a difficult decision, he often thought of Farragut and what he would do in the same situation. " . . . I confess that I was thinking of him the night that we entered [Manila] Bay. . . ." In those early morning hours of 1 May 1898, Dewey was confident that he was doing exactly what Farragut would have done, striking boldly and aggressively at the enemy.[17]

During the spring of 1863, two events occurred that almost cut short Dewey's naval career. At 2200 on 13 March, the *Mississippi* began the approach to Port Hudson with Farragut in order to cooperate with Farragut's plan to cut the Confederate naval support of Vicksburg, Mississippi. As the Union fleet attempted to pass Port Hudson, Confederate guns opened fire. Because of a critical mistake by her civilian pilot, the *Mississippi* grounded near the ninety-degree turn in the river at the base of the rebel fortifications. Despite repeated efforts to back off the sandbar, heavy fire concentrated on the disabled vessel forced Smith to order his crew to abandon ship. Using the few undamaged boats still able to float, Dewey, brandishing his pistol, made a reluctant boat crew return to the burning ship to rescue the remaining ship's crew and the captain. Although under fire since the grounding, Dewey was not one of the sixty-four casualties. In his report after the action, Smith wrote the Secretary of the Navy that "I should be neglecting a most important duty should I omit to mention the coolness of my executive officer, Mr. Dewey. . . ." In describing the event to his father, Dewey wrote that "such scenes make people Christians."[18]

If fortune was smiling on him that day, Dewey got a special dispensation a few weeks later. With the loss of the *Mississippi*, he briefly served as prize commissioner at New Orleans before being transferred to the *Monongahela* to continue the river campaign. While he was serving as executive officer in the steam sloop, a rebel shell "came through the bulwarks on the port quarter" and mortally wounded her captain, who was standing next to Dewey on the bridge. Dewey emerged from the incident unscathed and in command of the ship.[19]

On 10 July, Dewey received orders for the *Monongahela* to proceed with the *Essex* to White Hall Point to assist the *New London*, which had been disabled by shell damage to her boilers. On the trip upriver, enemy batteries shelled the vessels without effect. At White Hall Point, Dewey was able to pull the *New London* off the bank, "took her in tow on the port side," and moved her out into the river. He then attached tow lines from the *Monongahela* to the port side of the *Essex* so that the *New London* could be kept to the starboard of the two ships and, "thus sheltered," towed downriver past the enemy batteries. According to Commander Robert Townsend, captain of the *Essex*, Dewey "displayed coolness, skill, and judgment" in rescuing the *New London*, and he used his guns effectively on enemy batteries.

A few days later, Dewey was transferred to blockade duty on board the *Brooklyn* off Charleston, South Carolina, then was sent to the *Agawam* in the James River Squadron, and finally reported to the *Colorado*, in which he took part in the capture of Fort Fisher in North Carolina. During this period, Dewey had an opportunity to return to the Gulf, but he wrote to his father of his reluctance to accept such an assignment, saying, "if I go to the Gulf I shall have fighting and I have had quite enough of that."[20] He ended the war as a lieutenant commander on board the *Kearsarge*.

During the decade following the Civil War, Dewey took advantage of friendships to obtain such preferred assignments as serving as flag lieutenant to Admiral L. M. Goldsborough while he commanded the European Squadron, and teaching at the Naval Academy. Dewey also courted his future wife, Susan Boardman Goodwin, daughter of the governor of New Hampshire.[21]

The postwar era left much to be desired for naval officers eager for a career of promotions and leadership. Dewey was doomed, as were others, to endure service in an increasingly obsolete fleet with an overcrowded officer corps. Dewey's service during these long years of stagnation was somewhat moderated, however, by his rank at the end of the war and his financial position. His war experience gained Dewey promotion to lieutenant commander in 1865, which gave him a jump on other officers his age. Many of his classmates were still lieutenants and lieutenant commanders in the 1890s when Dewey had reached flag rank. Dewey was also fortunate to have a good income from his share of his father's insurance business. This insulated Dewey from the financial problems that plagued many officers, and it allowed him to take advantage of the social life of Washington, D.C., during his several tours of duty there.

In the years before the Battle of Manila Bay, Dewey slowly ascended the career ladder as he took advantage of his friendships in and out of the Navy. In 1875, he moved to Washington to serve as a member of the Lighthouse Board. For seven years he enjoyed the social seasons and developed his contacts within the Navy Department. "I found myself in Washington social life, with its round of dinners and receptions, which were a new and enjoyable experience to me, if exhausting physically."[22]

Dewey returned to sea in 1882 as commander of the sloop *Juniata*, bound for the Asiatic Station. As he traveled to the East, his health took a turn for the worse. He was hospitalized at Malta, where it was feared that he might not survive. His full recovery took almost two years. In 1884, Dewey was assigned command of the *Dolphin*, one of the U.S. Navy's first steel ships, still under construction. Growing frustrated at delays in the commissioning of the new ship, Dewey accepted transfer to command of the old steam sloop *Pensacola*, flagship of the European Squadron, the following March. He remained with the ship throughout her four-year cruise before returning to Washington for service at Navy Department headquarters.[23]

In 1889, Dewey succeeded Winfield Scott Schley as chief of the Bureau of

Equipment. In his autobiography, Dewey took great pains to convince his readers that before his attempt to capture the flag of the Asiatic Squadron in 1897, he had never used political influence to further his career. Obviously this was not true. Dewey had used his father's influence to gain acceptance to Annapolis, continued to use the good offices of friends for choice assignments in the postwar years, made use of Vermont political clout through his brothers to obtain the equipment post, and eventually would employ every means available to obtain the flag of the Asiatic Station in 1898.[24]

Dewey's service in the Bureau of Equipment coincided with the emerging new steel-hulled, steam-powered Navy. The United States was beginning to retire the outdated ships of the Civil War in favor of ships equipped with the new, modern technology. It was Dewey's responsibility to ensure that the fleet could steam at will wherever American foreign policy dictated. Perhaps here, Dewey's administrative abilities began to mature and to presage his later contributions to the Navy in the post-Philippines era.

Under Dewey, the bureau fitted the new ships with many of the inventions that the scientific officers were designing for the New Navy. Although not a producing member of that group, Dewey was not only receptive to progressive change but also enthusiastically endorsed many improvements. Spector assesses Dewey positively, saying that he had "done a creditable job in a rather routine assignment [and] had established a reputation as an energetic administrator and a friend of innovation." But Spector rejects the thesis that Dewey's three years as head of the bureau "marked" him for later advancement. Certainly Dewey's performance reflected the role that he would later play as Admiral of the Navy. As a facilitator of creativity, Dewey acted as a buffer to the more reluctant traditionalists who found new ideas difficult to accept.[25]

After his term in the Bureau of Equipment expired, Dewey remained in Washington as president of the Board of Inspection and Survey from 1895 to 1897. During this time he won promotion to commodore, a rank that "entitled [him] to the command of a squadron as soon as there was a vacancy." The first such vacancy occurred in the Asiatic Squadron. By the fall of 1897, Dewey had learned of the impending vacancy and knew that he and Commodore John A. Howell were the two contenders for the position. The appointment became more important in the context of American foreign policy decisions arising out of concern for Spanish depredations in Cuba. In any war with Spain, the Philippines would figure prominently with American success or failure. President William McKinley and Secretary of the Navy John D. Long wanted a reliable commander on the Asiatic who could supply the aggressive action necessary to prevent the Spanish fleet in the Philippines from reinforcing Spanish forces in the Caribbean region. It was up to Dewey to persuade them that he was their man.[26]

Dewey again turned to his political contacts for support. To one he complained that Arendt S. Crowninshield, the influential head of the Bureau of Navigation, disliked him and would "hardly recommend me to any command; and his advice had great weight with . . . the secretary of the navy." Dewey turned to his friend Theodore Roosevelt, then Assistant Secretary of the Navy, who supported Dewey for the command. Roosevelt informed him of a political letter already on file in support of Howell and urged that Dewey use all the political leverage he had to combat Howell's apparent advantage. Dewey next turned to Vermont Senator Redfield Proctor, a close family friend, and with his support obtained the assignment.[27]

Before leaving Washington to assume his command, Dewey studied everything he could find on the Philippines. He reached Japan and broke his flag on the *Olympia* in early January 1898, a time of increasingly strained relations between the United States and Spain. Knowing that any war with Spain would mean instant action for his small squadron, Dewey began preparing for operations against the Spanish Philippines. His first move was to shift his base of operations to Hong Kong because "it was evident that in case of emergency Hong Kong was the most advantageous position from which to move to the attack." By the time Dewey established his headquarters at Hong Kong, the *Maine* had been sunk in Havana harbor, and war appeared imminent. Theodore Roosevelt, briefly acting as Secretary of the Navy, sent him orders to "keep full of coal. In the event . . . of war . . . , your duty will be to see that the Spanish squadron does not leave the Asiatic coast, and then offensive operations in Philippine Islands."[28]

No such instructions were necessary. Dewey understood the strategic setting and was already preparing his fleet for hostilities. He knew that a state of war with Spain would cut him off from supply by the neutral British at Hong Kong. To ensure that he had enough coal and provisions, Dewey had purchased the *Zafiro* and the *Nanshan* to serve the fleet as supply ships. By April, he had his warships, four protected cruisers, two gunboats, and a small revenue cutter prepared for battle, their hulls cleaned and their white peacetime paint covered with gray. Crews drilled daily under Dewey's personal inspection; and, leaving as little to chance as possible, Dewey sent a spy to Manila to report on the Spanish fleet and fortifications and another into Hong Kong to obtain what information he could from travelers recently arrived from the Philippines.[29]

On 23 April 1898, the British at Hong Kong ordered Dewey to remove the American fleet from their waters, according to the rules of neutrality. This was Dewey's first notice that a state of war existed between the United States and Spain, but he had anticipated the order to leave and had arranged for a temporary anchorage in Chinese waters at Mirs Bay. Dewey ordered his squadron to move there the next day; a day later, on 25 April, he received a cable from

Long stating that war had been declared. Dewey was ordered to "proceed at once to the Philippine Islands. Commence operations at once, particularly against Spanish fleet. You must capture vessels or destroy. Use utmost endeavors."[30]

Dewey immediately cabled the American consul at Manila, Oscar F. Williams, and asked for the location of the Spanish fleet and the general situation in the archipelago. Williams quickly left for Mirs Bay with intelligence that the Spanish commander, Rear Admiral Patricio Montojo, planned to oppose Dewey at Subic Bay, north of Manila on the west coast of Luzon. On 27 April, Dewey set a course for Luzon, exercising his men en route in day and night battle drills, fire fighting, and damage control. All unnecessary woodwork was stowed below or thrown overboard to reduce the fire hazard.[31]

Arriving off the coast of Bataan and Corregidor on 30 April, Dewey ordered the *Boston* and *Concord* to reconnoiter Subic Bay to locate the enemy's fleet. When they returned without seeing any Spanish ships, Dewey concluded that Montojo had elected to position his ships near the city of Manila. Dewey was correct; the Spanish commander knew that his ships were no match for the Americans in a battle involving maneuvering, and had deployed his ships in an east-west line across Canacao Bay near Cavite, the Spanish naval base opposite the city of Manila. Montojo wanted to fight at anchor and use the shore batteries to support his ships while not putting the city of Manila in the line of fire.[32]

Manila was regarded by many as the "Gibraltar of the Far East," and mining of the passages into the bay was rumored to make it impregnable. Dewey was undeterred. Reasoning that the Spanish lacked the expertise to properly mine the deep channel into the bay, Dewey ordered his ships to enter Boca Grande Passage at 2330 on 30 April. Slipping past the gun emplacements on Corregidor, the fleet steamed into Manila Bay in column on a course for Manila. Before reaching the city, Dewey sent the two supply ships and the revenue cutter "into an unfrequented part of the bay in order that they should sustain no injury and that they might not hamper the movements of the fighting-ships."[33]

Once he was safely through the mouth of the bay, Dewey slowed the fleet down to four knots, to delay its arrival at Manila until he had daylight to assist him in determining the location of the Spanish fleet and identifying gun positions along the shore. At daybreak, Dewey's ship came into range of the shore guns. As he steamed in a slow arc across the Manila waterfront, it was apparent that no warships were at anchor there; so Dewey adjusted his course farther to the south and west and soon found the Spanish line of battle. At 0540 he came within five thousand yards of the enemy and told the commander of his flagship to open fire. The little American fleet steamed across the line of

Spanish ships, firing first from the port side and then, reversing its course, from the starboard. Dewey pressed his attack on the beleaguered defenders in a series of five passes in all, three to the west and two to the east, pouring a rapid fire into the hapless Spanish ships. Throughout the early morning hours the Spanish fire was inaccurate, while the Americans laid in a "continuous and precise fire at ranges varying from [five- to two-thousand] yards, countermarching in a line approximately parallel to that of the Spanish fleet."[34]

At 0730, Dewey received a report that his gunners were low on ammunition; he quickly moved the fleet beyond the range of the Spanish guns at Cavite. The artillery from Manila continued to fire from emplacements along the shoreline near the city. Dewey sent word that unless the firing stopped, he would order his captains to shell the city. The guns soon fell silent. The atmosphere was tense in the *Olympia*. Smoke engulfed the Spanish ships, but the Americans did not know the extent of the damage.[35] Dewey sent the men to breakfast while he investigated the problem of ammunition and considered what to do next. At 0840, he called a meeting of his captains and was much relieved to learn that none of his ships had been seriously damaged, and the report of an ammunition shortage was erroneous. Luckily, he also had sufficient coal to continue the battle; otherwise, there would have been serious complications. With neutral Hong Kong closed to American warships, the nearest fuel stocks were thousands of miles away, but, fortunately, the supply of coal on board would prove to be adequate.

As soon as the men finished eating, Dewey once again moved in for the attack, at 1116. Just over an hour later, his victory was complete. Several days later Dewey was to recall that "by this time the flagship and almost the entire Spanish fleet were in flames, and at [1230], the squadron ceased firing, the batteries being silenced and the ships sunk, burnt and deserted."[36] Spanish casualties numbered seven warships and 370 men killed. Dewey was able to report that no American ships were lost, no sailors had been killed in the action, and only eight were wounded.[37] The battle was a resounding success—a success secured by careful preparation, daring, and no small measure of luck. Whenever moved to reminisce, from that day on, Dewey often remarked that the Battle of Manila Bay was won in Hong Kong harbor where he prepared his squadron for battle.[38] Perhaps therein lies the best explanation for his master stroke.

For the time being, Dewey had accomplished his mission. No Spanish fleet from the Philippines could threaten the American coast or reinforce Cuba. He waited for the U.S. Army to bring sufficient troops to take and hold Manila and for the Navy Department to transfer additional ships and supplies to his small fleet off the coast. During the interim, Dewey used his guns to maintain control of the Manila region. One Hong Kong correspondent reported that "Com-

modore Dewey has exercised consummate judgement and rare ability in maintaining a distance at once safe for his fleet and deadly to the Spaniards."[39]

During the summer, as the American presence began to increase, Dewey
established a blockade patrol to bottle up the Spaniards, dealt with problems
arising out of a German plan to outmaneuver the Americans for the islands,
and organized a system of supply for his meager force.[40] He maintained a limited line of communications with Washington. Some critics suggest that
Dewey failed his superiors by not supplying adequate intelligence on the mood
of the Filipinos regarding independence or acceptance of the United States as
a colonial control.

This failure was not one of communication, but of analysis; he could not
discriminate between information sources and simply did not recognize accurate information regarding the Filipinos' position on independence. Although
he was on the scene, Dewey relied on unsubstantiated reports and the advice
of many individuals who were not privy to Filipino attitudes and plans. Further, he ignored available documents that clearly stated the Filipino position
on the American role in the post-Spanish period and the question of independence; and he failed to provide Washington with assessments of these documents. Thus, Dewey contributed little to the formulation of a viable policy for
the islands.[41] His greatest failure in the Philippines was not his failure to communicate information but his inability to correctly identify and to rely on
sources of intelligence that certainly were available to him.

By August 1898, just four months after Dewey's destruction of Montojo's
fleet, American military power had increased enough to pressure the Spanish
into surrendering Manila.[42] By the end of the year, the war with Spain was won,
and the Treaty of Paris transferred ownership of the islands to the United States.

By that time, the Americans had new opponents to subdue. During the fall
of 1898, following the surrender of Manila, tensions between the Americans
and the Filipinos led to open conflict. Dewey suggested later that the insurrection occurred because long-term tension had been allowed to develop that
altered the Filipinos' earlier acceptance of some kind of American government
for the islands. Whatever the error of earlier intelligence, Dewey received a report in November 1898 that began to change his original assessment of Filipino
attitudes. Two naval officers, Paymaster W. B. Wilcox and Naval Cadet
Leonard R. Sargent, traveled into the interior of Luzon on a fact-finding mission. They found firm resistance to the idea of American control, and military
preparations were under way for an insurrection should the United States attempt to establish a colonial government for the islands. Dewey dutifully reported this intelligence to Washington, but it was too late then to change the
minds of President McKinley and leaders in the War Department. They were
convinced of the rightness of the acquisition of the Philippines.[43]

On 4 February 1899, shots were fired and the Philippine Insurrection began. Shortly thereafter, Dewey's service in the Philippines ended. When he sailed for the United States on 20 May, he was grateful to leave behind the problems of dealing with the insurrection. "It is the responsibility that kills," he wrote. "A year is long enough in this climate for an old man, and I am glad to be permitted to rest."[44]

Dewey left the Philippines as Admiral of the Navy, a new rank created for him by Congress a week after the Battle of Manila Bay. His meteoric rise from commodore was due primarily to the wave of Deweymania that swept the United States following his success at Manila. Awaiting him at home were celebrations and the adulation of an adoring public, and even the opportunity to run for President in 1900.

Long before Dewey's departure from the islands there were Dewey-for-President "booms," led by men such as Joseph Pulitzer of the New York World and others who sought to transform Dewey's sudden fame into political leverage. Dewey would have none of it, saying he was "unfitted for it [the presidency], having neither the education nor the training." Even during the triumphal voyage from Manila he refused to consider the possibility, but public curiosity began to build as the Olympia sailed closer to home.[45]

When Dewey arrived in New York in October 1899, public celebrations began, and the interest in his political future intensified. During the next six months, Dewey refused to discuss politics, to commit himself as a candidate, or to take advantage of the political opportunities presented him. Instead, he watched as the crowds began to dwindle and his popularity waned, never fully understanding what was happening. His refusal to accept many of the invitations to local Dewey celebrations dampened the enthusiasm of many of his fans. Dewey committed the ultimate example of "ingratitude and ill-taste" when he gave his wife the house that public subscription had purchased for him in Washington. What once had been effusive and adoring oratory began to degenerate into disparagement and amusement.[46] In April 1900, Dewey's resolve to avoid politics wavered, and he issued an ill-timed statement indicating his willingness to become a candidate:

> If the American people want me for this high office, I shall be only too willing to serve them.
>
> It is the highest honor in the gift of this nation; what citizen would refuse it?
>
> Since studying this subject, I am convinced that the office of the President is not such a very difficult one to fill, his duties being mainly to execute the laws of the Congress. Should I be chosen for this exalted position I would execute the laws of Congress as faithfully as I have always executed the orders of my superiors.[47]

The response from the press was to attack and ridicule the admiral's candidacy and his view of the presidency. In May, the attacks were becoming more personal and biting. On 18 May 1900, Dewey announced that he was no longer a candidate and added, "I don't understand how I got the idea in the first place."[48] The brevity of the people's infatuation with him and the failure of his tentative move to enter politics left Dewey bewildered. His venture outside the confines of the U.S. Navy illustrated a certain naiveté that was ridiculed by some but admired by others, and it did not retard his naval career.

Plans to reorganize the Navy had been hotly debated for more than a decade. The most popular plan, advanced by Captain Henry C. Taylor, championed the establishment of a general staff that would control naval planning. The proposal met with opposition from Secretary of the Navy Hilary A. Herbert, a Democrat, and some hesitation from his Republican successor, John D. Long; both feared a shift of authority from civilian to military leaders.[49] Dewey distanced himself from the debate, but he could not avoid direct involvement in it when, in March 1900, Long established the General Board as an in-house advisory mechanism for the Secretary. The board, established by executive order, had no basis in law and was always controversial. Most civilians believed that it fulfilled the need for a body of serving officers to advise the Secretary on policy and coordinate the work of the Navy's bureaus, but many officers considered it only the first step in the establishment of a true general staff that could determine policy and direct operations. As senior ranking officer in the Navy, Dewey was appointed president of the board. In that position, he could exercise great influence on the membership of the board and its staff. Careful to include the brightest of the new young officers on the staff, Dewey brought together the best minds that the Navy had to offer.[50]

During the early years, Dewey and the board focused on the new empire so recently won from Spain. In a detailed communication to Dewey on 30 March 1900, Long ordered the General Board to make plans for all possible contingencies of war for the United States.[51] With Long's instructions in mind, Dewey and the board established a series of operational strategies and plans designed to protect the Philippines, Puerto Rico, and other American possessions and bases. At the heart of these plans was Germany. Dewey's distrust of Germans, at least partially because of his experiences with them in the Philippines, reflected the mood of many in the Navy. The United States was emerging as a major naval power at the turn of the century and encountering stiff competition from Germany. It was natural for both German and American naval planners to anticipate war between the two countries. Much has been made of Dewey's personal dislike of all things German, and certainly his influence on the board carried great weight. The settlement of most Anglo-American disputes and the aggressive actions of Germany, however, would have made Germany the primary target of the U.S. Navy's war plans even had Dewey not served on the board.[52]

Soon after Dewey's appointment to the General Board, the death of McKinley brought Theodore Roosevelt, a friend of the Navy, to the White House. His presidency changed Dewey's professional and personal life. In 1902, Secretary of the Navy Long was forced into retirement and replaced with William H. Moody, a strong proponent of the "Big Navy" and a logical selection by Roosevelt. As a capable and respected ex-congressman from Massachusetts, Moody performed a variety of political duties for the President while managing "to stay on top of his work [in the Navy Department]." Moody played an important role in pushing for "additional naval and coaling stations, more ships, and an increase of officers and men."[53] Unlike Long, Dewey's new superior was receptive to his counsel, and during the two years that Moody served in the top naval post, a "harmonious" spirit of cooperation existed between civilian and naval leadership.

Contributing to Dewey's increased influence was the departure of his long-standing nemesis Arendt S. Crowninshield, who left the Bureau of Navigation and was replaced with Henry C. Taylor, now a rear admiral. Compared with their predecessors, Dewey was perhaps more comfortable with Moody and Taylor, who shared his ideas regarding deficiencies in the Navy and what was required to establish the United States as a naval power second only to Great Britain.[54]

Facing Dewey and the General Board in the immediate future were important questions related to developing the American empire and the evolving Navy assigned to protect it. Naval construction, personnel expansion, naval bases and a strategy for the Pacific, and the role of naval power in American foreign policy were all on the agenda for Roosevelt's General Board.

In 1902, the board was forced to deal with its first important crisis when Britain, Italy, and Germany sent naval forces to blockade the coast of Venezuela and force that country to pay some long-standing debts. Roosevelt responded by shifting the site of previously scheduled naval maneuvers in the Caribbean to demonstrate his concern and to pressure the Europeans into negotiating a peaceful solution to the crisis. To further impress the blockaders with the gravity of the situation, he ordered Dewey to take personal command of the American forces.

Dewey's reputation for unilateral action and his success in the Philippines had the desired effect. His well-known dislike for Germany was designed to place additional pressure on the nation that Roosevelt considered most responsible for the crisis. Tempers eventually cooled, and a settlement was reached in which Germany gained no territory. Dewey's contribution to the resolution is difficult to pinpoint. His presence in the general area caused some concern for the Germans, but it is doubtful that Roosevelt used Dewey as any-thing more than a veiled threat. Through it all, the U.S. Navy received some favorable publicity, the public's perception of Dewey's reputation in battle was revived, and Roosevelt's role as a policeman in the hemisphere was more clear-ly defined.[55]

Much more came from the naval exercises than a resolution to foreign pol-icy problems. The maneuvers brought home the alarming fact that the At-lantic, European, and South Atlantic squadrons were unable to perform ac-ceptably when brought together to form a single fleet. The exercises pointed to "defects in fundamental organization of the squadrons, such as the want of homogeneity among vessels on the same station." Before fleet maneuvers could begin at Culebra, near Puerto Rico, the three squadrons had to be broken into groups of similarly classed vessels. The squadrons' organization prevented them from drilling as a unit during fleet-level maneuvers, to the detriment of their efficiency and achievement of battle objectives. The lessons learned at Culebra led to the reorganization of the U.S. fleet. In peacetime, cruisers would make up the squadrons in the Caribbean, Europe, and other distant stations, with the battleships divided between the Asiatic and North At-lantic Fleets. In time of war, the cruisers would be reassigned from their squadrons to act as "auxiliaries to the battleships."[56]

Stationing similar ships together allowed the commanding officers to con-duct maneuvers and coordinate gunnery practice. The Spanish-American War had demonstrated the need to keep the battle fleet together, but the Bureau of Navigation, which controlled the assignment of ships, refused to do so. Instead, it argued that the "specific" requirements of the various squadrons dictated the dispersal of ships to widely separated stations. The effect of this policy was to reduce the ability of the ships to function as a single unit and thus to reduce their power. The Venezuelan crisis did not end the debate, but it did force a compromise on the General Board between those who wanted all the battle-ships assigned to a single "strategic" location and those who wanted them dis-persed. The solution also represented a compromise between those factions on the General Board that saw the greatest danger in the growing Japanese navy and German imperialism in the Far East, and those that believed the greatest threat to American interests was in the Caribbean. This division of opinion continued until after World War I, and the argument over the stationing of battleships was not solved until the United States developed a two-battle-fleet navy.[57]

Both sides on the battleship deployment debate agreed that the future re-quired a battleship construction program that would enable the United States to field a full battleship fleet in both the Atlantic and the Pacific. Although there was some difference of opinion as to the number of battleships needed, the General Board submitted a request to Secretary Moody in February 1903 that called for construction of one battleship for each of the forty-eight states, one armored cruiser for every two battleships, and one scout cruiser and one large, seagoing, quick-turning torpedo destroyer for each battleship added to the fleet. In addition, the board recommended increases in the auxiliary fleet and naval personnel as needed for each year's appropriation.[58]

Congress, in the midst of enormous appropriations for domestic reforms, refused to accept the ambitious naval building program. In 1904, Congress authorized only one new battleship, and in 1905, only two—in contrast to the Navy's plan of four per year until all forty-eight had been funded. Even Roosevelt seemed to waver by 1905, when he suggested that the twenty-eight battleships and twelve armored cruisers currently in the fleet or under construction placed the United States "second only to France and Great Britain." Dewey and the General Board did not agree with his estimation on two grounds: (1) Roosevelt's assessment did not take into account Germany's plan for future construction, and (2) the President's estimate included seven ships completed before the Spanish-American War whose combat effectiveness was at best "debatable."[59]

In July 1904, the death of Admiral Taylor deprived Dewey of a close ally in his program of orderly change within the Navy. Taylor had continued to push for a general staff after the formation of the General Board; with his death, leadership in the movement was assumed by a group of more radical officers who clashed with the traditional leadership in the bureaus.[60] These young officers considered the Navy's poor administrative organization and its lack of a general staff to be the cause of all of its problems. As the "insurgents" grew more vocal and aggressive, and the gap between the reformers and their conservative opponents widened, Dewey found it increasingly difficult to effect compromise and, in his caution, edged closer to the conservative officers and their allies in the Navy's bureaus.

His first clash with the insurgents came when the young officers presented their plan for a general staff to the General Board without first discussing the plan with Dewey. As chairman of the board, Dewey thought that he should have been consulted; he considered their action a personal attack on his reputation and position. Even though the plan was similar to Taylor's of 1902, Dewey refused to support the proposal or even to attend meetings of the board, and some of his closest associates feared that he would resign. With Dewey so strongly against them, the insurgents backed down, and the plan died.[61]

Later, in 1909, plans for Navy Department reorganization were advanced from a different direction. As Roosevelt's attempts to get changes through Congress had failed, George von Lengerke Meyer, Secretary of the Navy in the new Taft administration, decided to act on his own authority. He ordered the department divided into four divisions, each to be headed by a senior naval officer answerable only to the Secretary. Although this reorganization did not fully satisfy the insurgents, it did reduce the power of the bureau chiefs and brought more centralized control to the service. When congressional critics began to question Meyer's authority to make such major changes within the department, Dewey lent his support to the reorganization, and it was put into effect.[62]

Another issue facing Dewey during his tenure as president of the General Board was the placement of a major naval base in the Pacific. Since the acquisition of the Philippines, the location of such a base had been an integral part of naval war planning. In 1900, the board "unanimously recommended" the establishment of the base at Iloilo in the Central Philippines, but Dewey must have had second thoughts because he later urged the formation of a commission to study both Iloilo and Subic Bay.

At the same time, Dewey pushed the government to secure another base somewhere on the Chinese coast, even though this violated the American Open Door policy. No consideration was given to his proposal for a Chinese base, however, and Dewey soon took the lead in supporting the Navy's choice of Subic Bay, rather than Manila Bay, which the Army demanded in order to concentrate all military and naval bases at Manila "to facilitate their defense." The Navy countered that the channels in the approach to Manila were too wide and deep to "be defended securely by either guns, mines or torpedoes or all of them," whereas the Army placed great emphasis on the ability of its Coast Artillery Corps to use Corregidor to defend Manila against any enemy approach. Dewey responded to this argument by suggesting that any such plan would leave "all the outworks and the natural base of the fleet, Subig, for the comfort and security of the enemy operating against Manila."[63]

The debate continued for more than three years; ultimately, neither group won. Little building was done anywhere because Congress refused to appropriate funds. Thus, Dewey failed to obtain for the Navy a base that he considered crucial to its fulfillment of its role in American defense.

During the same period, plans were being developed to defend American interests against Japan and Germany. Code named War Plan Orange, the plan for war with Japan predicted possible defeat for the United States if Japan struck in the Pacific while the fleet was in the Atlantic. The plan for war with Germany (War Plan Black) predicted similar results if the fleet were in the Pacific when Germany struck. There were only two solutions to the problem; either a two-ocean navy had to be built, an unlikely event in the near future, or a mechanism had to be developed to accurately predict the location of a war far enough in advance to allow the concentration of the fleet in the area. Dewey rejected a Naval War College proposal that called for a council made up of civilian heads of the services, members of Congress, and military leaders because he doubted its ability to make an accurate assessment of the possibility of war. Instead, he continued to stress the Navy's ability to meet any enemy if it were given proper resources.[64]

Preparedness was the best guard against a future war, and Dewey was convinced that Germany, which he believed posed the greatest threat, would not dare strike if the battle fleet were stationed in the Atlantic. This remained his view until the California legislature precipitated a war scare with Japan by debating a bill that would prohibit Oriental aliens from owning land in that state. The year was 1913, the eve of World War I, but even such a Germanophobe as Dewey admitted that "it looks as if the Japanese are determined to find a reason for declaring war on us, perhaps they want the Philippines and Hawaii."[65] In time, the crisis passed, but from that point on Dewey saw Japan in a different light and took the threat of Japanese aggression more seriously.[66]

The timing was ironic. Only a year later, World War I engulfed Europe. Beset by health problems and weakened by old age, Dewey realized that his influence was beginning to decline, but he remained a defender of the Navy against outside detractors as well as against those reformers within the service who he believed did the Navy a disservice by publicizing its shortcomings in order to gain support for changes that they deemed necessary.

In a 1916 interview published in the *New York World*, Dewey refuted charges that the U.S. Navy was inefficient, demoralized, in need of a general staff, and wholly inadequate. In a statement reflecting his pride, he told reporter George Creel: "The attacks that have been made upon the Navy are as false as many of them are shameful. . . . There is no demoralization. Both in material and personnel we are more efficient today than ever before. Our ships are as good as any, our officers are as good as any, and our enlisted men are the finest in the world."[67]

This was Dewey's last broadside at what he perceived to be the enemies of the Navy. On 11 January 1917, five months almost to the day after the interview, the Admiral of the Navy lost his final battle. Nearly two decades had passed since his victory at Manila Bay, a victory made certain by his thorough preparations and aggressive leadership. As a result, the United States had gained an empire, and its Navy immense new responsibility. Dewey remained firmly in control of what could be described as a moderate course of change, using traditional avenues to accomplish modernization and improvements in the Navy. He was often seen as an obstacle to progress by more radical and impatient officers, but more often than not, he supported their aims and goals. Dewey, who perhaps lacked the vision of other more capable men, allowed himself to be persuaded by personal bias along the way, and stretched the limits of his talents.

He had done his duty as he understood it and served his nation and his service well.

## FURTHER READING

Of the published works in the life of Dewey, only four rate a second look. Dewey's *Autobiography of George Dewey: Admiral of the Navy* (New York, 1913) was ghostwritten by Frederick Palmer and relies heavily on secondary sources. It does, on occasion, provide important clues to attitudes and the perspective of the admiral. Of the three biographies published in more recent times, Ronald Spector's *Admiral of the New Empire: The Life and Career of George Dewey* (Baton Rouge, La., 1974) is the best. Its section on Dewey's seventeen years on the General Board is the high point of all Dewey scholarship. Laurin Hall Healy and Luis Kutner's *The Admiral* (Chicago, 1944) and Richard S. West's *Admirals of the American Empire* (Indianapolis, 1948) are also of value. Based on more limited sources than Spector's biography, both include more detail in earlier periods of Dewey's career and draw often on the many popular accounts published soon after Manila Bay; Spector makes it a point to exclude many of these "Dewey Stories."

Other works containing important Dewey material include Vernon L. Williams, "The U.S. Navy in the Philippine Insurrection and Subsequent Native Unrest 1898–1906" (Ph.D. diss., Texas A&M University 1985), which discusses Dewey's encounters with the Spanish and the Germans and details his strategy for blockade and early operations against the Spanish and the Filipino insurgents. Philip Y. Nicholson's "George Dewey and the Transformation of American Foreign Policy" (Ph.D. diss., University of New Mexico, 1971) provides an interesting look at Dewey in the context of public policy, the Philippines, and his service on the General Board. A third dissertation, Daniel J. Costello's "Planning for War: A History of the General Board of the Navy, 1900–1914" (Ph.D. diss., Tufts University, 1968) contains the best account of the General Board.

The U.S. Naval Institute *Proceedings* of the era include a host of articles on various Dewey topics. Many relate to the Battle of Manila Bay, whereas others deal with the attempts at naval reorganization. Other articles of note include Thomas A. Bailey, "Dewey and the Germans at Manila Bay," *American Historical Review* 45 (1939): 59–81; James K. Eyre, "Japan and the American Annexation of the Philippines," *Pacific Historical Review* 11 (1942): 55–71; William R. Braisted, "The Philippine Naval Base Problem, 1898–1909," *Mississippi Valley Historical Review* 41 (1954): 21–40; and Paul T. Heffron, "Secretary Moody and Naval Administrative Reform," *American Neptune* 29 (1960): 30–53.

## NOTES

1. This assessment of Dewey's career before the War with Spain reflects the view of Ronald Spector, whose opening chapter in his biography of Dewey is titled "Obscurity." Ronald Spector, *Admiral of the New Empire: The Life and Career of George Dewey* (Baton Rouge, La., 1974), 1–39, especially 39.

2. George Dewey, *Autobiography of George Dewey: Admiral of the Navy* (New York, 1913), 4.

3. Spector, *Admiral of New Empire*, 4.

4. Laurin Hall Healy and Luis Kutner, *The Admiral* (Chicago, 1944), 23. Dewey's *Autobiography*, ghosted by the noted journalist Frederick Palmer, relies on many questionable anecdotes found in the immediate post-Manila Bay press.

5. Dewey, *Autobiography*, 12–13.

6. Ibid., 14–15.

7. Healy and Kutner, *The Admiral*, 39.

8. Dewey, *Autobiography*, 23–36; and George Dewey to Julius Y. Dewey, 13 June, 19 June, 8 July, and 11 August 1858. Dewey Papers, Vermont Historical Society (hereafter cited as VHS).

9. Dewey, *Autobiography*, 477–479; and Navy Department *Official Records of the Union and Confederate Navies in the War of the Rebellion*, ser. 1, vol. 16, 519–22, 525–26, 530–33, 540–51, 560–66, 574–75, 646–49, 676–77 (hereafter cited as ORN).

10. John Niven, "Gideon Welles, 5 March 1861–4 March 1869," in *American Secretaries of the Navy*, edited by Paolo E. Coletta, et al., 2 vols. (Annapolis, Md., 1980), 1:336–37.

11. *ORN*, ser. 1, 18:57; and Dewey, *Autobiography*, 50.

12. Dewey, *Autobiography*, 50–51.

13. *ORN*, ser. 1, 18:35, 139, 159–60.

14. William N. Still, Jr., "David Glasgow Farragut: The Union's Nelson," in *Captains of the Old Steam Navy*, edited by James C. Bradford (Annapolis, Md., 1986), 169; Dewey, *Autobiography*, 54; and *ORN*, ser. 1, 18:361.

15. Dewey, *Autobiography*, 60–64; and *ORN*, ser. 1, 18:151, 156, 171–72.

16. Dewey, *Autobiography*, 68–71; and *ORN*, ser. 1, 18:142, 154, 157, 206.

17. Dewey, *Autobiography*, 50.

18. *ORN*, ser. 1, 19:681, 684, 692; and George Dewey to Julius Y. Dewey, 29 November 1864, VHS.

19. Dewey, *Autobiography*, 106–12; and *ORN*, ser. 1, 20:33, 145, 360–61. Ronald Spector lists four officers killed in his account of the *Monongahela* firefight on 7 July. Dewey mentions only one death, that of Commander Abner Read. In a casualty report three weeks later, Navy Surgeon David Kindleberger listed one officer killed, one officer wounded, one enlisted killed, and three enlisted wounded. The log of the *Monongahela* confirms Kindleberger's report. Spector, *Admiral of the New Empire*, 18; Dewey, *Autobiography*, 111–12; and *ORN*, ser. 1, 20:335, 360.

20. *ORN*, ser. 1, 20:339, 361; and George Dewey to Julius Y. Dewey, 18 January 1865, VHS.

21. Dewey, *Autobiography*, 113–49.

22. Ibid., 150–51.

23. Ibid., 153–60, 163–64.

24. Ibid., 164, 167; George Edmunds to Charles Dewey (this letter was forwarded to George Dewey with a brief note from his brother Charles), 9 March, Dewey Papers, Manuscript Division, Library of Congress (hereafter cited as DPLC); Charles Dewey to George Dewey, 23 March 1889, DPLC; Redfield Proctor to Edward Dewey (this letter was forwarded to George Dewey with a brief note from his brother Edward), 18 March 1889, DPLC; and George Edmunds to George Dewey, 4 April 1889, DPLC. Senator Edmunds offered little assistance other than to "vouch" for Dewey if asked by the Navy Department. Edmunds explained that "in the last 12 years," he had found that

offering references only when requested by the appropriate agency had been beneficial to the "public interest." He suggested that Dewey or "his friends" use his name as a reference. Edmunds concluded his letter by stating that "Vermont is handicapped by having been given the Secretaryship of War which . . . should close our expectations [for Dewey's appointment]." William E. Chandler to George Dewey, 18 March 1889, DPLC; and Eugene Hale to George Dewey, 19 March 1889, DPLC.

25. Dewey, *Autobiography*, 164–66; and Spector, *Admiral of the New Empire*, 30.

26. Dewey, *Autobiography*, 166–67.

27. Ibid., 167–69. Again, Proctor was called on (see note 24) to bring political pressure to bear for Dewey. Proctor's letter of support as senator contained none of the hesitancy exhibited by George Edmunds eight years earlier. Proctor to George Dewey, 16 October 1897, DPLC. It appears that Theodore Roosevelt was aware of Dewey as early as 1889, but their friendship did not develop until Roosevelt's appointment as Assistant Secretary of the Navy in 1897. Dewey and other Army and naval officers became a part of Roosevelt's circle at the Metropolitan Club in Washington, where Dewey had enjoyed membership for some years. Theodore Roosevelt, *An Autobiography* (New York, 1913), 210–11; Leonard Wood, "Introduction," in Theodore Roosevelt, *The Works of Theodore Roosevelt*, 20 vols. (New York, 1926), 11:xiii.

28. Dewey, *Autobiography*, 169–72, 174, 178–79; *Annual Report of the Secretary of the Navy for the Year 1898*, 4–5 (hereafter cited as *Annual Report, 1898*); and Roosevelt, *Autobiography*, 214.

29. Dewey, *Autobiography*, 180, 186–95; and E. B. Potter, *Sea Power: A Naval History* (Annapolis, Md., 1981), 178.

30. Dewey, *Autobiography*, 193–96; and *Annual Report, 1898*, 6.

31. George Dewey to John Long, 4 May 1898, Record Group (RG) 45; Naval Records Collection of the Office of Naval Records and Library, Area 10 File, National Archives (hereafter cited as RG 45: Area 10 File).

32. Ibid.

33. Dewey, *Autobiography*, 211–12.

34. Dewey to Long, 4 May 1898, RG 45; Area 10 File. "Precise fire" was an overstatement. American fire was woefully inaccurate, registering fewer than two hundred hits out of almost six thousand fired. Luckily, the Spanish were even poorer, registering only fifteen hits.

35. Ibid. Joseph L. Stickney, "With Dewey at Manila," *Harper's New Monthly* 98 (February 1899): 476, said that "as we hauled off into the bay, the gloom on the bridge of the *Olympia* was thicker than a London fog in November."

36. Dewey to Long, 4 May 1898, RG 45: Area 10 File.

37. *Annual Report, 1898*, 6. Dewey lost one man to heatstroke during the earlier passage into Manila Bay. Philip Y. Nicholson, "George Dewey and the Transformation of American Foreign Policy," Ph.D. diss., University of New Mexico, 1971, 90.

38. Nathan Sargent, comp., *Admiral Dewey and the Manila Campaign* (Washington, D.C., 1947), 48.

39. *New York Times*, 9 May 1898.

40. For a description of naval operations in the Philippines following the battle, see Vernon L. Williams, "The U.S. Navy in the Philippine Insurrection and Subsequent Native Unrest, 1898–1906," Ph.D. diss., Texas A&M University, 1985, 94–131. For Dewey's encounter with the Germans in the Philippines, see ibid., 17–24; Lester B.

Shippee, "Germany and the Spanish-American War," *American Historical Review* 30 (1925): 754–77, 764; Thomas A. Bailey, "Dewey and the Germans at Manila Bay," *American Historical Review* 45 (1939): 61; T. F. Brumby, "Synopsis of Interview with Vice Admiral Von Diederichs on board the *Kaiser* at Manila," 7 July 1898, RG 45: Area 10 File; and Henry V. Butler, "Memorandum," 16 November 1930, ibid. For a discussion of the affairs of the Navy's occupation in the Philippines under Dewey's leadership, see Williams, "U.S. Navy," 24–35, 65–95.

41. Examples of Filipino statements forwarded by Dewey without comment include Emilio Aguinaldo, "Amados Paisanos Mios," 24 May 1898; "Filipinos," 24 May 1898, both in RG 45: Subject File VD, Box 2, National Archives.

42. For a discussion of the events surrounding the surrender of Manila, see Williams, "U.S. Navy," 39–43.

43. Ibid., 50–54; W. B. Wilcox and Leonard R. Sargent to George Dewey, 23 November 1898, RG 45: Subject File OH, Box 2, National Archives.

44. Quoted in Murat Halstead, *Life and Achievements of Admiral Dewey: From Montpelier to Manila* (Chicago, 1899), 446.

45. Healy and Kutner, *The Admiral*, 263; Adelbert Milton Dewey, *The Life and Letters of Admiral Dewey from Montpelier to Manila* (New York, 1899), 426.

46. Dewey later explained that he transferred ownership of the house to his wife for legal reasons. He wanted to ensure that his son would inherit the property. Dewey's explanation did not appease the disaffected public. Frederick Palmer, *With My Own Eyes* (Indianapolis, 1932), 127.

47. *New York World*, 4 April 1900. As quoted in Healy and Kutner, *The Admiral*, 266.

48. *New York Times*, 18 May 1900.

49. The General Board did not abolish the authority of the bureaus or establish a centralized authority within the Navy Department. Taylor saw the board as a start toward a general staff similar to that of the German navy. Taylor and Dewey continued to push for such a general staff until Taylor's death in 1904. For an account of the history of the General Board, see Daniel J. Costello, "Planning for War: A History of the General Board of the Navy, 1900–1914," Ph.D. diss., Tufts University, 1968.

50. Charles O. Paullin, "A Half Century of Naval Administration," pt. 10, U.S. Naval Institute *Proceedings* 40 (January–February 1914): 111, 116.

51. John D. Long to George Dewey, 30 March 1900, RG 80: Records of the General Board, 1900–1902, National Archives (hereafter cited as RG 80: General Board).

52. See Spector, *Admiral of the New Empire*, chap. 6, for a good analysis of the anti-German perspective of many officers in the U.S. Navy at the turn of the century.

53. Paul T. Heffron, "William H. Moody, 1 May 1902–30 June 1904," in Paolo E. Coletta, ed., *American Secretaries of the Navy*, 2 vols. (Annapolis, Md., 1980), 1:461–62.

54. Ibid., 462.

55. Seward W. Livermore, "Theodore Roosevelt, the American Navy, and the Venezuelan Crisis of 1902–1903," *American Historical Review* 51 (1946): 425–71, 453–56, 470–71.

56. *Annual Report of the Secretary of the Navy for the Year 1903*, 58th Cong., 2d sess., 1903, H. Doc. 3, 478, 648–49.

57. Harold Sprout and Margaret Sprout, *The Rise of American Naval Power*, 1776–1918 (Princeton, N.J., 1939), 246; and Robert Albion, *Makers of Naval Policy*, 1798–1917, edited by Rowena Reed (Annapolis, Md., 1979), 327–28.

58. General Board Minutes, 31 January 1903, RG 80: General Records of the Department of the Navy, General Board, 1:237–38. Also, see Dewey to Secretary of the Navy William H. Moody, 9 February 1903, and Frank Marble to the Chief Clerk, Navy Department, 2 March 1903, ibid.

59. Sprout and Sprout, *Rise of American Naval Power*, 260–61.

60. The young naval reformers included such officers as Bradley A. Fiske, Albert L. Key, William Sims, and Philip Andrews. Other more senior officers taking the radical position were such men as Stephen B. Luce, William J. Barnette, and William Swift. Spector, *Admiral of the New Empire*, 156.

61. Mildred Dewey Diary, 27 January 1906, Box 86, DPLC.

62. Meyer's term as Secretary of the Navy is briefly discussed in Paolo E. Coletta, "George von Lengerke Meyer, 6 March 1909–4 March 1913," in Coletta, *American Secretaries of Navy*, 1:496–98; M. A. De Wolfe Howe, *George von Lengerke Meyer* (New York, 1920), 466–70; and George Dewey to George A. Loud, 31 January 1910, DPLC.

63. Secretary of the Navy Long to William McKinley, 12 July 1900, General Board No. 25, RG 80: General Board. It was probably the prohibitive cost and certain geographical disadvantages of Iloilo that caused Dewey to shift his support for Subic early in the debate. For a discussion of the investigation of the Iloilo site and the General Board's early approval, see Williams, "U.S. Navy," 236–43; Dewey to Long, 27 June 1900, General Board No. 25, RG 80: General Board; Dewey to Long 10 October 1900, ibid.; and William R. Braisted, "The Philippine Naval Base Problem, 1898–1909," *Mississippi Valley Historical Review* 41 (1954): 24.

64. Dewey to Theodore Roosevelt, 4 August 1904, RG 80: General Board. Although this letter was written in 1904, Dewey stated in the letter that Subic Bay had been the desired site of the General Board (and his) for several years, and he outlined in concise terms the Navy's objections to Manila.

65. George Dewey to George Goodwin Dewey, 19 April 1913, George Goodwin Dewey Papers, Naval Historical Center.

66. George Dewey to President, Naval War College, 19 June 1913, RG 80: General Board.

67. *New York World*, 20 August 1916.

# ☆ William Sowden Sims
## ☆
## ☆ The Victory Ashore

*by David F. Trask*

ADMIRAL WILLIAM SOWDEN SIMS OUGHT TO HAVE COMMANDED A battle fleet. An aggressive personality in the Nelsonian tradition, he should have become a swashbuckling seafighter, but he never gained the opportunity to do so. He missed the War with Spain in 1898 because he was serving in Paris as a naval attaché, and during World War I he commanded a desk in London. Sims exercised only one responsibility at sea of special significance, the leadership of a destroyer flotilla (1913–1915). He captained two battleships — the *Minnesota* (from 1909 to 1911) and the *Nevada* (from 1915 to 1916) — before the United States intervened in World War I. In January 1917, he became the president of the Naval War College at Newport, Rhode Island.

Sims suffered from an unfortunate accident of birth: he was born while his American parents, Alfred William and Adelaide Sowden Sims, were living in Port Hope, Canada, in 1858. His pro-British bias was often ascribed to this circumstance, certainly an unfair accusation. He spent most of his childhood in Pennsylvania and often lived in Washington, D.C., thereafter.

A domineering presence who was forthright to a fault, Sims left no doubt about his views, although he was reticent in at least one respect; he postponed marriage until he reached his forty-eighth year. His bride, Ann Hitchcock, was the daughter of a prominent politician, Ethan Allen Hitchcock, a former diplomat who had served as Secretary of the Interior.

After graduating from the U.S. Naval Academy in 1880, Sims grew up with the "New Navy" that came into existence during the next decade. Although the United States built a modest steel fleet powered by steam, and later enlarged it somewhat, the frustrations of life in the U.S. Navy were certainly considerable. Promotions came slowly and challenging assignments were rare. To

escape sea duty in old wooden vessels, Sims spent a year (1888–1889) on leave in Paris to study French, developing a facility for the language that would serve him well later in his career. The "free security" that the United States enjoyed across the nineteenth century after the War of 1812 made construction of a great navy unnecessary and inhibited the professional development of the naval service as a warfighting institution. The Navy concentrated on peacetime missions, notably protection of the nation's limited overseas commerce and defense of unchallenged coastlines. The activist Sims more than once contemplated resignation from the Navy in order to pursue more challenging civilian opportunities.

During the 1890s, however, Sims recaptured his commitment to the naval profession, especially while serving in the Pacific in some of the new steel ships. When assigned to the cruiser *Charleston*, he developed a strong interest in the application of modern technology to naval warfare. He soon identified himself as one of the so-called reformers in the naval officer corps who advocated increases in the size and efficiency of the Navy to meet changing responsibilities in an era of revolutionary scientific and political change.

When the brief War with Spain took place in 1898, Sims was again in Paris, serving as the naval attaché at the American Embassy. The Navy Department's need for information about Spanish naval movements led to the development of a network of American espionage agents in Europe. Sims proved energetic in this respect and received valuable information from a number of agents whom he employed to spy in Madrid and elsewhere. The Naval War Board in Washington, whose leading member was the influential naval writer Captain Alfred Thayer Mahan, made good use of the information that Sims and other attachés in Europe sent to the Navy Department about the movements of two naval squadrons deployed from Spanish ports during the war: that of Admiral Pascual Cervera, who steamed to a disastrous defeat at Santiago de Cuba, and that of Admiral Manuel de la Cámara, who progressed no farther than the Suez Canal in an abortive effort to challenge Admiral George Dewey at Manila Bay.[1]

The War with Spain led to the acquisition of a little American empire in the Caribbean Sea and the Pacific Ocean, notably Puerto Rico and the Philippines, along with the annexation of the Hawaiian Islands and the creation of a protectorate over Cuba. This short-lived burst of expansion was part of a stimulus to a measurable enlargement of the U.S. Navy, the other influence, more significant, being a great naval armaments race between Great Britain and Germany that reflected a dangerous destabilization in western Eurasia.

These circumstances encouraged the reformers within the naval officer corps, of whom Sims was one of the most vocal, to advocate an improved naval force—fully professionalized and equipped—that could rival those of such nations as Great Britain, France, Germany, and Japan. Sims agreed with the officers, including Rear Admiral Bradley Fiske, who urged extensive naval building programs and favored creation of a naval general staff to guide the Navy. The latter step would diminish civilian interference with those measures required to build a great fleet of the kind that Captain Mahan advocated: one prepared to defeat any opponent and able to achieve general and lasting command of the sea.

Sims was certain that senior officers, wedded to the status quo, were the bane for those junior officers who, like himself, advocated enlightened progress. To a fellow officer, William S. Benson, also interested in naval efficiency, he wrote in 1908: "If you can imagine a service in which all of the upper officers would carefully study and easily comprehend all criticism, and cheerfully and openly acknowledge all defects for which they were either actively or passively responsible, then there could be no such condition as that which we deplore." His naval heroes, courageous senior commanders with vision such as Commodore Robert F. Stockton and Admiral Richard Wainwright, were "always a small minority."[2]

Sims first came to the attention of the nation as a persuasive advocate of improved gunnery in the fleet. During the War with Spain, despite the successes of Admiral Dewey at Manila Bay and Admiral William T. Sampson at Santiago de Cuba, the Navy's gunnery had proved woefully deficient. For example, Dewey's ships fired 5,859 shells but made only 142 hits, a success rate of 2.42 percent. While serving in the Pacific after the war, Sims became acquainted with the gunnery reforms that Sir Percy Scott had initiated in the Royal Navy. Forceful, even overbearing in manner, Sims fought effectively for the adoption of Scott's methods in the U.S. Navy as inspector of target practice from 1902 to 1909. More an advocate than a creative intellect, Sims did not add much to Scott's techniques; his energies went toward breaking resistance to changes in the fleet. In 1916, when he was asked to guide the gunnery of the fleet once again, he declined, noting: "I did not initiate any part of it [gunnery training]. It was taken bodily from Sir Percy Scott. . . . I was never anything of an expert in the development of the details of gunnery training."[3]

Sims's naval career received a distinct boost when President Theodore Roosevelt, a patron of naval expansion, assigned him to additional duties as his naval aide in November 1907, although Sims was disappointed when Roosevelt failed to support the more radical elements in the program of the naval reformers.

However progressive his outlook, Sims's advocacy of reform carried a sharp edge, reflecting inner turmoil that led him on occasion to immoderate and unprofessional behavior. A most notable example of this tendency to excess was an unguarded and unauthorized endorsement of Anglo-American solidarity during a speech delivered in London in 1910, an indiscretion that earned him a reprimand from President William Howard Taft. Sims had the knack of engaging the loyalty of younger officers, among them Dudley Knox, later to become a leading naval historian, and William V. Pratt, who eventually served as Chief of Naval Operations, but he demanded total fidelity, a requirement that sometimes alienated him from close associates who presumed to differ on one or another professional matter. In any event, Sims's behavior did not prevent his promotion to rear admiral on the eve of the American intervention in World War I, an event that gave him an opportunity to contribute importantly to American naval history.

After President Woodrow Wilson decided to declare war on the Central Powers but before Congress acted, Sims was called to Washington and asked to represent the U.S. Navy in Great Britain. Early Anglo-American naval cooperation was imperative. Germany had resumed unrestricted submarine warfare against noncombatant and neutral commerce with no concern about the prospect of American belligerency because German leaders assumed that undersea warfare would knock the Allies out of the war before the United States, largely unprepared, could hope to influence the outcome.

When Admiral William Shepherd Benson, Chief of Naval Operations, gave Sims this assignment, he took note of Sims's reputation as an Anglophile by cautioning against undue pro-British behavior. "Don't let the British pull the wool over your eyes. It is none of our business pulling their chestnuts out of the fire. We would as soon fight the British as the Germans." These were representative views then, especially in the Navy, that reflected the sturdy, bumptious nationalism of the era, frequent suspicions of British motives, and concern about the possibility that Germany might defeat the Allies, which would leave the United States to fight on alone; but they conflicted with Sims's conception of sound inter-Allied relations.

Proceeding to London, Sims immediately discovered the extent of the submarine crisis. About 540,000 tons of shipping had gone to the bottom in February, the first month of unrestricted submarine operations. In March the figure rose to more than 600,000 tons, and in April to 875,000 tons. German naval leaders predicted that losses of this magnitude would force a decision on the Allies within six months.

Sims soon began a series of dramatic reports to the Navy Department in which he described the danger of Germany's successes against Allied merchant ships and endorsed various naval measures advocated by the British Admiralty, some of which did not conform to inclinations in Washington. He agreed with the Admiralty's view that the United States should make an early entry into the naval war by supporting British antisubmarine operations to protect sea lines of communication between the Allied nations, especially naval escort of merchant ships gathered in convoys. This course would require the United States to postpone construction of a balanced battle fleet and concentrate instead on building antisubmarine craft, especially destroyers, and merchant ships. Moreover, to all intents and purposes it would commit American ships and crews to service under the command of British senior officers.

Some historians erroneously maintain that Sims pressed the adoption of the convoy system on the Admiralty, but modern scholarship has demonstrated that this measure came about when advocates of this tactic convinced Prime Minister David Lloyd George of its practicality, in April 1917. In this case, as in most others, Sims adjusted his views to conform with those of British naval authorities.[4]

As Sims conducted his initial investigations in London, a series of missions from the Allied nations, most importantly from Britain and France, visited Washington to arrange wartime cooperation, including naval coordination, with the United States. British naval representatives reinforced the recommendations that came from Sims. The Royal Navy believed that the Grand Fleet, maintaining a distant blockade in the North Sea, could contain the German high sea fleet in port, thus commanding the surface of the sea. This effort, however, limited the number of naval vessels available for antisubmarine operations. To augment the antisubmarine force, the head of the British mission, Foreign Minister Arthur James Balfour, urged the immediate dispatch of American destroyers to European waters.[5]

Admiral Benson, and others who opposed so much subservience to British desires, worried about larger British motive, and they were concerned about the consequences should the Germans force the Allies out of the war. Benson was anxious about protecting the long-term naval interests of the United States, which might well diverge from those of Great Britain at some future time. Sims discounted views of this type; he was convinced that British and American interests were complementary and would remain so indefinitely.

Sims's ideas prevailed, if only because President Wilson had no choice. The grave threat of the German U-boats limited his freedom of action; America must do what it could as soon as possible to help keep Germany from achieving victory through sea power before the U.S. Army could deploy to Europe and make a significant contribution to Germany's defeat.[6]

In many respects, Sims's position in London was unique in the nation's naval experience. Given the decision to place American antisubmarine craft under European commanders, he did not exercise direct operational command over ships at sea. Instead, he transferred his authority to such British officers as Vice Admiral Sir Lewis Bayly, who commanded the naval base at Queenstown, Ireland, whence destroyers sortied to protect convoys entering the submarine danger zone. Sims devoted his energies during 1917 almost entirely to urging the Navy Department to deploy all available antisubmarine reinforcements to Europe and to ensuring their effective use against the German U-boats. In constant contact with the Admiralty in London, which he considered the center of inter-Allied coordination, he generally supported British initiatives, a course that aroused growing irritation in Washington. Sims tried to allay such suspicions, on one occasion telling Secretary of the Navy Josephus Daniels that he realized his opinions might be considered suspect but that "It should be unnecessary to state that I have done everything within my ability to maintain a broad viewpoint." Such protestations proved useless.[7]

However equivocal his standing in Washington, Sims gained unrivaled prestige in Europe. Enjoying the full confidence of his British associates, he established the closest possible day-to-day contacts. At the same time, he built an efficient staff that provided effective support for expanding American naval activity, not only in the waters surrounding Great Britain but increasingly in other regions of the Atlantic Ocean and in the Mediterranean Sea where merchant ships and troop transports were exposed to enemy attacks. Sims's personal qualities and his professional skills served him well during 1917–1918. He was the right man in the right place at a supreme moment in the naval history of his country.

Benson and others were concerned about the defense of home waters, but Sims discounted this problem. He argued correctly that submarines would not operate frequently in waters so distant from bases. The long voyage across the Atlantic Ocean would keep U-boats that undertook it out of action for an extended time; they could spend only a short time on station. Moreover, Sims believed that "the most effective defence which can be afforded to our home waters is an offensive campaign against the enemy which threatens these waters . . . the place for protection of home waters is . . . where the enemy is operating and must continue to operate in force."[8]

President Wilson and Admiral Benson disdained what they believed to be undue British preferences for defensive measures. They both pressed for offensive action against bases that harbored the German submarines, such as those on the Belgian coast; but Sims supported British naval opinion, which during 1917 was decidedly resistant to such operations because they were deemed impractical and liable to disturb some of the Allies. Belgium, for example, opposed raids on German bases at occupied places such as Ostend because they might do extensive damage. These arguments caused much irritation in Washington, but Wilson and others lacked sufficient leverage to coerce the Admiralty to U.S. views.[9]

Like Admiral Benson, the General Board of the Navy was especially concerned about preserving the great naval building program of 1916, which envisioned a battle fleet capable of operating along Mahanian lines—one that could gain general and lasting command of the sea. Opposition to this course appeared to contradict Mahan's views, but Sims argued for the need to consider that the naval forces of the entire Allied coalition constituted an inter-Allied battle fleet, to which the United States was making an important contribution. Moreover, in sending antisubmarine craft to European waters, the American fleet was merely maneuvering its screen to a position at a considerable distance in advance of its capital ships. If necessary, the heavy vessels could close up later.[10]

Sims was eager to build a staff in London prepared to cope with the many administrative responsibilities that developed there. Seeking officers with whom he had developed close relations in the past, especially the "band of brothers" who had served in his torpedo flotilla, Sims found his desires frequently set aside. The Navy Department had good reasons for its reluctance. Experienced officers were in great demand; their assignments were intended to provide some leaven of experience in the much expanded Navy. Sims, however, characteristically chose to interpret his difficulties as the result of personal animosity or incompetence. Disputes over personnel were among the many incidents that fueled his growing alienation from officials in the Navy Department, especially Secretary Daniels and, to a considerable degree, Chief of Naval Operations Benson. Fortunately, Benson's assistant, Captain William V. Pratt, was one of Sims's most valued associates in the Navy. Pratt managed to mediate effectively, explaining the ways of each admiral to the other and providing Sims with information about the basis of the Navy Department's views on disputatious issues.[11]

Although the President and the Navy Department accepted Sims's arguments about the need to concentrate on antisubmarine operations, there was a considerable difference of opinion about their character. Sims believed that the prime consideration was protection of commerce supplying the Allies, whereas the Navy Department interpreted its first responsibility as the escort of transports ferrying the American expeditionary force to Europe. During 1917, this difference did not create tensions because few troops were as yet ready to go to France. When the American reinforcement began in earnest during the early months of 1918, however, it became a serious bone of contention. The Allies' need for manpower proved so extensive that eventually Great Britain was forced to accede not only to the American desire for strong escorts to guard troop convoys but also to a demand that Britain provide vessels for use as transports.[12] To cover the arrival of American troops in 1918, Admiral Benson sought to develop a great base at Brest, France, adjacent to the route of American transports, an action that would inhibit the expansion of submarine operations out of Queenstown intended to guard convoys of merchant ships bound for British ports.

By the outset of 1918, it had become clear that the Allies had succeeded in containing the undersea offensive sufficiently to maintain effective maritime communications, thus frustrating the German attempt to achieve a decision at sea. About 300,000 tons of merchant shipping were destroyed per month during 1918, but new construction, averaging about 500,000 tons per month, more than offset this loss. The failure of the maritime gambit forced Germany's high command to seek a decision on land before American help could flow to Europe in large quantities. A great German offensive materialized on the Western Front and lasted about four months, from March to mid-July 1918. Although the Germans gained a great deal of ground, the assault fell short of decisive objectives. French Marshal Ferdinand Foch then launched an inter-Allied counteroffensive that finally forced Germany to accept an armistice on 11 November. These land battles in France obscured the growing success of the Allied navies during the final year of the war.[13]

During 1918, Admiral Sims gave much of his attention to the frustrating question of naval warfare in the Mediterranean Sea. He shared the British view that the Italians were entirely too inactive in dealing with the Austro-Hungarian fleet, and with naval bases at Pola and Cattaro in the Adriatic Sea that harbored German submarines. After the western coalition formed an Allied Naval Council in December 1917, Sims represented the United States during its sessions. The council dedicated much of its energy to Mediterranean affairs. Making use of an American planning section that he had managed to establish in London, Sims busied himself with all manner of schemes to wage an effective antisubmarine campaign in the Mediterranean Sea where maritime losses remained at a high level. He came to appreciate the political tensions among the French, the Italians, and the British that precluded action. Sims's failure to achieve much in the Mediterranean was perhaps the principal setback that he encountered during his wartime service in Europe, although he and others largely ignored the subject in postwar writings.[14]

Two petty but highly irritating developments contributed to Sims's growing disgust with the Navy Department. The British government sought to make him and Benson honorary members of the Board of Admiralty, an unprecedented honor to foreigners, but Secretary Daniels and Admiral Benson were definitively opposed to it, and they decided the matter. When Sims, seeking to boost the morale of his command, proposed that European governments be allowed to present decorations to American sailors, Daniels objected.[15]

When the war suddenly approached a most unexpected end late in 1918, Sims went to Paris for meetings of the Allied Naval Council that were called to determine the naval terms of armistice. Unfortunately for Sims, Benson had journeyed to Paris with Edward M. House, the President's principal representative at pre-armistice discussions concerning inter-Allied policy. At House's insistence, Benson displaced Sims as the American representative on the Allied Naval Council, and Sims returned to London. After the Armistice of 11 November 1918, Benson remained in Paris as the naval adviser to the American peace commissioners, thereby preventing Sims from taking part in important naval negotiations that occurred during the postwar peace conference. Sims privately betrayed his disappointment. After noting that General John J. Pershing also had not been appointed a plenipotentiary, he confided snidely to a close friend: "As for our naval advisor [Benson] with the peace delegates he is exactly the kind of man they want; of course you know why!" Sims here adverted to the conviction of his circle that Benson, lacking independent views and special talents of his own, was a yes-man who kowtowed to civilians.[16]

Sims's accumulating frustration with the Navy Department continued to surface during the war and shortly afterward. On 13 August 1918, he commented portentously to Captain Pratt: "When the history of this war comes to be written there will be a number of features that will not be very creditable to the United States Navy. If hearings are held on the conduct of the war, a number of rather disagreeable facts must inevitably be brought out." He mentioned especially the Navy Department's failure to bring the most experienced naval officers to Europe. Much more devastating was his reaction to a report, which Captain Pratt drafted shortly after the Armistice, detailing the Navy's accomplishments during wartime. To Sims, this report indicated that the Navy Department claimed "to have always foreseen everything, planned everything and supported us up to the handle," thereby depreciating the accomplishments of the Navy overseas. To the contrary, he concluded that "the cablegrams exchanged between the Department and me during the first four months of our participation in the war will be, I think, pretty damaging testimony to the game played by the Department, and will make this Departmental letter . . . look pretty sick."[17]

Sims returned to the United States in high dudgeon. Maneuvering successfully for reappointment as president of the Naval War College, he resettled in Newport to write a memoir of his wartime service. Negotiating a lucrative contract with Doubleday, Page & Company, and arranging for the collaboration of the talented Burton J. Hendrick, an editor with that publisher, Sims prepared a detailed report of his activities that appeared initially as a series of articles in *World's Work*, a well-known magazine of the day, and later as a book titled *The Victory at Sea*. Hendrick drafted the entire text of this cogent account, which faithfully reflected Sims's criticisms to the degree that he cared to express them. Naval regulations prevented Sims from venting his spleen extensively in this publication; he dealt with his tormentors by ignoring them, and he hardly mentioned Daniels and Benson. *The Victory at Sea* did not sell as well as Sims and his publishers had hoped, but it achieved a succès d'estime, the award of the Pulitzer Prize in 1920, and it became the accepted comment on the Navy's participation in the war, however unfair it was in its failure to give due credit to the Navy Department.[18]

Meanwhile, Sims took advantage of opportunities to provoke a congressional investigation of naval policy during the war. In so doing he redeemed a pledge to Admiral William Fullam, another naval reformer of the day: "You may be sure . . . that at the proper time I will tell the whole truth as I understand it." In another communication, he added, "You know I entirely agree with you that the country has got to be informed as to the condition of the Navy in the immediate past and its condition now." Those responsible who had "camouflaged the subject cannot escape very long." The basis for a public controversy developed when Sims angrily refused to accept a postwar decoration, the Distinguished Service Medal, in December 1919 because he felt that the list of those honored did not fairly reflect the contributions of various officers during the war. On 7 January 1920, after the Senate decided to examine the list of decorations, Sims wrote to Secretary Daniels and outlined his indictment of the Navy Department. He stressed the department's failure to respond immediately to his recommendations from London during 1917, when the crisis over the U-boat campaign was at its height. Thus, Sims fulfilled a vow he made to his collaborator, Hendrick: "You may be sure that if in the course of these hearings I can pry the lid off I will do so. I am prepared to go to the limit."[19]

When he appeared before the Senate subcommittee that conducted the naval investigation, Sims provided a detailed exposition of the complaints that he had made in 1917 and of the Navy Department's alleged failure to respond appropriately. Daniels, Benson, and others, Sims charged, had not prepared for the war properly, and the Navy had not been able to meet its responsibilities. "We pursued a policy of vacillation, or in simpler words, a hand to mouth policy, attempting to formulate our plans from day to day, based upon an incorrect appreciation of the situation," he complained. Sims maintained that the Navy Department had cost the Allies half a million lives, two and a half million tons of shipping, and fifteen billion dollars in expenditures. His testimony included extensive reference to the cable exchanges that he had conducted with the Navy Department during 1917 over the nature of the American naval contribution.[20]

In response, the Navy Department offered a spirited defense of its actions, as Daniels, Benson, Pratt, and others testified at length. They admitted that the Navy had been less than fully prepared at the beginning of hostilities in 1917, but they offered explanations of the reasons why the Navy Department had responded as it did to Sims's requests.

Benson made the most explicit rejoinder to the burden of Sims's charges. As to prewar unpreparedness, he noted that he had desired readiness, but "this was not the attitude of the people of the United States and not the attitude of the Administration." Political decisions, to which he was subject, accounted for naval unpreparedness in April 1917. During the war, he had acted in terms of the national interest and he emphasized his duty "to safeguard American interests regardless of any duty to humanity or anything else." Nevertheless, the United States had responded handsomely to the desires of the Allies and in some ways had urged more ambitious measures than had been recommended from Europe.[21]

In a sweeping conclusion, Benson left no doubt of his views: The Navy Department met its obligations "with efficiency and success; . . . the policies we adopted and our plans in accordance therewith were thoroughly justified by events." He, his colleagues, and the entire Navy had "performed well a difficult task; cooperating from beginning to end with the Allies and rendering them every assistance in our power, and contributing very materially to the general result." This rosy evaluation surely overstated a generally reasonable case, thereby further obscuring the whole truth about the Navy's wartime record.[22]

Sims hoped that the hearings would catch the imagination of the American public, but the outcome proved a great disappointment to him. The Republican majority on the Senate subcommittee supported Sims, but the Democratic minority defended the Navy Department. No action was taken against Daniels or Benson, and the investigation was soon forgotten, although it caused a long-term rift within the Navy between Sims's advocates and his enemies. Instead of reviewing wartime events, during 1921 the nation engaged in a discussion about future security in the Pacific Ocean that led to naval disarmament, one aspect of the treaty system that emerged from the Washington Naval Conference.

Various circumstances account for Sims's discomfiture. Above all, the naval war had ended in a great victory, whatever problems might have emerged along the way. Sims's charges appeared to many as simply a quarrel among admirals, reminiscent of the Sampson-Schley controversy that followed the War with Spain. Second, the public had already tired of the war. Postwar exhaustion and disillusionment, reflected in the failure of the Senate to accept the Treaty of Versailles, certainly worked against Sims's efforts to arouse the American people.

Finally, Sims overplayed his hand. His proclivity to overpersonalize issues and to tendentiousness caught up with him in this climactic episode. After all, Sims's general views about the centrality of the inter-Allied antisubmarine effort and the need to postpone the American naval building programs had prevailed over those of Benson; and good reasons existed for the delays and modifications that the Navy Department made in response to Sims's strident demands in 1917. Sims fell victim to a common error: theater commanders, insufficiently mindful of the larger considerations that motivate higher authority, all too often view their activities from the narrow perspective of their own situations.

Perhaps Sims's admiration of Great Britain and the Royal Navy affected his judgment in some respects too; surely he erred in identifying too closely with the Republicans during the hearings, thus allowing his critics to accuse him of partisanship. During the presidential campaign of 1920 he sought an audience with the Republican candidate, Warren G. Harding, to press his views on naval matters, but he was unsuccessful. Any interest that he might have had in becoming Secretary of the Navy went glimmering when President Harding appointed a loyal Republican rather than a naval expert.

Sims retired from the U.S. Navy in 1922 in the rank of rear admiral. After retirement, he resided in Newport, from where he occasionally attempted to influence naval policy until his death in 1936. Noteworthy was his strong support of naval aviation, which led to a brief recall to active duty in 1925. Advancing age did not moderate the inveterate intemperance that had dogged Sims through most of his naval career and, in the end, compromised his success. Perhaps this failing was consistent with his performance as a naval reformer before the war. He failed to weigh his views carefully against those of his antagonists or to give them due consideration, and, in the process, he alienated many who otherwise might have rallied to him.[23]

In evaluating Sims's naval career it is important neither to underestimate nor to exaggerate its significance. Sims's reputation benefited greatly from his own *The Victory at Sea* and especially from an excellent biography, written by his son-in-law Elting E. Morison, that glorified the admiral as the exemplar par excellence of the modern U.S. Navy and fixed him in the minds of naval historians and others as the leading prophet of the naval future after World War I.[24]

A modern finding must deplore Sims's intolerance of those who disagreed with him, an unlovely trait that eventually compromised his advocacy of naval reform. It must also identify some significant negative characteristics of his outlook, especially his unwillingness to give sufficient recognition to the principle of civilian supremacy over the military establishment. Like many other officers of his day, Sims failed to come to terms with the constraints that a democracy necessarily places on its naval officers. Perhaps, finally, an accounting must recognize that Sims was often more a publicist than an originator of the reforms that he pressed so energetically.

In the end, however, Sims stands in the foremost ranks of those who led the U.S. Navy during the transitional years from the age of free security in the nineteenth century to an era of great international destabilization, a shift that forced the nation to create a powerful steel fleet that met Wilson's criterion—a navy second to none. More than most others, Sims discerned the basic security requirements of the new age. Most important, whatever his failing, he served with the greatest distinction in London during 1917–1918, steadfast in attention to duty and remarkably successful in the conduct of his enormous responsibilities as executor of the American naval contribution to the victory at sea in European waters. No other officer in the Navy of his time could have matched his performance in the crucible of total war.

FURTHER READING

For general accounts of the naval war, the most informative works are Arthur J. Marder, *From the Dreadnought to Scapa Flow: The Royal Navy in the Fisher Era*, 5 vols. (New York, 1961–1970), especially the last two volumes, which cover 1917 to 1918; Thomas G. Frothingham, *The Naval History of the World War*, 3 vols. (Cambridge, Mass., 1924–1926); Paul G. Halpern, *The Naval War in the Mediterranean, 1914–1918* (Annapolis, Md., 1987); Robert M. Grant's two volumes, *U-Boats Destroyed: The Effect of Anti-submarine Warfare, 1914–1918* (London, 1964) and *U-Boat Intelligence, 1914–1918* (London, 1969); and Holger H. Herwig and David F. Trask, "The Failure of Imperial Germany's Undersea Offensive against World Shipping, February 1917–October 1918," *Historian* 33 (1971): 611–36.

Articles on the role of the U.S. Navy include Dean C. Allard, "Anglo-American Naval Differences during World War I," *Military Affairs* 44 (1980): 75–81, and David F. Trask, "The American Navy in a World at War, 1914–1919," in *In Peace and War: Interpretations of American Naval History, 1775–1978*, edited by Kenneth J. Hagan (Westport, Conn., 1978), 204–20.

For the views of Admiral William S. Sims, see his *The Victory at Sea*, edited by David F. Trask, in the Classics of Naval Literature series (Annapolis, Md., 1984), a reprint of the original 1920 edition. Also, see the magisterial biography by Elting E. Morison, *Admiral Sims and the Modern American Navy* (Boston, 1942); Dean C. Allard, "Admiral William S. Sims and United States Naval Policy in World War I," *American Neptune* 35 (1975): 97–110; and David F. Trask, *Captains and Cabinets: Anglo-American Naval Relations, 1917–1918* (Columbia, Mo., 1972).

For other personalities, see Gerald E. Wheeler, *Admiral William Veazie Pratt, U.S. Navy: A Sailor's Life* (Washington, D.C., 1974); Mary Klachko, with David F. Trask, *Admiral William Shepherd Benson: First Chief of Naval Operations* (Annapolis, Md., 1987); Paolo E. Coletta, "Josephus Daniels: 5 March 1913–5 March 1921," in Coletta, *American Secretaries of the Navy*, 2 vols. (Annapolis, Md., 1980); and E. David Cronon, ed., *The Cabinet Diaries of Josephus Daniels, 1913–1921* (Lincoln, Neb., 1963).

For the record of the congressional inquiry into the Navy after World War I, see U.S. Congress, Senate, *Naval Investigations: Hearings before the Subcommittee of the Committee on Naval Affairs; United States Senate*, 2 vols., 66th Cong., 2d sess., 1920.

NOTES

1. For biograpical information, see Elting E. Morison, *Admiral Sims and the Modern American Navy* (Boston, 1942). A striking short sketch by Jeffery M. Dorwart is in

*Dictionary of American Military Biography*, edited by Roger J. Spiller, Joseph G. Dawson, and T. Harry Williams, 3 vols. (Westport, Conn., 1984), 3:1003–6. Dorwart measurably modifies Morison's highly favorable evaluation of Sims, an approach that is extended in this essay. For naval intelligence during 1898, see David F. Trask, *The War with Spain* (New York, 1981), 87–89, 143.

2. Quoted in Mary Klachko, with David F. Trask, *Admiral William Shepherd Benson: First Chief of Naval Operations* (Annapolis, Md., 1987), 18.

3. Quoted in ibid., 43.

4. See David F. Trask, *Captains and Cabinets: Anglo-American Naval Relations, 1917–1918* (Columbia, Mo., 1972), 72, 79–80, an interpretation first advanced by Arthur Marder.

5. For information about the Allied missions, see ibid., 62–64, 74–77.

6. A convenient collection of Sims's messages to the Navy Department during this critical period is found in the admiral's memoir of the war, *The Victory at Sea*, edited with an introduction by David F. Trask and reprinted in the Naval Institute's Classics of Naval Literature series (Annapolis, Md., 1984), 374–99. For accounts of the discussion between Sims and the Navy Department, see Trask, *Captains and Cabinets*, 61–101; and Klachko, *Benson*, 70–81.

7. Sims to Daniels, 16 July 1917, reprinted in Sims, *Victory at Sea*, 398.

8. Ibid., 396.

9. Trask, *Captains and Cabinets*, 131–32.

10. David F. Trask, "The American Navy in a World at War, 1914–1919," in *In Peace and War: Interpretations of American Naval History, 1775–1978*, edited by Kenneth J. Hagan (Westport, Conn., 1978), 209–10.

11. For information about Captain Pratt and his dealings with Benson and Sims, see Gerald E. Wheeler, *Admiral William Veazie Pratt, U.S. Navy: A Sailor's Life* (Washington, D.C., 1974), especially 71–126.

12. For this subject, see two articles by Dean C. Allard, "Admiral William S. Sims and United States Naval Policy in World War I," *American Neptune* 35 (1975): 97–110; and "Anglo-American Naval Differences during World War I," *Military Affairs* 44 (1980): 75–81.

13. For information on the course of the submarine war, see Holger H. Herwig and David F. Trask, "The Failure of Imperial Germany's Undersea Offensive against World Shipping, February 1917–October 1918," *Historian* 33 (1971): 611–36.

14. For an up-to-date study of the tangled naval situation in the Mediterranean area during World War I, see Paul G. Halpern, *The Naval War in the Mediterranean, 1914–1918* (Annapolis, Md., 1987).

15. Trask, *Captain and Cabinets*, 193–96.

16. Sims to William Fullam, 15 January 1919, as quoted in Klachko, *Benson*, 121, 131–32.

17. For the quotations and information concerning Sims's irritation, see Wheeler, *Pratt*, 147–48. Sims, of course, had complained regularly. Wheeler notes one such comment made to Pratt on 21 November 1917: "My great fear is that this war may be lost or that the Allies may be forced into a very unsatisfactory peace and that the subsequent examinations as to the causes of this condition may reveal the fact that we have not done our utmost to prevent it and that our military decisions in many cases have been unsound." Sims here reflected the plenary fears that emerged in the Allied nations as the

Germans began preparations for their great offensive of March 1918, but it may be of some significance that already he was thinking about the possibility of a postwar investigation of the American naval effort. Ibid., 147.

18. For the story of the writing of *The Victory at Sea*, see Trask, "Introduction," *Victory at Sea*, xx–xxvii.

19. For the preliminaries to the hearings of 1920, see Klachko, *Benson*, 170–71. Sims's comment to Hendrick is quoted in Trask, "Introduction," *Victory at Sea*, xxiii.

20. Klachko, *Benson*, 172–73. For the hearings, see U.S. Congress, *Naval Investigation: Hearings before the Subcommittee of the Committee on Naval Affairs, United States Senate*, 2 vols., 66th Cong., 2d sess., 1920. A spirited redefinition of Sims's views is in Tracy B. Kittredge, *Naval Lessons of the Great War: A Review of the Senate Naval Investigation of the Criticisms of Admiral Sims of the Policies and Methods of Josephus Daniels* (Garden City, N.Y., 1921).

21. U.S. Congress, *Naval Investigation*, 1920, as quoted in Klachko, *Benson*, 176.

22. Benson to Senator Frederick R. Hole, 28 May 1920, as quoted in Klachko, *Benson*, 178–79.

23. Sims, along with a number of other officers, including Admiral Benson, was restored to his wartime rank of full admiral in 1930.

24. Morison, *Admiral Sims*.

# ☆ William A. Moffett
☆
☆ Steward of the Air Revolution

*by Clark G. Reynolds*

IN THE GENERATION OF AMERICAN OFFICERS PRODUCED BY THE SAIL-steam, coastal defense navy, none played a more far-reaching leadership role during the transition to an air-centered fleet with a global reach than did William Adger Moffett. For twelve years, from 1921 to 1933, in spite of strong opposition by the ruling battleship men, Admiral Moffett wielded immense authority in forging the fledgling air arm of the U.S. Navy. His consummate managerial skill enabled him to lay the foundations of American naval striking power during World War II and for the ensuing half century. His epitaph, the "Father of Naval Aviation," is entirely appropriate.

In terms of national policy and naval strategy, Moffett consistently endorsed the philosophy of worldwide American maritime expansion advocated by Alfred Thayer Mahan and Theodore Roosevelt. Indeed, as a young lieutenant (junior grade), Moffett served under Captain Mahan's command in the protected cruiser *Chicago* from 1893 to 1895, and he attended the Naval War College in the summer of 1896, during Mahan's last tour there. By the time he became an admiral, in the 1920s, Moffett followed Mahan in the belief that the United States needed a revitalized merchant marine and additional colonial possessions as naval bases.

"All virile nations are naturally annexationists," Moffett argued, in favor of an American empire; and in 1930, he declared: "The United States should not have a navy inferior to any other. . . . I am also in favor of a merchant marine inferior to none." American warships, merchantmen, and overseas bases were essential, he argued, to fill the vacuum being created by the demise of the British Empire.

> I can not but feel that Great Britain has reached her pinnacle; that they have a glorious history and traditions but are living on traditions too

much. . . . They have traditions and what is generally called aristocracy, but while we are comparatively short on both, we have virility and are a young nation stepping out with vision and confidence, and nothing will stop our being the greatest nation in the world except what we do within ourselves.[1]

Typical of naval officers of his generation, Moffett had the manner of a cool professional devoted to his service. He developed his administrative talents as a line officer in the usual shipboard and shoreside assignments and was not dazzled by innovations in technology. For example, observing the bitter resistance of the line to absorbing engineers, Moffett learned to accept change by understanding and applying technological progress. He took the same attitude with aircraft. "My former service on and experience with steam and the attitude of the Navy toward it," he observed in 1933, "has been of great assistance to me being patient when endeavoring to do all that I could to assist in indoctrinating the Navy as a whole in regard to aviation and its importance."[2]

Moffett's sound intellect and controlled manner stemmed from the circumstances of his youth. Born of Scotch-Irish parents in the genteel and Civil War–devastated port city of Charleston, South Carolina, on 31 October 1869, Moffett grew up in the dual environment of maritime commerce and Southern Reconstruction society. His father, a merchant of the city and former Confederate officer, passed on to him a deep respect for and emulation of the mighty Robert E. Lee. And though the father died in the boy's fifth year, Moffett drew similar strength from his mother. His solid upbringing in a family of nine children (he was number seven) enabled him to become a family man himself, with six children of his own. Moffett's calm, Southern demeanor stood him in good stead in the public schools and at the U.S. Naval Academy, where he often had to defend the honor of the South against Yankee critics. A fairly mediocre student, he graduated rather far down in the Class of 1890.[3]

His early career reflected the technological changes that were transforming the U.S. Navy at the turn of the century: service in sailing and steam sloops, a gunboat once and a monitor twice, cruisers, and predreadnought, as well as dreadnought, battleships. On board the *Charleston*, a protected cruiser named after his hometown, Moffett participated in the capture of Guam and the Philippine city of Manila during the war with Spain. His skills were sufficient to lead the Ottoman navy to offer him a senior commission in 1900, when he was but a new lieutenant in the battleship *Kentucky* en route to the Far East. He declined that honor, but received increasingly responsible posts during the expansion of the Roosevelt Navy.[4]

Moffett's long seagoing service led him to command of the scout cruiser *Chester* late in 1913. As such, he personally delivered Admiral Henry T. Mayo's ultimatum to the Mexicans at Tampico in April 1914, an action culminating in the Vera Cruz intervention, in which his ship engaged Mexican shore batteries. That August, he was given command of the Great Lakes Naval Training Station near Chicago, Illinois, with additional duty of supervising the three naval districts in the region. His organizational and innovative genius shone brightly as he upgraded the training program, which led to his promotion to captain in 1916 and his retention in the post throughout America's participation in World War I. From a capacity of sixteen hundred trainees, Moffett increased the recruit accommodations to some fifty thousand, making Great Lakes the largest recruit training depot in the Navy. It produced nearly one hundred thousand sailors for wartime service. Moffett even brought in the renowned bandmaster John Philip Sousa to provide music for the station. In December 1918, Moffett's reward was command of the battleship *Mississippi* for two years.[5]

Like many of his peers, Moffett had been catapulted into the forefront of the managerial revolution sweeping American industry in peacetime as in war. At Great Lakes he not only streamlined the internal organization but learned the art of working effectively through local political and business leaders. He developed an especially close relationship with the chewing gum magnate William K. ("Bill") Wrigley, Jr. Moffett's fine diplomatic tact enabled him, at the head of a landing party from the *Mississippi*, to prevent a radical labor demonstration during President Woodrow Wilson's visit to Seattle in September 1919.[6]

Moffett's first real exposure to the new technology of naval aviation occurred early in 1913 when, as executive officer of the new dreadnought *Arkansas*, he went duck hunting at Guantánamo Bay, Cuba, with the young fliers of the U.S. Navy's first seaplane unit. But he took no interest in the crude flying machines. Reflecting the general attitude of his fellow officers, he remarked to the airmen's commander, Lieutenant John H. ("Jack") Towers: "Towers, you're such a nice chap, why don't you give up this aviation fad? You'll surely get yourself killed. Any man who sticks to it is either crazy or else a plain damned fool!"[7]

The use of military aircraft in the European war and the pressing need to train aviation mechanics at Great Lakes changed Moffett's attitude, however. Working closely with Wrigley, he established an aviation unit of more than 250 planes at the sprawling depot. By the time he assumed command of the *Mississippi*, Moffett had begun to appreciate the revolutionary promise of fleet aviation, particularly because Japan had suddenly reemerged as the major enemy across the vast Pacific.[8]

Following experiments on board the *Texas*, Moffett had a ramp installed over a turret on the *Mississippi* in order to launch scout planes to spot the fall of her shells. (The planes landed ashore.) During gunnery exercises in May and June 1920, these Sopwiths, Jennys, and F5L flying boats, under Captain

Henry C. Mustin and Commander Towers, transmitted the proper ranges by wireless to Moffett's gunnery officer, Commander William L. Calhoun. On one day alone, Moffett signaled the aviators: "Your aeroplanes were our salvation. We thank you." In fact, the planes enabled the *Mississippi* to attain scores so high that they almost equaled those of all the other battleships combined! Among three aerial spotters whom Moffett singled out for high praise was Lieutenant Commander Marc A. Mitscher, an officer who would earn his growing admiration over time and who, as Admiral Mitscher, would lead the famous Fast Carrier Task Force in the war against Japan.[9]

The senior admirals realized that naval aviation was maturing so rapidly that it needed its own bureau organization, their thinking stimulated in no small part by the growing crusade of Brigadier General William "Billy" Mitchell of the U.S. Army's Air Service. Mitchell publicly proclaimed that the Navy's air arm should be united with the Army's in a new, separate, and independent air force, geared to land-based strategic bombing. So uncompromising and outspoken was Mitchell that the director of naval aviation, the normally affable Captain Thomas T. Craven, finally refused even to speak to him. As intraservice efforts to create the Navy's own bureau of aeronautics accelerated over 1920 to 1921, a tactful but knowledgeable bureau chief was needed, and Moffett was the logical choice. At the urging of Mustin, Moffett approached Wrigley to ask Wrigley's support for his candidacy. Wrigley had become a major power in the Republican Party, and he was pleased to lend his support in recommending Moffett to lead naval aviation. President Warren G. Harding agreed, whereupon Moffett relieved Craven as director in March 1921, then fleeted up to become Chief of the new Bureau of Aeronautics (BuAer) upon its creation in July. The post carried the rank of rear admiral.[10]

Moffett's style and philosophy of leadership in naval aviation were immediately obvious and did not change in the twelve years that he held the office. A man of only medium build, the white-haired Moffett was nevertheless a commanding presence, with his erect bearing and quiet, confident manner. Energetic, neat, and well ordered, he drove about in the latest model LaSalle automobile. Though no flag-waving "prophet" like Mitchell, he was an impressive individual who had to be reckoned with. Indeed, Admiral William V. Pratt, his friend and Chief of Naval Operations (CNO), remarked to Moffett in front of Secretary of the Navy Charles Francis Adams in 1930 that, as Moffett recalled it: "I was the most insistent person he had ever known. I told him that when I felt I was right, I would insist to the end." And yet, to the aviation community, in the words of Towers, Bill Moffett was "beloved by all who had the privilege of really knowing him."[11]

The insistence that Pratt observed was Moffett's determination to gain for aviation the importance he firmly believed that it deserved within the Navy.

The rigid conservatism of the so-called Gun Club of battleship admirals stood in his way at nearly every turn. Moffett often noted that the problem of selling naval aviation was "lack of knowledge and lack of understanding," both of which he labored energetically to correct. His task was made more difficult by the outspokenness of younger pilots who proclaimed the obsolescence of the battleship, thus further arousing senior admirals already resentful of BuAer's budgetary and manpower needs in an era of stringent economy measures. Moffett's struggles were fought largely within the Navy, with colleagues—"the old timers in the Navy who don't appreciate Aviation," he called them. These adversaries held such key positions as CNO, Commander in Chief United States Fleet (CinCUS), and Chief of the Bureau of Navigation (BuNav). The BuNav chief controlled personnel assignments, a subject of major interest in Moffett's attempt to gain control of the assignment of its aviators for BuAer, a goal achieved in the latter years of his tenure as bureau chief. Moffett set out to make BuAer into a superbureau, just as the office of naval aviation had been during the war—that is, an agency reaching into the previously sacrosanct bureaus that had controlled personnel, engineering, weapons, and even medicine.[12]

Moffett thus worked within the system to "sell" naval aviation. Of him, Towers wrote, "I cannot recall any man who more loved a fight and who could think of more ways to win one." Moffett grew so adept at it that he came to be feared by the conservative battleship-weaned admirals. The infighting never let up during his dozen years at the helm of BuAer. Even when he won victories for aviation that became department policy, the criticism and antagonism toward him so intensified that he felt compelled to counterattack it with pointed letters. For example, in the spring of 1932, he chastised Admiral Frank M. Schofield for being "disloyal" to the Navy by criticizing its adoption of Moffett's much resented dirigible program. Not only was Schofield the reigning CinCUS, he had also been an academy classmate of Moffett's. Moffett then expressed his chagrin to Towers: "Battles are in progress, not daily but hourly. . . . I must say that when we find we are double-crossed here in the Department in regard to flight pay and other Aviation matters, it makes one wonder whether we should continue the fight."[13]

But continue he did. Instead of depending on his uniformed colleagues in the hope of gaining concessions, he quietly courted presidents and members of Congress for appropriations. His careful testimony in congressional hearings was especially effective, as expert advisers sat behind him to coach him with data. He made speeches to appropriate patriotic and interest groups and utilized the press whenever he believed it necessary, often corresponding with publishers, editors, and reporters whom he had befriended. (In 1925 he began a letter to Pulitzer Prize winner Herbert Bayard Swope with "Herbert, old man.") He entered naval planes and pilots in air shows to win public recognition. The best of these fliers were his special "pets," notably polar explorer Richard E. Byrd, altitude record holder C. C. Champion, and speed champion Alford J. Williams. He appointed the famous pioneer Naval Aviator Number One, Commander T. G. ("Spuds") Ellyson, to head his plans division more for Ellyson's considerable public image than for his ability. Moffett shepherded along the struggling aircraft manufacturers to provide ever better planes for the Navy, especially after the more efficient air-cooled engine had replaced the water-cooled design. He not only established aviation training at the Naval Academy but also succeeded in having regular training planes assigned there.[14]

Moffett concentrated on policy and politics; he allowed his officer advisers to attend to details. In so doing, he became a master at promoting the cause of aviation within the U.S. Navy. In contrast to Mitchell the crusader, Moffett acted as the steward of the fleet's growing air arm, as he was quietly and effectively overseeing a revolution in naval warfare from the administrative end. He became an organization man in the new age of machine weaponry. In fully appreciating the realities of warfare in the modern world, he placed himself squarely in the future.

To guarantee his own future and reappointment to successive four-year terms as Chief of BuAer, Moffett again solicited the support of his good friend Wrigley in Chicago. In 1925 and again in 1929, Wrigley prevailed upon the President (first Calvin Coolidge, then Herbert Hoover) to reappoint Moffett, a brand of politicking thoroughly resented by Moffett's peers and superiors. In both instances, Moffett rebuffed attempts by his superiors to send him to sea or shunt him off to the General Board. He would have enjoyed a seagoing flag command, but he realized that the position of naval aviation was too tenuous to be left to others with less political finesse and clout. In other words, Moffett made himself indispensable as head of naval aviation and won a resounding battle against Secretary of the Navy Curtis D. Wilbur, CNO Admiral Charles F. Hughes, CinCUS Admiral Samuel S. Robison, and BuNav Chief R. H. Leigh, who tried to have him reassigned in 1929. Such a triumph, however, led Moffett to take care thereafter, "for as the Good Book says 'Pride goeth before destruction and a haughty spirit before a fall.'"[15]

The closest point of contact between Moffett and the administrations he served was the Secretary of the Navy, to whom all bureau chiefs reported directly. Edwin Denby gave no particular personal attention to aviation during the formative years of Moffett's rule, but the accession of Wilbur in 1924 brought direct secretarial involvement. A graduate of the academy two years ahead of Moffett, Wilbur sided with his own classmate Admiral Hughes, CNO from 1927 to 1930, in trying to have Moffett transferred from command of BuAer.

Although the Assistant Secretary of the Navy figured somewhat in these relationships, the creation in 1926 of the new post of Assistant Secretary of the
Navy for Aeronautics granted naval aviation a unique position within the civilian hierarchy of the Navy. It also strengthened Moffett in his battle with the
CNO and BuNav because both men who filled the post were strong Moffett
supporters. The first appointee held impeccable credentials: Edward P. Warner was a respected aeronautical engineer and educator who quickly became a
forceful spokesman alongside Moffett in budgetary hearings. His successor, in
1929, was even more prominent—David S. Ingalls, who had been the Navy's
only fighter ace in World War I and who as a practicing pilot now personally
tested all new naval aircraft. His aeronautical knowledge and pleasing personality never failed to win over congressional inquirers. When Ingalls resigned
in 1932 to run for elective office, the post fell vacant as an economy measure,
but Moffett had the continued general support of Secretary Adams and Assistant Secretary Ernest L. Jahncke.[16]

In molding BuAer internally, Moffett surrounded himself with the best
available talent from the flying cadre. Because too few senior officers were
qualified in aviation to fill the senior billets, he instituted the naval aviation observers course at Naval Air Station (NAS) Pensacola, wherein captains and
commanders could learn the rudiments of flight and do everything—spotting,
navigating, operating the radio—except actually flying the plane. Moffett had
flown to Pensacola when time permitted to participate in the course during his
first year in office. In June 1922, after accumulating some 150 hours of flight
time, he was rated as a naval observer. He kept the program in existence for another ten years, until qualified pilots attained sufficient seniority to fill the increasing number of aviation command billets.[17]

Though only a stopgap solution, the observer program typified Moffett's
wise managerial ability to compromise where necessary. Ideally, however, he
preferred to have actual pilots advising him in order to tap their undisputed expertise. Consequently, he selected as his first Assistant Chief of Bureau the innovative pioneer Mustin. After Mustin's premature death in 1923, observer
Captain Albert W. Johnson stepped in for a year, to be followed by two pioneer
aviators, Commanders Kenneth Whiting and John Rodgers. The latter's fatal
plane crash in 1926 led to the appointment of observer Captain Emory S. Land.
Though highly talented, Land lacked close contact with the line officer community as a member of the Construction Corps. The three subsequent assistants, however, were aviators: Ernest J. King (from 1928 to 1929); Jack Towers
(from 1929 to 1931), as Naval Aviator Number Three, the most experienced and
able; and Arthur B. Cook (from 1931 to 1933). King and Cook were latecomers
to the aviation community as qualified pilots. All were superior men who held
or attained the rank of captain while in the job.

During his first term (1921 to 1925), Moffett and his advisers agreed that aviation's primary role was reconnaissance as the "eyes of the fleet," just as it had been in World War I. Naval aircraft should not only spot for the gunships but also fly antisubmarine patrols, conduct long-range scouting against enemy fleet units, and, like scouting ships, provide additional firepower in the form of light bombs and aerial torpedoes. The platforms for these functions were flying boats, shore-based dirigibles, and the experimental aircraft carrier *Langley*, commissioned in 1922.

Although this reconnaissance mission satisfied the conservative admirals, Moffett and his cohorts also believed that the carrier, flying boat, and airship would gain enhanced striking power as a new advanced generation of delivery systems replaced wartime technology. Thus, they planned to develop the air arm into an offensive force. Under their leadership, the 1920s became a period of transition for aviation, from employment in the traditional scouting role for battleships to its use as a primary attack element, which would ultimately—during the 1940s—replace the battleship altogether. The more apparent the future course became, the more antagonistic the Gun Club grew. Moffett proceeded cautiously in the face of such opposition; until the technology matured to develop its offensive role, he carefully insisted that the air arm must only support the battle line.

Between 1921 and 1925 the aircraft carrier moved to the forefront of Moffett's plans. During the Washington naval arms limitation conference of 1921–1922, Moffett welcomed a decision that allowed the United States to convert two uncompleted battle cruiser hulls into large 33,000-ton carriers. These vessels, the *Lexington* and *Saratoga*, took most of the decade to design, build, outfit, and provide with special aircraft and squadrons of trained pilots. Experiments with the tiny 11,500-ton *Langley* quickly showed just how powerful the two *Lexingtons* would be. As part of the war reparations from Germany, the Navy received the rigid dirigible *Los Angeles*, and then it constructed its own *Shenandoah*. Plans called for testing both airships as platforms foreshadowing fleet "flying aircraft carriers," capable not only of long-range reconnaissance alone, but also of operating with a few scout planes launched from a special trapeze mechanism.

The four years of Moffett's first term at BuAer were the most chaotic because of the uncertain promise of carriers and airships, the resentment of aviation within the Navy, and Mitchell's continuing assaults. Mitchell vociferously proclaimed that land-based strategic bombers had made armies and navies obsolete, an attitude that did not endear him to the conservative generals in the Army, much less to Moffett and the Navy. He also insisted on a separate, independent air force with control over all military aviation.

Moffett firmly believed that the Navy's air arm should remain an integral part of the fleet and not be left to the mercy of land-based zealots, as had occurred under the Royal Air Force in Britain. He thus remained a steadfast opponent of such a unified air force and battled Mitchell continuously in public and in private. When the American Legion endorsed the idea of a separate air force, Moffett wrote to the Legion: "I think that the establishment of a separate, independent air force would almost ruin the national defense." Furthermore, although the majority of the Navy's pilots advocated their own naval air corps within the Navy, Moffett opposed it because airplanes and ships must work in concert under one fleet command. He preferred to educate the fleet commanders on the proper use of aircraft alongside all ships.[18]

Part of the interservice problem was that no centralized authority existed to establish defense policy, and the Army had reverted to its traditional prewar role of defending the continental United States. In addition, its airmen insisted that the aerial defense of the coasts was their province rather than the Navy's. Moffett, by contrast, espoused the Navy's position, which was global:

> For the same reason that we need a Navy second to none to defend against attack from overseas, we need an adequate Navy to secure for us the freedom of the seas for trade and commerce. . . . The air defense of the country must be maintained a thousand or more miles at sea which will serve the double purpose of guarding us against attack and protecting our lines of commerce and communication with other nations.

Because the Army's bombers could reach out only 250 miles, the immense task had to remain with the Navy.[19]

Not only did the Navy's newer and better flying boats and carrier-borne planes promise to equal Army bombers in their ability to defend coastal areas, but Moffett also firmly believed that the dirigible could greatly extend the Navy's range. Ever since 1919, British and German rigids had been crossing the Atlantic; such nonstop staying power offered the fleet a unique observation platform. "The rigid airship today fills a gap in transportation need [sic] that can be filled up by no other means," Moffett declared in 1925, and he thus steadfastly insisted that experimentation continue to improve the rigids.[20]

Events in September 1925 marked a watershed in Moffett's tenure. The rigid *Shenandoah* crashed in a storm over Ohio, and many of the crew were killed. A PN-9 flying boat was lost at sea in an attempt to fly nonstop between San Francisco, California, and Hawaii (actually, the crew sailed it into the islands in a remarkable ten-day voyage). Mitchell condemned the government and, by implication, the Navy, for allowing these tragedies to happen, whereupon Moffett threw his energies into destroying Mitchell's credibility—a reaction shared by many of Mitchell's own superiors in the Army, who silenced him with a court-martial. President Coolidge appointed the Morrow Board of distinguished aeronautical and engineering experts to establish a national aeronautic policy. Moffett and his advisers, most importantly Towers, presented careful evidence that so impressed the legislators that Congress instituted a five-year plan for naval, Army, and commercial aviation, including the creation of Assistant Secretary of Aeronautics posts in both services.[21]

Moffett dusted off a long-range development scheme devised by the late Henry Mustin that became the basis for naval aviation's growth between 1926 and 1931. Under it, the Navy contracted for the purchase of a thousand new aircraft, a commensurate increase in pilot training, at least one new carrier, and two fleet dirigibles. With the support of his able assistants and department heads—who found that Moffett usually just signed anything they put in front of him without reading it—the airplane production goal was met one year ahead of schedule. This proved providential, because the onset of the Great Depression delayed construction of the fleet airships *Akron* and *Macon* and the carrier *Ranger* and also slowed other essential aviation programs. As to the coastal defense mission, CNO Pratt agreed in 1931 to let the Army have primary responsibility for it, a decision that angered Moffett and most of his fellow admirals, who continued to oppose and circumvent it all the way down to World War II.[22]

While Moffett fought the political wars in Washington, he depended upon the theoreticians at Newport and the airmen in the fleet to give him hard data showing exactly what aircraft could do at sea. Moffett corresponded with Admiral William S. Sims, who as president of the Naval War College tested the role of aircraft in war games. Through Sims, in 1922, Moffett had the first pilot assigned to the course and staff there: famed Commander Albert C. Read, who had commanded the NC-4 flying boat on the first transatlantic airplane flight three years before. Moffett wrote to and occasionally visited with successive U.S. Fleet commanding air admirals, who maneuvered their planes with the battleships in weekly exercises and the annual fleet problems. The most progressive of these men was Rear Admiral Joseph Mason Reeves, whose dramatic use of the *Saratoga* to attack the Panama Canal in Fleet Problem IX in 1929 demonstrated the offensive power of the carriers. Moffett and Reeves disagreed over many issues—for example, the location of an airship base in California—but they shared a mutual respect. Moffett was completely honest when he wrote Reeves in 1928 that "in this tactical work . . . I believe that you . . . can make more progress and accomplish more than anyone else." Reeves's successor, Rear Admiral Harry E. Yarnell, however, was a kindred soul to Moffett in every respect, and his expert chief of staff was Moffett's own protegé, Jack Towers.[23]

For both his knowledge of aeronautics and his diplomatic skills Moffett served as a member of the London naval arms conference in 1930, but he was chagrined to encounter complete apathy toward carriers on the part of all of his colleagues except Yarnell. Not only did they not want to build up to the treaty limit for more carriers—perhaps four more—Moffett also had to fend off British attempts to reduce overall carrier tonnage. He finally succeeded in enlightening his colleagues, though only three other senior admirals favored the treaty as a viable solution to avert an arms race. Moffett feared the consequences if the United States did not build up to the limits allowed by the treaty; in his view, the General Board "and the reactionaries . . . are sinking the Navy and doing much more harm than the Japanese ever have or ever will do." He believed that the United States should keep all of its battleships as long as Britain and Japan kept theirs, but he hoped that at the next conference he might scrap them all in favor of carriers and some cruisers. Moffett also came up with a compromise ship type, the "flying deck cruiser"—to him "the ship of the future"—to increase U.S. air strength at sea. The final treaty permitted it, but the U.S. Navy never adopted the idea.[24]

Unfortunately, the aftermath of the London conference left Moffett thoroughly disgusted with the Hoover administration. Because of the deepening depression, Hoover refused to build the Navy up to treaty limits—not only in carriers but in other ship types too. Moffett thus welcomed the election of Franklin D. Roosevelt late in 1932: "I believe that the stagnation that we have been going through in [the] Increase of the Navy will end soon after Mr. Roosevelt comes in. So much time has been lost by Mr. Hoover in trying to get Europe to disarm that we find ourselves in a position with nothing to trade." In February 1933 he elaborated on this theme by delivering an address to Naval Academy alumni titled "The Decadence of the Navy."[25]

Still in all, now nearing the end of his third term as Chief of BuAer, Moffett could take solace in the fact that he had achieved most of his goals, particularly in the knowledge that U.S. naval aviation was far ahead of Japan's. He had produced a strong cadre of trained pilots and had fought, with decreasing success, to retain their flight pay. The carriers had proved their worth and were equipped with new, powerful airplanes. The patrol-bombing flying boat had evolved to the Consolidated P2Y, the last step before the sturdy PBY to come a year later. All battleships and cruisers carried catapult-launched seaplanes as gunfire spotters for the battle line.

The dirigible remained an unknown quantity, however, although Moffett hoped it would prove its utility in operations with the fleet. In the face of almost universal opposition to the rigid airships within the Navy, Moffett once wrote that "Putting over Lighter-Than-Air has been the toughest job I ever undertook." Moffett loved to go for quiet soaring rides in the dirigible *Akron* out of NAS Lakehurst. During one such flight, on 4 April 1933, the big airship, unable to outmaneuver a violent storm, crashed into a cold night sea. Killed were most of its crew—and Admiral Moffett. The rigid airship program died with him.[26]

"Life is timing," Moffett had often remarked; he believed that one should leave a job "when the flags were flying and the bands were playing." And so he had done. He never experienced the dreary retirement he had expected on 1 November of that year. The new President had been disposed to reappoint Moffett later in April, although Roosevelt did not like the idea of such a short-term appointment for anyone. Moffett had wanted to stay on, especially to ensure the appointment of heir-apparent Towers as his successor. "I think all Aviation wants to see Towers here," Moffett had written to Congressman Carl Vinson in 1932; but that would have taken some doing. King, already selected for rear admiral, had the support of Moffett's opponents, whereas Towers was still a very junior captain.[27]

With Moffett's death, King won out as his successor—and he went on both to direct the entire World War II fleet and to personally conduct the antisubmarine air war against Germany in the Atlantic. Towers, however, brought naval aviation into that war as Chief of BuAer from 1939 to 1942, and then he shaped the Pacific Fleet's air doctrine for Chester W. Nimitz in the war against Japan.

William A. Moffett was indeed the father of modern naval aviation. Rooted in the golden age of the steel battleship but foreseeing the age of the Air Navy, he was a key transitional figure in bridging the two eras. As a peerless naval politician and manager, he had battled the service conservatism typical of naval hierarchies but had worked as much as possible within the system, where naval aviation belonged. His quiet, deliberate personality had impressed members of Congress repelled by Billy Mitchell's harangues; and the achievements of his racing and long-distance fliers had won over the public. By deeds rather than words, Moffett used his stewardship over the naval air revolution to lay the foundations of a Navy that would dominate the seas during succeeding generations.

## FURTHER READING

This essay was written before the publication of the definitive biography by William F. Trimble, *Admiral William A. Moffett: Architect of Naval Aviation* (Washington, D.C., 1994). Trimble's work supersedes the privately published biography by Edward Arpee, *From Frigates to Flat-Tops* (Lake Forest, Ill., 1953).

Two autobiographies add important insights into the admiral during the late 1920s: Eugene E. Wilson, *Slipstream: The Autobiography of an Air Craftsman*, 2d ed. (New York, 1965), and Admiral J. J. Clark, *Carrier Admiral* (New York, 1967). Both men were naval aviators who served closely with Moffett in Washington, the former in engine design, the latter as personal pilot. The most analytical examination is in Clark G.

Reynolds, *Admiral John H. Towers: The Struggle for Naval Air Supremacy* (Annapolis, Md., 1991); Towers served as Moffett's alter ego between 1928 and 1933, even when Towers was no longer at the Bureau of Aeronautics.

In order to understand Moffett's leadership role in the context of the interwar period, three sources are essential. Stephen Roskill's two-volume work *Naval Policy Between the Wars* (London, 1968 and 1976), which divides at 1930, covers U.S. and British naval developments equally well, plus the interrelationships between the two navies. Several chapters are devoted to naval aviation. Fred Greene, "The Military View of American National Policy, 1904–1940," *American Historical Review* 66 (1961): 354–77, succinctly treats the Navy's strategic differences with the Army. John F. Shiner, "The Air Corps, the Navy, and Coast Defense, 1919–1941," *Military Affairs* 45 (1981): 113–20, gives a balanced analysis of a very important aspect of this interservice rivalry.

NOTES

1. Moffett to H. Ralph Burton of the National Patriotic League, 3 June 1930; Moffett to inventor and Aeronautical Society member Hudson Maxim, 6 February 1923; Moffett to Congressman Burton L. French, 5 March 1930; Moffett to Captain John H. Towers, 17 February 1930. These documents, and all others not cited herein as belonging to other collections, are from the William A. Moffett Collection, Nimitz Library, U.S. Naval Academy. The author is indebted to Professors William Reynolds Braisted and Paolo E. Coletta for their assistance in obtaining source material.

2. Moffett to Commander C. H. McMorris, Department of English and History, U.S. Naval Academy, in March 1933, quoted in William A. Moffett, Jr., "For the Good of the Ship," *Shipmate* 48 (January–February 1985): 20; and Moffett to Captain Joseph Mason Reeves, 28 March 1926.

3. Moffett, "For Good," 19; and Edward Arpee, *From Frigates to Flat-Tops* (Lake Forest, Ill., 1953), 3–31. Moffett's father, George Hall Moffett, purchased arms for the Confederacy before enlisting and becoming aide-de-camp to Brigadier General Johnson Hagood in Lee's army. His mother was Elizabeth H. Simonton Moffett. Moffett stood thirty-first in a class of thirty-four, although forty-seven had failed to complete the course. His classmates included future senior admirals Frank H. Schofield, Jehu V. Chase, Montgomery Meigs Taylor, Charles B. McVay, Jr., John H. Dayton, L. A. Bostwick, and J. L. Latimer. He married Jeannette Beverly Whitton in 1902; all three of his sons graduated from Annapolis and became naval aviators. Livingston Davis, special assistant to Assistant Secretary of the Navy Franklin D. Roosevelt, noted in his diary, 8 May 1918, after dining with the Moffetts at Great Lakes Naval Training Station, that Mrs. Moffett "is perfectly charming" and the captain "as fine a man as I ever met," impressions shared throughout the Navy. Davis Diary, Franklin D. Roosevelt Library, Hyde Park, New York.

4. Moffett, "For Good," 19; and Arpee, *Frigates*, 32–44. Moffett's early ranks were passed midshipman, 1890, ensign, 1892, lieutenant (junior grade) and lieutenant, 1899, lieutenant commander, 1905, and commander, 1914. Early tours of duty: screw steamer *Pensacola*, 1890–1891; cruiser *Baltimore* 1891–1892; sloop *Portsmouth*, 1892–1893; monitor *Amphitrite*, 1895–1896, 1904; Naval War College, 1896, 1907–1908; sloop *Constellation*, 1896; schoolship *Enterprise*, 1896–1898; steam sloop *Mohican*, 1898; *Charleston*, 1898; practice ship *Monongahela*, 1900; *Kentucky*, 1900–1901; gunboat *Ma-*

*rietta,* 1901; sloop *St Mary's,* 1901–1902; cruiser *Minneapolis,* 1902; steam sloop *Lancaster,* 1903; battleship *Maine,* 1903–1904; commanding officer, Guantánamo Bay, Cuba, 1904–1906; Bureau of Equipment, 1906–1907; armored curiser *Maryland,* 1908–1910; lighthouse inspector, San Francisco, 1910–1912; and battleship *Arkansas,* 1912–1913, in Clark G. Reynolds, *Famous American Admirals* (New York, 1978), 221–22.

5. Moffett, "For Good," 19; and Arpee, *Frigates,* 45–51, 55–70. Although Moffett received the Medal of Honor for his part in the Vera Cruz affair, Congress extravagantly awarded the medal to large numbers of participants hardly deserving of it, Moffett among them.

6. Moffett even came to know the underworld figures of the crime-infested city of Chicago so well that he joked he could have had anyone "eliminated" had he so desired. Mrs. John H. Towers to the author, 9 December 1978.

7. Moffett quoted in Towers's unpublished reminiscences, John H. Towers Collection, Naval Historical Foundation, Library of Congress.

8. Arpee, *Frigates,* 66.

9. Moffett to William K. Wrigley, Jr., 29 July 1921; Arpee, *Frigates* 51–52; Henry C. Mustin Diary, April–June 1920, Mustin Collection, Naval Historical Foundation, Library of Congress; Theodore Taylor, *The Magnificent Mitscher* (New York, 1951), 68–69; and Elretta Sudsbury, *Jackrabbits to Jets* (San Diego, 1967), 63. Moffett to Lieutenant Commander M. A. Mitscher, 2 April 1929: "I have always felt greatly indebted to you not only for what you did yourself but for the advice and counsel you gave me" while serving at the Bureau of Aeronautics.

10. Admiral J. J. Clark, *Carrier Admiral* (New York, 1967), 36; and Arpee, *Frigates,* 83–96. Moffett relieved Craven on 7 March 1921, was designated Chief of BuAer by Harding on 25 July 1921, and assumed the post officially on 10 August 1921. Moffett to Captain Powers Symington, USN (Ret.), 16 February 1925: "When I relieved Craven, Craven wouldn't speak to him [Mitchell]." Also, Moffett to Wrigley, 11 June 1921.

11. Inglis M. Uppercu, President, Uppercu Cadillac Corp., New York City, to Moffett, 31 May 1929; Moffett to Towers, 17 February 1930; and Towers, review of Edward Arpee's *From Frigates to Flat-tops,* U.S. Naval Institute *Proceedings* 79 (October 1953): 1139. See Clark, *Carrier Admiral,* 35–36. To his friends, Moffett was known as both "Bill" and "Billy."

12. Moffett to Reeves, 22 March 1926; and Moffett to Wrigley, 7 May and 13 October 1928.

13. Towers, review of Arpee's *From Frigates to Flat-tops,* 1139; Moffett to Lieutenant Commander D. C. Ramsey, 19 November 1928; Moffett to Admiral Frank M. Schofield, 29 March 1932; and Moffett to Towers, 31 March, 29 April 1932.

14. George van Deurs, *Anchors in the Sky: Spuds Ellyson, the First Naval Avaiator* (San Rafael, Calif., 1978), 212; Clark, *Carrier Admiral,* 236–37; Eugene E. Wilson, *Slipstream: The Autobiography of an Air Craftsman,* 2d ed. (New York, 1965), 63–64; Moffett to Congressman Carl Vinson, 13 March 1932; and Moffett to Herbert Bayard Swope, 16 September 1925.

15. Wrigley to Moffett, 5 November 1924; Moffett to Wrigley, 7 May and 13 October 1928, 29 January and 26 November 1929; Moffett to Ramsey, 13 November, 7 and 11 December 1928; Moffett to Lieutenant Commander Claude Bailey, USN (Ret.), his academy roommate, 3 April 1929; and Arpee, *Frigates,* 114–19, 153–54. Moffett was reappointed Chief of BuAer on 13 March 1925 and 13 March 1929. He also battled over per-

sonnel with Leigh's predecessor, Rear Admiral William R. Shoemaker, and again with Leigh's successor, Rear Admiral F. Brooks Upham.

16. Moffett to Towers, 10 February 1930.

17. Moffett to Ramsey, 13 November 1928; Moffett to Rear Admiral H. E. Yarnell, 22 January 1932. Moffett was designated naval observer on 17 June 1921 and ordered to duty involving flying on 1 July 1922.

18. Arpee, *Frigates*, 88–100 and passim; Moffett to SecNav, "Naval Aeronautical Policy," 10 August 1922; Moffett to Charles W. Schick, 3 October 1931; Moffett to French, 5 March 1920; and Moffett to Symington, 16 February 1925.

19. Arpee, *Frigates*, 110–12; Moffett to Porter Adams of the National Aeronautic Association, 5 January 1925; Moffett to CNO, 8 April 1928; Moffett to Captain E. S. Land, 1 July and 11 August 1930; Moffett to Towers, 22 August 1931; Fred Greene, "The Military View of American National Policy, 1904–1940," *American Historical Review* 66 (1961): 354–77; John F. Shiner, "The Air Corps, the Navy, and Coast Defense, 1919–1941," *Military Affairs* 45 (1981): 114–18; and John F. Shiner, *Foulois and the U.S. Army Air Corps 1931–1935* (Washington, D.C., 1983), 52–54.

20. Moffett quoted in Arpee, *Frigates*, 200, 214–15.

21. Clark, *Carrier Admiral*, 16–17; and Arpee, *Frigates*, 102–4.

22. Wilson, *Slipstream*, 67–68; Moffett to Captain Adolphus Andrews, 24 February 1926; Moffett to Dwight Morrow, 2 March 1926; Shiner, "Coast Defense," 116–17; and Shiner, *Foulois*, 54ff.

23. Moffett to Rear Admiral William S. Sims, 28 February 1922; Moffett to Reeves, 23 February 1928; and Reeves to Moffett, 12 March 1926: "You have the hardest job in the Navy." Moffett had tried to have Rear Admiral John Halligan appointed to command the carriers in 1930, but Standley and Leigh reappointed Reeves for a second tour. Moffett to Rear Admiral J. L. Latimer, 3 May 1930. Reeves opposed Moffett, but in vain, on locating the new West Coast dirigible base at Sunnyvale rather than Camp Kearney near San Diego. Moffett to Captain J. H. Gunnell, 3 June 1930.

24. Statement by Moffett before the Senate Naval Affairs Committee, 22 May 1930; Raymond G. O'Connor, *Perilous Equilibrium: The United States Navy and the London Naval Conference of 1930* (Lawrence, Kan., 1962), 76–77; Arpee, *Frigates*, 169ff.; Moffett to Frank A. Tichenor of *Aero Digest*, 14 January 1931; and Moffett to Towers, 3 and 17 February, 31 March, and 2 April 1930. The only other admirals to favor the treaty were Pratt, Yarnell, and Arthur J. Hepburn. Moffett to Lieutenant Commander George D. Murray, 4 June 1930; Moffett to David S. Ingalls, 24 February 1930, 30 September 1931; and Moffett to Lieutenant A. R. Mead, his aide, 27 February 1930.

25. Moffett to Vice Admiral William H. Standley, 19 December 1932; and Moffett speech at annual dinner of the Naval Academy Graduates Association, New York, 17 February 1933. Also, see Arpee, *Frigates*, 164–65.

26. Moffett to Ingalls, 30 September 1931; and Arpee, *Frigates*, 232ff., 238ff.

27. Clark, *Carrier Admiral*, 50; Moffett to Towers, 9 and 25 July 1932, and 20 March 1933; Moffett to Ingalls, 26 July 1932; Moffett to Yarnell, 19 July 1932, Yarnell Collection, Naval Historical Foundation, Library of Congress; and Moffett to Vinson, 22 November 1932. Although Moffett preferred Towers, he held King in high regard, as in Moffett to King, 8 August 1930, and 18 November 1932. The date for Moffett's reappointment would have been 22 April 1933, the fourth anniversary of his last confirmation by the Senate.

# ☆
## ☆ Ernest J. King
### ☆ Commander of the Two-Ocean Navy

*by Lloyd J. Graybar*

RAMROD STRAIGHT AT AGE SIXTY, VICE ADMIRAL ERNEST J. KING EX-
perienced one of the most painful moments of his career when, on 15 March
1939, he walked over to congratulate his longtime acquaintance, Admiral
Harold R. Stark, on Stark's appointment as the U.S. Navy's next Chief of Naval
Operations. At his age, King did not expect a second opportunity to reach the
U.S. Navy's top position. His fears were confirmed later in 1939 when he was
appointed to the General Board, an aggregation of officers, nearing retirement,
whose wisdom could be culled for recommendations on such matters as proper characteristics for the next generation of ships or of sites for future base construction. The work was bound to be a disappointment to someone like King
who wanted to command, not to advise.[1]

Born in Lorain, Ohio, on 23 November 1878, King was the oldest of four
surviving children of James Clydesdale King and Elizabeth ("Bessie") Keam.
James King was born in the small town of Bridge-of-Weir, Scotland, and Bessie
was raised in Plymouth, England. Both were brought to the United States by
their parents. A man of outspoken integrity, James King held several jobs before settling down to work in the maintenance shops of the Cleveland, Lorain
and Wheeling Railroad in Lorain. Ernest, who often worked in the shops with
his father during summers and for one entire year as well, graduated as valedictorian of his high school class in 1897. He then gained an appointment to
the United States Naval Academy.[2]

Gifted in the classroom, King was also respected for his leadership by both
fellow students and administrators of the Naval Academy and was named batal-
lion commander for his first-class year, an auspicious culmination to his career
as a cadet. By the time King graduated fourth in his class in 1901, he already

had combat experience, for he was one of a handful of lower classmen who had finagled orders for sea duty during the War with Spain. His ship, the protected cruiser *San Francisco*, came under fire from Spanish fortifications at Havana hours before the war ended.[3]

Upon completing his studies at the Naval Academy, King went to sea as a passed midshipman in the survey ship *Eagle*. An eye affliction necessitated his hospitalization; on his release, he reported to the new battleship *Illinois*, which spent summers in European waters and the winter of 1902–03 on Caribbean maneuvers. Alert for assignments that were considered career enhancing, King accepted a transfer to the cruiser *Cincinnati* as a division and watch officer. The ship was at Culebra, Puerto Rico, when King joined her, but she was soon ordered to the Asiatic Squadron. King passed his ensign's examinations while on board the *Cincinnati*.[4]

During a 1905 leave, King married Martha ("Mattie") Egerton of Baltimore, his best girl during his cadet days. The couple would have seven children. King returned to sea shortly after the marriage to spend the final year (1905–06) of his initial five-year tour of sea duty in the battleship *Alabama*. His promotion to lieutenant in 1906 (most officers then skipped the grade of lieutenant junior grade) came as a great relief, for King had previously received four black marks for various infractions and was rightly, if belatedly, concerned whether they would be sufficient to block his promotion. After the fourth, he had resolved never to get another black mark, and he never did. He remained opinionated and abrasive, however, and continued to court the disfavor of superiors, with whom he disagreed, by speaking his mind. After three years as a drillmaster and gunnery instructor at the Naval Academy (for one year, he was co-supervisor of the new Bancroft Hall and its one thousand resident midshipmen), King received a choice assignment in 1909 as flag secretary to Rear Admiral Hugo Osterhaus, who had just been given a division of battleships in the Atlantic. King held the post for a year until Osterhaus went ashore. In 1910, King became chief engineer of the battleship *New Hampshire* and returned to Osterhaus's staff as flag secretary the following year when the admiral was named Commander-in-Chief, Atlantic Fleet. King then served (1912–14) as executive officer of the Engineering Experiment Station in Annapolis, Maryland. For a year, he also edited the United States Naval Institute *Proceedings*, a publication to which he contributed several thoughtful essays over the years.[5]

Promoted to lieutenant commander in 1913, King secured his first command, the destroyer *Terry*, in 1914 when the Navy rushed reinforcements to Mexican waters following a controversial incident at Tampico and President Wilson's decision to occupy the important port of Vera Cruz. King next commanded the *Cassin* in the Atlantic Destroyer Flotilla. For a while, he had additional duty as aide to Captain Williams Sims, commander of the flotilla and one of the most able, albeit opinionated, officers in the Navy. When the two men disagreed at a staff conference, Sims criticized King's views in a way that King thought was unnecessarily derogatory; the next day he requested to be relieved as Sims's aide. A year later, he was pleasantly surprised when Sims recommended that he be given command of the Sixth Division of Destroyers over several officers senior to King. Sims described King as "one of the ablest officers of his grade of my acquaintance."[6]

King recognized, however, that for his own advancement he would do well to have duty on the staff of another respected officer. His inquiries assured him that Admiral Henry Mayo, recently named commander of the Battleship Force, Atlantic Fleet, was just such a man. King, who had benefited from Osterhaus's patronage, secured appointment to Mayo's staff as engineering officer but was fortunate to spend much of his time dealing with tactical and strategic matters and became assistant chief of staff in 1915. King was also pleased to find that he could disagree with Mayo and have his own opinions validated if Mayo saw merit in them. Both men disliked excessive centralization and professed belief in the initiative of the subordinate. During King's subsequent career, however, he sometimes looked more closely over a subordinate's shoulders than he might have and, when provoked by incompetence or carelessness, flared up into a temper that became legendary in the Navy.[7]

King normally would have been rotated to shore duty in 1917, but war with Germany appeared imminent, and he was retained on Mayo's staff. Mayo had fleeted up to become commander of the Atlantic Fleet. For a time, King served Mayo as acting chief of staff and was delegated much responsibility that proved invaluable for King's own education in high command. Although the occasion did not arise for Mayo to take the fleet to sea for combat, King spent considerable time in England and France with Mayo. He met such luminaries as French Marshal Ferdinand Foch, U.S. General John J. Pershing, and British Admirals John Jellicoe and David Beatty, with whom Mayo conferred. From his contacts, King developed an enduring skepticism about the fighting capabilities of the Royal Navy and deep suspicion of the political motives of British leaders.[8]

King's promotion to captain (temporary) came through only weeks before the war ended. After a tour as head of the Postgraduate School of Annapolis (1919–21), King hoped to return to sea in destroyers, but he was too senior to have command of a destroyer group and too junior for command of a flotilla or a cruiser. He accepted command of the refrigerator ship *Bridge*. No cruisers were available in 1922 when King was made a captain on the permanent list, and he agreed to attend submarine school at New London, Connecticut, in order to qualify for command of a submarine division in the Atlantic. All told, King spent four years with the submarine force, first as a division commander and then as commander of the submarine base at New London, Connecticut. As base commander (1923–26), he lived comfortably with his large family and, as the Navy's senior officer in the state of Connecticut, represented the Navy on public occasions. For a time, he had detached duty to command the raising of submarine S-51 that had sunk in deep water off Block Island, Rhode Island. The difficult salvage operation went on for several months during the fall of 1925 and resumed in the spring of 1926. It won favorable publicity for the Navy and praise for King, who was awarded the Distinguished Service Medal. Two years later, he received another for directing the salvage of S-4.[9]

Again due for sea duty in 1926, King still could not obtain command of a cruiser. While he was mulling over his future, however, Rear Admiral William A. Moffett asked King if he would care to go into aviation. Moffett, once recognized as one of the surface navy's most able and aggressive officers, then headed the Bureau of Aeronautics, which was involved in virtually everything having to do with aviation. The linear system of promotion that still kept King from getting command of a cruiser also made it difficult for Moffett to find officers experienced in aviation with sufficient seniority to command naval aviation's major shore facilities and its ships. Because the new carriers *Lexington* and *Saratoga* soon would be completed, Moffett had decided to recruit men such as King. He offered them the chance to attend flight school at Pensacola, Florida, and qualify either as an observer, as he himself had, or take pilot's training if they preferred and could pass the physical requirements. King accepted Moffett's offer after careful consideration. His initial assignment was as captain of the seaplane tender *Wright*, whose attached pilots King badgered for flying lessons. He then interrupted his tour in the *Wright* to take the student aviator's course at Pensacola and earned his wings in May 1927. Although he and other officers who first entered aviation during their forties were regarded as Johnny-come-latelies by younger officers who had gone into flying at an earlier stage in their careers but who did not have the seniority in rank required to command carriers and seaplane tenders, King was proud that he had qualified as a pilot.[10]

King was now eligible for various appealing billets within Moffett's empire. He completed his tour in the *Wright* (1927–28), briefly served as commander of Aircraft Squadrons, Scouting Fleet (Atlantic), and next became assistant chief of the Bureau of Aeronautics (1928–29). He then had a disagreement with Moffett over whether Moffett, as head of the Bureau of Aeronautics, should control the assignment of aviators to billets. King's belief that the Bureau of Navigation should assign aviators, just as it assigned all other officers, led him to request a transfer. Moffett obliged him with a comfortable and important assignment, command of the Naval Air Station at Hampton Roads, Virginia. In

1930, King received command of the carrier *Lexington*, based at Coronado Roads, California, with her sister ship *Saratoga*. Though reputed to be a happy ship, the *Lexington* did not measure up to King's exacting standards. Well before his two-year cruise in her was over, King made the carrier into a taut ship. Such ships, he insisted, were the truly happy ones. Most important, King insisted that the personnel of the squadrons assigned to the *Lexington* were under his command, not just the ship's crew, as the aviators maintained.[11]

King left the *Lexington* in 1932 to take the senior course at the Naval War College. While there, he was notified that he would become a rear admiral as soon as a vacancy in that rank opened. The death of Moffett in an accident in April 1933 spurred King to seek assignment as Moffett's successor. He got the billet and, during his tour in Washington, presided over many improvements in naval aviation. For instance, he cooperated with Rear Admiral William D. Leahy, chief of the Bureau of Navigation, to recruit college graduates as naval aviation cadets needed to augment the few Annapolis men who were then entering aviation.[12]

King's assets, including intelligence and hard work, were partially offset by his liabilities—awkward public speaking and impatience with questions that he thought were elementary or just plain stupid. He never did become a gifted speaker, nor did he develop tactfulness. He did improve as a witness before Congress, however, thanks to the assistance of such able subordinates as Donald Duncan and Arthur Radford, both to become flag officers, and the aid of sympathetic congressmen, such as William Ayres and Carl Vinson, with whom he worked well in private.[13]

In a time of financial austerity, King was able to gain the appropriations to keep naval aviation going forward and made good use of the money. King knew, however, that he needed to complete a three-year tour at sea before turning sixty to have a chance at either of the navy's two top uniformed positions: Commander-in-Chief, United States Fleet, or Chief of Naval Operations. Accordingly, he sought relief from his post in Washington and in 1936 was named Commander, Aircraft, Base Force (Pacific), the so-called patrol plane command.[14]

Relying on the new Catalina patrol planes whenever possible, King cruised the Pacific in his flagship, the *Wright*, to identify atolls and even coral reefs where the tender and her flock of seaplanes could anchor. He drove his subordinates to improve naval aviation's performance and often shared risks with them. On one memorable occasion when the *Wright* was at French Frigate Shoals, some six hundred miles west of Oahu in the Hawaiian Islands, King ordered a squadron of seaplanes to take off in stormy weather from French Frigate Shoals for remote Kingman's Reef. The squadron commander, Walter F. Boone, later to become a four-star admiral, protested, but King ordered Boone to proceed. En route, Boone realized that the squadron would never reach its destination and secured King's permission by radio to divert to Honolulu. Despite the near calamity, King was delighted with the results, for it was the first time that a flight far from its base had received instructions by radio to alter its mission. If the timid were to transfer, reasoned King, the Navy would be better prepared for war.[15]

In 1938, King fleeted up to Commander, Aircraft, Battle Force, a highly coveted position that normally meant command of the navy's carrier operations. King's old friend, Admiral Edward Kalbfus, his immediate superior in Battle Force, often gave King a free hand to use the carriers as he wished in the important fleet exercises. King, in common with more experienced but younger aviators, such as Captain John Towers, maintained that the fast carriers needed to steam independently of the slow battle line to operate effectively. In Fleet Problem XIX held in 1938, King was at his best. Often writing his own orders, which were, in Boone's words, "the ultimate in clarity, brevity, and incisiveness," King had his squadrons practice night operations. Using a storm front to screen his carriers, King ordered planes from the *Saratoga* to "bomb" Pearl Harbor. The surprise attack demonstrated what the aviation community long had been arguing: audaciously led carriers could deal powerful blows with their air groups far beyond the reach of the battle line.[16]

In Fleet Problem XX, held in the Caribbean in March 1939, King did not perform as well. Although he was ruled successful in his "attack" on the Panama Canal, King bullied Rear Admiral William F. Halsey, who commanded a carrier division consisting of the new *Yorktown* and *Enterprise*, into paring his staff, and he antagonized the much admired Captain Marc A. Mitscher when he ruled that Mitscher's patrol plane mission against King's carriers had been a failure. Mitscher, who, like Towers, was a widely respected career aviator, believed otherwise. King also caused alarm when, irate at his flag signalman, he took control of the flag hoists himself, only to cause confusion among his ships' captains. Near collisions ensued.[17]

President Franklin D. Roosevelt attended these maneuvers and announced Stark's appointment as Chief of Naval Operations (CNO) at their conclusion. Yet, other factors were uppermost in Roosevelt's decision to select Stark. Evidence shows that King's name never reached the final slate of officers from whom Roosevelt selected the CNO. The Navy was not ready to give its top position to an aviator, nor were King's peers willing to ignore his well-known abrasiveness and his drinking (which he was able to curb when war began). Further, Stark was a longtime friend of Roosevelt's and King had apparently gone out of his way, while in Washington as a bureau chief, to avoid the appearance of cultivating the President's friendship. Ambitious as he was, King was still determined not to let it be said that he had "greased" his way to the top, nor, as military analyst Hanson Baldwin later wrote of him, could he "be had."[18]

Passed over for CNO, King was appointed to the consultative General

Board when his tour as Commander, Aircraft, Battle Force, ended in the summer of 1939. Service on the General Board did not turn out to be the twilight cruise that King had feared when he was informed of his appointment to it. When war broke out in Europe, the Roosevelt administration no longer could ignore America's naval forces in the Atlantic. In December 1940, dissatisfied with the performance of the Patrol Force (the name then given to the Atlantic command), Stark and Secretary of the Navy Frank Knox persuaded Roosevelt that King was the man to get the most from the motley collection of ships then in the Atlantic. Rescued from the backwaters of the General Board, King would again be at sea as the United States entered one of the most critical periods in its history, not yet at war, but the source of supplies that were vital to Great Britain. Although he transported Roosevelt to Argentia, Newfoundland, for Roosevelt's Atlantic Charter Conference with British Prime Minister Winston Churchill, King had little to do with the deliberations of the political and military leaders who attended the conference other than to listen and to think about what they portended for his command, which had already been upgraded, renamed the Atlantic Fleet, and designated a four-star billet. Despite the receipt of reinforcements, King realized by the summer of 1941 that his command, then responsible for patrolling the Western Atlantic from Brazil to Iceland, still had insufficient resources and that demands on it would probably grow. Three of his destroyers had well-publicized encounters with German U-boats as 1941 advanced, and King expected that more incidents would occur, probably leading to war with Germany.[19]

Shortly after the Japanese attack on Pearl Harbor and the U.S. entry into the war, King was summoned to Washington for one of his frequent conferences with Stark. He returned to the capital on December 15 to be informed by Stark and Knox that Chester W. Nimitz would assume command of the battered Pacific Fleet and that King was being named Commander-in-Chief, U.S. Fleet (CinCUS). This put him over both Nimitz and Royal Ingersoll, whom he selected as his successor in the Atlantic. King quickly decided to maintain his headquarters in Washington, rather than at sea, as his predecessors had done in peacetime, and to rename his position CominCh; the traditional CinCUS sounded too much like "sink us." He did have his own flagship, a converted yacht, that served as his floating home when at anchor in the Washington Navy Yard. His family lived in the Naval Observatory, but King had grown apart from his wife and confined his family visits to Sunday afternoons. As CominCh, King would have command authority over all operating forces of the Navy, as well as the responsibility for preparing current war plans. CNO Stark would prepare long-range war plans and have control over logistics. The two men cooperated, but, in March 1942, Stark advised President Roosevelt that he wished to be relieved as CNO and that King should assume the duties of that office in addition to those of CominCh. Roosevelt promptly agreed.[20]

In exercising his new authority, King had numerous conflicts with Secretary of the Navy Knox and Knox's successor, James V. Forrestal, as well as with his colleagues on the Joint Chiefs of Staff and the Combined Chiefs of Staff (CCS), the group that decided strategy for British and American forces. He also tried to get Roosevelt to give him control of the Navy's powerful bureaus, which reported to the Secretary of the Navy rather than to the uniformed head of the service, but he failed. Roosevelt reasoned that to make such a change might disrupt the usual procedures because the Bureau of Ordnance and the other agencies in question, such as King's former Bureau of Aeronautics, had responsibilities that required dealing with manufacturers. He therefore denied King's requests. Despite his failure to gain control of the bureaus, King was able to manage the Navy's Washington bureaucracy effectively with the aid of three men in particular: Vice Admiral Frederick Horne, who had charge of logistical planning and distribution and headed the Navy's shore establishment and shipbuilding programs; Rear Admiral Charles M. Cooke, Jr., who directed planning; and Admiral Richard Edwards, who served as King's chief of staff. King and Horne did not get along well personally, but King recognized Horne's administrative abilities and made good use of him for most of the war.[21]

Events in the Pacific during the first weeks of U.S. involvement in the war directed the attention of the CCS to Australia because Allied defenses to the north seemed likely to crumble. Although Australia had never received much attention from prewar American planners, King was obliged to spread his forces in that direction when the British chiefs declined responsibility. King insisted that New Caledonia, nine hundred miles due east of Australia, had to be vigorously defended and prevailed upon a reluctant George C. Marshall, the respected chief of staff of the U.S. Army, to assign a garrison to New Caledonia. King had already ordered Nimitz to defend the supply lines between the United States and Australia, and New Caledonia, along with bases in Samoa, Fiji, and the New Hebrides, would be essential.[22]

King's background in submarines and aviation helped him to put the sunken and disabled battleships at Pearl Harbor out of his mind and plan for the aggressive use of the assets remaining in the Pacific, namely, submarines that would be deployed as commerce raiders and carrier task forces used as mobile units. The latter would threaten enemy lines of communication that stretched ever farther into the South Pacific while they safeguarded the U.S. Navy's lines of communication then being established in the region.[23]

Already in December 1941, while King was winding up his tenure as Commander-in-Chief, Atlantic Fleet (CinCLant), the Navy had been driven from the Central Pacific and lost its bases on Guam and Wake Island. King seems to have concurred with Stark's decision not to chance a major fleet engagement over Wake. Although some American naval units, principally a few cruisers, some destroyers, and patrol planes that had been part of the Asiatic Fleet in the Philippines, would soon be engaging enemy forces in the hastily organized joint American-British-Dutch-Australia (ABDA) command, consisting primarily of Malaya, the East Indies, and the northern approaches to Australia, King regarded their efforts as sacrificial in nature. He was not one to accept continued retreat, however, and sought action where the circumstances offered some possibility of success. In March 1942, King explained to the Joint Chiefs of Staff that the fleet must fight the enemy "where he is to be found, to seek him out rather than to husband our fighting strength at home and await his coming. . . . The winner hits and keeps on hitting even though he has to take some stiff blows in order to be able to keep on hitting."[24]

Accordingly, King prodded Nimitz to use his three single-carrier task forces (all he then had available pending the transfer of the *Hornet* from the Atlantic) to raid Japanese bases at Rabaul on New Britain; Lae and Salamaua on New Guinea; on Wake Island; and on remote Marcus Island, about one thousand miles southeast of Tokyo. As a result, the *Lexington* force, which, in early 1942, carried much of the burden of the naval air war along with the *Yorktown* and *Enterprise*, was at sea for more than two months while it hit or threatened Japanese bases. Finally, in April 1942, King took his first major gamble by sending two carriers, commanded by Vice Admiral Halsey, on Lieutenant Colonel James H. Doolittle's Tokyo raid. The unprecedented use of Doolittle's twin-engine Air Force bombers that were temporarily based on the carrier *Hornet* allowed the United States, for the first time, to bomb the Japanese homeland, rather than simply sting the enemy on the peripheries of its far-flung empire. Historians disagree on whether these raids from the carriers had any strategic value or whether King unduly risked America's scant resources simply for the sake of appearing to do something. King's biographer, Thomas Buell, himself a retired naval officer, takes a dim view of King's orders, especially the Doolittle raid, but, more recently, historian Clark Reynolds whose knowledge of World War II carrier operations is unsurpassed, has argued that the Tokyo raid and other aerial attacks on Japan's Pacific bases did accomplish much of value. Not knowing when or where the Americans might strike, the Japanese redeployed ships, ceased sending replacement aircraft to forward areas that had already been hit by U.S. carriers or were exposed to such attacks, and postponed their effort to seize Port Moresby on the southeastern coast of New Guinea. In Japanese hands, Port Moresby could be used to disrupt the supply lines between the United States and Australia. Able to send two carriers into the Coral Sea in May (Halsey's task force had not yet returned from the raid on Tokyo), Nimitz's Pacific Fleet rewarded King's boldness by sinking one small Japanese carrier and decimating the air groups of two large carriers. Although the battle cost American forces the *Lexington*, the Japanese invasion fleet was recalled from the Coral Sea before it could disembark troops at Port Moresby.[25]

The question after Coral Sea was where Japanese forces would strike next. Lieutenant Commander Joseph Rochefort's communications intelligence office in Pearl Harbor convinced Nimitz that Midway was their target, but the Office of Naval Communications in Washington argued that Port Moresby or some other location in the South Pacific, perhaps New Caledonia, would be their objective. Logically, therefore, any move toward Midway Island would be a feint and responding to it might result in a setback in the South Pacific that could be ill afforded. King had doubts about Nimitz's judgment but decided that, as commander-in-chief in the Pacific, Nimitz had to be allowed to deploy his forces as he saw fit and that concentrating his three carriers to defend one location was sound thinking. It was a difficult decision on King's part, but one which paid rich dividends, the destruction of four Japanese carriers at Midway. King could now drop what Reynolds calls the "fleet-in-being" strategy that had hitherto characterized his planning in favor of an offensive-defensive strategy, by which American forces began the arduous effort to halt the Japanese advance through seizure of the recently constructed enemy bases on Tulagi and Guadalcanal in the lower Solomon Islands.[26]

The Guadalcanal campaign brought King some of his most difficult months of the war. To begin with, American strategy emphasized the defeat of Germany, the most formidable of the Axis powers. Although the Joint Chiefs of Staff had unanimously agreed that Australia should be saved, the question was hotly debated whether amphibious operations mounted against Tulagi and Guadalcanal were needed to safeguard Australia. King believed that they were; waiting too long to seize them, he later wrote, would only have allowed the enemy "to button up every exact button of their gaiters." Then, too, the Solomons had been assigned to the Southwest Pacific Theater commanded by General Douglas MacArthur. King and MacArthur saw eye to eye on few matters, and King refused to provide MacArthur the carriers and the Marines that the general wanted to strike directly at Rabaul, the linchpin in Japan's network of South Pacific bases. Instead, King instructed Nimitz to plan an invasion of Tulagi. MacArthur finally agreed that a campaign in the lower Solomons offered greater prospects of success than an immediate assault on Rabaul, but he demurred at the command arrangements that would give authority to the Navy, even though Tulagi and Guadalcanal were in his theater.[27]

King and Marshall conferred in person, rather than exchanging memoranda as they normally did, and decided to relocate the theater boundary so that Nimitz would have control of operations in the lower Solomons while MacArthur would have jurisdiction over any subsequent operations to the north. To succeed in the campaign, code-named Operation Watchtower, King also needed material and supplies from the Army. General Marshall and General Henry H. ("Hap") Arnold, chief of the Army Air Corps, however, were far more interested in the approaching landings in North Africa that were designed to strengthen the Allied hand in the Mediterranean by landing American and British forces in Morocco and Algeria. Marshall and King both preferred a cross-channel operation against German forces in France to a campaign in what they both considered a peripheral area, but the British would approve only the less risky North African campaign. Although King was committed to providing the naval support needed for these operations and appointed the able Rear Admiral Kent Hewitt to command the Moroccan landings, his colleagues on the CCS saw him as being more interested in undertaking offensives in the Pacific, operations for which Allied strategy had not expressly called.[28]

Marshall refused to divert men and equipment to the Pacific that might have to be sent to North Africa and that, in any event, were needed for the buildup in England that would eventually enable the Western Allies to overcome Germany. Thus, King launched Watchtower with only the limited resources of the Navy in August 1942. Although the Marines' landings on Guadalcanal were unopposed, the Japanese augmented their forces already on the ninety-mile-long island and bitterly contested the U.S. foothold throughout September and October. The numerous task forces that were sent to the Solomons to guard American supply lines and to interdict Japan's Tokyo Express supplying its forces on the island engaged in a series of battles that ultimately cost King two of his four fleet carriers and eight cruisers, as well as many other ships that suffered heavy damage. The press berated King and the Navy for managing the news to obscure the extent of American losses, for displaying poor leadership, and for blocking MacArthur from exercising overall leadership in the South Pacific. Not until October did Arnold and Marshall allow some of their forces to be redirected to Guadalcanal from elsewhere in the Pacific. The decision of King and Nimitz to replace Vice Admiral Robert Lee Ghormley, the Navy's South Pacific commander, with the aggressive Halsey also contributed to the ultimate U.S. triumph on Guadalcanal. To help strengthen his own position, King himself began to hold behind-the-scenes meetings with several senior Washington correspondents in a successful effort to explain the rationale of the Navy's operations and to place them in the context of Allied strategy. Never comfortable when speaking in a formal setting, King was at his best when meeting with this small group that called itself the "Arlington County Commandos."[29]

At almost the same time that American forces gained the upper hand on Guadalcanal, MacArthur won the first of his many victories on New Guinea. The triumphs of early 1943 provided King and MacArthur a chance to move northward toward Rabaul, and King was quick to seize the chance to maintain momentum in the Pacific. As his memoirs put it, "Japan was not likely to wait to be defeated at a time and place convenient to the Allies." King also realized that, to maintain the flow of men and supplies to the Pacific, he had to continue using the forces already there. With the Joint Chiefs sanctioning further offensives in the Pacific, Halsey, now operating under MacArthur's strategic direction, was able to continue moving up the Solomons, while predominantly Army forces under MacArthur moved northwestward along the New Guinea coast.[30]

As a member of both the Joint Chiefs and the CCS, however, King was also obligated to pursue coalition warfare. The British often found him difficult to deal with and, for that reason, appointed a four-star admiral as head of the British Naval Mission in Washington. This prompted Churchill, in a moment of pique, to complain about the need to "dance attendance" upon King. Despite his interest in the Pacific, King did not try to reverse the Germany-first strategy that his predecessor Stark had helped to formulate. Although he demurred with certain aspects of European strategy and wished to get ahead with a cross-channel operation that would bring maximal Anglo-American power to bear against German forces in western France, the most advantageous location for mobile warfare, he did provide the necessary shipping to make victory possible in the Battle of the Atlantic and to support the Sicilian and Italian campaigns of 1943.[31]

During the war's early months, King's conduct of the Battle of the Atlantic resulted in the greatest criticism that he received in World War II. German U-boats wreaked havoc on American coastal shipping during January and February 1942, but King resisted the use of convoys because he believed that he lacked sufficient escort vessels to make them effective and that the formation of convoys with inadequate escort would merely give the enemy larger targets. Not until the spring could King establish a day-and-night interlocking convoy system running from Newport, Rhode Island, to Key West, Florida. In the meantime, he was subject to scathing criticism from the British and several ill-conceived suggestions from President Roosevelt. By the end of 1942, the submarine threat to shipping in U.S. coastal waters was contained, and King was able to give closer attention to the Battle of the Atlantic by appointing himself commander of the newly established Tenth Fleet and turning over details of its operations to his able subordinate, Rear Admiral Francis Low. Although he kept control of the battle near at hand, King did not let its conduct and criticism of his handling of it blind him to the larger strategic picture. He recognized that he needed numerous destroyer escorts and escort carriers in the Atlantic, but there was no particular need in that theater for the many fast carriers that would be joining the fleet from 1943 onward. These could be sent to the Pacific.[32]

A student of military history and strategy, King had read in depth about the campaigns of Napoleon's marshals and of the American Civil War. Like

Stephen B. Luce and Alfred Thayer Mahan, he believed that, whether on the ground or on the sea, the art of military operations could be reduced to such principles as the initiative of the subordinate and the economy of force. He was also well versed in the thinking of other American strategists, including former Naval War College President Clarence Williams, who maintained that the most certain way to defeat Japan in the long-anticipated war was to cross the Pacific and seize advance bases in the Marshall and, possibly, the Mariana Islands. Increasingly, King articulated the view that naval air power could be best used to seize bases in the Central Pacific. Although he wanted Halsey to press on in conjunction with MacArthur in the South Pacific until Rabaul was taken (bypassed, as things turned out), he also wished Nimitz to initiate a campaign that would begin in the Marshalls and proceed through the Marianas until Luzon in the Philippines or Formosa could be taken and the Imperial Japanese Navy punished when it sortied to defend such strategically vital areas. King then foresaw additional campaigns to occupy and develop bases along the China coast. To facilitate his operations, he tried in vain to prod the British into reopening land communications with China via Burma. He hoped that, if the Japanese were tied down by a major effort in China, they would be unable to reinforce their Central Pacific garrisons. Rather than attack the Japanese in northern Burma, Churchill wished to mount amphibious operations against the Burma coast or Sumatra with the aim of liberating Malaya instead of linking up with our Chinese allies. Such policy differences revived the reservations about British imperialism first felt by King during World War I.[33]

Even without cooperation from the British in Burma, King remained convinced that the Japanese were vulnerable in the Central Pacific. Thus, he pushed hard for a new Central Pacific campaign that began at Tarawa in the Gilbert Islands in November 1943. Early in 1944, shortly before Nimitz's forces were to take the next step and land on Kwajalein Atoll in the Marshall Islands, King journeyed to San Francisco for one of his periodic meetings with his Pacific Ocean commander. When he left San Francisco, King believed that Nimitz concurred with his strategy but was shocked later to learn that both MacArthur and Nimitz were raising objections to his plans to invade the Marianas. MacArthur wished to see the American effort in the Pacific consolidated under his leadership with a single thrust along the New Guinea coast to the Philippines. Nimitz and his own planners were skeptical about the value of the Marianas, for the islands contained no suitable site for the large anchorage that the Pacific Fleet would require as it moved toward the Philippines. Yet, Nimitz agreed to attack the Marianas because the Army Air Force wanted the islands for the construction of air bases from which bombers could strike the Japanese home islands. Not until March 1944 did the Joint Chiefs rule in favor of continuing the dual advance, with one prong led by MacArthur and the other by

Nimitz, whose forces would land in the Marianas in June. From there, they would strike westward to support MacArthur's landings on Mindanao in the southern Philippines in November.[34]

So formidable had American power become that the U.S. Navy could commit large forces both to the D-Day landings in France and to landings in the Marianas. At the Marianas in June and in October at the Philippine island of Leyte, where MacArthur's land and air forces proceeded in lieu of Mindanao, American naval forces delivered grievous blows to Japanese seapower. The Japanese use of kamikazes (suicide planes), however, caused King and Nimitz much alarm. Nevertheless, King was sufficiently pleased with the progress of the war in the Pacific that, during Allied summit meetings at Yalta, Crimea, in early 1945 and at Potsdam, Germany, in July, he had almost nothing to say; he knew that the strategy previously determined was bringing victory over Japan closer. He did continue to believe that a large Soviet effort directed against Japanese forces in Manchuria would be helpful. At the conclusion of the Potsdam conference, he continued his habit of sightseeing, viewing not only the scenes of recent battles in and around Berlin but journeying to Bavaria to visit Hitler's retreat at Berchtesgaden. At Potsdam, King had been informed by General Marshall that the atomic bomb had been successfully tested and that President Harry S Truman had decided to use it against Japan. It is doubtful whether King wanted the war to end with the nuclear devastation of Hiroshima and Nagasaki, but when the news of the Japanese surrender reached him, he simply told his flag secretary, "Well, it's all over. I wonder what I'm going to do tomorrow."[35]

King left office in the middle of December, his final weeks as CNO embittered by his inability to get along with James Forrestal, who had been Secretary of the Navy since Knox's death in 1944. Awarded the five stars of a fleet admiral in December 1944, King never did retire from the Navy. For a time, he maintained an office in the Navy Department, where he began work on his memoirs. After the war, he received many other honors, but the onset of ill health in 1947 made the last decade of his life difficult. To receive the care that he required, he lived alternately in a suite of rooms at the Bethesda (Maryland) Naval Hospital and in the hospital at Portsmouth (New Hampshire) Navy Yard, where he could be more comfortable in the summer. He died in 1956 and was interred at the cemetery of the United States Naval Academy.[36]

Officially, no American naval officer had ever held more authority than King, and, of course, the prodigious size of American naval forces during World War II in personnel, ships, overseas bases, and shore establishments throughout the United States had never before (or has since) been equaled. King's greatest contribution to victory was as a strategist, especially in the Pacific, where much of the war effort bore the imprint of his thought. "If I were asked to single out any one thing in which I take deep satisfaction," he wrote to former Secretary of the Navy Josephus Daniels, "I think likely it would be the part I played in urging that the war in the Pacific should receive its due share of attention—and of 'ways and means.'" The campaigns in the Solomons and subsequently in the Marshalls and Marianas were attributable to King. He was not inflexible, however. Later, for instance, he yielded to the views of Nimitz and most of his ranking planners that the United States had insufficient forces to take Formosa and develop bases there, as King preferred. Rather than remain idle until the defeat of Germany released additional personnel for use in the Pacific, he accepted Nimitz's advocacy of proceeding to Iwo Jima and Okinawa prior to landing in Kyushu, the southernmost of the Japanese home islands. King remained hopeful that a combination of blockade and bombing could cause Japan to surrender, but he acknowledged that there was need to plan the invasion of Kyushu. In American hands, Kyushu could be used to tighten the vise on the faltering Japanese economy, but it could also serve as the springboard for the invasion of the main Japanese island of Honshu, which Army planners advocated.[37]

King had entered the Navy midway through the first generation of steel ships. No dreadnought had joined the American battle line, nor did submarines or aircraft carriers yet threaten it. During his first two decades in the Navy, his career profile was that of a conventional line officer, differentiated primarily by his uncommon quest for excellence and by his insistence that an officer's education must be furthered by continued reading and schooling. During World War I, King met both Beatty and Jellicoe of the Royal Navy and admired his own commander, Admiral Mayo, more than any officer he knew, but he was wise enough to take from Mayo only principles of planning and organization and not any faith in the battleship that had been the backbone of Mayo's Atlantic Fleet. Beginning in the 1920s, however, King's restless ambition led him to leave the "Gun Club" of the surface navy and to acquire more firsthand experience, initially with submarines, then with aviation, than any of his peers. His knowledge of strategy and of the widest range of naval capabilities would subsequently serve him and the Navy well. King's personality was not a pleasing one, but, in his single-minded devotion to duty, he continued to display throughout World War II the professionalism, intelligence, and intensity characteristic of his earlier years and culminated his service by leading the U.S. Navy to victory in its first two-ocean war.

FURTHER READING

Before his health deteriorated, King had begun work on his memoirs. He was unable to finish the work himself, but with the aid of the distinguished scholar and bibliophile, Walter Muir Whitehill, he was able to proceed with the project, *Fleet Admi-*

*ral King: A Naval Record* (New York, 1952). Whitehill later made available to Thomas B. Buell the records that he had compiled on King. Supplementing this material with his own research and numerous interviews with subordinates of King, as well as King's friends and family members, Buell completed *Master of Sea Power: A Biography of Fleet Admiral Ernest J. King* (Boston, 1980), which is likely to remain for some time the most thorough biography of King. Buell is not hesitant to make judgments about King's career and his difficult personality. Robert W. Love, Jr., has written two biographical essays on King: "Ernest Joseph King" in Love, ed., *The Chiefs of Naval Operations* (Annapolis, Md., 1980), and the derivative "Fleet Admiral King" in Stephen Howarth, ed., *Men of War: Great Naval Leaders of World War II* (London, 1992). Another essay on King is in Charles E. Pfannes and Victor A. Salamone, *The Great Admirals of World War II, Volume I: The Americans* (New York, 1983), a work intended for the general reading public.

Legions of books are available on the U.S. Navy and on strategic planning during World War II. Among the best are the fifteen-volume classic, Samuel Eliot Morison, *History of United States Naval Operations in World War II* (Boston, 1947–60); Patrick Abbazia, *Mr. Roosevelt's Navy: The Private War of the U.S. Atlantic Fleet, 1939–1942* (Annapolis, Md., 1975); Robert G. Albion and Robert H. Connery, *Forrestal and the Navy* (New York, 1962); Townsend Hoopes and Douglas Brinkley, *Driven Patriot* (New York, 1992); Clay Blair, Jr., *Silent Victory: The U.S. Submarine War against Japan,* 2 vols. (Philadelphia, 1975); Forrest C. Pogue, *George C. Marshall: Ordeal and Hope, 1939–1942* (New York, 1973) and *George C. Marshall: Organizer of Victory, 1943–1945* (New York, 1987); D. Clayton James, *The Years of MacArthur, 1941–1945* (Boston, 1985); Clark G. Reynolds, *The Fast Carriers: The Forging of an Air Navy* (New York, 1968); Grace Person Hayes, *The History of the Joint Chiefs of Staff in World War II: The War against Japan* (Annapolis, Md., 1982); and Lisle Abbott Rose, *The Ship That Held the Line: The USS Hornet and the First Year of the Pacific War* (Annapolis, Md., 1995).

Many books on wartime diplomacy, for instance those dealing with the wartime summit conferences, mention King. Not to be missed is Robert Dallek's thorough *Franklin D. Roosevelt and American Foreign Policy, 1932–1945* (New York, 1979).

In late 1942 when the protracted Guadalcanal campaign brought his leadership into question, King first met with a group of Washington correspondents. Comments were off the record, and King talked freely. He continued these meetings for the duration of the war. Glen C. H. Perry, one of the regular correspondents at the meetings, compiled his memoranda of them in *Dear Bart: Washington Views of World War II* (Westport, Conn., 1982).

Frank Knox and James Forrestal, Secretaries of the Navy with whom King worked closely, are the subjects of essays in Paolo E. Coletta, ed., *American Secretaries of the Navy,* 2 vols. (Annapolis, Md., 1980).

NOTES

1. Thomas B. Buell, *Master of Sea Power: A Biography of Fleet Admiral Ernest J. King* (Boston, 1980), 117–119; Ernest J. King and Walter Muir Whitehill, *Fleet Admiral King: A Naval Record* (New York, 1952), 291–94; B. Mitchell Simpson, III, *Admiral Harold R. Stark: Architect of Victory, 1939–1945* (Columbia, S.C., 1989), 1–2.

2. Buell, *Master of Sea Power,* 3–8; King and Whitehill, *Fleet Admiral,* 9–15.

3. Buell, *Master of Sea Power,* 8–14; King and Whitehill, *Fleet Admiral,* 16–34.

4. Buell, *Master of Sea Power*, 15–25; King and Whitehill, *Fleet Admiral*, 38–43.

5. Buell, *Master of Sea Power*, 26–42; King and Whitehill, *Fleet Admiral*, 46–87.

6. Sims quoted in King and Whitehill, *Fleet Admiral*, 95.

7. Buell, *Master of Sea Power*, 43–50; James C. Bradford, "Henry C. Mayo: Last of the Independent Naval Diplomats," in Bradford, ed., *Admirals of the New Steel Navy: Makers of the American Naval Tradition, 1880–1930* (Annapolis, Md., 1990), 253–281.

8. Bradford, "Mayo," 268–72; Buell, *Master of Sea Power*, 50–53; King and Whitehill, *Fleet Admiral*, 97–145.

9. Buell, *Master of Sea Power*, 54–70; King and Whitehill, *Fleet Admiral*, 146–85.

10. Clark G. Reynolds, "William A. Moffett: Steward of the Air Revolution," in Bradford, *Admirals of New Steel Navy*, 374–92; Buell, *Master of Sea Power*, 71–76; King and Whitehill, *Fleet Admiral*, 188–94.

11. Buell, *Master of Sea Power*, 78–93; King and Whitehill, *Fleet Admiral*, 206–33; William F. Trimble, *Admiral William A. Moffett: Architect of Naval Aviation* (Washington, D.C., 1994), 214–15; Eugene Wilson, "The Navy's First Carrier Task Force," U.S. Naval Institute *Proceedings* 76 (February 1950): 159–69; King to Walter Brennan, 3 January 1943, Box 9, King Correspondence, Manuscript Division, Library of Congress (hereafter cited as King Corr.).

12. Buell, *Master of Sea Power*, 94–97; King and Whitehill, *Fleet Admiral*, 242–43; Trimble, *Moffett*, 250–73.

13. Buell, *Master of Sea Power*, 98–100; King and Whitehill, *Fleet Admiral*, 247–63.

14. Buell, *Master of Sea Power*, 100–01; King and Whitehill, *Fleet Admiral*, 264–65.

15. Buell, *Master of Sea Power*, 102–28; King and Whitehill, *Fleet Admiral*, 266–78.

16. Clark G. Reynolds, *Admiral John H. Towers: The Struggle for Naval Air Supremacy* (Annapolis, Md., 1994), 270–81; Buell, *Master of Sea Power*, 108–13, Boone quote, 111; King and Whitehill, *Fleet Admiral*, 279–94; J. J. Clark, "Navy Sundowner Par Excellence," U.S. Naval Institute *Proceedings* 97 (June 1971): 54–59.

17. Reynolds, *Towers*, 287–89; Buell, *Master of Sea Power*, 113–17.

18. Buell, *Master of Sea Power*, 117–19; King and Whitehill, *Fleet Admiral*, 291–94. Baldwin quoted by Robert W. Love, Jr., "Ernest Joseph King," in Love, ed., *The Chiefs of Naval Operations* (Annapolis, Md., 1980), 179.

19. Simpson, *Stark*, 61, 128; Buell, *Master of Sea Power*, 123–50; King and Whitehill, *Fleet Admiral*, 310–46; Harry Sanders, "King of Oceans," U.S. Naval Institute *Proceedings* 100 (August 1974): 52–59; King to Frank Knox, 17 January 1941; King to Rear Admiral Frank Berrien, 9 February 1941; Commander H. R. Thurber to King, 6 March 1941; King to Thurber, 15 March 1941; General Thomas Holcomb to King, 10 March 1941; King to Rear Admiral D. M. LeBreton, 10 October 1941; and King to Chester Nimitz, 10 November 1941; all in Box 8, King Corr.; King to Walter Lippmann, 25 July 1940, Box 82, Series 3, Lippmann Correspondence, Sterling Library, Yale University (hereafter cited as Lippmann Corr.).

20. Simpson, *Stark*, 125–32; King and Whitehill, *Fleet Admiral*, 342–59; Buell, *Master of Sea Power*, 156–61.

21. Buell, *Master of Sea Power*, 153–55, 232–39, 406–09.

22. Edward S. Miller, *War Plan Orange: The U.S. Strategy to Defeat Japan, 1897–1945* (Annapolis, Md., 1991), 246–49; Buell, *Master of Sea Power*, 152–72; King and Whitehill, *Fleet Admiral*, 360–77; E. B. Potter, *Nimitz* (Annapolis, Md., 1976), 31–35; King to Field Marshal Sir John Dill, 3 April 1942, Box 10, King Corr.

23. Clark G. Reynolds, "The U.S. Fleet-in-Being Strategy of 1942," *The Journal of Military History* 58 (January 1994): 103–10.

24. Reynolds, "U.S. Fleet-in-Being Strategy," 110–18; King quoted in Buell, *Master of Sea Power*, 193; John F. Wukovits, *Devotion to Duty: A Biography of Admiral Clifton A. F. Sprague* (Annapolis, Md., 1995), 44–72; Grace Person Hayes, *The History of the Joint Chiefs of Staff in World War II: The War against Japan* (Annapolis, Md., 1982), 55–71; Lloyd J. Graybar, "American Pacific Strategy after Pearl Harbor: The Relief of Wake Island," *Prologue: The Journal of the National Archives* 12 (Fall 1980): 134–50; King to Wesley Winans Stout, 30 March 1942, copy in Box 82, Lippmann Corr.

25. Buell *Master of Sea Power*, 172–200; John B. Lundstrom, *The First South Pacific Campaign: Pacific Fleet Strategy, December 1941–June 1942* (Annapolis, Md., 1976), 28–34; Potter, *Nimitz*, 36–47; Reynolds, "U.S. Fleet-in-Being Strategy," 110–18.

26. Buell, *Master of Sea Power*, 200–04; King and Whitehill, *Fleet Admiral*, 377–89; Lundstrom, *First South Pacific Campaign*, 154–64; see also note 23.

27. King to General Merritt Edson, 29 September 1949, copy in Box 4, Correspondence of Adm. Charles N. Cooke, Hoover Institution, Stanford, Calif. (hereafter cited as Cooke Corr.); King to General George C. Marshall, 10 July 1942, copy in Box 10, Cooke Corr.

28. King and Whitehill, *Fleet Admiral*, 390–427; Potter, *Nimitz*, 173–80; King to Marshall, 3 September 1942, copy in Box 10, Cooke Corr.; Vivian Dykes to Lieutenant Colonel W. S. Sterling, 29 August 1942, and Sterling to Dykes, 29 September 1942, both in Cabinet 122/1582, Public Record Office, Kew, London, England (hereafter cited as PRO).

29. Buell, *Master of Sea Power*, 219–25, 258–63; Lundstrom, *First South Pacific Campaign*, 128–36; Lloyd J. Graybar, "Admiral King's Toughest Battle," *Naval War College Review* 32 (February 1979): 38–47; Roscoe Drummond and Glen Perry, "King of the Seven Seas," *Look* (22 December 1944): 42–49; Potter, *Nimitz*, 181–210.

30. Buell, *Master of Sea Power*, 278–81; King and Whitehill, *Fleet Admiral*, 428–44, quote, 442.

31. Buell, *Master of Sea Power*, 53; Sir John Slessor, *The Central Blue: Recollections and Reflections* (London, 1956), 491–99; Miller, *War Plan Orange*, 105–21; Captain Donald McIntyre, RN, *Fighting Admiral: The Life of Admiral of the Fleet Sir James Somerville* (London, 1961), 226–27, 253–57; Stephen Roskill, *Churchill and the Admirals* (New York, 1978), 237–78; Potter, *Nimitz*, 237–78; King to Nimitz, 8 February 1944, copy in Box 22, Cooke Corr. Also, Sir John Dill to Churchill, 7 March 1942, Prem 3/478/6; First Lord of the Admiralty A. V. Alexander to Chancellor of the Exchequer, copy dated 10 April 1943, Prem 3/478/4; Alexander to Churchill, 27 April 1943, Prem 3/478/4; Alexander to Churchill, 3 May 1944, Prem 3/478/5; Churchill to First Lord of the Admiralty, 21 May 1944, Prem 3/478/5; and "dance attendance" in Churchill to First Lord, 27 May 1944, Prem 3/478/5, all in PRO.

32. Buell, *Master of Sea Power*, 282–99; King and Whitehill, *Fleet Admiral*, 445–75; Ladislas Farago, *The Tenth Fleet* (New York, 1962), 91–108; Robert W. Love, Jr., *History of the U.S. Navy, II, 1942–1991* (Harrisburg, Pa., 1992), 64–83, 96–119, 191–92.

33. Buell, *Master of Sea Power*, 272–75; Miller, *War Plan Orange*, 114–21; H. P. Willmott, "Grave of a Dozen Schemes," *Joint Forces Quarterly* 1 (Spring 1994): 82–91. For a concise overview of King's strategy and the operations that implemented it, see the handsomely illustrated volume, Clark G. Reynolds, *War in the Pacific* (New York, 1990), 83–159.

34. Buell, *Master of Sea Power*, 438–47; Reynolds, *Towers*, 460–67; Winston Churchill, Observations on Chiefs of Staff minutes (44) 123, dated 14 February 1944, Prem 3/160/7, PRO.

35. Buell, *Master of Sea Power*, 463–79, 495–98, quote, 498; King and Whitehill, *Fleet Admiral*, 556–621; Henry H. Adams, *Witness to Power: The Life of Fleet Admiral William D. Leahy* (Annapolis, Md., 1985), 234–74; Ronald Schaffer, *Wings of Judgment: American Bombing in World War II* (New York, 1985), 172; Love, "King," 178; John Ray Skates, *The Invasion of Japan: Alternative to the Bomb* (Columbia, 1994), 247–57; Love, *History of U.S. Navy*, 2:253–77, 846; King to Admiral Sir Andrew Cunningham, 31 January 1945, Box 10, King Corr. Although historians are divided about whether President Truman sought King's concurrence in using the atom bomb against Japan (and evidence on this matter is both scant and contradictory), King recognized that, once it had been used, it was a military fact, and he made it clear during the last months of his watch that he favored testing the effects of the atom bomb against ships. For some of the ramifications of these tests that were held in the summer of 1946, see Lloyd J. Graybar, "The 1946 Atom Bomb Tests: Atomic Diplomacy or Bureaucratic Infighting?" *Journal of American History* 72 (March 1986): 888–907, and Jonathan M. Weisgall, *Operation Crossroads: The Atomic Tests at Bikini Atoll* (Annapolis, Md., 1994), 15–16, 246–316.

36. Buell, *Master of Sea Power*, 480–97; King and Whitehill, *Fleet Admiral*, 629–38.

37. Hayes, *History of Joint Chiefs*, 701–10, 722–29; Skates, *Invasion of Japan*, 36–83; Lundstrom, *First South Pacific Campaign*, 196–205; quotation in King to Josephus Daniels, 31 August 1945, Box 10, King Corr.

# ☆ Chester W. Nimitz
☆
☆ Victory in the Pacific

*by John B. Lundstrom*

TENSION MANIFESTED ALMOST A PHYSICAL PRESENCE IN FLEET HEAD-
quarters at Pearl Harbor on Oahu in the Hawaiian Islands for the first two days
of June 1942. During the past two weeks, Admiral Chester W. Nimitz, Commander-in-Chief, United States Pacific Fleet (CinCPac), had engineered a
drastic redeployment of his striking force in outright defiance, at least initially, of the orders of his superior, Admiral Ernest J. King. Nimitz recalled his
three aircraft carriers from the South Pacific, thousands of miles away, to the
Central Pacific to battle a massive offensive that he believed the Japanese Combined Fleet was about to unleash against Midway and also the Aleutian Islands
well to the north.

Nimitz acted solely on the basis of intelligence estimates derived from incomplete deciphering of Japanese fleet radio messages. They were served up
by the very same analysts who, six months before, could not warn Nimitz's predecessor, Admiral Husband E. Kimmel, that Japanese carriers would strike the
fleet at Pearl Harbor. The result then was the crippling of the battleship force.
The stakes now were much higher.

Until 3 June, Nimitz had to rely on his professional judgment, moral
courage, and a great deal of faith that his radio intelligence specialists had indeed predicted the place and time of the Japanese onslaught. Never did he reveal to his anxious staff a glimmer of doubt or worry over one of the more momentous decisions made by any commander during World War II. That
morning, however, sighting reports radioed by American search planes confirmed that the enemy appeared to be coming as expected.

Present with the admiral was the fleet intelligence officer, Lieutenant Commander Edwin T. Layton, who, along with code-breaker Commander Joseph

J. Rochefort, had championed the value of radio intelligence. Nimitz flashed to Layton "that brilliant white smile" that "just lights up."

"This ought to make your heart warm," Nimitz congratulated Layton. "This will clear up all the doubters now. They just have to see this to know that what I told them is correct."[1]

The ensuing Battle of Midway (4–6 June 1942) was one step, albeit perhaps the most important, that led to ultimate total victory over Japan. Pounded by bombs and gutted by fire, four Japanese carriers and a heavy cruiser slipped beneath the waves at the cost of one American carrier, one destroyer, and many brave aviators. The courage, skill, and sacrifice of the Pacific Fleet's flyers and the Midway defenders, along with the good fortune that is absolutely essential in warfare, completely vindicated Chester Nimitz's decision to risk an early decisive battle with the Japanese Combined Fleet and regain the initiative in the Pacific.

What sort of man was this admiral who so swiftly reversed the Pacific balance of power? Within the Pacific Fleet and the U.S. Navy as a whole, Nimitz inspired not only great respect for his skill and insight but tremendous affection for his congenial and considerate personality. Lacking bluster and imperiousness, he was the master of consensus and cooperation. In a biographical sketch, one prominent naval historian referred to Nimitz as the "principal Allied naval *administrator*" in the Pacific, that is, more of a "manager" than a warrior.[2] In fact, Nimitz made it look much too easy. His very success in nearly four years of bitter warfare obscured the obstacles that he had to surmount and his quick adaptation to new ways of naval warfare. His avuncular manner concealed a will of steel that he rarely needed to reveal except in times of extreme crisis, such as the spring of 1942 and in the Guadalcanal campaign later that year.

The grandson of German immigrants, Chester William Nimitz was born on 24 February 1885 in Fredericksburg, a small town in South Texas. He grew up in nearby Kerrville, where his parents, far from being well to do, ran a small hotel. Unable to gain an appointment to West Point, Chester successfully competed for a slot at the Naval Academy and, in the summer of 1901, enrolled as a member of the class of 1905.

Befitting the growing strength of the U.S. Navy, Nimitz's class, nearly twice as large as its predecessors, was the first to exceed 100 midshipmen. Even so, the number of nascent naval officers was small enough for everyone to get acquainted. During Nimitz's time at Annapolis, he served with all of his future key subordinates in World War II: William F. Halsey (1904); John H. Towers, Robert Lee Ghormley, and Frank Jack Fletcher (1906); Raymond A. Spruance (1907); and Richmond Kelly Turner (1908). In January 1905, Nimitz graduated 7th in his class of 114.

After nearly two years on the battleship *Ohio*, Nimitz reported in 1907 to the Asiatic Squadron as commander of the small gunboat *Panay*. That summer, at the age of twenty-two, Ensign Nimitz became skipper of the destroyer *Decatur* and took her throughout the Philippines and to Southeast Asia. Only one untoward incident marred an otherwise spotless tour of duty. In July 1908, he ran the *Decatur* aground and survived a charge of "neglect of duty."[3] Thereafter, Nimitz always gave young officers the benefit of the doubt for one mistake, provided they learned, as did he, from their error.

Nimitz returned home in January 1909 to serve, albeit reluctantly, in submarines. Only recently developed and certainly far from reliable, the small, rotund American "pigboats" were considered suitable mainly for harbor defense, and their gasoline engines made them dangerous to operate. Nimitz commanded three submarines in succession and, by September 1911, also led a division. A pioneer of diesel propulsion for submarines, Nimitz in early 1912 became skipper of the E-1 (*Skipjack*), the first American diesel-powered submarine, and took command of the Atlantic Submarine Flotilla that spring. In later life, he proudly wore the gold dolphin insignia subsequently adopted for officers who qualified in submarines.

Nimitz's expertise in diesel engines led to study in Germany and the job, as prospective executive officer and chief engineer, of helping to design and install diesels in the fleet oiler *Maumee*. In early 1917, the *Maumee* experimented with underway refueling and, in April, provided oil far out at sea for destroyers bound for the War in Europe.[4] That summer, Lieutenant Commander Nimitz became an aide to Captain Samuel S. Robison, commander of the Atlantic Fleet submarines. Nimitz spent the balance of World War I on staff duty, but he made the important transition from engineering, which would limit his career opportunities, to command. As his eminent biographer E. B. Potter wrote, Nimitz became "concerned less with machinery than with people, less with construction and maintenance than with organization, and thus he found his true vocation."[5]

In 1920, Commander Nimitz erected, virtually from scratch, a submarine base at Pearl Harbor, Hawaii, and took command. He attended the Naval War College in Newport, Rhode Island, in 1922 to study naval strategy, particularly the conduct of a naval war across the vast Pacific to defeat Japan (War Plan Orange). Nimitz also joined in tactical experiments on ship formations to devise something better than the cumbersome columns of ships used in 1916 by the British and German fleets at the Battle of Jutland. He helped to develop the circular formation with capital ships surrounded by concentric circles of screening vessels. In 1923, by a fortunate circumstance, Nimitz joined the staff of then Vice Admiral Robison, commander of the Battle Fleet, which enabled him to test the circular formation at sea. Two years later, Robison became

Commander-in-Chief, United States Fleet, with Nimitz as his assistant chief of staff and tactical officer. Although the Navy did not take immediately to the circular formation, the fleet was aware of its potential, particularly in connection with carriers, and revived it just prior to World War II, when it really counted.

Captain Nimitz demonstrated his "people" skills when he turned the Naval Reserve Officer Training Corps program at the University of California-Berkeley into an unqualified success. After several administrative posts, he gratefully returned to sea in October 1933 as commanding officer of the heavy cruiser *Augusta* with the Asiatic Fleet. Her crew reckoned themselves fortunate to have such a competent, yet genial captain. On voyages throughout the Far East, the *Augusta* became known as one of the finest ships in the Navy.

In 1935, the Navy brass had the opportunity to take the measure of Captain Nimitz when he reported as assistant chief to the Bureau of Navigation (predecessor to the Bureau of Naval Personnel) in Washington, D.C. They liked what they saw and only let him escape that hotbed of politics and red tape for a short interval. In July 1938, newly promoted Rear Admiral Nimitz assumed command of a light cruiser division, but illness forced his immediate relief. That September, he took over Battleship Division One at San Pedro, California, with his flag on the *Arizona*.[6] In January 1939, when most of the U.S. Fleet departed for the Caribbean and Fleet Problem XX, Nimitz was left as senior officer in the Pacific. He conducted gunnery and amphibious exercises, as well as more underway refueling tests, for the first time with heavy ships. In one of his few questionable calls, he recommended the stern-to-bow, rather than what became the standard beam-to-beam, refueling configuration, only to be overruled by Admiral William D. Leahy, Chief of Naval Operations (CNO).[7]

Nimitz returned to Washington in June 1939 to run the Bureau of Navigation under the new CNO, Admiral Harold R. Stark. Thus, he became a key player in President Franklin D. Roosevelt's vast expansion of the Navy to prepare for the war that Roosevelt felt to be inevitable after Europe erupted in conflict. Nimitz's superb administrative ability and political skills were put sorely to the test as he oversaw programs to acquire and train the greatly increased numbers of personnel required by the Navy. The urgency became more apparent in May 1941 after the President declared an unlimited national emergency. Faced toward Europe, Washington focused on what became an undeclared war with Germany in the North Atlantic, while discounting the growing threat of Japan in the Far East.

When war finally came on 7 December 1941, the principal blow landed neither in the Atlantic nor in the Far East, but where it was least expected, against the Pacific Fleet at Pearl Harbor. His reputation permanently scarred by the devastation of his battle line, Admiral Kimmel could no longer effectively exercise command. On 15 December, he offered Stark the names of seven admirals that he recommended to replace him as CinCPac.[8] Last on the list was Rear Admiral Chester Nimitz. Kimmel evidently was unaware that, in January 1941, the President had offered Nimitz the same post. Nimitz declined because he felt that he lacked seniority, and the job went to Kimmel. Now in the aftermath of disaster, Nimitz again stood first on the President's own list. On 16 December, Secretary of the Navy Frank Knox informed Nimitz of his promotion to admiral and his new command, then relayed Roosevelt's valedictory: "Tell Nimitz to get the hell out to Pearl and stay there till the war is won."[9]

Kimmel was relieved of command on 17 December by Vice Admiral William S. Pye, the Battle Force commander whose only significant (and correct) decision as caretaker CinCPac was to recall the carriers attempting to reinforce besieged Wake Island, which fell on 23 December. On 31 December, Nimitz assumed command of the Pacific Fleet in a ceremony conducted at Pearl Harbor on the deck of the submarine *Grayling*. He liked to joke that a submarine was the only vessel that the Japanese left for him there.

Why Nimitz? Of all the senior admirals, he had probably accumulated the least sea duty as a flag officer and had never exercised command in any of the massive fleet problems that so dominated the pre–World War II Navy. Since his stints at the Naval War College and on Robison's staff during the early 1920s, he had not moved within the inner councils that formulated fleet strategy and doctrine. On the positive side, Nimitz had acquitted himself superbly in all of his duty assignments. The President knew personally from Nimitz's performance as a bureau chief that he was clear thinking and innovative, an excellent administrator, calm, resolute, and unflappable under pressure. His gracious, cheerful personality seemed just the thing to revive sagging morale in Hawaii. Another possible plus in the President's mind was that Nimitz, not wedded to any particular faction in the Navy, would approach his daunting task with an open mind.

Perhaps the only concern regarding the new CinCPac was whether he really was a fighter. Only battle would tell the tale. Just appointed Commander-in-Chief, United States Fleet (CominCh), imperious Admiral Ernest J. King (whose pugnacity nobody doubted), was evidently unsure of his new subordinate. Deeply distrusting those he thought were political admirals, the "fixers" who supposedly owed their advancement to their proximity to the President, King was not about to keep Nimitz on anything but a short leash.[10] As to which of the two admirals was the more aggressive, however, the reader can judge. Throughout the war, their relations, while always correct, certainly were not cordial.

At Pearl Harbor, Nimitz discovered that his principal mobile fleet assets were the three carriers *Lexington*, *Saratoga*, and *Enterprise*, with a total of about 210 aircraft. Each flattop was the nucleus of a task force screened by two or three cruisers and about a half dozen destroyers.[11] Nimitz also controlled half of the fifty-odd submarines in the Pacific, with the rest under the Asiatic Fleet. He realized, far sooner than most admirals, that battleships were no longer the cynosure of naval warfare. Japanese carrier airpower, an order of magnitude more powerful than any American had understood, rendered what was left of Kimmel's proud battle line virtually irrelevant. The old battleships were far too slow to operate with the swift carriers and too poorly protected to face enemy aircraft alone. In January 1942, Nimitz relegated them to escorting convoys between the West Coast and Pearl Harbor in order to free up his cruisers. Later at Coral Sea and Midway, he deliberately kept them far away from the battle.[12]

Nimitz faced a frustrating situation during the first months of 1942 as he settled in as CinCPac. The disaster at Pearl Harbor and manifest Japanese naval strength prevented the Pacific Fleet from seizing the strategic initiative. Despite public expectations, there could be no dramatic rush westward to stem the tide of conquest in the Philippines and the Dutch East Indies. Equally unfeasible for the immediate time was the amphibious advance to the Marshall Islands long enshrined in the War Plan Orange studies. King harped on the need to divert enemy strength away from the collapsing Far East, but Nimitz felt that any significant target he could reach would prove too tough for the weak Pacific Fleet. Instead, he had to concentrate on holding Hawaii and Midway because the Japanese Combined Fleet appeared powerful enough to threaten America's strongholds in the Central Pacific. That left only swift, small-scale raids against outlying bases in the Central Pacific. Even so, they proved difficult to orchestrate. Finally, on 1 February 1942, Vice Admiral William F. Halsey's *Enterprise* and Rear Admiral Frank Jack Fletcher's newly arrived carrier *Yorktown* raided widely throughout the eastern Marshall and Gilbert Islands and provided a vital boost to American morale.

Within a month of taking command, Nimitz found himself in fundamental strategic disagreement with King, his difficult superior in Washington. In a 30 December 1941 directive, King had stated the obvious need to defend Hawaii and Midway but added that "only in small degree less important [is the] maintenance of communications [from the] West Coast to Australia."[13] That foreshadowed his growing interest in the South and Southwest Pacific that would decisively affect fleet deployment.

Passionately committed to fighting Japan in the Pacific, King battled both his colleagues in Washington and the Allied Combined Chiefs of Staff (CCS) within the constraints of the basic strategic question of Germany first. He feared that the Allies would effectively shut down offensive operations in the Pacific by shifting badly needed resources to the European theater. In January, King arranged with the CCS to set up, under his direct command and not Nimitz's, the so-called ANZAC Area to control U.S. and Allied naval forces in Australia and New Zealand and waters north of there. He matured plans to build up strength and create new bases in the distant South and Southwest Pacific to halt the enemy advance. That became crucial after 23 January when the Japanese invaded Rabaul on New Britain in the Bismarck Archipelago. From there, they threatened not only eastern New Guinea (and ultimately Australia itself) but also key South Pacific islands on the sea route between the United States, New Zealand, and Australia. Once the Allies could regain the initiative, King intended to launch his first counteroffensive in the South Pacific, rather than the Central Pacific.

Because the Allies lacked the strength to defend the South Pacific, King informed Nimitz that he must provide the requisite forces. Worry about the havoc the Japanese could wreak if they returned in strength to the Central Pacific precipitated vigorous debate at Pearl Harbor: "Are we going to gamble all upon securing Australia as a base of future operations against the enemy and leave our Pacific Area open to attack?"[14] In early February, King removed the *Lexington*, one third of CinCPac's striking force, from Nimitz's command and sent her south. Vice Admiral Wilson Brown, the task force commander, noted the lack of suitable friendly harbors in the remote South Pacific. He likened his mission to "jumping off into space."[15] The staff at Pearl Harbor agreed. Nimitz felt reluctant to disperse his meager forces in the South Pacific but slowly recognized its inevitability. On 21 February, the War Plans Section opined that the South Pacific region was "one in which our forces will meet advancing enemy forces, and we may be forced to make the move due to political or 'desperation strategical' consideration."[16]

King showed he meant business on 24 February when he also detached the *Yorktown* for the Southwest Pacific. That left Nimitz only the *Enterprise*, which he had committed to raids on Wake and Marcus Islands in the Central Pacific. (A submarine had torpedoed the *Saratoga* on 11 January, and Nimitz sent her limping back to the West Coast for repairs). On 19 March, Nimitz learned that King had again appropriated his carriers. In a grandstand play designed to appeal to President Roosevelt, CominCh decreed that, in April, the *Enterprise* and the new *Hornet* were to bomb Japan.

For Nimitz, the first three months as CinCPac proved disappointing, relieved only by brief triumph when the carriers fought. To those around him, the ever imperturbable, intensely private admiral managed to conceal his growing frustration, but, on 22 March, he confided to his wife Catherine:

> Ever so many people were enthusiastic for me at the start but when things do not move fast enough—they sour on me. I will be lucky to last six months. The public may demand action and results faster than I can produce.[17]

For most of this period Nimitz exercised little control over his carriers. Quite likely, he felt that King might never give him the latitude to lead his fleet and fight the enemy his own way. He could not know that the next three months would bring him glory.

King's strategy of projecting American naval power into the South Pacific was brilliant. On 10 March, the *Lexington* and *Yorktown* combined at Lae and Salamaua in northern Papua to deal the Imperial Navy its heaviest losses to date.[18] That compelled the Japanese to divert significant forces to further their own rather modest offensive plans in that region. Envisioning an enlarged ANZAC Area under his own and not Nimitz's command, King looked forward to directing his offensive through the South Pacific island chains straight to Rabaul; however, a great obstacle to his grand design appeared in the form of General Douglas MacArthur, just recalled from the Philippines and eager to lead the way back. Suddenly, Nimitz was back in the picture as a counterweight to MacArthur, whom King distrusted intensely. On 4 April, Nimitz learned that the entire Pacific command would soon be reorganized and the ANZAC Area abolished. As Commander-in-Chief, Pacific Ocean Areas, he would exercise direct control of the North and Central Pacific Areas and run the South Pacific Area (SoPac) through a subordinate. (Nimitz later nominated and King approved Vice Admiral Robert Lee Ghormley.) MacArthur became Supreme Commander, Southwest Pacific Area (SWPA). King saw to it that the boundary between SoPac and SWPA was blurred so that the Navy could control at least the opening stages of the assault on Rabaul.[19]

Finally, Nimitz could fight his fleet. Quite providentially, the increasingly efficient radio intelligence in April detected hints of major enemy moves in the Southwest and South Pacific set to begin in late April or early May. Actually, the code breakers had uncovered elements of Japanese plans for an offensive (the MO Operation) using three carriers to capture Port Moresby in Papua and the Solomon Islands. Yet, Nimitz's analysts thought that Port Moresby would be only the first stage of a wider rampage by as many as six or more enemy flattops against northeastern Australia, New Caledonia, Fiji, and Samoa. That would seriously threaten communications with Australia and delay any Allied offensive in the region.

Nimitz boldly proposed to counter the Japanese South Pacific onslaught by committing all four of his carriers and their three hundred aircraft to battle. Fletcher, with the *Yorktown* and *Lexington*, would tackle the first blow in early May against Port Moresby. About two weeks later, Halsey, back from the Tokyo raid with the *Enterprise* and *Hornet*, would join Fletcher and take command. Nimitz quickly recognized that, although the bombing of Japan, which went off spectacularly on 18 April, provided good propaganda, it ultimately harmed his strategy because it deprived him of half his carriers when he especially needed them.[20]

The traditional view is that Nimitz, cued by his superb radio intelligence, simply reacted to the enemy's moves and, in desperation, threw his forces into the path of the Japanese in the hope of an "incredible victory." Actually, Nimitz saw the defense of the South Pacific bases as a great opportunity to accomplish what he felt to be his primary mission—the destruction of the Japanese carriers. Since January 1942, the enemy had employed its flattops in the Dutch East Indies or the Indian Ocean, where the Pacific Fleet could not get at them. To Nimitz, the tremendous advantage of reading the enemy's naval ciphers went far to negate the fact that the Japanese enjoyed interior lines and held the initiative. Mobility and the concentration of forces became the keys to defeating them. Cautiously confident, Nimitz felt: "Because of our superior personnel in resourcefulness and initiative, and the undoubted superiority of much of our equipment, we should be able to accept odds in battle if necessary."[21] King approved the plan to use all four carriers in the South Pacific. Concerned as always with protecting his vital foothold, however, he ordered Nimitz to keep at least two carriers in the South Pacific until further notice.

In the Battle of the Coral Sea (4–8 May 1942), Fletcher fought the first carrier-versus-carrier duel in history.[22] It cost the Japanese the light carrier *Shoho*, damage to the big carrier *Shokaku*, and such severe aircraft losses that they called off the Port Moresby invasion. Coral Sea became the first Allied strategic victory in the Pacific. Unfortunately, the gallant *Lexington* succumbed to fires, while the *Yorktown* ran southward with bomb damage deep in her vitals. Racing down from Pearl Harbor, Halsey's two flattops reached the South Pacific too late to fight in the first battle.

Nobody expected the Japanese to give up after just one try for Port Moresby. Yet, by 10 May, Rochefort and Layton, Nimitz's radio intelligence analysts at Pearl Harbor, could find no evidence that strong enemy forces were indeed concentrating in the south. Instead, indications pointed to the Central Pacific as the next Japanese target. That was always the gravest danger to the Pacific Fleet. Rochefort's code breakers had detected elements of the plan by Admiral Isoroku Yamamoto, commander of the Combined Fleet, to capture Midway in early June and entice the Pacific Fleet into decisive battle.[23]

In contrast to their colleagues at Pearl Harbor, King's own intelligence specialists forecast another major enemy South Pacific assault and failed to see the growing danger to Midway and Hawaii. Deeply worried about the threat to his bases and shaken by the loss of the *Lexington*, King suggested to Nimitz on 12 May that the damaged *Yorktown* leave her planes (and the *Lexington's*) to help defend the South Pacific. His thoughts regarding the *Enterprise* and *Hornet* betrayed his fears over the next battle: "In order to preserve our carriers during such an attack on islands it may be better to operate one or more carrier air groups from shore."[24]

Restricting the mobility of his carrier striking force was the last thing Nimitz desired, especially now. He needed all of them back in the Central Pacific as soon as possible. Forcefully but tactfully, he tried to warn King that the Japanese were about to descend on Midway and possibly Hawaii. Even so, he took the extraordinary step of using a ruse to contravene King's direct orders to retain two carriers in the South Pacific until further notice. On 13 May, Nimitz sent an "eyes-only" order telling Halsey to let his carriers be sighted by the Japanese, both to deter the enemy and to give Nimitz the excuse to pull them back. Not waiting for CominCh's concurrence, Nimitz followed on 15 May with orders for Halsey and Fletcher to return immediately to Pearl Harbor. To King, he explained, "Will watch situation closely and return Halsey to Southward if imminent [enemy] concentration [in] that area is indicated."[25] CinCPac's faith in the validity of his radio intelligence gave him the courage to shift his carriers three thousand miles to the northeast.

On 17 May, King informed Nimitz of his general agreement with CinCPac's estimate of Japanese intentions. If he ever knew of Nimitz's subterfuge regarding Halsey, he never admitted it. Fully realizing the vital necessity of fighting for Midway, King nevertheless feared the possible cost. As Clark G. Reynolds shows, CominCh much preferred a "fleet-in-being" strategy to risking all his forces in one battle.[26] King urged Nimitz to: "Chiefly employ strong attrition tactics and not repeat NOT allow our forces to accept such decisive action as would likely to incur heavy losses in our carriers and cruisers."[27]

The Pacific Fleet staff situation estimate outlined the problem and suggested the tactics to be followed:

> Not only our directive from Commander-in-Chief, U.S. Fleet, but common sense dictates that we cannot now afford to slug it out with the probably superior approaching Japanese forces. We must endeavor to reduce his forces by attrition—submarine attacks, air bombing, attack on isolated units. . . . If attrition is successful the enemy must accept the failure of his venture or risk battle on disadvantageous terms.[28]

Despite all the pious talk about standing off and inflicting attrition, however, Nimitz knew full well that defending Midway still meant meeting the Combined Fleet in battle, where anything could happen. Expecting to do that without risking significant loss was like jumping into the water and hoping not to get wet. With typical sangfroid, Nimitz summed up his feelings in a 29 May 1942 letter to King: "We are very actively preparing to greet our expected visitors with the kind of reception they deserve, and we will do the best we can with what we have."[29]

By 2 June, Nimitz had deployed off Midway all three carriers, including, remarkably, the damaged *Yorktown*, as well as fifteen submarines. More than 120 aircraft crowded the tiny atoll. This time, the Pacific Fleet enjoyed superior reconnaissance and, because of superb radio intelligence, the priceless advantage of surprise. During the battle on 4 June, both Midway's airpower and the submarines proved much less effective than anticipated, but the carriers under Fletcher and Rear Admiral Raymond A. Spruance came through splendidly. Himself counting on surprise, Admiral Yamamoto had so contrived his plans that his four carriers, the *Akagi, Kaga, Soryu,* and *Hiryu,* led the Midway assault, but, in traditional fashion, his battleships were to deliver the coup de grâce to the U.S. Pacific Fleet. After his carriers were ambushed and crushed, however, he could only meekly withdraw the rest of his vast armada.[30]

Never again would Nimitz exercise such direct personal influence over the course of the Pacific War as he did during the period between 15 April and 15 June 1942. As was said of British Admiral Sir John Jellicoe during World War I, Nimitz literally could win or lose the war in an afternoon. Thereafter, he operated within the tight framework of policy and strategy formulated by the Joint Chiefs and CominCh. His overwhelming victory at Midway completely changed the complexion of the Pacific War. Japan's initial superiority dwindled to parity at best. Despite the benefits, one wonders if King ever quite forgave Nimitz for putting the fleet in jeopardy at Midway. He certainly allowed his communications bureaucrats, the Washington experts embarrassed when Rochefort and Layton were proved correct about enemy plans for Midway, to supplant their counterparts at Pearl Harbor. Rochefort was cast off, but Nimitz managed to save Layton.[31]

The way was open for the Allies to assume the initiative in the Pacific. Indeed, shortly after Midway, MacArthur suggested a direct amphibious assault, naturally under his command, against Rabaul. In late June 1942, King stepped in and secured the approval from the Joint Chiefs to begin his gradual advance to Rabaul via the southern Solomons. Ghormley, the new ComSoPac, assumed direct control of Operation Watchtower. These days, with such massive logistical efforts as Operation Desert Storm, it is hard to imagine how quickly the United States improvised and unleashed its first amphibious offensive of World War II. From 23 June, when King first alerted Nimitz, only forty-five days elapsed until 7 August when Marines stormed ashore on distant Tulagi and Guadalcanal, 3,500 miles southwest of Pearl Harbor. The Japanese responded more violently than either King or Nimitz expected. For the next five months, it became a race between Japan and the Allies to rush more ships, aircraft, and troops to eject the other from Guadalcanal.

Although King conceived the Guadalcanal offensive, Nimitz swiftly became its champion and did everything he could to support SoPac and build morale. A message on 25 August to Ghormley and Fletcher typified Nimitz's attitude throughout the long campaign: "Realize situation still critical but exchange of damage to date seems to be in our favor." On 1 September, he urged King: "Let's give Guadalcanal the wherewithal to live up to its name. Something for the Japs to remember forever."[32] Nimitz's visit on 30 September to Guadalcanal, a rare inspection by a commander-in-chief in a direct combat zone, provided him invaluable personal insight and ultimately led to the relief of the unfortunate Ghormley on 16 October. Halsey swiftly revitalized SoPac and very likely saved Guadalcanal. Cheered by the sentiments expressed in Halsey's first personal letter as ComSoPac, Nimitz wrote in the margin: "That is the spirit desired."[33] By December, victory at Guadalcanal was in sight, although the Japanese finally evacuated the island on 8 February 1943.

Like Midway, Guadalcanal provided another watershed of the Pacific War. Thereafter, enjoying increasing superiority in men and material, the Allies went irrevocably on the offensive. After 1942, Nimitz ran a Pacific Fleet whose numbers and combat power seemed to grow in geometric progression, along with the attendant problems in administering such a vast armada. Nimitz's management skills came to the fore, and Pacific Fleet/Pacific Ocean Areas became probably the most efficient wartime organization of its size and complexity. He put great store in cooperation between different branches of the Navy and Marine Corps and between the services themselves. His treatment of the Army troops under his command was always friendly and fair, and he worked hard to prevent or mitigate interservice disputes.[34]

Probably Nimitz's biggest row within the Pacific Fleet was with his naval aviators, personified by Vice Admiral John H. Towers (Naval Aviator No. 3), who became Commander, Air Force, Pacific Fleet, in October 1942. Obviously, carrier airpower had become central to the offensive mission of the Pacific Fleet; with full justification, the air admirals felt that they and not nonaviators should lead carrier task forces. They also campaigned to exclude nonaviators automatically from the top echelons of naval command, however, something that Nimitz would not tolerate. He brokered a series of compromises to see that the aviation viewpoint always would be represented. In 1944, Towers, a superb administrator who hankered for combat command, became Deputy CinCPac. Despite Nimitz's personal dislike of the ambitious Towers, the two worked together effectively.

Unlike his overbearing and devious neighbor MacArthur, Nimitz did not consider himself a prime initiator of strategy in the Pacific. That role he left to his irascible but astute superior, Admiral King, who hammered out policy with his colleagues on the Joint Chiefs of Staff. Once a plan was proposed, however, Nimitz gave it the closest scrutiny and did not hesitate to offer his informed opinion. He encouraged his subordinates to come forward with their ideas and particularly valued the keen insights of Raymond Spruance, one of the victors of Midway and his chief of staff in 1942–43; Captain Forrest P. Sherman, his war plans officer; and Rear Admiral Charles H. McMorris, Spruance's successor as chief of staff.

By late 1943, two general axes of advance had evolved to project Allied forces through the maze of Pacific strongholds to the vital centers of Japanese power. The first was the southern route, begun by SoPac in the Solomons and SWPA in Papua to capture or, at least, neutralize Rabaul. MacArthur extended it westward along the north coast of New Guinea toward the Philippines, his predominant goal. To his chagrin, he had to depend on Nimitz for the loan of naval support whenever he desired to leap forward.

Rather than get bogged down in the Solomons and New Guinea, King resurrected the traditional Navy concept of a Central Pacific offensive, which Nimitz placed under the command of Spruance, the subordinate whom he most respected and trusted. Fearing the Marshalls might be too strong as yet, Nimitz recommended the Gilbert Islands as the first objective. Spruance swiftly conquered the Gilberts in November 1943, despite suffering great losses at Tarawa. In December, he and the other planners recommended a cautious advance toward Kwajalein Atoll in the Marshalls. However, in one of the rare instances when Nimitz completely overruled his strategic brain trust, he ordered a direct and much earlier assault on Kwajalein. The ease in which Kwajalein fell in February 1944, one of the model amphibious operations of the war, vindicated CinCPac's judgment.[35]

Throughout 1944, debate raged among Washington, Pearl Harbor, and Australia as to the precise courses that the two Pacific offensives would take. To King's exasperation, Nimitz did not follow in lockstep his strategic proposals but kept an open mind and recommended what he thought was best. In early 1944, the way through Truk Atoll in the Carolines to the Philippines looked most attractive to Nimitz as the goal of the Central Pacific drive, but King persuaded him of the value of bypassing Truk and capturing the Marianas, both to threaten Japan directly and to isolate the many enemy-held islands south of there. King's desire to seize the Marianas coincided, for once, with the wishes of Joint Chiefs rival General Henry H. ("Hap") Arnold, head of the U.S. Army Air Forces, who needed bases for his huge Boeing B-29 heavy bombers to strike Japan. To Arnold, the Marianas became vital after efforts to base B-29s in China ran into trouble. On 15 June, Admiral Spruance's Fifth Fleet invaded Saipan and inflicted a devastating defeat on the Japanese fleet in the Battle of the Philippine Sea (19–20 June 1944). The Japanese defeat in the Marianas brought down Premier Hideki Tojo's government.

King wanted to jump northwest from the Marianas all the way to Formosa (now Taiwan) to cut off Japan from its southern resources and facilitate a foothold on the Chinese mainland. He hoped to substitute Formosa for MacArthur's long-bruited return to Luzon in the Philippines but lost out in July when the President decided in favor of MacArthur. For his own part, Nimitz had accepted the inevitability of MacArthur's Philippine crusade and instead urged King to accept a proposal by Spruance to capture two islands on the direct approach to Japan: Iwo Jima in the Bonin Islands and Okinawa in the Ryukyu Islands. Nimitz recognized the value of Iwo Jima as a fighter base to support the Army Air Force bombing offensive against Japan, and the capture of Okinawa would open the way for the assault on Kyushu, southernmost of the Japanese home islands. With King's concurrence, the way to final victory in the Pacific was open.

On 15 October, MacArthur's forces, supported by most of the Pacific Fleet, landed at Leyte in the Central Philippines. Blurred command responsibilities marred victory in the Battle of Leyte Gulf (24–26 October 1944), the biggest naval engagement in history and the one that finally crushed Japanese sea power. The Japanese responded with kamikaze (suicide) air attacks that presented the gravest threat to the Pacific Fleet since Guadalcanal. MacArthur's Luzon campaign began on 8 January 1945, and reconquering the vast Philippine archipelago kept him busy for the rest of the war.

In December 1944, Leahy, now chairman of the Joint Chiefs, King, and Nimitz were elevated to the new rank of Admiral of the Fleet (fleet admiral), with five stars like their General of the Army counterparts. To get closer to the action, Nimitz moved his headquarters to Guam in January 1945. Two of the bloodiest campaigns of the war followed shortly thereafter: Iwo Jima (16 February–26 March 1945) and the Okinawa Gunto (24 March–30 June 1945). Parked for months off Okinawa as Lieutenant General Simon B. Buckner's Tenth Army slowly advanced through the island's intricate defenses, Spruance's Fifth Fleet suffered under a blizzard of kamikazes. Worries about his fleet drew an unusually harsh reaction from Nimitz, who told Buckner on 23 April: "I'm losing a ship and a half a day. So if this line isn't moving within five days, we'll get someone here to move it so we can all get out from under these stupid air attacks."[36]

With the fall of Okinawa, planning proceeded apace for the direct invasion of Japan—Kyushu possibly in late 1945 and Honshu the next year. Nimitz thought (or at least hoped) that invasion would not be necessary. Army heavy bombers from the Marianas were incinerating Japan's cities and industry. Submarines, carrier strikes, and aerial mines had destroyed her merchant marine. Finally, on 15 August, after the agony of two atomic bombs, Japan sued for peace. On 2 September 1945, Nimitz joined MacArthur on the deck of the battleship *Missouri* to accept the unconditional surrender of Japan. No single other person did more than Fleet Admiral Nimitz to ensure final victory in the Pacific.

Nimitz had long aspired to become Chief of Naval Operations, which King had held concurrently with his job of CominCh. Now with King's impending retirement, the way seemed open except for the reluctance of Secretary of the Navy James V. Forrestal, who was wrestling with the question of service unification. Nevertheless, with President Harry S Truman's support, Nimitz became CNO on 15 December 1945. Originally a supporter of limited unification, mainly because it worked so well in the Pacific Ocean Areas, Nimitz backed off when he realized how the mission and best interests of the Navy would suffer at the hands of an executive who clearly was biased toward either the Army or the new independent Air Force about to be created. Along with Forrestal, who became the first Secretary of Defense in 1947, he tried to mitigate the effects of unification on the Navy. Nimitz defined sea power's vital role in the postwar age and forcefully denied the claims of the strategic airpower enthusiasts that the Navy should not exercise an offensive capability, either in the air or afloat.[37]

On 15 December 1947, Nimitz resigned upon completing his two-year term as Chief of Naval Operations. By law, as a fleet admiral, he remained on the active list. After serving with the United Nations as a plebiscite administrator for Kashmir and as a roving goodwill ambassador, he withdrew to private life. He died on 20 February 1966, just four days short of his eighty-first birthday. Fleet Admiral Chester W. Nimitz was the last officer of the United States Navy ever to wear the broad sleeve band and four stripes of his rank. This is fitting because no one will ever command a fleet as large, and, in this author's opinion, as fine as the Pacific Fleet of 1941–45.

FURTHER READING

The papers of Fleet Admiral Nimitz are in the Naval Historical Center in Washington, D.C., which also holds, among many other vital documents such as action reports and the "CINCPAC Greybook," a war diary kept by the War Plans Section on the CinCPac staff. The CinCPac Secret and Confidential Message File 1941–45 is on microfilm in Record Group 38 of the National Archives. Throughout his life, Nimitz hoped to avoid controversy and kept his personal opinions to himself. During World War II, he wrote daily to his wife Catherine, but only a few of these letters have been preserved. He was adamantly opposed to writing a memoir, but did act as an associate editor to a naval history textbook, E. B. Potter, Sea Power (Englewood Cliffs, N.J., 1960), a role that he took seriously and in which he offered suggestions to ensure proper assessment of the roles played by naval officers in the Pacific. The chapters dealing with World War II were also separately published as The Great Sea War: Story of Naval Action in World War II (Englewood Cliffs, N.J., 1960).

The best biography of Nimitz and an indispensable source on his life is E. B. Potter's Nimitz (Annapolis, Md., 1976). Memoirs by close associates of Nimitz include: Fleet Admiral Ernest J. King and Commander Walter Muir Whitehill, Fleet Admiral King: A Naval Record (New York, 1952); Fleet Admiral William F. Halsey and J. Bryan III, Admiral Halsey's Story (New York, 1947); Rear Admiral Edwin T. Layton, with Roger Pineau and John Costello, "And I Was There," (New York, 1985); Admiral James O. Richardson, On the Treadmill to Pearl Harbor: Memoirs of Admiral J. O. Richardson (Washington, D.C., 1973); and Vice Admiral George C. Dyer, The Amphibians Came to Conquer: The Story of Admiral Richmond Kelly Turner, 2 vols. (Washington, D.C.,

1971). Also extremely useful are four biographies of naval officers: Thomas B. Buell, *The Quiet Warrior: A Biography of Admiral Raymond A. Spruance* (Boston, 1974), and *Master of Sea Power: A Biography of Fleet Admiral Ernest J. King* (Boston, 1980); E. B. Potter, *Bull Halsey* (Annapolis, Md., 1985); and Clark G. Reynolds, *Admiral John H. Towers: The Struggle for Naval Air Supremacy* (Annapolis, Md., 1991). Robert W. Love, Jr., *Chiefs of Naval Operations* (Annapolis, Md., 1980) offers biographical sketches of the CNOs, including Nimitz.

Literature on World War II in the Pacific is vast, but the starting point is Samuel Eliot Morison, *History of United States Naval Operations in World War II*, 15 vols. (Boston, 1947–60). Two general histories are John Costello, *The Pacific War* (New York, 1981), and Ronald H. Spector, *Eagle against the Sun: The American War with Japan* (New York, 1985). Indispensable for understanding strategy is a once-classified study by Grace Person Hayes, *The History of the Joint Chiefs of Staff in World War II: The War against Japan* (Annapolis, Md., 1982).

The interpretation given here of Nimitz's strategy for the Battles of Coral Sea and Midway is based on this author's book, *The First South Pacific Campaign: Pacific Fleet Strategy December 1941–June 1942* (Annapolis, Md., 1976). For carrier operations in general in early 1942, see also John B. Lundstrom, *The First Team: Pacific Naval Air Combat from Pearl Harbor to Midway* (Annapolis, Md., 1990). The best accounts of the Battle of Midway are Walter Lord's classic *Incredible Victory* (New York, 1967) and Robert J. Cressman, ed., *"A Glorious Page in Our History": The Battle of Midway 4–6 June 1942* (Missoula, Mont., 1990). Richard B. Frank's *Guadalcanal* (New York, 1990) is indispensable for that campaign. Among the studies of later campaigns, Thomas J. Cutler's *The Battle of Leyte Gulf, 23–26 October 1944* (New York, 1994) stands out.

NOTES

1. E. B. Potter, *Nimitz* (Annapolis, Md., 1976), 91–92.

2. Clark G. Reynolds, *Famous American Admirals* (New York, 1978), 238.

3. Potter, *Nimitz*, 61–62.

4. Thomas Wildenberg, "Chester Nimitz and the Development of Fueling at Sea," *Naval War College Review* 46 (Autumn 1993): 52–62.

5. Potter, *Nimitz*, 130.

6. Paul Stillwell, *Battleship Arizona: An Illustrated History* (Annapolis, Md., 1991), 198–201.

7. James O. Richardson, *On the Treadmill to Pearl Harbor: Memoirs of Admiral J. O. Richardson* (Washington, D.C., 1973), 208.

8. Kimmel to Stark, 15 December 1941, cited in Robert J. Cressman, "A Magnificent Fight": *The Battle for Wake Island* (Annapolis, Md., 1995), 157.

9. Quoted in Potter, *Nimitz*, 9.

10. Thomas B. Buell, *Master of Sea Power: A Biography of Fleet Admiral Ernest J. King* (Boston, 1980), 197.

11. For the carriers in December 1941, see John B. Lundstrom, *The First Team: Pacific Naval Air Combat from Pearl Harbor to Midway* (Annapolis, Md., 1990), 47–48.

12. "CINCPAC Greybook," 21 January 1942, Record Group (RG) 38, National Archives; also, "Estimates of the Situation," 22 April 1942 and 26 May 1942 contained therein.

13. CominCh to CinCPac, message 301740, December 1941, in "CINCPAC Greybook," 121.

14. "Brief Estimate of the Situation," 5 February 1942, in "CINCPAC Greybook."

15. Vice Admiral Wilson Brown, "From Sail to Carrier Task Force," Wilson Brown Papers, Nimitz Library, U.S. Naval Academy, unpublished memoir, 12.

16. "CINCPAC Greybook," 21 February 1942.

17. Quoted in Potter, *Nimitz*, 47.

18. Lundstrom, *First Team*, 122–32.

19. Grace Person Hayes, *The History of the Joint Chiefs of Staff in World War II: The War against Japan* (Annapolis, Md., 1982), 96–103.

20. John B. Lundstrom, *The First South Pacific Campaign: Pacific Fleet Strategy December 1941–June 1942* (Annapolis, Md., 1976), 77–86.

21. "Estimate of the Situation," 22 April 1942, in "CINCPAC Greybook."

22. For a detailed account of the Battle of the Coral Sea, see Lundstrom, *First Team*, 167–282.

23. Lundstrom, *First South Pacific Campaign*, 137–40.

24. CominCh to CinCPac, Message 121950, May 1942, in "CINCPAC Greybook," 464.

25. Lundstrom, *First South Pacific Campaign*, 153–61; CinCPac to CominCh, Message 170407, May 1942, in "CINCPAC Greybook," 490.

26. Clark G. Reynolds, "The U.S. Fleet-in-Being Strategy of 1942," *The Journal of Military History* 58, no. 1 (January 1994): 103–18.

27. CominCh to CinCPac, Message 172200, May 1942, in "CINCPAC Greybook," 489–90.

28. "Estimate of the Situation," 26 May 1942, in "CINCPAC Greybook."

29. Nimitz to King, 29 May 1942, in Correspondence of FADM Nimitz with FADM King, Nimitz Papers, Naval Historical Center (hereafter cited as Nimitz Papers).

30. The best accounts of Midway are in Walter Lord, *Incredible Victory* (New York, 1976), and Robert J. Cressman, ed., *"A Glorious Page in Our History": The Battle of Midway 4–6 June 1942* (Missoula, Mont., 1990).

31. Edwin T. Layton, with Roger Pineau and John Costello, *"And I Was There"* (New York, 1985), 464–69.

32. CinCPac to ComSoPac, CTF-61, Message 242125, August 1942, and CinCPac to CominCh, Message 012331, September 1942, both in CINCPAC Secret and Confidential Message File, RG 38, National Archives.

33. Halsey to Nimitz, 31 October 1942, in Correspondence of FADM Nimitz with Commander, South Pacific, Nimitz Papers.

34. For an example, see Harry A. Gailey, *"Howlin' Mad" vs. The Army: Conflict in Command Saipan 1944* (Novato, Calif., 1986), 233–35.

35. Potter, *Nimitz*, 265–66; George C. Dyer, *The Amphibians Came to Conquer: The Story of Admiral Richmond Kelly Turner* (Washington, D.C., 1971), 2:738–42.

36. Quoted in Potter, *Nimitz*, 375.

37. See Jeffrey G. Barlow, *Revolt of the Admirals: The Fight for Naval Aviation, 1945–1950* (Washington, D.C., 1994), for a recent account of Nimitz's role in defending naval aviation.

# ☆ William F. Halsey
☆
☆ "To Find a Fight"

*by John F. Wukovits*

FROM THE MOMENT OF HIS BIRTH IN ELIZABETH, NEW JERSEY, ON October 30, 1882, William Frederick Halsey, Jr.'s life was dominated by the U.S. Navy. Seafaring men dotted the family tree, from Captain John Halsey, who attacked French shipping as an English privateer in Queen Anne's War (1703–13), to his own father, William Frederick Halsey, who graduated from the Naval Academy in 1873.

Thus, it was hardly any surprise when he decided to apply for admission to the Naval Academy in 1900. What distinguished Halsey was the determination that he exhibited to get there. Because the Navy constantly shuffled his father from post to post, the family had no permanent address, which made it more difficult for Halsey to receive an appointment. Rather than bemoan the fact, he immediately started writing letters to anyone who might help, including one plea directed to President William McKinley.

His grit paid dividends, and Halsey eventually graduated forty-third of the sixty-two students in the class of 1904. Although he did not exactly light up the academic world with his intellect, Halsey's pugnacious demeanor showed up both in sports, where he played for the football team, and in the social arena, where his friendly nature and zest for life made him a welcome figure.

After graduating from the Academy, Halsey spent most of his early career on board destroyers, where he earned a solid reputation as a commander. Instead of remaining in that area, however, he gravitated toward the newer branch of aviation. Though not the type to analyze any topic in depth—a tendency displayed throughout his career—Halsey inched toward aviation because he instinctively realized its potential. Hunches and gut feelings, not disciplined study, guided him in this and other key moments of his life.

While serving at the Naval Academy in the late 1920s, Halsey learned the rudiments of flying. He successfully completed the aviation observer's course in the mid-1930s before receiving command of the aircraft carrier *Saratoga*. By 1940, Halsey had risen to the post that he held when Japan hit Pearl Harbor, Commander, Aircraft, Battle Force, in which he shouldered responsibility for all aircraft carriers and their air groups operating in the Pacific.

Halsey's World War II service can be split into two distinctive segments, each containing its own flavor and carrying vastly different impacts. It is almost as though two separate Halseys existed, one for the years 1941–43 and the other for 1944–45. Although the latter segment brought controversy and bitterness, Halsey's words and deeds in the first portion guarantee his place among great naval leaders.

Fortunately for the U.S. Navy, Halsey and his flagship, the carrier *Enterprise*, were 150 miles out at sea when Japanese bombs poured down on Pearl Harbor. Typically, he immediately veered his unit north in a desperate attempt to locate the enemy and disregarded the fact that the Japanese might be vastly superior in numbers and destructiveness. His instincts told him to chase after the enemy, so he did. Years later, he wrote that no matter what one might say about him, "I have the consolation of knowing that, on the opening day of the war, I did everything in my power to find a fight."[1]

Those words—"to find a fight"—characterized Halsey's temperament over the war's four years. He was always ready to do battle. That pugnaciousness lifted him to hero status in the war's early going, then almost plummeted him to villain's role as the war progressed.

When Halsey guided his task force back to Pearl Harbor and received his first look at the damage, he shook in anger, especially when he saw the battleship *Utah*, sunk bottom up at her berth—"the berth the *Enterprise* would have occupied if we had not been delayed." Gazing at the incredible destruction about him, Halsey muttered, "Before we're through with 'em, the Japanese language will be spoken only in hell!"[2]

This was the first of Halsey's numerous wartime utterances that solidified his image as the "Bull" and helped to boost morale. In desperate times, people need someone who can look into the future and promise a better day. It does not matter whether or not the person's statement is true, but only that the words are said by someone in a position of authority and people believe that the person can follow through. Halsey's words helped the American public to maintain hope.

In the months following Pearl Harbor, Japanese forces overran every Pacific objective, most with ease. Guam and Wake Island fell. Hong Kong was subjugated. In the Philippines, Bataan and Corregidor succumbed. From the ashes of Allied defeat rose the image of a Japanese superman that could not be

corraled. Americans began to doubt their nation's ability to hold off the enemy. They needed someone to turn that attitude around. As the American spirit slumped after each successive blow by the Japanese, Halsey was there to pick
it right up with his bold words.

Sooner or later, however, words alone do not suffice. Action, symbolic or
real, is needed. In the weeks following Pearl Harbor, Americans began asking
why the U.S. Navy had not struck back at the Japanese. Correspondent Robert
J. Casey wrote at the time, "We began to feel as the dismal weeks piled up in
Honolulu that if the Navy ever got around to do anything in this war we were
going to be pleasantly surprised." Even "Tokyo Rose" taunted the Americans
by asking in her propaganda broadcasts from Japan, "Where, oh where, is the
United States Navy?"[3]

Halsey's February 1942 carrier raids on Kwajalein, Roi, and Jaluit in the Marshalls provided the answer. Although his aircraft did little real damage to Japanese installations, they gave people back home something to point to and thereby reassure themselves that the Navy was indeed guarding the gates. For his
role in these raids, Halsey received the Distinguished Service Medal from
President Franklin D. Roosevelt and acclaim back home as a fighter.

Halsey added to his luster two months later when his aircraft carriers transported Colonel James H. Doolittle's sixteen B-25 bombers within 600–700
miles of Japan and launched them on their dramatic bombing raid of Tokyo.
Again, little actual damage was done, but the raid electrified disheartened civilians back home and provided a taste of vengeance for Pearl Harbor.

The February air raids and the Doolittle bombing run propelled Halsey to
the forefront of American naval commanders in the eyes of Americans eager
for a hero. While many naval commanders were embroiled in controversy over
military disasters, Halsey reaped headlines for his offensive thrusts against the
hated Japanese. Rather than excuses, he delivered aggression.

If America needed a hero, Halsey was the perfect man for the job: he loved
the limelight, he carried the ideal nickname of "Bull," and he preferred to fight
first and think later. He seemed made for this phase of the Pacific conflict, a
time when bold actions and brash words carried more import than carefully
designed plans.

On top of that, he told the public exactly what it was thinking and what it
wanted to hear: the world existed only in black and white, good and bad, and
the United States represented the good. When he vented, as he frequently did,
that "the only good Jap is a Jap who's been dead six months,"[4] millions of heads
back home nodded in assent. Mothers and fathers of America's youth, who would
soon be placing their lives on the line to win the war, enthusiastically agreed with
Halsey's words that his main job was to "kill Japs, kill Japs, kill more Japs."[5]

Halsey perfected the "sound bite" years before that term came into use. He knew what words the public and his men wanted to hear, and he offered them in short, stirring phrases issued without ambiguity—he would strike at the hated Japanese and restore order to the Pacific. In building this image, however necessary that it was in 1942–43, that Halsey always could be counted on to chase after the enemy, he created a trap into which he would eventually tumble. The public and his men expected him to charge; therefore, he would. But, that would come later. In 1942–43, Halsey filled the hero's role so sorely demanded. Another Pacific war correspondent, Clark Lee, wrote as much in those dark, early days of the conflict. Halsey "was all the United States Navy needed," Lee stated. "It needed the confidence that comes with knowledge that you are attacking and not retreating; fighting aggressively instead of defensively."[6]

Halsey missed the next two Pacific naval encounters. When the Japanese built up their forces in the Southwest Pacific for a planned invasion of Port Moresby, New Guinea, north of Australia, Admiral Chester W. Nimitz, Commander-in-Chief, Pacific Fleet, ordered Halsey to meet with American naval units in the Coral Sea to counter the enemy. Because he had been in the North Pacific with Doolittle, however, Halsey was unable to reach the Coral Sea before the battle, which was the first major clash of opposing aircraft carriers in naval warfare.

If Halsey felt disappointment over missing the Battle of the Coral Sea, that word cannot begin to describe his feelings about his absence during the next contest—the epic carrier duel off Midway Island. After arriving in the South Pacific, he had developed a horrendous skin rash from the combination of heat, humidity, and stress. He resorted to trying oatmeal baths to reduce the itching, but nothing worked. He quickly lost twenty pounds and felt fortunate to get two decent hours of sleep at night. When he returned to Pearl Harbor to be briefed on an upcoming Japanese advance toward Midway, Nimitz sent him into the hospital for treatment.

Still chagrined about the Battle of the Coral Sea, Halsey watched from his hospital bed, where he lay covered with soothing ointment, as Admiral Raymond A. Spruance took the American carriers to sea. In early June, Spruance's aviators sank four Japanese carriers in a crucial struggle that turned the war in favor of the United States.

Though elated over the victory, Halsey was crushed to have missed the action. His ships, his men, and his aircraft carried the day off Midway while he was on the sidelines. "Instead of being allowed to fight it—and I would have been senior officer present—I was sent to the hospital." Halsey later labeled this "the most grievous disappointment in my career." His only consolation came in knowing that much fighting yet lay ahead. Certainly, he would get his crack at Japanese carriers—and when he did, he would be ready.[7]

Although he had missed out on Midway, Halsey still basked in the adulation of home-front civilians. Fortunately for Halsey's image, Spruance, who is called the "quiet warrior" by his biographer, Thomas B. Buell, cared little for public acclaim, even though he had won a momentous battle. Some commanders would have eagerly tried to grab a portion of the spotlight from Halsey, but Spruance was content with knowing that he had performed his duty. As a result, Halsey's star was in no way eclipsed by Spruance's victory. He remained the fighting admiral, the naval commander whom most people expected to take up the charge.

After a trip to Richmond, Virginia, for further treatment of his dermatitis, Halsey finally left Johnston-Willis Hospital on August 5. Later that month, he gave an illuminating speech at the Naval Academy. He let his fellow Americans know that he was back and raring to fight: "Missing the Battle of Midway has been the greatest disappointment of my life, but I am going back to the Pacific where I intend personally to have a crack at those yellow-bellied sons of bitches and their carriers."[8]

It was significant that, not only did he again employ words about the enemy that he knew his countrymen loved to hear, he also referred to its carriers. Those ships would dominate much of his thinking during the next few years.

Halsey flew to Pearl Harbor the next month. On September 22, at an award ceremony on board the damaged *Saratoga* in Pearl Harbor, Nimitz announced Halsey's return. "Boys," he told the assembled crew, "I've got a surprise for you. Bill Halsey's back!" The resultant cheers delighted Halsey, who was just as eager to get back to combat as the men were for him to be there.[9]

While Halsey was still in the states, U.S. Marines had landed on Tulagi and Guadalcanal, two islands in the Solomon chain northeast of Australia, to block Japanese construction of an airfield from which planes could threaten the vital supply lines from the United States to Australia. Although news of the offensive boosted home-front morale, the operation quickly bogged down in a series of disasters. During the battle of Savo Island, the Japanese sank four Allied heavy cruisers, damaged three other ships, and inflicted one thousand casualties in what became the worst defeat at sea ever suffered by the U.S. Navy. Vice Admiral Frank Jack Fletcher, commander of the expeditionary force, withdrew his carriers to the southeast to avoid further loss. Without protection from the carriers, Rear Admiral Richmond Kelly Turner, commander of amphibious forces, felt compelled to pull his transports out of Guadalcanal before they had put all of the supplies ashore. As a result, sixteen thousand Marines were stranded on Guadalcanal with inadequate supplies, insufficient naval support, and increasing bitterness. The fighting in the Solomons bogged down to a nip-and-tuck struggle for control of Guadalcanal and its precious airfield site.

Near the end of September, Nimitz flew on an inspection trip to the

Nouméa, New Caledonia, headquarters of Rear Admiral Robert Lee Ghormley, Commander, South Pacific Forces. He found a dispirited staff, exhausted commander, indecision, and defeatism. Correspondent Lee interviewed naval officers at this time and concluded that "some of our officers thought only of NOT [capitals are Lee's] losing more ships, and it was in that mood that we undertook our early operations in the Solomons." When Nimitz asked General Alexander A. Vandegrift, U.S. Marine commander on Guadalcanal, to list the problems he faced, Vandegrift bluntly replied, "Out here too many commanders have been far too leery about risking their ships."[10]

Nimitz decided to relieve Ghormley and name Halsey as his replacement. When Halsey learned of his new post, he exclaimed, "Jesus Christ and General Jackson! This is the hottest potato they ever handed me!"[11]

The effect, both at home and on the troops ashore, was electrifying. A Marine officer on Guadalcanal gushed, "I'll never forget it! One minute we were too limp with malaria to crawl out of our foxholes; the next we were running around whooping like kids."[12] A *New York Times* headline declared, "Shift to Offensive Is Seen in Selection of 'Fighting' Admiral Halsey as Commander in the South Pacific."[13]

Halsey lived up to expectations. In answer to a reporter's query about his strategy for Guadalcanal, he characteristically blustered, "Kill Japs, kill Japs, and keep on killing Japs," precisely the words that the weary Marines longed to hear. He promised Vandegrift that he would immediately send every available ship, supply, and man he could spare. He flew to Guadalcanal for a personal inspection; according to Vandegrift, this was "like a wonderful breath of fresh air."[14]

Most important, Halsey's combativeness permeated the men under him and led to a new spirit. As *Time* magazine reported in a cover story on Halsey in late November, instead of timorously striking at the Japanese and then pulling back, Halsey's Navy "came in slugging again and yet again" and tried to live up to Bull's battle cry of, "Hit hard, hit fast, hit often." This led to a series of engagements with the enemy that culminated in the momentous Battle of Guadalcanal in mid-November, which caused Japan to abandon its intention of reinforcing the island. Under Halsey's aggressive guidance, American aviators transformed the skies over the Solomons into a vast battlefield. In a series of determined assaults, they removed one of Japan's most heralded advantages—its core of expert aviators. Lacking adequate replacement pilots, Japanese airpower rarely posed a significant threat from the spring of 1943 until the introduction of the kamikaze attacks in late 1944.[15]

Once again, Halsey had been thrust into the limelight as a battler, as the man who, according to *Time*, "saved Guadalcanal." When the nation most needed its knight in shining armor, both in words and in deeds, Halsey rode in. Added to his previous exploits, Halsey attained a level of adulation that no other American naval commander could approach. In recognition of his outstanding performance during 1941–42, which alone guarantees that his name will forever reside with those of history's other great naval commanders, Halsey was promoted to full admiral. Only one nagging aspect plagued the hero— would he get a crack at Japanese carriers?

By the end of 1943, American forces under Halsey had driven the Japanese up the Solomon chain to Bougainville and had begun bombing the immense enemy installations at Rabaul on New Britain. By seizing Bougainville, the Americans acquired airfields to use in keeping Rabaul in check through air attacks, which might preclude the need to take it with a bloody assault. Instead of worrying about what the enemy would do and trying to prevent more territory from falling into Japanese hands, American forces could now switch to the offensive.

For two years, Halsey had stepped to the vanguard and injected boldness and purpose where little had existed. With Allied forces reeling in disaster and people clamoring for action, Halsey had thrown both vitriolic words and daring deeds at the Japanese.

Now, however, the Pacific war was entering a new phase less suited to his talents—an organizational war. American factories were sending a gigantic flow of ships, weapons, and supplies to the Pacific. Instead of desperation tactics that called for throwing at the enemy whatever was available, a planned approach was now required to achieve maximum utilization of hundreds of ships and aircraft. Halsey best loved fighting when his back was to the wall and he could rely on gut instinct. Careful thought and detailed planning were not his forte.

The manner in which the Pacific Fleet was divided illustrates this point. By the first half of 1944, with so much war material flowing out of American factories, the fleet had been divided into three commands designated the Third, Fifth, and Seventh Fleets. As the Seventh Fleet supported General Douglas MacArthur's offensive operations in the Southwest Pacific, Halsey's Third Fleet and Spruance's Fifth Fleet—in effect, the same ships under separate commands—would alternate operations in the Central Pacific drive for maximal employment. While Spruance was at sea with the ships, Halsey would plan his next operation and vice versa.

Although the Pacific war had solidified into a more rigid system, Halsey intended to operate his carriers in the same bold manner as he had during the desperate days of 1942. "I believe in violating the rules," he boasted. "We violate them every day. We do the unexpected. . . . But, most important, whatever we do—we do fast!"[16]

This was not the most effective way to command a fleet in 1944. Some officers griped that Halsey's tendency to act first and think later caused problems, especially when they compared his system to the organized conditions under Spruance. One officer mentioned that, working for Halsey, "you never knew what you were going to do in the next five minutes or how you were going to do it." Another added, "My feeling was one of confidence when Spruance was there and one of concern when Halsey was there." Even the Japanese unfavorably compared Halsey to Spruance. Captain Yasuji Watanabe, a staff officer for Admiral Isoroku Yamamoto, claimed that Spruance possessed an "air admiral's best character—strong, straight thinker, not impulsive fluctuating thinker."[17]

The situation was more apt to produce mistakes when one remembers Halsey's intense desire to battle with the enemy, carrier for carrier. Many of his contemporaries and even some subordinates had had their cracks at carrier duels. Halsey, the name that most Americans thought of when the word "fighter" came to mind, wanted his chance before the war ended.

An apparent chance for Halsey brewed east of the Philippine Islands in October 1944, when Halsey's Third Fleet supported other naval units involved in MacArthur's landings at Leyte. According to Operation Plan 8-44 from Nimitz's headquarters, Halsey's prime duty was to keep enemy air and naval forces away from Vice Admiral Thomas C. Kinkaid's Seventh Fleet, a conglomeration of more than seven hundred ships that would land MacArthur's troops and supplies and launch supporting missions from its eighteen small escort carriers.

There was nothing unusual in this setup. Standard assault procedure stipulated that, while one arm of the Navy landed troops and supplies, another arm shielded them from the Japanese. Nimitz, however, added a directive telling Halsey that if the Japanese fleet appeared and Halsey believed he could inflict serious damage to the enemy, "such destruction becomes the primary task" for his ships.[18]

This extra directive created havoc during a crucial portion of the upcoming battle. Although Nimitz did not intend that Halsey should completely abandon Kinkaid by removing all of his forces to go after the enemy fleet, the directive gave Halsey free rein to do precisely that. A more cautious commander might have juggled the two duties correctly, but, for an impetuous commander such as Halsey, who was eager to take on Japanese carriers, it became a green light to do whatever he thought proper.

As his fleet entered the Philippine operation, Halsey was determined that, should enemy carriers appear, he would go after them. He was courting disaster here because he was inclined to mold events to a predetermined pattern instead of examining them for what they truly were and selecting the best option. Carriers, not the Leyte beachhead, occupied his mind.

Halsey needed prudence off Leyte Gulf that would permit him to be alert for enemy carriers while not forgetting his responsibility to the men and supplies pouring ashore. Prudence, however, did not take him within six hundred miles of Tokyo in early 1942, sweep the enemy out of the Solomons, or dictate the audacious statements that he had issued to a victory-starved nation. Prudence was the last thing on his mind in October 1944.

This is exactly what the Japanese counted on. Their complex plan, called SHO-1, unleashed four separate naval forces on the Philippines. Two arms would steam through Surigao Strait and attack MacArthur's forces from the south, while a third, the vastly powerful First Striking Force under Vice Admiral Takeo Kurita, dashed through San Bernardino Strait and struck from the north.

The key to the entire plan, however, rested with the fourth arm—the four aircraft carriers and supporting ships of Vice Admiral Jisaburo Ozawa's Northern Force. If Ozawa could lure Halsey's potent Third Fleet away from the Leyte Gulf area, the other three arms might succeed in disrupting MacArthur's landing operations. Knowing Halsey's penchant for aggressive action, the Japanese dangled four aircraft carriers as bait. The carriers contained little offensive capability because American carrier airpower had shorn the Japanese Imperial Navy of its air arm in a series of engagements, most notably the Battle of the Philippine Sea where Spruance, not Halsey, had again commanded U.S. forces. The Japanese hoped that the Americans were unaware of their shortage of aircraft and that the mere appearance of Japanese carriers would lure Halsey north.

The early stages of the encounter, known as the Battle of Leyte Gulf, appeared to swing Halsey's way when his aviators hammered Kurita's First Striking Force in the Sibuyan Sea west of Leyte in five air strikes on 24 October. Halsey's aviators sank the huge battleship *Musashi* and knocked out of the battle a heavy cruiser, which caused a shaken Kurita to reverse course and temporarily head away from Leyte Gulf. An emboldened Halsey, fresh from tasting an easy victory, was more eager than ever to search for enemy carriers.

That afternoon, he issued directives detailing what the Third Fleet would do if Japanese carriers approached. He first ordered his subordinates to be prepared to form Task Force 34 should it be needed. This force of battleships, cruisers, and destroyers would be left behind to block San Bernardino Strait's eastern exit and prevent Japanese forces from swooping down on Leyte Gulf. Halsey meant this directive as an alert to his commanders—the force would be formed when the occasion demanded. To ensure that they understood this point, he sent a second message to them via TBS (talk between ship) emphasizing it. Almost every naval commander from the Philippines to Pearl Harbor, including Nimitz and Kinkaid, had intercepted Halsey's first message about forming Task Force 34, even though it was not intended for anyone other than Halsey's subordinates. Unfortunately, the other commanders could not pick up Halsey's second message transmitted over the short-range TBS. They assumed from the intercepted message that Halsey had already formed and placed Task Force 34 off San Bernardino Strait.

Less than two hours after sending his directive, Halsey learned that a force of enemy carriers was approaching from the north. He paid lip service to proper procedure and discussed with his staff whether he should take the Third Fleet away from Leyte Gulf, but, in reality, he had made up his mind long before. Three options faced him: (1) he could remain on station off Leyte Gulf with his entire force, (2) he could leave Task Force 34 behind and attack Ozawa with the rest of his Third Fleet, or (3) he could take everything he had and hit Ozawa with his full might.

Halsey quickly discounted the first two options. Even if Kurita broke through the strait and into Leyte Gulf, Halsey believed that Kinkaid's escort carriers contained enough strength to deflect him because Kurita had been badly mauled by Halsey's earlier air strikes. His choice was to take the entire Third Fleet with him and pursue the enemy carriers.

Halsey's judgment was blinded by his desire to command in a carrier encounter. He saw what he wanted to see, not what was actually unfolding. It had been no secret that the enemy planned to use a decoy sometime soon; however, when two intelligence officers on Halsey's flagship tried to argue that Halsey was being lured away, no one listened. Halsey and his staff irritated Third Fleet commanders throughout the entire night of October 24–25 by rejecting or ignoring all their advice to leave a unit off San Bernardino Strait.

When so many high-ranking subordinates disagree with their commander's action, it means that either the commander sees something that none of the other men notice or the commander is making a huge mistake. Halsey fell into the latter category because he wanted a carrier engagement too much. He also had become trapped by his own publicity, cranked out early in the war, that he was the "Bull," the fighting admiral. Halsey, the leader whom most Americans associated with aggressiveness and carrier airpower, was not about to let this opportunity slip away. Faced with either guarding a static strait or attacking enemy carriers, Halsey never hesitated. He swung north with the entire Third Fleet.

Thus the door to Leyte Gulf lay wide open for Kurita's potent force. When the Japanese commander barreled down on the unsuspecting escort carriers of Taffy 3, the support force stationed just off Leyte Gulf, Rear Admiral Clifton A. F. Sprague, their commander, bellowed in exasperation, "That son-of-a-bitch Halsey has left us bare-assed!" He and Kinkaid then commenced a lengthy series of messages to Halsey that begged him for assistance.[19]

These pleas angered Halsey, who wondered why Kinkaid's search planes had not spotted Kurita earlier or why eighteen escort carriers could not hold off a damaged Kurita until help arrived from naval units to the south. His Third Fleet was drawing close to striking range of Ozawa, yet he had to worry about fellow commanders.

"Here I was on the brink of a critical battle, and my kid brother was yelling for help around the corner," Halsey mentioned later. He had forgotten, however, that protecting his kid brother was precisely his mission.[20]

Nimitz finally prodded Halsey into turning back to Leyte Gulf by sending a question about the location of Task Force 34. Nimitz hoped that the message would nudge Halsey into sending the task force south, but Halsey misinterpreted its meaning. With padding added to confuse Japanese interceptors, Nimitz's dispatch read, "Where is RPT where is Task Force Thirty-Four RR the world wonders." The final three words should have been removed by communicators on the *New Jersey*, but they were retained in case they were part of Nimitz's message. When Halsey received the note, he instantly took it as a reprimand and exploded in anger.

"I was stunned as if I had been struck in the face," Halsey later wrote. "The paper rattled in my hands. I snatched off my cap, threw it on the deck, and shouted something I am ashamed to remember." His chief of staff finally had to come over, grab Halsey, and remind him to pull himself together. Halsey ordered his ships south, although by now they could do little to help Sprague and Kinkaid because they stood 350 miles away. "I turned my back on the opportunity I had dreamed of since my days as a cadet," he later mourned.[21]

Halsey's heated reaction to Nimitz's message indicates not only the depth of his desire to command in battle against Japanese carriers but also his guilt, conscious or not, that he placed a higher priority on the carriers than on protecting Leyte Gulf. A clear conscience enables one to react calmly, but Halsey's bitter reaction underscores his uncertainty over the propriety of turning north.

Because of the stirring defense put up by a courageous Clifton Sprague and Taffy 3, Kurita eventually turned away before entering Leyte Gulf but not before Sprague had lost four ships and hundreds of men. Both Nimitz and Chief of Naval Operations Ernest J. King concluded that Halsey should have guarded San Bernardino Strait, but Nimitz had seen the destructive effects of a Navy controversy earlier in his career, and he stifled public criticism of Halsey. Nimitz wanted to avoid a rift that might split the Navy, and both he and King realized that Halsey was too popular among his own men and with the American public to remove him.

Halsey's error in the latter part of the war was thus swept under the rug because of his actions during the earlier war years. Halsey could have handled both tasks of guarding the strait and chasing Ozawa by simply leaving one part of his immense force off San Bernardino. While his detached ships destroyed Kurita's ships piecemeal as they exited the strait, he could have gone after Ozawa with the remainder of his Third Fleet.

As it was, Halsey's Third Fleet sank Ozawa's aircraft-shorn carriers at a cost of Taffy 3 lives and ships off Samar. Attacking carriers that were devoid of any airborne punch made little difference to the battle or progress of the war, but, in chasing after them, Halsey almost opened the door to disaster through a monumental error in judgment.

As at Midway, where the spotlight remained fixed on Halsey because the quiet Spruance disdained publicity, the public again acclaimed Halsey after Leyte Gulf because another commander remained silent. Taciturn by nature and carrying a deep affection for the Navy, Sprague would do nothing openly to humiliate his branch of service. He died in 1955 without breaking his silence about the chaos off Leyte Gulf, thereby guaranteeing not only harmony but that Halsey would continue to reap public adulation while his own role received little notice. Even fifty years after the battle, Clifton Sprague's name is known by few Americans.

An incident at Ulithi in the Palau Islands illustrates not only that Halsey felt deeply indebted to Sprague and Taffy 3 for saving his reputation but that he realized he had erred in leaving the strait wide open. In a letter meant only for his wife's eyes and not made available to historians until fifty years later, Sprague described a chance meeting with Halsey. Calling Halsey "the gentleman who failed to keep his appointment last October," Sprague wrote that Halsey walked up to him and said, "I didn't know whether you would speak to me or not." When Sprague replied that he bore no anger toward him, Halsey added, "I want you to know I think you wrote the most glorious page in American naval history that day."[22]

Unfortunately, Halsey did not add to his luster in the war's closing months. Twice, his Third Fleet was battered by typhoons that sank three ships, damaged more than forty others, destroyed 250 aircraft, and took the lives of almost eight hundred men—heavier losses than many commanders suffered in battle. Separate courts of inquiry placed the blame on Halsey, who made "errors in judgment under stress of war operations," and urged that he be relieved, but Nimitz and King, recognizing the damage to morale that might occur should the popular admiral be dismissed, kept him at his post.

After the Japanese surrendered on board Halsey's flagship in September 1945, the old warrior requested his retirement. Promoted to fleet admiral in December 1945, Halsey officially retired on 1 March 1947. Twelve years later, on 1 August 1959, he died of a heart attack. After his body lay in state in Washington National Cathedral in Washington, D.C., for two days, Halsey was buried with full military honors at Arlington National Cemetery on 21 August 1959.

In spite of his spotty 1944–45 record, Halsey deserves his lofty place among naval greats for the dramatic turnaround that he helped to engender in 1942–43. The Navy will always need Halseys, fearless leaders who act aggressively in desperate times and never fail to find a fight.

FURTHER READING

To achieve a basic understanding of Halsey, one should begin with E. B. Potter's fine biography, *Bull Halsey* (Annapolis, Md., 1985), and Halsey's autobiography, written with J. Bryan III, *Admiral Halsey's Story* (New York, 1947). Whereas the former is an objective portrayal produced by one of the Pacific war's premier historians, the latter must be read with caution, as Halsey understandably presented his side of every issue, particularly in dealing with Leyte Gulf. Important supplements of these two books are James M. Merrill's biographical essay of Halsey in Stephen Howarth, ed., *Men of War: Great Naval Leaders of World War II* (London, 1992), and the splendid material on Pacific naval commanders found in Eric Larrabee's valuable work, *Commander in Chief* (New York, 1987).

Halsey's performances in his various Pacific encounters can be located in numerous places, particularly Samuel Eliot Morison's volumes dealing with the Pacific in his *History of United States Naval Operations in World War II*, 15 vols. (Boston, 1947–60). For Halsey's contribution to the Doolittle raid, James H. Doolittle's autobiography, *I Could Never Be So Lucky Again* (New York, 1991), provides fascinating detail.

To receive a critical view of Halsey's actions at Leyte Gulf, one should consult Gerald E. Wheeler, *Kinkaid of the Seventh Fleet* (Washington, D.C., 1995); E. B. Potter, *Nimitz* (Annapolis, Md., 1976); and John F. Wukovits, *Devotion to Duty: A Biography of Admiral Clifton A. F. Sprague* (Annapolis, Md., 1995).

NOTES

1. William F. Halsey and J. Bryan III, *Admiral Halsey's Story* (New York, 1947), 80.
2. Ibid., 81.
3. Robert J. Casey, *Torpedo Junction* (New York, 1942), 34; John Toland, *But Not in Shame* (New York, 1961), 103.
4. Quoted in John W. Dower, *War without Mercy: Race and Power in the Pacific War* (New York, 1986), 79.
5. Quoted in ibid., 55.
6. Clark Lee, *They Call It Pacific* (New York, 1943), 358.
7. Halsey and Bryan, *Admiral Halsey's Story*, 106–07.
8. Quoted in E. B. Potter, *Bull Halsey* (Annapolis, Md., 1985), 150.
9. Ibid., 155.
10. Lee, *They Call It Pacific*, 324; Vandegrift quoted in Potter, *Bull Halsey*, 179.
11. Halsey and Bryan, *Admiral Halsey's Story*, 109.
12. Quoted in Potter, *Bull Halsey*, 160.
13. Headline quoted by James M. Merrill in *Men of War: Great Naval Leaders of World War II*, edited by Stephen Howarth (London, 1992), 232.
14. Halsey quoted in "Hit Hard, Hit Fast, Hit Often," *Time*, 30 November 1942, 29–30; Halsey and Bryan, *Admiral Halsey's Story*, 123.
15. "Hit Hard," 29–30.

16. Quoted in C. Vann Woodward, *The Battle for Leyte Gulf* (New York, 1947), 29.

17. First quotation in Ronald H. Spector, *Eagle against the Sun: The American War with Japan* (New York, 1985), 423; second and third quotations in Eric Larrabee, *Commander in Chief* (New York, 1987), 391–93.

18. Potter, *Bull Halsey*, 279.

19. Vernon D. Hipchings, Jr., the *Fanshaw Bay*'s visual fighter-director officer, interview by author, 31 January 1994.

20. Quoted in Gilbert Cant, "Bull's Run: Was Halsey Right at Leyte Gulf?" *Life*, 14 November 1947.

21. Halsey and Bryan, *Admiral Halsey's Story*, 220–21.

22. C. A. F. Sprague to Annabel Sprague, 15 May 1945, Sprague Family Collection, possession of Courtney Sprague Vaughan.

# ☆ Arleigh Burke
☆
## ☆ The Last CNO

### by David Alan Rosenberg

AT THE TIME OF HIS DEATH, HALF A CENTURY AFTER THE END OF WORLD War II, Arleigh Albert Burke was best remembered by both naval officers and naval historians as the U.S. Navy's premier destroyerman.[1] His bold and innovative combat style as Commander, Destroyer Squadron 23 (DesRon 23), during the night engagements of Empress Augusta Bay and Cape Saint George in the Solomon Islands won him a Navy Cross and a permanent place in naval legend. Burke's contributions to twentieth-century American naval history, however, go far beyond his wartime exploits in destroyers. His multifaceted career began on battleships but finished with battles to build and maintain supercarriers, nuclear-powered submarines, the Polaris missile, and the Navy's role in space. Even during World War II, he spent more time on the staff of Commander, Fast Carrier Task Force 58, as he helped to shape naval aviation, than he did in destroyers. Burke commanded destroyers in the South Pacific from February 1943 through March 1944; during the last 5 months, he commanded DesRon 23. He was chief of staff to Vice Admiral Marc A. Mitscher in Fast Carrier Task Force 58/38 from March 1944 through June 1945.

During his 38 years of commissioned service, in fact, Burke spent more time ashore than at sea. He had command at sea for a total of only 2½ years before being selected for rear admiral in December 1949, and then served barely 17 more months in three subsequent seagoing flag command assignments. By contrast, Burke spent a total of 8 years in four shore tours with the Bureau of

*The author gratefully acknowledges the financial support provided by the Ford Foundation, the John D. and Catherine T. MacArthur Foundation, and Temple University in facilitating his research.*

Ordnance between 1929 and 1945 and 9 years in three different posts in the Office of the Chief of Naval Operations (CNO) after World War II. For the last 6 of these years, he was CNO, an unprecedented and unequaled three terms in the Navy's top uniformed post.

It is not surprising that Arleigh Burke's wartime surface combat exploits have overshadowed his postwar accomplishments of creating and defending navy strategy and programs. Valor in battle signals a strength of will and character that tend to grow larger as the years pass, plus success in combat conveys a sense of conclusive accomplishment. Peacetime achievements ashore are difficult to measure, and their impact is all too easily buried in paperwork, bureaucracy, and secrecy. Yet, physical courage in combat is not always accompanied by the strength of mind and moral courage needed to defend and advance both institutional interests and strategic principles in bureaucratic skirmishes over money, people, or ideas. As impressive as Burke's combat victories were, it was his long hours ashore in fighting bureaucratic battles where he achieved his most lasting impact on the Navy. His postwar service helped ensure that the nation would continue to exploit the strategic advantages of the oceans and that the Navy could keep its own counsel on budgets, programs, and personnel, if not operations. To a remarkable degree, in fact, the story of Arleigh Burke's naval career is the story of the U.S. Navy in the mid-twentieth century.[2]

## Technical Mastery

Burke became a naval officer under rather unusual circumstances and drove himself hard to prove he had not taken on more of a challenge than he could handle. Born on the family farm three miles east of Boulder, Colorado, on 19 October 1901, he was the grandson of a Swedish immigrant, Anders Petter Bjorkegren, who shortened his name to Gus Burke before becoming the first baker in Denver. Arleigh's father, Oscar, was a farmer who wanted his first-born son to inherit his property and his dreams. Burke's mother, Clara Mokler, was of Pennsylvania Dutch stock, and she put a high premium on education. She encouraged her son to follow his own destiny, rather than limit his vision to the 180 acres that Oscar owned or rented and hoped to buy. To his father's distress, young Arleigh went to State Preparatory High School in Boulder in 1916 and pursued a college course. Encouraged by his teachers, inspired by the history books he read, and stimulated by the outbreak of World War I, he developed an interest in a military career.

The flu epidemic of 1918 closed high school during his junior year. After a brief sojourn on a threshing crew, seventeen-year-old Arleigh decided to compete for an appointment to the Naval Academy. The night before his congressman's competitive examination, he rode into Boulder because it looked like snow the next day and slept in the stable with his horse. The snow became a blizzard. Many students who were academically far better prepared stayed home, but Arleigh took the test and received the appointment. With school still closed, he studied for the Academy entrance examination with the help of his teachers and some University of Colorado professors. For a few months, he attended a cram school run by a former congressman in Columbia, Missouri. He passed the examination and, barely escaping quarantine when his father contracted smallpox, boarded the train east. Burke entered the Naval Academy class of 1923 on 26 June 1919.

Midshipman Burke, the farm boy who had always hated the smell of cows, felt immediately at home in the Navy. He enjoyed competing "in just such an organization in which the rules were strict, known and observed."[3] Painfully aware of his inadequate schooling and the flukes that had brought him to the Academy, he threw himself into his studies, determined to make the grade. He was not an outstanding student, an uncommon athlete, or an obviously charismatic leader, but he quickly won the respect of his classmates. Energetic and dependable, he used his capacity for hard work and self-discipline to establish a solid record. At graduation, he stood a respectable 70th in a class of 412.

One notable success at Annapolis was the courtship that began on a blind date during his Third Class (sophomore) year. Roberta Gorsuch, born and raised in Kansas, was the daughter of a Washington, D.C., businessman, and Burke felt immediately drawn to her. She was pretty, playful, kind, candid, and easy to talk to. "Bobbie" stood only five feet tall, but in strength of character, intelligence, and determination, she was fully a match for the six-foot midshipman. She quickly came to occupy a great deal of Burke's free time and attention. Her puckish sense of humor could shake him loose from the black moods that sometimes plagued him, and her inner serenity and strength, rooted in a Christian Science faith that he admired but did not share, steadied and reassured him. Worried that duty at sea would take him from her side for too long, First Classman Burke even requested a commission in the Marine Corps in December 1922, following a rousing address by Major General Commandant John A. Lejeune. Bobbie's lack of enthusiasm for this abrupt change in plans and Burke's growing naval ambitions led him to withdraw the request a month later.[4] Arleigh and Bobbie were married on graduation day, 7 June 1923, and she was to prove a loyal and energetic partner and ally for more than seven decades.

The Navy that Ensign Burke entered was an institution in transition. In many ways, the U.S. Fleet that trained and exercised off America's coasts and concentrated in annual fleet problems for defense of the Caribbean, Panama Canal, West Coast, or Hawaii was a huge operational laboratory for the testing of technology and the training of the officer corps that would lead the Navy through World War II and beyond. The battle line reigned supreme in the beginning, but, through the 1920s and 1930s, carrier and patrol aviation, long-range fleet submarines, and the amphibious Fleet Marine Force would be adopted, evaluated, and improved. By the end of the interwar period, of 381 ensigns commissioned in 1923, only 193 remained on active duty; 40 had become naval aviators and 44 had qualified in submarines.[5] For Burke himself, however, gunnery, fire control, and explosives held sway, and he became a member of the so-called "Gun Club" of the Bureau of Ordnance.

Even before commissioning, Midshipman Burke had written his bride-to-be of the thrill he felt when the big guns had been fired during his summer midshipman cruise and of how he hoped to "get a full knowledge of ordnance so that we may have a chance to take a PG [postgraduate work]."[6] Like 80 percent of his classmates, Ensign Burke went to battleship duty as his first assignment so that he could receive "intensive education in the practice of [his] profession at sea."[7] Spending five years in the USS *Arizona*, he learned the basic skills of a seagoing officer. This modern-day "school of the ship" provided the 40 ensigns in the *Arizona*'s 60–line-officer wardroom with practice in deck seamanship, stream engineering, and gunnery and, as division officers, in leading American sailors. Battleship wardrooms at this time were among the largest single congregations of line officers in the Navy, surpassed only by the Office of the Chief of Naval Operations in Washington, with 65 on duty, and the Naval War College in Newport, Rhode Island, where 68 served, 14 as staff and 54 as students.[8] During Burke's tour in the *Arizona*, he grew impatient in his progress and flirted in 1925 with becoming qualified in lighter-than-air aviation and the following year with becoming a specialist in aerology. Dissuaded by his seniors, he kept working on his qualifications in gunnery, particularly fire control in the plotting room for the battleship's main armament and, in 1927, applied for postgraduate training in ordnance. Rejected, he transferred to the auxiliary *Procyon*, applied again, and was accepted in 1929 for PG work in ordnance engineering at the Navy's Postgraduate School at Annapolis.

After completing a year of classroom and laboratory work and being tutored in college chemistry to meet graduate admission requirements, Burke moved on to the University of Michigan, where he received a master of science in chemical engineering in June 1931. He then spent another year in touring Navy and Army ammunition and explosive production facilities before returning to the fleet as main battery officer on the heavy cruiser *Chester*. Burke's postgraduate training qualified him as a full member of the elite and influential corps of line technical specialists who staffed and led the Bureau of Ordnance (BuOrd). The bureau's senior leadership often ran not just the bureau but the Navy itself; two former chiefs of the bureau, William D. Leahy and Harold R. Stark, became CNOs during the interwar years. BuOrd designated Burke a design and production specialist in ordnance explosives and would largely control his service for the next decade. After eleven months in the *Chester*, Burke became assistant and then officer-in-charge of the Battle Force Camera Party recording fleet target practice and, during 1935–1937, ran BuOrd's ammunition section in Washington.

In May 1937, Burke began his first tour in (and a lasting love affair with) destroyers, when he became prospective executive officer of the *Craven*, then building in Quincy, Massachusetts. Battleships had been Burke's traditional sea-duty preference up to 1934, but dozens of new destroyers were being added to the fleet. These smaller ships offered more opportunities for command and significant new challenges in shiphandling and leadership. Burke spent two years in the *Craven* and then was appointed to his first command, the *Mugford*, another new destroyer. Lieutenant Commander Burke was one of only five officers selected early to command one of the new ships instead of a World War I four-stack destroyer. He was assigned to the division of a tough, veteran shiphandler and tactician, Commander F. E. M. ("Red") Whiting, who demanded audacity at sea as well as technical competence. Burke's command tour was a triumph. The ship won the Destroyer Gunnery Trophy for 1939–40 as a result of an unprecedented perfect score—thirty-six shots, thirty-six hits—in short-range battle practice and received the "E" in engineering competition and the "C" for communications. Whiting's last fitness report declared Burke to be "a leader of the highest type" and predicted "he will go far in the Navy."[9] For his part, Burke later told Whiting, "I think that I learned some very important lessons under your guidance, the most important one being that when you have got anything to do, the time to do it is right now. If you've got power, use it and use it fast, and the time to make a decision is as soon as the problem presents itself."[10]

The Bureau of Ordnance reclaimed Burke in May 1940 and sent him to the Naval Gun Factory in the Washington Navy Yard as an inspector of antiaircraft and broadside gun mounts. To Burke, this might have seemed like purgatory, but the job was critical to ensuring the success of the U.S. Navy that was now mobilizing for war. There were only 220 ordnance specialists in the entire officer corps, and Burke was one of only 46 who were specialists in design and production. More than 80 inspectors were needed ashore to run ordnance production; train officers; and inspect output in guns, torpedoes, and ammunition. Not even the attack on Pearl Harbor could break the gun factory's hold on Burke. He submitted a request for sea duty every week for more than a year after the United States had entered the war, only to be told each time that he could not be spared. Finally, on 10 January 1943, with a relief at last found and trained, Commander Burke left for the Pacific.

Burke had become a highly proficient naval officer during his nineteen-year career. A good deal smarter than he liked to let on, he had a tremendous capacity for hard work and overcame severe educational handicaps to rise to the technical peak of his profession as an ordnance specialist. His gunnery officer in the *Mugford* had noted that Burke "may have been endowed with gifts beyond other men, but that is not important, for he developed the numerous ones he had to a superb degree by continuous persistent application with a firm determination to do anything he did very well."[11] If war had not come in 1941, Burke still would have enjoyed a solid reputation in the service as an officer marked by his superiors as one of the Gun Club's future leaders. But, combat demanded more than the technical mastery of the interwar years. While Burke's seniors valued his technical abilities, his subordinates recognized his talent for command. Burke's engineer in the *Mugford* had evaluated his captain as follows: "One had to have an intimate knowledge of all line duties, engineering, gunnery, seamanship, navigation, shipbuilding, tactics, communications, up keep, repair, logistics. These are the ingredients for command. He had these plus a little extra: enthusiasm for, trust in, and loyalty to his subordinates."[12]

## Tactical Innovation

Despite his superb prewar performance in the *Mugford*, Commander Burke was unprepared for surface combat against the Japanese Imperial Navy and had a year's worth of combat lessons to learn. Assigned initially as Commander, Destroyer Division 43, he spent much of his first months in the South Pacific on his flagship *Waller*; he read action reports and talked with veterans of night actions in the bitter campaign for Guadalcanal, which had just ended. Ostensibly assigned as screen commander to Rear Admiral A. S. ("Tip") Merrill's cruiser task force, Burke's four destroyers were often dispersed on a variety of assignments in the Solomon Islands. As a unit, they spent long days on escort duty, where Burke relearned antiair and antisubmarine screening operations as modified by wartime experience. His first combat mission, bombarding the airfield at Vila in Kula Gulf with Merrill's cruisers on 6–7 March 1943, was a success, but Burke was chagrined that his command had not operated more smoothly because he had not worked through detailed combat procedures in advance with his flag captain. He set to work to create a night surface battle doctrine that would remedy such deficiencies.

By early May, building on the lessons of the Guadalcanal campaign and the views of Destroyer Division (DesDiv) 43's captains, Burke had developed a new approach to the use of destroyers in a cruiser task force. Standard practice was to station destroyers as a submarine screen at night and require them to scramble into battle formation ahead and astern of the cruisers only after the enemy was sighted. Burke proposed that all destroyers should be routinely stationed ahead of the cruisers, in battle formation, from just after sunset until shortly before sunrise, with permission to engage as soon as an enemy was sighted. Burke wanted his ships used as offensive weapons of opportunity, capitalizing on speed and surprise. He believed that if the destroyers were authorized to attack as soon as the enemy was sighted, they could disrupt or disable a small force or distract a superior one with torpedo salvoes to give the cruisers time to withdraw. The crucial problem was whether task force commanders would delegate the initiative in opening fire.[13] Admiral Merrill agreed to take the risk, but Burke was transferred before he could test his tactics in combat.

Burke took command of DesDiv 44 in late May and became Commander, Destroyer Squadron 12, in August. Again, he found his ships assigned to a variety of escort duties and was almost never able to operate them as a unit. By late July, his combat doctrine had further evolved. Burke now envisioned night engagements using two parallel columns of destroyers attacking sequentially. Alerted by radar, these columns would carry out successive torpedo attacks on an unsuspecting enemy by maximizing surprise. Burke was unable to implement his ideas in combat, but, in early August, his Naval Academy classmate Frederick Moosbrugger took Burke's plan and used it in the battle of Vella Gulf where six U.S. destroyers sank three Japanese destroyers without a loss.[14]

On 19 October, Burke was ordered as Commander, Destroyer Squadron 23, and rejoined Admiral Merrill's Task Force 39 in time for the invasion of Bougainville in the Solomons. Merrill agreed to allow Burke's now-proven tactical concepts to govern his night surface actions. The battle of Empress Augusta Bay on 1–2 November saw Merrill's four cruisers and Burke's eight new *Fletcher*-class destroyers confront four Japanese cruisers and six destroyers sent to disrupt the invasion. Burke's division of four destroyers stationed ahead of the cruisers opened the action by firing twenty-five torpedoes and then turned away while the cruisers opened fire. Burke then found it impossible to regroup and rejoin the cruisers as the battle turned into a melee. At one point, Burke mistook his other destroyer division for the enemy and fired several salvos at them, all of which missed. Despite its mishaps, the Americans sank two enemy ships and damaged four against one U.S. ship damaged and three Americans dead. The lessons of the battle, Burke observed, were the importance of surprise, the necessity of having a clear battle plan, and the importance of allowing destroyers to operate independently. In particular, "it is necessary that [commanders] realize the value of time. It's the only commodity which you can never regain."[15]

DesRon 23 spent November covering the amphibious forces in Empress Augusta Bay or escorting convoys up to the beachhead. During a brief respite, Burke and the skipper of his flagship *Charles Ausburne*, Commander L. K.

("Brute") Reynolds, spotted the painting of a little American Indian boy that a torpedoman was putting on his mount. Intrigued, they asked what it meant; after being told, "It was an American symbol," Burke asked to use it for the squadron. The *Ausburne's* crew had already begun calling themselves "beavers" because of their busy operations schedule. Someone suggested the Indian be named "Little Beaver," after Red Ryder's sidekick in the popular cowboy comic strip, and the nickname stuck. DesRon 23 forever after was known as the "Little Beavers." For Burke, the Colorado farm boy who had ridden horses since he was four, the nickname was a perfect match.

On the afternoon of 24 November, after repairs to a troublesome boiler on the destroyer *Spence* that had restricted ship (and squadron) speed to thirty knots, Burke reported to Admiral William F. Halsey's South Pacific headquarters that his ships were proceeding at his preferred nonbattle formation speed of thirty-one knots to a late-evening rendezvous southeast of Bougainville. In response to an ULTRA (code word for radio intelligence) report of a "transportation operation to Buka by destroyers" that night, Halsey's operations officer, Captain Ray Thurber, recalling Burke's previously impaired formation speed, prepared an operations order: "Thirty-One Knot Burke get athwart the Buka-Rabaul evacuation line about 35 miles west of Buka. If no enemy contacts by 0300 Love [Local Time], 25th, come south to refuel same place. If enemy contacted you know what to do." Prepared by prior messages and operations for such an action, Burke found the new orders "ideal . . . they gave us all the information we needed, and how we did the job was entirely up to us."[16]

The ensuing battle of Cape Saint George, where DesRon 23's five destroyers engaged five Japanese destroyers, began at 0141 on 25 November, when radar detected surface contacts 22,000 yards to the east. Burke led his three leading ships at the enemy at twenty-five knots, while the other destroyers stood by in support. Burke's attack came as almost a complete surprise. Two enemy screen destroyers were hit, and one sank immediately. Accelerating to thirty-three knots, Burke now began a stern chase after the three destroyer transports, and the two supporting destroyers finished off the Japanese ship still afloat. At 0215, on a hunch, Burke ordered a radical course change, thereby avoiding a Japanese torpedo spread. In an hour-long running gun battle, a third enemy destroyer was sunk. Unscathed but low on fuel and ammunition and closing Saint George's Channel leading to the enemy base at Rabaul on New Britain, Burke reversed course at 0400 and headed for home. The Thanksgiving Day victory made Burke and DesRon 23 famous. Congratulations poured in from Admirals Merrill, Halsey, Chester W. Nimitz, and Ernest J. King and General Douglas MacArthur, while the name of "31-Knot Burke" spread throughout America. A subsequent analysis by the Naval War College described Cape

Saint George as "an almost perfect action" and one "that may come to be considered a classic."[17]

After a year in the combat zone, Burke did not want to return to shore duty in BuOrd. He hoped to stay in DesRon 23 through the spring, but this was not to be. Burke was initially slated for shore duty at Pearl Harbor to train new destroyer skippers for combat and then a new surface command, possibly one of the new squadrons of 2,200-ton destroyers. His life changed forever as a result of a decision by Admiral King, Commander-in-Chief (CominCh), U.S. Fleet, on 11 March 1944. King directed that "aviator flag officers having surface officers under their command have non-aviator line officers as chiefs of staff."[18] Rear Admiral Marc A. Mitscher, Commander, Carrier Division Three and Fast Carrier Task Force 58, was given a list of four surface line captains, including Burke, from which to choose. Mitscher, a pioneer naval aviator and air combat commander, resented the order and refused to deal with it. Captain Truman Hedding, his existing chief of staff, picked Burke because of his combat record and on the advice of Mitscher's departing operations officer, Commander C. D. ("Don") Griffin, who had been Burke's shipmate in 1932–33.

Burke transferred to Mitscher's flagship, the carrier *Lexington*, on 27 March. Mitscher did little to make his new chief of staff feel welcome in his job. Burke wrote home, "I don't know my job and there are many things I should know I don't and I feel lost." With Hedding's encouragement, Burke threw himself into "learning the bird man's lingo." He flew as much as possible and got "lots of training in handling the Fleet." He struggled to "get into the habit of dealing with forces instead of ships—and planes instead of guns." It was not until early May 1944, however, that Burke "really cracked the ice" with the aviator admiral as a result of Burke's short, concise plans, tailored to the needs of those doing the fighting.[19] The admiral even began to permit Burke to introduce some innovative air tactics in the plans for coming operations. Burke still found the job tedious and longed to command destroyers again. He responded enthusiastically to a proposal by Commander, Destroyers, Pacific, to form a two-squadron force that Burke could lead on forays in the North Pacific, but the scheme never solidified. He later noted that, during his fifteen-month tour as Mitscher's chief of staff, "I have never worked so hard in my life, either before or since, and I don't believe any other person on that staff did either."[20]

As Burke proved himself, Mitscher let him handle nearly all details of Task Force 58's administration, planning, and operations. By the time the carriers began the Marianas campaign in June, the destroyer captain and aviator admiral cemented a relationship based on mutual respect and an aggressive combat spirit. They would stay together until the end of Mitscher's life. Burke shared the aviators' frustrations in June when Admiral Raymond A. Spruance, commanding the U.S. forces in the Battle of the Philippine Sea, failed to appreciate the capabilities of the fast carriers to operate west of the Marianas against the Japanese fleet while guarding against an end run by the enemy on the amphibious forces off Saipan and Tinian. When Halsey took tactical command of the fast carriers during the Leyte operation in October, there were new frustrations. Often bypassing Mitscher, Halsey failed to consult him during major strategic turning points during the Battle of Leyte Gulf. In preparation for the Iwo Jima and Okinawa campaigns, Burke co-authored a comprehensive set of instructions on fast carrier operations, the first of its kind, to guide the task force in the coming months. He survived the winter 1945 operations in support of the invasion of Iwo Jima and against the Japanese homeland and the bitter spring campaign for Okinawa, "the longest sustained carrier operation of World War II." From 18 March until late May, elements of Task Force 58 were "under almost continuous attack." "The complete course in suiciders, including the postgraduate course" drove Mitscher and Burke from the flagship *Bunker Hill* on 11 May, when two kamikaze hits killed 352 men, including 13 of Mitscher's staff. A kamikaze strike forced them off the *Enterprise* to the *Randolph* three days later.[21]

Mitscher found Burke's work outstanding and twice recommended that his chief of staff be promoted to rear admiral, at least four years ahead of his contemporaries. Both times, Burke objected because "in fairness to a lot of other people and to the Navy I feel that I do not deserve this promotion now" and because "I can't think of any way the Navy could get any more out of me if I wore two stars."[22] In November 1944, however, Burke was promoted to one-star rank as a commodore, a rank contingent upon his billet as Mitscher's chief of staff. By 1945, however, Burke was tired of pushing papers. He continued to feel out of place; the disdain of aviators for most surface officers galled him, although he was now convinced that carriers were the future of the Navy and was "resigned to a happy and early retirement." Before retiring, however, he wanted one more crack at the enemy in his own cruiser command and a postwar stint as Commandant of Midshipmen at the Naval Academy.[23]

After the Okinawa operation in June 1945, Burke was assigned to Fleet Admiral King's CominCh staff in Washington as part of newly formed Section F49 that was attempting to counter the kamikaze problem. When Japan surrendered, Burke was at a desk in Washington. The war had changed him and his prospects significantly. In 1941, Burke had been a promising technical officer, a member of the Navy's conservative brain trust in BuOrd. By 1945, he was one of the war's most successful surface combat commanders and also one of the very few "black shoes" (surface officers) accepted by the "brown shoes" of naval aviation. When Mitscher became Deputy CNO for Air in August, he asked Burke to be his deputy, but Burke declined. He argued that Mitscher needed a career aviator in the post, and that, even if he took flight training, he would always be resented as a usurper. He promised that he would be available to serve Mitscher when he went back to sea.

It was with that condition that Burke returned to BuOrd in the fall of 1945 as Director of Research and Development. His responsibilities included overseeing guided missile development and service on the military advisory committee to the head of the atomic bomb project. He remained there until early 1946, when Mitscher, now a full admiral, went to sea in command of the U.S. Navy's first postwar striking fleet. The new job entailed building a force to deploy to the Mediterranean waters in a crisis, and Mitscher and Burke took a revealing three-week tour of Western Europe that summer. In October 1946, Mitscher became commander-in-chief of the Atlantic Fleet, and Commodore Burke again went with him as chief of staff. There, Burke struggled to maintain readiness in the face of a rapidly shrinking, demobilized navy. Admiral Mitscher died in February 1947. By that time, Burke's service reputation was such that he was regarded by many, including Secretary of the Navy James V. Forrestal, as a potential chief of naval operations.

## Strategic Vision

Arleigh Burke's prewar technical and wartime tactical accomplishments did not necessarily equip him to take on the political and technical complexities of the emerging Cold War as a strategic planner. His only formal training in strategy and tactics was a Naval War College correspondence course in 1926–29. For the remainder of his career, however, Burke would be assigned to positions of increasing complexity and responsibility in strategic planning and programming. His engineering skills and operational experience, plus his wide array of connections across the Navy's technical and warfare communities, provided him with a solid foundation on which to build a comprehensive view of how a modern navy could contribute to national strategy. He encouraged his seniors and subordinates, through long working hours, to do the same, and incorporated their ideas and findings into an expanding strategic concept.

Burke's first planning assignment was a fifteen-month stint in 1947–48 as a member of the General Board, which advised the Secretary of the Navy on matters of high policy. He worked on a range of projects, from studies of the shore establishment and development of force requirements for the first Joint Chiefs of Staff long-range war plan to a project personally originated by Burke that was titled "The National Security and Navy Contributions Thereto." This last involved a broad-range survey of active and retired flag officers and selected civilian experts, and resulted in a report, substantially drafted by Burke himself, that laid out a comprehensive and pessimistic assessment of the service's responsibilities and prospects over the next decade, given a powerful continental power, the Soviet Union, and declining U.S. defense budgets. Following his tour with the General Board, Burke spent an enjoyable five months in command of the light cruiser *Huntington* on cruise to the Mediterranean and South Atlantic. In December 1948, he returned to Washington for his first tour in the Office of the Chief of Naval Operations (OpNav) as director of the Organizational Research and Policy Division (Op-23).

Burke's tour in Op-23 was arguably the most controversial of his naval career. It brought him face to face with the difficult and exasperating problems involved in the unification of the armed services and the resulting, often bitter competition over budget dollars, roles, mission prerogatives, and strategic concepts that he would fight throughout the remainder of his service in the Navy. Much of his work involved providing the CNO and the high command of the Navy with assessments of the reorganization schemes that resulted in the National Security Act Amendments of 1949, including a far-ranging analysis that strongly rejected the establishment of a national general staff. In the summer and early fall of 1949, however, Op-23 was assigned to support a high-level task force charged with preparing the Navy's testimony for the House Armed Services Committee hearings into charges that, possibly, there had been illegal conduct in the procurement of the Air Force's B-36 bomber, as well as testimony on the wider implications of the Truman administration's budget-constrained defense policy under unification. Working with Admiral Arthur Radford, Commander-in-Chief, Pacific, Op-23 coordinated the Navy's efforts to defend the Navy's and naval aviation's places in national defense and also challenged a developing national military strategy dependent on what the Navy believed was a flawed, inadequate, and immoral Air Force plan for an atomic air offensive against seventy Soviet cities to realize initial military objectives.

During the hearings on the B-36 and on Unification and Strategy (the latter came to be known as "The Revolt of the Admirals"), Burke was tarred in the press with accusations that he was running an antiunification, anti-Air Force "secret publicity bureau," and Op-23 was subjected to a Navy Inspector General investigation ordered by Secretary of the Navy Francis Matthews. The investigation showed no improper conduct, but, that December, after Burke was unanimously approved "below the zone" by the rear admiral selection board for promotion before officers senior to him, Matthews, with the apparent concurrence of Secretary of Defense Louis Johnson, requested that Burke's name be removed from the flag list and the name of a more senior officer substituted. It took the intercession of President Harry S Truman, at the behest of his naval aide and Burke classmate, Rear Admiral Robert Dennison, and the new CNO, Admiral Forrest Sherman, to have Burke's name reinstated.[24]

In June 1950, Rear Admiral Burke was serving as the Navy secretary of the Defense Research and Development Board, on what would prove to be his last engineering assignment, when the Korean War broke out. Admiral Sherman dispatched him to Tokyo to be his personal troubleshooter as deputy chief of staff to Commander, Naval Forces, Far East. There, Burke oversaw strategic and operational planning for exploitation of the Inchon invasion and the defeat of North Korea. After the Chinese intervention, he helped to plan the evacuation of U.S. forces under the Communist onslaught. Burke also initiated planning for the maritime rearmament of Japan, an effort that instilled in him an understanding of and increasing commitment to the development of maritime allies for the Cold War competition against the Soviet Union and its allies.

A stint as Commander, Cruiser Division Five, on the gun line off Korea in spring 1951 was cut short that July when he was assigned to the first United Nations delegation to the truce talks with the Chinese and North Koreans. The prolonged wrangling over agendas and demarcation lines, while Americans died in bitter battles, angered and frustrated Burke. In addition, he was dismayed to find that the secret Allied negotiating positions were repeatedly being anticipated—he believed as a result of espionage—by the Communists. This face-to-face confrontation made a lasting impression. The truce talks convinced him that "the only thing the Communists pay any attention to is power," and that sustaining the Cold War and waging and winning limited wars on the Eurasian periphery were as important to the success of U.S. military policy as deterring or fighting a general nuclear war with the Soviet Union.[25]

Burke returned to Washington in December 1951 to serve as director of the Strategic Plans Division of OpNav. This was one of the most important jobs open to a junior flag officer. Although many occupants of that post found themselves overwhelmed by the paperwork, Burke impressed both seniors and subordinates with the energy and initiative that he devoted to preparation of countless papers for consideration by the Joint Chiefs of Staff, the Office of the Secretary of Defense, the National Security Council, and Navy operational commanders worldwide. He directed the development of a rationale for U.S. aircraft carrier force levels for a prolonged Cold War; pushed the creation of options for naval operations to defeat the Soviet Union in the event of war; directed the preparation of a long-range strategic estimate that could be used to guide naval strategic and operational planning, which identified challenges short of all-out war with the Soviet Union as the greatest security problems facing the United States in the future; and personally drafted the Navy's critique of the Eisenhower administration's emerging policy of "massive retaliation" for the CNO in December 1953.[26]

In April 1954, the CNO, Admiral Robert B. Carney, ordered Burke back to sea as Commander, Cruiser Division Six. His two years in the Pentagon had left him both exhausted and disheartened about the direction of national strategy and the deteriorating state of the peacetime Navy. When a friend from his year at the University of Michigan offered Burke a civilian job, he seriously contemplated leaving the service. He was not sure he was suited to high command and doubted that he could do better than Carney at solving the myriad problems confronting the Navy. "I am not sure I would wish to be CNO, even if it were made available to me" he wrote his old division commander, Red Whiting.[27] Carney, on the other hand, saw Burke as an outstanding candidate for further promotion. In January 1955, he put him in command of the Atlantic Fleet Destroyer Force and was prepared to send him to Sixth Fleet in the Mediterranean the following year.

Burke's advancement came a good deal sooner than Admiral Carney expected. Secretary of the Navy Charles Thomas had decided not to reappoint Carney and wanted, as his replacement, a vigorous younger officer with a strong technical background and outstanding leadership skills to reenergize what he saw as a demoralized Navy. When flag officers were polled as to what admirals they felt were best qualified to be CNO, Burke's name turned up on every list. On 10 May 1955, Thomas offered the CNO position to Rear Admiral Arleigh Burke. Burke was startled and somewhat dismayed by the offer. There were ninety-two active-duty flag officers senior to him on the Navy Register, more than eighty of whom were potential candidates for the post, and he thought that his sudden rise might create bad feeling. In addition, he was not sure if he was suited to the job. He warned Thomas that he had a bad habit of speaking his mind, as during the "Admiral's Revolt" in 1949, which might land him in trouble, and he did not intend to give up this habit. Finally, he felt that he could not accept the post without Carney's full support. Carney had doubts about the wisdom of such an accelerated promotion but none about Burke's abilities, and he offered his warm endorsement. On 17 August 1955, Burke became the fifteenth Chief of Naval Operations.

His first few weeks were not propitious. The new CNO found himself at odds with Secretary of the Navy Thomas, Secretary of Defense Charles Wilson, and President Dwight D. Eisenhower over the issue of the draft. Burke was convinced that the draft was the only way for the Navy to meet its personnel goals, and he was unwilling to accept the Eisenhower administration's recent ruling that it would not be reinstated. He requested a White House meeting, where he presented his case. Eisenhower agreed to reverse his decision, but, after the meeting, he expressly warned Burke never again to put his commander-in-chief in such an embarrassing position. Eisenhower treated Burke with cool formality for many months afterward but eventually came to value the soundness of the new CNO's counsel, as well as the direct manner in which he was inclined to offer it. By the time Burke was reappointed to a second two-year term in 1957, he had become a valued and influential member of the Eisenhower team.

Burke served as CNO through 1 August 1961, an unprecedented and un-matched three terms and nearly six years in office. During that time, his con-tributions to the service ranged from the adoption of formal mess dress uni-forms for both male and female officers and the renovation of buildings at the Naval Academy, a few rooms at a time until complete funding could be achieved, to sponsoring nuclear power for aircraft carriers and surface com-batants, changing the submarine building programs to ensure that all future submarines would be nuclear powered, and starting the Polaris Fleet Ballistic Missile program. In particular, he fulfilled Secretary Thomas's goal of aggres-sively pursuing the development and procurement of advanced technology sys-tems, including surface-to-air, air-to-air, and air-to-surface missiles, and ad-vanced jet fighters and attack aircraft, including the F-4 Phantom, A-6 Intruder, and A-5 Vigilante, and he brought the Navy into the computer age with the development and initial procurement of the Naval Tactical Data Sys-tem (NTDS) for command and control of air and naval forces.

Much of what Burke accomplished as CNO was done within the context of the most intense competition among the armed services for peacetime de-fense funds in the nation's history. The Navy consistently came in second be-hind the Air Force, which received nearly half of all defense dollars during the Eisenhower years. Debates in the Joint Chiefs of Staff (of which Burke was now a member) over strategic plans for the use of U.S. forces in war, particularly general war with the Soviet Union, and over procurement objectives in sup-port of those plans were blunt and prolonged. More was at stake than just forces and funding; the central issue in the debates was nothing less than the Amer-ican approach to waging war.

The position taken by Burke and the Navy was fundamentally at odds with that of the Air Force and also differed in many ways from that of the Eisen-hower administration. Much of the nation's defense expenditure during the mid-1950s was being devoted to the problem of general nuclear war between East and West. U.S. war plans, which, through the early 1950s, had envisioned a U.S.–USSR war as a protracted multiphase conflict lasting months or years where naval forces could play an important role, had been changed in 1955–56 and now anticipated a rapid two-phase war, with a short, massively destructive thermonuclear first phase and a second phase of "indeterminate duration." As CNO, Burke worked hard to ensure that the U.S. Navy was at the forefront of development of the capability for fighting a nuclear conflict with the Soviet Union, including nuclear-tipped surface-to-air guided missiles and the ASROC, a rocket-powered nuclear depth charge. His highest priority was antisubmarine warfare. Building on the capabilities of the new and expanding SOSUS (sound surveillance system), a fixed passive low-frequency sonar detection system, the Navy planned to establish surface, maritime patrol aviation, and submarine barriers to prosecute Soviet submarines and deny the enemy navy access to the open oceans. In addition, as Burke wrote to British First Sea Lord Louis Mountbatten, "It will be one of the major tasks of carrier striking forces in the early days of a general war to find and destroy" Soviet "submarine hideaways" in "coves and bays away from any other profitable fixed targets" where he expected the Soviet Union to "deploy all of her operational submarines" and their tenders.[28]

Burke also believed, however, that the developing nuclear stalemate between the superpowers would lead to a situation where "it is my opinion that not even a mad Russian would think of starting a nuclear war unless he has some chance of profit and there is no chance of profit if his own country is largely destroyed in retaliation. The USSR would have nothing to gain and certainly the free nations would have nothing to gain."[29] Burke had "long felt that the ultimate solution of the Communist problem" would "come from internal strains and tensions which will so change the USSR, evolutionary or revolutionary, that it will cease to be an international threat." A "last desperate gamble by the dictators to retain their power" leading to global war had to be guarded against, but this could be prevented by maintaining a "deterrent force so carefully dispersed yet strategically concentrated that initiation of war will be Russia's suicide while the free world can survive with some residuum of people and power."[30]

The United States and its allies, Burke said, would be well advised to prepare for a broader set of military contingencies: "What is more apt to occur [than a general war with the Soviet Union] are local wars which both the Free World and the USSR will take great pains to prevent expanding into general war. This means precise delivery of weapons suitable under the circumstances existing. It will mean the quick positive delivery of sufficient force but not in excess of that required for a particular situation. It will mean accepting something less than unconditional surrender."[31]

Burke believed that the Navy held the key to both of these strategic challenges. A sea-based nuclear force would be much less vulnerable than the land-based bombers and missiles of the Strategic Air Command (SAC) and could achieve the same deterrent effect as the larger SAC force because its weapons would be harder to target and destroy. This would permit the Defense Department to shift resources from the general nuclear war mission into preparations for limited and local conflicts. Further, in the unlikely event that the United States was forced into a nuclear war, the relative invulnerability of sea-based missiles would mean that they could be withheld and used selectively, thus freeing the United States from the "use it or lose it" doomsday scenarios that dominated Air Force nuclear war planning. This strategy of "finite deterrence, controlled retaliation" was the fruit of Burke's years as a strategic planner and provided the context for many of his most important decisions as CNO.[32]

Long before "finite deterrence" was fully articulated, Burke took the first steps toward creating the tools to make it possible. Only two months after taking office, in October 1955, he moved to implement aggressively a tasking from the National Security Council and directed the Navy to proceed as rapidly as possible to achieve a sea-based intermediate-range ballistic missile. Burke's directive ran counter to the advice of many of his top subordinates in OpNav, who argued that such a project was too technically complex and too expensive to be justified. Confident that the technical difficulties could be overcome, he appointed Rear Admiral William F. Raborn to head a Special Projects Office that would work jointly with the Army in developing a liquid-fueled missile to be fired from converted merchant ships. The next summer, while the successful development of ballistic missiles was still far from assured, Burke directed the Navy staff to investigate a "minimal target system, the threat of destruction of which would deter the USSR." Burke would use the resulting study in the Joint Chiefs of Staff to argue against the escalating requirements of the Air Force for thermonuclear weapons to attack the Soviet Union, as well as for the bombers (and later intercontinental ballistic missiles) to deliver them.[33]

In the fall of 1956, as a result of progress made in developing solid fuel propulsion and lighter nuclear warheads, the Navy split off its Fleet Ballistic Missile Program, now code-named Polaris, from the Army's program and looked to development of a submarine-based missile force. Breaking with the long-standing practice of treating naval nuclear forces as threats against only "targets of naval interest," Burke directed in January 1957 that the developing Polaris system be considered a "national" deterrent system. That November, the Polaris development schedule was accelerated so as to produce a deployed submarine armed with 1,200-mile missiles by 1961. Finally, in early 1958, Burke released a long-range concept for "The Navy of the 1970 Era" that called for forty ballistic missile submarines to serve as the Navy's deterrent to all-out war, while fifteen attack carriers would be used as the service's "primary cutting tool" to forestall or fight limited conflicts.

By 1959, Burke clearly was looking to Polaris as a potential replacement for most of SAC's bomber and missile force but at a much reduced cost for the nation as a whole. A study of alternative targeting, which had the potential to move the nation's war plans away from a largely preemptive massive first strike effort aimed at Soviet military and civilian targets across the board toward an exclusively retaliatory target list of highest-priority targets only, was under way in the Joint Chiefs of Staff. If the "alternative undertaking" was adopted as the nation's primary strategy in war, finite deterrence might become a reality. The first Polaris submarine, the USS *George Washington* with its sixteen ballistic missiles, was on track to its first deployment in the fall of 1960, thereby setting the stage for development of a controlled retaliation strategy.

The cost to the Navy of implementing Burke's alternative to national nuclear strategy, however, was high. The Navy's annual budget hovered at $11–$13 billion through 1961, far short of the $16–$17 billion that Burke calculated would be needed to produce a modernized U.S. fleet by the 1970s. This meant that many promising programs, including the Triton and Regulus II cruise missiles and the P6M Seamaster long-range jet seaplane, had to be canceled. The necessity of such trade-offs troubled Burke. A 1957 study projected that Navy force levels would fall to 693 ships by 1971, far short of the 927 required for wartime missions, if funds were committed to developing Polaris, making all future-construction submarines nuclear powered, and introducing nuclear power into all future aircraft carriers and some surface combatants.[34] Nevertheless, the CNO was determined to press forward with the effort to broaden national military strategy.

Arleigh Burke understood that "we have to work hard to maintain the Navy as a viable instrument of power—power which is needed by the United States, which is understood, and which can grow and change." He told a fellow admiral, "We have to maintain in ourselves, and imbue our juniors with an ardor to keep our Navy in front. We must pass along a willingness to think hard—to seek new answers—to chance mistakes—and to 'mix it up' freely in the forums and activities around us to promote knowledge. From that knowledge we can inspire our country to have faith in us—not because the organization of the military forces is the only place to put our national faith, but because we have discharged our responsibilities in such a manner that we have justified confidence in the effective manner in which we operate."[35]

## "We Believe in Command, Not Staff"

Burke's persistence in challenging prevailing assumptions about the nature of the threats facing the United States and how best to confront them was based on a philosophy of leadership rooted in Navy traditions and experience. Naval officers achieved the pinnacle of their careers in command at sea, a role which necessarily required a high degree of individual initiative and responsibility. Because of this, the service had evolved a system of decision making more consciously decentralized than might have been workable in the other services. Many of Burke's initiatives as CNO were intended to encourage preservation of this leadership tradition.

Upon becoming CNO in 1955, he had established "Flag Officers' Dope," a monthly classified newsletter to all flag officers in the Navy, to acquaint them with important events and proposals, as well as the rationale behind his decisions and actions. In 1956, he instituted a multimedia "Spirit of the Navy" presentation to provide naval personnel with an understanding of the foundations of the service and its role in the nation's history. Appreciating the new power of television to reach the general public and improve the Navy's image, he encouraged service support of such classic television series as *Navy Log, Silent Service,* and *Men of Annapolis.* In 1958, he created the Naval Leadership Program, which emphasized the importance of individual responsibility and individual contributions in meeting the many challenges that faced the Navy. In addition, he took steps to encourage increased postgraduate education for all naval officers in the social sciences, as well as in the natural and technical sciences. At the Naval Academy, Burke established a postgraduate scholarship, later bearing his name, that allowed a few highly motivated, excellent midshipmen—following graduation and after one year at sea—to obtain their doctorates at civilian graduate schools.

In 1958, Burke wrote:

> We believe in *command,* not *staff."*
> We believe we have "real" things to do. The Navy believes in putting a
> man in a position with a job to do, and let him do it—give him hell if he
> does not perform—but be a man in his own name. We decentralize and
> capitalize on the capabilities of our individual people rather than centralize
> and make automatons of them. This builds that essential pride of service
> and sense of accomplishment. If it results in a certain amount of cockiness,
> I am for it. But this is the direction in which we should move.[36]

Nevertheless, he pointed out, "there has to be a good deal of conformity in any organization or it will go off in all directions." The challenge was to create a sense of common purpose, without stifling individual drive and initiative. This was not easy in the postwar Navy; rivalry between the different branches of the service was sometimes intense, especially in competition for high command. It was quite natural, Burke noted, for an outstanding naval aviator to "believe that there is no other group in the whole world that does as much for the defense of the United States," and for submariners committed to nuclear power and the Polaris program to "become a little too enthusiastic sometimes and believe that only they are really needed in a Navy." Such pride, he observed, was "fine as long as the aim to make the specialty better is based on the larger desire to make the whole Navy stronger. All these elements are essential and they are needed. If any one element of the Navy were to be eliminated the whole Navy would suffer and the enemy could concentrate on the one element which we did not have and win their war, regardless of what the other people could do."[37]

He knew that those who had to pick the service's future leadership "cannot afford the luxury of bias for or against any group of people." He hoped that "there would come a time" when "it will be possible to have [most Navy commands] commanded by any line officer—aviator, submariner or ordinary surface officer." He "personally believe[d] also that by the time a man makes Flag Officer he should lose his designation, no matter what it is, submarines, aviation, or anything else, and become a Flag Officer in the broadest sense of the term—one who can command forces."[38]

As CNO, Burke had only limited power to move the Navy in the directions he wanted. By the time he took office, the OpNav bureaucracy was large and unwieldy. In 1923, when Burke had received his commission, the Office of the CNO was staffed by 65 line officers plus a handful of staff officers and a few civilians. In 1955, there were more than 630 officer billets in OpNav. The same growth was evident at all levels. The Bureau of Ordnance in Washington had only 26 officers when Burke came to the Explosives Section in 1935; by the 1950s, every bureau employed hundreds of uniformed and civilian personnel. Burke was very much aware that he could not merely command things to happen in Washington. He had to exercise leadership, not just authority. The keys to such leadership were loyalty, communication, and delegation of responsibility.

Burke was part of a generation of naval officers who had been taught that loyalty was the most important of the "essential qualities of a naval officer," and "loyalty up and loyalty down" epitomized how naval officers should conduct themselves with both subordinates and seniors.[39] As CNO, he felt "thwarted by the absence of simple, undistorted communications downward, as well as up." He was "never fully as knowledgeable of any one subject as I feel I should be" and regretted that "I never seem to have time to get the full story from the action officers." In order to get things done in the Pentagon, Burke felt that "it is not wise for me to give a direct order. If I do, then I must do my damnedest to make sure that it is carried out." Instead, "what I try to do is to call the action officers up to my office. This causes some complications right away because I bypass people. The action officer is supposed to tell his people what has happened and tell them what I think should be done. If the action officer is alert and enthusiastic and also believes that it should be done, it will get done, because *he* will follow through and *he* will do the checking [emphasis in original]." This was "the main reason why," that, as CNO, Burke believed he could "influence things but I must get things done by persuasion and sometimes things do not get done which I think should be done."[40]

In spite of such constraints and frustrations, Burke was a remarkably effective leader, capable of inspiring and persuading his bureaucracy. A master of the memo, he was able to tweak, cajole, and encourage his subordinates with pointed commentary and teasing good humor. In an era before computers and satellite communications, he kept his fleet commanders informed of what they needed to know by message, "Flag Officers' Dope," or a lengthy letter, as appropriate. His top leadership in OpNav (as would future historians) benefited from his memoranda for the record of more than 150 meetings of the Joint Chiefs of Staff, Armed Forces Policy Council, and National Security Council that he circulated for information or for action. His occasional rages were legendary but infrequent. For the most part, he motivated his staff by his own example of hard work and devotion to the service and his willingness to share generously the credit for any successes that came his way.

Burke's approach to leadership and his strategic vision of the importance of naval power in waging the Cold War came together in his efforts to build strong and lasting relationships with the navies of countries allied with the United States. This strategy began to take shape in 1950–51; while serving as the deputy chief of staff to Commander, Naval Forces, Far East, in Japan, he was instrumental in helping to lay the groundwork for the establishment of the Japanese Maritime Self-Defense Force. His commitment continued to grow throughout his tour as director of OpNav's Strategic Plans Division in 1952–54, as he worked to provide friendly naval forces with loans or transfers of ships and equipment under the Mutual Defense Assistance Program. As CNO, he looked to supporting the West German, Japanese, Nationalist Chinese, and many South American navies through ship and equipment assistance. In 1959–60, Burke established the annual UNITAS cruise and at-sea antisubmarine warfare exercises with South American navies. He also built strong personal relationships with, among others, Admiral of the Fleet Lord Mountbatten, the British First Sea Lord and later Chief of the Defence Staff; Vice Admiral Friedrich Ruge, chief of the naval forces of the Federal Republic of Germany; Vice Admiral Zenshiro Hoshina of Japan; and Admiral Henri Nomy of the French navy. Believing there was a professional bond and code of conduct among naval officers that transcended nationality, Burke established the Naval Command College at the Naval War College in 1956. The Naval Command College, designed to bring together outstanding and rising senior officers from allied and friendly nations to study naval power, work out problems, and develop bonds of trust and understanding, is among Burke's most long-lasting accomplishments. It continues to thrive at Newport and to expand navy-to-navy contacts well beyond the end of the Cold War.

## The Last CNO

Arleigh Burke was the last CNO to command the fleets. As "executive agent" under the Joint Chiefs of Staff, Burke directed the Commanders-in-Chief of the Atlantic and Pacific Fleets (CinCLant and CinCPac) and Commander-in-Chief, U.S. Naval Forces, Northeast Atlantic and Mediterranean (CinCNELM) where to move their forces in times of peace, crisis, and war. Also, as CNO, he had direct control over the sensitive submarine reconnaissance operations that gathered intelligence on the Soviet Union and its navy.[41]

During the Suez Crisis in October-November 1956, when England, France, and Israel attacked Egypt in response to Egypt's nationalization of the Suez Canal, Soviet Premier Nikita Khrushchev, beset by rebellion in Hungary and turmoil in Poland, threatened to send "volunteers" to aid Egypt and rain nuclear rockets on Egypt's attackers. U.S. policy looked to end the conflict and defuse the potential NATO (North Atlantic Treaty Organization) crisis. When Burke ordered the Sixth Fleet into the Eastern Mediterranean, Fleet Commander Vice Admiral C. R. ("Cat") Brown inquired of the CNO, "Whose side am I on?" Burke shot back, "Take no guff from anyone."[42] Burke concluded from the crisis that "as usual, only naval forces could take the military action that was required when the situation broke" and that his direct operational control of the fleets maximized their ability to respond quickly.[43] The following year, Burke twice moved the Sixth Fleet into the Eastern Mediterranean to deal with crises in Jordan and Turkey. A Washington columnist observed of these operations, "Our armed forces divide the chores. Whenever trouble brews, the navy gets the first assignment—and the Air Force gets the first appropriation." A delighted CNO passed the newspaper clipping on to the military assistant to the Secretary of Defense with two comments: "We didn't plant it," and "It's true."[44]

During 1958, two crises occurring in rapid succession on opposite sides of the globe again demonstrated the value of naval forces that were ready to respond. In May 1958, President Camille Chamoun of Lebanon notified the United States that he might need U.S. help to defend against a possible Syrian invasion. Determined not to be caught unprepared, as were the British by the Suez crisis, Burke dispatched the Sixth Fleet to the Eastern Mediterranean and added two U.S. Marine battalion landing teams to the one already in the area. A coup in Iraq in mid-July led Chamoun to request immediate U.S. support. President Eisenhower's order to land the U.S. Marines allowed Burke only thirteen hours for implementation, rather than the twenty-four hours that he had said he needed. Nevertheless, the fleet put the first Marines ashore the next morning and sent in reinforcements over the next few days. The lesson of Lebanon, Burke believed, was that the command system worked:

> Since the CNO was in command of the Fleets, I was responsible to the JCS
> [Joint Chiefs of Staff] and to the President for the readiness and movement
> of the Fleets. I followed President Eisenhower's and the JCS directives but it
> was up to me to have the Fleets positioned and ready for action whenever
> and wherever they were needed.

So I moved the Sixth Fleet and made other necessary preparations including reinforcing it for any emergency—or at least for some of them. Naturally everybody was informed, but I did not have to wait until the end of
weeks of debate before getting ready. It was a very flexible command system
in which action could be taken very fast. It was a decentralized system.[45]

The second crisis, in Taiwan Straits, closely followed the operation in
Lebanon. In late August 1958, the People's Republic of China launched a
heavy artillery attack against the Nationalist Chinese–held islands of Quemoy
and Matsu, less than twelve miles off the coast of mainland China. Burke believed that the Nationalists could defend the islands against a protracted siege
if they had American aid and argued strongly that the United States was obligated to help. Despite criticism in Washington that the islands had little
strategic importance and their defense might lead to nuclear war, Burke argued that to refuse to defend them against the Communists was intolerable: "If
we retreat under fire and retreat under pressure, where does that leave us in
the eyes of the rest of the world—and our own eyes?"[46] Burke believed that the
United States had to be ready to use tactical nuclear weapons if Chinese forces
attempted to invade Quemoy, but he did not expect the crisis to go that far.
Shifting forces from the Mediterranean and the United States, the CNO
moved to reinforce the Seventh Fleet with three attack aircraft carriers, two
cruisers, additional destroyers, and more nuclear-strike aircraft. From August
until the end of the year American warships surveilled the mainland and escorted Nationalist convoys resupplying the islands. The shelling continued
into early October, but no invasion was attempted, and the crisis quietly faded.

Even as Burke was directing these critical operations in the Mediterranean
and Western Pacific, events were transpiring in Washington to bring an end to
the CNO's operational control of the nation's naval forces. Proposals for increased unification, or even merger, of the armed services and creation of an
American general staff had been presented by various individuals and organi-
zations throughout the 1950s. In April 1958, President Eisenhower had sent a
special message to Congress that called for reorganization of the Defense Department to consolidate the power of the Secretary of Defense and reduce the
authority of the civilian and military heads of the individual services. In particular, direct control of operating forces would be transferred from the service
chiefs to the President and the Secretary of Defense. The Joint Staff was to be
enlarged, and the chairman's power over it enhanced. The role of the Joint
Chiefs was to be redefined, so that they would function as a unit, with their primary responsibility being to act as joint advisers to the Secretary of Defense,
rather than as heads of their own services.

Burke acknowledged the need for reform measures to clarify the responsi-

bilities of the Joint Chiefs and the Secretary of Defense and increase coordination in combined operations. Nevertheless, he had serious reservations
about Eisenhower's plan. Burke was reluctant to see operational command of
the U.S. Navy removed from the control of the Chief of Naval Operations.
Only naval officers, he believed, were familiar enough with the unique requirements of operations at sea to direct them with the dispatch that was needed in far-flung crisis situations. He was deeply worried about the prospect of a
unified military service, in which command of naval forces might fall to an
Army or Air Force officer who knew nothing about seafaring. Too many mistakes would be made, which would threaten the success of complex and critical operations. In addition, Burke liked the existing structure of the JCS, which
he saw as a forum where diverse views were argued. A microcosm of democracy where balance was maintained, it prevented "singlemindedness, one concept domination, one interest, one strategy, one military posture, one
weapon."[47] He worried that expansion of the Joint Staff could eventually lead
to creation of a national general staff powerful enough to quash debate over
strategy and tactics and allow a move toward complete merger of the armed
services. Unable to convince Eisenhower to alter the plan, Burke offered as
much support as he could in hearings before Congress, but he also explained
his reservations freely enough to provoke a storm of criticism from those who
thought he owed the President an unqualified endorsement. Convinced that
he would not be reappointed when his term expired, Burke took a certain grim
pleasure in riding out the storm. He had no political ambitions and would not
mind being fired for defending the Navy, he explained to a friend, and that
"gives me a freedom of action which is quite a powerful asset."[48]

The Defense Reorganization Act of 1958 became law on 6 August, and its
provisions were gradually implemented into 1959. Despite its passage, Burke
was able to claim a minor victory in what the act did not do: it did not provide
for the de jure or de facto establishment of a national general staff, nor did it
lay the groundwork for eventual merger of the armed services. One important
battle was lost, but one that Burke had been resigned to losing. The CNO was
removed from direct operational control of the fleets, although his office did
retain control over planning operations and thereby continued to set operational parameters.

The loss of control over fleet operations created more of a problem for his
successors than it did for Burke. After his first difficult year, Burke enjoyed an
unusually close relationship with Eisenhower. He was an effective member of
the administration's foreign policy team and worked harmoniously with military commanders, as well as the State Department and the Central Intelligence Agency (CIA). As the voice for the Navy in foreign policy problems resulting from civil wars and domestic unrest in Indonesia (1957–58), Cuba

(1957–60), and the Congo (1960), he exercised considerable influence on foreign policy decisions. During military preparations for dealing with a potential Soviet and East German closure of Western access to Berlin in 1959, Burke proposed the possibility of naval countermeasures against Soviet maritime choke points in the Norwegian Sea, Baltic Sea, and Mediterranean Sea/Black Sea as a means of applying pressure on the Soviets from areas where the United States had military leverage. This proposal set in motion a plan for maritime contingencies that remained in effect through the unification of Germany in 1990.[49]

By 1958, even as Burke was raising questions about the Defense Reorganization Act, Eisenhower began sending notes addressed to "Arleigh." In February 1959, the President presented Burke with a bottle of scotch as congratulations for the launch of a Vanguard satellite. Burke's public affairs officer, Commander C. R. ("Buck") Wilhide, drafted a humorous reply, in which an increasingly inebriated Burke expressed his thanks for the gift. The final paragraph ended: "Mush quitnow an fine anodder bodel odish delic iuocius boos." When Wilhide next checked, he was horrified to find that Burke had signed the letter in a mock drunken scrawl and sent it to the White House. The President, rather than being offended, delightedly thanked Burke for "a much needed chuckle." Arleigh Burke was the last CNO to have such a personal relationship with a serving President of the United States.[50] In 1959, when Burke let it be known that he did not wish to be reappointed for a third term because he feared he might be getting into "a rut" after four years, which "doesn't help the Navy any," Eisenhower refused to part with him. He told Burke flat out that it was his duty to accept reappointment. He was an indispensable part of the team.[51]

Despite the President's respect for Burke, the Eisenhower administration continued to whittle away at the flexibility of U.S. military strategy, in direct opposition to the CNO's long-standing positions that diversity of weapon systems and flexibility in strategic planning were critical to national security. The strongest blow was delivered in the summer and fall of 1960 when Secretary of Defense Thomas Gates decided to consolidate nuclear war planning in a Joint Strategic Target Planning Staff (JSTPS) located at Strategic Air Command headquarters in Omaha, Nebraska. Gates, as well as the President, regarded the move as a compromise. The Air Force wanted operational control over all strategic nuclear delivery systems, including Polaris, in a combined strategic command dominated by the Air Force. Gates's decision was designed to address Air Force concerns by eliminating wasteful and dangerous duplication in war planning while stopping short of removing the Polaris from Navy control. Burke found the compromise unacceptable and said so to the President. The proposed JSTPS would put SAC in a position to dominate national war planning. Requirements for nuclear weapons would be based on SAC's first-strike targeting concepts, excessive criteria for damage to be attained in a war, and conservative operational factors. A firm floor would be established below which strategic forces requirements could not fall. When Eisenhower backed Gates in August, Burke quickly sent some of the Navy's best officers to Omaha to join the staff and try to guard against SAC's targeting excesses. Even with these efforts, however, the National Strategic Target List and Single Integrated Operational Plan, produced in the fall of 1960, basically doomed the Navy's "finite deterrence" concept and second-strike targeting "alternative undertaking" from ever controlling national nuclear strategy and policy. Burke feared that this would severely limit the nation's future strategic flexibility as ballistic missiles came of age and limited wars proliferated around the Eurasian periphery.

In the fall of 1960, Burke told President Eisenhower that he wanted to retire at the end of his third term as CNO. In early January 1961, before the Kennedy administration came to power, planning commenced for a CNO change of command that summer. Although John F. Kennedy asked Burke if he would consider serving another term, Burke was convinced that this "job was nothing I wanted to continue."[52] He respected the new President, as well as his brilliant, if inexperienced, Secretary of Defense Robert McNamara and his Secretary of the Navy John Connally, but Burke found himself uncomfortable with many of the policy assumptions of the new administration and its style of management. He was irked by the systems analysis approach to developing defense policy and strategy and by the arrogant attitudes of junior officials in the Defense Department, who seemed to feel, he thought, that civilian control of the military meant that any civilian was the superior of any military officer. Kennedy did away with many of the systems that Eisenhower had established for assigning responsibilities and communicating decisions because he found them too confining, but he never clearly specified what would take their place. Burke often found himself at a loss to understand just what the President wanted from him.

Two episodes in the spring of 1961 topped off Burke's sense of frustration. The first was the administration's conduct of the planning, execution, and subsequent investigation of the Bay of Pigs invasion of Fidel Castro's Cuba by CIA-backed and trained Cuban exiles. Burke and the other Joint Chiefs had serious doubts about the military feasibility of the CIA plan but were never given the opportunity to fully assess it, nor were they asked to approve it. Under pressure from Secretary of State Dean Rusk, the landing site was switched from a friendly and isolated village on Cuba's south coast to the Bay of Pigs. The Joint Chiefs did not like the switch, but, even though they reviewed the plan a number of times and commented on specific aspects, they did not object to the President. The Joint Chiefs felt that they had no choice but to do their best to make the plan work because that was what the President appeared to want. Kennedy, on the other hand, seems to have interpreted their silence as approval. The landing took place on 16–17 April 1961. After a last-minute decision to withhold supporting American air strikes in order to improve deniability, Burke, who had not been told of the decision until too late, now knew that the invasion was headed for disaster. To the CNO, it seemed intolerable that the United States was willing to send a fighting force into danger with totally inadequate support or logistical planning. Helpless to avert the debacle, all he could do was pray for the lives of the men doomed by American bungling.[53]

In part, Burke's anger over the Bay of Pigs reflected his firm belief that Communist governments could be overthrown by popular uprising if the spark could be successfully lighted. The invasion by Cuban exiles might have worked if the United States had been willing to stand behind them. In the spring of 1961, Burke pushed for such a national commitment to the defense of Laos against Communist pressure from the Pathet Lao. Training the Laotian people to defend themselves would be the first step, but, he argued, the United States must be prepared to intervene with its own forces, including tactical nuclear weapons, if necessary. The military difficulties involved in mounting an American war effort in a distant, landlocked country were enormous, but if the United States were committed to defeating Communism, it must be prepared to take the necessary risks. War is not a game to be dabbled in, Burke warned; it is a deadly serious business. Willingness to use all necessary military force might make the use of any military force unnecessary. Lack of commitment, on the other hand, would only encourage Communist expansion and make ultimate confrontation, or even ultimate defeat, inevitable. Burke's argument for intervention in Laos was not popular with either the Kennedy administration or the Congress, particularly in the wake of the embarrassing failure in Cuba. As it turned out, no American action was required. A cease-fire put an end to the immediate crisis, but tensions remained unresolved in the long term.

On 22 April, as the Laotian crisis was coming to a head, President Kennedy appointed the Cuban Study Group under General Maxwell Taylor to review the Bay of Pigs operation and make recommendations about how similar mistakes could be avoided in the future. Burke served on this committee as the JCS representative and used the opportunity to press for clarification of the U.S. commitment to intervene in local conflicts. The committee's report, sent to the President in June, called for restructuring lines of communication within the administration to ensure that the JCS assumed responsibility for planning both military and paramilitary operations. It also recommended establishment of an interagency group to plan and execute the kind of local Cold War operations deemed necessary to counter Communist expansion. Kennedy accepted and implemented many of the committee's recommendations, perhaps Burke's last major contribution to the shaping of American national policy.

Relieved as CNO by Admiral George W. Anderson, Burke retired from the U.S. Navy on 1 August 1961. He was tired, "completely frustrated," and "felt there was nothing I could accomplish."[54] He was concerned that the Kennedy administration would not wage the Cold War as aggressively or as competently as he thought necessary. Moreover, he was convinced that the Navy was facing a long-term crisis in its force levels and that, if ship construction were not increased over the 1961 level of 22 ships a year, the active fleet of 817 ships would decline to 440 within two decades. Nevertheless, after a few months of decompression, he plunged into his new civilian life with the same energy and dedication that he had brought to his naval career. He became a long-term member of several major corporate boards, including Newport News Shipbuilding and Drydock Company, Chrysler Corporation, Thiokol Corporation, and Texaco. In 1962, Burke helped to organize the Georgetown University Center for Strategic and International Studies. He served as its chairman, counselor, and executive committee member for fifteen years and helped to build it into a major Washington policy analysis institution. Although he had never been a Boy Scout and had no children of his own, Burke also served as president and member of the executive committee of the National Capital Area Council of the Boy Scouts of America from 1962 to 1974, one more expression of his strong personal commitment to building patriotism and citizenship.

Although he continued avidly to follow the fortunes of the Navy and was glad to do whatever he could for the service whenever his help was requested, Burke never interfered in current naval policy or practice and never criticized any of his CNO successors. Great honors continued to come to him for his postretirement service, including the nation's highest civilian honor, the Medal of Freedom, awarded by President Gerald Ford in January 1977. In November 1982, Secretary of the Navy John Lehman bestowed on Burke his most signal tribute by naming for him not just one ship but the entire class of the new DDG-51 guided-missile destroyers. Despite increasing infirmity, he and Roberta Burke attended the USS *Arleigh Burke*'s keel laying in 1986, her launching in 1989, and sea trials and commissioning in 1991. Burke was the only living American ever to see the ship named for him go to sea.

Arleigh Burke "slipped his chain" at Bethesda Naval Hospital from complications of pneumonia at 0530 on New Year's Day, 1996. His funeral at the Naval Academy chapel on 4 January brought more than two thousand people, including the past and present high commands of the U.S. Navy and the President of the United States to say goodbye. President William Clinton declared, "The Navy all Americans are proud of, the Navy that stood up to fascism and stared down communism and advances our values and freedom today—that Navy is Arleigh Burke's Navy."[55]

During his last years, Burke summed up his long life as follows: "Life has been good to me. I didn't die young. I wasn't killed in the war. I did most everything I wanted to do, and some things I didn't want to do. I had a job I liked and a woman I loved. Couldn't ask for more than that."[56] Burke was many things during his lifetime—chemical engineer, ordnance design and production specialist, wartime combat commander, staff officer, service chief, architect of national policy, and corporate officer. On his tombstone, however, he requested only one word to sum up his accomplishments: "Sailor."

FURTHER READING

Three books have been written about Arleigh Burke. The first two, Ken Jones, *Destroyer Squadron Twenty Three* (Philadelphia, 1959), and Ken Jones, with Hubert Kelley, *Admiral Arleigh (31 Knot) Burke: The Story of a Fighting Sailor* (Philadelphia, 1962) are long out of print. Jones, who died before completing the second book, did a great deal of interviewing for both books and also carried on correspondence with Burke's family and Navy colleagues. Unfortunately, the source data in both books cannot be reconstructed, and there are a number of factual errors in each. The most recent study, E. B. Potter, *Admiral Arleigh Burke, A Biography* (New York, 1989) was designed as a popular biography; it is thus heavy on World War II and very light (and often inaccurate) on Burke's postwar career. This author's essays, "Officer Development in the Interwar Navy: Arleigh Burke—The Making of a Naval Professional, 1919–1940," *Pacific Historical Review* 44 (November 1975); 503–26; "Arleigh Albert Burke," in Robert W. Love, Jr., ed., *The Chiefs of Naval Operations* (Annapolis, Md., 1980); and "Admiral Arleigh A. Burke, United States Navy," in Stephen Howarth, ed., *Men of War: Great Naval Leaders of World War II* (London, 1992), are a concise set of assessments of Burke's life and career based on interviews; access to Admiral Burke's papers, which was as complete as possible at the time of writing; and broad research in declassified official and unofficial papers in Navy, Joint Chiefs of Staff, and Defense Department files at the Navy's Operational Archives and the National Archives, and presidential papers at the Truman, Eisenhower, and Kennedy Libraries. The postwar history of the U.S. Navy is in desperate need of solid work. Michael Isenberg's nine-hundred-page opus, *Shield of the Republic: The United States Navy in an Era of Cold War and Violent Peace, 1945–1962* (New York, 1993) is colorful but filled with errors and omissions. The two best surveys are Robert W. Love, Jr., *History of the U.S. Navy, vol. 2, 1942–1991* (Harrisburg, Pa., 1992), and George Baer, *One Hundred Years of Sea Power: The U.S. Navy, 1890–1990* (Stanford, Calif., 1994), but both are based essentially on secondary sources. Solid studies based on primary sources for Burke's period are Jeffrey Barlow, *Revolt of the Admirals: The Fight for Naval Aviation, 1945–1950* (Washington, D.C., 1994); Gary Weir, *Forged in War, the Naval-Industrial Complex and American Submarine Construction, 1940–1961* (Washington, D.C., 1993); Richard G. Hewlett and Francis Duncan, *Nuclear Navy, 1945–1962* (Chicago, 1974); Thomas C. Hone, *Power and Change: The Administrative History of the Office of the Chief of Naval Operations, 1946–1986* (Washington, D.C., 1989); and this author's two essays, "The Origins of Overkill, Nuclear Weapons and American Strategy, 1945–1960," *International Security* 7 (Spring 1983), 3–71, and "Process: The Realities of Formulating Modern Naval Strategy," in James Goldrick and John B. Hattendorf, eds., *Mahan is Not Enough, the Proceedings of a Conference on the Works of Sir Julian Corbett and Admiral Sir Herbert Richmond* (Newport, R.I., 1993), 141–75.

NOTES

1. See the obituaries of Admiral Burke in *The New York Times, The Washington Post,* and *The Washington Times,* 2 January 1996; the special edition of *Surface Warfare Magazine* 16 (September-October 1991), commemorating the commissioning of the USS *Arleigh Burke* (DDG-51); and E. B. Potter, *Admiral Arleigh Burke, A Biography* (New York, 1989), which devotes eleven chapters to Burke's World War II service and three chapters to his six years as Chief of Naval Operations.

2. This essay is based primarily on the author's three essays on Burke's life and career: "Officer Development in the Interwar Navy: Arleigh Burke—The Making of a Naval Professional, 1919–1940," *Pacific Historical Review* 44 (November 1975): 503–26; "Arleigh Albert Burke," in Robert W. Love, Jr., ed., *The Chiefs of Naval Operations* (Annapolis, Md., 1980), 262–319, 417–29; "Admiral Arleigh A. Burke, United States Navy," in Stephen Howarth, ed., *Men of War: Great Naval Leaders of World War II* (London, 1992), 506–27; and on the author's ongoing research in Admiral Burke's papers for a full life-and-times biography. Unless otherwise noted, information in the current essay is drawn from the previous essays.

3. Burke to author, January 1973.

4. Burke to Roberta Gorsuch, 17 December 1922, 19 January 1923, 22 January 1923, Arleigh Burke Papers (hereafter cited as Burke Papers), Operational Archives, Naval Historical Center (NHA). Burke's Naval Academy Official Record in the Naval Academy Archives indicates that he withdrew his request for a Marine commission on 5 February 1923.

5. These figures are derived from data on the Class of 1923 in Department of the Navy, *Register of Commissioned and Warrant Officers of the U.S. Navy and Marine Corps, July 1, 1940* (Washington, D.C., 1940), 80–87.

6. Burke to Roberta Gorsuch, at sea, July 1922; 22 January 1923; and 6 February 1923, Burke Papers.

7. U.S. Department of the Navy, *Annual Report of the Secretary of the Navy, for the Fiscal Year 1923* (Washington, D.C., 1923), 596.

8. These statistics are from Bureau of Navigation, Navy Department, *Navy Directory, Officers of the United States Navy and Marine Corps, July 1, 1923* (Washington, D.C., 1923).

9. Fitness Report, October 1, 1939–May 9, 1940, by Captain F. E. M. Whiting, Burke Papers.

10. Burke to Whiting, 6 December 1946, Personal File (PF), Burke Papers.

11. Rear Admiral Robert Speck, USN (Ret.), to author, 15 August 1971.

12. Rear Admiral H. H. McIlhenny, USN (Ret.), to author, 17 August 1971.

13. Commander, Destroyer Division 43, to Commander, Task Force 19, Subject: Employment of Destroyers, Secret, Serial 37, 7 May 1943, PF, Burke Papers.

14. Commander, Destroyer Division 44, to Destroyers of Task Force 31, 22 July 1943,

and Battle Plan, 1 August 1943; Commander Rodger Simpson to Burke, 28 August 1943; and Burke to Roberta Burke, 8 August 1943, all in PF, Burke Papers.

15. Burke, narrative, Film 411-1, 31 July 1945, PF, Burke Papers, 13.

16. CinCPac RI Secret Message 240348 November 1943 in U.S. Navy Commander-in-Chief Pacific Intelligence Bulletins (No. 534–No. 655), 1 September–31 December 1943, SRMN-013, Part III, NHA; Burke, Battle of Cape St. George, narrative, Film 411-2, recorded 1 August 1945, Burke Papers, 2.

17. President, Naval War College, to Commander-in-Chief, U.S. Fleet, Serial 4181, 13 January 1944, PF, Burke Papers.

18. Commander-in-Chief, U.S. Fleet, to Commander, Carrier Division Three, Naval Message 111700, March 1944, PF, Burke Papers.

19. Burke to Roberta Burke, 4, 11, and 15 April 1944; and transcript of Burke interview by Stan Smith, 12 July 1965, all in PF, Burke Papers.

20. Burke, Carrier Forces Pacific, Battle of the Philippine Sea, narrative, Film 417, recorded 20 August 1945, PF, Burke Papers, 1–13.

21. Quotations, in order given, are in Commander Task Force 58, Action Report, 14 March to 28 May 1945, Serial 00222, 18 June 1945, NHA; Theodore Taylor, *The Magnificent Mitscher* (New York, 1954), 279; Burke to Roberta Burke, 19 May 1945, PF, Burke Papers.

22. Burke to Roberta Burke, 18 August 1944; and Burke to Rear Admiral J. L. Kaufmann, 12 August 1944, both in PF, Burke Papers.

23. Burke to Roberta Burke, 9 February 1945, PF, Burke Papers.

24. On the "Admiral's Revolt" and Burke's part in it, see Jeffrey Barlow, *Revolt of the Admirals: The Fight for Naval Aviation, 1945–1950* (Washington, D.C., 1994), 165–218.

25. Burke to Captain C. D. Griffin, 8 October 1951, PF, Burke Papers.

26. This paragraph is based on a review of the recently declassified Strategic Plans Division files, NHA.

27. Burke to F. E. M. Whiting (draft), 30 July 1954, and Burke to Whiting, 31 July 1954, PF, Burke Papers.

28. Burke to Admiral of the Fleet Lord Louis Mountbatten, 4 February 1958, Mountbatten Folder, CNO Personal Files (CNOPF), Burke Papers. On Cold War naval strategy, see this author's "American Naval Strategy in the Era of the Third World War: An Inquiry into the Structure and Process of General War at Sea, 1945–1990," in N. A. M. Rodger, ed., *Naval Power in the Twentieth Century* (Annapolis, Md., 1996), 242–54; "The History of World War III, 1945–1990: A Conceptual Framework," in Robert David Johnson, ed., *On Cultural Ground, Essays in International History* (Chicago, 1994), 197–234; and "Process: The Realities of Formulating Modern Naval Strategy," in James Goldrick and John B. Hattendorf, eds., *Mahan Is Not Enough, the Proceedings of a Conference on the Works of Sir Julian Corbett and Admiral Sir Herbert Richmond* (Newport, R.I., 1993), 141–75.

29. Burke to Mountbatten.

30. Burke to Captain Geoffrey Bennett, RN, 5 March 1957, CNOPF, Burke Papers.

31. Burke to Mountbatten.

32. For a detailed assessment of Burke's role in the making of nuclear strategy, see this author's "The Origins of Overkill: Nuclear Weapons and American Strategy, 1945–1960," *International Security* 7 (Spring 1983): 3–71.

33. Vice Admiral R. E. Libby to Op-00, memorandum: "Proposals Relative to

Atomic Operation Concept," Serial BM00043-57, 1 May 1957, File A16-10, Atomic Warfare Operations, Box 8, Chief of Naval Operations Op-00 Files, NHA.

34. Rear Admiral R. E. Rose to Chief of Naval Operations, memorandum: "Inadequacy of $1.5 Billion Shipbuilding Funds Level," Serial 0041P03, 13 September 1957, A1(1) unlabeled folder; and Rose to Chief of Naval Operations, memorandum: "Impact of Polaris Program on Shipbuilding and Conversion Program," Serial 034903B1, 13 December 1957, A-1(1) Shipbuilding and Conversion Programs folder, both in Box 1, Op-00 Files, NHA.

35. Burke to Rear Admiral Walter Schindler, 14 May 1958, CNOPF, Burke Papers.

36. Ibid.

37. Ibid.

38. Ibid.

39. Henry B. Wilson et al., *Naval Leadership with Some Hints to Junior Officers and Others* (Annapolis, Md., 1924), 29–35.

40. Burke to Rear Admiral Robert Goldthwaite, 13 October 1960, CNOPF, Burke Papers.

41. Burke to Admiral Arthur Radford, memorandum: "Submarine Patrols," Op-00/rw, 7 November 1956; and Chief of Naval Operations to Chairman, Joint Chiefs of Staff, memorandum: "Submarine Reconnaissance Patrols," Op-332C3/msm, Serial 000104P33, 7 November 1956, both in Ship and Aircraft Movements, folder A4-3, Box 3, Op-00 Files, NHA.

42. CNO to ComSixthFleet, Naval Message 020615, November 1956, cited in Jill M. Hill, "Suez Crisis 1956, Center for Naval Analysis Study CRC 262" (Arlington, Va., 1974), 66–67.

43. Burke to Vice Admiral Friedrich Ruge, FGN, 14 November 1956, CNOPF, Burke Papers.

44. Chief of Naval Operations to Military Assistant to Secretary of Defense, memorandum: "Potomac Fever" by Fletcher Knebel, Op-00 Memo 281-57, 26 April 1957, Originators File, CNO Papers, Burke Papers.

45. Arleigh Burke, "The Lebanon Crisis," in Arnold R. Shapach, ed., *Proceedings, U.S. Naval Academy: Naval History Symposium* (Annapolis, Md., 1973), 73.

46. Arleigh Burke, "The Important Things Are Intangible," interview by Robert J. Donovan, *ONI Review*, November 1958, 517–20, NHA. On Taiwan Straits, see also Joseph F. Bouchard, *Command in Crisis, Four Case Studies* (New York, 1991), 57–86.

47. Letter, Burke to Schindler.

48. Burke to Captain George H. Miller, 10 July 1958, copy courtesy of the late Rear Admiral Miller.

49. Burke's Berlin proposals are discussed in Joel J. Sokolsky, *Seapower in the Nuclear Age, the United States Navy and NATO, 1949–1980* (Annapolis, Md., 1991), 67; their continuing impact is seen in Deep Sea planning under the quadripartite Live Oak contingency planning effort described by Dr. Gregory Pedlow, SHAPE (Supreme Headquarters, Allied Powers Europe) historian, in a series of unpublished papers for the Berlin Crisis Project of the Nuclear History Program in 1991–93. Burke's role in shaping Eisenhower foreign policy has been most recently discussed in Audrey R. Kahin and George McT. Kahin, *Subversion as Foreign Policy, the Secret Eisenhower and Dulles Debacle in Indonesia* (New York, 1995), 90–91, 120–27, 148–52, 170; Richard E. Welch, Jr., *Response to Revolution, the United States and the Cuban Revolution,*

1959–1961 (Chapel Hill, N.C., 1985), 49; and Thomas G. Paterson, *Contesting Castro, the United States and the Triumph of the Cuban Revolution* (New York, 1994), 83, 137, 156–59.

50. Burke to President Dwight D. Eisenhower, 18 February 1959, Burke folder, name series, Box 3, Ann Whitman File, Eisenhower Papers as President, 1953–1961, Dwight D. Eisenhower Library; Eisenhower to Burke, 25 February 1959, Eisenhower folder, CNOPF, Burke Papers.

51. The quoted words appear in Burke to Admiral Felix Stump, 27 November 1957, CNOPF, Burke Papers.

52. Arleigh Burke, oral history interview by Joseph E. O'Connor, John F. Kennedy Presidential Library.

53. On the Bay of Pigs and Burke's part in it, see Trumbull Higgins, *The Perfect Failure, Kennedy, Eisenhower and the CIA at the Bay of Pigs* (New York, 1987), 122–69; and Lucien S. Vandenbroucke, *Perilous Options, Special Operations as an Instrument of U.S. Foreign Policy* (New York, 1993), 19–50.

54. Burke, oral history interview.

55. "Remarks by the President at the Funeral Service for Admiral Arleigh Burke," 4 January 1996, copy in author's possession.

56. Quoted in "Funeral Program in Memory of Admiral Arleigh Burke," copy in author's possession.

# ☆ Hyman G. Rickover
☆
## ☆ Technology and Naval Tradition

*by Francis Duncan*

ADMIRAL HYMAN GEORGE RICKOVER WAS FORCED TO GIVE UP HIS leadership of the naval nuclear propulsion program at the end of January 1982. At that time, the U.S. Navy had in operation 135 nuclear-powered ships: 88 attack submarines, 33 ballistic missile submarines, 1 deep-submergence research vehicle, 4 attack aircraft carriers, and 9 cruisers. Authorized or under construction were 21 attack submarines, 9 Trident missile submarines, and 1 attack carrier; 5 submarines had been decommissioned and 2 had been lost at sea. The propulsion plants of all these ships had been designed and developed by Rickover and his organization during the more than three decades that he had led the program. For good reason, he was called "Father of the Nuclear Navy." He was also one of the most controversial figures who had ever worn the U.S. Navy uniform.[1]

This essay surveys the relationship between Rickover and the Navy. It does not discuss his contributions to the development of atomic power for civilian use or his books on education and American history.[2]

Nothing in Rickover's background foretold a naval career. Born on 27 January 1900 of poor Jewish parents in Makow, then part of czarist Poland, he was brought to the United States at the age of six. His father, a tailor, failing to make a living in New York City, moved to Chicago, Illinois, in 1909 or 1910. Life was hard, and, from a very early age, Rickover helped his family by working at odd jobs. After grade school, he had to find work. Fortunately, Western Union opened a branch office in his neighborhood; by working as a messenger boy at

*Rickover's personal views noted in this essay are from many years of the author's frequent conversations with Rickover and his associates.*

night, he earned money to help his family and was able to go to high school during the day. Graduating in 1918, he was determined to continue his education; but the country was at war and he soon would be subject to the draft.

The war that threatened Rickover's education, however, unexpectedly gave him the means for continuing it. To meet its need for officers to serve in a rapidly expanding fleet, the Navy had increased the number of men who could enter the Naval Academy. Through the influence of a cousin's uncle who was on the local draft board, Rickover was nominated by the congressman of his district. Never having thought of a naval career, he was badly prepared. Just barely passing the entrance examination, he entered the Academy on 29 June 1918 and graduated on 2 June 1922. He stood 107 in a class of 540.

Looking back, Rickover felt that the Academy had done a good job in preparing him for the Navy of that day. Accustomed to working hard, studying long hours, and making his own decisions, he considered himself far more mature than most of his classmates. He had to endure hazing but not as much as some other midshipmen. He had friends, although he was not to maintain close contact with them. In addition, he found that his religious and social background gave him the valuable perspective of an outsider, one who could look into the operations of an institution and differentiate between what was essential to its purpose and what was not.

From 1922 to 1927, he served in the destroyer *La Vallette* and the battleship *Nevada* and quickly earned the reputation of an intensely competitive officer who was always working, eager to accept responsibility, and determined to master his profession. He took postgraduate work in electrical engineering from 1927 to 1929. Until then, his knowledge of engineering had come from shipboard experience; at Columbia University, Rickover learned the principles of engineering. Eager for early command, he applied for submarine duty, despite a warning that, as a senior lieutenant, he was quite late in applying. From 1929 to 1933, he was in submarines, most of the time in the S-48. Although qualifying for command on 4 August 1931 and recognized for his engineering ability, he was not given his own ship. He left with a low opinion of submarine officers but with great respect for the dangerous environment in which their ships operated.

During his next tour, 1933–35, Rickover was assistant to the inspector of naval material in Philadelphia, where he rewrote the manual on batteries. As assistant engineer on the battleship *New Mexico* from 1935 to 1937, he gained an outstanding reputation by bringing her to first place in the competition for engineering efficiency for two consecutive years. Reporting to the Asiatic Fleet in 1937, he was given command of the minesweeper *Finch*. Finding her dirty and in poor condition, he tried to bring her up to the standards of the Pacific Fleet. Ships from several nations had gathered off Shanghai to protect their interests during the fighting between the Japanese and Chinese. With smartness deemed so important, Rickover was criticized for the appearance of his ship. He resented the emphasis on appearance instead of reality. Because his earlier application for engineering duty had been accepted, he was relieved of command of the *Finch* on 5 October 1937.

Becoming an engineering duty only (EDO) officer was a major change in Rickover's career. Officers with this designation could not exercise command afloat but usually served in navy yards and in Washington, D.C.; if all went well, they might reach the rank of rear admiral. Rickover was proud to be accepted. EDOs, few in number, were recognized as an elite throughout the Navy. After a stint in the Cavite yard in the Philippines, he reported to Washington on 15 August 1939, only a few weeks before the outbreak of World War II, and was assigned as second in command of the Electrical Section in the Bureau of Engineering (soon to become part of the Bureau of Ships).

His later career cannot be understood without considering the work of the section. Responsible for the design, development, and procurement of electrical systems, lighting, electric cables, motor controllers, circuit breakers, switchboards, and panels, as well as miscellaneous equipment, the section was an excellent school for learning ship design, construction, maintenance, and repair—and the workings of the Bureau of Ships and American industry.[3]

Rickover soon clashed with the bureau hierarchy. German magnetic mines laid by aircraft threatened control of the coastal waters of the British Isles. By developing special floating cable and shipboard generators, the British had devised a means to detonate the mines by creating magnetic fields. General Electric Company began manufacturing a large number of these generators at Rickover's request and on his personal assurance of reimbursement. Briefly, he was in trouble for not following procurement procedures, but a few highly placed officers recognized his foresight and praised him greatly.

Becoming head of the Electrical Section in December 1940, Rickover quickly recruited engineers from industry and added a number of subsections. He created his own management system by assigning specific individuals the entire spectrum of design, development, and procurement in the areas of their responsibility. When things went wrong or schedules slipped, he knew exactly whom to call. He established a system of keeping track of what was going on by insisting that, at the end of each day, he have a copy of every outgoing letter, even if in draft or incomplete. By scanning the correspondence, he was able to spot some problems before they became serious, catch trends, foresee difficulties, and assess the weaknesses and strengths of individuals in the section.

Pearl Harbor was probably Rickover's first big test as section head. Of the eight battleships that were damaged during the Japanese attacks, two—the

*West Virginia* and *California*—were electric drive. They had to be returned to the West Coast for repair and modernization, but several feet of filthy, muddy harbor water covered their propulsion plants. Never before had the Navy confronted such a situation. Dispute broke out over two courses of action. One proposed by many engineers and experts at Pearl Harbor and Washington called for careful washing and cleaning of the electric motors and auxiliary equipment. In contrast, Rickover argued that rewinding the motors was the only way to get reliable power. He flew to Hawaii and, just after the *California* entered dry dock, went down into the still-damp propulsion compartments and moved his hands along the wiring. The insulation came off like putty. Washing down never could have removed the contaminants that had penetrated deeply into the insulation. Under their own power and with rewound engines, the ships reached Puget Sound Navy Yard.

Inspection of the damaged ships from Pearl Harbor and of British ships sent to the United States for repair revealed the necessity for better electrical equipment. The Navy needed electric cable that would not leak water, equipment that would resist moisture and water, and systems that would supply emergency power from one part of a ship to another when the normal source had been severed. Further, the impact of waterborne shock from torpedoes, depth charges, and near misses from bombs was far greater than had been anticipated before the war. Even when a ship's hull was not ruptured, shock jarred vital equipment off its foundations. Rickover took the lead in developing shock testing.[4]

Before the war, when few ships were under construction, standardizing electrical equipment and components had not been necessary. During the massive wartime construction program, however, the Electrical Section found itself redesigning equipment, setting specifications, and determining schedules for production and delivery, as well as establishing priorities. The unprecedented scale of amphibious warfare also increased demands on the section. Rickover became involved in new areas, such as development of silicone insulation, infrared signaling and detection, and the location of underwater objects.[5]

Under his leadership, the section became the largest in the bureau and, instead of focusing mainly on contract administration, schedules, and inspections, kept control of its technical work. Rickover came to know the leaders of the electrical industry and also some of its best young engineers. Tireless, demanding, hard to get along with, and often abrasive, abusive, and insulting, Rickover could not be ignored. He won the respect of his own people by loading them with work and giving them new assignments. Industry complained loudly about his intense pressure but found that he achieved results. His contemporaries in the bureau deeply resented the way that he encroached on their responsibilities and disregarded organizational charts. In the small world of EDOs, Rickover was making many enemies who would not forget.

After six years in the Electrical Section, Rickover, who had been a captain since 26 June 1943, wanted overseas duty. Because of his outstanding record, he was given his choice of assignments. He selected the position of commander of the Naval Repair Base on Okinawa. The base would handle ships damaged in the invasion of Japan, repair those that could be returned to combat, and place others in condition to reach a major base or the West Coast. Rickover was to have the base in operation by 1 November 1945, the date set for the landing on Kyushu. When he was detached from the bureau in Washington on 24 March 1945, the landing on Okinawa was only days away.

Okinawa was secured on 21 June 1945. After visiting other installations in the Pacific, Rickover landed there on 20 July. He found his work exhilarating. Starting from nothing, he had to organize the men as they arrived, get the equipment ashore, decide the best location for various facilities, and battle the intense dust, driving rain, and bottomless mud. The repair base was taking shape when the Army Air Force, on 6 August, dropped the first atomic bomb on Hiroshima and, three days later, the second on Nagasaki. Rickover was left with the job of taking care of what had been built until Washington decided on the role of Okinawa.

Even before the fighting stopped, he was troubled by what he had seen. Victory seemed to be due less to the skill of the Navy than the strength of American industry. The Navy ignored the special talents of officers who had joined from civilian life. The gulf between officers and enlisted men was bad: it appeared to Rickover that, far too often, constructing elaborate amenities for officers took priority over providing spartan facilities for enlisted men. Many in the enlisted ranks came from good homes, had good education, and, having good cause to resent the privileges that rank bestowed, would be hostile to the Navy on their return to civilian life.

One event on Okinawa had a personal impact. In the presence of other officers, Rickover had confronted Commodore Fred D. Kirtland, commander of the Naval Operating Base, over the choice of officer to command the boat pool. Rickover got his way, but the price was a bad fitness report.

Discouraged and uncertain of his future in the Navy and knowing no one in industry who would hire him, Rickover returned to the United States in November 1945. Temporarily, he was inspector general of the Nineteenth Fleet, which was charged with decommissioning and mothballing ships. In the spring of 1946, he learned that he might be sent to the Massachusetts Institute of Technology in connection with some aspect of atomic energy. A little later, he found he was to go to Oak Ridge, Tennessee, one of the major installations of the Army's Manhattan Engineer District, which had developed the atomic bomb.

In January 1939, American scientists had learned of the Hahn-Strassmann experiment that split an atom and released energy. Ross Gunn, a physicist at the Naval Research Laboratory, saw in atomic energy a potential means for propelling a true submarine, one that could operate independently of the earth's atmosphere. But the urgency of developing the atomic bomb and President Franklin D. Roosevelt's decision to limit severely Navy participation in the Manhattan Project had blocked pursuing the promise. With the war over, the Navy resumed its interest. In April 1946, the Bureau of Ships accepted an invitation to send to Oak Ridge a handful of engineers who, along with some from industry, would gain practical experience in the very new field of reactor technology.

To make the most of the opportunity, the bureau selected outstanding men—a captain and four other officers of lower rank. Vice Admiral Earle W. Mills, assistant chief of the bureau, substituted Rickover for the captain on the list. The reaction was immediate and stormy: Rickover could not be trusted; he would take control of the program; he would not be able to get along with the Army. Mills had seen Rickover in action in the Electrical Section and held fast, but he had to yield on one point. Rickover would have no control over the other four officers. Mills faced another problem. Rickover believed that the bureau was trying to ease him out of Washington and did not want to go to Oak Ridge. Mills, also quite forceful, persuaded him to go.

Rickover reported to Oak Ridge on 4 June 1946. He made an excellent impression on the Army and, by dint of his personality and his bureaucratic skill, gained control over the other four officers. Although the Manhattan Project had built reactors, they were for research and the production of plutonium and were completely unsuitable for ship propulsion. As a team, the five officers studied, attended lectures and seminars, interviewed anyone with knowledge of reactor technology, and wrote detailed reports to the bureau. They were certain that nuclear propulsion was feasible, but the technical problems were enormous.[6]

At Oak Ridge, Rickover had found a cause that would drive him for the rest of his career. To lead the Navy's nuclear propulsion program, he was willing to maneuver and scheme and to work endless hours to master the technology.

Three reactor types appeared to be the most promising—gas cooled, liquid metal cooled, and pressurized water moderated and cooled—although none had been built for producing power. All had fundamental problems in common: components had to operate reliably for long periods of time in an environment of intense radiation, systems had to be worked out to control the power output, and radiation shielding had to be devised to protect personnel. Each approach had its own technical difficulties; metals and materials had to be investigated and tested to determine if they could be fabricated and could maintain their integrity against radiation. Thousands of pounds of zirconium, for example, were needed in the pressurized water approach, but, in 1947, when Rickover decided to use it, only small amounts were available and it was very expensive. The liquid metal- and water-cooled reactors were carried to shipboard use.

Rickover reached some important conclusions. No one in the program or associated with it should receive, under the guise of military necessity, more radiation than the level established by civilian authority for civilian personnel. Nuclear propulsion could not be developed by scientists; they were too interested in research and lacked practical engineering sense. It could not be developed within the existing structure of the Bureau of Ships; the technical problems were too great and far beyond anything the bureau had ever handled. Put another way, nuclear propulsion could be best developed by an organization and a leader such as the Electrical Section had during the war. Whether Rickover would be the one to put these principles into effect was another matter. The bureau had sent other officers to other sites. In more than one shouting match, they challenged Rickover's claim to leadership.

The Navy, however, could not do much until the American people, the Congress, and the President determined how to control the power of the atom. From these forces came the Atomic Energy Act of 1946, which gave a monopoly of the development and use of atomic energy to a commission headed by five civilians. Assuming its responsibilities on 1 January 1947, the Atomic Energy Commission (AEC) struggled to build a stockpile of nuclear weapons and to convert the emergency wartime effort to a stable long-term program. Against these urgent priorities, a naval propulsion reactor had little weight.

Aided by some shrewd maneuvering by Rickover, Mills got the AEC to give official status to a naval reactor project. Mills had no intention, however, of letting Rickover head the effort. That assignment would fall to Rear Admiral Thorvald A. Solberg, an able and highly respected bureau officer who would serve as a liaison between the Navy and the AEC. At the last moment, Solberg received another assignment. On 16 July 1948, Mills, almost in an act of desperation, named Rickover to the post.

Even had the original plan gone into effect, Rickover unquestionably would have played a major role, if for no other reason than that no other officer knew so much of the technology. Under the changed circumstances, however, he could shape the program. He was further aided by the confusion that marked the AEC's reactor development effort. He would not be a liaison officer but, putting into effect an earlier idea he had proposed to Mills, Rickover would head a joint Atomic Energy Commission and U.S. Navy program and answer to both agencies. As an AEC official, he was responsible for the design and development of the Navy's reactors and for their safe operation. As a Navy officer, he had to make sure the ships were designed and built to meet the requirements of the propulsion plant. Probably no one, not even Rickover, could see how much power the dual responsibility was to give him.

Within limits, he could play one agency against the other. A good example of this technique occurred in 1950 when the Navy's General Board was considering the 1952 shipbuilding program. Rickover informed the General Board that the AEC was developing a submarine reactor. Therefore, the Navy had to have a submarine in the building program. If it did not, the AEC might turn its attention elsewhere. Because of this argument and some important support in the Navy, the *Nautilus* was included in the construction program. It should also be noted, parenthetically, that support from submarine officers enabled Rickover to win his contention that she should be a warship, not an experimental platform; otherwise, he believed, the Navy would not be convinced of the military significance of nuclear propulsion. When faced by opposition from the AEC and forced to fight for essential materials, he could point out that the reactor plant had to be ready for the submarine in the Navy's program.

In summary, the organization that he created was simple. He made the decisions. Obviously, he had to have help. For that purpose, he recruited engineers and sent them for training either to the Massachusetts Institute of Technology or to the reactor school that he had founded at Oak Ridge. Contractors, primarily Westinghouse Electric Corporation and General Electric Company, did the technical work and proposed courses of action and solutions to obstacles. Although true in essentials, this brief summary does not reflect the hectic and frantic activity of all concerned.

To force technical decisions early, Rickover built land prototype plants, complete with reactor and associated steam equipment arranged as if in a ship, while the submarines themselves were under construction. The pressurized water prototype was constructed in Idaho for the *Nautilus* as she was being built by Electric Boat Company at Groton, Connecticut. While the liquid metal prototype for the *Seawolf*, the navy's second nuclear-powered submarine, was being built at West Milton, New York, the ship was under construction at Electric Boat. Problems encountered in the prototypes were solved before they were met on the building ways. Constructing the prototypes gave essential training to the Navy, the AEC, the fabricators of reactor components, and Electric Boat.

Although the program was moving ahead rapidly and attracting national attention, Rickover was in trouble. The Navy's selection board had twice passed him over for promotion to rear admiral; therefore, he had to retire on 30 June 1953. Because the engineers on the board selected the engineers for promotion, the source of the opposition was clear. Early that year, Rickover's key personnel, most of them civilians, decided to fight. They went to Congressman Sidney R. Yates, who represented the Chicago district in which Rickover had once lived, and to Senator Henry M. Jackson of the Senate Armed Services Committee. In his speeches on the floor, Yates contrasted Rickover's accomplishments against the rigidity of the promotion system, and Jackson worked among his colleagues. In the face of their efforts and public response, the Senate Armed Services Committee held up the Navy's promotions. A new selection board, over the bitter opposition of the engineer officers, promoted Rickover to flag rank.

The struggle also involved a clash between two philosophies. Every few years, the Navy rotated an officer from one assignment to another so that the officer could gain broader experience in management and prepare for higher command. Rickover exemplified a different approach. Nuclear propulsion was too demanding and the results of a wrong decision could be too devastating for anyone to lead the program who did not thoroughly know the technology—a process that took years. Rickover had won, but the intervention of Congress widened the gulf between him and the rest of the Navy.

Progress was visible. President Harry S Truman laid the keel of the *Nautilus* on 14 June 1952. In Idaho, the land prototype began a one hundred-hour power run on 25 June 1953; for the first time, atomic energy produced power in the amount and with the reliability necessary to drive machinery. First Lady Mamie Eisenhower christened the submarine on 21 January 1954. A year later, on 17 January, Rickover took the *Nautilus* on sea trials. In one record-breaking voyage after another and in exercises with the fleet, she vividly demonstrated the revolutionary impact of nuclear propulsion on undersea operations and, so far as technology was concerned, proved the superiority of the pressurized water approach for ship propulsion.

In 1958, the *Nautilus* steamed, submerged, across the Arctic Ocean and beneath the North Pole. To celebrate the event, the White House held a reception for her captain and invited leading figures in the Navy and the AEC to attend. Unfortunately, Rickover was not asked, an omission the press gleefully picked up. Congress used this oversight to vote him a gold medal and to force his promotion to vice admiral. The Joint Committee on Atomic Energy, however, which counted powerful figures in both houses among its members, was already taking steps to advance Rickover. As rear admiral, Rickover would have to retire in January 1960; as vice admiral, he would retire in January 1962.

Congress supported, protected, and advanced Rickover and authorized and appropriated funds for the program because of the Cold War: in 1948, the Communists had seized control of Czechoslovakia, and the Soviet Union had blockaded Berlin; in 1949, the Soviet Union had detonated its first nuclear device; in 1950, the North Koreans had attacked the South Koreans; in 1957, the Soviet Union had launched the first man-made satellite. Some members of Congress declared that only in naval nuclear propulsion—because of Rickover—did the United States hold an unquestioned technological superiority over the Soviet Union.

Rickover was a brilliant witness before congressional committees. Often brash, often deferential, he was nonetheless always aware of political sensibilities, and he had the ability to make members of the committees, particularly those on the Joint Committee on Atomic Energy, feel that they were part of the program, closer to it, and more understanding of its goals than the AEC or the Navy. Because of his control over the effort, Rickover became the sole spokesman for the naval nuclear propulsion program before the committee. It was to him that committee members listened.

Applying nuclear propulsion to the surface fleet went much more slowly than it did for submarines. The beginnings were promising: the Newport News Shipbuilding & Dry Dock Company laid the keel of the aircraft carrier *Enterprise* in February 1958, and the Bethlehem Steel Corporation laid down the guided missile cruiser *Long Beach* in December 1957 and the guided missile frigate *Bainbridge* in May 1959. But, because nuclear-powered surface ships cost more to build, maintain, and operate than their oil-fueled counterparts, the pace slowed down. Nuclear submarines, too, cost more than diesel-electric submarines, but the unprecedented advantages of submerged long voyages at high sustained speeds were worth the cost. The case was not so clear for nuclear surface ships.

For surface ships, the greatest difference was in construction costs. In hearings held in October and November 1963, the Joint Committee on Atomic Energy and Secretary of Defense Robert S. McNamara argued over the value of nuclear propulsion for the carrier *John F. Kennedy*. Construction costs for the nuclear-powered version were estimated at $403 million; those for the oil-fired ship were $277 million. The difference of $126 million consisted of $32 million for the initial loading of nuclear fuel, $81 million for the nuclear propulsion plant, and $13 million for the larger size of the nuclear ship and a greater capacity for jet fuel. The $32 million for nuclear fuel was part of the construction cost because it was put in place as the ship was nearing completion. Fuel for the oil-fired carrier would be delivered over her lifetime and hence was not part of her construction cost. On the other hand, the nuclear version could operate for seven years without refueling and steam long distances at high speed, qualities enabling her to respond rapidly in a crisis. In McNamara's view, the greater cost was not worth the benefits. He won the fight over the *Kennedy* but, in the face of congressional opposition, had to yield on the subsequent attack carriers. All were to be nuclear powered.[7]

Rickover was exerting tremendous influence on naval affairs, far more than was warranted by his title of Assistant Chief of the Bureau of Ships for Nuclear Propulsion. Before congressional committees, he castigated systems analysts (the "Whiz Kids," whom McNamara had brought into the Pentagon) and ridiculed their studies and impugned their motives. At some point—the date is uncertain—McNamara sounded out L. Mendel Rivers, the powerful chairman of the House Armed Services Committee, on the possibility of courtmartialling Rickover. Bluntly, Rivers warned him not to do so; every member of Congress would oppose him.[8] For its part, the Navy wanted to take from Rickover the power to select officers and to train them and the enlisted personnel who would operate the nuclear propulsion plant.

Secretary of the Navy Paul H. Nitze tried to reach an agreement with the Joint Committee and the AEC to curb Rickover's power but succeeded with neither. The AEC saw the naval nuclear propulsion program as its greatest accomplishment in reactor development, and the Joint Committee felt strongly that the continued success of the effort depended on Rickover's leadership.

President Kennedy had extended Rickover's duty from January 1962 to January 1964, but the law permitted no further extension. Rickover did not want to leave and could count on the support of the AEC and the Joint Committee. Briefly, he toyed with the idea of staying on as an AEC civilian employee. The AEC was willing to accept the arrangement, for it meant that Rickover and the staff he had so carefully recruited and trained would remain. The Navy opposed the scheme because it did not want one of its major programs to fall into civilian hands, and the Joint Committee also thought that a Navy officer, as long as his name was Rickover, should lead the effort.

Nitze, now Deputy Secretary of Defense, worked out a solution under which Rickover retired but was immediately recalled to active duty with the same responsibilities and authority. At the end of two years, his future would be reconsidered. This arrangement became routine; every two years, the Secretary of the Navy received letters from the chairman of the AEC (or its successor agencies) and from the chairman of the Joint Committee on Atomic Energy (or its successor committees) reminding him it was time to extend Rickover's tour of duty.

The system continued for fifteen years because a number of individuals, especially congressional leaders, considered Rickover vital to the nation's nuclear power program. Under his mandate from the AEC, he was charged with training officers and men to operate the reactor plants. He personally selected all officers for the program. No officer could even hope to command a nuclear ship unless Rickover selected and trained him. After two or three years at sea as engineer officer of the watch, an officer returned to Rickover's office for oral and written examinations to qualify him to become the engineer officer. Later in his career, as a prospective commanding officer, he would spend three months assigned to Rickover's office. As long as Rickover had the support of Congress and the AEC, and as long as the nuclear ships operated well, he could remain head of the naval nuclear propulsion program. Congress saw that he was promoted to rear admiral in 1953, to vice admiral in 1958, and to full admiral in 1973. The Navy, both uniformed and civilian elements, and senior officials in the Department of Defense found him hard to control. In his own mind, Rickover considered engineering excellence the key to his strength — without that he would have nothing.

Rickover's relations with every Chief of Naval Operations (CNO) under whom he served as head of the nuclear propulsion program were tense, but those with Admiral Elmo R. Zumwalt, Jr., were especially strained. When he became CNO in July 1970, Zumwalt faced two urgent problems. In a time of financial stringency he had to build new ships to replace those that had seen hard service during World War II, the Korean War, the Vietnam War, and the several diplomatic crises that marked those years and to counter an increasingly aggressive and expanding Soviet navy. He also had to relieve the explosive racial and social pressures that were building up, particularly among the enlisted personnel. On both issues, Zumwalt and Rickover clashed; on both issues, the Navy itself was split.

Differences between the two men went back to May 1959 when Rickover interviewed Commander Zumwalt to be executive officer in the *Long Beach*, about to be launched at Quincy, Massachusetts. The interview system followed a set course. Interviews with Rickover's senior staff established technical qualifications, and the interview with Rickover determined whether the candidate had the mental ability to pierce the crust of conventional thinking, to respond to unexpected questions, and to answer them directly and without evasion. Such occasions were seldom pleasant, and Zumwalt's interview was no exception. Although Rickover accepted him, Zumwalt declined to enter the nuclear program because he had a chance at a command. Zumwalt had made extensive notes after the interview that afterward became public. Later in his career, Zumwalt became close to Nitze, whom Rickover disliked, and, even later, headed the Division of Systems Analysis, a discipline that Rickover detested.

While Zumwalt was CNO, he and Rickover worked together on a few issues. They joined forces to convince a doubtful Congress that the May 1972 agreements resulting from the Strategic Arms Limitation Talks (SALT) made the Trident missile submarine necessary, and both worked to quicken the pace of the nuclear carrier program. Their guarded cooperation, however, did not extend to building non-nuclear ships or to the Navy's personnel problems.

Zumwalt believed that the fleet was seriously unbalanced. Too much had been spent on highly capable, expensive ships, such as nuclear-powered attack and guided-missile submarines, attack aircraft carriers, guided-missile cruisers, and non-nuclear ships, such as the *Spruance* class of destroyers. In his opinion, the Navy needed to give priority to building a number of lower-cost, less capable ships to be used in low-threat areas. For this low part of the "high-low" mix, as Zumwalt called it, he proposed austere patrol frigates, small non-nuclear carriers, patrol hydrofoils, and a surface-effect ship that could skim the ocean surface at a speed enabling it to span the Atlantic in little more than a day.

Rickover never claimed that all surface ships should be nuclear powered, but he was convinced that the Navy should build the difficult and costly ships during peacetime and give priority to the nuclear-powered major combatants. For surface ships, he defined these as attack aircraft carriers and their escorts of cruisers, frigates, and destroyers, as well as ships designed for independent operation where unlimited high-speed endurance was of important military value.

As it turned out, neither man received what he wanted. Zumwalt did get his austere frigate, the *Oliver Hazard Perry* class, but little else of his low part of the mix. Rickover and his congressional allies were able to get into the Department of Defense Appropriation Act, signed on 5 August 1974, a declaration of policy stating that all future major combatant ships should be nuclear powered. Never enthusiastically accepted by the Senate, the provision was repealed in a few years. In the future, attack aircraft carriers would be the only surface ships built with nuclear propulsion.

Zumwalt's efforts to relieve the racial and social pressures in the Navy dealt mainly with getting rid of petty and often demeaning regulations governing enlisted men. He did so by his famous "Z-grams," which came directly from his office and bypassed the chain of command. He had to bring to a halt a deteriorating situation. Rickover, in contrast, by selecting, training, and monitoring the officers and men of the nuclear program since its beginning in 1949, had been able to maintain his standards. He was caustic of Zumwalt's approach and believed that it was weakening, rather than restoring, authority.[9]

Of the controversies that continued to encircle Rickover, one of the most troubling dealt with shipbuilding claims. The disputes were already serious during Zumwalt's tour but became even more bitter in later years. Much of the struggle focused on two shipyards: Newport News Shipbuilding & Dry Dock Company, which built aircraft carriers, cruisers, and the 688 attack submarines and was owned by Tenneco, a Houston-based conglomerate; and Electric Boat Company, which built the 688 attack and Trident missile submarines, and was a division of General Dynamics Corporation. Each company was essential to the Navy. Only Newport News could build nuclear surface ships, and only Electric Boat could build Trident submarines.

Under Rickover's influence the Navy had awarded the two shipbuilders fixed-price incentive fee contracts, which set a ceiling on the price that the Navy would pay for a ship. Rickover favored this type of contract because it en-

couraged the builder to increase its profits by lowering costs, improving efficiency, and cutting waste, and it also promised Congress that costs would not
get out of control. The contracts set schedules by which the work was to be performed within estimated manhours. They also contained escalation clauses to
protect the builders from inflation, as long as they met the target dates and kept
within the manhours.

To meet their commitments, the builders rapidly added to their work forces.
The new workers had to be trained in their jobs, which swamped yard organization. As productivity fell, schedules slipped and manhours soared. Tenneco,
as well as General Dynamics, incurred cost overruns that were not covered by
the escalation clauses and were not the responsibility of the Navy. To recover
their costs and to regain their profits, the two conglomerates declared the Navy
at fault because it furnished late or defective information and equipment, as
well as thousands of design changes while the ships were under construction.
Analysis showed that only a fraction of the claims could be substantiated. By
the end of 1976, the Navy faced claims totaling $2.765 billion; of this amount,
those of Newport News came to $902.6 million and those of Electric Boat to
$543.9 million.[10] The situation could not continue. It absorbed funds needed
for other purposes and badly strained relations between the builders and the
Navy, both in the administrative offices and on the building ways. Newport
News even announced that it was seriously considering withdrawing from
naval construction, and Electric Boat threatened to stop work on the 688 submarines.[11]

There was a way out. Public Law 85-804 (50 U.S.C. 1431–1435), enacted in
August 1958, authorized the Department of Defense to grant relief to defense
contractors, provided neither house of Congress disapproved. In colorful testimony, reported by the press, before congressional committees, Rickover fought
against use of the law by the contractors and the Department of Defense to
settle claims. He asserted that such claims had become a way of life for the
builders, a means for them to undermine the discipline of fixed-price contracts,
and a technique for them to make profits despite poor work and inefficient
management. Moreover, he suspected that many claims contained fraudulent
items. If the government bailed out the builders, he argued, the government
should take title to the yards. They could be operated by contractors in an
arrangement known as "government owned–contractor operated," a common
practice in some defense industries and widespread in the AEC. The government would not be at the mercy of builders who threatened to stop work on
ships that could not be completed elsewhere. Rickover's solution was politi-
cally impossible, and the claims were eventually settled on terms generally favorable to the builders.

For his part in thwarting the settlements, Rickover had added to the intensity of the opposition against him. At the same time, his defenses were crumbling. The atmosphere in Congress was changing, particularly in the Senate, where questions were raised about the need for large aircraft carriers and Trident submarines. In addition, some of the senators and representatives with whom he had shared so many battles and won so many victories were leaving the scene. Those who remained believed that it was time for him to go. He was aging; his health was good, but his short-term memory was losing its sharp edge.

When the Reagan administration took office in January 1981, Rickover was eighty-one years old. John F. Lehman Jr., the new Secretary of the Navy, was thirty-nine years old, ambitious, and determined to play an active role in shaping the Navy. Seeing Rickover as an obstacle, he quickly began lining up support in the administration, in Congress, and among contractors for his removal. Aware that his position was no longer as strong as it was, Rickover still hoped to continue.[12]

Rickover prided himself that he had conducted the initial sea trials of all nuclear-powered ships except two that took place when he was ill. A part of the trials was the "crash back," which entailed steaming submerged ahead at full power for four hours followed by reversing the engines and going astern at full power until the ship was dead in the water. Although the crash back placed tremendous strain on the propulsion plant, it showed officers and crew on the submarine that the plant more than met specifications. The maneuver required care; submarines were not designed to operate submerged in this manner, and, because so much of their weight was aft, they could take a downward angle by the stern if they gathered too much sternway. It was Rickover who always gave the order for the engines to go ahead when the ship was no longer moving through the water.

On 27 July 1981, he was in the *La Jolla*, a 688-class submarine built by Electric Boat. In her crash back, she began building up sternway and diving by the stern. Because of a mixup in communications, someone other than Rickover gave the order to go ahead. Rickover repeated the maneuver and again delayed going ahead. When the submarine surged forward, she went down by the bow, possibly the result of an error by the planesman. She never exceeded her depth level and was not out of control. On rare occasions, similar incidents had occurred but none of this magnitude. Nonetheless, Rickover should not have allowed the event to occur. Electric Boat, with whom Rickover was engaged in a fierce fight, promptly and publicly accused him of needlessly endangering the boat.[13]

Rickover continued to conduct sea trials. On his return from the *Boston's* trials on 9 November 1981, he learned of radio news reports that he would not be reappointed. The next day, Lehman saw Rickover and made the decision official. Rickover hoped, however, that President Ronald Reagan would overrule Lehman. On 8 January 1982, what the White House staff expected to be a congratulatory farewell meeting turned into a stormy session when Rickover learned that his professional career was indeed over.

Through the influence of Congress, he was given an office in the Washington Navy Yard and a small staff of enlisted personnel. From this base, he continued to fight as best he could for an investigation of possible fraud in the shipbuilding claims. In July 1984, the press revealed that Rickover, while head of the program, had taken gifts from Electric Boat. Most were trinkets, such as tie clasps, and were often given away to individuals who had helped the effort in one way or another or were bestowed on such occasions as launchings. A few were personal and more costly. On one thing, everyone agreed; he had shown poor judgment but had not allowed the gifts to influence his decisions. Rickover died on 8 July 1986 at his residence in Arlington, Virginia, and his ashes were interred in Arlington National Cemetery.

Rickover has been strongly criticized. It has been charged that his demand that officers in nuclear ships spend so much effort in overseeing the propulsion plant did not give them time to master the weapons systems and acquire skills in shiphandling. Critics, some military and some civilian, have alleged that his domination of the naval nuclear propulsion program prevented research that might have developed small, lightweight, cheap reactors. Many of them believed that his influence on the shipbuilding program has saddled the Navy with submarines that are less capable, more expensive, and larger than technology could have provided. Strong beliefs existed on either side of these questions and, as the issues were professional and in some instances classified, a layman could do no more than point out the differing views.

Rickover also has been strongly praised. Nuclear ships have performed exceedingly well. During the time that he led the program, 8,400 officers and 44,500 enlisted men received intensive training in nuclear technology, and many of his practices have been adopted in the non-nuclear fleet to increase its material readiness. He fought against reliance on management systems and organizational charts; he insisted that personal responsibility was the only course to excellence.

Nuclear propulsion was a revolution and, like all revolutions, had its casualties. Also, like all leaders of revolutions, Rickover always will be the subject of controversy, but one thing is clear: naval operations, naval tactics, and naval strategy were never the same after that cold morning of 17 January 1955 when the *Nautilus* got under way on nuclear power.

At first glance, Rickover and naval tradition have little in common—if tradition means a heritage held by a group of individuals dedicated to a common purpose and whose relationships with each other are governed by certain practices. As a young officer, he mocked and ridiculed, or at best tolerated, the practices. As head of the Electrical Section, he found that they hindered him in quickly getting the best equipment to the fleet. As leader of the naval nuclear propulsion program, he was convinced that the usually accepted practices were potentially dangerous in dealing with the huge leap forward in technology.

It would be easy to say that Rickover acted as he did because he was Rickover, but that view does not take into account that he remained in the service of an institution with which he fought almost constantly. Also, it does not explain how he attracted exceedingly high-caliber people for his organization or how he could levy the demands that he placed on them. The answer only can be his conviction that the Navy was, as it had been in the past, crucial to the nation's defense. For this reason, he stated over and over to commanding officers: "Your job is to keep your ships ready to fight." His belief in the importance of the Navy and the role of its officers are the keel on which naval tradition rests.

## FURTHER READING

In his personal life, Rickover was an intensely private man; consequently, there are no adequate biographies of him. Normal Polmar and Thomas B. Allen, *Rickover Controversy and Genius* (New York, 1982), suffer from the authors' lack of information on Rickover and must be used with caution. Two books dealing with the naval nuclear propulsion program and having much information on Rickover's official life are Richard G. Hewlett and Francis Duncan, *Nuclear Navy 1946–1962* (Chicago, 1974), and Francis Duncan, *Rickover and the Nuclear Navy* (Annapolis, Md., 1990). The authors were historians of the Atomic Energy Commission, Department of Energy, and these volumes were an official assignment undertaken at Rickover's request. An engineer who served in the program during its early years, Theodore Rockwell, in *The Rickover Effect* (Annapolis, Md., 1992), has a valuable personal but noncritical insight into Rickover. Ruth Masters Rickover, the admiral's first wife, in *Pepper, Rice, and Elephants, a Southeast Asian Journey from Celebes to Siam* (Annapolis, Md., 1975), provides some personal glimpses of her husband in nonofficial surroundings. Patrick Tyler, *Running Critical: The Silent War, Rickover, and General Dynamics* (New York, 1986), relates Rickover's fight with Electric Boat during his last years. Clay Blair, Jr., wrote *The Atomic Submarine and Admiral Rickover* (New York, 1954) with the assistance of Rickover and his staff, and his work is an uncritical account of the man and the early program. Heather M. David, *Admiral Rickover and the Nuclear Navy* (New York, 1970), contains useful information.

Over the years, Rickover testified before various congressional committees, and the published hearings contain program information and some occasional biographical snippets. A valuable list of the hearings and other official sources on the propulsion program and the Shippingport atomic power station can be found in U.S. Congress, Joint Economic Committee, *Economics of Defense Policy: Adm. H. G. Rickover*, hearing before the Joint Economic Committee, 97th Cong., 2d sess., 1982, pt. 1, Appendix 1,

94–103. Consisting of six parts, the joint committee hearing covered selected congressional testimony and speeches, as well as official correspondence on Navy contracts and government policies, shipbuilding claims, lawyers and legal ethics, cost accounting standards, independent research and development, and miscellaneous matters.

NOTES

1. U.S. Congress, Joint Economic Committee, *Economics of Defense Policy: Adm. H. G. Rickover*, hearing before the Joint Economic Committee, 97th Cong., 2d sess., 1982, pt. 1, 75; U.S. Department of Energy and U.S. Department of Defense, *A Review of the United States Naval Nuclear Propulsion Program — June 1987* (n.p., n.d.), 34–40.

2. Rickover's works include *Education and Freedom* (New York, 1959); *Swiss Schools and Ours: Why Theirs Are Better* (Boston, 1962); *American Education — A National Failure: The Problem of Our Schools and What We Can Learn from England* (New York, 1963); *Eminent Americans, Namesakes of the Polaris Submarine Fleet* (Washington, D.C., 1972); and *How The Battleship Maine Was Destroyed* (Washington, D.C., 1976).

3. *Electrical Section History* (1946), NAVSHIPS 250-660-24, Naval Historical Center, Washington, D.C.

4. Rickover's constant interest in shock is referred to in *Mechanical Shock on Naval Vessels* (1946), NAVSHIPS 250-660-26, Naval Historical Center, vi.

5. Herman A. Liebhafsky, *Silicones under the Monogram: A Story of Industrial Research* (New York, 1978), 224–26.

6. Richard G. Hewlett and Francis Duncan, *Nuclear Navy 1946–1962* (Chicago, 1974), remains the best source for Rickover and the program through 1962.

7. See U.S. Congress, Joint Committee on Atomic Energy, *Nuclear Propulsion for Naval Surface Vessels*, hearings before the Joint Committee on Atomic Energy, 30 and 31 October and 13 November 1963, 88th Cong., 1st sess., 1964, for the cost comparison, 71–72, and for McNamara's testimony, 152–96. For background and results of the hearing, see Francis Duncan, *Rickover and the Nuclear Navy* (Annapolis, Md., 1990), 129–46.

8. Rickover recorded the conversation between Rivers and McNamara in "Memorandum of Discussion between Mr. L. Mendel Rivers, Chairman of the House Armed Services Committee and VADM Rickover," 14 November 1967. Rickover gave a copy of the memorandum to the author, and, in a note to the author, McNamara wrote that he did not recall any such conversation with Rivers; both in author's personal file. His interviews with John R. Blandford, former Chief Counsel, House Committee on Armed Services; Rickover; and Rickover's senior staff convince the author that the episode did take place.

9. Elmo R. Zumwalt, Jr., *On Watch: A Memoir* (New York, 1976). Chap. 5 is titled "The Rickover Complication"; chaps. 7, 8, 9, and 10 deal with enlisted personnel problems. For the high-low mix, see the statements of Rickover; Zumwalt; and Vice Admiral Frank H. Price, Director, Ship Acquisition and Improvement Division, Office of the Chief of Naval Operations, in House Committee on Armed Services, *Hearings on Military Posture and H.R. 12564 Department of Defense Authorization for Appropriations for Fiscal Year 1975 before the Committee on Armed Services*, 93d Cong., 2d sess., 16 and 17 January; 5–7, 11–15, and 21 March; and 9 April, 1974, pt. 2, 1025–40, 1043–78, 1291–1357.

Rickover explained his opposition to small, light, cheap ships in House Committee on Appropriations, *Department of Defense Appropriations for 1974*, hearings before the Subcommittee on Department of Defense, 93d Cong., 1st sess., 1973, pt. 3, 155–57.

10. Joint Economic Committee, *Economics of Defense Policy*, pts. 1–6, and U.S. Congress, Joint Economic Committee, *Economics of Defense Procurement: Shipbuilding Claims*, hearings before the Subcommittee on Priorities and Economy in Government, 94th Cong., 2d sess., and 95th Cong., 1st sess., 1978, pt. 2, have an invaluable collection of documents on claims.

11. Because claims are a complicated issue, this brief account is greatly simplified. Rickover's views and those of the Navy, Newport News, and Electric Boat are in House Committee on Appropriations, *Department of Defense Appropriations for 1978*, hearings before the Subcommittee on Department of Defense, 95th Cong., 1st sess., 1977, pt. 4. The claims amounts are on 21. Patrick Tyler, *Running Critical: The Silent War, Rickover, and General Dynamics* (New York, 1986), has much on Electric Boat and claims.

12. John F. Lehman, Jr., *Command of the Seas* (New York, 1988), 1–8, 29–35. For a view of Rickover's retirement based on his papers, see the author's "Retiring a Legend," U.S. Naval Institute *Proceedings* 115 (April 1989): 94, 97, 99–100.

13. Tyler, *Running Critical*, 295–99.

# ☆ Elmo R. Zumwalt, Jr.
☆
☆ Hero or Heretic?

*by Thomas J. Cutler*

MANY IMPORTANT FIGURES IN HISTORY ARE EASILY CLASSIFIED AS either heroes or villains. Few but the iconoclastic historian would have difficulty categorizing the likes of George Washington or Adolph Hitler. Some historical entities, however, fall into a different category altogether. The names of these individuals are guaranteed to provoke a reaction, if rarely a predictable one. The mere mention of the name Douglas MacArthur, for example, will almost always bring forth hymns of praise or venomous fulminations but rarely anything in between.

Whether permanently condemned to this purgatorial characterization or merely waiting for the mellowing effects of time, Admiral Elmo R. Zumwalt, Jr., at the time of this writing, is one of these individuals. A history-making admiral merely by being the youngest U.S. Chief of Naval Operations (CNO), Zumwalt was not content to steer the familiar courses taken by his predecessors. From the very beginning of his tenure as CNO, he was a champion of change who dared to sail into the political mine fields sown by traditionalists and special interest groups and was ever willing to "rock the boat" in an attempt to correct what he perceived as the serious ills of the U.S. Navy during the early 1970s.

Because he was appointed to the Navy's highest military office over the heads of many more senior admirals, opposition to his policies might have been inevitable, but a more conservative approach on his part would surely have minimized it. By overturning strategic thinking, liberalizing the Navy's personnel policies and practices, daring to challenge the omnipotence of the Navy's long-standing nuclear czar, and using unconventional means to attempt many of these changes, Zumwalt was bound to earn either the profound respect or the fervid execration of those bearing witness to all of this revolutionary turmoil. Like MacArthur and other controversial figures before him, "Bud" Zumwalt is rarely the object of indifference, and he is frequently referred to as either the savior or the ruination of the Navy of the 1970s.

Zumwalt was born in San Francisco, California, on 29 November 1920. Both of his parents were medical doctors, and young Bud (the nickname came from a younger sister's mispronunciation of brother) was determined to follow in their footsteps. He was a good student who played varsity football, traveled with the debating team, and graduated as class valedictorian. But his mother's struggle with terminal cancer depleted the family money, which made college and medical school impossibilities for Bud. In addition, despite his fine academic record and obvious intelligence, Bud was "kind of wild," according to his parents. These factors made the U.S. Naval Academy attractive to the Zumwalts because it offered a free college education in a disciplined environment that might settle him down. At the same time, it appealed to Bud because service in the Navy promised adventure and travel. In 1939, Zumwalt left California for Annapolis to embark on an adventure that would take him to a world war, to command of forces in an unpopular limited war, and, ultimately, to the pinnacle of naval leadership.[1]

At the Naval Academy, although he graduated in the top 5 percent of his class and finished seventh militarily, Zumwalt was unimpressed with the education he received. He referred to the Academy as a "trade school rather than a college" and noted that "the events in the outside world were bound to pale anything that happened within academic walls. Germany invaded Poland early in my plebe year. France fell as that year was ending. . . . And halfway through my third year, the Japanese bombed Pearl Harbor."[2] These momentous world events resulted in the early graduation of the class of 1943, and Zumwalt and his classmates went to sea in June 1942.

Assigned to the Pacific theater, Zumwalt saw action in two of the more dramatic engagements of the war: the disastrous battle of Savo Island in the Solomons and the classic victory over the Japanese in Surigao Strait at Leyte Gulf in the Philippines.[3] Between battles, he spent the inevitable hours of wartime tedium in reading. He developed an acute interest in the Soviet Union, which he soon concluded was bent on "world hegemony as soon as possible and as brutally as necessary."[4] At war's end, Lieutenant Zumwalt was assigned as prize crew skipper of a captured Japanese gunboat, which he sailed up the Yangtze and Hwangpoo Rivers to Shanghai. He came into contact there with an enclave of White Russian émigrés who had escaped the tyranny of the Soviet regime and whose tales solidified his feelings about the dangers posed by the autocratic and hegemonic Soviet Union. There, too, he met Mouza Coutelais-du-Roche, whose French father had married her Russian mother in pre-Revolution Russia. A brief courtship ensued and culminated in a marriage that was to last more than a half century.[5]

When Zumwalt returned to the United States with his new wife, he was intent on leaving the Navy to go to medical school and follow in his parents' footsteps. But, a fateful and unlikely meeting in 1949 with General of the Army George C. Marshall, then in temporary retirement between his tours as Secretary of State and Secretary of Defense, changed Zumwalt's mind. Responding to the young naval officer's lamentations regarding the poor state of the Navy and the nation's reluctance to prepare adequately for military contingencies, Marshall responded:

> You have just defined the kind of conditions that lead to war. I am convinced that we shall soon be in one again. Young man, don't ever sell the American people short. They have vast reserves of hidden strength to use when the cause is clear. And when the time comes, your country will need dedicated career men like you.[6]

Zumwalt heeded Marshall's advice. He abandoned his dreams of becoming a doctor and remained in the Navy for the next quarter century. Equally significant, however, was the great statesman's advice about the American people, which Zumwalt would remember and which would become a source of antagonism between him and another Secretary of State two decades later.

The war predicted by Marshall came in Korea. Zumwalt saw action as navigator in the battleship *Wisconsin*, where he gleaned another life's lesson that would forever shape his thinking on the importance of military readiness. Years later, he summed up that lesson while sharing his views as one of the participants in the Chester W. Nimitz Memorial Lectures in National Security Affairs:

> As one who participated in the Korean War, I believe that history has failed to record an important lesson of our victory there. The basis of the remarkable resilience of U.S. forces in that war . . . was that we were fortunate enough to have vast reserves of munitions, aircraft, tanks, ships, etc. which had been stockpiled for only five years since the end of World War II. . . . Equally important, we had ample numbers of well-trained World War II veterans. . . . That war, in which we came near to defeat, was turned around quickly because of the peculiar circumstances of reserves and equipment and well-trained personnel.[7]

In the years following the Korean War, Zumwalt enjoyed the reputation of "front-runner," or "comer" in Navy argot. Many in the Navy saw in him a future admiral as he commanded several ships (including the U.S. Navy's first guided-missile frigate *Dewey*), attended both the Naval and National War Col-

leges, and served two tours in Washington, one as an aide to the Assistant Secretary of the Navy for Personnel and the other in the Bureau of Naval Personnel (BuPers). While at BuPers, he encountered an unofficial but very real policy that he found "most upsetting." During his orientation briefing, "the officer
I was relieving told me that the routine for assigning minority officers was to
send them to dead-end billets so that their promotion beyond middle rank
would be unlikely." Zumwalt "did not follow that prescription," but admitted
that beyond that covert response he could not "think of a way that a junior commander could alter a policy that, evil as it was, was clearly winked at or even
encouraged by the captains and admirals he worked for."[8] Years later, as CNO,
he would think of a way.

In 1962, fate again intervened to alter the course of Zumwalt's life. While at
the National War College working on a thesis titled "The Problem of the Next
Succession in the USSR," his work came to the attention of Paul H. Nitze, then
Assistant Secretary of Defense for International Security Affairs (ISA), who
happened to be visiting the War College when Zumwalt was presenting his
work to his peers. Nitze was favorably impressed by what he heard about
Zumwalt, particularly from the War College's commandant, and offered
Zumwalt a position in ISA. Despite some resistance from his detailer,
Zumwalt accepted the position.

Nitze had been a member of the policy planning staff of the State Department during the Truman administration and was acknowledged as the author
of the famous National Security Council Memorandum 68 (NSC 68), which
had been an important component of American policy during the early Cold
War years. His writings had appeared in such prestigious journals as *Foreign
Affairs* and his counsel was often sought by government leaders. President John
F. Kennedy had considered Nitze for the post of Secretary of Defense but eventually appointed him Secretary of the Navy. When he assumed that position,
Nitze took Zumwalt with him to serve as his executive assistant and senior
aide.[9]

"I have never made a better decision," Zumwalt later wrote of his alliance
with Nitze. The two men became friends, as well as colleagues, and Zumwalt
described his years with the statesman as earning "what I think of as a Ph.D.
in political-military affairs."[10] His association with Nitze gave him insight into
the inner workings of the Navy Department, taught him many of the secrets
of statecraft and policy making, and allowed him to see the detrimental effects
that the Vietnam War was having on the material readiness of the Navy. That
association also helped him to earn a promotion to rear admiral in July 1965,
two years before his class was technically eligible for promotion to flag rank.

In July 1965, Zumwalt returned to sea as Commander, Cruiser Division 7,
but the creation of the Navy's new Division of Systems Analysis brought him

a summons from Secretary Nitze and Chief of Naval Operations David L. McDonald to return to Washington to head the new organization. This cut Zumwalt's sea tour short by nearly two years.

The challenges facing him in his new task were not insignificant, but he learned a great deal about the state of the postwar Navy and was able to have some influence over the directions that the Navy would take in the future. At the time that he took the helm of the new division in 1966, most of the ships making up the U.S. fleet had been built during World War II. Replacement of these aging veterans was an obvious priority. Because the operational costs of the Vietnam War were consuming ever more of the available money, the task was a difficult one. A report titled "Major Fleet Escort Study," issued by the Division of Systems Analysis, established the basic characteristics of a class of destroyers to replace the aging workhorses of the fleet and emphasized essentials rather than "frills." The intent was to meet the requirements of a modern escort ship while keeping the costs down so that a sufficient number of vessels could be built. This intention was diluted during the various stages of design and construction so that, by the time the *Spruance*-class destroyers emerged, they were considerably more sophisticated than the original concept called for in the study. Consequently, they cost more and fewer could be built than originally intended.

Another study initiated by the division focused on placing surface-to-surface missiles on Navy ships, submarines, and aircraft, which eventually led to development of the Harpoon antiship missile. Zumwalt's group also participated in the STRAT-X study that led to the Trident submarine with its unique ballistic missile system. Even though he was a surface officer, Zumwalt's longstanding focus on the Soviet threat made him aware of the need for a strong strategic deterrent, and he crossed intraservice boundaries in his advocacy of both submarines and aircraft carriers.[11]

Shortly after the Tet offensive in early 1968, Zumwalt was ordered to Vietnam to command the in-country naval forces there. All previous Vietnam naval commanders had been rear admirals, but the assignment was offered with a third star this time. Zumwalt suspected that the promotion was an enticement to ensure that he would take the assignment. He believed that Chief of Naval Operations Admiral Thomas H. Moorer wanted Zumwalt in Vietnam because no admiral had ever gone to a career-enhancing assignment after commanding the naval forces there. Zumwalt later wrote, "This was Moorer's way of getting rid of me."[12] Nonetheless, Zumwalt pinned on his three stars—a vice admiral at the age of forty-seven—and went to Vietnam, where, once again, fate would intervene in his favor when his path crossed that of Secretary of Defense Melvin Laird.

Zumwalt arrived in Saigon in September 1968 and found that the Navy's role in Vietnam had stagnated. Earlier coastal surveillance, river patrol, and combined riverine operations had driven the enemy off the major rivers and minimized its littoral operations, but supplies were now coming in from the Cambodian sanctuary and traveling uninhibited along a network of tributary waterways deep into the strategically vital Mekong Delta. To counter this, Zumwalt called together his senior commanders and staff members to work out the details of a new strategic concept that he called SEALORDS (South-East Asia Lake, Ocean, River, and Delta Strategy). The new strategy consolidated the various elements of the Navy's in-country forces and redeployed them to interdict the flow of enemy supplies, thus placing the naval forces "in harm's way" and taking the fight to the enemy. This redeployment not only put new pressure on the enemy but had the added effect of injecting new life into the "brown water" forces, whose relegation to mere holding operations had seriously demoralized them. Ironically, as casualties went up, so did morale.[13]

Perhaps an even more significant contribution by Zumwalt to the war effort, however, came not on the battlefield but from a plan for the extrication of U.S. forces from Vietnam. By the time Zumwalt got to Vietnam, the United States had been actively fighting there for nearly four years, and it was clear that the patience of the American people was wearing thin. Zumwalt had long advocated turning the war over to the South Vietnamese, a process called "Vietnamization" in the argot of the day. He believed that this advocacy was a primary reason why he had been selected to command U.S. naval forces there. Arriving in Saigon in the midst of the 1968 presidential campaign, Zumwalt perceived that he would have three years to turn over the naval war to the Vietnamese if Richard Nixon were elected or one year if his opponent, Hubert Humphrey, won the election.[14] Zumwalt's plan for Vietnamization, which he called ACTOV (Accelerated Turnover to Vietnam) was well thought out and earned him the respect of General Creighton Abrams, commander of all U.S. forces in Vietnam.

ACTOV had a workable timetable that would remove U.S. naval forces from the "front lines" by turning over all American craft and responsibilities to the Vietnamese navy by 30 June 1970. The plan was also reasonable and innovative because it called for a gradual turnover that allowed on-the-job training while maintaining the mission. This was accomplished by first bringing on board one Vietnamese sailor to learn the job of an American counterpart. Once he was sufficiently trained to take over the American sailor's job, another Vietnamese sailor reported on board and began training to assume another American's role. This process continued until the entire crew had been replaced from the bottom up. The officer-in-charge was the last to be relieved, at which point the craft itself would be transferred to the Vietnamese navy.[15]

While he was commanding naval forces in Vietnam, Zumwalt made a de-

cision that would later bring tragedy to his life. Viet Cong forces had long relied on the heavy foliage along the waterways of the Mekong Delta for cam-
ouflage. To counter that advantage, the admiral ordered the employment of
chemical defoliants while his son, Lieutenant Elmo Zumwalt III, was serving
in Vietnam as part of the brown water navy. Evidence later suggested that those
chemicals had been carcinogenic. When the younger Elmo succumbed to
cancer, the admiral was faced with the terrible possibility that he might have
played a role in the death of his own son.

When the new Secretary of Defense Laird visited Vietnam in February
1969, he was so favorably impressed by his meeting with Zumwalt that, a year
later when it was decided that Admiral Moorer should vacate the job of CNO
in order to move up to Chairman of the Joint Chiefs, Laird nominated the
young vice admiral for the Navy's top post. Zumwalt was summoned to Washington for a series of interviews with several Nixon administration officials, during which he was told that he had been chosen as a candidate because Laird
and Secretary of the Navy John Chafee wanted a nonaviator as CNO for the
first time in nine years and that they wanted someone younger in the office to
"bring the Navy into the modern age."[16]

As Zumwalt prepared to take the helm, the U.S. Navy was headed for uncertain waters. Because he had been promoted over the heads of thirty-three
men more senior to him, the strengths and frailties of human nature were
called into play. Some of those he had bypassed would respond as true professionals and accept him as their new leader, but some would allow their personal disappointment to overshadow their dedication to the greater good and
become avowed enemies bent upon subverting his success. Although he
brought youth and a more dashing image to the office, Zumwalt also brought
less experience. Because of his accelerated promotions and unconventional
duty assignments, he had left his cruiser division assignment early and had never held a major fleet command. His critics would say this left him unqualified
to head the Navy. All of that notwithstanding, on 1 July 1970, in a ceremony at
the U.S. Naval Academy, Admiral Elmo R. Zumwalt, Jr., was sworn in as the
nineteenth Chief of Naval Operations. At age forty-nine, he was the youngest
CNO in the history of the U.S. Navy.

During his preappointment interview with Laird in April, Zumwalt had
promised to prepare an agenda for change within the first sixty days of his new
office. Appropriately dubbing it "Project Sixty," Zumwalt produced the document that was to serve as his navigational chart for the rest of his tenure and
presented it to the Secretaries of the Navy and Defense on 10 September. Project Sixty was unprecedented in that the document served as a blueprint for
what the new CNO hoped to achieve while in office.[17] Admiral Worth Bagley
later acknowledged its significance when he confided that "there wasn't one

single policy paper I can remember in three-and-a-half years there in which it wasn't perfectly clear from the Project Sixty work the direction of decision that should be taken."[18]

Many new initiatives were proposed in Project Sixty. They included redefinitions of missions and their priorities, early retirement of obsolescing forces to make way for badly needed modern replacements, new emphasis on research and development, and high priority to "people programs" that would enhance recruiting and retention among naval personnel.

Also included in this unusual document was the young admiral's philosophy regarding institutional change, which generally embraced revolution rather than evolution. His three decades of experience with the U.S. Navy had taught him that traditional methods of change often led to the slow death of an initiative and that nontraditional ideas were usually swallowed up by a slow process of approval made slower by the reluctance of conservative senior commanders. While executive assistant to Nitze, Zumwalt had played a role in producing a set of dramatic recommendations to enhance personnel retention. He was disappointed to find that, once those recommendations were entrusted to the "system" for implementation, "so few of them were put into effect, and so slowly, that the impact to morale and retention that the whole package would have had was lost."[19] Zumwalt came to believe that ideas going against the grain of tradition could survive only if they were suddenly brought into the open where they could not be ignored.[20] This philosophy soon brought unprecedented changes to the Navy but had the corollary effect of creating vehement factions.

Most controversial of Zumwalt's methods were his so-called "Z-grams." The majority of these were designed to counter personnel retention problems in the Navy. Responding to the mandate given him by Laird and Chafee to "bring the Navy into the modern age" and keeping to his philosophy that unconventional changes needed unconventional methods of implementation if they were to succeed, Zumwalt used the Z-gram method as a means of simultaneously communicating his changes directly to all personnel in the Navy.

Even though the Navy was itself a volunteer force, it nonetheless indirectly benefitted from national conscription, and the coming end to the draft placed additional emphasis on the need for the Navy to retain its people. Zumwalt created a number of retention study groups to poll the Navy's personnel to identify the major obstacles to retention. Acting on the advice of these groups, he began issuing a series of numbered Z-grams to counter these obstacles: 10 were issued in August 1970, 23 in September, and 14 in October, most of them inspired by the findings of the retention study groups. The changes brought about included less stringent grooming regulations, the allowing of civilian clothes on board ship for fleet sailors, the creation of Wives

Ombudsmen, a more liberal liberty policy for forces afloat, a shiphandling competition for junior officers, an action telephone line to deal with personnel problems, changes in medals and award policies, major changes to the enlisted uniform, and significant modification to quarterdeck watch-standing procedures. Before Zumwalt was finished, 121 Z-grams had been issued; they covered a myriad of topics and caused a virtual revolution in the Navy's personnel policies.[21]

The personnel changes wrought by the Z-grams were generally popular among the younger officers and enlisted personnel but less so among more senior personnel. Some senior officers and petty officers felt that their authority had been undermined by the method and the content of the Z-grams. Others lauded the changes but resented the use of so unconventional a method of bringing them about.

The results, however, were indisputable. Never in the history of the U.S. Navy had such sweeping changes taken place. Gone were many of the so-called "chicken regs" (rules that seemed to have no purpose other than creating rigid discipline for its own sake) that had long been a point of contention among naval personnel. Suddenly, the family and the individual had taken on new significance. During Zumwalt's first year in office, first-term reenlistments rose from 10 percent to 17 percent. In the spring of 1971, a polling of the fleet showed that 86 percent of enlisted personnel and 80 percent of officers approved of the Z-grams and what they were accomplishing. Even among captains, commanders, chief warrant officers, and chief petty officers—the more senior personnel—the approval rating was 77 percent and among the most junior officers, 93 percent.[22] Zumwalt had succeeded in transforming the Navy from its image of a "humorless, tradition-bound, starchy institution."[23] In fact, he had been so successful that his efforts captured the attention of the national media, put him on the cover of *Time* magazine, landed him an interview in *Playboy*, and made him the most famous admiral since Halsey and Nimitz had captured the attention of the American public during World War II.

Remembering—and abhorring—the prevailing attitudes regarding minority officers that he had encountered in the Bureau of Personnel years before and recognizing that the U.S. Navy was still something less than an "equal opportunity employer," Admiral Zumwalt took aim at the problem with Z-gram No. 66, titled "Equal Opportunity in the Navy." Z-66, he said, "told the world that when it came to racial affairs Secretary [of the Navy] Chafee and I meant business."[24] It began by acknowledging that the Navy did indeed have problems in this area and went on to establish a number of measures to alleviate the situation. Among the changes mandated was the establishment of a special assistant for minority affairs at every base, on every ship, and in all aircraft squadrons. Each of these special assistants was to have direct access to the commanding officer and would be consulted on all matters involving minority personnel. Z-66 also directed Navy exchanges, commissaries, and barber shops to carry products and provide services frequently requested by minority personnel and decreed that a CNO's special assistant for minority affairs would be visiting major naval activities to identify problems. This groundbreaking Z-gram concluded with the words, "There is no black Navy, no white Navy—just one Navy—the United States Navy."[25]

Taking on the Navy's archaic but traditional regulations and attempting to rectify racial policies and practices would seem more than enough to incite a revolution and foment a counterrebellion, but Zumwalt tossed more fuel on the fire (or oil on the water, depending on the interpretation) when he issued Z-116. This Z-gram prepared the siege against another old bastion of naval tradition and parochialism by liberalizing naval policy toward women personnel. It opened up many areas previously barred to women by calling for their assignment to "the full spectrum of challenging billets, including those of briefers, aides, detailers, placement/rating control officers, attachés, service college faculty members, executive assistants, special assistants to CNO, military assistance advisory groups/missions, senior enlisted advisors, etc." Z-116 also provided opportunities for women to become chaplains and civil engineers and to command shore installations, thus creating paths that would ultimately lead to flag rank. In addition, it created a pilot program that placed women on board the hospital ship USS *Sanctuary* not just as nurses but as part of the ship's company and laid the groundwork for other policy changes that would come later, with the "ultimate goal" of "assignment of women to ships at sea."[26]

Reaction to this radical new policy centered on the *Sanctuary* program and evoked a wide range of dire predictions that included talk of seagoing orgies and the ultimate demise of the Navy family. In his memoirs, Zumwalt records President Nixon's reaction: "I guess I can put up with this race thing, but don't push so hard for women."[27]

While Admiral Zumwalt was CNO, the roles of women in the Navy indeed changed. The first female chaplain was commissioned; half a dozen women earned their wings as aviators; and, for the first time in American naval history, a woman pinned on the stars of an admiral. More significantly, a new course had been set, one that would not change after Zumwalt was gone. Since Z-116, progress has not always been smooth, but women have made great headway in the Navy and taken on more and more of the roles that for centuries had been the exclusive domain of men.

Ironically, at the same time that a CNO was finally attempting much needed race reforms, the lid blew off. Three racial incidents occurred on fleet units that eventually captured the attention of the national media and brought

Zumwalt's enemies out in force. Black sailors staged protests that, to alarmists, bordered on mutiny in the carrier *Kitty Hawk* on 12 October 1972, in the oiler *Hassayampa* on 16 October, and in the carrier *Constellation* on 3 November. The first two incidents, although indicative of underlying racial problems in the fleet, were relatively minor in nature and, more significantly, were handled by the effective employment of normal naval disciplinary measures. The *Constellation* affair, however, was much more dramatic; 144 protestors, both black and white, staged a media-covered confrontation that included clenched-fist salutes and utter defiance of naval authority. Zumwalt's conservative opponents pointed to these outbreaks as proof that the iconoclastic CNO's personnel reforms had eroded naval discipline and fostered anarchy in the fleet. President Nixon was outraged by the apparent breakdown in discipline and irrationally called for the immediate dishonorable discharge of all offenders, a reaction that was blatantly illegal if not patently hysterical. Several retired admirals convinced their conservative allies in Congress to call for an investigation (a maneuver that was reported in *Time* magazine's 27 November issue as "admirals . . . show[ing] their own lack of discipline by campaigning for Zumwalt's ouster").[28]

A combination of Zumwalt's support among liberals in Congress and the emergence of the Watergate crisis prevented any serious damage to Zumwalt and his policies. He emerged from the congressional hearings relatively unscathed, and the resulting investigative report, although frustratingly obtuse regarding the real issues at hand, received little attention.

It is difficult to assess the significance of Admiral Zumwalt's personnel policies. He was CNO at a time when all of American society was in turmoil, when such terms as "countercultural revolution" were commonplace, when racial tensions and dissensions over the Vietnam War had skewed perceptions and erected barriers to reasoned debate. In truth, much of what he was attempting to achieve in the Navy was mirrored in the other armed services but with much less flourish and without a personalized target such as he had become. It is quite probable, but impossible to be certain, that such incidents as those on board the *Kitty Hawk, Hassayampa,* and *Constellation* would have been more widespread and far worse without the implementation of his racial policies. Indeed, Zumwalt's unusual measures might well have served as a safety valve rather than an igniter. It is equally difficult to discern what the effects might have been had he not come along at a time when chicken regs and a countercultural society were on a collision course. His opponents see him as the instigator of permissiveness and the destroyer of discipline within the Navy, whereas his advocates see him as the "man of the hour" and the "savior of the Navy." Both views are certainly arguable, and the truth probably lies somewhere in between.

At the same time that he was struggling to reform naval personnel practices, Zumwalt was also trying to both modernize the fleet and revolutionize the Navy's strategy. This aspect of his tenure as CNO is often overlooked or, at least, overshadowed by the sensationalism associated with his personnel policies.

The Navy's ships had aged significantly during the Vietnam War, and operational requirements consumed greater and greater proportions of a relatively fixed budget. When Zumwalt became CNO, the problem of replacing World War II vintage ships was not yet solved. He had begun work on the problem while head of the Division of Systems Analysis and so knew the direction that he wanted to steer the Navy when he assumed its top uniformed position. Characteristically, Zumwalt took an innovative—heretical, some would say—approach to modernizing the fleet. First, he continued the work he had begun on surface-to-surface missile development to increase the offensive punch of U.S. warships and to match Soviet surface ship capabilities. Second, and far more controversial, he moved to alter the types of ships that would compose the fleet of the 1980s and beyond. Such changes in ship types and weapons systems would alter the course of American naval strategic thinking in a profound way.

The U.S. Navy had placed a heavy emphasis on aircraft carriers and submarines since the end of World War II. This was not hard to understand considering the vital roles each had played in the victory at sea. Zumwalt believed, however, that this postwar emphasis had placed too much importance on power projection, the main function of carriers and submarines, to the detriment of sea control. Zumwalt urged that both of these components of sea power were important, particularly in light of the growth of the Soviet navy that was then under way.

Zumwalt also believed that the reliance on sophisticated and highly specialized elements of naval warfare was contributing to "unionization" among officers and sailors and forcing them to compartmentalize themselves within a particular community if they were to have a successful career. This narrowed their focus and parochialized their operational vision in a way that could prove detrimental to strategic thinking.

To correct this strategic shortcoming and to replenish the fleet with appropriate replacement units in a time of tight budgetary constraints, Zumwalt devised what he called a "high-low mix" of fleet units. Defining the attack carriers and ballistic missile submarines as high-end ships ("high-performance ships and weapons systems that were also high cost"), he called for the addition of less expensive low-end vessels ("moderate-cost, moderate-performance ships and systems that could be turned out in relatively large numbers") for the sea control mission. The idea was to build a greater number of less expensive ships in lieu of fewer more sophisticated—and therefore more costly—ones. Zumwalt envisioned that "in most cases seven or five or even three ships of moderate capability would contribute far more to the success of this mission than one supership." To achieve this, he proposed decommissioning many of the older ships to free up funds and allowing the fleet to function for a time with less than the optimal number of units. Zumwalt deemed such a calculated risk necessary for the ultimate achievement of his long-term goals.[29]

A shift in strategic emphasis as great as Zumwalt proposed was bound to encounter opposition. The aviation admirals were generally opposed, and it was no surprise when the Navy's nuclear czar, Admiral Hyman G. Rickover, mounted the ramparts to thwart this perceived siege on his domain. In retrospect, this opposition seems largely unwarranted because the new concept did not call for an elimination of the high end, but merely advocated a sharing of resources to expand the Navy's mission capabilities. Indeed, an impartial examination of the record reveals that Zumwalt actively and successfully campaigned for the fourth U.S. nuclear carrier, the USS *Carl Vinson* and was a strong advocate of the Trident missile and submarine system that eventually replaced the older Polaris and Poseidon systems.[30]

A less parochial view opposed the high-low mix because it was believed that the low-end ships would lack the flexibility needed to respond in a modern multithreat environment. This argument, although certainly not lacking in validity, failed to take into account the necessity for cost reduction brought about by the political and fiscal effects of the Vietnam War.

In the end, Zumwalt's high-low concept achieved mixed results. It succeeded in acquiring the patrol frigate, a moderately priced and moderately capable escort ship that emerged as the *Oliver Hazard Perry* class, later described by Secretary of the Navy John F. Lehman, Jr., as one of the most successful shipbuilding programs in history.[31] Zumwalt failed to acquire his cherished "sea control ship," an envisioned seventeen-thousand-ton, twenty-five knot vessel capable of carrying fourteen helicopters and three VSTOL (vertical and short takeoff and landing) aircraft over vast expanses of the ocean. Although missile-carrying patrol hydrofoil vessels were built and deployed, the concept was eventually abandoned because of their limited sea-keeping abilities. The "surface effect ship," a five-thousand-ton vessel that could skim above the ocean surface at eighty to one hundred knots, never saw fruition in the original concept but eventually led to the building, on a much smaller scale, of air-cushioned landing craft for the Marine Corps.[32]

Growing out of the high-low mix and Zumwalt's strategic vision were several other tactical, technological, and organizational innovations that improved fleet readiness and mission preparedness. During his watch as CNO, the mission capability of aircraft carriers was expanded, Marine Corps air squadrons were incorporated into carrier air wings, helicopters were effectively placed on many surface ships, the CAPTOR mine (a deep-moored sensing device that detects an enemy submarine and fires a Mk 46 torpedo) was developed and deployed, attack submarines were employed as task group escorts, secure communications capability among fleet units was dramatically improved, antiship missile defense capabilities were greatly enhanced, and research and development budgets (particularly in antisubmarine warfare) were markedly increased.[33]

One of Admiral Zumwalt's most significant achievements was in the development of surface-to-surface missile (SSM) capability. When he first was appointed CNO, the U.S. Navy was significantly "outgunned" by the Soviets' vastly developed SSM capability, both short and long range. Development in this area not only would match an already existing Soviet threat but would reduce the dependence on carrier-based aircraft. In the years immediately following World War II, the Navy had embarked on SSM development when it began work on the Regulus missile, but it had abandoned the program when planners decided that the effectiveness of carrier aircraft had obviated the need for SSMs. Zumwalt called this "the single worst decision about weapons [the Navy] made during my years of service."[34] Building on the work that he had started while heading the Division of Systems Analysis, Zumwalt initiated a number of programs leading to the development of the sixty-mile Harpoon and one thousand-mile Tomahawk cruise missiles. These missiles eventually became major components in the armament of most of the surface units in the U.S. Navy. Proof of their importance was reflected in a 1988 letter to retired Admiral Zumwalt from Admiral William J. Crowe, Jr., then chairman of the Joint Chiefs of Staff, that began:

> Dear Bud,
> I just returned from a trip to the Persian Gulf where I had the opportunity to visit the Commander Joint Task Force Middle East, as well as some of the ships that took part in the at-sea engagement against Iranian naval forces on 18 April. . . . As I reflected on the events of the eighteenth, I couldn't help but recall the battle you waged in gaining acceptance for the HARPOON missile. Every HARPOON fired that day performed exactly as advertised. Without it we would not have been nearly as successful as we were. I just wanted you to know, Bud, that the system you personally championed had such a profound effect on our engagement with the Iranians, and will no doubt serve us equally well for a long period into the future. The Navy and the Nation are most grateful for your success with the HARPOON.[35]

The reference to serving well in the future was upheld during the war with Iraq just 2½ years later, when cruise missiles were employed in significant quantities against the forces of Saddam Hussein.

As Zumwalt's tour as CNO entered its last year, he found himself more and more at odds with the power foci of the administration. Nixon himself was less than pleased with his CNO and was pressuring the Secretary of Defense either to control Zumwalt or to dismiss him. Although Zumwalt had emerged from the *Constellation*-inspired Congressional hearings relatively unscathed, Nixon had been outraged by the affair and apparently held his CNO at least partially responsible. More significant was the enmity that had developed between Zumwalt and Secretary of State Henry Kissinger, one of Nixon's closest advisers. Zumwalt later revealed that Kissinger had privately told him that "the West was a civilization which had passed its historic high point and was on the wane, and that it was facing in the Soviet empire the rising empire of the next century, and his [Kissinger's] job was to preside over the smooth transition into inferiority."[36] This was very different from the philosophy imparted by George Marshall so many years before, and the rift between Kissinger and Zumwalt grew until it was impossible to breach.

Years later, during a lecture at the Institute of International Studies in Berkeley, California, retired Admiral Zumwalt told his audience, "I have a wonderful list of friends and a wonderful list of enemies, and am very proud of both lists."[37] Included in the latter list was Admiral Rickover, head of the Navy's nuclear power program for decades. Zumwalt believed that Rickover held too much power and influence over the Navy and that his views were much too parochial. The two admirals locked horns on several occasions, most significantly during the 1974 congressional appropriation hearings. Zumwalt had believed, in 1970, that he and Rickover reached an agreement under which Zumwalt would support the accelerated purchase of submarines for three years while new surface vessels were being designed and tested and that Rickover would not oppose the development of such vessels—the patrol frigates, hydrofoils, small carriers, and other vessels of the low end of Zumwalt's high-low mix. When it came time for funding the small carrier, a key part of Zumwalt's plan, in the 1974 budget, Rickover mustered support in Congress against the program that ultimately killed it.

Zumwalt's continued support for low-end ships earned him not only an enemy in Rickover himself but also enemies among leaders in the military-industrial complex who depended on Rickover's programs to keep them supplied with multimillion-dollar shipbuilding and weapons procurement contracts.

Zumwalt's enemies eventually were numerous and powerful enough that, had he not been nearing the end of his tour as CNO, it is quite likely that he would have been fired. Secretary of Defense James M. Schlesinger later told Zumwalt that, three days before the CNO change of command, he had been ordered to fire Zumwalt.[38] Schlesinger ignored the order and, on 29 June 1974, the tumultuous tenure of the Navy's nineteenth Chief of Naval Operations came to a close in a ceremony at the U.S. Naval Academy. At the end of the ceremony, at Admiral Zumwalt's request, the Navy band played "The Impossible Dream." Retirement did not bring an end to the dreams of Zumwalt. He continued to address various groups on topics of defense and foreign affairs and, at one time, sought a seat in the U.S. Senate from Virginia.

In an interview some years later, former Secretary of the Navy and then Senator John Warner described Zumwalt as having the courage to "raise his head above the ground" even at the risk of getting "it shot off."[39] There can be no doubt that Elmo Zumwalt did not hesitate to go "in harm's way" in order to implement what he perceived as badly needed changes. When faced with congressional hearings on the *Constellation* affair—a time when his job was clearly at stake—Zumwalt "considered the tumult not as a warning to take a defensive posture, but as an opportunity to nail equal treatment for minorities and women so firmly into the Navy that anyone would have trouble removing it."[40] Zumwalt was clearly an innovative thinker and a risk taker. His methods were unquestionably radical and provocative, but they also achieved what had not been done before. Zumwalt's contention that traditional methods were prone to failure when revolutionary changes were needed makes sense, as viewed historically. The evaluation proffered in a 1993 study conducted by the Center for Naval Analyses that "the Zumwalt strategic revolution would have achieved greater success had Admiral Zumwalt not believed it necessary to carry out the personnel revolution simultaneously" is intriguing and probably true.[41] Yet, Zumwalt did believe that his personnel revolution was necessary, even to the detriment of his strategic initiatives. Looking back, he later wrote:

> I was certain to turn over to my successor a navy in which all kinds of important business was unfinished: strategic analysis, ship construction, weapons development, relations with other parts of the government, and so forth, ad infinitum. But if it was within my power, I was determined to turn over to him a navy that had learned to treat its men and women, enlisted and commissioned, in a manner that recognized that, regardless of the peculiar demands military life made upon them, they were citizens of a free country in the last quarter of the twentieth century.[42]

In hindsight, it appears that Zumwalt's vision had been properly aimed. The strategic situation that he and the U.S. Navy faced in the early 1970s has changed tremendously, but the most important element of the Navy remains its people.

FURTHER READING

The most obvious source of information about Admiral Zumwalt is his *On Watch: A Memoir* (New York, 1976). Zumwalt pulls no punches in this account, and, when the author asked him in a 1995 interview if he would change anything in his memoir, he declined. Some additional insight is provided in Zumwalt's A *Global Military-Political Perspective: Past and Future* (Berkeley, Calif., 1989), which is actually a transcription of a series of lectures he gave at the Institute of International Studies at the University of California. A more personalized account is found in Elmo Zumwalt, Jr., and Lieutenant Elmo Zumwalt III, with John Pekkanen, *My Father, My Son* (New York, 1986), which focuses on the tragic death of the admiral's son. Some unbiased and revealing analysis is provided by Jeffrey I. Sands in a special study sponsored by the Center for Naval Analyses, *On His Watch: Admiral Zumwalt's Efforts to Institutionalize Strategic Change* (Alexandria, Va., 1993). A brief but revealing look at Zumwalt by one of his contemporaries is found in Andy Kerr, *A Journey amongst the Good and the Great* (Annapolis, Md., 1987). An excellent synoptic look at Zumwalt's entire career appears in Robert W. Love, Jr., ed., *The Chiefs of Naval Operations* (Annapolis, Md., 1980) in an essay titled "Elmo Russell Zumwalt, Jr." by Norman Friedman, and thought-provoking analyses of Zumwalt's career are found in Kenneth Hagan, *This People's Navy* (New York, 1991); Robert W. Love, *History of the U.S. Navy*, 2 vols. (Harrisburg, Pa., 1992); Stephen Howarth, *To Shining Sea* (New York, 1991); John F. Lehman, Jr., *Command of the Seas* (New York, 1988); and, most recently, George Baer, *One Hundred Years of Sea Power: The U.S. Navy, 1890–1990* (Stanford, Calif., 1994).

NOTES

1. Elmo R. Zumwalt, Jr., *On Watch: A Memoir* (New York, 1976), 23–24; Elmo Zumwalt, Jr., and Lieutenant Elmo Zumwalt III, with John Pekkanen, *My Father, My Son* (New York, 1986), 7–10.

2. Zumwalt, *On Watch*, 24.

3. Norman Friedman, "Elmo Russell Zumwalt, Jr.," in Robert William Love, Jr., ed., *The Chiefs of Naval Operations* (Annapolis, Md., 1980), 365.

4. Zumwalt, *On Watch*, 25; Elmo R. Zumwalt, Jr., interview by author, August 1995.

5. Zumwalt, *On Watch*, 3–22.

6. Quoted in Elmo R. Zumwalt, Jr., *A Global Military-Political Perspective: Past and Future* (Berkeley, Calif., 1989), 5.

7. Ibid., 6.

8. Zumwalt, *On Watch*, 198.

9. Andy Kerr, *A Journey amongst the Good and the Great* (Annapolis, Md., 1987), 163–63.

10. Zumwalt, *On Watch*, 29.

11. Friedman, "Elmo Zumwalt, Jr.," 366–67.

12. Zumwalt and Zumwalt, *My Father, My Son*, 41.

13. Thomas J. Cutler, *Brown Water, Black Berets: Coastal and Riverine Warfare in Vietnam* (Annapolis, Md., 1988), 285–88.

14. Zumwalt, *Global Military-Political Perspective*, 9.

15. Cutler, *Brown Water, Black Berets*, 344–45.

16. Zumwalt, *On Watch*, 43–46.

17. Jeffrey I. Sands, *On His Watch: Admiral Zumwalt's Efforts to Institutionalize Strategic Change* (Alexandria, Va., 1993), 19.

18. Worth Bagley, *Reminiscences by Staff Officers of Admiral Elmo Zumwalt, Jr.* (Annapolis, Md.), U.S. Naval Institute Oral History Collection, 241.

19. Zumwalt, *On Watch*, 170.

20. Zumwalt, interview by author.

21. The Z-grams and their subjects are listed in Zumwalt, *On Watch*, 530–32.

22. Ibid., 248.

23. Ibid., 178.

24. Ibid., 204.

25. Ibid., 204.

26. Ibid., 262–65.

27. Ibid., 265.

28. Stephen Howarth, *To the Shining Sea* (New York, 1991), 526.

29. Zumwalt, *On Watch*, 71–74.

30. George Baer, *One Hundred Years of Sea Power: The U.S. Navy, 1890–1990* (Stanford, Calif., 1994), 410.

31. John F. Lehman, Jr., *Command of the Seas* (New York, 1988), 392.

32. Sands, *On His Watch*, 108–09.

33. Ibid., 93–109.

34. Zumwalt, *On Watch*, 81.

35. William J. Crowe, Jr., to Elmo R. Zumwalt, Jr., 10 May 1988, letter in Zumwalt's possession.

36. Zumwalt, *Global Military-Political Perspective*, 27.

37. Ibid., 25.

38. Zumwalt, *On Watch*, 511.

39. Quoted in Sands, *On His Watch*, 21.

40. Zumwalt, *On Watch*, 248.

41. Quoted in Sands, *On His Watch*, 9.

42. Zumwalt, *On Watch*, 247–48.

# Contributors

JAMES C. BRADFORD teaches early American and naval history at Texas A&M University. He has been a visiting professor at the Air War College. His publications include a microfilm edition of *The Papers of John Paul Jones*; essays on Jones, French and American privateering, and Henry T. Mayo; and the three volumes, *Command under Sail, Captains of the Old Steam Navy*, and *Admirals of the New Steel Navy*, from which part of the essays in this volume are drawn.

THOMAS J. CUTLER currently serves as Director, Walbrook Maritime Academy, in Baltimore, a federally funded project designed to keep at-risk, inner-city youth in school and to provide them with a career-focused education. A career naval officer, he taught history at the U.S. Naval Academy and is the author of *Brown Water, Black Berets: Coastal and Riverine Warfare in Vietnam* and *The Battle of Leyte Gulf: 25–26 October 1944*.

FRANCIS DUNCAN is retired from the historians' office of the Atomic Energy Commission and its successor agencies, where he worked from 1962 to 1986. He won the Theodore and Franklin D. Roosevelt naval history prize for his *Rickover and the Nuclear Navy*. He and his co-author, Richard G. Hewlett, won the David D. Lloyd prize in history for their *Atomic Shield, 1947–1952*, volume two of *A History of the United States Atomic Energy Commission*. Duncan and Hewlett also wrote *Nuclear Navy, 1946–1962*.

WILLIAM M. FOWLER, JR., is professor of history at Northeastern University and editor of the *New England Quarterly*. His extensive works about the early Navy include *Rebels under Sail: The American Navy during the Revolution; William Ellery: A Rhode Island Politico and Lord of Admiralty; Jack Tars and Commodores:*

*The American Navy, 1783–1815;* and *Under Two Flags: The American Navy in the Civil War.*

LLOYD J. GRAYBAR is professor of history at Eastern Kentucky University. A diplomatic and military historian, his publications include "Admiral King's Toughest Battle" in *Naval War College Review,* "American Pacific Strategy after Pearl Harbor: The Relief of Wake Island" in *Prologue,* and "The Atomic Bomb Tests: Atomic Diplomacy or Bureaucratic Infighting?" in *The Journal of American History.*

JOHN B. HATTENDORF is Ernest J. King Professor of Maritime History at the Naval War College. He is the author or editor of more than twenty books on naval history, including *On His Majesty's Service: Observations in the British Home Fleet from the Diary, Reports and Letters of Joseph H. Wellings; The Writings of Stephen B. Luce; Sailors and Scholars: A Centennial History of the Naval War College; Maritime Strategy and the Balance of Power* (co-editor); *Mahan Is Not Enough;* and *British Naval Documents, 1204–1960* (co-editor).

HAROLD D. LANGLEY is the former curator of naval history, National Museum of American History, Smithsonian Institution, and adjunct professor of history at the Catholic University of America. He is the author of *Social Reform in the U.S. Navy, 1798–1862,* and *A History of Medicine in the Early U.S. Navy;* the co-editor of *Roosevelt and Churchill: Their Secret Wartime Correspondence;* and editor of *So Proudly We Hail: The History of the United States Flag.* His numerous articles and book chapters include studies of Winfield Scott Schley, the War of 1812, and four Secretaries of the Navy.

JOHN B. LUNDSTROM is curator of American and Military History at the Milwaukee Public Museum. His books *The First South Pacific Campaign: Pacific Fleet Strategy, December 1941–June 1942, The First Team: Pacific Air Combat from Pearl Harbor to Midway,* and *The First Team and the Guadalcanal Campaign* analyze American conduct of the early phases of the Pacific War. His most recent book, *Fateful Rendezvous* (written with Steve Ewing), is a biography of Edward H. (Butch) O'Hare, and he has begun work on a command study of Frank Jack Fletcher.

JOHN K. MAHON is retired from teaching history at the University of Florida. A former civilian historian for the Office of the Chief of Military History and Visiting Professor of Military History at the U.S. Army Military History Institute, Carlisle Barracks, Pennsylvania, he is the author of twenty-five journal articles and four books, including *The War of 1812* and *History of the Second Seminole War, 1835–1842.*

CLARK G. REYNOLDS is professor of history at the College of Charleston. He has taught at the U.S. Naval Academy, University of Maine, and U.S. Merchant Marine Academy. He is the author of several naval and maritime history studies, including *The Fast Carriers: The Forging of an Air Navy*; *Command of the Sea: The History and Strategy of Maritime Empires*; *Famous American Admirals*; *The Fighting Lady*; and *Admiral John H. Towers: The Struggle for Naval Air Supremacy*.

DAVID ALAN ROSENBERG teaches history at Temple University. During 1996–1998 he will hold the Maritime Strategy Chair at the National War College. The author of dozens of articles, book chapters, and monographs on post–World War II military and naval history and strategy, he was the first military historian awarded a John D. and Catherine T. MacArthur Fellowship. A commander (special duty, intelligence) in the U.S. Naval Reserve, he serves as a consultant to the Office of the Chief of Naval Operations and the Office of the Secretary of the Navy and chairs the Secretary of the Navy's Advisory Subcommittee on Naval History. He is currently writing a biography of Arleigh A. Burke.

JOHN H. SCHROEDER is professor of history and Chancellor of the University of Wisconsin–Milwaukee. He is the author of *Mr. Polk's War: American Opposition and Dissent, 1846–1848*, and *Shaping a Maritime Empire: The Commercial and Diplomatic Role of the American Navy, 1829–1861*. He is currently working on a biography of Matthew C. Perry.

ROBERT SEAGER II taught at the U.S. Naval Academy, the University of Maine, the University of Baltimore, and the University of Kentucky before retiring. His publications include *And Tyler Too*, a biography of the tenth president, as well as the biography titled *The Letters and Papers of Alfred Thayer Mahan*, in three volumes. He has edited *The Papers of Henry Clay*, volumes 7 through 9, and is currently writing a biography of Henry Clay.

TAMARA MOSER MELIA SMITH was a historian at the Naval Historical Center and taught at the Naval War College. Her publications include volume two of *The Naval War of 1812* (co-editor) and *Damn the Torpedoes: A Short History of U.S. Naval Mine Countermeasures, 1777–1991*. She is currently completing "Desert Slash: A History of U.S. Mine Warfare during Desert Storm."

WARREN F. SPENCER is retired from teaching history at the University of Georgia. A specialist in nineteenth-century French diplomatic history, his publications include *The Confederate Navy in Europe* and *The United States and France: Civil War Diplomacy* (co-author). He has just completed *Raphael Semmes: A Philosophical Mariner*.

WILLIAM N. STILL, JR., is retired from East Carolina University, where he was a professor of history and director of the Program in Maritime History and Underwater Research. He has written extensively on naval aspects of the Civil War, including *Iron Afloat: The Story of the Confederate Ironclads, Confederate Shipbuilding, American Sea Power in the Old World: The United States Navy in European and Near Eastern Waters,* and *Why the South Lost the Civil War* (co-author).

DAVID F. TRASK, a freelance historian, taught at Boston University, Wesleyan University, University of Nebraska at Lincoln, and State University of New York at Stony Brook before becoming director of the Office of the Historian, U.S. Department of State, and later the chief historian of the U.S. Army Center for Military History. His ten volumes include six on World War I, among them *The United States in the Supreme War Council; Captains and Cabinets: Anglo-American Naval Relations, 1917–1918; World War I at Home;* and *Admiral William Shepherd Benson: First Chief of Naval Operations* (co-author).

VERNON L. WILLIAMS is professor of history at Abilene Christian University. He is the author of *Lieutenant Patton and the American Army on the Punitive Expedition, 1915–1916* and several chapters on naval history. He is curently completing a biography of Marine Corps Major General Littleton W. T. Waller.

JOHN F. WUKOVITS, is a teacher and writer from Trenton, Michigan. His more than one hundred publications include *Devotion to Duty,* a biography of Vice Admiral Clifton A. F. Sprague, and essays on the battle of Okinawa and on Admiral Raymond Spruance.

# Index